THE PROTECTION OF THE UNDERWATER CULTURAL HERITAGE:
AN EMERGING OBJECTIVE OF THE CONTEMPORARY LAW OF THE SEA

Publications on Ocean Development

Volume 23

*A Series of Studies on
the International, Legal, Institutional and Policy Aspects
of Ocean Development*

General Editor: Shigeru Oda

The Protection of the Underwater Cultural Heritage: An Emerging Objective of the Contemporary Law of the Sea

ANASTASIA STRATI

MARTINUS NIJHOFF PUBLISHERS

THE HAGUE / LONDON / BOSTON

Library of Congress Cataloging-in-Publication Data

```
Strati, Anastasia.
   The protection of the underwater cultural heritage : an emerging
objective of the contemporary law of the sea / by Anastasia Strati.
      p.   cm. -- (Publications on ocean development ; v. 23)
   Includes bibliographical references.
   ISBN 0-7923-3052-8 (hardbound : acid-free paper)
   1. Underwater archaeology--Law and legislation.  2. Cultural
property, Protection of (International law)  3. Maritime law.
I. Title.  II. Series.
K3791.S77  1995
341.7'677--dc20                                         94-22723
```

ISBN 0-7923-3052-8

Published by Kluwer Law International,
P.O. Box 85889, 2508 CN The Hague, The Netherlands.

Sold and distributed in the U.S.A. and Canada
by Kluwer Academic Publishers,
101 Philip Drive, Norwell, MA 02061, U.S.A.

In all other countries, sold and distributed
by Kluwer Academic Publishers Group,
P.O. Box 322, 3300 AH Dordrecht, The Netherlands.

Typeset by Anne-Marie Krens – The Netherlands

Printed on acid-free paper

To my parents
and my uncle *Bey*

CONTENTS

Chapter 2 - Underwater Archaeology   35

Chapter 3 - International and Regional Instruments
Protecting the Cultural Heritage   69

FOREWORD

At the beginning of "The Tempest," Shakespeare's late and great play, a splintering shipwreck only sets the stage for a human drama. The King of Naples must have lost some valuable trinkets in the wreck. Ariel's song advises Ferdinand, however, that at "full fathom five thy father lies; of his bones are coral made." No mention is made of any sparkling jewels. The shipwreck in "Twelfth Night" plays a similar stage-setting role.

The law governing underwater cultural heritage is gradually moving toward Shakespeare's viewpoint. What counts, more and more, is the human dimension. The *dramatis personae* includes recreational and commercial divers, salvors, marine archaeologists, historians, financiers, insurance companies, lawyers, museum officials, government officials and the public. Their competing interests overshadow the traditional maritime rules of "finders, keepers" and "marine peril," which have served mostly to help empty the treasure from Davy Jones' locker. Gradually, cultural integrity is emerging as a guiding principle: even the most disintegrated shipwrecks are time capsules full of human history.

Dr. Strati acknowledges the competing interests in her flagship survey of the emerging law. She does not, however, advocate some kind of interest-balancing to avoid and resolve disputes. Instead, she emphasizes the significance of the underwater cultural heritage in terms of scientific exigencies, education, cultural patrimony and sustainable public access. The law should serve the function of archaeology "to draw conclusions about past societies by discovering, recording, interpreting and preserving the material evidence they have left behind."

This definitive book leaves very little behind. It thoroughly examines the inadequacies of the traditional regime and the contours of an emerging body of international and regional (mostly European) law. Although Dr. Strati repeatedly addresses the inadequacies of this new regime, she provides good reasons for proceeding full steam ahead in its wake.

So far, the emerging regime has been less significant in actually protecting the underwater heritage than in expressing a sea-change of thinking about it and the need for international cooperation. Fifteen or twenty years ago a study of this scope would have been impossible. The law was at sea. Until recently, it was little more than the flotsam and jetsam of national antiquities laws that were poorly enforced and adversarial proceedings that simply divided up the loot without regard to the public interest. Counter-productive statutes and judicial imbroglios rather than sound management ruled the waves, and still do to a great extent. In the United States, for example, decision-making was largely abdicated to the admiralty courts, which usually applied the laissez-faire rules of salvage. Under these cir-cumstances, it is small wonder that virtually the entire heritage off the French coast and the Florida Keys has been plundered. The looting of the *Espiritu Santos* off Padre Island in the Gulf of Mexico is another tragedy.

Too often the human dimension, in any enlightened sense, has been mis-sing in our approach to the underwater heritage. Our common heritage has been ignored. Unfortunately, the all-too-human dimensions of greed and adventurism have not been missing. I remember participating in a panel discussion in Miami on underwater heritage law, with a focus on the rampant plunder of Spanish galleons off the nearby Florida Keys. It was January 1988, just after the United States Congress had finally enacted the Abandoned Shipwreck Act. The states thereby assumed title to manage underwater resources, replacing the jurisdiction of admiralty courts, which have been so detrimental to the heritage. I was confident that the new legislation marked the vaunted sea-change in public philosophy. Reality quickly returned, however, when a swashbuckling, treasure-hunting member of our panel showed up, sporting a heavy necklace of doubloons from his famous discovery, *Nuestra Señora de Atocha*. In the ensuing months, television features and advertising by jewelry stores throughout the United States trumpeted the new consumerism in Our Lady's treasure: You, too, could have a necklace of gold doubloons. The media's treatment of the *Titanic* tragedy is another example. The sinking of the *Titanic* may have been a Night to Remember, in Walter Lord's memorable words, but the reappearance in 1987 of its passenger's possessions during a ghoulish publicity stunt on television was a night to forget. Such spectacles have inhibited our capacity to peer into "the dark backward and abysm of time."

Invention of the aqualung made possible the massive plunder of the last few decades. More recently, robotic and teleoperated equipment for locating shipwrecks and reducing them to legal possession have highlighted both the need and the opportunities for international conservation and management of the underwater heritage. No longer can we afford to rely on simplistic principles, such as freedom of the seas or *res nullius,* to govern decisions over the cultural commons. Nor should we be predisposed against the extension of coastal-state jurisdiction in every instance. Nor ought we to rely on salvage laws or admiralty courts. National laws and institutions are indispensable, but must be harmonized and guided by a better and stronger international regime.

This book provides a reliable compass to orient the reader in the journey ahead. Although a new regime of international protection, management and dispute resolution is still taking shape, its broad outlines are apparent. Its coordinates lie at the intersection of cultural heritage law and the law of the sea.

Drafters of the 1982 United Nations Convention on the Law of the Sea took a tack in the right direction. Article 303 of the 1982 Convention establishes a general duty to protect archaeological and historic objects found at sea and affirms coastal State jurisdiction to prohibit removal of objects from its contiguous zone. Article 149 proclaims the common heritage of objects found in the seabed area and establishes residual preferential rights for States of origin. As Dr. Strati convincingly demonstrates, however, these provisions are just the beginning. They provide little more than the vocabulary of a new commitment, a general duty to protect the common heritage, and preferential rights for States of origin. On the negative side, the terms are ambiguous, the restriction of coastal state protection to 24-mile contiguous zones is problematic, the toleration of salvage rules unfortunate, and the lack of implementing provisions debilitating. Similarly, international cultural property law provides some guidance but little authority for an effective regime to conserve and manage the underwater heritage. European and UNESCO conventions, in particular, point in the right direction, but the sailing then gets very rough.

At the end of this volume are several beacons of hope. In particular, Dr. Strati introduces the Buenos Aires Draft Convention on Protection of the Underwater Cultural Heritage, which was approved by the International Law Association in August 1994 for transmittal to UNESCO. This instrument forthrightly encourages coastal States to establish cultural heritage zones, displaces the law of salvage, provides a jurisdictional scheme to facilitate protection of the heritage and avoid competing claims, and incorporates scientifically acceptable standards into delineations of state responsibility. In a narrow sense, the human dimension is manifest, for example, in the Buenos Aires Draft Convention's non-applicability to warships, which generally remain under flag-State jurisdiction lest their human remains be disturbed. In a broader sense, however, the human dimension is celebrated in the Draft Convention's potential to reconcile competing interests and maximize the opportunities for historical revelation, education, and public access to the underwater heritage.

This book plumbs the depths of transnational law to find the means for fulfilling our guardianship of the underwater heritage. Only by such means can the past become prologue for us and future generations.

James A.R. Nafziger

ACKNOWLEDGEMENTS

The origins of this book lie in my PhD thesis which was submitted to the University of Wales in 1988. I should like to express my deep gratitude to my supervisor, Professor E.D. Brown, University of Wales, for his unfailing support and expert guidance during my years of postgraduate research, without which this work would not have been possible.

Another person to whom I am profoundly indebted, is Dr. Theodore Halkiopoulos, Special Legal Advisor to the Ministry of Foreign Affairs of Greece, who provided me with substantive information concerning the negotiations at the Third United Nations Conference on the Law of the Sea and the Council of Europe on the underwater cultural heritage issue, and has willingly offered constructive advice over the years.

Special thanks are also due to the following persons for their helpful co-operation: Dr. Robert G. Critchlow, The Steamship Mutual Underwriting Association Limited; Ms. Angela Croome, Deputy Editor and Reviews Editor of the International Journal of Nautical Archaeology; Lady Fox QC, General Editor, International and Comparative Law Quartely; Professor Krateros Ioannou, Democritus University of Thrace; Mr. Carsten Lund, Head of Cultural History Division, Ministry of the Environment, Denmark; Dr. Patrick J. O' Keefe, Consultant on National Cultural Heritage Law; Professor Lyndel V. Prott, Chief of the International Standards Section, Cultural Heritage Division, UNESCO; Professor Emmanuel Roucounas, University of Athens, and Professor Alfred H.A. Soons, Director of the Netherlands Institute for the Law of the Sea. In particular, I should like to thank Professor James A.R. Nafziger, Wilammette University, for our most stimulating discussions and, above all else, for his invaluable help and encouragement.

The staff of the following libraries also deserve my gratitude for their assistance and tolerance: UWIST Law Library, The Institute of Advanced Legal Studies, University College London, Department of Classics, and the National Museum of Wales.

Finally, I am grateful to Ms. Annebeth Rosenboom, Martinus Nijhoff Publishers, for her patience and understanding while I was preparing the manuscript for publication.

ABBREVIATIONS

A.B.A. Jour.	American Bar Association Journal
A.J.I.L.	American Journal of International Law
A.L.J.R.	Australian Law Journal Reports
All E.R.	All England Reports
AMC	American Maritime Cases
Annuaire de l'AAA	Yearbook of the Association of Attenders and Alumni of the Hague Academy of International Law
A/RES	Resolution of the UN General Assembly
Arizona L. Rev.	Arizona Law Review
A.Y.B.I.L.	Australian Yearbook of International Law
BGHZ	Entscheidungen des Bundesgerichthofs in Zivilsachen
Brooklyn J. Int'l L.	Brooklyn Journal of International Law
B.Y.I.L.	British Yearbook of International Law
c.	Chapter
CAHAQ	*Ad Hoc* Committee of Experts on the Underwater Cultural Heritage
Capital University L. Rev.	Capital University Law Review
Calif. W. Int'l L.J.	California Western International Law Journal
Case W. Res. J. Int'l L.	Case of Western Reserve Journal of International Law
Ch.D	Law Reports, Chancery Division
C.F.R.	Code of Federal Regulation
Cir.	Circuit
C.M.A.S.	World Underwater Federation
Colum. J. Transnat'l L.	Columbia Journal of Transnational Law
1982 Convention	UN Convention on the Law of the Sea
CHS	Geneva Convention on the High Seas (1958)
CSC	Geneva Convention on the Continental Shelf (1958)
ECJ	European Court of Justice
EEZ	Exclusive Economic Zone
Eng. Rep.	English Reports
E.P.I.L.	Bernhardt, R. (ed.), Encyclopedia of Public International Law
Europ. T.S.	European Treaty Series
Ex.D.	Law Reports, Exchequer Division
F. Cas.	Federal Cases
F.2d	Federal Reporter Second Series
Fla. L. Rev.	Florida State Law Review

F. Supp.	Federal Supplement
Georgia J. Int. Comp. L.	Georgia Journal of International and Comparative Law
Hague Recueil	Recueil des Cours, Académie de Droit International de la Haye
Hag. Adm./Hagg.	Haggard's Admiralty Reports
H.L.	House of Lords
Harvard Int'l L.J.	Harvard International Law Journal
H.R.L.J.	Human Rights Law Journal
ICJ	International Court of Justice
I.C.O.M.	International Council of Museums
ICNT	Informal Composite Negotiating Text
ICNT/Rev.1	Informal Composite Negotiating Text/Revision 1
ICNT/Rev.2	Informal Composite Negotiating Text/Revision 2
I.J.N.A.	International Journal of Nautical Archaeology and Underwater Exploration
ILC	International Law Commission
ILM	International Legal Materials
I.L.R.	International Law Reports
INA	Institute of Nautical Archaeology
Indian J. Int'l Law	Indian Journal of International Law
International Arbitrations	Moore, J.B., History and Digest of the International Arbitrations to which the United States has been a Party, 5 vols., 1898
Int'l & Comp. L.Q.	International and Comparative Law Quarterly
IOC	Intergovernmental Oceanographic Commission
ISNT	Informal Single Negotiating Text
I.Y.I.L.	Italian Yearbook of International Law
J. Arts Mgmt & L.	The Journal of Arts Management and Law
JFA	Journal of Field Archaeology
J. Mar. Law & Com.	Journal of Maritime Law and Commerce
J.O.	Journal Officiel
Law. Ed.	Lawyer's Edition, United States Supreme Court Reports
Loy. L. Rev.	Loyola Law Review
Lloyd's L.R.	Lloyd's Law Reports
L.N.T.S.	League of Nations Treaty Series
Marit. Pol. Mgmt	Maritime Policy and Management
Mich. L. Rev.	Michigan Law Review
Mod. L. Rev.	Modern Law Review
New L.J.	New Law Journal
N.Y.I.L.	Netherlands Yearbook of International Law
N.Y.J. Int'l & Comp. L.	New York Journal of International and Comparative Law
N.Y.U.J. Int'l Law & Pol.	New York University Journal of International Law and Politics
OAS	Organisation of American States
Ocean Dev. & Int'l L.	Ocean Development and International Law

P.	Probate division
PL	Public Law
P.Y.I.L.	Polish Yearbook of International Law
R.G.D.I.P.	Revue Général du Droit International Public
R.I.A.A.	United Nations Reports of International Arbitral Awards
RSNT	Revised Single Negotiating Text
San Diego L. Rev.	San Diego Law Review
Seton Hall L. Rev.	Seton Hall Law Review
Southwestern L.J.	Southwestern Law Journal
Stanford L. Rev.	Stanford Law Review
ST/LEG/SER.B/1	United Nations, Laws and Regulations on the Regime of the High Seas, vol. 1. (United Nations Legislative Series, ST/LEG/SER.B/1, 11 January 1951)
ST/LEG/SER.B/15	United Nations, National Legislation and Treaties Relating to the Territorial Sea, the Contiguous Zone, the Continental Shelf, etc. (United Nations Legislative Series, ST/LEG/SER.B/15, 1970)
ST/LEG/SER.B/16	United Nations, National Legislation and Treaties Relating to the Law of the Sea. (United Nations Legislative Series, ST/LEG/SER.B/16, 1970)
ST/LEG/SER.B/18	United Nations, National Legislation and Treaties Relating to the Law of the Sea. (United Nations Legislative Series, ST/LEG/SER.B/18, 1976)
ST/LEG/SER.B/19	United Nations National Legislation and Treaties Relating to the Law of the Sea. (United Nations Legislative Series, ST/LEG/SER.B/19, 1980)
Syracuse J. Int'l L. & Com.	Syracuse Journal of International law and Commerce
Texas Int'l L.J.	Texas International Law Journal
T.L.R.	Times Law Reports
TSC	Geneva Convention on the Territorial Sea and the Contiguous Zone (1958)
U.C.L.A. L. Rev.	U.C.L.A. Law Review
U. Fla. L. Rev.	University of Florida Law Review
UN GAOR	United Nations, General Assembly Official Records
U. Miami L. Rev.	University of Miami Law Review
UNCLOS I, Off. Rec.	First United Nations Conference on the Law of the Sea, Official Records
UNCLOS I, Off. Rec.	Third United Nations Conference on the Law of the Sea, Official Records
UNESCO	United Nations Educational, Scientific and Cultural Organisation
U.N.T.S.	United Nations Treaty Series
U.S.C.A.	United States Code Annotated
V. J. Transnat'l L.	Vanderbild Journal of Transnational Law
V.O.C.	Vereenigde Oostindische Compagnie
V.J.I.L.	Virginia Journal of International Law

W.L.R.   World Law Reports
Wm. & Mary L. Rev.   William and Mary Law Review
Wall   Wallace
ZaöRV   Zeitschrift für ausländisches öffentliches Recht und
                          Völkerrecht

Introduction

"It is probable that a greater number of monuments of the skill and industry of man will, in the course of ages, be collected together in the bed of the ocean than will exist at any other time on the surface of the continents."

Sir Charles Lyell (1872)[1]

The marine environment is an almost ideal surrounding for the preservation of artefacts and, until relatively recently, it also provided complete protection from destruction by man. However, the invention of the aqualung in 1943 made underwater sites accessible with the result that most archaeological remains in shallow water were plundered. Modern advances in deep seabed technology may prove to be equally detrimental to deepwater archaeological sites; unless proper precautions are taken, these too will be looted. There is an obvious need for immediate international action to preserve the man-made environment alongside the natural environment.

The enunciation of legal rules to protect the underwater cultural heritage is a complex legal issue involving a matrix of interests and laws at both international and national level. The different bodies of laws involved have been described as a legal labyrinth[2] and they must be co-ordinated if any conflict of objectives is to be resolved. At national level, the main bodies of laws involved are legislation concerning the protection of the cultural heritage, either general or specifically dealing with underwater relics, property law, admiralty law (wrecks and salvage law), taxation and laws concerning import and export, laws related to national parks, reserves and environmental protection and, finally, conflicts of law.[3] However, an adequate legal framework cannot be based on national legislation only. It must be supplemented by rules of international law. To date, the only international instruments specifically dealing with the protection of underwater cultural property are Recommendation 848 (1978) of the Parliamentary Assembly of the Council of Europe on the Underwater Cultural Heritage[4] and the Draft European Convention on the Protection of the Underwater Cultural Heritage (1985).[5] Other international instruments are relevant to the protection of the underwater cultural heritage, although they are either applicable to all cultural heritage or directed at special situations, i.e., the protection of cultural property in time of war prevention and or the punishment of offences against cultural property. Examples of regional instruments affording some protection for underwater cultural heritage are the 1982 Protocol concerning Mediterranean Specially Protected Areas, which includes "sites of particular importance because of their scientific, aesthetic, historical, archaeological, cultural or educational interest" among the range of protected areas[6], the European Convention on Offences relating to Cultural Property (1985)[7] and the European Convention on the Protection of the Archaeological Heritage (revised) (1992).[8]

The mere location of relics on and under the seabed brings them within the scope of the law of the sea, although they differ fundamentally - in terms of their nature and value - from other marine resources. The question, therefore, arises as to whether this body of international law has the appropriate means to regulate underwater cultural property effectively, considering that its safeguarding involves protection not only against the effects of time and nature, but also against theft and illicit traffic. The present study is devoted to the examination of these rules. At first sight, the preservation of the underwater cultural heritage appears to be one of the less controversial law of the sea issues. However, there is one aspect of its protection which causes concern to the maritime powers; it may provide a basis for extending coastal jurisdiction over the continental shelf for non-resource related purposes. The archaeological issue is, therefore, entangled within the general conflict between the interests of coastal States in promoting the expansion of their competence over extended ocean areas off their coasts, and those of maritime powers in defending the freedom of the high seas. In this context, the UN Convention on the Law of the Sea (1982)[9], the first codification of the law of the sea to provide for "objects of an archaeological and historical nature found at sea", failed to adopt a coherent scheme of protection. The desire for consensus did not always promote clarity of law and the solution provided for by the Convention is far from satisfactory.

Nevertheless, the role of the law of the sea should not be overestimated as it can only deal with certain aspects of the protection of the underwater cultural heritage, in particular with jurisidiction. *Jurisdiction* and *ownership* are the two core issues in the protection of the underwater cultural heritage. Questions of ownership of submerged cultural property can be enormously complex. Comparative legal research would reveal that the legal status of historic shipwrecks and their cargoes is entangled within the various wreck, salvage and heritage laws which differ between national legal systems. The absence of international principles on the question of ownership of cultural property indicates the reluctance of the international community to regulate this controversial issue, which is left open to domestic legislation. Although the means of asserting control depend on the legal and political system of each State, in respect of underwater cultural property, State ownership appears to offer the most efficient scheme of protection.

The effectiveness of any scheme of protection depends to a considerable extent on the co-operation of the public, particularly that of interest groups, such as underwater explorers and hobby-divers. Since legal action has its limits; educating the public may prove to be more effective than the enactment of draconian measures which cannot be enforced. It is, therefore, important that positive action is taken not only in the legislative sphere, but also to ensure that the public is properly educated and the law is rigorously enforced. The underwater cultural heritage is of sufficient importance to the international community so as to warrant an effective regime of protection. One would at least expect the accommodation of underwater cultural property in accordance with its nature and needs. When traditional principles are not useful, new ones have to be developed. The limited cultural resources of the oceans, which have been endangered recently by the development of advanced underwater technology, call for the adoption of such protective measures.

NOTES

1 Text quoted in Lenihan, D.J., "Rethinking Shipwreck Archaeology: A History of Ideas and Considerations" in Gould, R.A. (ed.), *Shipwreck Anthropology*, A School of American Research Book, University of New Mexico Press, 1983, pp. 37-64 at p. 39.
2 Korthals Altes, A., "Submarine Antiquities: A Legal Labyrinth", 4 *Syracuse J. Int'l. L. and Com.* (1976) pp. 76-96.
3 See also Prott, L.V. and O'Keefe, P., *Law and the Cultural Heritage,* vol. 1, *Discovery and Excavation,* Professional Books Ltd., Abingdon 1984 at p. 108.
4 Council of Europe, Parliamentary Assembly, *Texts adopted by the Assembly*, sessions 30-32 (1978-81). Reprinted in Council of Europe, Parliamentary

Assembly, *The Underwater Cultural Heritage*, Report of the Committee on Culture and Education, Doc. 4200-E, Strasbourg, 1978, pp. 1-4.

5 Council of Europe, *Ad Hoc* Committee of Experts on the Underwater Cultural Heritage (CAHAQ), "Final Activity Report", *Doc. CAHAQ(85)5*, Strasbourg, 23 April 1985.

6 Text reprinted in Simmonds, K.R. (ed.), *New Directions in the Law of the Sea [New Series]*, J.20, Release 84-1, September 1984 and in Burhenne, W.E. (ed.), *International Environmental Law: Multilateral Treaties*, Berlin, 1982, No. 26, pp. 11-18.

7 *Europ. T.S.* No. 119. The Convention has not entered into force.

8 *Europ. T.S.* No. 143. The Convention has not entered into force.

9 The official text of the UN Convention on the Law of the Sea 1982 and the Final Act of UNCLOS III are published in United Nations, *The Law of the Sea* (UN, New York 1983, Sales No. E.83.V.5).

PART ONE

CHAPTER 1

The Notion of the Underwater Cultural Heritage

DEFINITION

The concept of cultural heritage

There is no generally acceptable definition of the concepts of "cultural heritage" and "cultural property"[1] despite the frequent appearance of these terms in UN and UNESCO Conventions and Recommendations. Each instrument has employed a different definition drafted for its specific purposes. Similarly national heritage legislation employs a wide variety of methods to delimit its scope of application, ranging from the use of very general language to the specific nomination of what is protected. The terminology used reflects different ideological points of view regarding such property. As States are primarily concerned with their own national heritage, the definitions which they have adopted reflect the specific characteristics of their cultures.[2] Often a distinction is made between tangible (material) and intangible (non-material) cultural heritage. This division is largely conceptual: "There is no basic difference between the material manifestation of abstract concepts of form and function fossilised in the attributes of artefacts and the social manifestations of similar concepts ephemerally translated into social activities."[3] The data studied by archaeologists are aspects of the phenomenon of hominid culture, which "consists of learned modes of behaviour and its material manifestations, socially transmitted from one generation to the next and from one society or individual to another".[4] Monuments are an expression of the creativity of the past and a source of valuable information; they reveal, apart from material evidence, spiritual values created by man in the process of socio-historical practice. The notion of archaeological heritage is primarily related, though not restricted, to the material evidence of the past which, once preserved, can ensure access to it.[5] To date, legal protection, both at national and international level, is almost exclusively confined to the protection of tangible cultural heritage, e.g., monuments, individual items and sites. Very little attention has been paid to intangible cultural heritage.[6]

One may also identify universal content and specific national features in any national culture and its manifestations. Every national culture is endowed with common content belonging to everyone. Universal culture does not exist in its "pure" form beyond national cultures. "The general exists in and through the particular: the particular being the necessary form of the manifestation of the general, a mode of its existence."[7] This distinction is of particular significance to the general question of restitution of cultural property. Cultural objects which reveal the specific national features of original civilisations should belong to the people who created them. If they are no longer accessible to those who created them, provision should be taken for their restitution or return to the State(s) of origin. However, the cultural heritage is also significant to the international community as it manifests universally shared values and by revealing and respecting the specific national features of different original civilisations promotes understanding between nations. Article 1(3) of the Declaration of the Principles of International Cultural Co-operation (1966) reads: "In their rich variety and diversity, and in the reciprocal influences they exert on one another, all cultures form part of the common heritage belonging to all mankind."[8]

National heritage versus common heritage?

Up to the present time, the concept of the "common heritage of mankind"[9] has been viewed in terms of preservation and protection; a view that, although adhering to the idea of a State's position of custodian, does not in fact challenge its property rights.[10] The Hague Convention for the Protection of Cultural Property in the Event of Armed Conflicts (1954)[11] declares in its Preamble that damage to cultural property belonging to any people whatsoever is "damage to the cultural heritage of all mankind, since each people makes its contribution to the culture of the world." In time of peace, the Convention for the Protection of the World Cultural and Natural Heritage (1972)[12] recognises the duty of the international community as a whole to co-operate in the conservation of a heritage which is of outstanding universal value. However, the duty of ensuring its protection lies primarily with the State in whose territory it is situated.[13] In this context, national cultural heritage is not diminished and a State is considered to be responsible for the protection of property situated on its territory for the common good.[14] There is, however, a more radical approach which calls for the establishment of a *distinct* international cultural heritage, a new sort of property, administered by an international agency, and made available to all persons to enjoy.[15] This notion is open to objection on the grounds that the cultural heritage is always associated with a given people - the people who created it - and it is not possible to consider it outside this context. Cultural property is the product of given socio-economic and political processes and should, therefore, be considered in terms of social realisations rather than aesthetic appreciations. Historically and socially it is related to a particular human group, whether this is a whole nation or a minority group within it. Cultural property has cultural and spiritual importance for the people who created it which is quite distinct from its value as antiquities or works of art.[16] The idea of a distinct international cultural heritage does not appear to take into account the socio-economic basis of national heritage and, to a certain extent, devalues it by considering it as having the same cultural, historical and spiritual importance to all peoples, irrespective of origin.[17] Nowadays, where technology and mass communication means tend to create an "international" culture, it is of primary importance to identify "national" cultural heritage. "The co-existence of separate cultures is inevitable and it is precisely this co-existence of the various cultures which can furnish the substructure of a universal culture."[18] All peoples have a cultural heritage that is worthy of safeguarding in its own right, and if of exceptional interest it should be preserved as a component of the world heritage.[19]

The concept of "regional" cultural heritage, such as "Latin-American" or "European" cultural heritage, should also be viewed in terms of the intimate cultural and historical links between countries of a particular geographical area and the need for greater unity between them. The Council of Europe, however, has elaborated the concept of "European cultural heritage" in a more concrete form. Resolution 808 (1983) of the Parliamentary Assembly on the Return of Works of Art distinguishes claims for the return of cultural property within the European cultural area from claims for the return of property outside this area, and asks "member governments to co-operate fully on a bilateral basis, and where appropriate through the mechanisms provided by UNESCO, for the return of certain cultural property to countries *outside* the European area" (emphasis added).[20] In other words, the notion of a European cultural heritage belonging to all Europeans has been used as a basis to prevent the return of cultural property to European States.[21]

The Treaty on European Union adds a seperate title on culture (Title IX, to the Treaty establishing the European Economic Community ("EEC Treaty", now called "European Community (EC) Treaty"), which consists solely of article 128. Article 128(1) reads: "The Community shall contribute to the flowering of the cultures of the Member States, while respecting their national and regional diversity and at the same time bringing the common cultural heritage to the fore". Under para. 2, "action by the Community shall be aimed at encouraging cooperation between Member States and, if necessary, supporting or supplementing their action in the following fields, including the conservation and safeguarding of cultural heritage of *European significance*" (emphasis added). However, the promotion of European culture has not been included in the list of objectives of the refurbished article 2 of the EC Treaty.[22] Article 128 allows for the development of a European cultural policy, while leaving ample room for the Member States to pursue policies aimed at the preservation of their national cultures.[23]

The concept of the underwater cultural heritage

The concept of the underwater cultural heritage refers to that part of the cultural heritage which is found underwater. The term "underwater" should be understood in its widest sense so as to apply to both seas and inland waterways. The concept of the "underwater cultural heritage" first appeared in Recommendation 848 (1978) of the Council of Europe[24] and was further elaborated by the Draft European Convention on the Protection of the Underwater Cultural Heritage (1985). For the purposes of the Draft Convention, "all remains and objects and any other traces of human existence located entirely or in part in the sea, lakes, rivers, canals, artificial reservoirs or other bodies of water, or recovered from any such environment, or washed ashore, shall be considered as being part of the underwater cultural heritage, and are hereinafter referred to as 'underwater cultural property'".[25] The UN Convention on the Law of the Sea (1982) employs the term "objects of an archaeological and historical nature found at sea" in order to describe the cultural property to be protected. Since this formula is not defined, it is very difficult to identify the items that fall within its scope. An interpretation of these terms is attempted in Chapter 5.

The underwater cultural heritage as a common heritage of mankind

In a formal submission of the Council of Nautical Archaeology to the Committee on Culture and Education of the Council of Europe (dated December 1977) it was stated that: "The human heritage in extraterritorial waters is, if anything, more of a common heritage than the land archaeological heritage or that in territorial waters."[26] This raises the question whether a more concrete concept of the common heritage of mankind should be applied to cultural property found in marine spaces beyond the limits of national jurisdiction than that applied to cultural property found on land. While it is not desirable to have two different concepts of cultural heritage, with respect to underwater remains due consideration must be given to the following factors

a. A vast area of the oceans is not subjected to national jurisdiction. As a result, a considerable number of underwater sites are located beyond State jurisdiction and control, while archaeological sites on land are always found within national boundaries.
b. Even within marine spaces that fall under national jurisdiction, the location of underwater sites - the majority being shipwrecks - is accidental.
c. International nature of seafaring: seafaring involves economic and operational links between different countries. A sunken wreck may, thus, be of importance to the State of origin of the ship, the State of origin of the cargo (if different), the coastal State on whose continental shelf the ship was found, and, possibly, to other third States that were involved in the trade in question.

Under these circumstances, which State(s) should be recognised as competent to deal with cultural property found in extraterritorial waters[27] and on what legal basis? Setting up an international or a regional organ to exercise effective supervision over cultural property found in international waters would be essential if any protection measures were to be agreed upon and enforced. The same idea underpins the proposal that the Mediterranean be declared a "sea of human civilisation". As explained, the purpose of this proclamation would be "to enable effective supervision to be exercised over all matters concerning the underwater heritage of the Mediterranean found outside the territorial waters of the coastal States".[28] However, the location of cultural property in marine spaces beyond the limits of national jurisdiction should not be allowed to obscure the fact that the latter originates from a specific country and may be of particular significance to its history and the cultural identity of the people who created it. It is, therefore, important to emphasise the understanding of the notion of the common heritage of mankind in terms of preservation and protection, as there is room for confusion.

In conclusion, the application of the concept of the common heritage of mankind in the field of underwater cultural property differs from its application to land antiquities as regards the machinery and nature of protection. A distinction should, however, be made between cultural property found landward and seaward of the territorial sea boundary. Sites found within the territorial sea may be protected as part of the world heritage under the terms of the 1972 Convention, provided that they are of outstanding value. Given the territorial scope of application of this Convention[29], the protected cultural heritage is confined to sites within national territories. Sites found seaward of the territorial sea boundary fall outside the ambit of the 1972 Convention and the notion of the world heritage contained therein. It is with respect to these sites that wider ranging protective measures need to be undertaken. At this stage, it is sufficient to note that the establishment of an international or a regional body to deal with cultural property in international waters should be accompanied by the recognition of the interests of the State(s) of origin in the discovered objects.

CLASSIFICATION OF UNDERWATER REMAINS

Two broad categories of underwater cultural property may be distinguished: shipwrecks and submerged settlements.[30] Geographical features of historical significance may also fall within the notion of the underwater cultural heritage. However, national heritage laws reveal a tendency to protect human remains only.[31]

Shipwrecks and isolated objects

Of all underwater archaeological sites, wrecks are the most important in terms of their numbers, volume and variety. There are great differences in the size and complexity of the vessels involved[32] as well as in the degree of destruction suffered. On the one hand, one finds vessels, such as the

Swedish warship of Wasa, which was raised substantially intact, while, on the other, there are wrecks of which very little survived.[33] The actual quality of the remains depends on a number of factors, in particular on the manner in which the vessel was wrecked and the nature of the seabed on which it landed. It is noteworthy that no intact vessels have yet been found in Norwegian waters because of the rocky seabed and the damaging effect of shipworms.[34] Most of the cargoes discovered are of *amphorae* used in the wine trade that was carried out for centuries in the Mediterranean. Cargoes have also come to light containing Bronze Age artefacts, works of art, architectural components, sarcophagi, millstones, tiles, crockery, marble blocks, iron bars, copper and lead ingots, as well as minerals.[35] It is not surprising, therefore, that the classical image of shipwreck archaeology is based on the *amphora* wrecks of the Mediterranean and the Spanish wrecks of the Armada of 1588, that is on wrecks of great classical or historical antiquity and of limited scale. However, shipwreck archaeology is not confined to the ancient past. It has a wider scope which includes wrecks of all kinds - ancient and modern, prehistoric and historic, European-derived and non-Western.[36] Underwater sites of cultural importance are scattered all around the world. The main areas are obviously those areas which had been busy traffic areas in the past, such as the Mediterranean,[37] the Baltic Sea, the coasts of America (shipwrecks in the wake of Columbus) and the Caribbean Sea. Shipwrecks of great significance have also been located in Mombasa,[38] off the Western Australian coasts[39] and on the south-western coast of the Republic of Korea.[40]

Wrecks are not only found at sea; archaeological traces of commercial seafaring or sea battles are also left on the beds of rivers. The potential of *riverine archaeology* is great as in the past rivers constituted one of the most important forms of communication between different communities.[41] Isolated objects found in the water should be considered too. A number of these objects were intentionally cast into the water as part of ritual sacrifices, while others were lost from ships at anchor or at sea.[42]

Submerged sites

In the distant past many places that are now part of the oceans were dry land. Scientists believe that even 8000 years ago the coastlines lay at around the present 30.5 metre (100 ft) contour below sea level.[43] "During the Ice Age, when the sea level was much lower than it is now, early man undoubtedly migrated between land masses by walking across land bridges. Travel by sea came later."[44] Many caves and stone huts of late Ice-Age man are now deep under the water.[45] The main causes of submergence were land subsidence, rise of water level or a combination of both. Low-lying ancient cities and their associated harbour works, particularly in the Mediterranean, have been especially vulnerable to subsidence.[46] However, the gradual inundation of land sites has not always been the case. Some cities have become submerged as a result of earthquakes, such as the earthquake at Port Royal (Jamaica) in 1962, which resulted in the sinking into the sea of 90 per cent of the town.[47]

Submerged sites are also found in lakes. Some of them originate from habitation sites on low ground beside the lakes, while others from habitations built on islands in the middle of the lakes, inundated and subsequently preserved by silt.[48] Finally, one should consider underwater shrines[49] and the "cenotes", the sacred wells found in the Maya country on the Yucatan peninsula.[50]

SIGNIFICANCE OF THE UNDERWATER CULTURAL HERITAGE

Archaeological and historical value

The underwater cultural heritage is an essential source of non-documentary evidence of social and economic history. Besides distributing foods and other materials, boats (and later ships) have helped disseminate ideas and spread discoveries from place to place, while submerged prehistoric sites provide useful information about our ancestors.[51] The development of boats as a form of transport has been described "as notable an evolutionary advance as man's control over fire". In effect they formed the "leading edge" of the technologies of most pre-industrial societies from the Mesolithic (Middle Stone Age) period onward.[52] Boats and ships are "microcosms" of the technologies that created them and of the societies that used them.[53] Ship-wrecks are often described as "time capsules"[54] since the ship is sealed at the time of wreck and becomes a "closed deposit", if no later disturbance has taken place.[55] Each shipwreck presents the archaeologist with a wide range of evidence concerning:

a. The original vessel and her equipment: The hulls of the ships reveal the state of the art of naval architecture and shipbuilding.[56] However, some commentators have objected to the deduction of "overall traditions of naval architecture from wreck-site evidence." They argue that wrecked ships are unlikely to be typical of their time and place; for instance the Wasa might have sunk and, therefore, survived because she had a design fault.[57]

b. The ship's ancillary fittings and equipment, such as the remains of propulsion, anchors, rigging and steering arrangements.[58]

c. The vessel's original purpose: cargo in a merchant ship, armaments in a warship, and specialised gear if the ship was designed for a specialised purpose such as fishing.[59]

d. The society on board: utensils required for living, weapons and working tools, as well as the personal possessions of the passengers and the crew and the furnishings of the ship itself provide useful information about the everyday life of a past civilisation.[60] For example, the cargo of an exploratory or colonising vessel could clearly indicate the priorities that the parent culture "saw" in its overseas involvements, as all goods on board intended for use at the target destination must have been chosen selectively due to constraints of space.[61]

However, shipwrecks are not only individual sources of social, economic and technological information; seafaring involves economic and operational links between countries and regions in which ships themselves form only an element.[62] They should, therefore, be considered in the context of the greater system at large, which involved docking and harbour facilities, building and repair yards, warehouses, markets and port cities.[63] The potential contribution of shipwrecks to the study of human behaviour will be limited so long as research formulated to answer broader questions is not initiated.[64] Shipwrecks present an extraordinary data base which should be recognised and investigated by "anthropologically oriented archaeologists."[65]

Artistic value

The artistic value of objects recovered from the seabed is often great. The *Youth from Antikythera*, the two bronze statues found off Riace in Calabria, the *Zeus* from Cape Artemission and, finally, the bronze statue of a young athlete, the first discovery of an original by Lysippos, off Fano on the

Adriatic coast, are amongst the most famous finds.[66] Since most distance travel was made over water and looting/trading were integral parts of exploration/colonisation, it is very likely that art treasures rest on the sea floor. For example, most of the statues mentioned were part of the cargo of ships containing collections of works of art, usually as loot.[67]

Specific cultural value

Underwater remains have special cultural value for the people who created them and may even be essential to the affirmation of the cultural identity of a specific nation. In particular, one should consider the historical and national importance of warships lost in naval battles, the so-called war-graves.[68] The spiritual/religious significance of individual items found underwater should also be taken into account. As noted, a small group of artefacts found at sea or on the seabed of rivers and lakes were intentionally cast into the water as part of a ritual.

Educational benefits

The educational benefits to be derived from the safeguarding of the underwater cultural heritage are significant not only for archaeologists, historians and other scientists of related fields, but also for the public at large, including future generations.

Commercial value

The underwater cultural heritage should primarily be viewed in terms of cultural and historical importance. However, its pecuniary aspect should not be neglected:

Exchange value (intrinsic economic worth).[69] The huge profits made from the salvage of some historic wrecks combined with the publicity given by the media has resulted in an unprecedented "underwater goldrush".[70] Despite the fact that not all shipwrecks contain marketable treasures, "the popular myth" drives modern treasure-hunters and their investors forward.[71] It would be true to say that, considering archaeologically rich countries, the majority of the accessible underwater sites have already been looted.[72]

Potential benefits from tourism (extrinsic economic worth). Underwater finds, whether preserved *in situ* or in a museum's collection, attract tourists and visitors and thus contribute economically to the State's budget. It has, therefore, been suggested that the best way to attract political attention to the fate of the cultural heritage is to emphasise its importance for tourists.[73]

THE UNDERWATER CULTURAL HERITAGE AS A CULTURAL RESOURCE OF THE OCEANS

If resource means "a means of supplying some want or deficiency; a stock or reserve upon which one can draw when necessary",[74] then the underwater cultural heritage could be characterised as a *sui generis* resource or as a "cultural resource", which derives its transcendent value as a repository of cultural information.[75] It is, obviously, different from a natural resource, which may be defined as "any material in its native state which, when extracted, has economic value."[76] Nevertheless, since underwater cultural property is located on and under the seafloor, there have been attempts to interpret it as a non-living natural resource and, thus, subject it to either the continental shelf regime and the exclusive competence of the coastal State or the international deep seabed regime (Area). The interpretation of cultural property as a natural resource of the seabed is fundamental from a jurisdictional point of view. However, this issue can only be dealt with within each specific regime and its rules. As will be seen in Part Two, cultural property does not qualify as a natural resource of the seabed, whether it is found within or beyond the limits of national jurisdiction. Its main features are:

Accidental location of underwater remains. With the exception of fixed remains, the *location* of archaeological material on a specific part of the seabed is accidental. Underwater cultural resources do not constitute an organic part of the seabed, nor is their value estimated in terms of exploitation and contribution to the economic development of a nation. This consideration may be of importance to the legitimisation of coastal claims over archaeological remains found on the continental shelf and/or the recognition of the rightful interests of the State of origin.

The underwater heritage is a non-renewable resource. Underwater cultural property is an irreplacable, non-renewable resource, which provides essential non-documentary information about past societies and seafaring that goes well beyond the parameter of each individual case. Once destroyed, the invaluable information it carries, sometimes throughout centuries, is lost for ever. The recent development of advanced underwater technology has escalated the devastation of sites by souvenir collectors, treasure hunters and salvage companies. In addition, many underwater sites of archaeological significance are being ruined by dredging and landfill operations as well as by trawlers, fishing nets and deep seabed operators. Indiferrence has also resulted in the loss of valuable information.[77]

Claims related to underwater cultural property. Submerged remains once *had an owner.* As a result, issues such as succession in ownership, salvage remuneration claims and claims of insurance companies (in the case of relatively recent wrecks) may arise. For a wrecked vessel to be considered *res derelictae* so that ownership can be acquired by possession by a finder/salvor, an effective act of abandonment by the original owner must be proven.[78] The requirements of abandonment differ between jurisdictions, although abandonment is very difficult to prove in both common and civil law systems if the wreck has not been expressly abandoned by the owner or his successors. If the relic is found in marine spaces, which fall under coastal sovereignty, the sovereign State may claim ownership on the basis of its legislation.

The *State(s) of origin* may also enter the dispute and claim the recovered cultural property as part of its national cultural heritage. Since every State is entitled to undertake archaeological research in international waters, the likelihood of underwater cultural property being found by or coming into the possesion of a State other than the State(s) of origin is vastly increased. Would third States be under an obligation to return recovered items to the identifiable State of origin? Claims made by the latter should be distinguished from the proprietary rights of the identifiable owner(s), as they cannot be justified as a property right, but rather as an expression of the right of a State to its cultural heritage.

CONFLICTING INTERESTS IN THE PROTECTION OF THE UNDERWATER CULTURAL HERITAGE

The identification of the different interests involved in the preservation of underwater cultural heritage is essential as the formulation of national cultural policies, which in turn dictate the international legal position of States on cultural matters, is largely determined by those interests.

At national level, the main interest groups are the identifiable owners, archaeologists, commercial salvors, hobby-divers, collectors, auctioneers and the State, which represents the common interest.[79] The exploitation of submerged cultural resources by private companies and individuals for personal financial benefit is opposed by the preservationist community, which argues that underwater cultural property should be placed under the control of a more protective agency.[80] The cultural heritage is an eminently public resource; it reveals shared values and "bears witness to the history of a culture and of a nation whose spirit it perpetuates and renews."[81] It should, therefore, be preserved for the benefit of people at large. In systems, where there is a strong tradition of private ownership, the State will be more reluctant to intervene and deprive the *identifiable owners* of their title or to exclude the salvaging of underwater cultural property from the private sector. Heritage laws, especially the ones that invest ownership of underwater relics to the State, pose legal and philosophical problems as to the *rationale* behind the public policy to exclude individuals from the sphere of salvaging archaeological objects or even to divest them of ownership. The issue goes to the heart of property acquisition theory and the relationship between government and the individual.[82] Treasure seekers and sport divers naturally favour free access to shipwrecks. The pecuniary interests of *salvors* are best satisfied by the swift recovery of spectacular objects, while the sport divers' desire for unrestricted access to shipwrecks for recreational purposes, conflicts both with the salvor's interest for exclusive use of the wreck and the archaeologists' concern for ordered collection. Finally, *auctioneers and collectors* are simply interested in the acquisition of "sunken treasures", irrespective of the manner in which they have been acquired, and despite the dispersal of unique archaeological collections. The hearings in the U.S. Congress on the passage of legislation to protect historic shipwrecks, now the Abandoned Shipwrecks Act of 1987 (ASA), are illustrative of the conflicting interests in the preservation of the underwater cultural heritage.[83]

At international level, the main interests involved are those of the *flag State* of the wreck, the *coastal State* on whose continental shelf the relics lie, the *flag State* of the vessel, which undertakes research or recovery operations, the *State of origin*, if different from the coastal or flag State and, finally, the *international community*, which has recently shown an increased interest in the preservation of the underwater cultural heritage. One should also consider the conflict between *art-exporting* and *art-importing* States, which has dominated the field of cultural heritage law during the last years. The strong influence of art-importing countries is one of the main reasons for the failure to adopt drastic and efficient measures against the illicit international trade in artefacts. With respect to underwater cultural property, this conflict acquires a different character as a considerable number of archaeological sites lie in international waters, beyond national jurisdiction. If States are unable to enforce their heritage laws in their territories and prevent the export or import of protected cultural property on land, it is very unlikely that they would be able to control the activities of their nationals at sea.

NOTES

1   For a discussion of terminology, see Merryman, J.H., "Protection of Cultural "Heritage"?", 38 *American Journal of Comparative Law* (1990) pp. 513-522; O' Keefe, P.J. and Prott, L.V., "Cultural Property", 9 *E.P.I.L.* (1986) pp. 62-64, and Prott, L.V. and O'Keefe, P.J., "Cultural Heritage" or "Cultural Property"?", 2 *International Journal of Cultural Property* (1992) pp. 307-320; The denotation of "property" has been challenged by those who feel that it is not sufficiently broad to encompass the range of items for which protection is sought, such as folklore. "Heritage" has been suggested as an alternative term, which has the further advantage of not carrying along with it either civil or common law legacies of property values and most importantly, it incorporates concepts of duty to preserve and protect.

2   There are two main approaches in defining the cultural property that is to be protected: a broad definition would include all objects of cultural value (maximalist solution), while a selective definition includes objects that are of outstanding value or of real importance for the respective countries or the international community (minimalist solution). Dicke, D.C., "The Instruments and the Agencies of the International Protection of Cultural Property" in Council of Europe, *International Legal Protection of Cultural Property, Proceedings of the Thirteenth Colloquy on European Law*, Delphi, 20-22 September 1983, Strasbourg 1984, pp. 17-43 at pp. 19-20. See further N'Daw, A. et al., "Towards a definition of culture - Discussion" in UNESCO, *Cultural rights as human rights,* Studies and documents on cultural policies, 1970, pp. 15-23; Fraoua, R., *Le traffic illicit des biens culturels et leur restitution: Analyse des réglementations nationals et internationals critiques et propositions,* Travaux de la Faculté de Droit de l'Université de Fribourg, Suisse, 68, Editions Universitaires Fribourg Suisse, 1986, at pp. 5-33; Prott, L.V., "Problems of private international law for the protection of the cultural heritage", *Hague Recueil* (1989-V) pp. 215-317; ID, "The definition of the archaeological heritage". Paper presented at the *Athens*

Conference on the Protection of the Archaeological Heritage, organised by the Institute of Hellenic Constitutional History and Constitutional Law, November 26-27, 1992; Prott, L.V. and O'Keefe, P.J., *Law and the Cultural Heritage*, vol. 3, *Movement*, Butterworths, 1989 at pp. 26-36 and Reichelt, G., "International protection of cultural property (second study)" *Uniform Law Review* (1988-I) pp. 53-131 at pp. 83-91.

3   Clarke, D.L., *Analytical Archaeology*, Methuen, London, 1968 at p. 20. See also Muckelroy, K. (ed.), *Archaeology under Water: An Atlas of the World's Submerged Sites*, McGraw-Hill Book Company, New York, London 1980 at p. 7, who describes artefacts as tangible forms of archaeological information.

4   *Ibid* at p. 19.

5   See also Prott, L.V. and O'Keefe, P.J., *Law and the Cultural Heritage*, vol. 1, *Discovery and Excavation*, Professional Books Ltd., Abingdon, 1984 at p. 10.

6   Notable exceptions are the Republic of Korea's Cultural Properties Protection Act wholly amended by Law No. 3644 of 31 December 1982, and the Japanese Law No. 214 for the Protection of Cultural Properties of 30 May, 1950, amended on July 1975, which distinguish between "tangible" and "intangible" cultural property. UNESCO, *The Protection of Movable Cultural Property, Collection of Legislative Texts, Republic of Korea*, 1985, CLT-85/WS 37, and ID, *The Protection of Movable Cultural Property: Compendium of Legislative Texts*, vol. ii, 1984, pp. 112-148 (Japan). See also the UNESCO Recommendation on the safeguarding of the traditional culture and folklore (1989).

7   Mshvenieradze, V., "Cultural interaction as a factor influencing cultural rights as human rights", UNESCO, *op. cit.* note 2, pp. 42-45 at p. 44.

8   Declaration of the Principles of International Cultural Co-operation, adopted at the fourteenth session of the General Conference, 4 November 1966. Text reprinted in UNESCO, *ibid*, pp. 123-125.

9   On the application of the concept of the common heritage of mankind in the cultural field see Fraoua, *op.cit.* note 2, pp. 163-166; Kiss, A-Ch., "La notion de patrimoine commune de l'humanité", 175 *Hague Recueil* (1982-II), pp. 99-256; Nahlik, S.E., "L'intérêt de l'humanité à protéger son patrimoine culturel", 37/38 *Annuaire de l' AAA* (1967/68) pp. 156-165; Stocker, W., *Das Prinzip des "Common Heritage of Mankind" als Ausdruck des Staatengemeinschaftsinteresses im Völkerrecht,* Schweizer Studien zum Internazionalen Recht, Band 81, Schulthess Polygraphischer Verlag, Zürich, 1993; Williams, S.A., *The International and National Protection of Movable Cultural Property: A Comparative Survey*, Oceana Publications Inc., Dobbs Ferry, New York, 1978, pp. 52-63; Wyss, M.Ph., *Kultur als eine Dimension der Völkerrechtsordnung*, Schweizer Studien zum Internazionalen Recht, Band 79, Schulthess Polygraphischer Verlag, Zürich, 1992.

10   Williams, *ibid* at p. 55.

11   294 *U.N.T.S.* 215.

12   11 *ILM* (1972) at p. 1358.

13   Article 4.

14 Williams, *op. cit.* note 9 at p. 57. See also the UNESCO Recommendation for the Protection of Movable Cultural Property (1978), adopted by the General Conference at its twentieth session, Paris, 28 November 1978, which declares in its Preamble that "movable cultural property representing the different cultures forms part of the common heritage and that every State is therefore morally responsible to the international community as a whole for its safeguarding". The text of the Recommendation is reprinted in UNESCO, *Conventions and Recommendations of UNESCO concerning the protection of the cultural heritage*, 1985 at pp. 211-223.

15 Williams, *ibid* at pp. 201-202. See also ID, "Recent Developments in Restitution and Return of Cultural Property", 3 *International Journal of Museum Management and Curatorship* (1984) pp. 117-129 at pp. 117-118; "Protecting the archaeological heritage: can the "new world order" protect the old?". Paper presented at the *Athens Conference on the Protection of the Archaeological Heritage*, November 26-27, 1992 at p. 5.

16 See also Philippaki, B., "Greece", 31 *Museum* (1979) pp. 15-17 at p. 15: "Objects of cultural property are the *species differentiae*, the elements that distinguish one nation from another. They are products of experience lost over the centuries, of unique biological mixtures, as well as ways of life created under distinctive geographic, climatological, social, religious and political conditions and, therefore, they belong to the people who created them and who now claim them as a right, no matter if they are more or less of interest to humanity as a whole".

17 According to Williams, *op. cit.* note 15 at p. 117: "Should cultural property be seen in transcending normal conceptions of ownership and, being a medium for all nations equally, would not questions of restitution and return recede in importance so long as the property remains in the public domain, perhaps supervised by an international body set up for the purpose?" In her opinion, however, this type of international collaboration would not be an impediment on the cultural identity of States as it would in effect improve the means of disseminating the expression of the populations of States. Prof. Koumantos wonders whether it would be advisable to institute a sort of third degree of ownership of cultural property which would belong to the international community: "Why should we not establish an obligation on States to preserve the cultural property belonging to them and, possibly, to ask for the assistance of the regional or international community to that end? Would this be an admission that even States are only the custodians of the cultural property on their territory and are second degee owners in regard to such property? Must we institute a sort of third degree of ownership of cultural property which would belong to the international community? I think that this is an idea .... which might provide food for thought in the future." Koumantos, G., "International Legal Protection of Cultural Property: Introductory Report" in Council of Europe, *International Legal Protection of Cultural Property, op. cit.* note 2, pp. 12-16 at p. 14. In his opinion, the concept of "second degree ownership" (property belonging to the nation or the people) is needed to explain some legal phenomena concerning the protection of cultural property, even though it does not satisfy the dogmatic

requirements of a concept worked out with a view to civil law on ownership. *Ibid* at p. 12. One may, therefore, distinguish between three degrees of ownership: (a) civil ownership, (b) "second degree ownership" by the nation or people and (c) "third degree ownership" by the international community. It should be noted, however, that the proposed "third degree ownership" does not necessarily coincide with the aforementioned notion of a distinct international cultural heritage. Prof. Koumantos is primarily concerned with the possibility of intervention to prevent destruction "which would reduce the common cultural heritage of the whole human race". See also Kiss, who argues that "the very nature of common heritage seems to imply a form of trust: the trustee may be the international community through the intermediary of an international organ or one of several States which have agreed to act on the community's behalf. The selection of the best solution is a matter of policy". Kiss, A-Ch., "The common heritage of mankind", 59 *Revista Juridica de la Universidad de Puerto Rico* (1990) pp. 773-777. A similar approach is adopted by Fraoua, *op. cit.* note 2.

On the two competing theories of "cultural nationalism" and "cultural internationalism" ("common heritage of mankind") see Bator, P.M., "An essay on the international trade in art", 34 *Stanford L. Rev.* (1982) pp. 275-384; Merryman, J.H., "The protection of partimony" in Duboff, L.D. (ed), *Art Law: Domestic and International*, F.B. Rothman & Co, 1975, pp. 255-261; ID, "International art law: from cultural nationalism to a common cultural heritage", 15 *N.Y.U.J. Int'l L. & Pol.* (1983) pp. 771-787; ID, "The retention of cultural property", 21 *University of California Davis Law Review* (1988) pp. 477-513; ID, "The public interest in cultural policy", 77 *California Law Review* (1989) pp. 339-364; Merryman, J.H. and Elsen, A.E., "Hot art: a re-examination of the illegal international trade in cultural objects", 12(3) *J. Arts. Mgmt. & L.* (1982) pp. 5-31; Monden, A. & Wils, G., "Art objects as common heritage of mankind", XIX *Revue belge de droit international* (1986) pp. 327-338; Moustakas, J., "Group rights in cultural property: justifying strict inalienability", 74 *Cornell Law Review* (1989) pp. 1179-1227; Nafziger, J.A.R., "Comments on the relevance of law and culture to cultural property law", 10 *Syracuse J. Int'l L. & Com.* (1983) pp. 323-331; Prott and O'Keefe, *op. cit.* note 2, at p. 838 *et seq.*; Thomason, D.N.,"Rolling back history: The United Nations General Assembly and the right to cultural property", 22 *Case W. Res. J. Int'l L.* (1990) pp. 47-96; Warren, K.J., "A philosophical perspective on the ethics and resolution of cultural properties issues" in Messenger, Ph. M. (ed), *The Ethics of Collecting Cultural Property: Whose Culture, Whose Property?*, Albuquerque, 1990, pp. 1-25; Williams, *ibid.* The question of restitution is central in this debate. It is, therefore, important that the most recent UN GA Resolutions on the Restitution or Return of Cultural Property to the Countries of Origin refer to "representative collections" that each State should have of its cultural heritage. The idea of "representative" collections was mentioned for the first time in the 1979 Resolution: "Aware of the importance attached by the countries of origin to the return of cultural property which is of fundamental spiritual and cultural value to them, so that they may constitute collections *representative* of their cultural heritage". As argued: "The history of General Assembly Resolutions reflects the tension between the doctrines of the common heritage of mankind and national patrimony. The earlier resolutions were almost entirely driven by a belief in national patrimony. In the ensuing resolutions there is a constant movement towards principles allied with a common heritage perspective. The calls for the creation of museum infrastructures in the Third World, the acceptance of the principle of "representative collections", the endorsement of bilateral long-term exchanges, all represent a fusion of the once divergent principles of common heritage and national patrimony". Thomason, *ibid* at p. 95.

18   N'Daw, *op. cit.* note 2 at p. 19.

19   In this respect see the 1972 World Heritage Convention, *op. cit.* note 12. See also Fraoua, *op. cit.* note 2 at pp. 164-166, who is in favour of the integration of the notion of the "benefit of mankind as a whole" ("intérêt de l'humanité tout entière") into positive international law. In his opinion, the notion of common cultural heritage should encompass only cultural property of universal value, while the State in whose territory the property is situated should be considered as "trustee" ("dépositaire") of the cultural heritage of humanity.

20   Resolution 808 of 3 October 1983, paras. 9 and 11 in Council of Europe, *Texts Adopted by the Assembly*, Thirty-fifth Ordinary Session (Second Part), 26 September-6 October 1983, Strasbourg, 1983.

21   See further "Report on the return of works of art" (Rapporteur Mr. Tummers), Doc. 5111, 15 September 1983 in Council of Europe, Parliamentary Assembly, *Documents-Working Papers,* vol. III, Thirty-fifth Ordinary Session (Second Part) 26 September-6 October 1983, and the joint debate on this report and the report on the movement of art objects, 19th Sitting, 3 October 1983 in Council of Europe, Parliamentary Assembly, *Official Report of Debates,* Vol. II, Thirty-fifth Ordinary Session (Second Part), 29 September-6 October 1983, Strasbourg, 1984, pp. 537-547. One of the reasons for the refusal to accept the Greek claim for the return of the Parthenon Marbles (also known as the "Elgin Marbles"), presently held in the British Museum, was the fact that "this request by Greece would appear to overlook the extent to which ancient Greece forms part of the common basis and therefore heritage of European civilisation. Modern Greece should feel the force of this argument and realise that it is itself *no more and no less* than most of Europe the descendant of civilisations based geographically in Greece, Italy and the Near East" (emphasis added). *Ibid* (Report) at p. 9.

22   See also article 3: "For the purposes set out in Article 2, the activities of the Community shall include, as provided in this Treaty and in accordance with the timetable set out therein: (p) a contribution to education and training of quality and to the flowering of the cultures of the Member States". It is notable that the Commission in its Communication to the Council on the Protection of National Treasures Possessing Artistic, Historic or Archaeological Value stated that "the ideal solution [for the Community's cultural policy] would be to develop the idea of a common European heritage". *Communication from the Commission to the Council on the Protection of National Treasures Possessing Artistic, Historic or Archaeological Value: Needs Arising from the Abolition*

of Frontiers in 1992, COM (89)594 final at p. 1. For a discussion see, *inter alia,* Loman, J.M.E., Mortelmans, K.L.M., Post, H.H.G., Watson, J.S., *Culture and Community Law. Before and After Maastricht,* Kluwer Law and Taxation Publishers, 1992; Post, H.H.G., "The protection of archaeological property and community law: framework and new developments". Paper presented at the *Athens Conference on the Protection of the Archaeological Heritage,* organised by the Institute of Hellenic Constitutional History and Constitutional Law, November 26-27, 1992; Roberts, E.L., "Cultural policy in the European Community: a case against extensive national retention", 28 *Texas Int'l L. J.* (1993) pp. 191-228; Shackelton, M., "The European Community between three ways of life: a cultural analysis", XXIX *Journal of Common Market Studies* (1991) pp. 575-601; Smith, A., "National identity and the idea of European unity", 68 *International Affairs* (1992) pp. 55-76, and Wyss, *op. cit.* note 9 at pp. 60-67. See also Oreja, M., "European cultural identity and protection of the European cultural heritage", XXXIV *European Yearbook,* (1986) pp. 1-11.

23   Even after 1992 and the establishment of the internal market, the Member States retain the right to define their national treasures and to take the necessary measures to protect them within the limits of article 36 of the EEC Treaty. The latter justifies prohibitions or restrictions on the free movement of goods, *inter alia,* for "the protection of national treasures possessing artistic, historic or archaeological value"; such derogating national measures must not constitute a means of arbitrary discrimination or a disguised restriction on trade. However, the Member States are no longer able to carry out their customs controls and formalities at the Community's internal frontiers. The return of cultural objects unlawfully removed from the territory of a Member State is regulated by Directive 93/7/, *OJ L* 74 of 27.3.1993 at p. 74, which, however, has no retroactive effect; it applies exclusively to objects unlawfully removed from the territory of a Member State on or after the 1 January 1993 (article 13). Article 13 prevents the possibility of eventually applying the Directive to the case of the return of the Parthenon Marbles. For further discussion see *infra* chapter 3, p. 83. It is interesting to note that Roberts, *ibid,* at pp. 217-219 argues that the Directive shows disregard for the cultural heritage of mankind. In his opinion, it ignores both the interests involved in the formation of the Community's cultural policy, interests which extend beyond the borders of the internal market, and the existence of a universal patrimony. As a result, it threatens mankind's interest in the preservation of and access to Europe's cultural heritage.

24   Council of Europe, Parliamentary Assembly, *Texts Adopted by the Assembly,* sessions 30-32 (1978-81).

25   Article 1(1). Final Activity Report, *Ad Hoc* Committee of Experts on the Underwater Cultural Heritage (CAHAQ), *Doc. CAHAQ(85)5,* Council of Europe, Strasbourg, 23 April 1985. As explained by the Draft Explanatory Report: "The term "property" was chosen because it was more comprehensive then the term "object", which might be deemed to include only movable goods and not immovable property, such as sites and installations (e.g. a port). With regard to the latter two categories of underwater cultural property, it should be stated clearly that the expression "any other traces", appearing at the beggining of

paragraph 1, was intended to embrace in addition to those categories, geographical features of historical significance". Special mention should be made to the definition of "underwater cultural heritage" adopted by the ILA Draft Convention on the Protection of the Underwater Cultural Heritage. Article 1 reads: "Underwater cultural heritage means all underwater traces of human existence including: (a) sites, structures, buildings, artefacts and other human remains, together with their archaeological and natural contexts; and (b) wreck such as a vessel, aircraft, other vehicle or any part thereof, its cargo or other contents, together with its archaeological and natural context". See *infra* Appendix at p. 438.

26 Council of Europe, Parliamentary Assembly, *The Underwater Cultural Heritage*, Report of the Committee on Culture and Heritage (Rapporteur Mr John Roper), Doc.4200-E, Strasbourg, 1978, pp. 178-182 at p. 182.

27 By the late 1970s, coastal jurisdiction over underwater cultural property was recognised over the territorial sea but archaeological sites found seaward of the territorial sea limit remained unprotected. The 1982 Convention expands coastal jurisdiction to cover archaeological objects found within 24 miles from the coast, while a number of States have extended their competence over cultural property found on the continental shelf. See *infra* chapters 5 and 7.

28 The declaration of the Mediterranean as a "Sea of Human Civilisation" was proposed by Mr. Papathanasopoulos (Greece) in the course of the negotiations of the Council of Europe for the drafting of a European Convention on the underwater cultural heritage. See Council of Europe, *op. cit.* note 26, Appendix IV, Individual Submissions at p. 157. The proposal was incorporated in the Recommendations of the Final Report on the Legal Protection of the Underwater Cultural Heritage, *ibid* at p. 82.

29 See *infra* chapter 3 at p. 73.

30 The classification of underwater remains as "mobile" (ships) and "fixed" (towns, harbours, prehistoric sites) has been proposed by Muckelroy, in Muckelroy, K. (ed.), *Archaeology Under Water: An Atlas of the World's Submerged Sites*, McGraw-Hill, New York 1980. Despite the fact that this classification has been criticised by other scholars as over-simplified, it is useful for the purposes of this work as it corresponds to the legal distinction between "movable" and "immovable" cultural property. According to Watters, however: "Some authorities have linked the search for an all-encompassing term to the classic cases of comparing apples and oranges or forcing the square peg into the round hole .... This has the advantage of putting all apples together under "mobile" but leaves a wide variety of different oranges under "fixed"." Watters, D.R., "Terms and Concepts Related to Marine Archaeology", 28 *Oceanus,* No. 1, Spring 1985 pp. 13-17 at p. 17. Borhegyi differentiates between four types of underwater archaeological sites: (a) "refuse sites"; (b) "shrines" or sacred localities; (c) submerged or inundated settlements or human habitations; (d) shipwrecks, while Henderson categorises the main areas of archaeological study underwater as: submerged settlements, harbour works, refuse deposits and shipwrecks. See Borhegyi, S.F., "The Challenge, Nature and Limitations of Underwater Archaeology" in Holmquist, A.D. and Wheeler, A.H., *Diving into the Past: Theories, Techniques and Applications of Underwater Archaeology*, Minnesota

Historical Society and the Council of Underwater Archaeology, 1964, pp. 1-9 at p. 2 and Henderson, G., *Maritime Archaeology in Australia*, University of Western Australia Press, 1986 at pp. 10-15 respectively. Finally, the notion of the underwater cultural heritage as defined by the ILA Draft Convention, *op. cit.* note 25, includes wrecks of aircraft and other vehicles within the protected cultural property.

31 It is, therefore, important that the Draft European Convention (1985) enables the inclusion of geographical features of historical significance within the scope of protection. On the importance of "natural objects" to the cultural heritage and their protection see Prott and O'Keefe, *op. cit.* note 5 at pp. 157-158 and pp. 176-177.

32 Wrecks from the little 10m coaster to the great 36m Roman cargo boat have been discovered. The oldest dates back to 1200 B.C. and the Roman era, including the Byzantine Empire, are very well represented. Dumas, F., "Ancient wrecks" in UNESCO, *Underwater Archaeology: a nascent disipline*, Museums and Monuments XIII, Paris, 1972, pp. 27-34 at p. 28. One should specifically mention, the Late Bronze Age shipwreck at Kas, Turkey, dating to 1300 B.C. and the Early Bronze Age cargo wreck at Dhokos, Greece, which is the oldest wreck ever excavated, dating to 2150-2200 B.C.

33 Muckelroy, K., "Introduction" in Muckelroy (ed.), *op. cit.* note 30, pp. 6-11 at p. 7.

34 Molaug, S., "The Norwegian Maritime Museum organises underwater archaeology", 137 *Museum* (vol. XXXV, No. 1) 1983 pp. 57-61 at p. 60.

35 Dumas, *op. cit.* note 32 at p. 28.

36 Gould, R.A., "Looking Below the Surface: Shipwreck Archaeology as Anthropology" in Gould, R.A. (ed.), *Shipwreck Anthropology*, A School of American Research Book, University of New Mexico Press, Alburquerque, 1983, pp. 3-22 at p. 3.

37 The Center of Maritime Studies of Haifa, Israel, has undertaken an ambitious project off the coasts of Caesarea (*Caesarea Maritima*) which has revealed a number of significant underwater sites, such as sunken settlements, ship cargoes, ancient anchors and material of ancient shipping. There have been important excavations of Arab wrecks in the Red Sea, Phoenician cargoes of wine containers and clay figurines, hoards of bronze objects and helmets of Babylonian origin, Byzantine wrecks and more. Raban, A., "Archaeology in Israel", 28 *Oceanus,* No. 1, Spring 1985 pp. 59-64.

38 On the background of the Mombasa Wreck, see Piercy, R.C.M., "Mombasa Wreck Excavation", 137 *Museum* (vol. XXXV, No. 1) 1983.

39 A number of those wrecked vessels were part of a fleet of ships belonging to the Dutch East India Company Vereenigde Oostindische Compagnie (V.O.C.) which sailed from the Netherlands for the Indies in 1628. See further, Green, J.N., "The excavation and reconstruction of the Batavia, Western Australia", 137 *Museum* (vol. XXXV, No. 1) 1983 pp. 30-33; ID, *The loss of the Vereenigde Oostindische Compagnie Jacht Vergulde Draeck, Western Australia 1656,* BAR *Supplementary Series* 36, 1977; ID, *Australia's Oldest Wreck,* BAR *Supplementary Series* 27, 1977.

40 Ki-Woong, K., "The Shinan Shipwreck", 137 *Museum* (vol. XXXV, No. 1) 1983 pp. 35-37.

41 Martin, C., "Archaeology in an underwater environment" in UNESCO, *Protection of the underwater heritage*, Technical handbooks for museums and monuments 4, 1981, pp. 15-133 at p. 21. An illustrative example is provided by the York River Shipwreck Project 1978, which resulted in the location and study of eight shipwrecks associated with the British Fleet of Lord Cornwallis. Three of these shipwrecks were in excellent condition. See further Broadwater, J.D., "The York River Shipwreck Project: Results from the 1978 Survey" in Cockrell, W.A. (ed.), *In the Realms of Gold: the Proceedings of the Tenth Conference on Underwater Archaeology*, Fathom Eight, California, 1981, pp. 33-44 at p. 41.

42 Ruoff, U., "Archaeological discoveries in lakes and rivers", 137 *Museum* (vol. XXXV, No. 1) 1983, pp. 64-57 at p. 64.

43 Van Meurs, L. H., *Legal Aspects of Marine Archaeological Research*, Special Publication of the Institute of Marine Law, University of Cape Town, Publication no. 1, 1985 at p. 7.

44 Martin, C., Flemming, N., "Underwater Archaeologists" in Flemming, N. (ed.), *The Undersea*, Cassel & Company Ltd., London 1977 pp. 203-230 at p. 203.

45 In Gibraltar, there are partly submerged caves that were occupied from Neolithic to Roman times, while investigations along the Selsey peninsula in Sussex, United Kingdom, revealed submerged sites from prehistoric times to the present. *Ibid.* See also Taylor, J., Du Plat and others, "The Future" in Taylor, J. du Plat (ed.), *Marine Archaeology,* edited for CMAS, Hutchinson of London, 1965, pp. 190-201 at pp. 194-198. A fascinating array of artefacts from every age sine Neolithic times has also been discovered in Belgium in the underground caves of Han-sur-Lesse. See Prott, L.V. and O'Keefe, P.J., "International legal protection of the underwater cultural heritage", 14 *Revue belge de droit international* (1978-79), pp. 85-103 at p. 87, and Van Meurs, *op. cit.* note 43 at p. 7.

46 Martin, *op. cit.* note 41 at p. 21. Examples are *Cenchreae* in Saronicos Gulf and *Halieis* on the eastern coast of the Peloponese (Greece), the harbours of Tyros and Sidon, *Carthagena, Civitavecchia*, the port of Rome, the medieval city of Danwich, off the east coast of Britain and finally, coastal dwellings in the Black Sea. See Roucounas, E., "Cultural Treasures on the Seabed", 23 *Review of Public and Administrative Law* (1979) pp. 10-37 at p. 13 (in Greek), Bacon, R.C., "Underwater exploration at Dunwich, Suffolk", 3 *I.J.N.A.* (1974) pp. 314-318 and Blawatsky, V.D., "Submerged sectors of towns on the Black Sea coast" in UNESCO, *op. cit.* note 32, pp. 115-122.

47 Martin, *ibid* at p. 21. See further Aarons, A.C., "Port Royal, Jamaica: from cataclysm to renaissance", 138 *Museum* (vol. XXXV, No 2) 1983, pp. 114-118; Marx, R., "The submerged remains of Port Royal, Jamaica" in UNESCO, *op. cit.* note 32, pp. 139-145. *Appolonia* in the Greek island of Samos is also believed to have sunk as a result of an earthquake, while in *Pythagorio* the harbour works of Polykrates are only 10m below the surface of the sea, Roucounas, *ibid.* Finally, a number of ancient harbours situated at river mouths have become silted up so that their excavation by normal land methods is possible.

Two well-known examples are the Roman harbour built by Tiberius at *Ostia* at the mouth of the Tiber, and *Leptis Magna* in North Africa. See various authors, "Ports, Harbours and Other Submerged Sites" in Taylor (ed.), *op. cit.* note 45, pp. 160-189 at p. 160.

48   Martin, *op. cit.* note 41 at p. 21. The best known examples are in Switzerland, dating from the Neolithic period (c.30 B.C.) to the Early Iron Age (c.500 B.C.), in Scotland and in England (Flag Flen, Peterborough), where a Bronze Age lake village was discovered. Blackman, D.J., "Archaeological Aspects" in Council of Europe, *op. cit.* note 26 pp. 27-44 at p. 30. See further, Pryor, F., "Flag Fen", 96 *Current Archaeology*, April 1985, pp. 6-8.

49   Underwater shrines are found in Lake Chapala in Mexico, Dzibilchatum in Yucatan, Lake Amatitlan and Lake Detén Itzá in Guatemala, and Guatavita Lagoon in Colombia. See Borhegyi, *op. cit.* note 30 at p. 2.

50   The best known of which is Chichén-Itzá. Romero, P.B., "The sacred well of Chichén-Itzá and other freshwater sites in Mexico" in UNESCO, *op. cit.* note 32, pp. 147-151.

51   Given the fact that during the Ice Age man migrated between land masses by using "land bridges", then even the finding of one small site would provide valuable data about the first human occupation of the Americas. Roberts, M., "Comment II", 8 *JFA* (1981) pp. 233-235 at p. 233.

52   Martin and Flemming, *op. cit.* note 44 at p. 202. In any pre-industrial society, from the upper palaeolithic to the 19th century A.D., a boat (or later a ship) was the largest and most complex machine produced... Improvements in shipbuilding have also led to new inventions in other fields; there is a clear connection between 18th century advances in casting cannons for the Royal Navy and the development of efficient cylinders for steam engines. Muckelroy, *op. cit.* note 30 at pp. 3, 24-25.

53   Martin, *op. cit.* note 41 at p. 20. See also Murphy, L., "Shipwrecks as Data Base for Human Behavioural Studies" in Gould (ed.), *op. cit.* note 36, pp. 65-89 at p. 83: "While perhaps not correctly termed a microcosm, the ship does carry and represent aspects of the parent culture, which can produce analytically useful perspectives on social processes if the proper questions are posed during wreck excavation and analysis". Bascom argues that nearly any B.C. wreck will contain new information about the life and times when it sailed. Bascom, W., *Deep Water, Ancient Ships: the Treasure Vault of the Mediterranean,* David & Charles, Newton Abbott, 1976 at p. 7. Shipwrecks offer unique possibilities for historical studies as answers to questions in the narrow field of Greek prehistory alone should be startling. Bass, G.G., *Archaeology Under Water. Ancient Peoples and Places*, Daniel, D., general editor, Thames & Hudson, London, 1966 at p. 165.

54   Martin, *ibid* at p. 21. The concept of "time-capsule", however, must be used with caution as underwater sites are as liable to contamination by later activities as any site on land. See further Muckelroy, K., *Maritime Archaeology*, Cambridge University Press, 1978 at p. 56. "It should also be noted that the time capsule effect is dependent on the shipwreck site being well defined in

nature and on there being little chance of confusing later or earlier cultural activity with the wreck under study. Unfortunately, the real world does not always present such an ideal situation. There are many cases in the literature where shipwrecks have tended to cluster owing to a particular hazard that has been extant in the area for as long as there has been shipping (e.g., submerged reefs) or because there have been 'wrecking' activities traditionally carried out in the region." Lenihan, D.J., "Rethinking Shipwreck Archaeology: A History of Ideas and Considerations for New Directions" in Gould (ed.), *op. cit.* note 36, pp. 37-64.

55 Blackman, *op. cit.* note 48 at p. 31. See also Martin, *op. cit.* note 41 at p. 21: "The fact that all the objects which sink with a ship were in use up to the moment of disaster (though, some, of course, may have been older than others when they were lost) gives such a collection further archaeological value concerning dating objects also found on land." They can only be compared to landsites that were buried by a volcanic eruption, such as *Pompeii* or *Herculaneum.* Ropert, J., "Explanatory Memorandum" in Council of Europe, *op. cit.* note 26, pp. 1-26 at p. 6. According to Muckelroy: "The ship is the event by which a highly organised and dynamic assemblage of artefacts are transformed into a static and disorganised state with long-term stability". Muckelroy, *ibid,* at p. 157. Three are the main aspects of a ship: "(a) as a machine designed for harnessing a source of power in order to serve as a means of transport; (b) an element in a military or economic system, providing its basic *raison d'être*; (c) a closed community, with its own hierarchy, customs and conventions." *Ibid* at p. 216. It should be emphasised, however, that "the ship is not a totally closed community because it can be 'open' on both ends of a journey, during visits to numerous ports on a voyage, while in contact with other vessels at sea, and also by discarding material overboard. Normally aboard a vessel during a voyage there is little activity not directly related to ship operation and mission objective. The nature of activity aboard would vary according to the purpose of the voyage." See Murphy, *op. cit.* note 53 at p. 86.

56 Bascom, W., "Deepwater Archaeology", 174 *Science* (1971) pp. 261-269 at p. 262.

57 Muckelroy, *op. cit.* note 54 at p. 28.

58 Martin, *op. cit.* note 41 at p. 20.

59 *Ibid* at p. 20. See also Muckelroy, *op. cit.* note 54 at p. 28.

60 Bascom, *op. cit.* note 53 at p. 260.

61 Lenihan, *op.cit.* note 54 at p. 57.

62 Martin, *op. cit.* note 41 at p. 20. According to Leone, anthropologically useful questions about variability in human behaviour in relation to shipwrecks and remains connected with seafaring can be approached effectively on a regional basis. See Gould, *op. cit.* note 36 at pp. 12-13, and Leone, M.P., "Land and Water, Urban Life and Boats: Underwater Reconnaissance in Chesapeake Bay", in Gould (ed.), *ibid*, pp. 173-188.

63 Schmidt, P.R. and Mrozowski, S.A., "History, Smugglers, Change and Shipwrecks" in Gould (ed.), *ibid*, pp. 143-171 at p. 143. The primary aim should be "the pursuit of general principles which can be extended beyond the parame-

ters of a certain case study and which incorporate a concern for important historical problems". *Ibid* at p. 144.

64 Murphy, *op. cit.* note 53 at p. 88. "The practical limitations in our knowledge of the past are not inherent in the nature of the archaeological record; the limitations lie in our methodological naivete, in our lack of development for principles determining its relevance of archaeological remains to propositions regarding processes of events of the past." Binford, L.R., "Archaeological Perspectives" in Binford, L.R. (ed.), *An Archaeological Perspective*, New York, Seminar Press, 1972 at p. 76. Text cited in Murphy, *ibid* at p. 89.

65 Gould, *op. cit.* note 36 at p. 22.

66 See further Blackman, *op. cit.* note 48 at p. 32 and Roucounas, E., "Laws Protecting Underwater Finds", 8 *Archaeology* (1983) pp. 8-15 at pp. 8-11 (in Greek). On the history of the discovery of the bronze statue of the school of Lysippos, which ended up in the Paul Getty Museum in California, see Prott and O'Keefe, *op. cit.* note 45 at pp. 98-99.

67 Blackman, *ibid;* Kazazis, A. "Thefts, donations or sales?", 87 *UNESCO Courier*, September/October 1984 at p. 91. One should also consider the wreck of the Medina which sunk off Devon and contained a unique collection of oriental art. The latter belonged to Lord Carmichael, who was returning to Britain in 1917, after three years in India as Governor of Bengal and Madras. The Medina treasure was raised in 1987 by an Anglo-Danish consortium. See further Lycett, A., "Sea gives up its treasures", *The Times*, Tuesday, April 28, 1987, p.12, col. 3; *ibid,* Thursday April 16 1987, p. 2, col. 7.

68 Human remains can exceptionally be found several hundreds years after a sinking. This was the case with a 17th century warship discoverd off the coast of Scotland. See further Dromgoole, S. and Gaskell, N., "Who has a right to historic wrecks and wreckages?", 2 *International Journal of Cultural Property*, (1993) pp. 217-273, at p. 230.

69 The "intrinsic economic worth" could be defined as the price that an artefact would bring in an open market. Merryman and Elsen, *op.cit.* note 17 at p. 10.

70 See further Fenwick, V., "Editorial", 16 *I.J.N.A.* (1987) p. 1.

71 Cockrell, W.A., "The Trouble with Treasure: A Preservationist View of the Controversy", 45 *American Antiquity* (1980) pp. 333-339 at p. 334.

72 Back in 1973, Bass reported the looting of almost every accessible wreck off the Turkish coast, while Throckmorton notes that, in both Italy and Greece, most sites in waters up to 100 feet have been looted. The same applies to France and Spain, where perhaps 9 out of 10 underwater sites in reach of divers have been destroyed. See Bass, G.F., "Turkey. Survey for Shipwrecks, 1973", 3 *I.J.N.A.* (1974) pp. 335-338 at p. 338 and Throckmorton, P., "Marine Archaeology", 28 *Oceanus* No. 1, Spring 1985, pp. 2-12 at p. 4.

73 Prott and O'Keefe, *op. cit.* note 5 at p. 19. See also Recommendation 1133 (1990) of the Parliamentary Assembly of the Council of Europe on European tourism policies, which reads, *inter alia:* "The cultural aspects of tourism should be integrated in tourism policies... Greater attention should be given to marrying tourism with the promotion of culture". The potential benefits from tourism

also constitute one of the main reasons why museums are reluctant to satisfy claims for the return of cultural property to the country of origin, even if it can be demonstrated to have been exported or acquired illegally. In this respect see the *Ethics of Aquisition,* adopted in 1970 by the International Council of Museums (ICOM), the 1977 ICOM Study on the Principles, Conditions and Means for the Restitution or Return of Cultural Property in View of Reconstituting Dispersed Heritages, and the most comprehensive *Code of Professional Ethics* adopted at the fifteenth General Assembly of the ICOM held in Buenos Aires, 4 November 1986.

74 *The Shorter Oxford English Dictionary,* 3rd edition revised with addenda, Clarendon Press, Oxford, 1966 at p. 1716.

75 Lawrence, A., "State antiquity laws and admiralty salvage: protecting our cultural resources", 32 *U. Miami L. Rev.* (1977) pp. 291-338 at p. 291.

76 *Black's Law Dictionary,* 5th ed., St. Paul Minn., West Pub. Company, 1979 at p. 925.

77 For example, back in 1972 Sotheby's auctioned part of the most valuable antique treasure yet recovered from an historic shipwreck around the British Isles, and despite expensive publicity in the months before, in which the value of the part of the treasure was estimated at £ 100.000, not one museum approached the divers to discover what they have found... The wreck was the Dutch East Indian Hollandia lost off the Isles of Sicily in 1743. Marsden, P., "Archaeology at sea", 46 *Antiquity* (1972) pp. 198-202 at p. 198.

78 Miller is, therefore, oversimplistic by arguing that "maritime artefacts under both comon law and civil law are considered *res derelictae* or abandoned property". Miller, H.C., *International Law and Marine Archaeology,* Academy of Applied Sciences, Belmont, Mass., 1973 at p. 18. According to Korthals Altes three categories of maritime antiquities should be distinguished: "(1) *res nullius,* nobody's property which can either be *res derelictae,* vis. truly abandoned and therefore became *res nullius;* or objects which are known to have no owner, generally because they never had an owner at all, and therefore have always been *res nullius,* and also because all ayant-droit (interested parties) are known to be dead (known in the UK as *bona vacantia*); (2) objects of which simply the owner is unknown, but which may still be private property; (3) objects, never formally abandoned by their owner, and over which he or his successors may still after a long lapse of time exercise his rights." Korthals Altes, A., "Submarine Antiquities and the Law", 44 *Annuaire de l'AAA* (1974) pp. 127-141 at p. 132; ID, "Submarine Antiquities: A Legal Labyrinth", 4 *Syracuse J. Int'l L. and Com.* (1976) pp. 77-96 at pp. 84-85. See further Lawrence, *op. cit.* note 75 at pp. 292-296 and Matysik, S., "Legal problems of recovery of historical treasures from the sea-bed" in Frankowska, M. (ed.), *Scientific and Technological Revolution and the Law of the Sea,* Warsawa, Ossolineum, 1974, pp. 141-153 at p. 146.

79 See further Prott and O'Keefe, *op. cit.* note 45 at pp. 99-103; ID, *op. cit.* note 35, pp. 15-27, Giesecke, A.G., "Management of Historic Shipwrecks in the 1980's", 12 *JFA* (1985) pp. 108-115 at p. 108; ID, "Shipwrecks: The Past in

the Present", 15 *Coastal Management* (1987) pp. 176-195 at pp. 181-182; Runyan, T.J., "Shipwreck legislation and the preservation of submerged artifacts" *22 Case W. Res. J. Int'l L.* (1990) pp. 31-45.

80 Runyan, *ibid* at pp. 32-33.

81 See M'Bow, A-M., (then) Director-General of UNESCO "Plea for the return of an irreplaceable cultural heritage to those who created it", 31 *Museum* (1979) p. 58. See further Arnold, I.B., "Underwater Cultural Resources and the Antiquities Market", 5 *JFA* (1978) p. 232 and Fish, P.R., "Federal Policy and Legislation for Archaeological Conservation", 22 *Arizona L. Rev.* (1980) pp. 677-699 at pp. 682-683, 686 and 695-697.

82 See further Meenan, J.K., "Cultural resources preservation and underwater archaeology - some notes on the current legal framework and a model underwater antiquities statute", 15 *San Diego L. Rev.* (1978) pp. 623-662 at pp. 626-628, and Prott and O'Keefe, *op. cit.* note 5 at p. 317.

83 More specifically, see Herscher, E., "97 Congress, 1st session HR 132", 10 *JFA* (1983) pp. 107-113; ID, "Hearings Held on Historic Shipwreck Legislation", 11 *JFA* (1984) pp. 79-96 and Giesecke, *op. cit.* note 79.

CHAPTER 2

Underwater Archaeology

NATURE AND HISTORY OF THE DISCIPLINE

Use of the terms "underwater" and "marine"

The function of archaeology is to draw conclusions about past societies by discovering, recording, interpreting and preserving the material evidence they have left behind.[1] The term "underwater", when applied to archaeology, emphasises the fact that the field-work of this body of archaeology is carried out under water. Underwater archaeology has been defined by Coggin as "the recovery and interpretation of human remains and cultural materials of the past from underwater by archaeologists."[2] Many archaeologists, however, use terms, such as "nautical", "maritime" or "marine", to describe their discipline.[3] The use of the term "marine archaeology" has been recommended on the basis that "it encompasses research that revolves around a particular body of water, the ocean", while "underwater archaeology refers to the locale where research is conducted".[4]

For the purposes of this study, both terms "marine" and "underwater archaeology" will be used. The latter corresponds to the broader concept of "underwater cultural heritage" which, as defined by article 1 of the Draft European Convention, encompasses cultural property found in fresh water, objects which are partly or sometimes underwater, objects washed ashore as well as objects which were formerly located underwater and have now been recovered. The *rationale* behind this broad definition is that all these categories of cultural property raise similar problems.[5] Alternatively, when the context demands, i.e. in relation to issues which are confined to activities at sea, such as comparison of archaeological research with salvage operations or recognition of archaeological endeavour as a new use of the seas, the term "marine archaeology" is used.

Evolution of underwater archaeology

For the archaeologist whose site lies underwater, the main problem is working in an alien environment. In the past, it was believed that diving and
archaeology were two separate activities and that the presence of an archaeologist on the surface supervising the activities of a diving team was sufficient.[6] This belief proved to be fatal as sometimes divers failed to survey
or to record the investigated site in the required manner; wrecks were
destroyed in the search for artefacts, while only a few careful drawings were
made. In this way a lot of data was lost for ever.[7] The situation changed
in 1958 when Throckmorton and, shortly afterwards Bass, undertook "classi-
cally correct underwater excavations, including three-dimensional surveys
of ship and cargo, and established a technology for precise excavation of
wrecks in shallow waters".[8] These operations constituted an important
landmark in the development of underwater archaeology, which had already
expanded since the Second World War due to the development of convenient
and efficient subaquatic equipment.[9] Underwater archaeology is, therefore,
a relative new discipline, approximately 36 years old. As a result, only a
few projects have actually been completed, while archaeologists have not
had time to reach solutions to many operational and research problems.

As it exists today, marine archaeology derives from several distinct sources,
such as marine salvage, maritime history, classical archaeology, archaeometry
and cultural resources management.[10] Recent years have seen a tendency
to consider shipwreck archaeology as part of social sciences: "What makes
it a science is not the use of scientific techniques and apparatus, but an
organised process of reasoning based on the application of certain rules of
science, such as the testing of alternative hypotheses, the principle of par-
simony, the need of repeatability of results and the ability to extend the
results from a particular case to the realm of general propositions about the
nature of variability in the behaviour of the human species in a convincing
manner."[11] With a decreasing number of historical shipwrecks available
in future years, "there must be a more inter-disciplinary nature to the studies
carried out on shipwrecks, especially when heavy impact to the site (i.e.,
excavation) is anticipated".[12]

The operation of an underwater archaeological project

The operation of an archaeological project underwater consists of a number of different research activities.The only unifying element is the use of underwater technology.[13]

Search for and location of underwater sites
Finding a site
Chance discoveries. Wrecks and submerged settlements in shallow water have generally been found accidentally by fishermen, sponge- and sport divers. The disadvantages of such an accidental location by non-archaeologists, even when it is reported to the authorities, have already been pointed out. However, chance discoveries will always be important underwater as indeed they have remained on land.[14] In this context, the establishment of the duty to report the accidental location of underwater relics to the competent authorities is essential, especially when considering that the development of advanced underwater technology has broadened the scope of chance discoveries.[15]
Detective work. Two phases may be distinguished at this early stage: studying documents in archives (archival research), and systematically searching the seafloor. There exists a variety of methods of locating position at sea; these can be used either to locate the position of a particular archaeological site or to help define the area that has been covered when searching for archaeological sites.[16] Searching need not be limited to finding previously unknown sites. A systematic search around the core of a known site under investigation is also important. Projects have been left incomplete because those concerned did not undertake proper investigations.[17]

The search itself
Electronic search. The quickest way to scan a large seabed area is by electronic remote-sensing devices. Both echo sounders and side-scan sonars record the shape of the seabed and are useful for locating wrecks on a general flat bottom.[18] Sub-bottom profilers, on the other hand, record the various strata below the seabed.[19] For locating post-medieval vessels containing cannons, anchors and other large metal objects, magnometers and, generally, metal-detectors are particularly useful.[20] The latter reveal metal objects as anomalies (or variations) in a local magnetic field.
Visual search. Under water, plain visual search is slow and difficult. Visibility is rarely more than 50m even in shallow water. An important

substitute for a visual search is the use of photographic or video systems, which are either towed behind a surface craft or mounted on some kind of submarine (these cameras can produce permanent pictures).[21] The most important visual search techniques are the swimline, the towed search, remote operating vehicles, manned submarines, one atmosphere diving suits and aerial photography.[22]

In both electronic and visual search the main problem is to know exactly which part of the area is being scrutinised at any moment. An effective search programme is one where no area is scanned twice or missed altogether. Obviously, scanning a large part of the seabed is an expensive and time-consuming operation. In small-scale searches of limited areas, a great deal of time is devoted to laying buoys and controlling lanes, while in larger areas the main problem is to establish the position of the sensing devices that are trailed behind the surface craft.[23]

Pre-disturbance survey
An axiom of archaeological research is that exploration should precede excavation.[24] As already seen, the initial discovery of a target will normally be made by the recognition of a limited number of features which reveal the existence of a deposit, without, however, indicating its precise position and volume. It is obvious, therefore, that before any disturbance takes place, a preliminary survey should be carried out in order to determine the nature and the extent of the site.[25] A variety of methods may be used, such as two-dimensional surveying techniques (i.e., trilateration, distance-angle measuring, rectangular measuring systems, computers and electronic distance measuring systems), three-dimensional survey techniques, profiling, levelling and sub-surface survey (i.e., close-plot magnetometer survey, metal detector survey and probe survey).[26] In reasonable visibility, photogrammetry would appear to provide the most economical means of surveying the remains that can be seen.

Excavation and recovery techniques
Today excavation is but one link in the chain of scientific activities that make up archaeological research. There has been a major switch from concentration on excavation on the utilization of a wide range of techniques - geophysical, prospecting, processing of satellite pictures - in studying the past life of mankind. Information is the primary goal of the archaeologist, who will justify excavation only when it is absolutely necessary.[27] Excava-

tion is undertaken, if at all, with the greatest reluctance and extreme care.[28] As frequently reported by archaeologists, the primary purpose of excavation is deducing facts through recorded observation, and not recovering spectacular artefacts.[29] In this process of deduction artefacts are an important element, but they are only significant, if seen in the context of their environmental matrix and in their association with neighbouring finds.[30] The actual carrying out of excavation is a difficult and laborious operation which often involves the removal of concretion and sand.[31] Due to the limited period that the diver can stay under water, underwater archaeology is more costly, both in time and in money, than land archaeology.

Finds drawing and photography
All that must be recorded under water, is a find's precise location and level as well as its orientation and relationship to other neighbouring finds. With the exception of fixed remains and substantial elements of ship structure which may be drawn *in situ*, the finds are drawn in detail when they are brought to the surface.[32] The most efficient method of recording information underwater, is photography and photogrammetry.[33] Underwater video cameras and remotely operated vehicles have only recently been used on archaeological sites.

Documentation and publication
Systematic and detailed documentation as well as labelling of the finds is essential for later identification and further research. The same applies to publication which should aim at presenting, as clearly and objectively as possible, the fundamental nature of the evidence within a wider context of research.[34] It has been argued that "an unpublished excavated site has been destroyed or mutilated as surely as if it had been bulldozed."[35]

Conservation, restoration and display
As argued, "excavation without conservation is tantamount to vandalism."[36] Unless the recovered material is rapidly and skilfully treated, it will suffer, when lifted, irreparable damage, and loss of scientific (and commercial) value.[37] Two stages of conservation activities are distinguishable: on-site conservation and laboratory conservation. The lack of museum facilities may result in the corrosion of the recovered artefacts, while their treatment by inexperienced persons is likely to do more harm than good.[38] Marsden argues that valuable antiquities have often been mishandled by salvors even when they were in the custody of the Receiver of Wrecks.[39]

The museums that accept underwater material face considerable problems; the conservation treatment is expensive and time-consuming, while the museum's funds and facilities may be limited.[40] If resources are just adequate to complete an excavation, it will be possible to meet subsequent museographical costs, especially the costs of restoration and surveillance of the material on display.[41] This final stage is vital as part of the process of *educating the general public*.[42] In this context, the more meaningful museums are those based on complete shipwreck excavations; the public can appreciate the potential of underwater archaeology, while the complete collection of artefacts recovered from a specific wreck-site is a useful tool for future researchers.[43] The Roskilde Museum (Denmark), the Wasa Museum (Sweden), the Kyrenia Museum (Cyprus), a travelling exhibit of the remains of the 1554 fleet wrecked off Padre Island (Texas, U.S.A.), the Museum of Underwater Archaeology (Turkey) and the Mary Rose Tudor Ship Museum (United Kingdom) are among the most famous maritime museums of the world.[44]

MARINE ARCHAEOLOGY AS A NEW USE OF THE OCEANS

Marine archaeology has been a neglected issue. This is not surprising as it was underestimated by archaeologists, let alone lawyers, until the late 1950s. The main reason for this lack of interest in the legal regime of marine archaeology seemed to be the absence of underwater technology, which made the recovery of artefacts far too remote to create jurisdictional problems. Bettini offers one of the new examples where archaeology underwater is mentioned as a use of the oceans. He includes "the identification of zones of archaeological interest" among the principal forms of utilisation of seas, oceans and submerged lands.[45] Probably the first comprehensive study on the legal problems of marine archaeology in the English language was that by Miller[46] in 1973. One should not overlook, however, the various papers presented by archaeologists in regional or international conferences or those published in specialised journals[47] and dealing with various aspects of underwater archaeology.

A "Study on International Machinery" presented to the Seabed Committee on 26 May 1970 by the Secretary-General of the United Nations, recognised marine archaeology as a new use of the oceans, its being something more than traditional salvage operations.[48] The 1982 Convention, in turn, adopted two articles on the regime of archaeological and historical objects found at sea. However, it does not consider marine archaeology as an independent use of the oceans nor does it establish a comprehensive regime of protection of underwater cultural property. Article 303(2) simply refers to the removal of archaeological and historical objects from the bed of the contiguous zone, while article 149 provides for their preservation and disposal for the benefit of mankind as a whole.

Since the protection of the underwater cultural heritage has emerged as an objective of the contemporary law of the sea, archaeology underwater should be considered as a new use of the seabed and be treated according to its nature and needs. The international regime of marine archaeology should not, therefore, be limited to the recovery of cultural items from the seabed, as it covers a broad range of activities, from the initial search for wrecks and submerged sites to the actual publication of the evidence acquired. The informative nature of archaeology should be reflected in the legal regime of protection which should stress, *inter alia*:[49] (i) the need for protection of wrecks of all kinds, not only those related to major historic events within the much-studied areas of the Mediteranean and the Caribbean; (ii) the obligation to report the accidental discovery of underwater cultural property; (iii) greater explicitness in planning and carrying out research; (iv) systematic sampling and survey methods; (v) the *in situ* protection of underwater cultural property; (vi) a strong conservation ethic, given the limited number of the cultural resources of the oceans; (vii) the need for documentation and publication of the data acquired; (viii) the need for proper conservation and restoration; (ix) public access to the recovered material. In addition to these guidelines on substantive law, the *extension* of coastal *competence* beyond the territorial sea is equally important. For the successful operation of an archaeological project underwater, a substantial degree of control of the area in question is required. Without being necessarily related to claims of sovereignty, the expansion of coastal jurisdiction appears to be essential for the establishment of an effective scheme of protection.

Recent years have seen an increased interest in the protection of the underwater cultural heritage, both in State practice and in doctrine. A number of States have enacted specific lesiglation to protect underwater remains, and/or others have expanded their competence to regulate access to underwater sites outside the territorial sea. Marine archaeological research now features among the discussed topics in international conferences, and legal scholars appear to be more interested in the problems that the preservation of the underwater heritage poses to the law of the sea.[50] This increased interest should not be considered in isolation but as part of the general interest of the international community in the protection of the cultural heritage which has also resulted in the development of a new body of law, the law of cultural heritage.[51]

MARINE ARCHAEOLOGY AS DISTINCT FROM MARINE SCIENTIFIC RESEARCH AND SALVAGE OPERATIONS

Exclusion of marine archaeology from the notion of marine scientific research

By definition, the exploration of the seabed for the location, investigation and excavation of archaeological remains is scientific research. Underwater archaeology is a scientific discipline, which derives from, and contributes to, a wide range of applied and social sciences. Both the scientific knowledge acquired and the employment of scientific method in archaeological research tend to suggest that it should qualify as marine scientific research. However, within the sphere of the law of the sea, archaeological endeavour does not constitute marine scientific research, which is confined to the natural environment and its resources.

Despite the fact that the Geneva Convention on the Continental Shelf (1958) (CSC) does not deal specifically with the regime of marine scientific research, the examination of its records shows that archaeological research was not intended to be included within the notion of "research concerning the continental shelf and undertaken there" and the consent regime of the coastal State. Similarly, the recently established regime of marine scientific research by the 1982 Convention does not refer to archaeological research; it neither excludes nor includes it. Nonetheless, in the light of the *travaux préparatoires* of the Conference, which emphasised the distinction between "natural resources" and "objects of an archaeological and historical nature", the interpretation of the study of human remains as marine scientific research is not permissible. This is confirmed by a number of informal proposals submitted during the negotiations of UNCLOS III, which confined the content of marine scientific research to the investigation of the marine environment. No reference was made to archaeological exploration.[52] Similarly, the definition of marine scientific research under both the Interim Single Negotiating Text (ISNT)[53] and the Revised Single Negotiating Text (RSNT)[54] read: "Marine scientific research means any study or related environmental work designed to increase man's knowledge of the marine environment." These provisions, however, did not find their way into the Final Text of the Convention. If the drafters of the 1982 Convention had intended to subject archaeological research to the legal regime of marine scientific research, there would be no reason for the separate regulation of "objects of an archeological and historical nature" in articles 303 and 149. The failure of these provisions to include archaeological exploration within their scope, does not imply that the latter are to be governed by Part XIII of the Convention dealing with marine scientific research. Within the general framework of the 1982 Convention such an interpretation is not permissible.[55]

In contrast, Castagné argues that archaeological exploration of the seabed is purely scientific research in the light of the knowledge acquired and the advanced techniques involved.[56] The interpretation of archaeological exploration as marine scientific research may, indeed, be advantageous as the coastal State would be granted the necessary competence to regulate access to sites found on the continental shelf. However, this approach can be misleading in that it suggests that existing regimes should apply to underwater cultural property. Instead, the primary aim should be to agree upon *new principles* that will govern this new ocean use efficiently rather than the expansion of existing rules, which have been developed to accommodate fundamentally different activities. For example, the interpretation of marine archaeology as marine scientific research could result in differentiation between the legal regimes of archaeological exploration and excavation, as it is very unlikely that the removal of artefacts from the seabed would be included within the notion of "research".

Marine archaeology and the law of salvage

The concept of salvage
The term "salvage" implies two different components: the act of salvage and the reward for that act. The laws of salvage have evolved from Roman law doctrine which awarded compensation from the owner to those who voluntarily preserved, protected or improved another's property.[57] "A right to salvage arises when a person acting as a volunteer (without any pre-existing contractual or other legal duty so to act) preserves or contributes to

preserving at sea any vessel, cargo, freight or other recognised subject of salvage from danger. In the absence of a binding agreement fixing the amount of remuneration, the salvor upon the property being salved and brought to a place of safety is entitled to recover salvage remuneration not exceeding the value of the property salved assessed as at the date and the place of the termination of the salvage services. The salvor's rights may be enforced by an action *in rem* or *in personam* (when the property is *res nullius*, then only by an action *in rem*)".[58]

Sunken vessels and their cargoes as salvagable objects. The raising of sunken treasure has been accepted as being amenable to salvage award since the earliest maritime history. The Rhodian Maritime Code stated in article XLVII that: "If gold or silver, or any other thing be drawn up out of the sea eight cubits deep, he that draws it up shall have one third, and if fifteen cubits, he shall have one half, because of depth."[59] The salvagable character requirement which led to certain exemptions in the spectrum of the items eligible for salvage awards (e.g., mail, bills of exchange, personal property and wearing apparel of both passengers and crew) has been argued not to apply in the case of ancient sunken wrecks because of the labour and extreme peril involved with their recovery.[60] Even coins embedded in the seashore sand were presumed to have come from a wrecked vessel[61] so that the law of wreck rather than treasure trove would apply. Salvaging wrecks for "non-utilitarian" purposes is primarily a modern-day phenomenon. Lenihan reports that one of the earliest examples of shipwreck salvage for antiquarian purposes was the raising in 1822 of a 16th century ship, which had been found on the River Rother in Sussex. The remains were put on display near London.[62] Similarly, in 1863, a vessel apparently from the 4th century A.D., was excavated from a peat bog in Schleswig and restored by the Danish archaeologist Conrad Engelhardt.[63]

Requirements for a salvage award. To sustain a claim to salvage the three following incidents must be satisfied:[64] (i) marine peril; (ii) service voluntarily rendered; (iii) success in whole or in part. The concept of "possession" is also central to the operation of salvage. The salvor must be able to attain possession of the object concerned so as to exclusively occupy the site during salvage and to take action against the property recovered to secure payment of the salvage award.[65] In case of abandoned property, the salvor in possession may even acquire ownership, if the legislation so permits.

Assessment of the award. Salvors are highly regarded by admiralty and it is believed that a generous remuneration is an insurance against acts of dishonesty.[66] The various factors that may influence the award were outlined back to 1869 in *the Blackwall:*[67] (i) The degree of danger from which the lives and property are rescued; (ii) The value of the property saved; (iii) The risk incurred by the salvors in securing the property from the impending peril; (iv) The promptitude, skill and energy employed by the salvors; (v) The value of the property employed to render the service; (vi) The time and labour expended by the salvors. In abandoned and derelict situations awards have been high due to the labour and extreme danger involved.

Application of the law of finds in salvage cases

The law of salvage assumes that the salved property is owned and that the owner is never divested of his title.[68] A number of U.S. admiralty courts, however, have rejected the salvage law theory that title to property can never be lost and have instead applied the law of finds, which grants title to the first party to discover and reduce to possession objects, which have never been owned, or property which is long lost or abandoned.[69] It is important to distinguish between the two concepts: a proper salvage claim will vest only a possessory, not an ownership, interest in the object salved, while the law of finds will vest in the finder an absolute ownership interest in the object found.[70] The U.S. courts have applied the law of finds in cases involving ancient shipwrecks, where no owner is likely to come forward under the doctrine of *animus revertendi* (the owner has no intention of returning).[71] This approach has been criticised on the grounds that it would encourage lawlessness and piracy on the high seas. Fry stresses the technical superiority of salvage law for the purpose of granting injunctive relief in relation to wrecks found in international waters. In his view, an injunction based upon the common-law doctrine of the law of finds is not as likely to be acceptable to other countries as the doctrine of salvage which is part of international maritime law.[72] Salvage law should, thus, be applied in all cases, with an *in specie* award being granted were appropriate.[73]

Evaluation of the law of salvage in terms of protecting the underwater cultural heritage

The essence of the law of salvage lies in the compensation of the salvor for the rescuing of maritime property in distress. The protection of the underwater cultural heritage has never been an objective of this ancient maritime law. There is no motivation for the salvor to excavate in an archaeologically responsible manner, nor to come before a court of admiralty to share his finds with the public.[74] Lohrey, for example, wonders whether salvors or finders have a superior right to the property than the owner (since he is unknown to them) so that they may retain it, instead of turning it over to the custody of the admiralty court to be claimed by the owner or the State.[75] The salvor works for profit and this is reflected in the manner in which salvage operations are conducted. Indeed, good salvage practice may well dictate that a marine archaeological site is destroyed "piecemeal", or that finds are not recorded.[76] It is notable that in certain cases the only existing documentation of artefacts, coins and other items found in an underwater site, is that provided by the records of the auctioneer in whose possession the valuable artefacts end. Salvors are not willing to spend the vast amount of money and time necessary for proper exploration and excavation projects, nor do they possess the required knowledge and experience to deal with the site efficiently. Salvage law, which apportions awards to those who rescue ships using factors, such as degree of succession or recovery and time and labor expended, does not allow the consideration of the archaeological or the historical value of the located remains.[77] Similarly unsuited is the use of the "finders-keepers" principle to determine the ownership of wrecks which might have considerable historical or cultural value. "Even the salvors who are conscientious, responsible and have a genuine interest in preserving this portion of our heritage may not have the necessary knowledge or training to safely remove old objects and artefacts. To the untrained eye a small piece of pottery or a chipped bit of metal may seem of little significance, but it is often these prepossessing, seemingly valueless objects which yielded important knowledge about the past."[78] For the archaeologist, common place has the same value with the spectacular. Objects of great aesthetic value are of no archaeological interest when they are considered outside their context. Even in relation to protected marine archaeological sites, it is arguable that if the legislation does not provide for the preservation of the material from the wreck in a collection it does not, in fact, protect the wreck as in many cases such excavations are financed by the sale of the material.[79] Unique collections may, thus, be dispersed and it will never be possible to be reassembled or studied in the future. In contrast, excavation is the ultimate purpose of the salvor. Although the archaeologist would prefer to leave an underwater archaeological site intact until proper preservation facilities are available, the salvor will proceed with the recovery of artefacts as soon as he discovers them, without worrying about protection measures. It is not surprising, therefore, that salvage law has been said to be "the basis from which treasure hunters justify to the courts and to the public their depredations upon our collective cultural heritage."[80] Salvage law is disfunctional and provides one of the most inappropriate means to regulate access to and control of underwater archaeological sites. For these reasons, the exclusion of the law of salvage from the regime governing underwater cultural property has been recommended.[81] It is, therefore, important that the International Convention on Salvage (1989)[82] provides in article 30(1) that: "Any State may, at the time of signature, ratification, acceptance, approval or accession, reserve the right not to apply the provisions of this Convention: (d) when the property involved is maritime cultural property of prehistoric, archaeological or historical interest and is situated on the seabed".

However, this approach is not shared by all. Owen, for example, criticised the holding of the U.S. district court of Maryland in *Subaqueous Exploration and Archaeology Ltd. v. The Unidentified, Wrecked and Abandoned Vessel*[83] that salvage law is not applicable to an ancient, abandoned wreck on the basis that "the law of marine salvage performs a valuable sociable function". In his opinion, the distinction between "ancient, abandoned wrecks" and "recently wrecked or damaged vessels" should not become a part of general maritime law.[84] Furthermore, Davies argues that: "The exclusion of the rights to salvage would deter enterprising professional salvors from doing the necessary preliminary enquiries. It is unlikely that the limited resources of Government and local body archaeological services in New Zealand would be able to investigate sea wrecks while so much land based archaeological work remains."[85] In Braekhus' view even when a State acquires title to an historic wreck on the basis of its heritage legislation, finders should have the alternative right to claim salvage remuneration.[86]

Since salvage law is ineffective as a means of protecting underwater cultural property, the following questions arise: (a) whether, in the first place, salvage law could be considered as inapplicable on the grounds that the requirements for a salvage award, e.g., danger, service voluntarily rendered and success in whole or in part, are not satisfied, and (b) whether it is possible for admiralty to incorporate marine archaeological principles so as to oblige salvors to carry out salvage operations in an archaeologically responsible manner.

Inapplicability of salvage law to underwater cultural property. Archaeologists have frequently pointed out that ancient wrecks are safe and well-preserved in salt water and that when in equilibrium with their environment there is little danger of deterioration. It is the disturbance of this equilibrium through removal or recovery from this stable environment which starts further decomposition.[87] A ship lying for hundreds of years at the bottom of the sea does not, and should not, qualify as a distressed vessel. The only peril to such sites, if any, is the unskilled and ignorant salvor. Regrettably, the majority of courts have not only held salvage law applicable to ancient wrecks but, in their attempt to do so, they have also expanded traditional salvage principles. A notable exception is the ruling of the High Court of Singapore in *Simon v. Taylor*[88] over the recovery of a cargo of mercury from the wreck of a German submarine sunk in the straits of Malacca in 1944. In the court's view, the mercury which had been lying on the seabed for 28 years, was not "exposed to an imminent or pending danger" at the time when it was raised and, therefore, the salvors, who in addition were not motivated to salve for the benefit of the owners but solely for their own benefit, were not salvors and were not entitled to salvage award.[89] The Singapore Court based its decision on the definition of salvage services in Halsbury's Laws of England.[90] A different view was taken by Mason, J. and Stephen, J. of the High Court of Australia in *Robinson v. The Western Australian Museum*[91], who argued that the presence of "imminent or pending danger" is not essential for the application of the law of salvage: "It is sufficient to ground a claim for salvage that the salvor gave the ship, its cargo or apparel from the perils of the sea or that he recover the ship, its cargo or part thereof. Salvage is not limited to recovery of property in or from a ship which is actually in distress; it extends to recovery of property in or from a ship which has lain at the bottom of the sea for a long time."[92] In their decision, the two judges relied on the English cases of *The Tubantia*[93] and *Morris v. Lyonesse Salvage Company Ltd.*[94]

In the United States, the threshold issue of the applicability of salvage law to historic shipwrecks found within the territorial sea has finally been settled by the enactment of the ASA, which specifically excludes salvage and finds law from its scope. Before the enactment of this law, the marine peril element of salvage claims was addressed in a number of cases. In *Treasure Salvors I*[95] and in *Platoro Ltd. v. Unidentified Remains of a Vessel*[96] the courts were satisfied that the shipwrecks were still in peril and applied salvage law, while in *Subaqueous,* salvage law was held inapplicable on the grounds that "an ancient, abandoned shipwreck does not constitute a marine peril for purposes of stating a valid salvage claim."[97]

Application of archaeological principles in salvage operations. Recent decisions in the U.S.A. reveal a tendency for admiralty courts to take into consideration the archaeological significance of a wreck and sometimes even to decline to apply maritime law when the salvor has failed to act in good faith to preserve the archaeological provenance. A positive development can be traced from *Platoro's* judgement which declined to hold the salvor to the standard of expertise required by marine archaeologists, to the finding of the Court of Appeals, Fourth Circuit, in *Columbus-America,* that "the degree to which the salvors have worked to protect the historical and ar-chaeological value of the wreck and the items salved", should be added as a *seventh factor* to be taken into account by admiralty courts when fixing an award for salvage.[98] The future will show whether and to what extent archaeological principles will be incorporated in the salvage standards of admiralty and be implemented in practice.[99] It is notable that in the *Cobb Coin* the district court of Florida was satisfied that the salvor had adequately documented archaeological provenance in their salvage operations, despite Texas' contention to the contrary.[100] Although in the preliminary injunction it appeared that the court would award a portion of the finds to the State of Florida as custodian for the people,[101] in its final judgment it, never-theless, rewarded the salvors *in specie.*[102] It seems, therefore, that the best solution to the archaeological issue would be the exclusion of the law of salvage from the protected underwater cultural property: "It is not that scientific work cannot be done by treasure hunters. Obviously techniques for proper scientific recovery and preservation can be learned or a trained archaeologist could be employed. But the treasure hunter works for profit, and this motive is not compatible with the requirements of historical preser-vation."[103]

The same applies to the *law of wreck.*[104] The Receiver of Wrecks to whom property found at sea or washed upon the shore is normally delivered cannot ensure proper conservation facilities, nor does the procedure disposing of unclaimed wrecks guarantee public access to the recovered material or the keeping together of archaeological collections. It is notable that in the United Kingdom ordinary wreck law continues to apply to sites designated under

the Protection of Wrecks Act, 1973. Artefacts recovered from designated
sites by licencees constitute "wreck" and are, therefore, subject to the provisions of Part IX of the Merchant Shipping Act 1894. This is a major disadvantage which limits considerably the effectiveness of the 1973 Wrecks
Act.[105]

NOTES

1   Martin, C., "Archaeology in an underwater environment" in UNESCO, *Protection
     of the underwater heritage*, Protection of the cultural heritage - Technical hand-
     books for museums and monuments 4, 1981, pp. 15-76 at p.18.
2   Borhegyi, S.F., "The Challenge, Nature and Limitations of Underwater Archaeo-
     logy" in Holmquist, J.D. and Wheeler, A.H. (eds), *Diving into the Past: Theo-
     ries, Techniques and Applications of Underwater Archaeology*, Minnesota
     Historical Society and the Council of Underwater Archaeology, 1964, pp. 1-9
     at p. 1. Underwater archaeology is self explanatory and covers all types of
     archaeology if submerged, but excludes the archaeological investigation of boat
     finds on land such as Sutton Hoo. Dean, M., *Guidelines on acceptable standards
     in underwater archaeology*, Scottish Institute of Maritime Studies, University
     of St. Andrews, 1988 at p. 25.
3   A definition of these terms, all of which have slightly different meanings, is
     to be found in Muckelroy, K., *Maritime Archaeology,* Cambridge University
     Press, 1978. Muckelroy has objected to the assertion of the dominance of
     underwater remains in these studies on the grounds that a considerable number
     of finds related to maritime activities are terrestrial, i.e., boats and ships that
     have been excavated above water, maritime equipment which has been deposited
     in graves, remains of craft which have been deliberately abandoned or even
     sites originally under water which have been artificially drained or otherwise
     removed from a marine environment. He admitts, however, that "nearly all the
     evidence must come from submerged sites, so that the constraints of the under-
     water environment can reasonably be said to be one of the main characteristics
     of this sub-discipline." *Ibid* at pp. 8-10. In his opinion, the most suitable term
     is "maritime". Maritime archaeology may be defined as "the scientific study
     of the material remains of man and his activities in the sea". The two main
     features of the discipline are: (a) the primary object is man and not the ships,
     cargoes, fittings or instruments with which the researcher is immediately con-
     fronted, and (b) maritime archaeology is a disciplined search for knowledge
     as opposed to the "aimless delight of curiosities". *Ibid* at p. 4. See also Green,
     J., *Maritime Archaeology: A Technical Handbook,* Academic Press Ltd, 1990
     at pp. 1-5.
4   Watters, D.R., "Terms and concepts related to marine archaeology", 28 *Oceanus,*
     No 1, Spring 1985 at p. 14. Others have questioned the status of underwater
     archaeology as an independent discipline on the basis that the term "underwater"
     simply describes an environmentally imposed technique. In 1966 Bass argued

that: "Archaeology underwater, of course, should be called simply archaeology. We do not speak of those working on the top of Nimrud Dagh in Turley as mountain archaeologists. Is the study of an ancient ship and its cargo, or the survey of toppled harbour walls somehow different?" Bass, G.F., *Archaeology Under Water, Ancient Peoples and Places*, General Editor Daniel G., Thames and Hudson, London, 1966 at p. 15. This approach has been objected to on the grounds that "general theory, analytical methods and field techniques are all interconnected; a subject which tries to do without the first two cannot succeed in practising the third alone". Muckelroy, *ibid* at p. 248.

5   See Draft Explanatory Report on the Convention on the Protection of the Underwater Cultural Heritage, Doc. CAHAQ (85)5, Strasbourg, 23 April 1985, Appendix IV, pp. 24-32 at p. 25.

6   Martin, *op. cit.* note 1 at pp. 18-19.

7   Bascom, W., "Deepwater Archaeology", 174 *Science* (1972) pp. 261-269 at p. 263. If it is considered that, in fact, most underwater sites have been discovered by chance by non-archaeologists, such as sponge divers, fishermen or hobby divers, the number of cases where valuable evidence has either been lost or destroyed increases dramatically. A few examples of early discoveries are the following: Back in 1832, the 5th century bronze Apollo, which is now in the Louvre, was brought up by a trawler from the waters off the island of Elba. In 1901, a wreck off Antikythera was accidentally discovered by sponge fishermen, who reported their find to the government and an expedition was launched. Many statutes were salvaged amongst which was the already mentioned famous *Youth from Antikythera*. Greek sponge divers also found a wreck at Mahdia in the Bay of Tunis in 1907, while Greek trawler fisherman brought up in their nets parts of bronze statues from Cape Artemision in 1926. *Ibid* at p. 262.

8   *Ibid*. In the past, shipwreck archaeology did not attract the attention of classical archaeologists. The reasons for this lack of interest were: (a) the lack of information about old vessels, before underwater excavation became possible; (b) seafaring communities were less attractive subjects than urban or agricultural communities due to their low status; (c) classical archaeologists did not feel that "random" finds of ships were important in defining societies and cultures. See further Muckelroy, K., "Techniques and Approaches" in Muckelroy, K. (ed.), *Archaeology under Water: An Atlas of the World's Submerged Sites*, McGraw-Hill Book Company, New York, London 1980, pp. 12-31 at p. 25 and Bascom, *op. cit.* note 4 at p. 263.

9   It was the Congloué operation in 1952, which attracted the attention of the international community to a new source of historical material, the underwater cultural heritage. In this excavation, the Cousteau group pioneered the use of television, air lift and the aqualung. See further Bascom, *ibid* and Bass, G.H., "Marine Archaeology: A Misunderstood Science", 2 *Ocean Yearbook* (1980) pp. 137-152. It should be noted, however, that the first scientific dives employing mechanical equipment were made almost 100 years earlier by Henry Milne Edwards, a French professor of zoology in 1844. This operation took place two years after the first successful salvage job, using the (then) newly developed Siebe German helmet apparatus, was made. Throckmorton, P., *Diving for*

Treasure, Thames & Hudson Ltd., London, 1977 at p. 30. However, as Green, *op. cit.* note 3 at p. 2, comments: "The 1950's marked the start of two seperate developments that were to affect the future of maritime archaeology: the diving archaeologist and the "looter".

10   Lenihan, D.J., "Rethinking Shipwreck Archaeology: A History of Ideas and Considerations for New Directions" in Gould, R.A. (ed.), *Shipwreck Anthropology,* A School of American Research Book, University of New Mexico Press, Albuquerque, 1983, pp. 37-64 at p. 38.

11   Gould, R.A., "Looking Below the Surface: Shipwreck Archaeology as Anthropology" in Gould (ed.), *ibid*, pp. 3-22 at p. 16.

12   Lenihan, *op. cit.* note 10 at p. 64.

13   *Ibid* at p. 37. See also Blackman, D.J., "Archaeological Aspects" in Council of Europe, Parliamentary Assembly, *The Underwater Cultural Heritage,* Report of the Committee on Cultural and Education (Rapporteur Mr. John Roper), Doc. 4200-E, Strasbourg, 1978, pp. 27-44 at p. 35. The future of marine archaeology is inextricably linked with the development of advanced technology. The application of saturation diving techniques and, most importantly, the use of computers, satellite mapping systems and remote-operated and deep tow-vehicle technology have already increased considerably the effectiveness and range of archaeological endeavour. Keith, D.H., "Excavation of a third century B.C. shipwreck at La Secca de Capistello, Italy: a pioneer application of saturation diving techniques in nautical archaeology" in Arnold, I.B. (ed.), *Beneath the Waters of Time: Proceedings of the Ninth Conference on Underwater Archaeology*, Texas Antiquities Committee Publication No. 6, 1978, pp. 3-14. Cousteau has built an experimental village beneath the Red Sea at a depth of 300m. See further Muckelroy, *op. cit.* note 8 at p. 164. For an overview of current marine technology see Green, *op. cit.* note 3, Mazel, C., "Technology for Marine Archaeology", 28 *Oceanus,* No. 1, Spring 1985, pp. 85-89 at p. 88 and Verlaan, A.Ph., "Marine Archaeology: A Trojan (Sea) Horse?", *Ocean Yearbook*, (1989), pp. 231-253 at pp. 243-250.

14   Muckelroy, *op. cit.* note 3 at p. 14.

15   Today, archaeological remains may be discovered in the course of the following offshore operations: (i) exploration and exploitation activities on the continental shelf; (ii) use of the seabed for peaceful purposes, such as cable-laying of cable- or pipelines; (iii) use of the seabed for military purposes, and (iv) deep seabed mining. Roucounas, E., "Laws Protecting Underwater Finds", 8 *Archaeology*, August 1983 pp. 8-15 at p. 10 (in Greek).

16   Green, *op. cit.* note 3 at p. 15 *et seq.* Recently, there has been an important development in position fixing systems. By utilising more than one navigational sattelite, it is possible to obtain high positional accuracy anywhere over the surface of the earth (Global Positioning System, GPS). If two GPS instruments are used in a comparative mode survey, an accuracy of decimetres over distances of ten kilometres can be obtained. *Ibid* at pp. 35-36.

17   Muckelroy, *op. cit.* note 3 at p. 14.

18 Rozencrantz, D.M., Klein, M. and Edgerton, H.E., "The uses of sonar" in UNESCO, *Underwater Archaeology: A Nascent Discipline*, Museums and Monuments XIII, 1972, pp. 257-270 at p. 257. Side scanning sonars offer the most efficient searching tool for locating non-metallic wrecks which protruded above the seabed, while the vertical sonar is used for locating completely buried wrecks.

19 *Ibid* at pp. 264-265. See also Martin, *op. cit.* note 1 at p. 39.

20 Muckelroy, *op. cit.* note 3 at p. 14.

21 *Ibid* at p. 15.

22 Green, *op. cit.* note 3 at pp. 39-44. See also Verlaan, *op. cit.* note 13 at pp. 243-249.

23 Muckelroy, *op. cit.* note 3 at p. 15.

24 Taylor, J. du Plat and others, "The Future" in Taylor, J. du Plat (ed.), *Marine Archaeology*, edited for C.M.A.S., Hutchinson of London, 1965, pp. 190-201 at pp. 191-192.

25 Martin, *op. cit.* note 1 at p. 40.

26 Green, *op. cit.* note 3 at pp. 53-84. See also Blackman, *op. cit.* note 13 at p. 36, and Hall, E.T., "Wreck prospecting by magnometer" in UNESCO, *op. cit.* note 18, pp. 285-293.

27 "Excavation should be justified only when it could help to solve problems that are culturally important to us as a people or to the people whose cultural heritage is mostly linked to the archaeological evidence". Schmidt, P.R. and Mrozowski, S.A., "History, Smugglers, Change and Shipwrecks" in Gould (ed.), *op. cit.* note 10, pp. 143-171 at p. 147. See also Cockrell, W.A., "Some Moral, Ethical and Legal Considerations in Underwater Archaeology" in Cockrell, W.A. (ed.), *In the Realms of Gold: The Proceedings of the Tenth Conference on Underwater Archaeology,* Fathom Eight Special Publication No. 1, California, 1981, pp. 215-220 at pp. 217-129. One may therefore distinguish the operation of a deliberate project from *rescue* archaeology: "'Rescue job' must be done at once or not at all", while "deliberate projects" must not be done unless fully backed financially. Blackman, D.J. and others, "Discussion" in Blackman, D.J. (ed.), *Marine Archaeology*, Colston Papers, vol. xxiii, Butterworths, London 1973, pp. 517-520 at p. 517.

28 Blackman, *op. cit.* note 13 at p. 18. Since excavation techniques and methods will almost certainly improve, sites should perhaps be left for the time undisturbed, unless they are threatened in some way, e.g., by sandbank movements or dredging activities. Consideration should be given to the possibility of protecting certain wrecks *in situ* rather than excavating now or simply postponing excavation until resources are available. See Dromgoole, S., "Protection of Historic Wrecks. The UK Approach Part II: Towards Reform", 4 *International Journal of Estuarine and Coastal Law* (1989) pp. 95-116 at p. 107.

29 It has been argued that: "Excavation without systematic purpose or adequate recording is destruction which cannot under any circumstances pass for archaeology." Martin, *op. cit.* note 1 at p. 46.

30 Context can be investigated on any scale, from the relationship between two objects on one site to the relationship between groups of sites across the world. Muckelroy, *op. cit.* note 8 at p. 7. An artefact without provenance has lost at least half of its value. See further Arnold, J.B., "Underwater Cultural Resources and the Antiquities Market", 5 *JFA* (1978) p. 232.

31 Blackman, *op. cit.* note 13 at p. 36. Among the machinery used, one should mention the work platforms, the airlift, the water dredge, the water jet, the water or air probe and propwash systems. See further Green, *op. cit.* 3 at pp. 133-138.

32 Martin, *op. cit.* note 1 at p. 58.

33 *Ibid* at p. 67. See also Green, *op. cit.* note 3 at pp. 87-127.

34 *Ibid* at pp. 71-75.

35 Barker, P., *Techniques of Archaeological Excavations*, Batsford, London, 1977 at p. 228. Text cited in Muckelroy, *op. cit.* note 3 at p. 253.

36 Pearson, C., "On-site Conservation Requirements for Marine Archaeological Excavation", 6 *I.J.N.A.* (1977) pp. 37-46 at p. 45.

37 Blackman, *op. cit.* note 13 at p. 36. See also Pearson, C., "Conservation of the underwater heritage" in UNESCO, *op. cit.* note 1 at pp. 77-123.

38 Marsden, P., "Archaeology at Sea", 46 *Antiquity* (1972) pp. 198-202 at p. 199.

39 *Ibid.*

40 Blackman, *op. cit.* note 13 at p. 37. See also Harrison, P.F., "Museological problems associated with the underwater heritage" in UNESCO, *op. cit.* note 1 at pp. 135-163.

41 It is notable that in some cases the wrecks are burried under sand after being studied.

42 Blackman, *op. cit.* note 13 at p. 37.

43 Bass, G.F., "The promise of underwater archaeology in retrospect", 35 *Museum* (vol. XXXV, No. 1) 1983, pp. 5-8 at p. 8.

44 See also Johnston, P.F., "Treasure salvage, archaeological ethics and maritime museums", 22 *I.J.N.A.* (1993) pp. 53-60, who discusses the operation of existing private "treasure" or "salvage" museums, either profit or non-profit.

45 Bettini, E., "Possible Future Regimes on the Seabed Resources" in Sztucki, J. (ed.), *Symposium on the International Regime of the Sea-Bed. Proceedings*, Academia Nazionale dei Linzei, Rome, 1970, pp. 319- 342 at pp. 321 and 329.

46 Miller, H.C., *International Law and Marine Archaeology*, Academy of Applied Sciences, Belmont, Mass. 1973.

47 *The International Journal of Nautical Archaeology and Underwater Exploration (I.J.N.A.)* published for the Nautical Archaeology Society (United Kingdom) and the *Cahiers d' Archéologie Subaquatique (C.A.S.)* (France) are the two major journals specialising in underwater archaeology.

48 Doc.A/AC.138/SC.1/L.2 reprinted in "Report of the Committee on the Peaceful Uses of the Sea-Bed and the Ocean Floor Beyond the Limits of National Jurisdiction, 25 *UN GAOR Supp. No. 21* (A/8021), Annex III, pp. 61-123 at pp. 110-111. Para. 117 reads: "Besides the functions and powers referred to above, consideration may also need to be given to functions and powers relating to other uses of the seabed... exploration and recovery of sunken ships and lost

objects - both from the point of view of archaeology with regard to which UNESCO performs a variety of functions and as regards salvage operations."

49 Gould, *op. cit.* note 11 at p. 21 and Schmidt and Mrozowski, *op. cit.* note 27 at p. 147.

50 More specifically see: Alexander, B.E.,"Treasure salvage beyond the territorial sea: an assessment and recommendations", 20 *J. Mar. Law & Com.* (1989) pp. 1-19; Arend, A.C., "Archaeological and Historical Objects: The International Legal Implications of UNCLOS III", 22 *V.J.I.L.* (1982) pp. 777-803; Caflisch, C., "Submarine Antiquities and the International law of the Sea", 13 (XIII) *N.Y.I.L.* (1982) pp. 3-32; Castangé, A., "L'archéologie sous-marine et le droit" in Société française pour le droit international, *Actualités du droit de la mer*, Colloque de Montpellier, 25-27 Mai 1972, Pedone, A. éditions, Paris 1973, pp. 164-183; Cycon, D.E., "Legal and Regulatory Issues in Marine Archaeology", 28 *Oceanus* No. 1, Spring 1985 pp. 78-84; Korthals Altes, A., "Submarine Antiquities and the Law", 44 *Annuaire de l'A.A.A.* (1974) pp. 127-141; ID, "Submarine Antiquities: A Legal Labyrinth", 4 *Syracuse J. Int'l L. and Com.* (1976) pp. 77-96; Lindabloom, S.J., "Historic Shipwreck Legislation: Rescuing the Titanic from the Law of the Sea", 13 *Legislation* (1986) pp. 92-111; Lund, C., "Patrimoine culturel subaquatique", 12 *Jus Gentium* (1985) pp. 60-74; ID, "Report on Protection of the Underwater Cultural Heritage - The Rules of UN Law of the Sea Protection" in Council of Europe, Parliamentary Assembly, *Parliamentary Conference on the UN Convention on the Law of the Sea*, Palermo, 2-4 November 1983, *AS/JUR/MAR/CONF.35(7)*, pp. 1-10; Meurs (van) L., "Legal Aspects of Marine Archaeological Research", *Acta Juridica* (1986) pp. 83-124; ID, *Legal Aspects of Marine Archaeological Research*, Special Publication of the Institute of Marine Law, University of Cape Town, Publication Number 1, 1985; Michael, M.D., *The Archaeological and the Historical Objects of the Continental Shelf - International Law and the Aegean*, Saccoulas Publishing Co., Athens, 1983 (in Greek); Meenan, J.K., "Cultural Resources Preservation and Underwater Archaeology: Some Notes on the Current Legal Framework and a Model Underwater Antiquities Statute", 15 *San Diego L. Rev.* (1978) pp. 623-662; Miller, *op. cit.* note 46; Migliorino, L., "Submarine Antiquities and the Law of the Sea", 4 *Marine Policy Reports*, No. 4 (1982) pp. 1-5; ID, *Il recupero degli oggetti storici ed archeologici sommersi nel diritto internazionale*, Studi e documenti sul diritto internazionale del mare, 15, Dott. Giuffrè, A. editore, Milano 1984; Münch (von) I., "Schiffwracks Völkerrechtliche Probleme", 20 *Archiv des Völkerrechts* (1982) pp. 183-198; Nafziger, J.A.R., "Finding the Titanic: beginning an international salvage of derelict law at sea", 12 *Columbia - VLA Journal of Law & the Arts* (1988) pp. 339-351; O'Keefe, P.J., "Maritime Archaeology and Salvage Laws: Some Comments following Robinson v. The Western Australian Museum", 7 *I.J.N.A.* (1978) pp. 3-7; Prott, L.V. and O'Keefe, P.J., "International Legal Protection of the Underwater Cultural Heritage", 14 *Revue belge de droit international* (1978-79) pp. 85-103; ID, "Final Report on Legal Protection of the Underwater Cultural Heritage" in Council of Europe, Parliamentary Assembly, *The Underwater Cultural Heritage,*

Report of the Committee on Cultural and Education (Rapporteur Mr. John Roper) Doc. 4200-E, Strasbourg, 1978, Appendix II, pp. 45-90; ID, "Law and the underwater heritage" in UNESCO, *op. cit.* note 1, pp. 165-200; ID, *Law and the Cultural Heritage,* vol. 1, *Discovery and Excavation,* Professional Books Ltd., Abingdon, 1984, pp. 89-107; Passalacqua, J.L.A. (de), "Propriedad del partimonio cultural sumergido bajo las aguas territoriales del Estado Libre Asociado de Puerto Rico", 21 *Revista Juridica de la Universidad Interamericana de Puerto Rico* (1987) pp. 597-604; Ronzitti, N., "Stato costiero, archeologica sottomarina e tutela del patrimonio storico sommerso", *Il diritto marittimo* (1984) pp. 3-24; Roucounas, E., "Laws Protecting Underwater Finds", 8 *Archaeology,* August 1983 pp. 8-15 (in Greek); ID, "Cultural Treasures on the Seabed", 23 *Review of Public and Administrative Law* (1979) pp. 10-37 (in Greek); Runyan, T.J., "Shipwreck legislation and the preservation of submerged artifacts" 22 *Case W. Res. J. Int'l L.* (1990) pp. 31-45; Shore, H., "Marine Archaeology and International Law: Background and Some Suggestions", 9 *San Diego L. Rev.* (1972) pp. 668-700; Starkle, G., "Les épaves de navires en haute mer et le droit international: Le cas de Mont-Louis", 18 *Revue belge de droit international* (1984/85) pp. 496-528; Treves, T., "Stato costiero e archeologia sottomarina", *Rivista di diritto internazionale* (1993) pp. 698-719; Tubman, M., "Submarine Archaeological and Historical Objects: A Watery Legislative Limbo", 2 *International Hindsights* (1986) pp. 85-90; Watters, D.R., "The Law of the Sea Treaty and Underwater Cultural Resources", 48 *American Antiquity* (1983) pp. 808-816; Zhao, H., "Recent Developments in the Legal Protection of Historic Shipwrecks in China", *23 Ocean Dev. & Int'l L.* (1992) pp. 305-333. See also the papers presented at the *European Conference on the Protection of the Underwater Cultural Heritage,* organised by the Third Greek Presidency and the Ministry of Culture at Vouliagmeni, April 7-8, 1994, and the *Seminario: La protezione del partimonio culturale subacqueo nel Mediterraneo,* organised by the Università degli Studi di Roma 'Tor Vergata', Anacapri, 1 October 1994.

51 See also Prott, L.V., "Problems of private international law for the protection of the cultural heritage", *Hague Recueil* (1989-V) pp. 215-317 at pp. 301-305; Prott, L.V. and O'Keefe, P.J., "'Cultural heritage' or 'cultural property'?", 1 *International Journal of Cultural Property* (1992) pp. 307-320 at p. 318: "Now it is well accepted that this highly specialised field is an area of law *sui generis,* where public and private law intersect, and the prospective purpose of the law, relying on scientific evidence and impact assessment, has produced its own special technique and means of protection".

52 *Trinidad and Tobago*: Draft articles on marine scientific research. Article 1: "(a) Marine scientific research is any study of investigation of the marine environment and experiments related thereto." Doc. A/CONF.62/C.3/L.9 (5 August 1974), *UNCLOS III, Off. Rec.,* vol. III at p. 252. *Austria, Belgium, Bolivia, Botswana, Denmark, Germany (Federal Republic of), Laos, Lesotho, Liberia, Luxembourg, Nepal, Netherlands, Paraguay, Singapore, Uganda, Upper Volta and Zambia*: Draft articles on marine scientific research. Article 1: "'Marine scientific research' means any study of and related experimental work

in the marine environment, excluding industrial exploration and other activities aimed directly at the exploitation of marine resources, designed to increase man's knowledge and conducted for peaceful purposes." Doc. A/CONF.62/C.3/ L.19 (23 August 1974), *ibid* at p. 267. *Bulgaria, Byelorussian SSR, Czechoslovakia, German Democratic Republic, Hungary, Mongolia, Poland, Ukrainian SSR and USSR*: Draft articles on marine scientific research. Article 1. Definition of marine scientific research: "'Marine scientific research' means any study of, or related experimental work in, the marine environment that is designed to increase man's knowledge and is conducted for peaceful purposes". Doc. A/CONF.62/C.3/L.26 (3 April 1975), *UNCLOS III, Off. Rec.* vol. IV at p. 213. *Colombia, El Salvador, Mexico and Nigeria*: Draft articles on marine scientific research. Article 1. Definition of marine scientific research: "For the purpose of this Convention 'marine scientific research' means any study and related experimental work conducted in the marine environment designed to increase mankind's knowledge there of." Doc. A/CONF.62/C.3/L.29 (6 May 1975), *ibid* at p. 216. Similarly none of the official proposals on marine scientific research submitted to Sub-Committee III of the Seabed Committee referred to archaeological exploration. A number of these proposals are reprinted in Soons, A.H.A., *Marine Scientific Research and the Law of the Sea*, T.M.C. Asser Institute - The Hague, Kluwer Law and Taxation Publishers, 1982, Annex II, pp. 326-340, and Oda, S., *The International Law of Ocean Development. Basic Documents*, vol. II, Sijthoff, Leyden, 1975, pp. 416-437.

53   Article 2, Part III (Part II) of ISNT, Doc.A/CONF.62/ WP.8 (7 May 1975), *UNCLOS III, Off. Rec.*, vol. IV at p. 177.

54   Article 48, Part III (Chapter II) of ISNT, Doc.A/CONF.62/ WP.8/Rev.1 (6 May 1976), *UNCLOS III, Off. Rec.,* vol. V at p. 180.

55   According to Prof. Soons: "Marine archaeology does not involve the study of the natural environment, but involves the study and recovery of man-made objects present on and in the seafloor which are relevant from a historical point of view". Soons, *op. cit.* note 52 at p. 275, footnote 38. Similarly, Caflisch argues that the term "'scientific research' taken in its ordinary meaning, certainly does not include historical research on or in the seabed." Caflisch, *op. cit.* note 50 at p. 23.

56   Castangé, *op. cit.* note 50 at p. 172. See also Zhao, *ibid.* at p. 317: "Although such conceptualization is not rooted in the *travaux préparatoires* of UNCLOS, neither the *travaux* nor the UNCLOS text excludes marine archaeological research from marine scientific research. On the contrary, most of the provisions of Part XIII regarding marine scientific research may apply to marine archaeological research".

57   Norris, M., "Misconduct of Salvors", 18 *Brooklyn L. Rev.* (1952), pp. 247-262 at p. 247.

58   Brice, G., *Maritime Law of Salvage*, Stevens & Sons Ltd., London, 1983 at p. 7.

59   See *Justice: Sea Laws*, vol. 1, p. 231, 3rd ed. (1705). Text cited in Norris, M.J., *Benedict on Admiralty*, vol. 3A, *The Law of Salvage*, 7th ed., Matthew Bender,

New York, 1983, para. 1-7. See further Ashburner, W., *The Rhodian Sea-Law*, Clarendon Press, Oxford, 1909 pp. cclxxxviii-ccxciii at p. cclxxxix.

60 Koenig, R.A., "Property Rights in Recovered Sea Treasure: The Salvors Perspective", 3 *N.Y.J. Int'l & Comp. L.* (1982) pp. 271-305 at p. 281.

61 *Talbot v. Lewis*, 172 *Eng. Rep.* 1383 (Ex. 1834).

62 Lenihan, *op. cit.* note 10 at p. 40.

63 *Ibid.*

64 *The Sabine*, 101 *U.S.* 384 (1880).

65 See further O'Keefe, *op. cit.* note 50 at pp. 4-6. See also *Columbus-America Discovery Group v. Unidentified, Wrecked and Abandoned Sailing Vessel Believed to Be the S.S. Central America*, 1989 AMC 1955, where the district court held that in the deep ocean, exercise of effective control is achieved not through physical presence, but through a combination of live imaging coupled with the capability to manipulate the environment through tele-operated or robotic vehicles. Effective possession of an object is attained in this unique environment by: 1) locating the object searched; 2) real time imaging of the object; 3) placement or capability to place teleoparated or robotic manipulators on or near the object; 4) present intent to control the location of the object (so-called "telepresence" and "telepossession").

66 Back in 1869 it was held that: "If a salvor was liberally rewarded his every temptation to embezzlement and dishonesty would be removed". *The Blackwall*, 77 *U.S.* (10 Wall) 1, 14 (1869).

67 *Ibid.* See also article 13 (criteria for fixing the reward) of the International Convention on Salvage (1989). Text reprinted in *Lloyd's Maritime and Commercial Law Quartely* (1990) 54.

68 "Should a vessel be abandoned without hope of recovery or return, the right of property still remains in her owner; he does not acquire ownership or title to the salved property." Norris, *op. cit.* note 59, para. 150, 11-1, 2.

69 This is the so-called "American rule", under which title to recovered property or treasure vests in the finder absent of legislative exercise of sovereign prerogative (as is the case with the ASA, see *infra* at pp. 65 and 126). The English common law approach to the law of finds is that title to abandonded property found on the seas is the prerogative of the Crown. As will be discussed, however, in chapter 6, this rule has been held to apply only within the territorial waters. The Crown has no right to abandoned wrecks in extraterritorial waters; title to wrecks by occupancy applies on the high seas. Similar provisions exist in the national legislation of other States. As argued, finds law should be applied in situations where the previous owners are found to have abandoned their property. "Intent to relinquish title may be proven according to the three methods of proof: express notice from the owner, implication from an owner's inaction, or passage of time and the lack of an identifiable owner. An involuntary physical abandonment, as in the case of a shipwreck or goods lost overboard, will not of itself establish legal abandonment. If the requirement of proving intent to relinquish title is not then satisfied, any object recovered would be subject to the law of salvage and not of finds." Del Bianco, H.P., "Underwater Recovery Operations in Offshore Waters: Vying for Rights to Treasure", 5 *Boston Univer-*

sity International Law Journal (1987) pp. 153-176 at p. 161. In *Columbus-America Discovery Group v. Unidentified, Wrecked and Abandoned Sailing Vessel Believed to Be the S.S. Central America*, 1990 *AMC* 2409, the district court held: "The common law of finds, rather than maritime salvage law, applies to artifacts recovered from a 133-year old wreck discovered 1 1/2 miles below the ocean surface, some 160 miles east of Charleston, S.C. Because the property had been abandoned, the finder is entitled to full ownership ... Cargo underwriters, claiming to have insured gold aboard vessel when she sank in 1857, abandoned their claims by destroying all records and by failing to make any salvage efforts even after the technology became available to locate and retrieve the gold." However, the Court of Appeals, Fourth Circuit, reversed the decision by holding that the district court erred in applying the common law of finds and awarding the entire treasure to the salvor. Admiralty salvage law governs, and evidence did not establish any intent by the underwriters to abandon their interest in the gold. *Columbus-America Discovery Group v. Atlantic Mutual Insurance Company et al and Unidentified, Wrecked and Abandoned Sailing Vessel Believed to Be the S.S. Central America*, 1992 *AMC* 2705. According to the Court of Appeals, "such abandonment must be proved by clear and convincing evidence, though, such as an owner's express declaration of abandoning title. Should the property encompass an ancient and longlost shipwreck, a court may infer an abandonment. Such an inference would be improper though, should a previous owner appear and assert his ownership interest; in such a case the normal presumptions would apply and an abandonment would have to be proved by strong and convincing evidence". *Ibid* at p. 2722. See also *Zych v. The Unidentified, Wrecked and Abandoned Vessel Believed to Be the S.S. "Lady Elgin"*, 1991 *AMC* 1254, where it was held that marine underwriters, who in 1869 had paid for vessels' sinking following the Lake Michigan collision, did not abandon their title by failing to take any action to salvage the wreck during the succeeding 130 years.

On the application of the law of finds to abandoned property at sea see also Owen, D.R., "The Abandoned Shipwreck Act of 1987: Good-bye to Salvage in the Territorial Sea", 19 *Journal of Maritime Law and Commerce* (1988), pp. 499-516 at pp. 510-512, Norris, *op. cit.* note 59, para. 158, Koenig, *op. cit.* note 60 at pp. 293-299, Stevens, T.T., "The Abandoned Shipwreck Act of 1987: finding the proper ballast for the States", 37 *Villanova Law Review* (1992) pp. 573-617, at pp. 579-588, Dromgoole, S., and Gaskell, N., "Who has a right to historic wrecks and wreckage?", 2 *International Journal of Cultural Property* (1993) pp. 217-273 and Fry, J.P., "The treasure below: jurisdiction over salving operations in international waters", 88 *Columbia Law Review* (1988), pp. 863-881 at p. 877: "The law of finds requires that the finder have located the wreck, be stationed above it in the process in salving it, have the present ability to continue to salvage the wreck, and have reduced a significant quantity of artifacts to possession. If the finder suspends his ongoing efforts to reduce the artifacts to possession and removes himself from the vicinity from any reason, the court may consider the artifacts once again to be in a state of nature". In *Indian Recovery Co. v. The China*, 645 *F. Supp.* 141 (D. Del. 1986), 1989 *AMC*

50, the Court pointed out that demonstration of possession and control of abandoned property is the prerequisite to an award of title under the law of finds.

70 Under the common law of finds, ownership of abandoned property is generally assigned without regard to where the property is found. There two exceptions to this rule: first, when the abandoned property is embedded in the soil, it belongs to the owner of the soil; second, when the owner of the land, where the property is found (whether on or embedded in the soil) has constructive possession such that the property is not "lost", it belongs to the owner of the land. *Joan M. Klein v. Unidentified Wrecked and Abandoned Sailing Vessel (Believed to have sunk in 1740)*, 1985 *AMC* at 2974, 758 *F.2d* at 1514.

71 *Joan M. Klein v. Unidentified, Wrecked and Abandoned Vessel (Believed to have sunk in 1740)*, 568 *F. Supp.* 1562 at p. 1569, 1984 *AMC* 1897 at p. 1901 (S.D. Fla. 1983), aff'd 758 *F2d* 1511 (11th Cir. 1985); Prisbe, J.T., "Law determining ownership of shipwreck in the United States: Klein v. Unidentified and Abandoned Sailing Vessel", *Lloyd's Maritime and Commercial Law Quarterly* (1987) pp. 24-29. See also *Wiggins v. 1100 Tons, More or Less, of Italian Marble*, 186 *F. Supp.* 452 (1960): "Although lapse of time and non-user are not sufficient, in and on themselves, to constitute abandonment, where sunken ship and cargo had remained in exact location for 66 years, they were abandoned"; *Hener v. United States*, 1982 *AMC* 847: "Despite preference for the law of salvage, court may apply law of finds where all parties assume property has been abandoned and no prior owner is likely to appear"; *Treasure Salvors, Inc. v. The Unidentified Wrecked and Abandoned Sailing Vessel ("Treasure Salvors I")* 569 *F.2d* 330, 336 (5th Cir. 1978): "To apply the law of salvage, by creating the fiction of continuing ownership even after the property has long been abandoned, is rather absurd, especially when the law of finds provides a rational method for determining rights in property"; *Chance v. Certain Artifacts Found and Salvaged from the Nashville*, 660 *F. Supp.* 801, 804 (S.D. Ga. 1984), 1985 *AMC* 609, aff'd 775 *F.2d* 302 (11 Cir. 1985), 1986 *AMC* 1216; *Jupiter Wreck v. The Unidentified, Wrecked and Abandoned Sailing Vessel*, 1988 *AMC* 2705; *Martha's Vineyard Scuba Headquarters v. The Unidentified, Wrecked and Abandoned Steam Vessel Etc.*, 1988 *AMC* 1109: "District judge properly applied the law of finds to salvaged artifacts lost for so long that any realistic claim of original title had disappeared. Hence, salvor, who retrieved property from wreck of vessel, which sank almost 80 years before, was entitled to assert a prime claim"; *Commonwealth of Massachusetts v. Maritime Underwater Surveys*, 1989 *AMC* 425, 429. See also Norris, *op. cit.* note 59, para. 158, 11-17, 18: "This author would limit the doctrine of "find" relative to marine disasters to long-lost wrecks, such as the *Nuestra Señora de Atocha* or where the owners of maritime properties have publicly abandoned them".

72 Fry, *op. cit.* note 69 at p. 880; Korthals, Altes, A., "Antiquities: A Legal Labyrinth", 4 *Syracuse J. Int'l L. and Comm.* (1976) pp. 77-96. Norris, *ibid* at para. 158, argues that "were publicly abandoned marine property discovered on the high seas - international waters - regarded at law as a 'find', it could well be

that violent and lawless acts of the eager or desperate 'finders' would be thus encouraged". See also Barrowman, E., "The recovery of shipwrecks in international waters: a multilateral sulution", 8 *Michigan Yearbook of International Legal Studies* (1987) pp. 231-246 and Larsen, D.P., "Ownership of Historic Shipwreck in U.S. law", 9 *The International Journal of Marine and Coastal Law* (1994) pp. 31-56 at p. 38. Larsen argues that "the law of salvage allows the court to control the excavation of the wreck... Therefore, if the court feels that the salvor acted inappropriately, the court may withdraw the salvor's right to exclusive salvage... In contrast, under the law of finds, once the court awards title, all control and rights rest in the finder leaving the court powerless to control the excavation". See, however, *infra* note 98.

73   The *in specie* award was first advanced in *Cobb Coin Company Inc. v. The Unidentified Wrecked and Abandoned Sailing Vessel (Cobb Coin II)*, where it was held that under the rather unusual circumstances of the salvage of ancient wrecks, the salvage award herein "should differ from traditional awards. It should be given *in specie* because the property salved is uniquely and intrinsically valuable beyond any monetary value." 549 *F. Supp.* 540, 561 (S.D. Fla. 1982); 1983 *AMC* 1018, 1046. A similar approach was adopted in *Treasure Salvors, Inc. v. The Unidentified, Wrecked and Abandoned Sailing Vessel, et al ("Treasure Salvors IV")*, 556 *F. Supp.* 1319, 1985 *AMC* 136 (S.D. Fla. 1983), and in *MDM Salvage, Inc. v. The Unidentified, Wrecked and Abandoned Sailing Vessel, etc.*, 631 *F. Supp.* 308, 1987 *AMC* 537. However, the Fifth Circuit rejected this approach in *Platoro Limited Inc. v. The Unidentified Remains of a Vessel, Her Cargo, Etc.*, 695 *F.2d* 893 (5th Cir. 1983); 1984 *AMC* 2288, which vacated the district court's award of the *res* because of the artifact's historical significance to the State of Texas. The award "should be in a dollar amount and limited to the value of the artifacts recovered, net of the State's expense for cleaning, preserving and cataloguing them." Similarly, in *Chance v. Certain Artifacts*, 1985 *AMC* 609, 618-619, the district court stated that: "Since an admiralty salvage award does not confer title to the salved property, no *in specie* award may be granted in respect of artifacts recovered from the sunken wreck, especially when they were subjected to a greater rate of deterioration after their removal from the river bed in which they were embedded". "Although title to the *res* rests with the State, the *Klein rationale* permits consideration of a salvage award. Plaintiffs must prove that: (1) Their services were voluntary; (2) They successfully salvaged the articles; (3) The artifacts are in marine peril". In the court's opinion, the salvors did not undertake adequate steps to ensure conservation of the artifacts and, therefore, were not entitled to a salvage award. Finally, in *Columbus-America*, 1992 *AMC* 2729, the Court of Appeals held that: "As for the logisitcs in making a salvage award, we believe that in a case such as this, an award *in specie* would be proper. Also because salvaging efforts have not been completed, the lower court might want to consider denominating the award as a percentage of the total recovery, rather than as a monetary amount. Should a specific monetary amount be too high, the underwriters could end up receiving nothing, while if an award is too low,

Columbus-America would have a discentive to complete recovery of the gold".
Columbus-America was awarded 90% of the salvaged gold and the underwriters
10%, see *Columbus-America Discovery Group v. Unidentified, Wrecked and
Abandoned Sailing Vessel Believed to Be the S.S. Central America*, U.S. District
Court (E.D. Virginia), 18 November 1993.

74   Lawrence, A., "State antiquity laws and admiralty salvage: protecting our
     cultural resources", 32 *U. Miami L. Rev.* (1977) pp. 291-338 at p. 336.

75   Lohrey, T.E., "Sunken vessels, their cargoes and the casual salvor", 20 *JAG
     Journal* (1965) pp. 25-29 at p. 28. "Of course, the only proper way to acquire
     title to salved property, whatever it may be, is by resort to the courts. As a
     practical matter, however, it is felt that such would not be necessary in the case
     of the casual salvor who salvages some trinket or relic from the ocean floor."
     Ibid at p. 29. On the contrary, archaeologists urge the need to establish the duty
     to report the accidental recovery of individual items as the latter may reveal
     the existence of a wreck site or a submerged settlement. It is, therefore, impor-
     tant that the relic should not be removed by unqualified divers.

76   See further Prott and O'Keefe, *op. cit.* note 50 at pp. 90-91, and *infra* chapter
     7, note 86.

77   Recently, however, admiralty law does seem to have begun to acknowledge
     the public interst of States in the preservation of historic wrecks off their coasts.
     The notion that salvors must act to preserve the archaeological provenance of
     a wreck has been recognised in a number of U.S. cases; even being described
     as an emerging doctrine in maritime law. See also King, M., "Recent Develop-
     ments", 31 *Harvard Int'l L.J.* (1990) pp. 313-321 and *supra* at p. 49.

78   Statement by Rep. Bennett, "Hearings Held on Historic Shipwreck Legislation",
     11 *JFA* (1984) pp. 79-96 at p. 81.

79   Green, J. and Henderson, G., "Maritime Archaeology and Legislation in Western
     Australia", 6 *I.J.N.A* (1977) pp. 245-248 at p. 247.

80   Arnold, J.B., "Some thoughts on salvage law and historic preservation", 7
     I.J.N.A (1978) pp. 173-176 at p. 173.

81   The exclusion of the law of salvage appears amongst the minimum requirements
     of the legal protection of the underwater cultural heritage at national level
     adopted by Recommendation 848 (1978) of the Council of Europe. See further
     Prott, L.V. and O'Keefe, P.J. "Final Report on Legal Protection of the Underwa-
     ter Cultural Heritage", *op. cit.* note 50 at pp. 69-70 and Shallcross, D.B. and
     Giesecke, A., "Recent Developments in Litigation Concerning the Recovery
     of Historic Shipwrecks" *Syracuse J. Int'l L. and Com.* (1983) pp. 371-404. See
     also article 4 of the ILA Draft Convention on the Protection of the Underwater
     Cultural Heritage, which reads: "Underwater cultural heritage to which this
     Convention applies shall not be subject to the law of salvage".

82   *Op. cit.* note 67. Also, the U.S.A. and Canada have formally agreed that article
     II of the Treaty on Wrecking and Salvage, signed 18 May 1908, does *not* apply
     to historic shipwrecks. See 23 *I.J.N.A.* (1994) p. 60.

83   577 *F. Supp.* 597, 1984 *AMC* 913 (D.Md. 1983) aff'd by the U.S. Courts of
     Appeals, Fourth Circuit 4/26/1985, No. 84-2170, 765 *F.2d* 139. This case was
     decided before the ASA was passed.

84 Owen, D.R., "Some Legal Troubles with Treasure: Jurisdiction and Salvage", 16 *J. Mar. Law & Com.* No. 2 April, 1985 pp. 139-179, at p. 175. "In principle, it is unworkable because there is no objective test as to what is 'ancient' and what is 'recent'. Under the *Subaqueous dictum* the law of marine salvage does not apply to the recovery of a vessel or cargo sunk 'approximately two hundred years ago'. But does the law apply to vessels sunk in 1863? 1918? 1942?"

85 Davies, P., "Wrecks on the New Zealand Coast", *N.Z.L.J.* (1983) pp. 202-205 at p. 205.

86 Braekhus, S., "Salvage of Wrecks and Wreckage - Legal Issues arising from the Runde Find", 20 *Scandinavian Studies in Law* (1976) pp. 39-68 at p. 62. Braekhus' argument concerns the relation between the Norwegian Protection of Antiquities Act of 1961, as amended in 1963, and the Administration of Wrecks Act of 1893. Finally, Davis has made the rather unusual proposal to apply salvage doctrines to conflicts raised by wartime dispersion of cultural property and its subsequent restoration. Davis, A.J., "Beyond Repatriation: A Proposal for the Equitable Restitution of Cultural Property", 33 *U.C.L.A. L.Rev.* (1985) pp. 642-663 at pp. 658-663. In her opinion, the application of salvage principles and military law would be both "fair to the individuals involved and sensitive to the broader public interest in cultural property." *Ibid* at p. 661. Davis' remarks concern exclusively the need to compensate those individuals who acted at great personal risk to salve property in danger of either capture by a belligerent force or destruction. Consequently, their relevance to the evaluation of ancient wrecks as salvage objects is limited. Davis' proposals were inspired by *Abrams v. Sotheby Parke Bernet, Inc.* concerning the sale by the auction house of Sotheby Parke Bernet of "Highly Important Hebrew Printed Books and Manuscripts" formerly owned by a leading Jewish institution (Hochschule) dissolved by the Nazis in 1941. As owner of the manuscripts appeared the wife of Dr. Guttman, an eighty two year old professor who was offered the papers in exchange for smuggling them out of Germany and who had transferred title to the manuscripts to his wife. After the entry into the dispute of the Anti-Defamation League of B'nai B'rth and the Jewish Restitution Successor Organisation (JRSO) the New York Attorney-General commenced legal action against Sotheby's and challenged Dr. Guttman's right of ownership of the manuscripts. In Davis' opinion: "The facts surrounding Dr. Guttman's manuscripts parallel the circumstances in which salvage awards traditionally have been granted. Dr. Guttman acted in the face of great danger to the Hochschule property and at great personal risk. There existed at least a reasonable apprehension of destruction of the manuscripts or, alternatively, the danger of capture by a belligerent force. If ML 59 (Military Law 59) and salvage principles were used to resolve Abrams, the JSRO would take title to the manuscripts subject to payment of a salvage award to Dr. Guttman." *Ibid.* It is notable that the litigation ended in 1985 with an out-of-court settlement, whereby the auction house agreed to recall the manuscripts that it had already sold, waive profits from the sale and redistribute the manuscripts to institutions. *Ibid* at p. 642.

87 Arnold, *op. cit.* note 80 at p. 124; Bascom, *op. cit.* note 4 at p. 174. "The degree of preservation of a ship in shallow water apparently becomes stabilised after about a dozen years, and then seems to remain unchanged for centuries. One has good reason to hope for much less deterioration in deep water, both in those first years and afterward." See also Lawson, E., "In Between: The care of artifacts from the seabed to the conservation laboratory and some reasons why it is necessary" in Arnold (ed.), *op. cit.* note 13, pp. 69-91 at p. 70.

88 (1975) 2 *Lloyd's L.R.* 338.

89 *Ibid* at pp. 344-345.

90 *Halsbury's Laws of England,* 3rd ed., vol. 35 at p. 731, para. 1109.

91 [1977] 51 *A.L.J.R.* 806.

92 *Ibid* at p. 825.

93 [1924] *P.* 78.

94 [1970] 2 *Lloyd's L.R.* 59. According to O'Keefe, however, neither the *Tubantia* nor *Morris v. Lyoness Salvage Company Ltd* addressed the question at issue. "Each case proceeded on the unquestioned basis that the persons operating on the wreck were salvors in spite of the fact that there was no immediate danger to the objects they so sought." O'Keefe, *op. cit.* note 50 at p. 4.

95 569 *F.2d* 330, 337 (5th Circ. 1978), 1978 *AMC* 1404, 1412 aff'd in part and rev'd in part, on other grounds, sub. nom. *Florida Department of State v. Treasure Salvors, Inc.,* 458 *U.S.* 670, 1983 *AMC* 144 (1982).

96 518 *F. Supp.* 816 (W.D. Texas 1981), aff'd 695 *F2d* 893 (1983).

97 577 *F. Supp.* 611, 1984 *AMC* 932.

98 1992 *AMC* at 2728. See also the holding of the district court: "Courts may decline to apply the maritime law of finds to shipwrecks of substantial historical or archaeological significane, where a salvor has failed to act in good faith to preserve the scientific, historical, and in the limited situations where applicable, archaeological provenance of the wreck and artifacts. This emerging maritime doctrine finds its roots in the admiralty principle that a salvor may not conduct so as to despoil property at sea. *Whether applying the law of finds at sea, or the law of salvage,* maritime law requires the salvor to come into court with clean hands" (emphasis added), (1989 *AMC* 1955, 1957). The court was satisfied that in addition to achieving effective possession: "Columbus-America has met the threshold requirement for application of the law of finds to abandoned shipwrecks having historical or archaeological significance. It has scrupulously avoided acts which might destroy important scientific or historical data. It has developed new technologies and applications of protecting the scientific and historical provenance of the wreck. It has created two new scientific subdisciplines to assist its efforts. It has preserved information and artifacts for future generations. It has disseminated its research. It intends to continue its efforts" (*Ibid* at p. 1959). Platoro's holding was also rejected in *Joan M. Klein v. Unidentified Wrecked and Abandoned Sailing Vessel (Believed to have sunk in 1740), 568 F. Supp.* 1562, 1984 *AMC* 669 (S.D. Fla. 1983); aff'd 1985, *op. cit.* note 72, and *Chance v. Certain Artifacts,* 1985 *AMC* 609 (S.D. Ga. 1984), which denied a salvage award, *inter alia*, because the salvors had used unscien-

tific methods. In *Klein, op. cit.* note 71 at p. 1515, the U.S. Court of Appeals affirmed the holding of the district court that: "The plaintiff was not a trained, qualified archaeologist, and his salvage efforts employed no procedures to protect or preserve the archaeological and historical significance of the artifacts he removed from the site. Unfortunately, the plaintiff's unauthorised disturbance of one of the oldest shipwrecks in the Park and his unscientific removal of the artifacts did more to create a marine peril than to prevent one" (568 *F. Supp.* at p. 1568). As argued by the district court, "archaeological provenience is not only important for the historical information that it provides, but it also adds to the value of artifacts for donation or sale to interested buyers." *Ibid* at p. 1564. In *Cobb Coin Co. v. Unidentified, Wrecked and Abandoned Sailing Vessel, Preliminary Injunction (Cobb Coin I)*, the district court held that: "There can be no suggestion that federal admiralty procedures sanction salvaging methods which fail to safeguard items and the invaluable archaeological information associated with the artifacts salvaged" (525 *F. Supp.* 186, 208 (S.D. Fla. 1981); 1983 *AMC* 966, 999), and that: "It is in the salvor's best interest to record all such data accurately both to enhance the historical value of a piece and to enhance an artifact's value for purposes of sale". *Ibid* at pp. 1014-1015. "Extra expenses involved will be taken into account in fixing the amount of the salvage award". *Ibid* at p. 1018. In its final judgment *(Cobb Coin II)* the court held that: "In order to state a claim for a salvage award on an ancient vessel of historical and archaeological significance, it is an essential element that the salvor document to the Admiralty Court's satisfaction that it has preserved the archaeological provenance of a shipwreck. To leave this element merely for consideration of a salvage award would not provide, per force, sufficient initiative to salvors to ensure that the information is obtained". 549 *F. Supp.* at p. 559, 1983 *AMC* at p. 1043. Finally, in *MDM Salvage*, the Southern District of Florida held that "there can be no suggestion that federal admiralty procedure sanction salvaging methods which fail to safeguard items and the invaluable archaeological information associated with the artifacts salved." "No party in this action has engaged in independent historical research ... nor has any party made a real effort to preserve the archaeological integrity of the purported wreck site..... Archaeologial preservation, on site photography, and the marking of sites are particularly important in the instant context, as the public interest is compelling in circumstances in which a treasure ship, constituting a window in time, provides a unique opportunity to create a historical record of an earlier era. These factors constitute a significant element of entitlement to be considered when exclusive salvage rights are considered". 1987 *AMC* at 539; 631 *F. Supp.* at 310.

99   Under U.S. law, the law of finds and the law of salvage will still be applicable to shipwrecks which do not fall within the ambit of the ASA. In other words, they will still be applicable to shipwrecks which are 'situated on the submerged lands of a State, but which are neither embedded nor included in the National Register as well as to most wrecks beyond the three mile limit. See *infra* chapter 4, at pp. 120 and 145 (note 33). See further Lawrence, *op. cit.* note 74 at pp. 336-337, who considers methods by which admiralty could become more responsive to the problems of marine antiquities.

100 1983 *AMC* at p. 1015 ("Cobb Coin I").

101 *Ibid* at p. 1014.

102 In the court's opinion, "the State's possession of a representative cross-section of recovered 1715 artifacts makes it inappropriate to award further artifacts to the State at this point. This finding is without prejudice, however, to the right of the Division of Archives, History and Records Management to intervene in future, salvage award determinations before this court to assert an interest on behalf of its citizency to particular artifacts which are not represented in its present inventory and which it feels are essential to the preservation of people's heritage". 1983 *AMC* at p. 1048 ("Cobb Coin II").

103 Statement by Prof. Fred Wendorf in "Hearings Held on Historic Shipwreck Legislation", 11 *JFA* (1984) pp. 79-96 at p. 83. A good example of contrast between the treatment given to historic shipwrecks by treasure hunters and that given by a scholarly study is provided by the wreck of the *Espirito Santu*, which suffered a lot of damage due to inexperienced and careless salvors and that of the *San Esteban* excavated under the sponsorship of the Texas State Antiquities Committee, *ibid*, pp. 83-84. The State of Texas spent a considerable amount of money which exceeded by far anything that might have been recovered by the sale of the artefacts on the antiquities market. "For this reason such a course of action will never be followed by commercial treasure hunters". *Ibid* at p. 84. In contrast, Matthewson, who was the archaeologist employed by Treasure Salvors in the recovery operations of the Spanish vessels of the Atocha and Santa Margarita argues that: "The Atocha project demonstrates that archaeologists should learn to use the profit motive to preserve the integrity of wreck sites being legally salvaged by commercial companies". Green, J., Book review: The Treasure of the Atocha by Matthewson, D., 16 *I.J.N.A.* (1987) pp. 73-75 at p. 75. Mathewson's attitude and, in general, the recruitment of "contract archaeologists" by treasure-hunters "to provide a veneer of archaeological technique" so that salvage contracts may be more easily obtained from countries with underwater heritage legislation has been strongly criticised. See Fenwick, V., "Editorial", 16 *I.J.N.A.* (1987) p. 1. The question has been also raised whether museums should boycott sales of artefacts and agree with other public institutions to restrict access to information on historic wrecks. There has been considerable debate within marine archaeological circles over codes of ethic, especially in relation to the question of dispersal of collections. In some cases the sale of the collection finances the excavation work, and by necessity the material must be sold in order to carry on working. The purists argue that the collection is unique, and, if dispersed, the information will be lost for ever. Therefore, no excavation should take place unless the material can be conserved and then preserved. The pragmatists state that sites will be excavated or looted and, unless the material is recorded, it will be totally lost. Green, *op. cit.* note 3 at p. 4. See also Johnston, *op. cit.* note 44, who discusses maritime museum and museum association positions on treasure hunting and explores some of the issues and possible solutions to what is becoming one of the most significant and controversial problems in the profession (i.e., minimum conditions a concsientious archaeologist might impose upon a salvor, if the two were to work

succesfully on a wreck site). Johnston uses the destruction of the wreck of the 18th-century British warship *De Braak* as an example to illustrate the new trend in the U.S.A., wherein salvors who have obtained permits to recover artefacts from significant shipwrecks later lose interest or financing before completing their projects, and simply abandon the ships and associated artefacts of little monetary value. In this case, ownership has diverted to the State of Delaware which is now forced to manage these resources without dedicated funding or staffing commitments. *Ibid* at p. 57. See also Miller, E.M., "A time for decision on submerged cultural resources", 31 *Oceanus*, Nov. 1988, pp. 25-34 at p. 28, who argues that the salvor's recovery of the wreck pathetically validates the 1978 Council of Europe Report that the "motivation of profit dictates a speed and efficiency in salvage which is inevitably irreconcilable with the painstaking recording and controlled investigation of a site which archaeological standards require".

104 See further Prott and O'Keefe, *Law and the Cultural Heritage, op. cit.* note 50 at pp. 127-128.

105 Protection of Wrecks Act, 1973, *c*.33. See further Department of Trade, *Historic Wrecks, The Role of the Department of Trade:* London, 1979 at p. 3. The need to devise new means of protection has often been urged by those concerned with the preservation of Britain's maritime remains. C/f. "Medina Treasure", *The Times*, Saturday, May 30, 1987; Letters to the Editor, *ibid* at p. 9. See also Dromgoole, S., "Protection of Historic Wrecks: The UK Approach Part I: The Present Legal Framework", 4 *International Journal of Estuarine and Coastal Law* (1989) pp. 26-51, who discusses the weaknesses and limitations of the present legal framework of protection of historic wreck in the United Kingdom. As argued: "The obvious and major failing of the 1973 Act is that it does not in any way update the 1894 wreck law provisions relating to handling and disposal in order to cater for the special requirements of historic wreck... in 1988, 400 artefacts from the designated wreck *HMS Invincible* were auctioned at Christie's in London. The sale raised £60.000 towards the further excavation of the wreck for which a licence had been granted. By insisting that designated sites are excavated archaeologically and then by allowing (and in some cases prescribing) the sale of finds, the present UK legislation creates an absurd situation. It seems clear that comprehensive reform of the system is required". *Ibid* at pp. 50-51. In this respect see ID, *op. cit.* note 28.

CHAPTER 3

International and Regional Instruments
Protecting the Cultural Heritage

There is a considerable number of international Conventions and Recommendations protecting the cultural heritage. The question, therefore, arises as to whether these instruments provide a satisfactory basis for protecting underwater cultural property.

INTERNATIONAL AND REGIONAL INSTRUMENTS PROTECTING THE CULTURAL HERITAGE IN GENERAL

International Protection of Cultural Property in Time of War

The Hague Convention for the Protection of Cultural Property in the Event of Armed Conflict (1954).[1]
The Hague Convention deals with the protection of movable and immovable property of great importance to the cultural heritage of every people, irrespective of origin or ownership.[2] For the purposes of the Convention, the protection of the cultural heritage comprises the safeguarding of, and respect for, such property.[3] In time of peace, the State in whose territory the cultural property is situated will take all the appropriate measures for its safeguarding against the foreseeable effects of an armed conflict.[4] During armed conflicts, both the territorial State and its enemies have the duty to respect the protected property; they should refrain from any use of the property and its immediate surroundings, which are likely to expose it to destruction or damage, and from any act of hostility directed against it.[5] Furthermore, States parties undertake to prohibit, prevent and, if necessary, put a stop to any form of theft, pillage or misappropriation of, and any acts of vandalism directed against cultural property.[6] Finally, provision is made for special protection of cultural property of very great importance and of the refuges intended to shelter it.[7]

In addition to the Hague Convention, the International Conference convened by UNESCO in 1954 adopted *Regulations for the Execution of the Protection of Cultural Property in the Event of Armed Conflict,*[8] *a Protocol and three Resolutions.*[9] Under the 1954 Protocol, the high contracting parties undertake to prevent the exportation of the protected cultural property from occupied territories and to take into their custody such property imported into their territories. In case cultural property is exported from an occupied territory, at the close of hostilities, this property must be returned to the competent authorities of the territory previously occupied. Such property shall never be retained as war reparations. The contracting party whose obligation was to prevent such exportation shall pay an indemnity to the holders in good faith of any cultural property which has to be returned.

International Protection of Cultural Property in Time of Peace

Cultural Conventions
The UNESCO Convention on the Means of Prohibiting and Preventing the Illicit Import, Export and Transfer of Ownership of Cultural Property (1970).[10]

The 1970 Convention, which followed the adoption of the 1964 Recommendation on the Means of Prohibiting and Preventing the Illicit Export, Import and Transfer of Ownership of Cultural Property,[11] aims at putting an end to the illegal trade and transfer of ownership of cultural property. Primary responsibility has been given to exporting countries (countries of origin), which should protect their cultural property by establishing national services and by maintaining export controls. In particular, they should establish and keep up to date national inventories of protected property, organise the supervision of archaeological excavations, ensure the preservation *in situ* of certain cultural property, protect certain areas reserved for future archaeological research, and establish, for the benefit of those concerned (curators, collectors, antique dealers etc.), rules in conformity with the ethical principles set forth in the Convention.[12] So far as export controls are concerned, the States parties undertake: (a) to introduce an appropriate certificate, in which the exporting State would specify that the export of the cultural property in question is authorised; (b) to prohibit the exportation of cultural property from their territory unless accompanied by the aforementioned export certificate; (c) to publicise this prohibition by appropriate means.[13]

Regrettably, the 1970 Convention did not introduce a corresponding import control system that could ensure an efficient scheme of protection. Importing countries shall only co-operate in the recovery and retrieval of cultural property, which has been illegally exported *after* the entry into force of the Convention. More specifically, they undertake: (a) to take the necessary measures, consistent with national legislations, to prevent museums within their territories from acquiring cultural property which has been illegally exported, (b) to prohibit the import of cultural property stolen from a museum or a public institution, and (c) at the request of the State of origin, to recover and return any such cultural property imported after the entry into force of the Convention.[14] The concept of restitution under the 1970 Convention is very restrictive as it covers only property stolen from another State's museums or public institutions *after* the entry into force of the Convention. Finally, States parties undertake, consistent with their laws: (a) to prevent by all appropriate means the transfer of ownership of cultural property likely to promote the illicit export of such property, (b) to ensure the earliest possible restitution of such property to the rightful owner, (c) to admit actions for recovery of lost or stolen items of cultural property brought by or on behalf of the rightful owners, and (d) to recognise the indefeasible right of each State party to classify and declare certain cultural property as inalienable and, therefore, unexportable.[15]

The definition of cultural property for the purposes of the 1970 Convention is wide enough to include underwater relics. Article 1 reads:

> "The term 'cultural property' means property which, on religious or secular grounds, is specifically designated by each State as being of importance for archaeology, prehistory, history, literature, art or science and which belongs to the following categories:
> (c) products of archaeological excavations or discoveries;
> (d) elements of artistic or historical monuments or archaeological sites which have been dismembered;
> (e) antiquities more than one hundred years old, such as inscriptions, coins and engraved seals;
> (f) objects of ethnological interest;
> (g) property of artistic items, such as: (ii) original works of statuary art and sculpture in any material."

Accordingly, not only sunken wrecks, but also elements of submerged sites and individual items found at sea may be protected, if they are specifically designated to be so. The same applies to objects of ethnological interest found in wells and submerged caves. However, since the scope of application of the 1970 Convention is confined to the territories of States parties,[16] the designation of archaeological remains in international waters as protected cultural property is not permissible. Underwater cultural property found in extraterritorial waters falls outside the scope of the Convention.[17]

The UNESCO Convention concerning the Protection of the World Cultural and Natural Heritage (1972).[18]
The 1972 Convention recognises both the interest and the duty of the international community to participate in the protection of the cultural and natural heritage of outstanding universal value. However, the duty of ensuring the protection of such heritage belongs primarily to the State on the territory of which it is situated.[19] In this respect, the States parties shall establish national services, develop scientific research and take all the necessary measures for the identification, protection, conservation, presentation and rehabilitation of this heritage.[20] International protection of the world cultural and natural heritage should be read as the establishment of a system of international co-operation and assistance to support States parties to the Convention in their efforts to conserve and identify this heritage.[21] In this respect, the 1972 Convention establishes an Intergovernmental Committee for the Protection of the Cultural and Natural Heritage of Outstanding Universal Value, the "World Heritage Committee".[22] On the basis of the inventories submitted by States, the World Heritage Committee shall establish, keep up to date and publish under the title of "World Heritage List", a list of properties forming part of the cultural and natural heritage protected by the Convention.[23] Whenever circumstances so require, the Committee shall establish, keep up to date and publish, under the title of "List of World Heritage in Danger", a list of the property appearing in the World Heritage List for the conservation of which major operations are necessary and for which assistance has been requested under the Convention.[24] The fact that a property belonging to the cultural and natural heritage has not been included in either of the two mentioned lists does not mean that it lacks outstanding universal value for purposes other than those resulting from inclusion in these lists.[25]

For the purpose of this Convention, as "cultural heritage" shall be considered:

"*monuments*: elements or structures of an archaeological nature, cave dwellings and combinations of futures, which are of outstanding universal value from the point of view of history, art or science; groups of buildings or connected buildings which, because of their architecture, their homogeneity or their place in the landscape, are of outstanding value from the point of view of history, art or science;
sites: works of man or the combined works of nature and man, and areas including archaeological sites which are of outstanding universal value from the historical, aesthetic, ethnological or anthropological points of view" (article 2).

Underwater archaeological sites of outstanding universal value[26] may also be protected as part of the world cultural heritage, if they satisfy the following conditions: first, they must be registered in the inventory of the State in whose territory they are situated, and second, and most importantly, they must be included in either the "World Heritage List" or the "List of World Heritage in Danger" drawn up on the basis of the inventories of States parties. Obviously, such sites should be located landward of the outer limit of the territorial sea. The territorial scope of application of the Convention is expressed in article 3, which reads: "It is for each State party to this Convention to identify and delineate the different properties situated on its territory". Along the same lines, natural features of the seabed, such as coral reefs, may also qualify as part of the world natural heritage protected by the UNESCO Convention.[27]

Resolutions and Recommendations[28]

The UNESCO Recommendation on International Principles Applicable to Archaeological Excavations (1956).[29] The 1956 Recommendation refers specifically to relics found underwater. According to article 1:

"For the purpose of the present Recommendation, archaeological excavations is meant any research aimed at the discovery of objects of archaeological character, whether such research involves digging of the ground or systematic exploration of its surface or is carried out on the bed or in the subsoil of inland or territorial waters of a member State."

The Recommendation applies to all remains whose preservation is in the public interest from the point of view of history or art and architecture, each member State being free to adopt the most appropriate criterion for assessing the public interest of objects found on its territory: "In particular, the provisions of the present Recommendation should apply to any monuments and movable or immovable objects of archaeological interest considered in the widest sense".[30] Each member State should ensure the protection of its archaeological heritage and apply certain common principles to all national archaeological services.[31] Further, the Recommendation advocates principles governing excavations and international collaboration, assignments of finds, scientific rights and obligations of the excavator and trade in antiquities. With regard to the controversial question of restitution, it simply suggests the mutual assistance of excavation services and museums in order to facilitate the recovery of objects derived from clandestine excavations or theft and objects exported in infringement of the legislation of the country of origin; "it is desirable that each member State should take the necessary measures to ensure this recovery".[32] Finally, in the event of armed conflict, any State occupying the territory of another State should refrain from carrying out excavations in the occupied territory.[33]

The UNESCO Recommendation concerning the Preservation of Cultural Property Endangered by Public or Private Works (1968).[34] The 1968 Recommendation acknowledges the duty of governments to ensure the protection and the preservation of the cultural heritage of mankind as well as to promote social and economic development. In an attempt to harmonise the preservation of the cultural heritage with the changes that follow from social and economic development, it recommends the extension of preservation measures over the whole territory of States and the establishment of national inventories.[35] The main principles are twofold: (a) preservation of an entire site from the effects of private or public works, and (b) salvage or rescue of cultural property, if the area in which it is found is to be transformed by public or private works.[36] Member States should give due priority to measures required for the preservation *in situ* of the endangered cultural property. When overriding economic or social conditions require that cultural property be transferred, abandoned or destroyed, the salvage or rescue operations should include a careful study of such property and the preparation of detailed records.[37] The procedures to preserve and to salvage cultural property include: (a) the making or the starting of the new work conditional on preliminary archaeological excavations, or even the delay of the work, and (b) the zoning or scheduling of archaeological reserves.[38] The broad definition of the protected cultural property enables the application of the 1968 Recommendation to property found within marine spaces that fall under the sovereignty of the coastal States.[39]

The UNESCO Recommendation concerning the Protection at National Level of the Cultural and Natural Heritage (1972).[40] The 1972 Recommendation purports "to integrate into an overall policy the achievements of our time, the value of the past and the beauty of nature". In this respect, each State should formulate, develop and apply, as far as possible, a policy to co-ordinate and to make use of all the resources available to secure the effective protection of the cultural and natural heritage.[41] For the purposes of the Recommendation, "monuments of special value from the point of view of archaeology, history, art or science, groups of buildings of special value from the point of view of history, art or science, and sites of special value from the archaeological, historical, ethnological or anthropological point of view" are considered as "cultural heritage".[42] The cultural or natural heritage should be regarded as a homogeneous whole, comprising not only works of great intrinsic value, but also more modest items that have, with the passage of time, acquired cultural or natural value.[43] The broad definition of the protected property in combination with the consideration that "the protection, conservation and presentation of the wealth that the cultural and natural heritage represents, impose responsibilities on the States in whose territory it is situated",[44] permits the application of the 1972 Recommendation to underwater sites found landward of the outer limit of the territorial sea. Unlike the World Heritage Convention, the aim of which is to preserve sites of universal importance, this Recommendation is intended to induce States to safeguard all the components of their cultural and natural heritage.

The UNESCO Recommendation for the Protection of Movable Cultural Property (1978).[45] The 1978 Recommendation promotes the adoption of a series of measures aimed at the improvement of security systems in museums and similar institutions, a better protection for private collections, religious buildings and archaeological sites, the prevention of risks during transport and temporary exhibition and the punishment of offences relating to cultural property. For the purposes of this Recommendation,

> "'movable cultural property' shall be taken to mean all movable objects which are the expression and testimony of human creation or of the evolution of nature and which are of archaeological, historical, artistic, scientific or technical value and interest, including items in the following categories:
> (i) products of archaeological exploration and excavations conducted on land and under water."

The territorial scope of the Recommendation is clearly indicated in section 2 which states that: "Each member should adopt whatever criteria it deems most suitable for defining the items of movable cultural property within its territory which should be given the protection envisaged in this Recommendation by reason of their archaeological, historical, artistic, scientific or technical value." In other words, underwater cultural property found in the territorial sea may fall within the scope of the 1978 Recommendation.

UN *General Assembly Resolutions on the Return or Restitution of Cultural Property to the Countries of Origin.*[46] The General Assembly of the United Nations has since 1973 adopted a series of biennial Resolutions on the restitution of works of art to their countries of origin. The most recent ones invite, *inter alia*,

> "member States engaged in seeking the recovery of cultural and artistic treasures from the seabed, in accordance with international law, to facilitate by mutually acceptable conditions the participation of States having a historical and cultural link with those treasures."

The significance of the UN Resolutions is twofold: first, they recognise the continuing interest of the State of origin in cultural property recovered from the sea, and second, the accommodation of those interests is regarded as part of the general question of the return of cultural property to the countries of origin. Although the general language of the text permits its application to sites found both within and beyond the territorial sea limit, there is no reference either to the scope or nature of the "participation" of the States concerned in the recovery operations. The whole issue is to be dealt with by mutually acceptable conditions and in accordance with international law.

Regional Protection of Cultural Property

The Council of Europe
The European Cultural Convention (1954)[47]
The European Cultural Convention was concluded as early as 1954. The Convention pursues a policy of common action to safeguard and encourage the development of European culture. Article 5 provides that each contracting party shall regard the objects of European cultural value placed under its control as integral parts of the common cultural heritage of Europe, shall take appropriate measures to safeguard them and shall ensure reasonable

access thereto. In addition, contracting parties undertake to promote cultural activities of European interest and to facilitate the movement and exchange of persons as well as of objects of cultural value.[48] The broad language of article 5, which refers to objects of European cultural value "under the control" of contracting parties, allows an extensive interpretation of the 1954 Convention so as to extend the scope of its application to areas outside the territorial sea. As will be discussed in Chapter 5, article 303(2) of the 1982 Convention places archaeological and historical objects found on the bed of the contiguous zone under the control of the coastal State.

The European Convention on the Protection of the Archaeological Heritage (1969).[49]
The 1969 Convention declares that the first step towards protecting the European archaeological heritage is the application of the most stringent scientific methods to archaeological research and discoveries. In this context and with the object of ensuring the protection of deposits and sites, contracting parties shall: (a) delimit and protect sites and areas of archaeological interest,[50] (b) create reserve zones for the preservation of material evidence for future research,[51] and (c) give full scientific significance to archaeological excavations. More specifically, the parties shall prohibit and restrain illicit excavations, entrust excavations only to qualified persons and ensure that control and conservation of the results are obtained.[52] They will also establish national inventories of publicly-owned and, where possible, privately-owned archaeological objects as well as facilitate the circulation of archaeological objects for scientific, cultural and educational purposes.[53] However, the international circulation of archaeological objects shall in no way prejudice the protection of the cultural and scientific interest attaching to such objects. In this respect, the parties undertake to take the necessary measures: (a) to prevent museums and other similar institutions which are under their control from aquiring archaeological objects suspected of having originated from clandestine excavations or of coming unlawfully from official excavations, (b) to spare no effort to obtain the support of museums and institutions that are not under their control for the principles set out above, and (c) to give consideration to any question of identification raised by any other contracting party and to co-operate therefor.[54] However, "the provided measures cannot restrict lawful trade in or ownership of archaeological objects, nor affect the legal rules governing the transfer of such objects".[55]

For the purposes of this Convention,

> "all remains and objects, or any other traces of human existence, which bear witness to epochs and civilizations for which excavations or discoveries are the main source or one of the main sources of information, shall be considered as archaeological objects".[56]

Since underwater archaeological excavations provide new information about past societies, lost civilizations and seafaring, a considerable number of underwater sites should fall within the ambit of article 1.[57] Despite the fact that the Convention is silent on the scope of its application, in the light of the nature of the measures adopted, which assume the undiscretionary authority and the exclusive competence of contracting States, it would be reasonable to conclude that it applies only to archaeological objects found within national territories. In other words, archaeological remains found in extraterritorial waters fall outside the scope of the Archaeological Convention.

The European Convention on Offences relating to Cultural Property (1985).[58]
Under the 1985 Convention, the member States of the Council of Europe recognise their common responsibility and solidarity in the protection of the European cultural heritage and agree to take all the necessary measures, both criminal and administrative, to prevent and punish offences against cultural property. More specifically, they undertake: (a) to take measures to enhance public awareness of the need to protect cultural property,[59] (b) to co-operate with a view to the prevention of offences against cultural property,[60] (c) to acknowledge the gravity of any act or omission that affects cultural property, and (d) to take the necessary measures for adequate sanctioning.[61] However, the main part of the Convention deals with the restitution of cultural property.[62] "The Parties undertake to co-operate with a view to the restitution of cultural property found on their territory which has been removed from the territory of another party subsequent to an offence relating to cultural property committed in the territory of a Party".[63] In this respect, provision is made for different notifications on the cultural property that was removed or found on the territories of parties and for the execution of "letters rogatory".[64]

So far as the competence to prosecute such offences is concerned, article 13(1) reads:

"Each Party shall take the necessary measures in order to establish its competence to prosecute any offence relating to cultural property:

a. committed on its territory, including its internal and territorial waters, or in its airspace;

b. committed on board a ship or an aircraft registered in it;

c. committed outside its territory by one of its nationals;

d. committed outside its territory by a person having his/her habitual residence on its territory;

e. committed outside its territory when the cultural property against which that offence was directed belongs to the said Party or one of its nationals;

f. committed outside its territory when it was directed against cultural property originally found within its territory."

Provision is also made for conflicts of competence and the *ne bis in idem* rule attached to judicial decisions.[65] The scope of the protected cultural property is rather wide so as to include underwater cultural property. Amongst the categories of cultural property enumerated in Appendix II (para. 1), the "products of archaeological exploration and excavation (including regular and clandestine) conducted on land and underwater" are included.[66]

To sum-up, the Cultural Offences Convention is applicable to cultural property found on the bed of the internal waters and the territorial sea of States parties. In case such property is the victim of an offence falling within the scope of the Convention and it is subsequently removed to the territory of another party, it should be handed over to its lawful owners.[67] In addition, the Convention enables States to prosecute offences relating to cultural property when they are committed on the high seas by one of its nationals/residents on board of ships flying its flag, or when they are directed against cultural property originally found within its territory or belonging to one of its nationals.[68] Although the Convention does not refer specifically to high seas areas, the expression "outside the territory" adopted by article 13 (1) c, d, e, f may be interpreted so as to include them. This is confirmed by article 13(1)a which encompasses the territorial sea within the notion of "territory".

Convention for the Protection of the Architectural Heritage of Europe (1985).[69]

The 1985 Convention protects the architectural heritage which "constitutes an irreplaceable expression of the richness and diversity of Europe's cultural heritage, bears inestimable witness to our past and is a common heritage of all Europeans". For the purposes of the Convention, the expression "architectural heritage" shall be considered to comprise the following permanent properties:

> "*Monuments*: all building and structures of conspicuous historical, archaeological, artistic, scientific, social or technical interest, including their fixtures and fittings;
> *Groups of buildings*: homogenuous groups of urban or rural buildings conspisuous for their historical, archaeological, artistic, scientific, social or technical interest which are sufficiently coherent to form topographically definable units;
> *Sites*: the combined works of man and nature, being areas which are partially built upon and sufficiently distinctive and honogenuous to be topographically definable and are of conspicuous historical, archaeological, artistic, scientific, social or technical interest".[70]

Each State party undertakes, *inter alia*: (a) to identify the properties to be protected through the establishment and maintenance of national inventories;[71] (b) to take statutory measures to protect the architectural heritage;[72] (c) to provide financial support for maintaining and restoring it;[73] (d) to support scientific research for identifying the harmful effects of pollution;[74] (e) to adopt intergrated conservation policies;[75] (f) to develop public awareness of the value of conserving the architectural heritage;[76] (g) to promote training in the various occupations and craft trades involved in the conservation of the architectural heritage.[77] Although the 1985 Architectural Convention is not particularly relevant to the protection of underwater sites, the latter may be covered under its scope provided of course that they are found within the territories of States parties.[78] The Convention specifically states that its provisions shall not prejudice the application of more favourable measures concerning the protection of the architectural heritage as embodied in the 1972 World Heritage Convention and the 1969 Archaeological Convention.

The European Convention on the Protection of the Archaeological Heritage (revised) (1992)[79]
The revised Convention replaces the original 1969 Archaeological Heritage Convention, by incorporating concepts and ideas which now have become accepted practice. According to article 1(1), the aim of the revised Convention is to protect the archaeological heritage as a source of the European collective memory and as an instrument for historical and scientific study. To this end, shall be considered to be elements of the archaeological heritage,

> "all remains and objects and any other traces of mankind from past epochs:

i. the preservation and study of which help to retrace the history of mankind and its relation with the natural environment;

ii. for which excavations or discoveries and other methods of research into mankind and the related environment are the main sources of information; and

iii. which are located within the jurisdiction of the parties.

The archaeological heritage shall include structures constructions, groups of buildings, developed sites, moveable objects, monuments of other kinds as well as their context, whether situated on land or under water" (article 1(2) and (3)).

The broad definition of the archaeological heritage adopted by article 1, enables the protection of all remains and objects and any other traces of mankind from past epochs together with their context, whether situated on land or underwater. So far as the protection of the underwater cultural property is concerned, the Convention constitutes an important landmark in that it expands the scope of its application so as to include "any area within the jurisdiction of the parties". As explained: "In itself, this is merely stating what is inherent in any international convention. Here it emphasises that the actual area of State jurisdiction depends on the individual States and in respect of this there are many possibilities. Territorially, the area can be coextensive with the territorial sea, the contiguous zone, the continental shelf, the exclusive economic zone or a cultural protection zone. Among the members of the Council of Europe some States restrict their jurisdiction over shipwrecks, for example to the territorial sea, while others extend it to their continental shelf. The revised Convention recognises these differences without indicating a preference for one or another".[80]

Each party undertakes, *inter alia:* (a) to institute a legal system for the protection of the archaeological heritage, making provision for the maintenance of an inventory, the creation of archaeological reserves and the mandatory reporting to the competent authorities of chance discoveries;[81] (b) to ensure that archaeological excavations and prospecting are undertaken in a scientific manner by qualified specially authorised persons;[82] (c) to implement measures for the physical protection of the archaeological heritage,[83] and (d) to ensure that environmental impact assessments and the resulting decisions involve full consideration of archaeological sites and their settings.[84] Provision is also made for the financing of archaeological research and conservation, the collection and dissemination of scientific information, the promotion of public awareness, the prevention of the illicit circulation of elements of the archaeological heritage, and for mutual technical and scientific assistance.[85]

Recommendations and Resolutions
There is a considerable number of Resolutions and Recommendations of
the Committee of Ministers and the Parliamentary Assembly of the Council
of Europe concerning the protection of cultural property.[86] Among them,
*Recommendation 883 (1984) of the Parliamentary Assembly on the United
Nations Convention on the Law of the Sea* suggests that the Committee of
Ministers do whatever is in its power to accelerate the drawing up and
implementation of a European Convention on the protection of the underwater cultural heritage and promote continued European co-operation in this
field, in particular on such questions as relations between professional and
amateur interest in the underwater heritage, and means of ensuring that
cultural heritage protection has precedence over salvage, and *Recommendation 997 (1984) of the Parliamentary Assembly on regional planning and
protection of the environment in European coastal regions* invites, *inter alia,*
States parties to promote the drawing up, ratification or implementation of
European Conventions on the architectural, archaeological and underwater
cultural heritage.

The European Union

*Council Regulation (EEC) No. 3911/92 of 9 December 1992 on the export
of cultural goods.*[87]
Council Regulation No. 3911/92 deals with the issues of the circulation of
cultural goods within the Community after the aboliton of the internal
borders and the establishment of the internal market in 1992. Whereas, under
the terms and within the limits of Article 36 of the EEC Treaty, the Member
States retain the right to define their national treasures and to take the
necessary measures to protect them in this area without frontiers, in view
of the completion of the internal market, rules on trade with third countries
were needed for the protection of the cultural goods. According to article
2, the export of all cultural goods outside the customs territory of the Community shall be subject to the presentation of an export licence. The export
licence shall be issued by a competent authority of the Member State in
whose territory the cultural object in question was lawfully and definitively
located on 1 January 1993, or, thereafter, by a competent authority of the
Member State in whose territory it is located following either lawful and
definitive dispatch from another Member State, or importation from a third
country, or reimportation from a third country after lawful dispatch from
a Member State to that country. Among the categories of cultural objects

covered by this Regulation, feature archaeological objects more than 100 years old which are the products of land or underwater excavations.[88]

Council Directive 93/7 of 15 March 1993 on the return of cultural objects unlawfully removed from the territory of a Member State.[89]
For the purposes of the Directive, cultural objects mean those objects which are classified, before or after their unlawful removal from the territory of a Member State, among the "national treasures possessing artistic, historic or archaeological value" under national legislation or administrative procedures within the meaning of Article 36 of the EEC Treaty, and belongs to one of the categories listed in the Annex, or form an integral part of public collections listed in the inventories of museum, archives or libraries' conservation collection and the inventories of ecclesiastical institutions. A cultural object is unlawfully removed from the territory of a Member State if it is removed in breach of either that Member State's rules on the protection of national treasures or the aforementioned Regulation (EEC) No 3911/92 or it is not returned after lawful temporary removal. The requesting State may initiate, before the competent court in the requested Member State, proceedings against the possessor or failing him the holder with the aim of securing the return of a cultural object which has been unlawfully removed for its territory. The return proceedings may not be brought more than one year after the requesting State became aware of the location of the cultural object and of the identity of its possessor or holder. Such proceedings may, at all events, not be brought more than 30 years after the object was unlawfully removed from the territory of the requesting Member State, or 75 years in the case of objects forming part of public collections and inventories of ecclesiastical institutions. Where return of the objects is ordered, the competent court shall award fair compensation to the possessor, provided that he exercised due care and attention in acquiring the object. Such compensation shall be paid by the requesting Member State upon return of the object. The Directive does not have a retroactive effect; it applies only to cultural objects unlawfully removed from the territory of a Member State on or after 1 January 1993.[90] Among the categories of cultural objects listed in the Annex and as a result protected under the Directive, feature "archaeological objects more than 100 years old which are the products of land or underwater excavations or finds". The adoption of Directive 93/7 raised a lot of opposition from the southern Member States, the art exporting countries of the European Union.[91]

The Organisation of American States (OAS)

Convention on the Protection of the Archaeological, Historical and Artistic Heritage of the American Nations (1976).[92]
The purpose of the San Salvador Convention is to identify, register, protect, and safeguard the property making up the cultural heritage of the American nations, so as to prevent illegal exportation or importation of cultural property, and to promote co-operation among the American States for mutual awareness and appreciation.[93] In this context, it is emphasised that regulations on ownership of cultural property and its transfer within the territory of each State shall be governed by domestic legislation.[94] Amongst the proposed measures, the following are included: (a) registration of collections and of transfer of protected cultural property, (b) registration of transactions by establishments engaged in the sale and purchase of such property, and (c) prohibition of imports of cultural property from other States without appropriate certificate and authorisation.[95] Furthermore, the establishment of inventories and records of cultural property,[96] the delimitation and protection of archaeological sites and places of historical and artistic interest,[97] and the prevention of unlawful excavations are declared.[98] For purposes of compliance with the objectives of the Convention, the General Secretariat of the OAS is charged, *inter alia*, with ensuring its enforcement and effectiveness, establishing an Inter-American Registry of cultural property, arranging technical co-operation and promoting the exchange of cultural property amongst parties.[99]

In the light of articles 5, which provides that "the cultural heritage of each State consists of property mentioned in article 2 found or created in its territory and legally acquired items of foreign origin", and 2 which adopts a broad definition of the cultural property to be protected, the 1976 Convention may be applied to relics found landward of the outer limit of the territorial sea. Article 2 reads:

"The cultural property referred to in the preceding article is that included in the following categories:
a. Monuments, objects, fragments of ruined buildings, and archaeological materials belonging to American cultures existing prior to contact with European culture, as well as remains of human beings, fauna and flora related to such cultures;
b. Monuments, buildings or ... objects of an artistic, utilitarian and ethnological nature, whole or in fragments from the colonial era and the Nineteenth century;

d. All objects originating after 1850 that have been recorded as cultural property, provided that they have given notice of such registration to other parties to the treaty;
e. All cultural property that any of the States parties particularly declares to be included within the scope of this Convention."

The definition of cultural property under the San Salvador Convention is more precise than most of the definitions featuring in similar regional or international Conventions. The same applies to the envisaged scheme of restitution, which covers all cultural property illegally exported. According to article 11, the State petitioned shall employ all available lawful means to recover and return the cultural property claimed, including judicial action if its laws so require. The petitioning State is also entitled to institute appropriate judicial action in the State petitioned in order to bring about such recovery. As soon as the latter is in a position to do so, it shall return to the petitioning State the cultural property that has been removed.[100]

INTERNATIONAL AND REGIONAL INSTRUMENTS PROTECTING THE UNDERWATER CULTURAL HERITAGE

Regional protection

Protocol concerning Mediterranean Specially Protected Areas (1982).[101]
The parties to the 1982 Protocol, which are also parties to the 1976 Barcelona Convention for the Protection of the Mediterranean Sea against Pollution,[102] agree to take all the appropriate measures to protect the marine areas that are important for the safeguarding of the natural resources and natural sites of the Mediterranean Sea Area, as well as for the safeguarding of their cultural heritage in the region. In this respect, they will establish protected areas to preserve "sites of particular importance because of their scientific, aesthetic, historical, *archaeological, cultural or educational interest*" (emphasis added).[103] The protection of a protected area may be strengthened by the establishment of one or more buffer areas in which activities are less severely restricted, while remaining compatible with the purposes of the protected area.[104] The parties agreed to adopt common guidelines and standards on the selection, establishment, management and notification of information on protected areas, and, in conformity with international law, progressively to take the measures required. The latter may include: (a) the regulation of the passage of ships and any stopping

or anchoring, (b) the regulation of any archaeological activity and of the removal of any object which may be considered as an archaeological object, and (c) the regulation of trade in and important export of "archaeological objects which originate in protected areas and are subject to measures of protection."[105]

The encouragement and development of scientific and technical research on the protected areas,[106] the information of the public of the gained scientific knowledge,[107] and the promotion of co-operation programs and programs of mutual assistance and of assistance to those developing countries which express a need,[108] are the main objectives of the Protocol. So far as administration is concerned, information on the establishment of protected and buffer areas will be given to the Organisation designated in article 13 of the Barcelona Convention, which shall compile and keep up to date a directory of protected areas in the area to which the Protocol applies.[109] This area shall be the Mediterranean Sea Areas as defined in article 1 of the Barcelona Convention, namely "the maritime waters of the Mediterranean Sea proper, including its gulf and seas, bounded to the west by the meridian passing through Cape Spartel lighthouse, at the entrance of the Straits of Gibraltar, and to the east by the southern limits of the Straits of the Dardanelles between Mehmetcik and Kumkale lighthouses."

For the purposes of the present Protocol,

> "the area shall be limited to the territorial waters of the parties and may include waters on the landward side of the baseline from which the breadth of the territorial sea is measured and extending, in the case of watercourses, up to the freshwater limit. Wet lands or coastal areas designated by each of the parties may also be included".[110]

In other words, the 1982 Protocol is not applicable to archaeological sites found either in lakes and rivers or in international waters.[111] Finally, provision is made for the situation where a party (or a non-party) intends to establish a protected area contiguous to the frontier or to the limits of the zone of national jurisdiction of another party (or non-party respectively).[112]

Recommendation 848 (1978) of the Parliamentary Assembly of the Council of Europe on the underwater cultural heritage[113]
This Recommendation recognises the historical and cultural significance of the underwater cultural heritage and suggests: (a) the drawing up of a

European Convention, (b) the declaration of 200 mile protection zones wherever that limit is in keeping with geographical realities, (c) the administration, in co-operation with UNESCO and ICOM, of the application of the convention at regional level, (d) the setting up of a European Group for Underwater Archaeology and, finally, (e) in an Annex, the minimum legal requirements that should be incorporated in national legislation.[114] Recommendation 848 (1978) constitutes the first attempt to establish regional principles on the protection of the underwater cultural heritage and to address the controversial jurisdictional issue of coastal State jurisdiction over underwater cultural property. It is a brave and scientifically sound attempt based on recommendations made by marine archaeologists.

Draft European Convention on the Protection of the Underwater Cultural Heritage (1985).[115]

The initiative for the work carried out on the Draft European Convention was taken by the Parliamentary Assembly of the Council of Europe, which, as already seen, adopted in 1978, Recommendation 848 on the protection of the underwater cultural heritage. The Committee of Ministers subsequently decided at its fifth meeting at deputies level (November 1979) to set up an *Ad Hoc* Committee of Experts on the Underwater Cultural Heritage with terms of reference to draft a European Convention on the Protection of the Underwater Cultural Heritage. The *Ad Hoc* Committee of Experts finalised the preparation of the draft Convention on the Protection of the Underwater Cultural Heritage and the draft Explanatory Report on the Convention in March 1985 and submitted them to the Committee of Ministers for approval. No decision was taken to open the Convention for signature due to Turkey's objection to its territorial scope of application. This is rather unfortunate as the latter provides the most comprehensive scheme yet for the protection of the underwater cultural heritage.

Article 1 of the Draft Convention defines the protected underwater cultural property as:

> "1. ... all remains and objects and any other traces of human existence located entirely or in part in the sea, lakes, rivers, canals, artificial reservoirs or other bodies of water, or in the tidal or other periodically flooded areas, or recovered from any such environment, or washed ashore...
>
> 2. Underwater cultural property being at least 100 years old shall enjoy the protection provided by this Convention. However, any contracting State may provide that such property which is less than 100 years shall enjoy the same protection."

In other words, the contracting States remain free to lay down a lower age-limit or a criterion of intrinsic cultural value so as to protect more recent property. The parties undertake to protect underwater cultural property and to co-operate therefor.[116] In case the specific underwater cultural property is of particular interest to other contracting States, the parties will consider providing information about its discovery and collaborating in the excavation, conservation and cultural promotion of the property to the extent permitted by its legislation.[117] The advocation of the fundamental principle to protect underwater cultural property *in situ*, is accompanied by the obligation of the parties to take all appropriate measures to conserve recovered property as well as to record fully the finds.[118] Discoveries of underwater cultural property within the area of a contracting State should be reported to the competent authorities, the discoverers being required to leave the property where it is situated. The parties, however, may require their nationals to notify the competent authorities about discoveries made in places where no State exercises control over such property.[119] The Draft Convention also provides for the official registration by each party of available information on underwater cultural property discovered or otherwise known to be located in its area[120] and the diffusion of relevant scientific information.[121]

Contracting States shall take appropriate measures to ensure the documentation and conservation of the recovered property, to promote public appreciation of the underwater cultural heritage and the need to protect it and to further underwater research.[122] Authorisations to carry out survey, excavation or recovery operations may also be granted to private persons subject to certain scientific considerations.[123] The control of traffic in underwater cultural property and the restriction of its illicit circulation is also one of the fundamental objectives of the Convention. In this respect, each party shall make available evidence on any lawful export of such property[124] and notify the other contracting States about the illegal recovery or export of underwater cultural property.[125] So far as restitution is concerned, a moderate solution is provided by article 14 which reads that:

> "Each contracting State shall take all practicable measures towards the restitution of underwater cultural property located within that State, which has been illegally recovered in the area of another Contracting State or illegally exported from such a State.'"

The obligation of parties to return such property is qualified by the words "all practical measures". Underwater cultural property illegally recovered or exported will be returned to the State of origin only when the domestic legislation of contracting parties permits it and it is considered practicable under the circumstances. Where damage has been caused to underwater cultural property in the area of a contracting State, contracting States shall co-operate, if so requested, with that State so as to discover the authors of that damage.[126] The most controversial provision of the Draft European Convention is article 2, which defines the territorial scope of its application. Article 2 is drafted on the basis of article 303(2) of the 1982 Convention and extends coastal jurisdiction over underwater cultural property in the contiguous zone. This provision will be discussed in chapter 5 together with article 303(2). The same applies for article 17 of the Draft Convention which enables contracting States to take all the appropriate measures to protect underwater cultural property in exercising their resource jurisdiction on the continental shelf (see *infra* chapter 7).

Finally, the Draft Convention provides that it will not interfere with property rights, the law of salvage or laws and practices with respect to cultural exchanges. Nor will it prejudice any jurisdiction or rights which contracting States may otherwise have under international law in respect of the protection of the underwater cultural property.[127] The implementation of the Convention will be kept under review by a Standing Committee.[128]

Bilateral Arrangements

Agreement between The Netherlands and Australia concerning Old Dutch Shipwrecks (1976).[129]
The 1976 Agreement concerns vessels which belonged to the Dutch "Vereenigde Oostindische Compagnie", known as the V.O.C., and which were wrecked off the coast of Western Australia. The two parties, having regard to the fact that the Netherlands is the present legal successor to the V.O.C. by virtue of article 274 of the 1798 Constitution of the Batavian Republic, agreed that the Netherlands should transfer to Australia all its rights, title and interest in and to wrecked vessels of the V.O.C. lying on or off the coast of the State of Western Australia and in and to any articles[130] thereof to Australia which should accept such rights, title and interest.[131] Australia agreed to make no claim on the Netherlands for reimbursement of any cost incurred,[132] while, at the same time, it recognised the continuing interest of the latter, particularly for historical and other cultural purposes, in articles recovered from any of the vessels. To give effect to this, it was agreed that

a Committee should be established to determine the disposition and subsequent ownership of the articles between the Netherlands, Australia and the State of Western Australia.[133] In this context, the sharing of material from an archaeological site should be considered as the accommodation in several localities of a corporate entity, rather than its division into parts.

The Committee shall determine the disposition of the recovered articles in accordance with the principles attached to this document.[134] The aim of the Committee will, thus, be the deposition of representative collections in the museums of the Netherlands and Australia. The remainder of the material would be held in the Western Australia Museum. Since sites are no longer regarded as a source of important individual items, but as a body of material whose collective value outweighs the importance of the individual pieces, the sharing of material from an archaeological site should be considered as the accommodation in several localities of a corporate entity, rather than its division into parts. In case the contents of an archaeological site are to be apportioned between two or more institutions, the following principles will be applicable. First, the total assemblage should be capable of re-assembly to allow further research. In this context, unnecessary splitting of a sample of closely similar objects capable of statistical treatment should be avoided. Second, where unique or rare objects themselves form a meaningful assemblage within the whole, this assemblage should not be split or, if split, perfect replicas be made to complete the assemblage.[135] "The Committee shall ensure that representative series of statistical samples and sufficient examples of the rarer objects will be deposited in the museums of the Netherlands and Australia to convey the variety and contents of each wreck to both the public and to scholars while, at the same time, ensuring that major projects of scholarly research will not be impeded by overfragmentation of the collection."[136] The Australia/Netherlands agreement constitutes one of the most important, if not unique, attempts to regulate the dispersal of archaeological material from shipwrecks and should be used as a basis for the modelling of other similar inter-State agreements.[137]

EVALUATION OF THE PROTECTION ACCORDED TO UNDERWATER CULTURAL PROPERTY UNDER THE CULTURAL CONVENTIONS

The vast majority of international and regional cultural conventions apply a territorial jurisdictional theory with respect to law making and enforcement.[138] As a result, if they were interpreted to apply to underwater cultural property, their application would be confined to sites found landward of the outer limit of the territorial sea. Notable exceptions are the 1985 European Convention on Offences Relating to Cultural Property and the 1992 European Convention on the Protection of the Archaeological Heritage (revised).

The most common measures of protection are the following:

1 Registration of the cultural property that constitutes the cultural heritage of contracting States.
2 Creation of national inventories.
3 Delimitation of archaeological sites.
4 Application of scientific standards for excavations.
5 Prohibition of illicit excavations.
6 Prevention of illegal exportation and importation of the protected property.
7 Duty to report the accidental recovery of such property.
8 Promotion of co-operation and assistance among States.

Such measures, however, are not capable of providing solutions to problems specifically related to marine archaeology, such as conflicts between salvage law and heritage legislation, the extent and scope of coastal jurisdiction over underwater cultural property, the enforcement at sea of heritage legislation and, most importantly, the protection of cultural property found in international waters. Even the few instruments which do make some reference to underwater cultural property do not provide a satisfactory scheme of protection as, first, they cover only certain aspects of the archaeological issue, and, second, they deal exclusively with problems which are common to land and underwater cultural property. That said, it would be absurd to expect a convention dealing with a specific aspect of the archaeological heritage to offer a comprehensive regime for the protection of underwater cultural property. For example, consider the 1985 European Cultural Offences Convention; within the limits of its scope, it offers the best possible solution. It not only includes underwater remains within the cultural property which is protected, but it also adopts the active and passive personality principle of jurisdiction as bases for prosecution in respect of offences committed outside the territories of contracting States; i.e. on the high seas. The same applies for the 1992 Archaeological Convention (revised) which linked together the protection of the archaeological heritage found on land and under water into a single instrument. Only international conventions specifically protecting the underwater cultural heritage can offer a more comprehensive regime of protection. At present, with the exception of the 1982 Protocol concerning Mediterranean Specially Protected Areas and the legally non-binding Recommendation 848 (1978) of the Council of Europe, there are no positive rules of international law regarding specifically the protection of underwater cultural property.

Finally, it is notable that none of the cultural conventions incorporate provisions in relation to the thorny question of *ownership* which is, thus, left open to domestic legislation. A number of them simply state that national laws are not to be affected; States are, therefore, free to adopt whatever principle they prefer.[139] Only the Draft European Convention specifically upholds the rights of the identifiable owners. The main choice is between State ownership and restriction on private ownership. It has been argued that, in relation to the protection of cultural heritage in general, State ownership is not necessary as the identity of the owner of a relic at the time of its discovery does not dictate the degree of protection offered to it. This is evidenced by the fact that the same types of control are utilised by both States with a strong commitment to private ownership and those favouring public ownership. However, State ownership of cultural property found underwater is preferable both in terms of the protection afforded to unexcavated sites and the rights of the State in case of illicit excavation or theft of the recovered items. The vesting of title to all antiquities in the State enables competent authorities to control underwater cultural property without any delay caused by ownership claims. In addition, it provides a "neat solution" to the problem posed by the difficulty in proving the origins and ownership of ancient shipwreck.[140]

NOTES

1   294 *U.N.T.S.* 215. As at 30 October 1994, 85 States were parties to the Convention. On the historical evolution of legal rules concerning the protection of cultural property in the event of armed conflict, see Solf, W.A., "Cultural Property, Protection in Armed Conflict", 9 *E.P.I.L.* (1986) pp. 64-68. See also Clément, E., "Some Recent Practical Experience in the Implementation of the 1954 Hague Convention", 3 *International Journal of Cultural Property* (1994 pp. 11-25.

2 *Ibid.* Article 1.
3 *Ibid.* Article 2.
4 *Ibid.* Article 3.
5 *Ibid.* Article 4(1).
6 *Ibid.* Article 4(3).
7 *Ibid.* Chapter II: Special Protection.
8 UNESCO, *Conventions and Recommendations of UNESCO concerning the Protection of the Cultural Heritage*, 1985 at pp. 32-43.
9 *Ibid* at pp. 44-47 and 48-49 respectively. As at 30 October 1994 73 States were parties to the Protocol.
10 10 *ILM* (1971) at p. 271. As at 31 April 1994, 81 States were parties to the 1970 Convention. One should also mention the Agreement between the Socialist States on Co-operation and Mutual Aid concerning the Means of Detention and the Return of Cultural Property Illicitly Transported Across State Borders (1986) and the Draft Unidroit Convention on Stolen or Illegally Exported Cultural Objects. For a discussion see Prott, L.V., "The preliminary draft Unidroit Convention on stolen or illegally exported cultural objects", 41 *Int'l & Comp. L.Q.* (1992) pp. 160-170. The most recent Unidroit draft is the one adopted at the Fourth Session of the Committee of Governmental Experts on the International Protection of Cultural Property in Rome, 29/9-8/10/1993.
11 Adopted by the General Conference at its thirteenth session, Paris, 19 November 1964.
12 *Op. cit.* note 10, Article 5.
13 *Ibid.* Article 6.
14 *Ibid.* Article 7. In addition, article 9 provides that when the cultural property is in jeopardy from pillage of archaeological or ethnological materials, the State in question may call upon other Staties parties who are affected, to control the flow of the jeopardised property by carrying out the necessary concrete measures, including the control of imports and exports ("emergency provision".)
15 *Ibid.* Article 13.
16 This is revealed in the overall scheme of protection, which provides both for export and import controls and the establishment of inventories of protected cultural property within the territories of States parties, and in article 4, which reads: "For the purpose of the Convention property which belongs to the following categories forms part of the cultural heritage of each State: (a) Cultural property created by the individual or collective genius of nationals of the State concerned, and cultural property of importance to the State concerned created *within the territory* of that State by foreign nationals or stateless persons resident within such territory; (b) cultural property found *within the national territory"* (emphasis added).
17 As already seen, however, the protection under the 1970 Convention is limited. For an item to be protected a dual standard must be met, the "definitional" test, and the "connection" test. The definitional test has two parts: first, the property must "on religious or secular grounds be specifically designated by each State as being of importance...", and, second, the protected objects must belong to one of the enumerated categories (article 1). The connection test requires that

the particular item must not only be cultural, but it must also be sufficiently connected to the interested country so as to give that country preference over other countries (article 4). It is notable that the Convention itself does not provide any means for determining priorities in case of conflicting factors. See further Gordon, J.B., "Comment: The UNESCO Convention on the Illicit Movement of Art Treasures", 12 *Harvard Int'l L.J.* (1971) pp. 537-556 at pp. 542-546.

18   11 *ILM* (1972) at p. 1358. As at 30 October 1994, 139 States were parties to the 1972 Convention.

19   *Ibid.* Article 4.

20   *Ibid.* Article 5(b), (c), (d).

21   *Ibid.* Article 7.

22   *Ibid.* Article 8(1).

23   *Ibid.* Article 11(2).

24   *Ibid.* Article 11(4).

25   *Ibid.* Article 12.

26   The Convention does not define the notion of "outstanding universal value". However, this is elaborated in the Operational Guidelines for the Implementation of the World Heritage Convention, WHC/2/Revised December 1988, which specify criteria on the basis of which cultural property is considered to be of "outstanding universal value".

27   Out of the 358 properties which the World Heritage Committee has included in the World Heritage List (as at January 1992), 260 are cultural sites, 84 natural sites and 14 mixed sites in 84 States. Among these, one should mention the Galapagos Islands (Ecuador).

28   The following Recommendations have been adopted by UNESCO on the protection of the cultural heritage: (1) Recommendation of International Principles Applicable to Archaeological Excavations (1956); (2) Recommendation concerning the Most Effective Means of Rendering Museums Available to Everyone (1960); (3) Recommendation concerning the Safeguarding of the Beauty and Character of Landscapes and Sites (1962); (4) Recommendation on the Means of Prohibiting and Preventing the Illicit Export, Import and Transfer of Ownership of Cultural Property (1964); (5) Recommendation concerning the Preservation of Cultural Property Endangered by Public or Private Works (1968); (6) Recommendation concerning the Protection at National Level of the Cultural and Natural Heritage (1972); (7) Recommendation concerning the International Exchange of Cultural Property (1976); (8) Recommendation concerning the Safeguarding and Contemporary Role of Historic Areas (1976); (9) Recommendation for the Protection of Movable Cultural Property (1978); (10) Recommendation for the Safeguarding and Preservation of Moving Images (1980); (11) Recommendation on the safeguarding of the traditional culture and folklore. See UNESCO, *op. cit.* note 8. In addition, one should mention the considerable number of UNESCO and UN Resolutions on the restitution and return of works of art to countries victims of expropriation, and the Resolutions of the Intergovernmental Committee for Promoting the Return of Cultural Property to its Countries of Origin or its Restitution in Case of Illicit Appropriation. In this

section, only those Recommendations which are significant to underwater cultural property will be examined.

29 Adopted at the ninth session of the General Conference, 5 December 1956; UNESCO, *ibid* at pp. 101-114.

30 *Ibid.* Article 2.

31 *Ibid.* Articles 4 and 6.

32 *Ibid.* Article 31.

33 *Ibid.* Article 32.

34 UNESCO, *op. cit.* note 8 at pp. 147-161.

35 *Ibid.* Articles 3 and 4.

36 *Ibid.* Article 5.

37 *Ibid.* Article 9.

38 *Ibid.* Articles 23 and 24(a) respectively.

39 Article 1: "For the purpose of this recommendation, the term 'cultural property' applies to: (a) immovables, such as archaeological and historic or scientific sites, structures or other features of historic, scientific artistic or architectural value; (b) movable property of cultural importance including that existing in or recovered from immovable property and that concealed in the earth..". As noted, the scope of application of the Recommendation is confined to the territories of Member States.

40 UNESCO, *op. cit.* note 8 at pp. 163-180.

41 *Ibid.* Article 3.

42 *Ibid.* Article 1.

43 *Ibid.* Article 5.

44 *Ibid.* Article 4. See also article 18: "Member States should ... take all necessary measures to ensure the protection of the cultural and natural heriatge in their territories".

45 UNESCO, *op. cit.* note 8 at pp. 209-224.

46 Resolution 38/34 of 25 November 1983: 38 *UN GAOR Supp.* No. 47 (A/38/47) at p. 24; Resolution 40/19 of 21 November 1985, 40 *UN GAOR Supp. No. 53* (A/40/53) at p. 23; Resolution 42/7 of 22 October 1987, 42 *UN GAOR Supp.* No. 49 (A/42/49) at p. 10; Resolution 44/18 of 6 November 1989, 44 *UN GAOR Supp.* No. 49 (A/44/49) at p. 30; Resolution 46/10 of 22 October 1991, 46 *UN GAOR Supp.* No. 49 (A/46/49) at p. 14; Resolution 48/15 of 2 November 1993, 48 *UN GAOR Supp.* No. 49 (A/48/49) at p. 19.

47 218 *U.N.T.S.* 139; *Europ. T.S.* No. 18. The Convention entered into force on 5.5.1955. As at 30 October 1993, 41 States were parties to the 1954 Convention.

48 *Ibid.* Article 3 and 4.

49 *Europ. T.S.* No. 66. The Convention entered into force on 20.11.1970. As at 30 October 1994, 23 States were parties to the 1969 Convention.

50 *Ibid.* Article 2(a).

51 *Ibid.* Article 2(b).

52 *Ibid.* Article 3.

53 *Ibid.* Article 5(a).

54 *Ibid.* Articles 6(1), (2)a, 2(b)ii and 7.

55 *Ibid.* Article 8.
56 *Ibid.* Article 1.
57 The restriction of the scope of "archaeological objects" to those where excavations or discoveries are the "main source or one of the main sources of information" has been criticised by Prott and O'Keefe: "In certain instances, it would be debatable whether excavations are the main sources of information, even if they are useful in understanding the historical event." Prott, L.V. & O'Keefe, P.J., *The Law and the Cultural Heritage*, vol. 1, *Discovery and Excavation*, Professional Books Ltd., Abingdon, 1984 at p. 170.
58 *Europ. T.S.* No. 119. The Convention has not entered into force. As at 1 March 1994, 6 States had signed the 1985 Convention.
59 *Ibid.* Article 4.
60 *Ibid.* Article 5.
61 *Ibid.* Article 12.
62 *Ibid.* Part IV.
63 *Ibid.* Article 6.
64 *Ibid.* Articles 7-11.
65 *Ibid.* Part V. Articles 17-19.
66 With respect to property listed in Appendix II (para. 1), the implementation of the Convention is mandatory. However, the scope of the latter may be enlarged so as to include one or more of the categories of property listed in para. (2), or property not listed in Appendix II but declared to be protected by a contracting State. *Ibid,* article 2(2) and (3). According to article 26, the rule of reciprocity is applicable in both these instances. The same applies to the scope of the offences relating to cultural property. The implementation of the Convention is obligatory over offences listed in Appendix III (para. 1), with potential extension to offences listed in para. (2) or declared to be so by any contracting State. *Ibid,* article 3.
67 According to the Explanatory Report, "restitution" presupposes that: (a) the cultural property was found on the territory of a party (State A); (b) the cultural property had been removed from the territory of another party (State B), and that (c) this removal was the result of an offence against cultural property committed in the territory of a party (State C), it being understood that State C can be a third State or the same as either State A or State B. See *Explanatory Report on the European Convention on Offences relating to Cultural Property*, Council of Europe, Strasbourg, 1985 at p. 11, as well as article 6.
68 Under the qualifications provided by article 13(2): In the cases where an offence was committed outside the territory of a party by a person having his/her habitual residence on its territory or it was directed against cultural property originally found within its territory, the party shall not be competent to institute proceedings unless the suspected person is on its territory.
69 *Europ. T.S.* No. 121. The Convention entered into force on 01.12.1987. As at 30 October 1994, 22 States were parties to the 1985 Convention.
70 *Ibid.* Article 1.
71 *Ibid.* Article 2.

72 *Ibid.* Articles 3 and 4.
73 *Ibid.* Article 6.
74 *Ibid.* Article 8.
75 *Ibid.* Article 10.
76 *Ibid.* Article 15.
77 *Ibid.* Article 16.
78 Under article 24, any State may at the time of signature or when depositing its instrument of ratification, acceptance approval or accession, specify the territory or territories to which this Convention shall apply.
79 *Europ. T.S.* No. 143. The Convention has not entered into force. As at 30 October 1994, 24 States had signed the 1985 Convention, while 3 had ratified it. See further Vedovato, G., "La tutele du partimoine archéologique subaquatique dans une Convention du Conseil de l'Europe". Paper submitted at the *66th ILA Conference in Buenos Aires,* 14-20 August 1994.
80 *Explanatory Report on the European Convention on the Protection of the Archaeological Heritage (revised),* Provisional edition, MPC (91)8.
81 *Ibid.* Article 2.
82 *Ibid.* Article 3.
83 *Ibid.* Article 4.
84 *Ibid.* Article 5(iii).
85 *Ibid.* Articles 6-12.
86 See, *inter alia, Parliamentary Assembly*: (i) Recommendation 589 (1970) on the European Conference of Ministers responsible for the preservation and rehabilitation of the cultural heritage of monuments and sites; (ii) Recommendation 612 (1970) on a draft outline law for the active protection of immovable property in Europe; (iii) Resolution 598 (1975) on the social aspects of architectural conservation; (iv) Recommendation 848 (1978) on the underwater cultural heritage; (v) Recommendation 872 (1979) on industrial archaeology; (vi) Recommendation 880 (1979) on the conservation of the European architectural heritage; (vii) Recommendation 921 (1981) on metal detectors and archaeology; (viii) Resolution 808 (1983) on the return of works of art; (ix) Recommendation 1042 (1986) on protecting the cultural heritage against disasters; (x) Recommendation 1072 (1988) on the international protection of cultural property a the circulation of works of art; (xi) Resolution 916 (1989) on redundant religious buildings; (xii) Recommendation 1171 (1992) on the situation of the cultural heritage in Central and Eastern Europe. *Committee of Ministers*: (i) Resolution (76)28 concerning the adaptation of laws and regulations to the requirements of intergrated conservation of the architectural heritage; (ii) Recommendation No R (88)5 of the Committee of Ministers to member States on control of physical deterioration of the architectural heritage accelerated by pollution; (iii) Recommendation No R (89)5 of the Committee of Ministers to member States concrning the protection and enhancement of the archaeological heritage in the context of town and country planning operations; (iv) Recommendation No R (89)6 of the Committee of Ministers to member States on the protection and enhancement of the rural architectural heritage; (v) Recommendation No R (91)6 of the Committee of Ministers to member States on measures likely to promote the

funding of the conservation of the architectural heritage; (vi) Recommendation No R (91)13 of the Committee of Ministers to member States on the protection of the twentieth-century architectural heritage.

87   *OJ L* 395 of 31.12.1992 at p. 1. See also Commission Regulation (EEC) No 752/ 93 of 30 March 1993 laying down provisions for the implementation of Council Regulation (EEC) No 3911/92 on the export of cultural goods, *OJ L* 77 of 31.3.1993 at p. 24.

88   The items covered by the Regulation are listed in an Annex.

89   *OJ L* 74 of 27.3.1993 at p. 74. For a discussion see Post, H.H.G., "The protection of archaeological property and community law: framework and new developments". Paper presented at the *Athens Conference on the Protection of the Archaeological Heritage*, November 26-27, 1992; Sico, L., "Le norme internazionali e comunitarie concernenti l'illecita rimozione dei beni culturali rinvenuti sul fondo marino". Paper presented at the *Seminario: La protezione del partimonio culturale subacqueo nel Mediterraneo,* organised by the Università degli Studi di Roma 'Tor Vergata', Anacapri, 1 October 1994 and Voudouri, D., "The idea of a common European cultural heritage in view of the abolition of the internal frontiers", *ibid.* See also Frigo, M., "The proposed (EEC) Council Directive on the Return of Unlawfully Exported Cultural Objects", 2 *International Journal of Cultural Property* (1993) pp. 73-80.

90   *Ibid.* Article 13. According to article 15, the Directive shall be without prejudice to any civil or criminal proceedings that may be brought, under the national laws of the Member States, by the requesting State and/or the owner of a cultural object that has been stolen. Finally, under article 18, Member States shall bring into force the laws, regulations and administrative provisions necessary to comply with this Directive within nine months of its adoption, with the exception of Belgium, Germany and the Netherlands which must conform with this Directive at the latest twelve months from the date of its adoption.

91   The effectiveness of the measures adopted will indeed be limited, especially in relation to cultural objects which are not classified, such as the products of underwater excavations or finds, since it will be extremely diffficult for a Member State to prove the time of unlawful removal from its territory. As already seen, under article 1(1), a cultural object may be classified "among the national treasures possessing artistic, historic or archaeological value" *before* or *after* its unlawful removal from the territory of a Member State. The southern member States have also strongly objected to the limitation period for return proceedings adopted by the Directive in article 7.

92   15 *ILM* (1976) at p. 1350.

93   *Ibid.* Article 1.

94   *Ibid.* Article 7.

95   *Ibid.* Article 7(a), (b) and (c).

96   *Ibid.* Article 8(c).

97   *Ibid.* Article 8(d).

98   *Ibid.* Article 9.

99   *Ibid.* Article 17.

100 *Ibid.* Article 12.
101 Text reprinted in Simmonds, K.R. (ed.), *New Directions in the Law of the Sea [New Series]*, J.20, Release 84-1, September 1984 and in Burhenne, W.E. (ed.), *International Environmental Law: Multilateral Treaties*, Berlin, 1982, No.26, pp. 11-18.
102 15 *ILM* (1976) at p. 290.
103 *Op. cit.* note 101. Article 3(2)b.
104 *Ibid.* Article 5.
105 *Ibid.* Article 7.
106 *Ibid.* Article 10.
107 *Ibid.* Article 11.
108 *Ibid.* Article 15.
109 *Ibid.* Article 8.
110 *Ibid.* Article 2. It is noteworthy that article 1 of the Barcelona Convention expressly excludes the internal waters from the scope of its application.
111 See, however, article 1(2) which states: "Nothing in this Protocol shall prejudice the codification and development of the law of the sea by the United Nations Conference on the Law of the Sea ..., nor the present or future claims and legal views of any State concerning the law of the sea and the nature and extent of coastal and flag State jurisdiction".
112 *Ibid.* Article 6.
113 Council of Europe, Parliamentary Assembly, *Texts adopted by the Assembly*, sessions 30-32 (1978-81). Reprinted in Council of Europe, Parliamentary Assembly, *The Underwater Cultural Heritage*, Report of the Committee on Culture and Education, Doc. 4200-E, Strasbourg, 1978, pp. 1-4.
114 (i) There should be no loopholes in the system of protection; (ii) Protection should cover all objects that have been beneath the water for more than 100 years (with the possible exclusion of less important objects or inclusion of more recent significant objects); (iii) individual objects should also be protected; (iv) national jurisdiction should be extended up to the 200 mile limit; (v) salvage and wreck law should not apply to any items protected; (vi) compulsory reporting of finds; (vii) establishment of a single authority dealing with both land and underwater finds; (viii) establishment of a single authority dealing with both land and underwater finds.
115 *Doc. CAHAQ(85)5.* Publication of the full text of the Draft Convention in an annex is not possible, due to restrictions imposed by the Council of Europe.
116 *Ibid.* Article 3.
117 *Ibid.* Article 4.
118 *Ibid.* Article 5.
119 *Ibid.* Article 6.
120 *Ibid.* Article 7.
121 *Ibid.* Article 8.
122 *Ibid.* Articles 9 and 10.
123 *Ibid.* Article 11.
124 *Ibid.* Article 12.

125 *Ibid.* Article 13.
126 *Ibid.* Article 15.
127 *Ibid.* Article 18.
128 *Ibid.* Articles 19 and 20.
129 Schedule 1 to Australian Historic Shipwrecks Act, 1976 in *Acts of the Parliament of the Commonwealth of Australia*, 1976, Australian Government Publishing Service, 1978 at pp. 1613-1616.
130 The expression "articles" means any part of the said vessels that has become or has been detached or removed therefrom, as well as the fittings, goods and other property, wherever situated, that were installed or carried on those vessels. *Ibid.* Article 2.
131 *Ibid.* Article 1.
132 *Ibid.* Article 3.
133 *Ibid.* Article 4.
134 *Ibid.* Article 6.
135 Arrangement Setting Out the Guiding Principles for the Committee to Determine the Deposition of Material from the Shipwrecks of Dutch East India Company Vessels off the Coasts of Western Australia: General Principles. This document was signed at the same time with the Agreement.
136 *Ibid.* Operating Principles.
137 For a discussion of the Agreement see Prott and O'Keefe, *op. cit.* note 57 at pp. 278-291 and Korthals Altes, A., "Submarine antiquities: a legal labyrinth", 4 *Syracuse J. Int'l L. and Comm.* (1976) pp. 77-96 at p. 86.
138 Bassiouni, M.C., "Reflections on criminal jurisdiction in international protection of cultural property", 10 *Syracuse J. Int'l L. & Com.* (1983) pp. 281-322 at p. 303.
139 The Preliminary Report of the Director-General of UNESCO on the 1956 UNESCO Recommendation on International Principles Applicable to Archaeological Excavations, is illustrative of this atittude. On the issue of ownership, para. 24, reads: "Any recommendation cutting across the property laws in force in each State would meet with strong opposition and that therefore it was best to leave States complete free to adopt whatever principle they thought preferable". *GUA/ 68*, 9 August 1955.
140 Prott, L.V. and O'Keefe, P.J. "Final Report on Legal Protection of the Underwater Cultural Heritage" in Council of Europe, *The Underwater Cultural Heritage, op. cit.* note 113, Appendix II at p. 68; ID, *op. cit.* note 57 at pp. 189-202. Against this, it is argued that the automatic assertion of State ownership will encourage illicit excavation of underwater sites. It is suggested that, where possible, the State should award a portion of the finds to the excavator. Shore, H., "Marine Archaeology and International law: Background and Some Suggestions", 9 *San Diego L. Rev.* (1972) pp. 668-700 at p. 696. See also Church, J., "Evaluating the effectiveness of foreign laws on national ownership of cultural property in U.S. Courts", 30 *Columbia Journal of Transnational Law* (1992) pp. 179-229 at p. 207 *et seq.*, who argues that: "The U.S. courts should not accept wholesale declarations of national ownership. This is particularly impor-

tant because a foreign national's rights to both private ownership of property and liberty are affected. National cultural property ownerhip laws create, as a result of their enactment, the crime of stealing national cultural property. In some countries, punishment for the violation of a national ownership law or an export regulation by a foreign national can result in a long prison term, life imprisonment or even death". On the other hand, "State ownership of selected cultural property of particular significance has never been disputed. It is the application of blanket ownership laws to items like property, coins, etc., that commentators feel is unacceptable". See also Merryman, J.H., "The nation and the object", 3 *International Journal of Cultural Property* (1994) pp. 61-76. The importance of private banking has also been emphasised, especially in respect of archaeologically rich countries which are unable to either undertake or complete successfully archaeological projects. This argument has a basis in reality. However, as privately backed excavations are often financed by the sale of the recovered artefacts, such practices may end up in the dispersal of significant archaeological collections.

PART TWO

INTRODUCTION

The Law of the Sea

The division of the oceans into functional jurisdictional zones precludes one from making a single comprehensive statement of the law that applies to marine archaeology.[1] In order to determine the applicable law it is necessary to examine each one of these zones to ascertain its legal status in relation to cultural property found within its bounds. As underwater relics are always located on and/or under the seabed, the legal regime of the latter is clearly of primary importance to the study of marine archaeology. Within the territorial sea limit, the legal status of the seabed is the same as that of the superjacent waters, namely territorial sovereignty. Beyond the territorial sea limit, the existence of functional zones urges their separate examination. The ensuing discussion of the jurisdictional zones of the oceans is divided into three sections. The first section examines the respective regimes as envisaged by the Geneva Conventions (1958)[2], the second section deals with the UN Convention on the Law of the Sea (1982)[3], and the third section discusses customary international law. The four *Geneva Conventions (1958)* do not provide a satisfactory basis for protecting the underwater cultural heritage. Since none of them makes specific reference to underwater cultural property, only those provisions which may have a bearing on the protection of the cultural heritage of the oceans will be considered. These Conventions are still in force and State parties to them will remain bound until they lawfully denounce them or become parties to the UN Convention on the Law of the Sea (1982), which is expressly stated to prevail over them (article 311).

The *UN Convention on the Law of the Sea (1982),* which will enter into force on 16 November 1994, is the first codification of the law of the sea to regulate objects of an archaeological and historical nature found at sea. It is interesting to look back at the manner in which the archaeological issue was dealt with by the Third UN Conference on the Law of the Sea (UNCLOS III). Within UNCLOS III, underwater archaeology was not considered *per se*.

Instead, in the course of the discussions of the various ocean regimes, regard was paid to the accidental location of submerged archaeological and historical objects. Initially, the discussion of the archaeological issue was limited to relics found on the seabed beyond the limits of national jurisdiction. This is not surprising as UNCLOS III had its origins in the Sea Bed Committee which dealt with the deep seabed.[4] The result was the adoption of article 149 providing for historical and archaeological objects found in the Area. In 1979, various proposals were made in the Second Committee of the Conference to include provisions defining the legal status of archaeological and historical objects situated on the continental shelf and/or the bed of the exclusive economic zone (EEZ). When suggestions were made for a general duty to protect these relics wherever found, the debate was passed on to the Plenary of the Conference, which adopted article 303 among the General Provisions of the Convention. The regime of archaeological and historical objects found at sea was thus discussed by two (three, if the Plenary of the Conference is also included) different Committees. The fact that three separate bodies were concerned with the same issue, even successively, had far reaching consequences. For a considerable period of time, there was even a differentiation in the *formulae* employed to define the protected items. Draft article 149 referred to "objects of archaeological and historical nature", while draft article 303 referred to "archaeological objects and objects of historical origin". It was the drafting Committee in 1982 which removed this inconsistency. Disputes over archaeological and historical objects concern the interpretation or application of the Convention and would, therefore, fall under the general scheme on the settlement of disputes (Part XV).[5] As will be seen in chapter 8, deep seabed archaeological activities do not qualify as "activities in the Area" and as a result they are not subject to the dispute system envisaged by the Convention for the international deep seabed (Part XI, section 5). The provisions of the recently adopted Agreement Relating to the Implementation of Part XI of the 1982 Convention on the Law of the Sea[6] make no adjustment in article 149 or in the dispute settlement procedures set out in the Convention.

In the sphere of *customary international law*, there is less certainty on the legal regime of underwater cultural property, epecially that found in extra-territorial waters. Since articles 303 and 149 of the 1982 Convention constitute a progressive development of the law,[7] the question arises as to whether they have acquired a customary status in the years following the adoption of the Convention.[8] However, some scholars doubt whether third States can selectively claim rights derived from the 1982 Convention as rules of custom. In their view, the 1982 Convention was adopted as a package, and, therefore, particular provisions which were included as part of the overall package may not be singularly acceptable. It has been argued that the package nature of the 1982 Convention modified the application of the traditional treaty-custom rules identified by the ICJ in the *North Sea Continental Shelf Cases (1969)*.[9] According to Caminos and Molitor, the legal effect of the package deal is confined to those provisions that had not acquired customary status at the time that the Convention was formally adopted; both the innovative provisions that achieved customary status while the negotiations were being held, and those provisions which were carried over directly from the 1958 Conventions and which reflected customary law prior to UNCLOS III are excluded from its effect.[10] However, this is not the prevailing approach in doctrine. Most authorities recognise that a very complex interaction between treaty law and customary law exists in the sphere of the contemporary law of the sea. Whereas many of the provisions of the Convention undoubtedly restate existing law, in other cases, the position is not so clear as there is less than uniform State practice.[11] As argued, it would be futile to discuss the correspondance to customary law of the Convention as a whole; such correspondance must be ascertained for each rule, or group of closely connected rules, in the Convention. In this respect all relevant factors of international practice will be taken into account, not excluding positions taken at the Conference, but certainly including positions taken outside the Conference especially after its conclusion.[12] Thus, a third State will not be precluded from claiming particular provisions of the 1982 Convention as part of customary law, if they have been generally assumed as such. In such cases the rule contained in article 38 of the Vienna Convention on the Law of Treaties is applicable.[13]

NOTES

1   Arend, A.C., "Archaeological and Historical Objects: The International Legal Implications of UNCLOS III", 22 *V.J.I.L.* (1982) pp. 777-803 at p. 782.

2   Doc.A/CONF.13/L.52-L.55 and Misc. No. 15 (1958), Cmnd. 584. The four Conventions are reprinted in Brownlie, J. (ed.), *Basic Documents in International Law*, 2nd ed. Clarendon Press, Oxford 1982, pp. 77-115. See also Convention on the Territorial Sea and the Contiguous Zone (TSC), 516 *U.N.T.S.* 205; Convention on the Continental Shelf (CSC), 499 *U.N.T.S.* 311; Convention on the High Seas (CHS), 450 *U.N.T.S.* 82; Convention on Fishing and Conservation

of Living Resources on the High Seas, 559 *U.N.T.S.* 285. The latter is of no relevance to the protection of the underwater cultural heritage.

3 Under article 308(1), the Convention will enter into force 12 months after the date of deposit of the sixtieth instrument of ratification or accession. The sixtieth instrument of ratification was deposited by Guyana on 16 of November 1993. United Nations *Report of the Secretary-General on the Law of the Sea: Addendum* (UN Doc.A/48/527/Add.1), 30 November 1993, p. 1.

4 In 1967, the UN General Assembly established the Sea Bed Committee to examine the question of the deep seabed lying beyond the limits of national jurisdiction over the continental shelf, following a proposal by Dr. Arvid Pardo, the Maltese ambassador. In the course of its work, the Committee realised that the question of the deep seabed was closely related to other unresolved issues of the law of the sea and proposed to the UN General Assembly the convention of a Conference on the law of the sea on a broad range of issues. The result was Resolution 2750 (1970) under which the General Assembly decided to convene a Conference on the law of the sea in 1973 and authorised the Seabed Committee to examine the existing conditions of the law of the sea to draw its conclusions therefrom and to present certain proposals of legal nature. See 25 *UN GAOR Supp.* No. 28 (A/8028) at p. 26. The Sea Bed Committee changed its character and was then engaged in Preparatory Work for the Conference (1971-1973). While the Seabed Committee was engaged in Preparatory Work, the archaeological issue was dealt with by the First Sub-Committee. Since the holding of the Conference, the negotiations took place in front of the First Committee. The Conference itself, as was the Sea Bed Committee, was organised in three Committees: The First Committee (I), corresponding to Sub-Committee I of the Sea Bed Committee, dealt with issues pertaining to the deep seabed. The Second Committee (II) dealt with the territorial sea, the contiguous zone, the continental shelf, the exclusive economic zone (EEZ), the high seas as well as with specific aspects of those regimes such as straits and archipelagos. The Third Committee (III) dealt with the preservation of the marine environment and marine scientific research. Finally, the General Provisions of the Convention were discussed by the Plenary of the Conference.

5 Part XV is divided into three sections: section 1 declares the general obligation to settle disputes by peaceful means, while preserving the right of States parties to settle such disputes by peaceful means of their own choice; section 2 deals with the compulsory procedures entailing binding decisions, and section 3 with the limitations and exceptions to the compulsory procedures. If no settlement is reached by recourse to section 1, under article 286, the dispute must be submitted, at the request of any party to the dispute, to the court or tribunal having jurisdiction under section 2. More specifically, article 287(1) enables States parties to choose by means of written declaration one or more of the following courts: (a) The International Tribunal for the Law of the Sea, established in accordance with Annex VI; (b) The International Court of Justice; (c) An arbitral tribunal constituted in accordance with Annex VII; (d) A special tribunal constituted in accordance with Annex VIII. If the parties to a dispute have made no such declaration, or they have not accepted the same procedure,

the dispute must be submitted to arbitration in accordance with Annex VII unless the parties otherwise agree. Finally, according to article 288(1) "a court or tribunal referred to in article 287 shall have jurisdiction over any dispute concerning the interpretation or application of this Convention ...". "All the dispute settlement procedures ... shall be open to States Parties" (article 291(1)).

6   The Agreement, which was adopted on 28 July 1994 at an extraordinary session of the General Assembly of the United Nations is the result of the Secretary General's informal consultations with representatives of a number of developed and developing countries from 1990-1994. These took place in an attempt to re-evaluate Part XI in the light of recent political and economic developments and thus enable universal participation in the 1982 Convention.

Article 2 provides that the provisions of the Agreement and Part XI will be interpreted and applied together as a single instrument, but in the event of any inconsistency, the provisions of the Agreement will prevail. After the adoption of the Agreement, any instrument of ratification or formal confirmation or accession to the Convention shall represent also consent to be bound by the Agreement (article 4). The Agreement shall enter into force 30 days after the date when 40 States have established their consent to be bound, provided that such States include at least seven States referred to in para. 1(a) of Resolution II of UNCLOS III of which at least five must be developed States (article 6). If on 16 November 1994 the Agreement has not entered into force, article 7 provides for its provisional application pending its entry into force. Provisional application shall terminate upon the date of its entry into force, or on 16 November 1998 if on that date the requirement in article 6 of consent to be bound by this Agreement by at least seven States (of which at least five must be developed countries) has not been fulfilled. For a discussion see Anderson, D., "Legal effects of mechanisms for adjusting Part XI". Paper presented to the *18th Annual Seminar of the Center for Oceans Law and Policy, University of Virginia, School of Law*, Rhodos 22-25 May 1994; Treves, T., "The Agreement completing the Law of the Sea Convention: formal and procedural aspects", *ibid.*

7   Although the line between codification and progressive development of the law of the sea under the 1982 Convention is a shadowy one, the provisions dealing with archaeological and historical objects are undoubtedly new, there being no such law prior to the negotiations.

8   In the *North Sea Continental Shelf Cases (1969), I.C.J. Reports* (1969) p. 3 the ICJ at pp. 39 (para. 63) and 42 (para. 72) recognised that a multilateral convention, even if it does not in all respects codify existing customary law, may lead to the crystallization of customary law or influence its subsequent adoption. The Court has confirmed this statement in the *Case concerning Military and Paramilitary Activities In and Against Nicaragua (Nicaragua v. United States of America), I.C.J. Reports* (1986) p. 14 at p. 95 (para. 177). See however, Butler who argues that: "In this case, the multilateral treaty is not in force. The issue therefore is not whether the 1982 Convention provisions are or have become customary rules of international law, but whether customary rules of international law exist or are coming into being which happen to have a counterpart in the Convention awaiting the requisite minimum of ratifications

to enter into force". Butler, W.E., "Custom, Treaty, State Practice and the 1982 Convention", 12 *Marine Policy* (1988) pp. 183-186 at p. 185; 81 *American Society of International Law Proceedings* (1987) pp. 84-88. Nevertheless, the ICJ in a number of cases has resorted to the 1982 Convention to establish whether there existed a rule of customary law even before its entry into force: see, *inter alia*, the Tunisia/Libya Continental Shelf Case, *I.C.J. Reports* (1982) p. 18, where, however, the two parties particularly instructed the court to take into account the "new accepted trends in UNCLOS III"; the Nicaragua Case, *ibid*, and the Case concerning the Delimitation of the Maritime Boundaries between Canada and the United States in the Gulf of Maine, *I.C.J. Reports* (1984) p. 246. A similar approach was adopted by the Arbitral Tribunal in the Case concerning the Delimitation of the Marine Boundaries between Guinea and Guinea Bissau, 25 *ILM* (1986) p. 252. See futher Danilenko, G.M., *Law Making in the International Community,* Martinus Nijhoff Publishers, 1993, at pp. 152-153, Lee, L.T. "The Law of the Sea Convention and third States", 77 *A.J.I.L.* (1983) pp. 541-568, Wolfrum, R., "Entry into force of the Law of the Sea Convention: legal effect for parties and non-parties". Paper presented to the *18th Annual Seminar of the Center for Oceans Law and Policy, University of Virginia, School of Law*, Rhodos 22-25 May 1994 at pp. 22-24.

9   Caminos, H. & Molitor, M.R., "Progressive Development of International Law and the Package Deal", 79 *A.J.I.L.* (1985) pp. 871-890 at pp. 886-887. See also the remarks addressed to the Final Session of UNCLOS III in December 1982 by the President of the Conference, T.T. Koh; United Nations, *The Law of the Sea*, 1983 (Sales No. E. 83. V. 5), pp. xxxiii-xxxvii, and Butler, *ibid* at p. 86: "Under this view, the legislation of signatory States implementing convention provisions before the convention enters into force, is not generating customary norms outside the convention; rather it is anticipatory of the 'package' rights and obligations during the intermediate stage between signature, ratification and entry of the convention into force".

10 *Ibid* at pp. 887-888. In their view, the future of the package lies in the hands of the future States parties: "The extent to which the future States parties feel bound to the package deal, and act accordingly in not acquiescing in the creation of customary norms, will determine which, if any, of the majority of the innovative provisions in the 1982 Convention will enter into the general *corpus* of international law". *Ibid* at p. 889. See also Butler, *ibid* at p. 183: "In principle, however, it would seem to be within the capacity of the parties to a treaty to restrict expressly the passage of treaty norms into customary law to those situations where all the treaty obligations are assumed", and Kolodkin, A.L., Andrianov, V.V. and Kiselev, V.A., "Legal implications of participation or non-participation in the 1982 Convention", 12 *Marine Policy* (1988) pp. 187-191 at pp. 189-190: "As agreed during the Conference, the package agreement excludes the selective application of Convention provisions, which means that no State except a State party may claim any right or require the execution of obligations by other States... Non-ratification or non-participation in the Convention will place a State in the position of a third State with respect to the Convention. After the Convention enters into force, the third State cannot use conventi-

on rights and advantages granted for State parties there for the first time." See, however, Wolfrum, *op. cit.* note 8 at pp. 29-30, distinguishes between rights and obligations created by the 1982 Convention exclusively for States parties, and rights and obligations for all States. In his view, "third States may, in accordance with articles 35 and 36 of the Vienna Convention on the Law of Treaties, accept the rights and obligations enshrined in the Convention on the Law of the Sea. Such acceptance may take different forms and does not necessarily require a direct reference to the Convention .... Such rights can only be accepted while at the same time submittimg to the corresponding obligations... One may even go as far as to argue that since all regulations of the law of the sea are closely interrelated, the invocation of a particular right which has not become customary international law does not only entail the acceptance of the directly corresponding obligations, but of all rights and obligations addressed to all States". For further discussion see Lee, *op.cit.* note 8.

11 See, for example, MacRae, L., "Customary International Law and the United Nations Law of the Sea Treaty", 13 *Cal. W. Int'l L.J.* 181 (1983); Gamble, J.K. and Frankowska, M., "The 1982 Convention and Customary Law of the Sea: Observations, a Framework and a Warning", 21 *San Diego L. Rev.* (1984) pp. 491-511, and Iguchi, T., "Remarks", 81 *American Society of International Law Proceedings* (1987) pp. 98-102. One should equally oppose attitudes, such as that of the United States, which states that the non-seabed portions of the Convention represent customary international law, and that all non-signatory States are able to benefit from those rights and obligations. See further Larson, D.L, "When will the UN Convention on the Law of the Sea come into effect?", 20 *Ocean Dev. & Int'l L.* (1989) pp. 175-202 at pp. 176-177; ID, "Conventional Customary, and Consensual Law in the United Nations Convention of the Law of the Sea", 25 *Ocean Dev. & Int'l L.* (1994) pp. 75-85, and *Restatement (Third) of Foreign Relations Law of the United States, Part V (The Law of the Sea).* The failure of the drafters of the Restatement to provide supporting evidence for declarations about customary law has been widely criticised in doctrine. See, *inter alia*, Burke, W., "Customary Law of the Sea: Advocacy or Disinterested Scholarship?", 14 *Yale Journal of International Law* (1989) pp. 508-527; ID, "Remarks", 81 *American Society of International Law Proceedings* (1987) pp. 75-84 and Simmonds, K.R., "The Law of the Sea", 24 *The International Lawyer* (1990) pp. 930-956. For further discussion see "The Law of the Sea: Customary Norms and Conventional Rules", 81 *American Society of International Law Proceedings* (1987) pp. 77-104; Bernhardt, R., "Custom and Treaty in the Law of the Sea", *Hague Recueil* (1987-V) pp. 249-330; Carty, A., "Towards a critical theory of general custom as a source of international law", 12 *Marine Policy* (1988) pp. 211-218; Lee, *op.cit.* note 8; Mendelson, M.H., "Fragmentation of the law of the sea", 12 *Marine Policy* (1988) pp. 193-200, and Allott, P., "*Mare Nostrum*: A New International Law of the Sea", 86 *A.J.I.L.* (1992) pp. 764-787.

12 Treves, T., "Remarks", 81 *American Society of International Law Proceedings* (1987) pp. 93-98 at p. 95. See further ID, "Codification du droit international et pratique des états dans le droit de la mer", *Hague Recueil* (1990-IV) pp. 9-302.

13 According to article 38, a rule set forth in a treaty may become binding upon a third State as a customary rule of international law, if it is recognised as such.

CHAPTER 4

Marine Spaces Under the Sovereignty of the Coastal State

INTERNAL WATERS

THE GENEVA CONVENTION ON THE TERRITORIAL SEA AND THE CONTIGUOUS ZONE (1958)

Article 5(1) of the TSC defines internal waters as "waters on the landward side of the baseline of the territorial sea". These waters include rivers, lakes, bays, ports and canals within the land area of the State. Within the internal waters, the coastal State exercises territorial sovereignty,[1] which extends both to the seabed and the subsoil thereof and the air space above. Relics found on the bed or in the subsoil of internal waters are exclusively governed by the laws of the coastal State, whether it concerns their discovery, removal or trade.[2] The only exception to the unlimited territorial jurisdiction of the sovereign State is self-limitation or limitations imposed by international law.[3] Flag States cannot, as a matter of strict law, demand any rights for their vessels. The law of the coastal State, however, might allow for the application of the admiralty rules of the flag State of a foreign ship removing archaeological or historical objects from the bed of the internal waters or its subsoil.[4]

A particular problem arising in connection with marine archaeology is the *access to, and use of, ports.* As a general rule, foreign shipping searching for or recovering underwater remains use local ports as bases of operations. The successful completion of a research project depends to a large extent upon the possibility of calling at such ports. In the absence of express provisions to the contrary, there are no additional requirements for the call of archaeological research vessels at foreign ports.[5] Ports are presumed to be open unless entry is restricted or prohibited.[6] However, difficulties may be encountered in practice as the whole issue lies within the discretionary authority of the coastal State, which may make entry to its port dependent upon compliance with conditions concerning the removal of cultural property. The right of coastal States to prescribe conditions for access to their ports can be regarded as a rule of custom, as it is confirmed firmly by State practice over centuries.[7] This means that vessels wishing to conduct archaeological operations in international waters from a foreign port may have to secure the permission of the coastal State. The main disadvantage of this scheme is that the enforcement jurisdiction of the coastal State is confined to its ports. If a ship does not enter the port, it lies beyond the authority of the coastal State.[8] In closed areas, such as the Mediterranean, where distances between States are small, research vessels will have the alternative of using a foreign port where entry requirements are less of a burden. Still, in the absence of a more effective regime of protection, the prescription of conditions for entry into ports may provide a basis for regulating access to archaeological sites found in extraterritorial waters. Even though the coastal State is not entitled to extend its heritage laws to protect such sites, the requirement of its permission for the undertaking of archaeological research may ensure a substantial degree of control. In open sea areas, where the alternative use of foreign ports is not possible, the effectiveness of this regime will be greater.

While in port, ships are fully subjected to the laws and regulations of the port State. In practice, however, port States tend to enforce their laws only in cases where their interests are engaged.[9] Local jurisdiction will, thus, be asserted when the offence affects the peace or good order of the port either literally (for example, customs or immigration offences) or in some constructive sense.[10] Customs laws are particularly relevant to research vessels. These laws can either facilitate their operations or make the movement of personnel and equipment extremely difficult. Foreign shipping must also comply with export laws that incorporate protective measures against the illicit trade of artefacts. Illicit transactions taking place on board of ships will invoke the criminal jurisdiction of the port State.

THE UN CONVENTION ON THE LAW OF THE SEA (1982)

There are no significant differences between the legal regime of internal waters envisaged by the TSC and that provided for by the 1982 Convention. The only differences are minor verbal modifications necessary to correspond with the establishment of two new jurisdictional zones, the archipelagic waters and the EEZ.[11] Like the TSC, the 1982 Convention does not regulate access to ports. However, the coastal right to make entry dependent on conditions is strengthened by article 211(3). Although its purpose is to prevent pollution coming from vessels, article 211(3) is based on the assumption that the port State has the discretionary authority to permit or deny entry of foreign shipping into its maritime ports. The same idea was expressed in a proposal made during the negotiations of UNCLOS III concerning coastal rights over archaeological objects found in extraterritorial waters; it was suggested that the coastal State should be entitled to make access to its maritime ports dependent on conditions relating to the removal of such objects.[12] Despite the fact that this proposal did not find its way into the Final Text of the Convention, it may still be used as a basis to protect the underwater cultural heritage unilaterally. Since the underlying purpose of such measures is the safeguarding of underwater archaeological sites, their adoption should be regarded as an expression of the duty to protect archaeological and historical objects found at sea under article 303(1).

The 1982 Convention introduced radical innovations to port State jurisdiction on pollution matters. Articles 218(1) and 220(1) extended the enforcement jurisdiction of the port State by enabling it to undertake investigations and, when the evidence so warrants, to institute proceedings against a vessel which is voluntarily within its ports or at an offshore terminal "in respect of any discharge from that vessel outside the internal waters, territorial sea or exclusive economic zone of that State in violation of applicable international rules and standards established through the competent international organisation or general diplomatic conference" and "in respect of any violation of its laws and regulations adopted in accordance with this Convention or applicable international rules and standards for the prevention, reduction and control of pollution from vessels when the violation has occurred within the territorial sea or the exclusive economic zone of that State" respectively.

This raises the question whether these provisions could be used as a basis for protecting the underwater cultural heritage. In other words, would port States be entitled to exercise enforcement jurisdiction against foreign vessels which have plundered marine archaeological sites and are voluntarily within their ports? In order to give an answer to this question a distinction should be made between sites within the territorial sea and the contiguous zone and sites in international waters. As will be discussed in Chapter 5, under the 1982 Convention, the coastal State is entitled to expand its competence over archaeological and historical objects found in the 24-mile contiguous zone. There is no reason why the coastal State should not be entitled to institute proceedings against a vessel that has violated its laws within the 24-mile zone and is voluntarily within one of its ports or at an offshore terminal. However, if such damaging acts have occurred beyond the 24-mile limit, the coastal State will not be empowered to take legal proceedings against the responsible vessel. It should always be borne in mind that the enlarged enforcement jurisdiction envisaged by article 220(1) corresponds to extensive coastal rights over the prevention of pollution in the EEZ (c.f. article 211), while the coastal State does not enjoy such powers over underwater cultural property in this area. Similarly, article 218, which enables the port State to take legal proceedings against a vessel which has discharged polluting matter outside that State's internal waters, territorial sea or EEZ, cannot be applied by analogy to damaging acts against underwater cultural property, as it is an exception to the general rule that port State enforcement jurisdiction does not extend to acts committed on the high seas and should be interpreted restrictively. Nor does the establishment of the general duty to protect objects of an archaeological and historical nature by article 303(1) provide the basis for the justification of such claims.

CUSTOMARY INTERNATIONAL LAW

The exercise of coastal sovereignty in internal waters has long been recognised by the international community. As far back as 1876, in the United Kingdom, it was unanimously accepted that common law operated on the landward side of the low-water mark which formed the littoral boundary of a county and the commencement of the high seas.[13] The nearer one moves landwards, the truer becomes the *dictum* of the ICJ in the *Fisheries Case (United Kingdom v. Norway) (1951)* that: "It is the land which confers upon the coastal State a right to the waters off its coast."[14]

Artefacts found on the bed or the subsoil of these waters would thus be exclusively governed by coastal law. The coastal State is also entitled to prescribe conditions for access to its maritime ports by foreign shipping. This right may be used as a basis for imposing limited control on ships undertaking archaeological operations on the high seas; unless coastal permission is obtained, there will be problems of customs and taxes on objects brought in on the ship. It is notable that in an attempt to prevent the salvaging of the wreck site of the *Titanic* by the French Institute for Maritime Research and Exploration (IFREMER), the U.S. Congress considered a ban on the importation for commercial gain of any object from the wreck. The bill, which was never enacted, provided for termination of the embargo whenever the U.S. became bound by international agreement governing the exploration and salvage of the *Titanic*.[15]

THE TERRITORIAL SEA

THE GENEVA CONVENTION ON THE TERRITORIAL SEA AND THE CONTIGUOUS ZONE (1958)

In the past, the sovereignty doctrine was not shared by all States as a considerable number of them were claiming separate jurisdictional zones for different purposes and of different widths. The recognition of the territorial sea as part of the territory of the State was broadly accepted at the time of the Hague Conference in 1930.[16] Nowadays, coastal sovereignty over the bed and the subsoil of the territorial sea is beyond dispute and is considered as one of the fundamental principles of the law of the sea.[17] Article 2 of the TSC reads: "The sovereignty of the coastal State extends to the air space over the territorial sea as well as its bed and subsoil." Consequently, all activities related to cultural property found on the bed of the territorial sea fall within the plenary jurisdiction and control of the coastal State.

Coastal jurisdiction over foreign vessels

The jurisdiction of the coastal State in the territorial sea is subject to certain limitations due to the existence of a *right of innocent passage*. The right of innocent passage is enjoyed by all ships regardless of their nature, i.e., whether they are research vessels or not. The coastal State is obliged not to interfere with the innocent passage[18] of foreign shipping through its territorial sea (article 15(1)), which is considered to be innocent so long as it is not prejudicial to the "peace, good order or security" of the coastal State (article 14(4)).

Two cases may thus be distinguished: (a) with respect to foreign ships that are not engaged in passage or they have stepped outside the right of innocent passage, the coastal State enjoys full legislative and enforcement jurisdiction; (b) with respect to foreign ships that are engaged in innocent passage, the enforcement jurisdiction of the coastal State is limited (c.f. articles 19 and 20).[19] The limited enforcement jurisdiction is exercised only when passing ships fail to comply with coastal laws and regulations enacted in conformity with article 17.[20] The failure to comply with these laws does not mean that passage is non-innocent; it will always be a question of determining whether such failure has been prejudicial to the "peace, good order or security" of the coastal State for the passage to be non-innocent.

Archaeological surveys as an exercise of the right of innocent passage

Since the right of innocent passage provides the only means for promoting the freedom of research within the territorial sea, there have been numerous attempts to interpret it extensively.[21] However, any proposals for an extensive interpretation of the right of innocent passage in the interests of freedom of research, must be considered in the light of the TSC, which gives the coastal State a large margin of discretion as to what activities are prejudicial to the peace, good order or security of the coastal State. By definition, the right of innocent passage is confined to the superjacent waters. As a result, archaeological research conducted on the seabed cannot be considered as a legitimate exercise of innocent passage.[22] A further limitation should be made in relation to activities that demand stopping or anchoring, as these operations would exceed the limits set by article 14(3): "Passage includes stopping and anchoring, but only in so far as the same are incidental to ordinary navigation or are rendered necessary by *force majeure* or by distress." In this context, the discussion of archaeological research as an exercise of innocent passage is limited to survey activities and the operation of electronic remote-sensing devices. Is it permissible to consider the running of such instruments as incidental to the passage of ships through the territorial sea?

It has been argued that a ship making gravity measurements or investigating the properties of the sea-floor and using echo-sounder or a sonic bottom profiler for this purpose may well be considered as exercising the "ancient right of innocent passage", so long as it is in conformity with "laws and regulations relating to transport and navigation" and "it is not prejudicial to the peace, good order or security of the coastal State."[23] *Prima facie*, these suppositions appear to be compatible with the notion of innocent passage as elaborated by the TSC. However, it would be unrealistic to expect the adoption of an extensive interpretation of the right of innocent passage. Political and security reasons would not allow it.[24] In most cases, the operation of electronic remote-sensing devices would be considered as prejudicial to the security of the coastal State. Concerning archaeological research, the additional reason exists that operating vessels normally navigate in a grid of survey lines; such manoeuvring cannot be regarded as "traversing" the territorial sea.[25] It seems, therefore, that the undertaking of archaeological surveys will render the operating vessel outside the notion of passage and within the full jurisdiction of the coastal State. The failure of the vessel to report the conduct of such research could also be considered to be "prejudicial to the peace, good order or security" of the coastal State, in which case the passage would be non-innocent.

Operation of national heritage laws

In relation to municipal law, the problem arises as to whether the legislation of the coastal State applies automatically to activities taking place in the territorial sea. This issue cannot be discussed in terms of international law exclusively. International law secures only recognition of coastal sovereignty over territorial waters; it does not determine the extent and the degree of the authority that each sovereign exercises in the territorial sea. This is something to be dealt with by municipal law. The pattern of national heritage legislation varies considerably between States. As noted, two types of heritage laws may be distinguished: general heritage legislation, and legislation dealing specifically with underwater remains.[26] A general heritage legislation would apply to relics found on the bed of the territorial sea, if it expressly extends its geographical scope so as to include them[27] or it may be interpreted so as to apply to underwater remains.[28] In addition, a number of general heritage laws include specific sections on shipwrecks.[29]

Complications may arise in relation to federal States as to whether the States or the Federal Government has jurisdiction over cultural property found within the territorial sea. In the U.S.A., until recently, there was such a controversy over responsibility for managing historic wrecks. Although the Federal Submerged Lands Act[30] gives jurisdiction over submerged lands within territorial waters to the States, the enactment of State legislation to control activities relating to underwater cultural resources was, in substance, nullified as States were held not to be entitled to displace federal salvage law by their own legislation. In a number of cases, federal courts held that cases involving shipwrecks were within their exclusive admiralty jurisdiction and applied either the law of finds or the law of salvage to adjudicate the disputes over them. *Cobb Coin Company Inc. v. Unidentified, Wrecked and Abandoned Sailing Vessel (Cobb Coin I)* was the first case to challenge the authority of States for the recovery of historic shipwrecks.[31] Subsequent judgments in this field created a jurisdictional conflict between the authority of State government and the federal court to control the excavation of State land for the purpose of recovering shipwrecks.[32] In an attempt to clear the confusion, the ASA was enacted. Under its provisions, the U.S. asserts title to any abandoned shipwreck which is: (a) embedded in submerged lands of a State; (b) embedded in coralline formations protected by a State on submerged lands of a State, or (c) on submerged lands of a State and is included in or determined eligible for inclusion in the National Register. This title is being transferred to the State in or on whose submerged lands the shipwreck is located.[33] The constitutionality of the ASA was recently questioned on the basis that it represents impermissible interference with admiralty jurisdiction.[34] Nevertheless, in *Harry Zych v. Unidentified, Wrecked and Abandoned Vessel, Believed to Be the "Seabird" ("Seabird II")*, the district court of Illinois upheld ASA's constitutionality.[35] Similar problems are encountered in other federal States, such as Canada, where the Federal Government has jurisdiction over navigation and shipping (including the removal and disposal of wrecks), while property rights fall within the exclusive power of Provinces. However, provincial practice has not been challenged at federal level.[36]

Finally, some scholars criticise the exclusive competence of coastal States to regulate access to archaeological sites found within the territorial sea, as leading to a considerable lack of uniformity and uncertainty in such rights of access. As an alternative, the establishment of international principles regulating these rights is proposed.[37] The co-ordination of national heritage laws, through the adoption of an international convention, will, undoubtedly, eliminate considerably differences in requirements upon rights of access to underwater archaeological sites. However, this should not take place by imposing informal sanctions against the State that arbitrarly denies access to archaeological sites[38] or by employing arguments, such as "the territorial sovereignty over a coastal State's adjacent waters is not so fundamental to State existence" and that "it is apparent that the oceans are continuous bodies of water whose resources and phenomena know no artificial boundaries. This is of great consequence to marine archaeology, since exploration and excavation may well lead the scientists across artificial territorial boundaries in the seas."[39] There can be little doubt that the artificial division of the seas in legal zones is detrimental for more than one sea use, let alone the environmental protection and the ecological balance of the oceans. In this context, co-operation between States is essential. At the same time it is important to appreciate the potential difficulties posed by the fact that territorial sovereignty constitutes one of the fundamental principles of the law of the sea. Recent years have seen an expansion of coastal jurisdiction over wide ocean areas. It would be absurd to expect the recognition of the freedom of research or other activities, unrelated to international navigation, within the territorial sea. The fact that marine archaeology has "no distinct commercial or military objective" is inconsequential, as coastal States will always be suspicious of research vessels operating in their waters. It is notable that the 1985 Draft European Convention does not impose any restrictions on coastal authority to control access to archaeological sites found within the cultural heritage zone. The implementation of its provisions has been entrusted to a Standing Committee which is a purely consultative and co-ordinating body.

THE UN CONVENTION ON THE LAW OF THE SEA (1982)

Marine archaeology and the right of innocent passage

The notion of innocent passage
The 1982 Convention set the maximum breadth of the territorial sea at 12 nm (c.f. article 3) and elaborated the notion of innocent passage in a more precise and concrete way. First, the rule of "not hanging around" is strengthened by article 18(2) which reads that passage shall be "continuous and expeditious", and second, article 19(2) offers a more helpful definition, as in addition to the general 1958 formula, it specifies the notion of "non-innocent" to certain activities committed during passage. The commission of any of these acts renders passage non-innocent, without being necessary to show that the latter is prejudicial to the "peace, good order or security" of the coastal State.

Under article 19(2)j, the carrying out of "research or survey activities" will render passage non-innocent automatically; the language used is broad enough to include archaeological research.[40] In addition paragraph (k) excludes from the notion of innocent passage all activities "not having a direct bearing on passage", and paragraph (g) "the loading or unloading of any commodity contary to the customs and fiscal regulations".[41] Can underwater cultural property be interpreted as a "commodity" so that its loading or unloading contrary to the customs and fiscal laws of the coastal State would render passage non-innocent? In the light of the judgment of the European Court of Justice (ECJ) of 10 December 1968 in *Commission of the European Communities v. Italian Republic,*[42] the answer should be in the positive. The Court held that by goods within the meaning of Article 9 of the EEC Treaty, there must be understood products which can be valued in money and which are capable, as such, of forming the subject of commercial transactions.[43] Despite the fact that the interpretation of "goods" by the ECJ concerns exclusively the EEC Treaty, it does shed some light on the more general issue of the definition of cultural property and its distinction from other goods or articles of general use. The adoption of the philosophy of the ECJ would allow the interpretation of cultural property as a commodity, since it fulfils the two criteria suggested by the court: (a) it can be valued in money, and (b) it is capable as such of forming the subject of commercial transactions.

Exercise of coastal jurisdiction during innocent passage
Article 21 of the 1982 Convention provides that:

> "The coastal State may adopt laws and regulations in conformity with the provisions of the Convention and other rules of international law, relating to innocent passage through the territorial sea, in respect of all or any of the following:
> (g) marine scientific research and hydrographic surveys;[44]
> (h) the prevention of infringement of the customs, fiscal, immigrations or sanitary laws and regulations of the coastal State."

Contrary to article 17 of TSC, article 21 introduces a limitation to the legislative jurisdiction of the coastal State *ratione materiae;* laws other than those included in article 21 must not be extended to passing ships. The breach of these laws and regulations will result in the exercise of the criminal and civil jurisdiction of the coastal State subject to the limitations of articles 27 and 28. Clearly, coastal States retain their right to unlimited jurisdiction in relation to ships found within territorial waters, but not engaged in innocent passage, i.e., vessels conducting archaeological research.

Prima facie, article 21 does not appear to be relevant to the protection of underwater cultural property, in that it deals with the exercise of jurisdiction during innocent passage which excludes archaeological research from its ambit. However, it may be of interest to the international trade of artefacts. Under paragraph (h), the coastal State is entitled to adopt laws and regulations relating to innocent passage so as to prevent the infringement of its customs and fiscal regulations. The failure of passing vessels to comply with these regulations and the repeated willingness to do so, may be considered prejudicial to the "peace, good order or security" of the coastal State in which case passage will be non-innocent. It is beyond dispute that each State has "an absolute right to enforce its customs and revenue laws within its territorial waters. The passing of these laws is a matter for municipal legislation".[45] The 1982 Convention explicitly upheld the right of the coastal State to adopt legislation in order to prevent the infringement of its customs and revenue laws by ships exercising the right of innocent passage.[46] The only qualification provided is that, in the application of these laws, the coastal State must not impose any requirements that would have the practical effect of denying or impairing the right of innocent passage (c.f. article 24 1(a)).

Conflict between marine archaeology and the right of innocent passage
Archaeological research in the territorial sea is governed exclusively by the municipal law of the coastal State. The only limitation that international law confers to the exercise of coastal sovereignty in this area, is the obligation "not to hamper" the right of innocent passage. If, under the circumstances, archaeological operations impair the passage of foreign vessels through the territorial sea or *vice versa,* the question arises as to whether the protection of underwater cultural property will acquire priority over the needs of international navigation.

Prima facie, the exercise of coastal sovereignty over the territorial sea would seem to weigh the balance in favour of the coastal State. However, international law acts as a restraining factor and requires that innocent passage should not be hampered. In this context, the coastal State will be entitled to take the necessary measures to facilitate the carrying out of marine archaeological operations, but will not be entitled to hamper innocent passage unjustifiably. Under article 21(1)a, "the coastal State may adopt laws and regulations relating to innocent passage through its territorial sea, in respect of the safety of navigation and the regulation of maritime traffic."[47] For safety reasons, the coastal State may adopt legislation under which foreign shipping should keep clear of the area in question by using an alternative route.[48] The failure of passing vessels to comply with such measures will involve the exercise of the limited criminal and civil jurisdiction of the coastal State. In addition, if a shipwreck constitutes "danger" to international navigation, the coastal State will be responsible for taking all the precautions to avoid accidents and, if necessary, to remove the wreck in question.[49] With respect to ancient shipwrecks, it is rather unlikely that such a situation will occur as they are normally buried under thick layers of sand and sediments.

In case the conflict between innocent passage and archaeological operations is *unavoidable*[50], two factors should be weighed against each other: (a) the damage to the need of the international community for freedom of navigation, and (b) the damage to the coastal State caused by the failure to protect the cultural property in question. However, the State which pursues archaeological research and preserves the underwater cultural heritage is acting in an interest wider than its own national interest; it is also acting in the interest of the international community in the protection of the cultural heritage. Could one, therefore, argue that it has the right to suspend innocent passage as a means of resolving the conflict? The answer would seem to be in the negative. Both under article 16(3) of the TSC and article 25(3) of the 1982 Convention, the coastal State is entitled to temporarily suspend innocent passage, "if it is essential for the protection of its security". An extensive interpretation of the term "security" so as to include the interests of coastal States in the protection of the underwater cultural heritage is not permissible as, in effect, it would abolish the very institution of innocent passage. Consequently, in case of unavoidable conflict between the right of innocent passage and marine archaeology, the coastal State will be entitled to take the necessary measures to regulate traffic so as to avoid interference of passing vessels with archaeological operations, but will not be entitled to suspend innocent passage on these grounds.

Effect of article 303 on cultural property found within the territorial sea

Duty to protect objects of an archaeological and historical nature (article 303(1))
Under the 1982 Convention, the coastal State is not only entitled to regulate access to archaeological sites found within the territorial sea boundary, but it has also the duty to protect them. Clearly, within marine spaces that fall under coastal sovereignty, the onus of responsibility for ensuring the protection of underwater cultural property lies upon the coastal State. One hopes that those coastal States which have not yet adopted legislation to protect their underwater heritage will do so on the basis of article 303(1). The latter should be given the broadest possible meaning so as to embrace the whole spectrum of activities related to the underwater cultural heritage.[51] Article 303(1) may thus be read as: (i) the obligation to report the accidental discovery of archaeological sites to the competent authorities; (ii) the obligation to take the necessary *interim* protective measures for the preservation of an underwater site before the arrival of marine archaeologists or even to suspend construction projects; (iii) the need to preserve *in situ* the located remains and to avoid unnecessary excavation; (iv) the need for conservation, proper presentation and restoration of the recovered items. A similar

approach should be adopted in relation to the second duty established by article 303(1), the duty of co-operation. It should also be interpreted extensively so as to promote, *inter alia*, the exchange of scientific information, the undertaking of joint archaeological projects as well as the co-ordination of the fight against the illicit trade of artefacts which has expanded dramatically in the last years.

Reservation of the rights of the identifiable owners, the law of salvage and other rules of admiralty[52] (article 303(3))
As pointed out, the law of salvage provides one of the most inappropriate means to regulate access to marine archaeological sites. By reserving it, article 303(3) paves the way for conflict and confusion, as the latter often conflicts with coastal heritage legislation. However, within the territorial sea, where the admiralty laws of the coastal State prevail over those of flag States, the question whether salvage law is excluded or not will be determined on the basis of national law alone.[53] It would be absurd to argue that a general provision reserving admiralty law and the rights of the identifiable owners can confer a considerable limitation to the sovereignty of the coastal State by excluding those archaeological provisions that vest title of ownership of underwater relics in the State, or, in case of conflict between salvage law and antiquities legislation, by rendering salvage law applicable. The coastal State will, thus, be entitled if it wishes to exclude salvage law from the regime of the underwater cultural heritage.

So far as *rights of ownership* are concerned, almost all jurisdictions provide that the owners do not lose their property rights simply by the sinking of their vessel. Instead, the question of title depends on whether the owners have abandoned the wreck or not. The requirements of abandonment differ between jurisdictions, although abandonment is very difficult to prove in both common and civil law systems if the wreck has not been expressly abandoned by the owner or his successors. To overcome this problem, a number of States have enacted legislation, which vests ownership of shipwrecks and their cargo to the State after the passage of a very short period of time. For example, Spanish legislation provides that the State becomes the owner of any sunken ship and its cargoes after three years, if the owners do not exercise their rights,[54] while in France the owner's rights can be terminated by a declaration made by the Ministre de la Marine Marchande.[55] In other words, the acquisition of title to the wreck by the State is done by way of deemed abandonment. The exercise of State prerogative over abandoned goods or goods belonging to unidentifiable persons is rather common. This rule, which fundamentally differs from the otherwise predominant concept of the acquisition of property rights by occupation, vests title to the wreck in the sovereign State. In common law systems, the rule of sovereign prerogative - known as the "English rule" - was incorporated for the first time in the Merchant Shipping Act 1894.[56] Even in 1798, it was held that it is "the general rule of civilised countries that what is found derelict on the seas is acquired beneficially for the sovereign, if no owner shall appear" (*The Aquila*).[57] In contrast, the majority of the courts in the U.S.A. vested title of abandoned wrecks to the salvor/finder (the "American rule"). The American courts recognised the inherent power of the U.S. to assert ownership over artefacts recovered from the sea, but denied that Congress had exercised its sovereign prerogative in respect of abandoned property found at sea.[58] The ASA altered this position by giving a prerogative to the State in or on whose submerged lands the abandoned shipwreck is located.

The enactment of a general heritage law or one specifically dealing with underwater remains, superimposes a new legal regime on these traditional rules of maritime law. A number of these laws vest ownership of protected items to the State; some provide for State ownership under the assumption that no owner is known or can be identified,[59] while others provide for an automatic transfer of ownership of all antiquities to the State.[60]

CUSTOMARY INTERNATIONAL LAW

With the exception of the right of innocent passage, the coastal State has exclusive jurisdiction over all acts committed in its territorial sea.[60a] As a result, the conduct of archaeological activities in this area would always require its permission. Since innocent passage relates to continuous navigation through the territorial sea, archaeological research cannot be regarded as incidental to its exercise; under the circumstances, its conduct may passage non-innocent.

Finally, State practice provides evidence of the settlement of the maximum breadth of the territorial sea to 12 nm. As of 16 November 1993, one hundred and nineteen (119) States have claimed 12nm territorial seas.[61]

STRAITS USED FOR INTERNATIONAL NAVIGATION

Geographically speaking, a strait means a narrow water passage connecting two seas or large bodies of water. The legal status of the waters that constitute the strait determines the respective rights of the riparian and flag States. If the waters are high seas, namely if the territorial seas of the riparian States leave a navigable channel of high seas in the strait, then freedom of navigation applies. If the strait is comprised of the territorial seas of the riparian States, problems may arise as to the nature of the rights of passage by foreign shipping.

THE GENEVA CONVENTION ON THE TERRITORIAL SEA AND THE CONTIGUOUS ZONE (1958)

According to article 16(4) of the TSC: "There shall be no suspension of the innocent passage of foreign ships through straits which are used for international navigation between one part of the high seas and another part of the high seas or the territorial sea of a foreign State". The only difference between the general right of innocent passage through the territorial sea and the right of passage through straits is the non-suspendable nature of the latter. The exercise of coastal sovereignty over the strait is not affected in any other respect. Consequently, underwater cultural property found in this area would fall within the plenary authority of the riparian State. Similarly, the undertaking of archaeological surveys cannot be considered as a legitimate exercise of the right of passage through international straits.

THE UN CONVENTION ON THE LAW OF THE SEA (1982)

Legal status

The 1982 Convention envisages four types of straits: (a) special convention straits, the legal regime of which remains unaffected (article 35(c)); (b) straits with central area of high seas or an EEZ (article 36); (c) straits subject to the regime of transit passage: these are straits between one part of the high seas or an EEZ and another part of the high seas or an EEZ (article 37); (d) straits subject to the regime of innocent passage: these are straits which are formed by an island and its mainland and there exists seaward of the island a high seas route or an EEZ route of similar convenience (article 45(1)a), and straits between a part of the high seas or an EEZ and the territorial sea of a foreign State (article 45(1)b).

Marine archaeology and the right of transit passage

The notion of transit passage
Article 34(1) emphasises the fact that the regime of transit passage "shall not in other respects affect the legal status of the waters forming such straits or the exercise by the States bordering the straits of their sovereignty or jurisdiction over such waters and their air space, bed and subsoil". In the light of article 38(2), which defines transit passage as "the exercise in accordance with this Part of the freedom of navigation and overflight solely for the purpose of continuous and expeditious transit", the conduct of archaeological surveys in the course of transit passage cannot qualify as a legitimate exercise of this right. This is confirmed by article 40, which requires prior authorisation of the States bordering straits for the carrying out of any research or survey activities by foreign ships, including marine scientific research and hydrographic survey ships, during transit passage, and article 39(1)a and c which provide respectively: "Ships and aircraft shall proceed without delay through or over the strait", and "Ships should refrain from any activities other than those incident to their normal modes of continuous and expeditious transit, unless rendered necessary by *force majeure* or by distress." These provisions are clear enough to disperse any doubts over the exclusion of marine archaeological research from the notion of transit passage. The *rationale* of both innocent and transit passage is to facilitate navigation and not to give flag States access to coastal waters for the carrying out of other activities unrelated to international shipping. For military and security reasons, coastal States would firmly object to any alterations to the nature and scope of these regimes. The conduct of archaeological research during transit passage will render passage non-innocent with the consequent implications.[62]

Exercise of coastal jurisdiction during transit passage
The exercise of the legislative jurisdiction of States bordering straits in relation to transit passage is confined to the limited number of cases envisaged by article 42.[63] Among them features the "loading or unloading of any commodity, currency or person in contraversion of the customs, fiscal, immigration or sanitary laws and regulations" (para. (1)d). As already seen, an extensive interpretation of the term "commodity" so as to include underwater cultural property is possible. Since the legislative competence of the

coastal State in relation to transit passage is limited, article 42(1)d may be used as a basis for regulating the trade of artefacts during transit passage.

Finally, the 1982 Convention is silent on the enforcement jurisdiction of the riparian State during transit passage. As a result, the general territorial sea regime on innocent passage applies, where enforcement jurisdiction should only be exercised when the good order of the coastal State is disturbed or the flag State requests assistance.

Conflict between marine archaeology and transit passage
According to articles 44 and 45(2), both transit and innocent passage through international straits are non-suspendable. In case of absolute conflict[64] between archaeological operations and transit passage, the priority lies clearly in favour of the latter. Riparian States are not entitled to stop the passage of foreign shipping even for security reasons.[65] The temporary suspension of transit passage for the conduct of archaeological operations will raise the international responsibility of the riparian State. Only when a sunken wreck constitutes danger for international navigation does the riparian State enjoy the right to suspend transit passage without committing an international illegitimacy. Necessity requires that passage should be suspended for so long as it is necessary for the recovery of the wreck in question.[66] Otherwise, the prohibition of suspension is absolute.

CUSTOMARY INTERNATIONAL LAW

Rights of passage through international straits constitute one of the most controversial issues of the contemporary law of the sea. In 1949, in the *Corfu Channel Case* the ICJ held that: "It is, in the opinion of the Court, generally recognised and in accordance with international custom that States in time of peace have a right to send their warships through straits used for international navigation between two parts of the high seas without the previous authorisation of a coastal State provided that the passage is innocent" and that "there is no right for a coastal State to prohibit such passage through straits in time of peace."[67] The Court's *dictum* referred to straits between two parts of the high seas. Rights of passage through straits between one part of the high seas and the territorial sea of a foreign State were not addressed by the Court. As already seen, under the TSC, passage through such straits is assimilated to passage through the territorial sea, with an additional non-suspension guarantee. It is highly questionable whether the regime of transit passage envisaged by the 1982 Convention, which confers a more serious limitation to coastal sovereignty than the right of innocent passage, has acquired the status of a customary rule.[68] Nevertheless, this debate is of no interest to the international regime of marine archaeology in that the latter cannot be considered to be a legitimate exercise of the general right of passage through the territorial sea. Underwater cultural property found in straits falling under the territorial seas of the riparian States is exclusively governed by the respective national legislation.

ARCHIPELAGIC WATERS

THE GENEVA CONVENTION ON THE TERRITORIAL SEA AND THE CONTIGUOUS ZONE (1958)

In the past archipelagic States demanded a special regime for their waters based on the need to safeguard the unity of the nation and to promote the economic and cultural development. The TSC does not provide specifically for archipelagic waters. Nevertheless, the enclosure of *coastal archipelagos* can take place on the basis of article 4(2), which recognises the right of the coastal States to draw straight baselines around islands fringing a coast.[69]

THE UN CONVENTION ON THE LAW OF THE SEA (1982)

The 1982 Convention promoted the claims of the archipelagic States[70] into a new jurisdictional zone, the archipelagic waters. The regime of archipelagic waters coincides with neither the internal waters nor the territorial sea; it is a *sui generis* regime which falls under the sovereignty of the archipelagic State. According to article 49, the sovereignty of the archipelagic State extends to the airspace above the archipelagic waters as well as to their bed and subsoil and the resources contained therein. So far as rights of passage through archipelagic waters are concerned, flag States enjoy both the right of innocent passage[71] and the right of archipelagic sea lanes passage.[72] The definition of the archipelagic sea lanes passage as "the exercise of the rights of navigation and overflight in the normal mode solely for the purpose of continuous, expeditions and unobstructed transit between one part of the high seas or an exclusive economic zone and another part of the high seas or an exclusive economic zone," and the *mutatis mutandis* application of the relevant articles regulating transit passage,[73] do not allow an extensive interpretation of the archipelagic sea lanes passage so as to consider archaeological surveys as its legitimate exercise.

Consequently, the conduct of archaeological research within archipelagic waters falls within the plenary jurisdiction and control of the archipelagic State. In case of conflict between archaeological operations and archipelagic sea lanes passage, the priority is clearly in favour of the latter. Contrary to the exercise of innocent passage through archipelagic waters, archipelagic sea lanes passage is non-suspendable.[74]

CUSTOMARY INTERNATIONAL LAW

To date, fifteen (15) States appear to have claimed archipelagic waters: Antigua and Barbuda, Cape Verde, Comoros, Fiji, Indonesia, Kiribati, Marshall Islands, Papua New Guinea, Philippines, Saint Vincent and Grenadines, São Tomé e Príncipe, Solomon Islands, Trinidad and Tobago, and Vanuatu.[75] Tuvalu has made provision for the possibility of the future declaration of "archipelagic waters"[76], while Mauritius has not claimed archipelagic waters but has, nonetheless, delimited its maritime zones from straight lines drawn around the Chagos archipelago referred to as "straight baselines".[77] The concept of archipelagic waters is also recognised by the South Pacific Nuclear Free Zone Treaty (1985), which states in article 1(b) that "'territory' means internal waters, territorial sea and archipelagic waters, the seabed and subsoil beneath the land territory and the airspace above them",[78] and in a number of bilateral agreements, such as the Treaty between Malaysia and the Republic of Indonesia relating to the Legal Regime of Archipelagic State and the Rights of Malaysia in the Territorial Sea, Archipelagic Waters and the Territory of the Republic of Indonesia Lying between East and West Malaysia (1982).[79]

A number of scholars have questioned the status of archipelagic waters under customary law,[80] while others tied its general recognition to the fate of the 1982 Convention.[81] It has also been argued that the compromise of archipelagic waters was "sold" to non-archipelagic States by the guarantee of innocent passage and archipelagic sea lanes passage. Movement of this compromise into the realm of customary international law could, therefore, be inferred from the care taken to reach the compromise and the paucity of objections to the result.[82] The validity of this argument which advances the theory of instant customary law is doubtful.[83] Whether the concept of the archipelagic waters is now part of customary law depends upon evidence of State practice recognising the relevant principles as they are elaborated in the Convention. Since State practice is not always in conformity with the regime envisaged by the 1982 Convention, it would be more reasonable to refer to the *general* concept of the archipelagic waters as a customary rule.[84] It is noticeable that a number of States, such as Australia, Denmark, Ecuador, Portugal and Spain, have drawn archipelagic baselines, although they do not qualify as "archipelagic States".[85]

So far as cultural property is concerned, it can be safely assumed that it falls under the sovereignty of the archipelagic State irrespective of whether existing national legislation makes specific reference to it.[86]

CONCLUSION

The protection of underwater cultural property found landward of the outer limit of the territorial sea, does not create considerable problems of international law. The sovereignty of the coastal State extends over the bed of *internal waters* and brings within its plenary jurisdiction all activities related to the search for and recovery of underwater archaeological remains. Maritime ports are normally presumed to be open for archaeological research vessels, the port State having the right to restrict or even prohibit entry. If a coastal State makes entry to its ports dependent on conditions concerning the removal of underwater cultural property, its permission will be required for archaeological operations conducted from its ports, even when the latter take place in international waters. The prescription of such conditions has limited practical significance in that the enforcement jurisdiction of the coastal State is confined to its ports. However, in the absence of a more effective legal regime of protection, it may provide a basis for regulating access to archaeological sites in extraterritorial waters unilaterally.

Within the *territorial sea,* coastal States have the right to regulate both access to marine archaeological sites and the conduct of exploration and excavation activities. The conditions under which archaeological research takes place depends entirely on coastal laws and regulations. However, archaeological operations conducted in coastal waters must not interfere with the exercise of *innocent passage* by foreign shipping. Otherwise, the coastal State will break its obligation "not to hamper" innocent passage through the territorial sea. In case of conflict between archaeological operations and innocent passage, the priority lies in favour of the latter. The coastal State will be entitled to adopt legislation under which passing vessels should keep clear of the area in question by using an alternative route of similar convenience; it will not be entitled, however, to suspend innocent passage for these reasons, even temporarily. The temporery suspension of innocent passage can be justified only if it is essential for the security of the coastal State. Finally, archaeological surveys cannot be considered as a legitimate exercise of innocent passage through the territorial sea. Under the TSC, the conduct of archaeological research will render passage non-innocent, only if it is considered to be prejudicial to the "peace, good order or security" of the coastal State. Under the 1982 Convention, the undertaking of research activities during passage renders it non-innocent automatically.

Similarly, archaeological research cannot be considered as a legitimate exercise of *transit or archipelagic sea lanes passage*. The *ratio* of these regimes is to serve the needs of international navigation and not to promote the freedom of research and other, unrelated to international shipping activities, within marine spaces that fall under coastal sovereignty. The 1982 Convention emphasises the fact that both the regime of transit passage through straits for international navigation and the regime of archipelagic sea lanes passage through archipelagic waters, do not affect the exercise of coastal sovereignty and jurisdiction over the respective waters, their airspace and the seabed. The conduct of archaeological research by foreign ships in the territorial sea without the prior authorisation of the coastal State will invoke the exercise of its civil and criminal jurisdiction. The coastal State will thus be entitled to exclude the vessel in question and, if the requirements of the right of "hot pursuit" are fulfilled, it may pursue it and arrest it on the high seas.[87]

Finally, the duty of the coastal State to protect underwater cultural property found landward of the outer limit of the territorial sea should be considered as an emerging rule of custom. Each State is responsible for the protection of cultural heritage situated within its territory. Both in time of peace and war, cultural property should be respected. This tentative conclusion is confirmed by the 1982 Convention which establishes the duty to protect archaeological and historical objects found at sea. Recent years have seen an increased interest in the protection of the underwater cultural heritage. A group of States have enacted specific underwater heritage legislation, while others have made specific reference to underwater relics in their general heritage laws. In addition, an increased number of regional Protocols concerning the protection of the marine environment have included the "historic and touristic attractions of coastal areas" among the protected interests.[88]

NOTES

1   The coastal State exercises complete sovereignty over internal waters, as complete as over its land. This is implied by both the wording of article 1 of the TSC: "The sovereignty of a State extends, *beyond its land territory and its internal waters*, to a belt of sea...", and the exclusion of a right of innocent passage through these waters, except in the case where the establishment of straight baselines along an indented coast has the effect of enclosing as internal waters areas, which previously had been considered as part of the territorial sea or of the high seas (c.f. article 5(1)).

2   There are two types of heritage laws: (a) general heritage legislation, and (b) legislation dealing specifically with underwater remains. Since the internal waters form an integral part of the territory of the coastal State, heritage laws should be applicable even if there is no particular reference to cultural property found under water. See further Prott, L.V. and O'Keefe, P.J., "Law and the underwater heritage" in UNESCO, *Protection of the underwater heritage. Protection of the cultural heritage. Technical handbooks for museums and monuments*, 4, 1981 pp. 165-200 at pp. 169-170; ID, *Law and the Cultural Heritage*, vol. 1, *Discovery and Excavation*, Professional Books Ltd., Abingdon, 1984 at pp. 90, 111-115.

3   Sovereignty is not a discretionary power which overrides the law, but rather the competence of a State as defined and limited by international law. See further Larson, A., Jenks, C. and others, *Sovereignty within the Law*, Oceana Publications Inc., Dobbs Ferry, New York, 1965.

4   Caflisch, L., "Submarine Antiquities and the International Law of the Sea", 13 *N.Y.I.L.* (1982) pp. 3-32 at p. 10, footnote 28.

5   However, the ability of research ships to conduct undetected research or even espionage within coastal waters, might induce port States to demand additional requirements for their entry. In this respect, the legal nature of the vessel, namely whether it is a private or a public research vessel, will play an important role. According to Soons, "private research vessels appear to be generally considered as merchant vessels for this purpose. This means that entry is usually permitted as a matter of routine, and clearance requests are handled informally. For public research vessels (not being warships) and for warships (temporarily) employed as research vessels diplomatic clearance will be required". Soons, A.H.A., *Marine Scientific Research and the Law of the Sea*, T.M.C. Asser Institute-The Hague, Kluwer Law and Taxation Publishers, 1982 at p. 91. See also Redfield, M., "The Legal Framework for Oceanic Research" in Wooster, W.S.(ed.) *Freedom of Oceanic Research*, Crane, Russak & Company Inc., New York, 1973 pp.41-95 at p. 43; Caflisch, L. and Piccard, S., "The Legal Regime of Marine Scientific Research and UNCLOS", 38 *ZaöRV* (1978) pp. 848-901 at p. 854. In contrast, Burke argues that the consent of the coastal State would

be required for both public and private research vesels. Burke, W.T., *A Report on International Legal Problems of Scientific Research in the Oceans*, Clearinghouse for Federal Scientific and Technical Information, Doc. PB-177-724 at p. 5. *Ibid.*

6   The TSC does not deal specifically with rights of access to ports. However, the exercise of territorial sovereignty over national ports and the absence of a general right of passage through internal waters would seem to preclude the assertion of a right of entry by foreign ships. The vast majority of scholars recognise the full authority of the coastal State over access to ports and its competence to exclude entry by foreign vessels, virtually at will. An historical account of the minority view, from Grotius to recent scholars can be found in McDougal, M.C. and Burke, W.T., *The Public Order of the Oceans - A Contemporary International Law of the Sea*, Yale University Press, New Haven/London, 1962 at pp. 103-117. See further Hydeman, L.M. and Berman, W.H., *International Control of Nuclear Maritime Activities*. Atomic Energy Research Project, The University of Michigan Law School, Ann Arbor, 1960 at p. 131 *et seq*. The minority point of view based on, or just supported by, an arbitral decision (the *Aramco Arbitration* of 1958), claims that flag States may demand access to ports of other States as a matter of right. See *Saudi Arabia v. Arabian American Oil Company (Aramco)*, 27 *I.L.R.* 117. "According to a great principle of public international law, the ports of every State must be open to foreign merchant vessels and can only be closed when the vital interests of the State so require". This interpretation is not justifiable under customary international law: "Even the most extreme supporter of freedom of the seas would hardly deny the legal right of a State to exclude aliens and alien vessels from its ports or insist on the opposite. Today the littoral State has, if not a right of arbitrary exclusion, at least its equivalent in rights of regulation." Potter, P.B., *The Freedom of the Seas*, London, 1924 at p. 84. Text quoted in McDougal and Burke, *ibid* at pp. 107-108. See also *the Poggioli Case (1903) [Italian-Venezuelan Commission]*, X *R.I.A.A.* 669 at p. 670: "No allowance will be made for the closure of a port, whatever reasons may have induced it, when no contract relations between the government and the claimant are in question"; *the Orinoco Steamship Company Case [Opinion American Commissioner]*, (1903) IX *R.I.A.A.* 180: "Closure of ports and waterways during revolt by constituted authorities cannot be considered as a blockade unless the rebels have been recognised as belligerents. The right to close portions of the national territory to navigation is inherent in all governments"; *the Faber Case (1903) [German-Venezuelan Commission]*, X *R.I.A.A.* 438: "States through the territory of which navigable schemes flow, although these streams rise in the territory of other States, have the right to close the rivers to navigation at their discretion, and no appeal will lie therefrom. This doctrine would seem to apply even though these rivers emptied directly into the sea instead of debouching into an inland lake, as in the case under consideration, wholly within the territory of the State seeking to control the navigation of these rivers. This doctrine being applicable to their

inhabitants of the State at the headwaters of the streams is all the more applicable to domiciled foreigners".

Since international law fails to impose any limitations to the exercise of coastal sovereignty in internal waters, this right would seem to lie within the exclusive competence of the port State. The only exceptions to the authority of the coastal State are the privileges of ships in distress, which enjoy both the right of free access to national ports and, while in port, certain immunities from local jurisdiction. See e.g., *the Creole Case (1853)* reprinted in Moore, J.B., 4 *International Arbitrations* 4375; *Kate A. Hoff (The Rebecca) Case,* (1929) IV *R.I.A.A.* p. 444. "Peace, good order and security" are undoubtedly good reasons for the closure of ports as the coastal State is entitled to prohibit passage through the territorial sea when these interests are prejudiced (article 14(4) of the TSC). *A fortiori*, therefore, it must have the right to close its ports for the same reasons. In the *Faber case, ibid* at p. 463, it was held that States have the right to prohibit temporarily navigation on rivers which flow at sea and close their ports, where it is "necessary to the peace, safety and convenience of its citizens." However, despite the absence of a right to entry under international law, in practice, most States enjoy such rights. There seems to be a presumption that designated ports are open to foreing vessels in the absence of express provisions to the contrary made by the port State. This is confirmed by numerous bilateral treaties regulating access to ports, e.g., the 1968 Treaty of Navigation Between the Federal Republic of Germany and the Spanish State, *ST/LEG/SER.B/16* at p. 401, the 1923 Geneva Convention and the Statute on the International Regime of Maritime Ports, 58 *L.N.T.S.* 285, and the needs of navigation. See further Lowe, A.V., "The Right of Entry into Maritime Ports in International Law", 14 *San Diego L. Rev.* (1977) pp. 597-622.

7   See, for example, *Patterson v. Bark Eudora*, (1903) 190 *U.S.* 169 at p. 178: "Indeed, the implied consent to enter our harbours may be withdrawn, and if this consent may be wholly withdrawn, it may be extended upon such terms and conditions as the government sees fit to impose", and the cases cited in note 6. The ICJ in the *Nicaragua Case* recognised that "it is by virtue of its sovereignty that the coastal State may regulate access to its ports"; *I.C.J. Reports* (1986) 14 at p. 101, para 213. The coastal right to make entry to its ports dependent on conditions belongs to the exclusive domestic jurisdiction of the coastal State unfettered by international law. Any arguments opposing the establishment of those conditions as an illegal limitation of the freedom of the high seas are not valid. As already pointed out, the only exceptions to the authority of the coastal State are the privileges of ships in distress. It should be admitted, however, that the right of regulation is not unlimited and that it should be exercised within the limits of the principle of *abus de droit*. See Lowe, *ibid* at p. 608 and citations in footnote 38.

8   Under the TSC, it is not permissible for the port State to impose on foreign shipping obligations that have to be complied with throughout the voyage and then to enforce these rules on the high seas. Such practices would exceed the limits of enforcement jurisdiction which is based on the assumption that visiting

ships owe "temporary allegiance" to the territorial sovereign. McDougal and Burke, *op. cit.* note 6 at p. 110. See also, Lowe, *ibid* at pp. 600-604.

9   Coastal States do not interfere with matters of internal discipline of the ships found within internal waters - the so-called "internal economy" of the ship - unless their assistance was invoked or the peace was compromised. This self-limitation is mainly confined to criminal matters. With respect to civil matters, the ships which are found within internal waters are fully subjected to local jurisdiction. See further, Brierly, J.L., *The Law of Nations. An Introduction to the International Law of Peace*, 6th ed. Clarendon Press, Oxford, 1963 at pp. 223-226.

10 Churchill, R.R. and Lowe, A.V., *The Law of the Sea*, 2nd revised edition, Manchester University Press, 1988 at p. 55.

11 C.f. article 8(1) and (2) respectively.

12 Treves, T., "Rassegne: La nona sessione della conferenza sul diritto del mare", 63 *Rivista di diritto internazionale* (1980) pp. 432-463 at p. 441.

13 *R v. Keyn (The Franconia) (1876)*, 2 *Ex D.* 63 at p. 1689. See also *R v. Forty-Nine Casks of Brandy (1836)*, 3 *Hag. Adm.* 257 at p. 289.

14 Judgment of December 18th, 1951, *I.C.J. Reports* (1951) p. 116 at p. 133. See also Schwarzenberger, G., *International Law*, vol. 1, Stevens & Sons Ltd., London, 1957 at p. 195.

15 S. 1581, 100th Cong., 1st Sess., 133 *Cong. Rec.* S.11150-51 (Aug. 3, 1987). See also *Ocean Policy News*, April 1987 at p. 3, and Nafziger, J.A.R., "Finding the Titanic: beginning an international salvage of derelict law at sea" , 12 *Columbia - VLA Journal of Law & the Arts* (1988) pp. 339-351 at pp. 349-350. The U.S. Congress also considered a ban on any for-profit display of the objects. See *Sunday Times,* 8 November 1987, p. 19, col.7, and Prott, L.V. and O'Keefe, P.J., *Law and the Cultural Heritage*, vol. 3, *Movement*, Butterworths, 1989 at p. 599: "Clearly, it was intended that the closing off of the lucrative United States market would deter speculative attempts to retrieve objects from the *Titanic*." On the discovery of the *Titanic* see "The Titanic: Lost and Found", 28 *Oceanus* No. 4 Winter 1985/86 (special issue); Ryan, P.R., "The Titanic revisited", 29 *Oceanus,* No. 3, Fall 1986, pp. 2-15; Ballard, R.D., *The Discovery of the Titanic: Exploring the Greatest of all Ships,* A Hodder & Stoughton/ Madison Press Book, 1987.

16 Although the divergence of views within the First Conference for the Progressive Codification of International Law at The Hague (March 12 - April 12, 1930) rendered the conclusion of a convention on the territorial sea impossible, the recognition of coastal sovereignty over the territorial sea would seem to be widely acceptable. See further Reeves, J.S., "The codification of the law of territorial waters", 24 *A.J.I.L.* (1930) pp. 486-499. See also the Harvard Law School Draft on "Convention on Territorial Waters", 23 *A.J.I.L.* (1929) at pp. 243-245, the Amended Draft Convention communicated to various Governments by the League of Nations Committee of Experts for the Progressive Codification of International Law with Questionnaire No. 2, January 29, 1926 (League of Nations Document C.196.M.70 1927 V. p.72), *ibid*, pp. 366-368 and the League

of Nations Documents C.74.M.39, 1929 V and C.351(b)M.145(b) 1930 V, reprinted in Rosenne, S. (ed.), *League of Nations-Conference for the Codification of International Law [1930]*, vol. 2, pp. 219-421 (with supplements) and vol. 4, pp. 1203-1423 respectively. For a discussion of the development of the doctrine of the territorial sea, see further O'Connell, D.P., *The International Law of the Sea*, vol. 1, Clarendon Press, Oxford, 1982 at pp. 59-123.

17 Early practice and doctrine were not concerned as much with the submerged areas as with the superjacent waters, because of the lack of any significant interest in use of them. As a result, the rule for the bed and the subsoil was conceived later than the corresponding rule for the superjacent waters and airspace, although the "subsequent crystallization process resulted in a unitary customary rule and not three separate rules." Marston, G., "The evolution of the concept of sovereignty over the bed and the subsoil of the territorial sea", 48 *B.Y.I.L.* (1976/77) pp. 321-332 at p. 332.

18 Under article 14(2), "passage" means "navigation through the territorial sea for the purpose of traversing that sea without entering internal waters, or of proceeding to internal waters, or of making for the high seas from internal waters".

19 Article 19 deals with the exercise of the criminal jurisdiction of the coastal State and article 20 with the exercise of civil jurisdiction. Under article 19 coastal States *should not* enforce their laws in respect of crimes committed on passing ships, unless the consequences extend to the coastal State, or disturb the peace of the country or the good order of the territorial sea, or coastal State intervention is requested by the flag State or to surpress drug trafficking. Enforcement jurisdiction is excluded only when the crime was committed before the ship entered the territorial sea and the ship is merely passing through the territorial sea without entering internal waters. Similarly, article 20 provides that passing ships should not be stopped or diverted in order to exercise civil jurisdiction against a person on board. The arrest of ships for civil proceedings is also prohibited except in relation to obligations or liabilities assumed by the ship itself in the course of or for the purpose of its voyage through the teritorial sea. However, coastal jurisidction is reserved in the case of ships lying int he territorial sea or passing through it after laeving internl waters.

20 Article 17 confers no limitations to the legislative jurisdiction of the coastal State in relation to vessels exercising the right of innocent passage.

21 See, for example, the 1968 UNESCO Report on Legal Questions Related to Scientific Investigations of the Oceans: "The view was also expressed that the Group might concentrate on new interpretation of existing law as well as attempting to define new law or principles since it might be possible to facilitate research through such interpretations. For example, 'innocent passage' might be defined as including the right to run continuous recording instruments (which can be done anyway virtually undetectably) or take a few samples." UNESCO/IOC Summary Report of Working Group on Legal Questions Related to Scientific Investigations of the Ocean (First meeting, Paris 16-20 Sept. 1968), *Doc. AVS/9/ 89 M(8)*, December 1968 at p. 7. Text reprinted in Brown, E.D., "Freedom of

Scientific Research and the Legal Regime of Hydrospace", 9 *Indian J. Int'l Law* (1969) pp. 327-380 at pp. 377-378.

22 Article 14(2) is in accordance with past developments which did not recognise the exercise of this right on the seabed. According to Marston, "the fragmentary development of the sovereignty of the coastal State over the territorial sea is still reflected in the fact that the right of innocent passage is impliedly confined to passage on the surface or through the water mass and does not include passage through the subsoil or airspace". *Op. cit.* note 17 at p. 332. In addition, article 14(6) requires that all submarines and underwater vehicles must navigate on the surface.

23 Revelle, R., "Scientific Research on the Sea-Bed; International Co-operation in Scientific Research and Exploration of the Sea-Bed" in Sztucki, J.(ed.), *Symposium on the International Regime of the Sea-Bed. Proceedings*, Academia Nazionale dei Linzei, Rome, 1970, pp. 649-663 at p. 660.

24 The practice of certain maritime powers to employ trawlers and other environmental research ships for espionage provides a further justification for the rejection of such an extensive interpretation. The *Pueblo* incidence even if not directly related to innocent passage, provides one of the most illustrative examples of the political aspects of science. The *Pueblo* was an electronic surveillance ship which had been described by the U.S. Defence Department as an "environmental ship." When captured by the North Koreans for espionage, the captain of *Pueblo* claimed that the ship was engaged in oceanographic research including the study of sun spots. For further discussion see Knauss, A.J., "Development of Freedom of Scientific Research Issue of the Third Law of the Sea Conference", 1 *Ocean Dev. & Int'l. L.* (1973) pp. 93-120 at p. 95.

25 According to Miller, the methodical exploration of the seabed would seem to be "more comparable to mapping exercises than to the passage of a vessel". Miller, H.C., *International Law and Marine Archaeology,* Academy of Applied Sciences, Belmont, Mass., 1973 at pp. 16-17.

26 The vast majority of States still apply their general heritage laws to underwater relics, while a small number have enacted legislation which specifically regulates aspects of the underwater cultural heritage. Others have legislation which falls into more than one of these categories. See, for example, *Italy: Law No. 1089 of 1 June 1939 on the Protection of Objects of Artistic and Historic Interest*; *Code of Navigation of 1942* including special provisions for objects of artistic, historic, archaeological and etnographic interest; *United Kingdom: Ancient Monuments and Archaeological Areas Act 1979*, c.46. Sec. 53(1): "A monument situated in, on or under the seabed within the seaward limits of United Kingdom's *territorial waters* adjacent to the coasts of Great Britain ... may be included in the Schedule under section 1(3) of this Act, and the remaining provisions of the Act shall extend accordingly to any such monument which is a scheduled monument (but not otherwise)"; *Protection of Wrecks Act, 1979, c.36.* The legislative approach towards the protection of underwater remains is far from unified. However, this is unimportant provided there are no loopholes in the legislative schemes which leave part of the cultural heritage unprotected.

Underwater cultural property should enjoy the same level of protection as cultural property on land. As argued: "For jurisdictions which have a wealth and variety of relics underwater there are a number of practical reasons in favour of a dual legal regime - one law applicable to relics on land; the other applying to those underwater. The major advantage is that of easy recognition by persons not skilled in the law; other advantages are association by name, concise statement of rights and duties and absence of need to refer to other legal provisions....In all cases, the best protection of the underwater cultural heritage lies in education and in persuasion of the diver, fisherman, oil worker or cable layer of the cultural value of what is found. This will be done more easily if reference can be made to a single piece of legislation which is easily accessible physically and associated by name: one in which rights and duties are set out concisely, without ambiguity or the need to refer to other legal provisions". Prott and O'Keefe, *op. cit.* note 2 at p. 114.

27   See, for example, *Algeria*: Ordinance No. 67-281 of 20 December 1967 on Excavations and the Protection of Historic and Natural Sites and Monuments. The definition of "historic monuments" includes movable and immovable property of national historic, artistic or archaeological importance (articles 19 and 57). Under article 14, "the State acquires by right any movable property discovered during the course of excavations or fortuitously in the Algerian *territorial waters*" (emphasis added). See also Burnham, B., *The protection of cultural property - Handbook of National Legislations,* ICOM, 1974, pp. 30-31. *Chile*: Law No. 17,288 of 27 January 1970 on National Monuments, amended by Laws No. 17,341 of 9 September 1970 and No. 17,577 of 14 December 1970 and by Decree Law No. 1 of 5 May 1979. Article 1: "National monuments, which shall remain in the custody and under the protection of the State are ... anthropo- archaeological, palaeontological pieces or objects or natural formations, which exist on or below the national territory or within Chilean *territorial waters*, the preservation of which is of historical, artistic or scientific interest" (emphasis added). UNESCO, *The Protection of Movable Cultural Property -Compendium of Legislative Texts,* vol. 1, 1984, pp. 85-101 at p. 86. *Cyprus*: Antiquities Law 1935 as amended by Laws No. 48 of 1964 and No. 32 of 1973. The Cypriot Antiquities Law provides a good illustration of a general antiquities legislation gradually extending to include archaeological remains found on the bed of the territorial sea. Article 2 of the original Antiquities Law (1935) read: "'Land' includes land (with the grazing rights, and all water and rights on, over or under such land), buildings, trees, easements and standing crops." This definition was amended by article 3(b) of the Law to Amend the Antiquities Law of 10 September 1964 (No. 48 of 1964): "Section 2 is hereby amended as follows: [b]y the insertion immediately after the interpretation of land of the words following: 'and also includes the territorial waters of the Republic'." A further amendment was made by article 2 of the Antiquities (Amending) Law of 8 June 1973 (No. 32 of 1973): "Section 2 of the principal law is amended as follows: by numbering the existing part thereof as subsection (1) and by adding the following amendments thereto: (b) by the repeal of the amendment to the definition of land made by section 3(b) of Law 48 of 1964

and the insertion immediately after the definition of the word land, of the words 'and includes the territorial waters of the Republic'." Section 2 now reads: "Antiquity" means any object, whether movable or part of immovable property, which is work of architecture, scultupre, graphic art, painting and any art whatsoever, produced, scultupres, inscribed or painted by human agency, or generally made in Cyprus earlier than the year A.D. 1850 in any manner and from the sea within the *territorial waters* of Cyprus and includes any such object or part thereof which has at a later date been added, reconstructed, readjusted or restored: Provided that in the case of such works of ecclesiastical or folk art of the highest archaeological, artistic or historical importance, the year A.D. 1900 shall be taken into account in place of the year A.D. 1850" (emphasis added). UNESCO, *The Protection of Movable Cultural Property, Collection of Legislative Texts, CLT-85/WS 22*, 1985. *Egypt:* Law No 117 of 1983 promulgating the Law on the Protection of Antiquities. Article 5: "The Organisation shall be responsible for exploration for antiquities above the ground, under the ground and the inland and *territorial waters*" (emphasis added). *Kenya:* The Antiquities and Monuments Act No. 2 of 1983. Section 3 declares that the application of this Act shall extend to monuments and antiquities on the seabed within the *territorial waters* of Kenya. *CLT-85/WS 29*, 1985. *Libyan Arab Jamahiriya:* The Antiquities Law (No 40 of 1968). Article 4(1): "All antiquities whether immovable or movable in or on the ground or in the ground or in the *territorial waters* shall be considered to be public property" (emphasis added). Article 39: "Archaeological excavations means any activity or activities undertaken with a view to discovering movable or immovable antiquities, by means of excavations, of topography or of exploration in water courses, the beds of lakes and gulfs or in any part of the depths of *territorial waters*" (emphasis added). *Qatar:* Law No. 2 of 1980 on Antiquities. Article 2: "Antiquities are of two kinds: movable and immovable; the latter includes sites of ancient buildings and their annexes, such as ruins of ancient cities and buildings, as well as mounds, grottoes, caves, citadels, ramparts, forts, religious places, schools and so forth, whether they are above or under the ground, or submerged by inland or *territorial waters*. Movable antiquities are antiquities which, by their nature, are not made to be attached to the ground and can be deplaced without being damaged" (emphasis added). *CLT-85/WS 36*, 1985.

See also *Brunei*: Antiquities and Treasure Trove Enactment 1967. Article 1 defines antiquity as "any object, movable or immovable or any part of the soil or of the bed of a river or lake or of *the sea*" (emphasis added). Burnham, *ibid* at pp. 43-44; *Greece:* Codification of the provisions of Act 5351, together with the relevant applicable provisions of Acts BXM/7, 2447, 491 and 4823 and of the legislative Decree of 12/16 June 1926, into a single legislative text bearing the number 5351 and entitled "The Antiquities Act" and dated 24 August 1932; *CC-87/WS 5*, 1987. Article 1: "All antiquities whether movable or immovable, from ancient or subsequent times found in Greece and any national possessions in rivers, lakes and the *depths of the sea*, and on public, monastic and private land, shall be the property of the State" (emphasis added). *CC-87/WS 5*, 1987, and *Turkey*: Cultural and Natural Objects (Conservation) Act, No. 18113 of 23 July 1983 as amended by Law No. 3386 of 17 June 1987. Article 3(a)(2): "Cultural objects are all movable and immovable objects above or below ground or *under water,* prehistoric or of historical times, of scientific, cultural, religious or artistic value" (emphasis added).

28 See, for example, *Albania:* Decree No 4874 of 23 September 1971 on the Protection of Cultural Monuments, Historic Monuments and Rare Natural Objects; Regulations of the Ministry of Education and Culture of 18 October 1972 for the Protection of Cultural and Historical Monuments; Regulations concerning the Protection of Cultural Monuments promulgated by the Decision of the Council of Ministers No 130 of 9 April 1955. In Albania a new law is under preparation. The draft legislation makes specific reference to antiquities found in rivers, lakes or under the sea and vests title of all antiquities in the State. As it stands it adopts a very general definition of the protected cultural property, including objects of 40 years old. Information kindly provided by Mr Guri Pani, Ministry of Culture, Youth and Sport, Tirana; *Lebanon:* Order No 166 LR of 7 November 1933 prescribing Regulations on Antiquities; Order No 255 LR of 28 September 1934 prescribing Regulations on the Suppression of Offences Relating to Antiquities and Historic Monuments.

29 *Finland*: Act of Archaeological Remains 1963 regulates "Ship Discoveries" in Chapter 3 (article 20). The Act, which is confined to Finland and its territorial waters, was kindly provided by Ms. Marianna Kaukonen, Curator, National Board of Antiquities, Helsinki; *Ireland:* National Monuments Act of 1930 as amended in 1954 and in 1987 by the National Monuments (Amendment) Act, 1987, No. 17 of 1987: An Act to make further provision for the protection and preservation of national monuments and archaeological objects, including provision for the regulation of the use and possession of detection devices, to make provision for the protection and preservation of historic wrecks, to amend and extend the National Monuments Acts, 1930 and 1954, and to provide for connected matters (sec. 3); *Norway*: Cultural Heritage Act of 1978, Act No. 50 of 9 June 1978 regulates "Ship's Finds" in Chapter IV (article 14), *CC-87/WS 7,* 1987; *Sweden:* Act No. 350 of 12 June 1942 concerning Ancient Monuments and Finds as amended by Act No. 77 of 17 March 1967 and Act No. 589, 30 June 1971, applies to "shipwrecks and objects found in the vicinity of such wreck and being connected thereto" (sec. 9(a)); see Prott, L.V. and O'Keefe, P.J., "Analysis of Legislation in Individual Countries" in Council of Europe, Parliamentary Assembly, *The Underwater Cultural Heritage*, Report of the Committee on Culture and Education (Rapporteur Mr. John Roper), Doc. 4200-E, Strasbourg, 1978, Appendix III, pp. 91-135 at pp. 125-126.

30 43 *U.S.C.* para. 1301 (1970).

31 1983 *AMC* 1003. The Florida Archives and History Act was held invalid as unconstitutional on the basis that it conflicted with federal principles of admiralty and maritime law, and the federal interest affected was substantial. In the opinion of the court, the case was not like those validating State police power regulations, which merely affect maritime concern, as the Florida statute interferes with substantial existing federal maritime rights: it prohibits salvors from

exploring sites in State waters without a permit, it grants exclusive rights for a fixed period regardless of the licencee's diligence in conducting operations, and it provides for a fixed salvage compensation unrelated to risk and merit. *Cobb Coin I* constituted a major obstacle to the protection of cultural resources as most of the regulatory programs of the twenty-five States, which had enacted underwater antiquities legislation at the time, were similar to the Florida Archives and History Act and could, therefore, be held invalid. These were: Alaska, Arizona, Colorado, Florida, Georgia, Hawaii, Indiana, Louisiana, Maine, Massachussetts, Michigan, Minnesota, Mississippi, Montana, New Hampshire, New York, North Carolina, North Dakota, Rhode Island, South Carolina, Texas, Vermont, Virginia, Wisconsin, Northern Mariana Islands. See further Throckmorton, P., "Introduction: Marine Archaeology", 28 *Oceanus,* No. 1 Spring 1985, pp. 2-12 at p. 3, and Shallcross, D.B. and Giesecke, A.G., "Recent Developments in Litigation concerning the Recovery of Historic Shipwrecks", 10 *Syracuse J. Int'l L. & Com.* (1983) pp. 371-403 at p. 400. It is notable that more than 35 cases were pending in 1983.

32 There were, however, a number of federal court admiralty cases, which decided in favour of State regulation of historic shipwrecks and revealed a tendency to address the controversial issue of the protection of underwater cultural resources in a more responsible manner. These were: *Maritime Underwater Surveys Inc. v. The Unidentified, Wrecked and Abandoned Sailing Vessel,* 717 *F.2d.* 6 (1st Circ. 1983). In this case, the First Circuit held that the Eleventh Amendment barred adjudication of a State's interest in artifacts found within its coastal waters, absent the State's consent, and dismissed salvor's action for title to and possession of a 1717 wreck in Massachussett's waters, since the Commonwealth was obviously the plaintiff's principal adversary, even though not named as a defendant in the *in rem* complaint. Although the district court held that Massachussett's claim of title to the vessel was colorable, the First Circuit did not reach the issue of colorability of title: "Because this is not a claim against a named State official and because of the Eleventh Amendment's flat prohibition of suits against States regardless of their merit, we need not reach the colorability of the Commonwealth's claim (although we have no doubt that Commonwealth's claim is at least colorable, see note 1). We merely hold that when a State asserts title to antiquities lodged within the seabed under its authority, the Eleventh Amendment bars federal adjudication of State's interest, absent its consent." It seems, therefore, that a different framing of the complaint, or the participation of State officials to the salvage operations of Maritime Surveys which would have waived the defence of the Eleventh Amendment, might have led to a different holding. It is on these grounds that the overall significance of Maritime Surveys had been questioned. "The practical effect of Maritime Surveys will not be to discourage salvors from conducting recovery operations on historic shipwrecks, but it will simply shift legal battles from the federal courts to State courts". *Ibid* at p. 404. As a matter of fact, in 1986 the Supreme Court declared that title to the vessel is vested in Maritime and that since the Commonwealth's statutory scheme conflicts with federal maritime law, Maritime was not obliged to comply with the statute's requirements,

Maritime Underwater Surveys Inc. v. The Unidentified, Wrecked and Abandoned Sailing Vessel, 1987 *AMC* 2590. The judgment was affirmed by the Supreme Judicial Court, *Commonwealth of Massachusetts v. Maritime Underwater Surveys*, 1989 *AMC* 425, which held that the federal maritime law of finds and not State statutory scheme for protection of underwater archaeological resources governs right to salvage the wreck of a 18th century pirate vessel lying in Mass. State waters (see also *Richard Fitzerald v. The Unidentified Wrecked and Abandoned Vessel*, 1989 *AMC* 1075, which was held to be indistinguishable from Maritime Underwater Surveys. However, in *Elias Lopez Soba, Executive Director of the Institute of Puerto Rican Culture v. Richard Fitzerald, et al*, 1993 *AMC* 120, the Supreme Court of the Commonwealth of Puerto Rico, affirmed the decision of the Superior Court that under applicable Puerto Rican legislation, objects recovered from a sunken shipwreck in Puerto Rican waters belong to the Commonwealth, and there is no need to apply maritime salvage law. It is notable that in 1987 Puerto Rico did pass legislation to protect underwater archaeological resources (Act No. 7), under which all artifacts found in Puerto Rican waters are public property, but the events in controversy took place before its enactment);

Subaqueous Exploration & Archaeology Ltd. v. The Unidentified, Wrecked and Abandoned Vessel, 577 *F. Supp.* 597, 1984 *AMC* 913 (D.Md. 1983). In this case, the Federal Court provided another solution to this problem by holding that the law of marine salvage and finds is applicable only to "recently wrecked or damaged vessels" and not to "an ancient, abandoned shipwreck." The court also held that Maryland had a colorable claim to the vessels on the basis of the Submerged Lands Act of 1953 and the Maryland statute passed originally in 1968, and that therefore the Eleventh Amendment barred the maintenance of the proceedings; *Klein v. Unidentified, Wrecked and Abandoned Sailing Vessel*, 568 *F. Supp.* 1562 (S.D. Fla. 1983), 1984 *AMC* 1897, aff'd 758 *F2d* 1511 (11th Cir. 1985). In this case the historic shipwreck was found on submerged lands within the Key Biscayne National Monument, in other words, on lands owned by the United States. The court held that the shipwreck, which was embedded in submerged land, owned by the United States and administered and controlled by National Park System, belonged to the United States, and the alleged finder was not entitled to salvage award where government was in constructive possession of the shipwreck; *Chance v. Certain Artifacts, etc.* 1985 *AMC* 609 (S.D. Ga. 1984), where the U.S. District court upheld Georgia's claim that the wreck was embedded on State property and that consequently title to the vessel rests with the State. In *Jupiter Wreck v. The Unidentified, Wrecked and Abandoned Sailing Vessel, Her Tackle etc*, 1988 *AMC* 2705, the U.S. district court held that Florida Statutes giving the State ownership of property found in State-owned submerged lands, neither conflict with nor are preempted by federal maritime salvage law. Federal question jurisdiction exists only where the issue appear on the face of a "well-pleaded" complaint and may not be predicated on a federal admiralty law defense raised only in defendant's answer. The Southern District of Florida remanded the State of Florida's court action brought to enjoin salvor from continuing unlicensed activity forbidden by State law governing the exploration of wrecks in State waters. It was irrelevant that the federal court had already taken jurisdiction in an *in rem* action by the salvor against such a wreck. The court applied the common law of finds with the result that the owner of the soil has title to abandoned property found beneath it. Since the *res* is embedded in soil, which is owned by the State, it belongs to the latter. *Ibid* at 2716. Finally, in *People v. Massey*, 137 *Mich. App.* 480; 358 *NW2d* 615 (1984), the Michigan Court of Appeals declared that the 1929 Michigan Aboriginal Records and Antiquities Act, as amended in 1980 which gives the State of Michigan jurisdiction over all articles of historical and recreational value within the territorial borders on the Great Lakes' bottomlands, is constitutional, and the Michigan Supreme Court denied leave to appeal. Although the court recognised that all cases of admiralty and maritime matters were within the Federal Government's jurisdiction, it concluded that federal authority extends only to matters and issues relevant to navigation through the Great Lakes, and not to beds or bottomlands of navigable waters. See further Barrows, R.T., "Ownership of Submerged Lands and Rights to Articles found Thereon", 66 *The Michigan Bar Journal* (1987) pp. 886-893 and Grigg, J.W., "The Michigan Aboriginal Records and Antiquites Act: a Constitutional Question", 65 *Michigan Bar Journal* (1986) pp. 432-437.

33   Pub. L. No 100-298, 102 *Stat.* 432 (1988); 43 *U.S.C.* para. 2101-2106 (1988). At the time the ASA was being considered, 28 States had enacted legislation to protect historic shipwrecks off their coasts. In *Commonwealth of Massachusetts v. Maritime Underwater Surveys*, *ibid* at p. 413, the Supreme Judicial Court held that while the ASA by its terms does not affect any legal proceedings prior to the law's enactment, its provisions are consistent with the view that title to or rights in ancient wrecks were *not* conveyed in the SLA and that the constitutional power to take control of and assert title to abandoned wrecks remained in the Federal Government. Thus, until enactment of the ASA, Federal Government retained dominion over ancient wrecks lying in the seabed within the three-mile territorial limit. See also Owen, D.R., "The Abandoned Shipwreck Act of 1987: Good-Bye to Salvage in the Territorial Sea", 19 *J. Mar. Law & Com.* (1988) pp. 499-516. Although the U.S. territorial sea now extends to 12nm (c.f. Proclamation of the President on 27 December 1988), the ambit of the ASA is still confined to 3nm, as the former expressly provides that Federal and State law remains unaltered. A new bill to deal with this issue is being prepared. For a discussion of the ASA, see Fisher, M.A., "The Abandoned Shipwreck Act: the role of private enterprise", 12 *Columbia - VLA Journal of Law & the Arts* (1988) pp. 373-377; Giesecke, A.G., "The Abandoned Shipwreck Act: Affirming the role of the States in historic preservation", 12 *Columbia - VLA Journal of Law & the Arts* (1988) pp. 379-389; Hewitt, N.M., "The proposed Abandoned Shipwreck Acts of 1987 - archaeological preservation and maritime law", 12 *Suffolk Transnational Law Journal* (1989) pp. 381-393; Stevens, T.T., "The Abandoned Shipwreck Act of 1987: Finding the Proper Ballast for the States", 37 *Villanova Law Review* (1992) pp. 573-617 and Runyan, T.J., "Shipwreck legislation and the preservation of submerged artifacts", 22 *Case W. Res. J.*

Int'l L. (1990) pp. 31-45. The ASA also anticipates the preparation of guidelines, which shall seek to maximize the enhancement of natural resources, foster a partnership among sport divers, fisherman, archaeologists, salvors and other interests to manage shipwreck resources of the States and the United States, facilitate access and utilization by recreational interests and recognize the interests of individuals and groups engaged in shipwreck discovery and salvage. See Abandoned Shipwreck Act Guidelines, 54 *Fed. Reg.* 13642-13658 (1989) published in corrected form as *Final Guidelines* in December 1990. See further Croom, A., "The United States' Abandoned Shipwreck Act goes into action - a report", 21 *I.J.N.A.* (1992) pp. 39-53, and Nelson, R.H., "Guiding the Ocean Search Process: Applying Public Land Experience to the Design of Leasing and Permitting Systems for Ocean Mining and Ocean Shipwrecks", 20 *Ocean Devel. & Int'l L.* (1989) pp. 577-600, who discusses the different parameters that should be taken into consideration when designing new leasing and permitting systems for ocean shipwrecks. As of 4 December 1990, there were 142 shipwrecks listed in or determined eligible for listing in the National Register.

34   *Harry Zych v. Unidentified, Wrecked and Abandoned Vessel, Believed to Be the "Seabird" ("Seabird I")*, 941 *F.2d* 525 (7th Cir. 1991), 1992 *AMC* 532. There is a close question whether the enactment of the ASA divested federal courts of their admiralty jurisdiction over claims relating to embedded shipwrecks. However, the U.S. Court of Appeals, Seventh Circuit did not deal with the issue of constitutionality. In its view, before deciding whether the ASA is constitutional, remand was required so that the distict court can determine whether the wreck was in fact embedded and, if so, whether the Act is constitutional to allow its application. Specific finding that the shipwreck is embedded in submerged lands within the meaning of the ASA was necessary in order to preclude the claimant from invoking the law of finds or the law of salvage; the conclusion of the district court that the shipwreck was "likely" embedded was insufficient (*Harry Zych v. Unidentified, Wrecked and Abandoned Vessel, Believed to Be the "Seabird"*, 746 *F. Supp.* 1334; 1991 *AMC* 359; the district court also held that the constitution does not prohibit Congress from altering substantive maritime law so long as that law continues to be applied by federal courts, and that the enactment of ASA did not constitute impermissible interference with the uniformity of federal maritime law by making the common law of finds rather than maritime salvage law applicable to wrecks embedded in State submerged lands). As argued: "It is of course preferable that a suit be resolved on the first appeal. However, we will not question the constitutionality of a federal statute on the mere assumption that it might be relevant. If the ASA applies to the *Seabird* because it is embedded, our discussion regarding the issues to be considered in determining the ASA's constitutionality will be available to the parties and the district judge". *Ibid* at p. 534.

35   811 *F. Supp.* 1300 (N.D.Ill. 1992). The district court concluded that the Congress, in enacting the ASA, acted in a manner consistent with the recognised limits in its power to alter or modified federal admiralty jurisdiction.

36 See further Langley, S.B.M., "Canadian Archaeology and the Law" in Langley, S.B.M. & Unger, R.W.(eds.), *Nautical Archaeology: Progress and Responsibility, BAR International Series* No. 220, 1984, pp. 18-31, and Runyan, T.J., "Shipwreck legislation and the preservation of submerged artifacts", 22 *Case W. Res. J. Int'l L.* (1990) pp. 31-45 at p. 41.

37 Shore, H., "Marine Archaeology and International law: Background and Some Suggestions", 9 *San Diego L. Rev.* (1972) pp. 668-700 at p. 673. "The freedom of marine archaeologists to conduct exploration and excavation of submarine sites within the territorial jurisdiction of coastal States will not ordinarily conflict with the goals inhering to the exercise of national sovereignty over coastal waters, where such 'freedom' is properly managed ... It is not suggested that coastal States relinquish their control over marine archaeological research conducted in areas otherwise subject to their jurisdiction. What is being urged is that States, by international convention, define the nature and extent of such control so as to uniformly harmonise the potentially conflicting interests of marine archaeology and coastal State sovereignty". *Ibid* at p. 680.

38 "Marine archaeologists wishing to explore or excavate submarine sites would be required to register a 'Certificate of Intent' with the Commission [i.e., a suggested International Marine Archaeological Commission, which would serve as an international source of information on marine archaeological research] ... after the Certificate is filed with the Commission and the marine archaeologists have applied for a deed of concession from the coastal State in whose waters they intend to conduct the research, the coastal State would have a specified period of time to determine whether it would be necessary to deny the scientists access ... the coastal State would have the final say. Continual arbitrary denial of access, however, could lead *to informal sanctions* by other States and individuals who could, for example, deny technical assistance to or participation by, the objecting State in foreign expeditions" (emphasis added). *Ibid* at pp. 681-682. It should be noted, however, that under Shore's proposal the coastal State would not be relinquishing its authority to grant deeds or concession to marine archaeologists; it would be merely agreeing to grant them according to uniform international principles ... the 'competent authority' would still be the concerned coastal State, but the conditions would now be subject to certain international principles. *Ibid* at p. 684. Furthermore, she argues that: "A coastal State shall not arbitrarily deny, nor unfairly restrict ... the right of qualified marine archaeologists to explore for and excavate submarine archaeological sites within coastal waters over which such State has jurisdiction". "Such denial shall not be considered arbitrary if it is considered necessary by the coastal State for the protection of more pressing interests unrelated to marine archaeology."

39 *Ibid* at p. 678.

40 State practice will indicate whether and to what extent the interpretation of research will create difficulties. According to Soons, the correct view is that article 19(2) refers only to research activities carried out without coastal authorisation. As article 19(2) does not specify the opposite one could argue that it also encompasses the research carried out with the permission of the coastal State.

However, such an extensive interpretation would seem to be absurd. *Op. cit.* note 5 at pp. 149-150.

41 See further Migliorino, who discusses the question whether article 19(2)e and f dealing with the "launching, landing or taking on board of any aircraft" and the "launching, landing or taking on board of any military device" respectively, provides a basis for arguing that the removal of archaeological and historical objects during the exercise of innocent passage is permissible. The author concludes, correctly, that such an argument goes beyond the *rationale* of article 19(2)e and f, which provides that even the taking on board, let alone the removal, of aircraft or military devices would render passage non-innocent. Migliorino, L., *Il recupero degli oggetti storici ed archeologici sommersi nel diritto internazionale,* Studi e documenti sul diritto internazionale del mare, 15, Dott. Giuffrè, A. editore, Milano, 1984 at pp. 58-59.

42 *Reports of Cases Before the Court* (1968) pp. 432-434. In this case, the Commission brought before the Court, under article 169 of the EEC Treaty, an application for a declaration that the Italian Republic by continuing, after 1st January 1962, to levy the progressive tax provided for in article 37 of Law No. 1089 of 1st June 1939 on the export to other member States of articles having an artistic, historical, archaeological or ethnographical value, has failed to fulfil the obligations imposed on it by article 16 of the Treaty establishing the EEC. The Court held that Italy had indeed failed to fulfil its obligations under article 16.

43 In the Court's opinion, article 36 of the EEC Treaty which permits restrictions on exports justified on grounds of the protection of national treasures possessing artistic, historic or archaeological value, constitutes an exception to the fundamental principle of the elimination of all obstacles to the free movement of goods between member States, and should be construed strictly. As a result, it could not apply by analogy in the sphere of charges having an effect equivalent to a customs duty on exports. *Ibid* at p. 427. The rules of the Common Market applied to articles possessing artistic or historic value subject only to the exceptions provided for by the Treaty. *Ibid.*

44 There seems to be an inconsistency between article 21 and article 19(2). If article 19(2) is interpreted so as to consider that the carrying out of marine scientific research during passage automatically renders it non-innocent, then the inclusion of marine scientific research in the list of article 21 which enumerates the subjects on which the coastal State may adopt laws and regulations relating to innocent passage, is incomprehensible. Article 19(2) should therefore, be interpreted as specifying those activities with respect to which the presumption exists that they make passage non-innocent. The coastal State, however, may destroy this presumption and hold otherwise. Under this interpretation, a ship carrying out marine scientific research during passage through the territorial sea in accordance with coastal laws enabling such research or, in the absence of such laws, with prior express consent of the coastal State, is still exercising the right of inocent passage. See further Soons, *op. cit.* note 5 at p. 148.

45 Colombos, C.J., *The International Law of the Sea*, 6th ed., Longman Group Ltd., London, 1967 at p. 136. Back in 1927, Schücking stated that national legislation, international practice and codifications projects are all in general

agreement with the right of customs inspection as formulated by M. Fauchille in his "Traité de Droit International Public": "The coastal State is authorised to establish in its territorial waters a customs supervision which includes the right of enforcement over vessels, the inspection and detention of ships and boats suspected of contraband, the seizure of prohibited articles and their forfeiture and punishment by way of fines and confiscation." League of Nations Document, *C.196.M.70 1927 V* pp. 29, 51. Text quoted in Whiteman, M.M., 4 *Digest of International Law* 1965 at p. 391.

46 By comparison, the TSC does not enumerate the laws and regulations of the coastal State that are applicable to ships exercising the right of innocent passage. However, article 17 of the TSC retains the unlimited *ratione materiae* jurisdiction of the coastal State over ships exercising the right of innocent passage. It is notable that in the ILC list of issues on which laws and regulations might be enacted by the coastal State, "the observance of rules relating to security and of customs and health regulations" was included. The list is mentioned in the ILC's Commentary on draft article 18. See Report of the International Law Commission to the General Assembly (Doc. A/3159), "Commentary to the articles concerning the law of the sea", II *ILC Yearbook* (1956) at pp. 273-274.

47 See also article 17 of the TSC and the aforementioned list of the ILC's Commentary on draft article 18, *ibid*, which includes the "safety of traffic and the protection of channel and buoys" amongst the matters on which laws and regulations might be enacted.

48 Along these lines, the 1982 Protocol Concerning Mediterranean Specially Protected Areas provides in article 7 that within the protected areas established in accordance with this Protocol, State parties will be entitled to take, in conformity with international law, the measures required to regulate the passage of ships and any stopping or anchoring. Article 303(1), which reads that "all States have the duty to protect objects of an archaeological and historical nature found at sea and shall co-operate for this purpose", provides another basis for the adoption of coastal measures. The coastal State is, therefore, not only entitled to adopt protective legislation in order to avoid interference of innocent passage with marine archaeological operations, but it also has the duty to do so. Furthermore, article 303(1) may be used as a basis for requiring flag States to comply with coastal legislation. Since all States are under the obligation to protect archaeological objects and to co-operate therefor, flag States should respect the coastal measures taken in this duty.

49 Article 15(2) of the TSC and article 24(2) of the 1982 Convention read: "The coastal State is required to give appropriate publicity to any dangers to navigation of which it has knowledge, within its territorial sea." Since the duty to remove a wreck that creates danger or obstructs navigation lies with the owner, the coastal State would be entitled to either order the owner or the flag State to remove it, or remove it itself and charge them with the necessary costs. See Münch (von) I., "Schiffwracks: Völkerrechtliche Probleme", 20 *Archiv des Völkerrechts* (1982) pp. 183-198 at p. 196. On the need to limit the liability for the removal of wrecks see Luksic, B., "Limitation of Liability for the raising and removal of ships and wrecks: A comparative survey", 12 *J. Mar. Law &*

Com. (1981) pp. 50-64. Recent amendments to the U.S. Wreck Removal Act (Pub. L. 99-662, Nov. 17, 1986, 100 *Stat.* 4199; 33 *U.S.C.* para. 409, 414-415), however, removed the distinction between negligent and non-negligent owners and made all such owners strictly liable for the costs of removing sunken vessels. See Quinby, C. & Owen, D.R., "Recent Amendments to the U.S. Wreck Removal Act", *Lloyd's Maritime and Commercial Law Quartely* (1989) pp. 15-20.

50 It is rather unlikely that an absolute incompatibility between the two activities will occur, as, under normal circumstances, deviation off the scheduled sea route will be sufficient to avoid conflict.

51 As argued: "It is a positive duty; it goes beyond just passing legislation; it goes beyond imposing penalties. It requires a positive program of management both to extract and preserve information". O' Keefe, P.J., "The law and nautical archaeology: an international survey" in Langley & Unger (eds.), *op. cit.* note 36 at pp. 9-17.

52 According to the Report of the President on the work of the informal plenary meeting of the Conference on general provisions, the term "rules of admiralty" should be understood to mean commercial maritime law: "It was also decided that in translating the term 'rules of admiralty' from the original English into other languages account should be taken of the fact that this was a concept peculiar to Anglo-Saxon law and the corresponding terms in other legal systems should be used to make it clear that what was meant was commercial maritime law." Doc. A/CONF.62/L.58, *UNCLOS III, Off. Rec.* vol. XIV, p. 128 at p. 129.

53 The question has been posed whether the reservation covering admiralty rules and laws and practices on cultural exchanges, also extends to domestic legislation specifically regulating the salvage, protection and preservation of submarine antiquities as distinguished from ordinary wrecks and their cargoes. Caflisch, *op. cit.* note 4 at pp. 20-21. A distinction should be made between States that have enacted specific underwater antiquities legislation and States that have incorporated such protective measures in their salvage laws. For example, in France, Decree No. 61-1547 contains a whole chapter on wrecks which present an archaeological, historic or artistic interest (Chapter V of Decree No. 61-1547 of 26 December 1961 establishing the regime of shipwrecks, (*J.O.* du 12 janvier 1962). Chapter V was not modified by Decree No. 85-632 of 21 June 1985 amending Decree No. 61-1547 of 26 December 1961 establishing the regime of shipwrecks, 59 *Semaine Juridique* (1985) PTS 2-4, para. 57335. See also Chabert, J. "How underwater archaeology is regulated in France" in UNESCO, *Underwater Archaeology: A Nascent Discipline*, Museums and Monuments XIII, Paris, 1972, pp. 297-303. The reservation made by article 303(3) may be construed extensively so as to cover protective measures incorporated in admiralty laws. In contrast, heritage laws should be excluded from the ambit of paragraph (3) even if they deal exclusively with historic shipwrecks.

54 See Law 60/1962 of 24 December 1962 on the regime of salvage and findings, "Regimen de auxillio, salvamentos, remolques, hallazgos y extracciones maritimas", article 29 (Jefatura del Estado, B.O. 27) in XXI Aranzari, *Nuevo Diccionario de Legislacion* RENT-SEGU, 26404-27245, editorali Aranzari, Pamplona,

1977, para. 27006. See also Decree 984/1967 of 20 April 1967 approving Regulations for the Application of the Law of 24 December 1962, (Mo Marina, B.O., 17 mayo), *ibid*, para. 27008.

55 See article 12 of the Decree No. 85-632 of 1985 (*op. cit.* note 53) and article 1 of Law No. 61-1262 of 24 November 1961 on the Control of Shipwrecks. Similarly, in Greece the State aquires ownership of a sunken wreck, if there is no identifiable owner, or the identified owner fails to raise the wreck within three years from the date of the judgment declaring his right of ownership (or if an attempt is made to raise the wreck, which is interrupted for three successive years). The Abandoned Wreck Law of the Cayman Islands (revised in 1977) provides that a wreck which "has remained continuously upon the seabed within the limits of the islands for a period of 50 years and upwards before being brought to shore" belongs to the State. "All wreck found in the possession of any person within the islands shall be deemed to be abandoned wreck until the contrary is proved to the satisfaction of a Magistrate or the Commissioner of Wreck and any person found in the possession of abandoned wreck shall be presumed to have brought it ashore, unless he has some satisfactory explanation of the manner in which it came into his possession."

56 57 & 58 *Vict., c.60* para. 523 (Right of Crown to unclaimed wreck).

57 165 *Eng. Rep.* 87 (Adm. 1798) at p. 89. The *Aquila* involved a Swedish ship found floating at sea. The vessel was returned to the owners, but the cargo remained unclaimed and was disputed between the finders and the Crown. According to Blackstone, property in wrecks and chattels thereby rested are originally and solely vested in the Crown, without any transfer or derivative assignment either by deed or law from any former proprietor, as they are inherent to the sovereign by the rules of law. Blackstone, W., *Commentaries on the Laws of England*, Oxford, Clarendon Press, M.DCC LXV vol. I, ch. 7 at pp. 280-284. The earliest codification of the common law notion of sovereign prerogative was in 1275 by the Statute of Westminster, which limited the King's right to property at sea to "wrecks". In 1601, however, in the *Constable's Case* the King's right to property found at sea was interpreted to include flotsam, jetsam and lagan. On the development of the British rule see Kenny, I.J. and Hrusoff, R.R., "The ownership of the treasures of the sea", 9 *Wm. & Mary L. Rev* (1967) pp. 383-401 at pp. 384-392.

58 In particular see *United States v. Tyndale,* 116 *F.2d* 820 (2st Cir. 1902) and *Thompson v. United States*, 62 *Ct. Cl.* 516 (1926). For a discussion of these cases see Lipka, L.J., "Abandoned Property at Sea: Who Owns the Salvage 'Finds'"?, 12 *Wm. & Mary L. Rev.* (1970) pp. 97-110 at pp. 103-104, and Kenny and Hrusoff, *ibid* at pp. 394-395.

59 Under article 2 of *French* Law No 89-874 of 1 December 1989 on Maritime Cultural Property amending Law of 27 September 1941 regulating Archaeological Excavations, "maritime cultural property situated in the maritime public zone whose owner cannot be located shall be the property of the State. Property whose owner has not been located within three years following the date on which their discovery was made public shall be the property of the State".

United Nations, *Law of the Sea: Current Developments in State Practice,* No.
III, Office for Ocean Affairs and the Law of the Sea, 1992, pp. 39-43. Note
that "property" has been substituted for "assets" which appears in the U.N.
English translation of the French Law. See also article 511 of the *Italian* Code
of Navigation, promulgated by Royal Decree No. 327 of 30 March 1942, which
provides that objects of artistic, historic, archaeological or ethnographic interest
found in the sea, whose owner does not claim them, belong to the State, and
sec. 14 of the *Norwegian* Cultural Heritage Act, *op. cit.* note 29, which provides
that: "The State shall have right of ownership of boats more than 100 years
old, hulls, gear, cargo and all else that has been on board, or parts of such
objects, when it is clear that *it is no longer reasonably possible to find out if
there is an owner or who is the owner"* (emphasis added). Similarly, sec. 28(1)
of the *Danish* Museum Act No. 291 of June 6, 1984, with later amendments,
reads: "Objects, including wrecks of ships, which at any time must be assumed
to have been lost for more than 100 years ago, shall belong to the State, unless
somebody proves to be the rightful owner, if the object is found in territorial
waters and on the continental shelf, however, not beyond 24 nautical miles ....".
Finally, article 20 of the *Finnish* Act on Archaeological Remains, 1963, *op.
cit.* note 29, provides that "items discovered in wrecks envisaged in paragraph
1, or which evidently originate from such wreck go to the State without redemp-
tion, and otherwise the provisions concerning movable archaeological items
shall apply to them, where relevant". According to paragraph 1: "Wrecks of
ships or other craft discovered in the sea or in inland waters, which can be
expected to be more than one hundred years old, or parts of such wrecks, are
protected ...". See also the *Irish* National Monuments (Amendment) Bill 1993,
No. 52a of 1993, which reads in article 2(1): "Without prejudice to any other
rights howsoever arising in relation to any archaeological object found before
the coming into operation of this section, there shall stand vested in the State
the ownership of any archaeological object found in the State after the coming
into operation of this section where such object has no known owner at the time
when it was found".

60   In this respect consider the *Greek* Antiquities Law of 24 August 1932 (article
1), *op. cit.* note 27, and the *Chinese* Protection of Cultural Relics Law of 1982
(article 4) and the Regulation on Protection and Administration of Underwater
Cultural Relics of 1989 (article 3) For a discussion of the Chinese legislation
see Zhao, H., "Recent Developments in the Legal Protection of Historic Shipwrecks in China", 23 *Ocean Dev. & Int'l L.* (1992) pp. 305-333. See also the
Turkish Cultural and Natural Objects (Conservation) Act, 1983 as amended in
1987, *op. cit.* note 27 (articles 5 and 23) and the *Italian* Law No. 1089 of 1
June 1939 on the Protection of Objects of Artistic and Historic Interest (articles
44 and 49 vest title to antiquities which are fortuitously discovered or which
are discovered in the course of excavations to the State). The application of
blanket ownership laws is being criticised by some scholars on the basis that
it encourages illicit excavation of archaeological sites and the crime of stealing
national property. For further discussion see *supra* chapter 3 at pp. 92, 100-101.

60a In the Nicaragua case, *op.cit.* note 7 at p. 101, para 212, the ICJ stated: "The
basic legal concept of State sovereignty in customary international law ... extends
to the internal waters and territorial sea of every State and to the air space above
its territory... The Court has no doubt that these prescriptions of treaty-law (note:
the TSC and the 1982 Convention) merely respond to firmly established and
longstanding tenets of customary international law". The Court also acknowledged that article 18(1)b of the 1982 Convention dealing with the right
of innocent passage for the purposes of leaving or entering internal waters "does
no more than codify customary international law on this point". *Ibid* at p. 101,
para 213.

61 This number does not include Turkey which claims 12nm for the Mediterranean
and Black Sea. See United Nations, *The Law of the Sea: Practice of States at
the Time of Entry of the United Nations Convention on the Law of the Sea,*
Division for Ocean Affairs and the Law of the Sea, Office of Legal Affairs,
1994 at p. 215. If one adds Germany to the list of States claiming 12 nm
territorial seas, their number rises to one hundred and twenty (120). Five States
claim territorial seas of 3nm, two States territorial seas of 4nm, three States
territorial seas of 6nm, one State territorial sea of 20nm, two States territorial
seas of 30nm, one State territorial sea of 35nm, one State territorial sea of 50nm,
and eleven States territorial seas of 200nm.

62 This is due to article 38(3) which states: "Any activity which is not an exercise
of the right of transit passage through a strait, remains subject to the other
applicable provisions of this Convention", and article 19(2)j, which provides
that the carrying out of research and survey activities will render passage non-
innocent automatically. It should be noted, however, that with regard to transit
passage the practical problems in discovering ships engaged in research activities
are increased. This is due to article 39(1)c which does not require submarines
to navigate on the surface.

63 Under article 19(2)j, the carrying out of research and survey activities during
innocent passage is prohibited. Article 42 is, in all, less numerous that the
relevant article on innocent passage. However, the significance of this extended
ratione materiae limitation of the legislative jurisdiction of riparian States is
moderated when it is seen in the light of the aforementioned articles 39(1)c
and 38(3).

64 If it is considered that a strait is a narrow water passage and that, therefore,
the availability of alternative shipping routes is low, there is seemingly an
increase in incompatibility between freedom of passage and other coastal
activities.

65 See further Migliorino, *op. cit.* note 41 at pp. 67-70 and footnotes 77, 78, 79,
80.

66 *Ibid* at pp. 69-70.

67 *Corfu Channel Case*, Judgment of April 9, 1949, *I.C.J. Reports* (1949) p. 4,
28.

68 The customary law position on this question, supported mainly by the major
maritime powers, is the weakest and the most difficult to defend. See, for
example, the *Restatement (Third) of Foreign Relations Law of the United States,*

Part V (The Law of the Sea), which declares that the provisions of the Convention dealing with transit passage are also customary law, but offers no independent reference to or an assessment of the basis in State practice that it appears to believe to exist. See further Burke, W., "Remarks" in "The Law of the Sea: Customary Norms and Conventional Rules", 81 *American Society of International Law Proceedings* (1987) pp. 75-104 at pp. 75-84. In favour of the U.S. position are, among others, Wainright, R., "Navigation through three straits in the Middle East: effects on the United States of being a non-party to the 1982 Convention on the Law of the Sea", 18 *Case W. Res. J. Int'l L.* (1986). pp. 361-414, and Burke, K., DeLeo, D., "Innocent passage and transit passage in the United Nations Convention on the Law of the Sea", 9 *Yale Journal of World Public Order* (1983) pp. 389-408. Others have expressed the opinion that the conventional regime would influence the State practice even before the entry into force of the Convention. In this respect, the Joint Declaration by the Government of the United Kingdom and the Governmnet of the French Republic is mentioned, which recognises an unimpeded transit passage in the Straits of Dover. See further Nandan, S.N., Anderson, D.H., "Straits used for international navigation: a commentary on Part III of the United Nations Convention on the Law of the Sea", 60 *B.Y.I.L.* (1989) pp. 159-204.

69　Mid-ocean archipelagos do not fall within the ambit of article 4. See further Brown, E.D., *Passage Through the Territorial Sea, Straits Used for International Navigation and Archipelagos,* David Davies Memorial Institute of International Studies, 1974.

70　According to article 46(a), "'archipelagic State' means a State constituted wholly by one or more archipelagos and may include other islands." Consequently, metropolitan States are not entitled to apply the scheme provided by the 1982 Convention to their mid-ocean archipelagic dependencies.

71　Article 52.

72　The latter is exercised in sea lanes and air-routes specifically designated by the archipelagic State or, in their absence, in routes normally used for international navigation. See article 53(1) and (12).

73　See articles 39 (duties of ships and aircraft during transit passage), 40 (prior authorisation of the States bordering straits for the undertaking of research and survey activities) and 42 (application of laws and regulations of States bordering straits).

74　Under article 52(2): "The archipelagic State may, without discrimination on form or in fact among foreing ships, suspend temporarily in specific areas of its archipelagic waters the innocent passage of foreign ships if such suspension is essential for the protection of its security. such suspension shall take effect only after having been duly published". Concerning the exercise of archipelagic sea lanes passage, article 54 requires the *mutatis mutandis* application of article 44, which, in turn, reads that riparian States do not enjoy the right to suspend transit passage through international straits.

75　*Antigua and Barbuda*: Territorial Waters (Amendment) Act 1986; *Cape Verde*: Decree No. 126/77 of 31 December 1977, United Nations, *The Law of the Sea: Practice of Archipelagic States*, Office for Ocean Affairs and the Law of the

Sea, 1992, pp. 17-20; *Comoros*: Law No. 82-005 relating to the delimitation of the maritime zones of the Islamic Federal Republic of Comoros, 28 July 1982, *ibid*, pp. 20- 22; *Fiji:* Marine Spaces Act, 1977; Interpretation (Amendement) Act, 1977; Marine Spaces (Amendment) Act, 1977; Marine Spaces (Archipelagic Baselines and Exclusive Economic Zone) Order, 1981, and Marine Spaces (Territorial Seas) (Rotuma and its dependencies) Order 1981, *ibid*, pp. 23-44. See also Smith, R.W., *Exclusive Economic Zone Claims: An Analysis and Primary Documents,* Martinus Nijhoff Publishers, Dordrecht, 1986, pp. 129-146; *Indonesia*: Act No. 4 concerning the Indonesian Waters of 18 February 1960, *Limits in the Seas* No. 35 (1971); *Kiribati:* Marine Zones Act (Declaration) Act 1983 (No. 7 of 1983) in Smith, *ibid*, pp. 245-249; *Marshall Islands:* The Marine Zones (Declaration) Act 1984; *Papua New Guinea:* National Seas Act, 1977 in Churchill, R. and others (eds.), *New Directions in the Law of the Sea*, vol. VII, p. 485; *Philippines:* Act No. 3046 of 17 June 1961 to define the Baselines of the Territorial Sea of Philippines, as amended by Act No. 5446 of 18 September 1968; *ST/LEG/SER.B/15* at p.105; *Limits in the Seas* No. 33 (1971); *St. Vincent and Grenadines:* Maritime Areas Act, 1983 (Act. No. 15) in Smith, *ibid*, pp. 399-403; *São Tomé e Príncipe:* Decree-Law No. 14/78 of 16 June 1978; *ST/LEG/SER.B/19* at p.101; Decree-Law No. 48/82 of 2 December 1982; *Limits in the Seas* No. 36 at p. 147; *Solomon Islands:* Delimitation of Marine Waters Act, Act No. 32 of 1978 in Smith, *ibid* at pp. 413-416; Declaration of Archipelagos of Solomon Islands, 1979, and Declaration of Archipelagic Baselines, 1979, *ST/LEG/SER.B/19* at pp. 106-107; *Trinidad and Tobago:* Ministry of Foreign Affairs Notice, No. 500 of 1983, *ibid* at pp. 455-457; Act No. 24 of 1986, Archipelagic Waters and Exclusive Economic Zone Act, *Law of the Sea Bulletin*, No. 7 April 1987 at p. 6; *Vanuatu:* Maritime Zones Act No. 23 of 1981 in Smith, *ibid* at pp. 471-476; *Law of the Sea Bulletin,* No.1 (1983) at p. 64.

76 Marine Zones (Declaration) Ordinance 1983, Explanatory Memorandum in Smith, *ibid* at pp. 459-464.

77 Maritime Zones Act 1977 and Notice No. 194 of 1984; Smith, *ibid* at pp. 288 and 292.

78 South Pacific Nuclear Free Zone Treaty (1985). Adopted at Raratonga, Cook Islands, August 6; 24 *ILM* (1985) p. 1442.

79 United Nations, *op. cit.* note 75 at pp. 144-155. For a discussion see Hamzah, B.A., "Indonesia's archipelagic regime: implications for Malaysia", 8 *Marine Policy* (1984) pp. 30-43. See also Treves, T., "Codification du droit international et pratique des états dans le droit de la mer", *Recueil des Cours* (1990-IV), pp. 9-302 at p. 79, who argues that certain provisions of the Treaty on Delimitation of the Territorial Sea, Continental Shelf and Exclusive Economic Zone between the Netherlands Antilles and Venezuela in the Caribbean Sea (1978) are drafted so as to take into account future proclamation of archipelagic waters by the Antilles, once independent.

80 O'Connel, for example, argued in 1982 that: "Although seven mid-ocean archipelagic States have legislated for archipelagic baselines (Fiji, Solomons, Philippines, Indonesia, Mauritius, Micronesia and Papua New Guinea), there is as yet no overwhelming trend towards the emergence in customary international law of a special regime for archipelagos, independent of the application of the particular case of archipelagos of the ordinary straight baseline principle". *Op. cit.* note 16. Similarly, in Treves' view in 1980: "Though the Law of the Sea Conference has agreed on the main features of archipelagic waters, there is room for doubt about the status of the concept under international law, as it stands today. Nonetheless, especially (but perhaps not exclusively) if the Law of the Sea Conference adopts a treaty with provisions on archipelagic waters along the lines of the negotiating text, and the most directly involved States do not dissent, it seems likely that ... custom would grow out of accepted compromise." Treves, T., "Military Installations, Structures and Devices on the Seabed", 74 *A.J.I.L.* (1980) pp. 808-857 at p. 829. It is notable, however, that Treves, *op. cit.* note 79 at pp. 77-83, accepts today the principle of archipelagic waters as part of customary law. Finally, Lentsch comments that: "It appears from the foregoing that the employment of the straight baseline as a method of delimitation for archipelagic States seems to be generally recognised, albeit within reasonable limits. A certain degree of jurisdiction of the archipelagic State over the enclosed waters between the islands of the archipelago and the superjacent airspace consequently has to be accepted. It is doubtful, though, whether there is general recognition of the claim to these waters as 'internal' waters, over which the archipelagic State has complete and exclusive sovereignty, including the superjacent airspace." See Lentsch, P. (de Vries), "The Right of Overflight over Strait States and Archipelagic States: Developments and Prospects", 14 *N.Y.I.L.* (1983) pp. 165-225.

81 Brown, E.D., "Exclusive Economic Zones: The Legal Regime and the UN Convention on the Law of the Sea" in *Exclusive Economic Zones - Resources, Opportunities and the Legal Regime. Advances in Underwater Technology, Ocean Science and Offshore Engineering,* vol. 8, Graham & Trotman, London, 1986, pp. 15-35 at p.17.

82 Gamble, J.K. and Frankowska, M., "The 1982 Convention and customary law of the sea: observations, a framework and a warning", 21 *San Diego l. Rev.* (1984) pp. 491-511 at p. 501.

83 For a discussion of the concept of instant customary international law see Cheng, B., "United Nations Resolutions on Outer Space: 'Instant' International Customary Law?", 5 *Indian J. Int'l L.* (1965) pp. 23-48 and Danilenko, G.M., *Law-Making in the International Community,* Martinus Nijhoff Publishers, 1993 at pp. 97-98, who argues that the creation of customary law presupposes duration of custom-generating practice over a certain period of time. In contrast, see Alvarez, J.E., "Book review: G.M. Danilenko, Law-Making in the International Community", 15 *Michigan Journal of International Law* (1994) pp. 747-784 at p. 774 *et seq.*

84   For example, both the Philippines and Indonesia have not modified their archipe-
     lagic legislation, which was enacted before the adoption of the 1982 Convention
     and is incompatible with its provisons. The Preamble to the Republic Act No.
     3046 of 17 June 1961 (Philippines) states: "All the waters around, between and
     connecting the various islands of the Philippine archipelago, irrespective of their
     width of dimension, have always been considered as necessary appurtenances
     of the land territory forming part of the island or internal waters of the Philip-
     pines". A similar approach has been adopted by Cape Verde, which claims the
     enclosed waters as internal waters. See also Ku, Ch., "The Archipelagic States
     Concept and Regional Stability in Southern Asia", 23 *Case W. Res. J. Int'l L.*
     (1991) pp. 463-479 at pp. 473-474, who discusses the closing of Sunda and
     Lombook straits by Indonesia in 1988. Indonesia justified the action on its
     "sovereign right to close the straits", precisely the kind of unilateral action the
     1982 Convention tried to foreclose in article 53. She maintained that it need
     not concern itself with the obligations of the 1982 Convention because it was
     not yet in force. Treves, *op. cit.* note 79, wonders whether the tolerance existing
     today towards the claims of archipelagic States not complying with the provisi-
     ons of the Convention will be consolidated after its entry into force. There are,
     of course, States, such as Antigua and Barbuda, Fiji, Papua New Guinea, Sao
     Tome e Principe, the Solomon Islands, Trinidad and Tobago and Vanuatu, which
     have drawn archipelagic waters in accordance with the provisions of the 1982
     Convention. The same applies to the enabling legislation of Kiribati, St. Vincent
     and Tuvalu, which, however, have not yet drawn the necessary archipelagic
     baselines.

85   *Australia (Houtman Abrplhos Islands)*: Proclamation of 4 February 1983, *Com-
     monwealth of Australia Gazette* No. 29 of 9 February 1983; *Denmark (Faroes):*
     Order No. 598 of 21 December 1976 on the Fishing Territory of the Faroes
     in Churchill, R. and others (eds.), *New Directions in the Law of the Sea*, vol.
     V at p. 111; *ST/LEG/SER.B/19* at p. 1920; Order No. 599 of 21 December 1976
     on the Boundary of the Sea Territory of the Faroes, *ibid* at p. 1102; *Ecuador*:
     Supreme Decree No. 959-A of 28 June 1971 establishing archipelagic baselines
     for Galapagos Archipelago, *Limits in the Seas*, No. 42 (1972); *ST/LEG/SER.B/18*
     at p. 15; *Portugal (Madeira and Azores)*, Decree-Law No. 495/85 of 29 Novem-
     ber 1985, Treves, *op. cit.* note 79 at p. 83; *Spain:* Law No. 15/78 of 20 February
     1978 on the Economic Zone, *ST/LEG/SER.B/19*, p. 250; Smith, p. 425, and
     Royal Decree No. 2510/1977, *ST/LEG/SER.B/19*, p. 112. See further Churchill,
     R.R. and Lowe, A.V., *The Law of the Sea*, Manchester University Press, 2nd
     edn., 1988 at pp. 106-108, who argue that such claims could still be valid *vis-à-
     vis* those States which have acquiesced in them. It may be noted that the United
     States protested against the Portuguese claim in a 1986 diplomatic note. See
     United States Department of State, *Limits in the Seas,* No. 112, 1992 at p. 27.

86   To the extent that the sovereignty of the archipelagic State is recognised over
     the archipelagic waters, underwater cultural property found within this area
     would fall within the plenary authority of the archipelagic State. Ecuador, for
     example, has declared, "the water column, the seabed, and the marine subsoil

of the sea located within the interior of the Galapagos Archipelago, along with a band of 15 nautical miles surrounding the said baselines" to be a marine resource reserve: c.f. President's Decree on Galapagos Marine Resource Reserve, *The Official Register of Ecuador*, No. 434, May 13 1986, reprinted in 30 *Oceanus* No. 2, Summer 1987, pp. 28-29. As already seen, the Galapagos Archipelago features among the 358 properties which are included in the World Heritage List envisaged by the 1972 UNESCO Convention on the Protection of the World Natural and Cultural Heritage (see *supra* chapter 3 at p. 94).

87   According to article 23 of the CHS and article 111 of the 1982 Convention, the hot pursuit of a foreign ship may be commenced from the internal waters or the territorial sea only when the following requirements have been satisfied: (1) the competent authorities have good reason to believe that the ship has violated the laws and regulations of the coastal State (in this case, the antiquities legislation or any relevant customs and fiscal laws regulating the export/import of archaeological and historical objects); (2) the pursuit may only be commenced after a visual or auditory signal to stop has been given and ceases as soon as the ship pursued enters the territorial sea of its own country or of a third State; (3) the right of hot pursuit may be exercised only by warships or military aircraft or other ships or aircraft on government service specially authorised. Hot pursuit is not deemed to have begun, unless the pursuing ship has satisfied itself by such practicable means, as may be available, that the ship pursued, or one of its boats, are within the limits of the territorial sea.

88   In particular see the 1981 Protocol to the Convention for Co-operation in the Protection and Development of the Marine and Coastal Environment of the West and Central African Region of 23 March 1981. Text reprinted in Simmonds, K.R. (ed.) *New Directions in the Law of the Sea [New Series], J.5, Release 83-1,* issued July 1983, and the 1982 Protocol concerning Regional Co-operation in Combating Pollution by Oil and Other Harmful Substances in Cases of Emergency, adopted by the Contracting Parties to the Regional Convention for the Conservation of the Red Sea and Gulf of Aden Environment, *ibid, J.19, Release 84-1*, issued September 1985. Similarly, the 1981 Convention for the Protection of the Marine Environment and Coastal Area of the South-East Pacific provides in its Preamble: "Convinced of the economic, social, *cultural* value of the South-East Pacific as a means of linking the counrties of the region...." (emphasis added), *ibid, J.18, Release 84-1*, issued September 1984. It is noteworthy that the Director of the Office of Ocean Law and Policy, U.S. Department of State, stated before the House Merchant Marine and Fisheries Committee, 29 October 1985 that: "In concluding my testimony I would like to emphasise that customary international law supports co-operation among States to protect objects of an archaeological and historical nature found at sea." Hoyle, B.J., "U.S. Position on Titanic Memorial Site", 28 *Oceanus*, No. 4, Spring 1985, pp. 45-46 at p. 46.

CHAPTER 5

The Contiguous Zone

THE GENEVA CONVENTION ON THE TERRITORIAL SEA AND THE CONTIGUOUS ZONE (1958)

Legal status

Article 24(1) of the TSC reads:

> "In a zone of the high seas contiguous to its territorial sea, the coastal State may exercise the control necessary to
> (a) prevent infringement of its customs, fiscal, immigration or sanitary regulations within its territory or territorial sea;
> (b) punish infringement of the above regulations committed within its territory or territorial sea."[1]

The contiguous zone is now firmly established in international law. However, both the scope and the precise nature of the powers of the coastal State in these waters have often given rise to doubts. Even the concept of the contiguous zone as a separate institution has been argued to be a literary invention of legal scholars and a product of collective efforts of codification.[2] The origins of the contiguous zone are generally traced back to the British "Hovering Acts" in the eighteenth century, which claimed jurisdiction over customs matters from one league to one hundred leagues from the shore. These claims, however, were made at a time when the three-mile limit territorial sea was not established in State practice. The modern contiguous zone "is the product of a nineteenth century notion that a coastal State had jurisdiction beyond its territorial sea for the purpose of protecting its revenue against smuggling and its public health against disease."[3] The concept of the contiguous zone as an independent institution of international law was brought into existence by the Hague Conference in 1930. Both within the preparatory work and in the Hague Conference itself there was an overall tendency towards recognising the enforcement rather than the legislative jurisdiction of coastal States and towards the general acceptance of the zone as being in principle a part of the high seas.[4] This approach was inconsistent with State practice, where there was no evidence that these functional zones were limited to enforcement jurisdiction. On the contrary, States extended both their legislative and enforcement jurisdiction for limited purposes into the marginal seas.[5]

Coastal powers in the contiguous zone
Contrary to State practice, the TSC adopted a zone of limited practical significance, where coastal States enjoy powers of control for customs, fiscal, immigration and health purposes. Under article 24, the infringement of customs, fiscal, sanitary and immigration regulations should occur within the territory or the territorial sea of the coastal State. The application of these laws is, thus, confined to the territorial sea where the coastal State exercises dominion. An extensive interpretation of article 24 so as to recognise the exercise of the legislative jurisdiction of the coastal State over the contiguous zone is not permissible within the general framework of the TSC.[6] Coastal powers in the contiguous zone are *preventive*, i.e., to prevent eventual infringement of the enumerated laws in the territorial sea,[7] and *punitive*, i.e., to punish the infringements that have already been committed,[8] while the enumeration of the purposes for which it may be established is exhaustive. Since the residual regime is that of the freedom of the high seas, the concept of the contiguous zone is of exceptional nature and should, therefore, be interpreted restrictively.

The nature of coastal jurisdiction within the contiguous zone was discussed in Italian courts. In 1959 in the case of *Re Martinez,*[9] the court of Criminal Cassation held that: "Although in theory it may seem as if in the contiguous zone only police and preventive measures may be taken, because this zone forms part of the open sea rather than the territorial sea, a different view must be taken when one considers that the draft code of the Institute of International Law on the contiguous zone clearly recognises the right to exercise jurisdiction".[10] Similarly, a number of scholars argue that even under article 24, coastal States should be entitled to exercise their authority as exercisable in the territorial sea for limited purposes.[11] According to Judge Oda, a restrictive interpretation of article 24 would contradict article 23 of the CHS, which in relation to the exercise of the right of hot-pursuit in the contiguous zone provides that the pursuit may only be undertaken, if there has been a violation of the rights of the protection of which the zone was established.[12] However, there is nothing in the wording of article 23 of the CHS to prohibit its interpretation in the light of article 24 of the CHS, which requires that the violation of the enumerated laws should take place within the territory or the territorial sea of the coastal State. In this context, the right of hot pursuit can only be exercised against outgoing vessels;[13] incoming vessels cannot be pursued on the high seas, since they have not violated any coastal laws within the territorial sea.[14]

As drafted, article 24 cannot ensure an effective scheme of protection of the rights in relation to which a contiguous zone may be established.[15] Nevertheless, under the TSC, it is not permissible to argue that the coastal State exercises legislative jurisdiction in the contiguous zone. Both the restrictive language of article 24(1), and the rejection, in the Plenary Session of the Geneva Conference in 1958, of a Polish text deleting the reference to "infringements within the territorial sea",[16] do not allow such an interpretation.

Effect of article 24 on cultural property found on the bed of the contiguous zone

As the limited number of purposes for which a contiguous zone may be declared is exhaustive, the establishment by analogy of an archaeological contiguous zone is not permissible. However, article 24 may be used as a means to control the international trade of artefacts in cases where foreign ships attempt to import or export underwater cultural property into, or from, the territory or the territorial sea of the coastal State in contravention of its customs and fiscal laws.[17] By contrast, article 24 does not apply to items which are found, and remain, outside the territorial sea.[18] The same applies for the 1970 UNESCO Convention. Since the scope of its application is confined to the national territories of States parties, coastal States are not entitled to apply its provisions in the contiguous zone.[19] However, they will be entitled to exercise control in order to prevent or punish the infringement within their territory or the territorial sea of their customs laws incorporating the protective measures of the 1970 Convention.

THE UN CONVENTION ON THE LAW OF THE SEA (1982)

The concept of the contiguous zone envisaged by article 33 of the 1982 Convention is almost identical to that provided for by article 24 of the TSC.

The only differences are: (a) the maximum breadth of the contiguous zone, which is now settled at 24 miles; (b) the omission of the reference to the high seas[20], and (c) the lack of a delimitation formula. It seems, therefore, that the drafters of the 1982 Convention adopted the restrictive interpretation of the concept of the contiguous zone.[21] However, article 33 is not the only provision of the 1982 Convention to deal with the contiguous zone. Article 303(2) specifically provides for archaeological and historical objects found on the bed of the 24-mile zone.

Genesis and development of article 303

The discussions that led to the adoption of article 303 started at a relatively late stage of the Conference, in 1979. Initially, they took place before the Second Committee as they concerned objects found within the EEZ and/or the continental shelf. Later, when suggestions were made for a general duty of States to protect these relics wherever located, the debate was passed on to the Plenary of the Conference.

Geneva eighth session (1979). During the first part of the eighth session, the Greek delegation submitted an informal proposal, which suggested the inclusion of a provision regulating antiquities found "on the seabed and subsoil of the exclusive economic zone/on or under the continental shelf". The following text was proposed as a new paragraph 3 to article 56 and a new paragraph 5 to article 77 of the Informal Composite Negotiating Text (ICNT), which dealt with the EEZ and the continental shelf respectively:[22]

> "(a) The coastal State exercises sovereign rights over any object of purely archaeological or historical nature on the seabed and subsoil of its exclusive economic zone/on or under its continental shelf for the purpose of research and salvaging.
> (b) However, regarding archaeological or historical objects originating from a State or country or from a State of cultural origin other than the coastal State, the State of the primary origin will have, in case of disposal, preferential rights."

New York resumed eighth session (1979). During the resumed eighth session, Greece amended its proposal and, together with Cape Verde, Italy, Malta, Portugal, Tunisia and Yugoslavia, jointly sponsored the following text as a new paragraph to article 77 of ICNT[23]:

> "The coastal State exercises sovereign rights over any object of purely archaeological and historical nature on or under its continental shelf for the purpose of research,

salvaging, protection and proper presentation. However, the State or country of origin, or the State of cultural origin, or the State of historical and archaeological origin shall have preferential rights over such objects in case of sale or any other disposal".

Five days later the same delegations introduced a revision of their proposal.[24] The language of the text was identical apart from the inclusion of a concluding phrase which read: "However, the State of origin or or the State of cultural origin, or the State of historical and archaeological origin shall have preferential rights over such objects in case of sale or any other disposal, resulting in the removal of such objects out of the coastal State". This modification restricted even more the scope of the preferential rights of the State of origin, which were now to be exercised only in case the disposal or sale of the particular items resulted in their removal out of the coastal State.

New York ninth session (1980). During the ninth session, the same States introduced another draft proposal, the language of which was very similar to the previous one.[25] Later on in the session, the same countries introduced a draft which read:[26]

"The coastal State may exercise jurisdiction, while respecting the rights of identifiable owners, over any object of an archaeological and historical nature on or under its continental shelf for the purpose of research, recovery and protection. However, particular regard shall be paid to the preferential rights of the State or country of origin, or the State of cultural origin, or the State of historical and archaeological origin, in case of sale or any other disposal, resulting in the removal of such objects out of the coastal State."

The seven States retreated from the assertion of "sovereign rights" to the more modest "jurisdiction".[27] The less strong character of jurisdiction was also revealed in the language of the draft text; the initial proposal read "the coastal State exercises sovereign rights", while the amended draft provided that the "coastal State *may* exercise jurisdiction". Provision was also made for the rights of the identifiable owners, which were to be respected by the coastal State in the exercise of its jurisdiction over archaeological objects on the continental shelf. The modified proposal acquired a lot of support from the other delegations.[28] Nonetheless, strong opposition by the United States, the United Kingdom and the Netherlands did not permit its inclusion in the then adopted ICNT/Rev.2 of 11 April 1980. The reasons for this objection were, as the U.S. Delegation Report explained, the following. First, the seven-nation proposal would upset the delicate balance between coastal State rights and obligations and the rights and obligations of other States; second, the text was vague and, if adopted, could have led to disputes between States with no guidelines to their solution.[29] It seems that the main reason for the rejection of the seven-State proposal was the fear that the extension over the continental shelf of a set of rights which bore no relation to natural resources would favour creeping jurisdiction and alter overtime the conceptual character of the regime applicable to this area.[30]

In an attempt to dissociate the archaeological issue from the regime of natural resources, the U.S. delegation made a proposal[31] to the Plenary of the Conference suggesting the establishment of a general duty to protect archaeological objects found at sea:

> "All States have the duty to protect objects of an archaeological and historical nature found in the marine environment. Particular regard shall be given to the State of origin, or the State of cultural origin, or the State of historical and archaeological origin of any objects of an archaeological and historical nature found in the marine environment in the case of sale or any other disposal, resulting in the removal of such objects from a State which has possession of such objects".

Geneva resumed ninth session (1980). The subsequent informal meetings between the U.S. and the Greek delegations were not successful. There seemed to be no compromise solution and the three-week time limit for the submission of the amendments was almost over, when the Greek delegation made a decisive compromising step and proposed to the Plenary of the Conference a new draft, which read:[32]

> "1. All States have the duty to protect in a spirit of co-operation, objects of archaeological or historical value, found in the marine environment.
> 2. Nothing in this Convention shall be deemed to prevent coastal States from enforcing, in an exclusive manner, their own laws and regulations concerning such objects up to a limit of 200 nm from the baselines from which the breadth of the territorial sea is measured, while respecting the rights of identifiable owners.
> 3. The State or country of origin, or the State of cultural origin, or the State of historical or archaeological origin of the object shall enjoy preferential rights in case of sale or any other disposal resulting in its removal from the State where it is situated."

The proposal was discussed the same day and was supported by the Tunisian[33] and the Portuguese delegates. Clearly, this text had a less radical character than the previous drafts: first, there was no reference to the continental shelf or to the EEZ; second, "jurisdiction" was substituted by the "enforcement of laws and regulations in an exclusive matter". Nevertheless, even this modest proposal was not accepted by the United States, arguably on the basis that "since a two hundred mile area is coterminous with the exclusive economic zone, the draft would have meant an expansion of coastal State rights within that zone."[34] The result was that the President asked the interested parties to negotiate with each other and present to the Plenary of the Conference a commonly acceptable draft within two days.

At this stage, the negotiations were conducted among the Greek, the Tunisian and the U.S. delegations. The controversial issue was always the nature of the rights that coastal States were to be granted and the geographical area over which these rights were to be exercised.[35] Finally, the following text was adopted:[36]

> "1. States have the duty to protect archaeological objects and objects of historical value found at sea and shall co-operate for this purpose.
> 2. In order to control traffic in such objects, the coastal State may, in applying article 33, presume that their removal from the seabed in the area referred to in that article without the approval of the coastal State would result in an infringement in its territory or territorial sea of the regulations of the coastal State referred to in that article.
> 3. Nothing in this article affects the law of salvage or other rules of admiralty, or laws and practices with respect to cultural exchanges."

Later a fourth paragraph was added:[37]

> "4. This article is without prejudice to other international agreements and rules of international law regarding the protection of archaeological objects and objects of historical origin."

Analysis of article 303(2)

The agreed formula is substantially different from what the initial proposals of Greece and the other six States had intended, namely the recognition of sovereign rights over the continental shelf for the purpose of protecting archaeological objects. Article 303(2) attributes only a presumption in favour of the coastal State that the removal of objects of an archaeological and historical nature from its contiguous zone would result in an infringement of its fiscal and customs regulations within its territory or the territorial sea. This is the combined effect of articles 303(2) and 33;[38] customs and fiscal laws are the only laws from those mentioned in article 33 that may be relevant to the removal of archaeological objects or to the control of their traffic. The reason for the adoption of this obscure provision is to be found in the negative attitude of the major maritime powers which were willing to accept only an application of existing rules. As the Vice-Chairman of the U.S. delegation explained, "when we want to avoid the procedural and substantive risks and complications of a doctrinal change, we take refuge in the minor premise: we presume the facts and leave the principle intact".[39] Nevertheless, the precise scope of coastal rights over archaeological objects in the contiguous zone creates interpretation problems.[40]

Presumption or legal fiction?
By definition, a fiction assumes something that is known to be false, while a presumption assumes something that may "possibly" (conclusive) or "probably" (rebuttable) be true.[41] This distinction is not as clear and straightforward, since the application of a presumption always involves, to a variable degree, a legal fiction.[42] No presumption can be wholly non-fictitious, unless it is freely rebuttable and establishes an inference justified by common experience.[43] In this sense, every presumption is a distortion of reality, but this probably does not justify the application of the term fiction; the latter is reserved for those distortions of reality that are outstanding and unusual.[44]

Under article 303(2), the removal of relics from the bed of the contiguous zone is presumed to result in the infringement of coastal customs and fiscal regulations within the territory or the territorial sea. This presumption distorts reality to such a degree that it amounts to a fiction. First, article 303(2) requires only the removal of archaeological objects from the contiguous zone; the relics concerned are, therefore, presumed to have been removed from the territory or the territorial sea of the coastal State.[45] Second, article 303(2) assumes that such removals will infringe the customs and fiscal regulations. It is very difficult to perceive the relevance between the two: "Appearing as it does in a public law convention of organic character, the conceit ought (for better or worse) to be treated as a true fiction - a rule of law - rather than as a rule of evidence."[46] If this interpretation is not acceptable, article 303(2) should at least be read as being based on a conclusive (absolute) presumption. To argue that the presumption in question is rebuttable, is not only unjustifiable in the light of the *travaux préparatoires* of article 303(2), but would also minimise the effectiveness and overall significance of this provision. It would then be a matter of examining each individual case in order to determine whether the coastal State enjoys any rights over the removal of archaeological objects from the contiguous zone. The authority of the coastal State would thus be challenged by the removing State; if the latter could prove that the removal of relics will not result in the infringement of coastal customs and fiscal regulations within the territory or the territorial sea, the coastal State would be deprived of all of its rights. However, there is nothing in article 303(2) to indicate that the presumption is rebuttable: "It nowhere states - as it would have to if the presumption were rebuttable - that such removal is presumed to have occurred in the territorial sea, unless the contrary is proved".[47]

Scope of coastal rights over archaeological objects in the 24-mile zone
There are two possible approaches to interpreting article 303(2).[48] Under a grammatical interpretation, the coastal State would be granted enforcement jurisdiction to control the removal of archaeological objects from the contiguous zone. Under a teleological interpretation, article 303(2) establishes a 24-mile archaeological zone. The primary end of treaty interpretation is to give effect to the intentions of the parties. However, eliciting the intentions of the parties is not normally a task which can be performed exclusively by means of logical or grammatical interpretation.[49] So far as article 303(2) is concerned, it seems that the same language was used because a straightforward solution could not be agreed. A number of the delegations were in favour of limited coastal rights over archaeological objects found in the contiguous zone, while others were in favour of the creation of a full-fledged archaeological zone. The obscure language of article 303(2) caters for both interpretations.[50]

Extention of the legislative competence of the coastal State. The fiction established by article 303(2) appears to extend the *legislative* competence of the coastal State over the 24-mile zone. In the first place, article 303(2) attributes to the coastal State a certain degree of legislative competence by enabling it to prescribe that the removal of archaeological objects from the bed of the contiguous zone without its consent is illegal. Since such removals are presumed to result in the infringement of customs and fiscal regulations within the territory or the territorial sea of the coastal State, the scope of application of fiscal and customs regulations expands over the 24-mile zone. Under article 303(2), prevention of the removal of archaeological objects from the contiguous zone is incidental to prevention of their removal from the teritorial sea. Consequently, the scope of coastal powers over archaeological objects in the 24-mile zone is wider than the limited powers of policing recognised in a general contiguous zone. Even under a restrictive interpretation of article 303(2), the coastal State would enjoy punitive measures against removing vessels as the infringement of fiscal and customs laws is deemed to take place within the territorial sea.[51] For the same reasons, coastal States would enjoy the right of hot pursuit against removing vessels.[52]

In any case, it would be absurd to argue that article 303(2) grants the coastal State only limited powers of control. Otherwise, there would be no reason for its adoption. The inclusion of article 303(2) in the 1982 Convention must have introduced some changes to the existing regime of archaeological resources in the contiguous zone. Under article 303(2), the scope of application of coastal customs and fiscal regulations is *de facto* expanded over the 24-mile zone. Does the heritage legislation of the coastal State also apply to this area?

Creation of a 24-mile archaeological zone distinct from the general contiguous zone. Prima facie, the wording of article 303(2) appears to preclude the application of coastal heritage laws in the 24-mile zone, as it confines coastal rights to the removal of archaeological objects with the aim of controlling their traffic. However, if the coastal State is the only State competent to regulate the removal of archaeological objects from the contiguous zone, the recognition of more extended rights is possible. In authorising such removals, the coastal State can impose whatever conditions it considers to be necessary for the protection of the objects recovered. Article 303(1), which advocates the general duty to protect archaeological and historical objects, allows the application of the heritage legislation of the coastal State under the conditions provided by paragraphs (3) and (4). The coastal State is, thus, by the operation of article 303(1) and by the recognition of its competence to control traffic in archaeological objects *in substance* authorised to extend its laws to the area concerned for the purpose of protecting them.[53]

However, this *de facto* establishment of an archaeological zone, contiguous to the territorial sea, does not result in the transformation of the general contiguous zone into a full jurisdictional zone. The 24-mile archaeological zone has an independent character that enables its autonomous declaration.

Article 303(2) should not be understood to establish the declaration of a general contiguous zone as a prerequisite for its application, despite the fact that the 1982 Convention relates article 303(2) to article 33. First, article 303(2) forms part of the General Provisions of the 1982 Convention and not of the specific section dealing with the contiguous zone. Second, the duty of States to protect archaeological objects found at sea precedes article 303(2); it is permissible, therefore, to extract from article 33 only the elements that are necessary for its implementation, i.e., the geographical scope and the rights for the protection of which a contiguous zone may be established. A confirmation of this conclusion is provided by the text of article 303(2) which refers to "the area referred to in that article" and not to the contiguous zone. Third, the independent character of the archaeological zone is revealed in the different juridical nature of the two zones. The 24-mile archaeological zone is a full-jurisdictional zone, while in a general contiguous zone the coastal State enjoys limited enforcement jurisdiction.

Right to conduct archaeological research in the 24-mile zone. Does the failure of article 303(2) to provide for the search for archaeological objects on the bed of the contiguous zone, imply that flag States are entitled to undertake archaeological research in this area without the approval of the coastal State? If this assumption is correct, foreign ships would be entitled to pursue archaeological research, but would not be entitled to remove located remains. Only the interpretation that article 303(2) establishes an archaeological zone may avoid this awkward situation. Otherwise, archaeological exploration would be governed by either the principle of the freedom of the high seas or article 59, if the coastal State concerned has declared an EEZ. As will be seen in Chapter 7, within the EEZ coastal States do not enjoy any priority in conducting archaeological operations. In case of doubt, the question will be resolved on the basis of equity and in the light of all the relevant circumstances, taking into account the respective importance of the interests involved to the parties as well as to the international community. It seems, however, that within the contiguous zone, where the coastal State has already been granted jurisdiction to prevent the removal of archaeological objects, the balance would weigh in its favour at least with regard to the right to conduct archaeological exploration. Alternatively, article 303(1) may be employed as a basis for recognising limited powers of control over archaeological research in the contiguous zone. Since the coastal State has the duty to protect archaeological and historical objects found at sea, it could impose control over research activities so that the archaeological heritage is protected.[54] Even though the carrying out of archaeological research does not need the consent of the coastal State, provision should be made that the finds are not damaged by inexperienced persons.[55]

In conclusion, the recognition of a full-fledged archaeological zone under article 303(2) will bring within coastal jurisdiction both the right to search for and the right to excavate archaeological sites in the contiguous zone. If this interpretation is not acceptable, article 303(1) may be employed as a basis for recognising limited coastal control over archaeological exploration. The recognition of such rights will be more easily acceptable if the coastal State in question has declared an EEZ.

Comparison of article 303(2) with article 2 of the Draft European Convention

The debate in the Council of Europe on the drafting of a European Convention on the Protection of the Underwater Cultural Heritage reveals the two opposing approaches in interpreting article 303(2). As noted, the Draft European Convention has adopted a provision similar to article 303(2) in order to define the territorial scope of its application. Article 2 reads:

> "1. For the purposes of this Convention, the 'area' of a contracting State means its territorial sea and, in respect of a contracting State which has established it, the zone referred to in paragraph 2.
> 2. A contracting State which has established a contiguous zone in conformity with international law may presume that removal of underwater cultural property from the seabed in that zone without its approval would result in infringement within its territory or territorial sea of laws and regulations applied in that zone."

There is, however, an important difference between article 303(2) and article 2 of the Draft Convention. The latter requires the prior establishment of a general contiguous zone, while, as argued, article 303(2) does not establish the declaration of the contiguous zone as a prerequisite for its application. The drafting of article 2 generated considerable reaction. It was argued that: (a) article 303(2) cannot form the basis for the elaboration of the far more substantial rights envisaged by the Draft European Convention; (b) article 2 introduces fundamental changes to the scope and nature of the contiguous zone; (c) the expansion of coastal powers over underwater cultural property in the contiguous zone may give rise to serious practical problems, especially when the delimitation of the continental shelf between opposite or adjacent States is involved.[56]

As drafted, article 2 of the Draft European Convention establishes a full-fledged archaeological zone. However, this regulation does not bring any changes to the concept of the general contiguous zone. Both under the 1982 Convention and the Draft European Convention the archaeological "contiguous" zone has an independent, autonomous character. The fact that it "borrows" the width of the contiguous zone does not mean that it coincides with the notion of the latter.[57] It is noteworthy that the Treaty on the Prohibition of the Emplacement of Nuclear Weapons and Other Weapons of Mass Destruction on the Seabed and the Ocean Floor and the Subsoil Thereof (1971)[58] has also employed the concept of the contiguous zone in order to define the geographical scope of its application. Contrary to the TSC, which deprived the traditional concept of the contiguous zone of most of its substance by adopting a functional zone limited to enforcement jurisdiction, the 1982 Convention breathed new life into it by incorporating it in the scheme provided for archaeological objects. The protective measures adopted by the Draft European Convention should be understood as an analytical description of the general duty of protection established by article 303(1). As already seen, under article 303, the coastal State does not only enjoy limited powers to regulate traffic in archaeological and historical objects. It also has the right and the duty to implement the protection accorded by paragraphs (1) and (2). In this respect, a positive programme of management of underwater cultural property like that provided by the Draft European Convention is required.

Effect of article 303 (3) and (4) on coastal rights over the 24-mile zone

Reservation of the law of salvage and other rules of admiralty
The reservation of the law of salvage should not be interpreted extensively so as to exclude the application of the heritage legislation of the coastal State. The purpose of article 303 is the protection of archaeological objects and not the declaration of the application of the law of salvage on underwater cultural property. Within marine spaces that fall under coastal sovereignty, the admiralty laws of the coastal State prevail over the admiralty rules of flag States. Potential conflicts between salvage and heritage laws would, therefore, be resolved on the basis of the municipal law of the coastal State.

With respect to cultural property found in the contiguous zone, the issue arises as to which laws are applicable, those of the coastal or the flag State. There are two approaches: According to the first, article 303(3) should be read as "the rule expressed in paragraph (2) - coastal State jurisidiction over antiquities in the contiguous zone - will not affect the application of the admiralty rules of the coastal State."[59] Despite the absence of a priority in favour of coastal admiralty law in the contiguous zone, such an argument is essential; otherwise, article 303(2) will be deprived of most of its substance.[60] The second interpretation offers a moderate solution to this problem. Without accepting the exclusion of coastal laws by the admiralty laws of third States, it holds that whatever the applicable law is, this should not abolish the law of salvage. In practice, it will be the *lex fori* which will determine the applicable law, which can be the law of either the coastal or the flag State.[61] Obviously, this approach does not recognise the exclusive application of coastal heritage laws within the 24-mile zone. Since it will be a matter of examining each individual case in order to determine the applicable law, the situation will not differ from that existing on the high seas. The first approach, which ensures coastal jurisdiction in the 24-mile zone, is preferable by far; potential conflicts between salvage and heritage law would be settled on the basis of the national law of the coastal State. However, one may raise the question whether such an interpretation is permissible within the general framework of the 1982 Convention, where coastal admiralty law does not appear to enjoy any priority over the admiralty law of flag States beyond the territorial sea. In addition to the aforementioned explanation, namely that this is the only effective interpretation of article 303(2), the recognition of more extensive coastal rights in the 24-mile zone will be more easily acceptable, if a coastal State has declared an EEZ. Conflicts over residual rights would then have to be solved on the basis of article 59, which establishes the rules of equity and the consideration of the relevant interests of the parties, including those of the international community, as the main criteria of dispute settlement. Under these circumstances, the balance would appear to weigh in favour of the coastal State.

Another issue that demands attention is the scope of application of salvage law. Is there room for arguing that the drafters of the 1982 Convention were in favour of a legal regime of protection based on the incorporation of archaeological principles by admiralty or that ordinary maritime law applies to historic shipwrecks? This interpretation is far too extreme. In Arend's view: "By explicitly excluding from its reach objects covered by the law of salvage, article 303 avoids the confusion that might result if the provisions dealing with archaeology were applicable to objects with identifiable owners."[62] Thus, article 303(1) sheds light on the interpretation of the expression "objects of an archaeological and historical nature": "At a minimum, the objects must be old enough that the laws of salvage do not apply to them. That is, that there can be no person, legal or natural, who might be able to claim title to the objects in question."[63] The interpretation of "objects of an archaeological and historical nature" is considered below; nevertheless, it would be interesting to have a brief look at the assumption that the drafters of article 303 intended to separate salvage from heritage law by confining the latter to ancient items. There is nothing in article 303 or in its *travaux préparatoires* to suggest such an interpretation. On the contrary, an extensive interpretation of "archaeological" and "historical" is both desirable and permissible within the general framework of the 1982 Convention. If it is considered that admiralty courts tend to uphold salvage law applicable even to old wrecks, then, under an extensive interpretation of article 303(3), the scope of application of the heritage legislation may be limited considerably. Even if there is no identifiable owner, the question whether the law of salvage and other rules of admiralty prevail would still arise. In this context, the determination of the scope of application of salvage law is essential, especially if the priority of coastal admiralty law in the 24-mile zone is unacceptable.

The purpose of article 303 is the protection of archaeological and historical objects found at sea. To argue that the protected items should be interpreted restrictively so as to avoid interference with the law of salvage, in effect, reverses the situation and outweighs the balance in favour of the latter. Article 303 simply emphasises the fact that the proposed scheme of protection will not abolish the law of salvage. There is nothing in article 303 to indicate that the commercial interests of private salvage companies should be given more weight than the protection of the underwater cultural heritage. In this respect, the use of a fixed period of 100 years as a qualifying factor of protection is a reasonable time limit for both the determination of the scope of salvage law[64] and the interpretation of "archaeological" and "historical". The reservation of the law of salvage should be construed in a way that nullifies neither the jurisdictional rule of article 303(2) nor the duty of protection established by article 303(1). With respect to archaeological objects found within 24 miles off the shore, this reservation has been argued to find its limit in the public interest of the coastal State. Only the recognition of the legislative and judicial competence of the coastal State can ensure an effective scheme of protection.[65]

Reservation of the rights of the identifiable owners
Under article 303(3), the rights of the identifiable owners must be taken into consideration by the coastal State when applying its laws in the 24-mile zone. Article 303(3) should be read as a disclaimer of any effect on private law rights[66] and not as a repudiation of the duty to protect archaeological objects.[67] Archaeological and historical objects with identifiable owners should be also protected.[68] Nevertheless, coastal States will not be entitled to assert title to at least, wrecks of foreign origin, if their owner can be found or is known.[69] In relation to coastal rights over archaeological objects in the contiguous zone, international law acts as an enabling force and determines their scope *ratione materiae*.

Reservation of laws and practices with respect to cultural exchanges
The policy of cultural exchanges has often been recommended at the international level.[70] The 1969 Archaeological Convention promotes "the circulation of archaeological objects for scientific, cultural and educational purposes",[71] while the 1976 San Salvador Convention invites States parties to facilitate "the circulation, exchange and exhibition for educational, scientific and cultural purposes of cultural property from other nations and of their own cultural property abroad, when authorised by the pertinent governmental agencies."[72] The 1992 Archaeological Convention (revised) also promotes "the national and international exchange of elements of the archaeological heritage for professional scientific purposes", under the condition that all the appropriate steps are being taken to ensure that such circulation in no way prejudices the cultural and scientific value of those elements.[73]

There is, however, only one international instrument dealing specifically with cultural exchanges, the UNESCO Recommendation concerning the International Exchange of Cultural Property (1976).[74] The 1976 Recommendation advocates the lawful circulation of cultural property amongst cultural institutions in different countries. States are suggested to take all the necessary measures, including the adoption of new legislation or regulations on inheritance, taxation and customs duties, to carry out: (a) the definitive or temporary import or export of cultural property; (b) the transit of cultural property, and (c) the transfer of ownership or derestriction of cultural property belonging to a public body or a cultural institution.[75] Special consideration is given to the coverage of the risks to which cultural property is exposed throughout the duration of loans. In particular, the introduction of government guarantee and compensation systems for the loan of objects of great value is strongly recommended.[76] For the purposes of the Recommendation, "cultural property" shall be taken to mean items, which are the expression and testimony of human creation, and the evolution of nature, which, in the opinion of the competent bodies in individual States, are, or may be, of historical, artistic, scientific or technical value and interest, including archaeological objects.[77] Although this definition is broad enough to include underwater cultural property, the overall scheme of cultural exchanges, which is confined to exchanges of cultural property between cultural institutions, is not relevant to its removal from the contiguous zone. Furthermore, the underlying purpose of cultural exchanges being the enrichment of the world's cultural heritage and the promotion of understanding between nations, there is no room for conflict between the reservation laid down by article 303(3) and the general duty of protection under article 303(1). The protection of the property involved is implicit in the notion of cultural exchanges.

It seems, therefore, that laws and practices with respect to cultural exchanges are not directly related to the removal of archaeological objects from the ocean floor. They may be relevant to the circulation of the recovered archaeological material. The coastal State should promote their international exchange provided that all the necessary measures are taken to ensure that their cultural and scientific value is not prejudiced. However, its authorisation will always be required. It is very difficult to perceive a situation, where foreign missions would be entitled to remove archaeological objects from the contiguous zone on the basis of these laws, without the approval of the coastal State.[78]

Reservation of other international agreements and rules of international law regarding the protection of objects of an archaeological and historical nature
Article 303(4) should not be understood to refer exclusively to existing international agreements. It primarily promotes the elaboration in the future

of more comprehensive schemes of protection of underwater cultural property. As the international protection of the underwater cultural heritage is presently limited to archaeological sites found landward of the outer limit of the territorial sea, there is an urgent need to draft new agreements dealing specifically with underwater relics. The only exception is the 1992 Archaeological Convention (revised) which enables the application of its provisions within the contiguous zone in case the particular State party has expanded its jurisdiction over this area. With regard to the reservation of other "rules of international law", the question arises whether existing customary law governing the removal of archaeological objects from the contiguous zone is also included within its scope. The answer should be in the negative; otherwise, the overall significance of article 303(2) would be minimised. Under customary law, cultural property found in the contiguous zone falls within the freedom of the high seas regime and flag State jurisdiction. The purpose of article 303(2) is precisely to modify this law because it cannot ensure a satisfactory scheme of protection.

In this context, it would be absurd to argue that its drafters included a reservation which, in effect, nullified the expansion of coastal jurisdiction in the 24-mile zone. Article 303(4) should be interpreted so as to refer to future international agreements and rules of international law regarding the protection of archaeological objects.[79] Ronzitti argues that article 303(4) enables States to stipulate derogatory provisions without following the procedure of article 311(3). Article 303(4) prevails over article 311(3) either as *lex specialis* or as being implicitly contained in article 311(5): "This article shall not affect international agreements expressly permitted or preserved by other articles of this Convention."[80]

Interpretation of the term "objects of an archaeological and historical nature"

The Convention has failed to define the term "objects of an archaeological and historical nature" and is, therefore, difficult to identify the items that fall within its scope. First, there are no guidelines for the interpretation of "archaeological" and "historical" nor is there any explanation given for the necessity for their juxtaposition.[81] Second, the word "object" raises interpretation problems as to whether or not it encompasses immovable cultural property.

The notion of "archaeological" and "historical"
The interpretation of these terms will be oriented by setting, if possible, time limits, which are essential in determining the scope of underwater cultural property. Although age is not a determining factor of the notion of cultural heritage, e.g. even recent items may be of cultural importance, in certain cases its use is necessary in order to avoid conflicts with other bodies of laws. Regarding shipwrecks, the establishment of a time limit is of utmost importance in that it determines clearly the application of heritage legislation from that of salvage law. However, this approach should not result in a rigid conceptualisation of the terms. A flexible definition of cultural property should always provide for the discretionary inclusion of more recent items of historical importance or the exclusion of old, but less important objects. The overall goal is to offer the maximum possible protection to a wide range of items that reveal human past and are endangered by the development of advanced underwater technology. Under the rules set forth in the Vienna Convention on the Law of Treaties (1969), the object of treaty interpretation is to give the "ordinary" meaning to the terms of the treaty in their context and in the light of its object and purpose in good faith. There shall be taken into account, together with the context: (a) any subsequent agreement between the parties regarding the interpretation of the treaty or the application of its provisions; (b) any subsequent practice in the application of the treaty which establishes the agreement of the parties regarding its interpretation; (c) any relevant rules of international law applicable in the relations between the parties.[82] Resort to *travaux préparatoires* as a supplementary means of interpretation is allowed either to confirm an interpretation arrived at by literal or teleological methods, or to achieve an interpretation when pursuant to such methods, the treaty would remain ambiguous or obscure or the result would be manifestly absurd or unreasonable.[83]

Ordinary meaning of the words "archaeological" and "historical". Archaeologists often stress the fact that archaeology is not synonymous with prehistory even though it contributes mainly to areas and periods without written records. It has a wider scope, "which stretches beyond the perimeter of prehistoric studies and includes classical, medieval, recent colonial and industrial archaeology".[84]

"Any find that throws light on ways of life, techniques in construction or shipbuilding, methods of travel and travel routes can have an archaeological value, irrespective of how far back these date. For our practical purposes let us assume the most recent time of our 'archaeological period' of *100 years*. Certainly, when talking of ships, this becomes quite an important time. For this was the era of transition from sail to steam, from wooden hulls to steel and, more to the point, it was the time when the art of shipbuilding began its change to the true 'science of shipbuilding'. From about this period, far more detailed drawings of actual construction were used and have been retained. Consequently, naval historians have a fair degree of detailed knowledge of the shipwrights' methods after that time, whereas from the earlier times only rudimentary details can be gleaned from contemporary writings and from artists' drawings." (emphasis added)[85]

If it is considered that the above definitions concern the interpretation of the term "archaeological", then the notion of "historical" should be at least as extensive. In relation to the British Protection of Wrecks Act 1973, an eminent archaeologist, Muckelroy, argued that "in general terms 'historic' wreck means anything dating from before about AD 1800 and more recent finds which are particularly interesting".[86] It seems, therefore, that the ordinary meaning of the terms "archaeological" and "historical" is broad enough to include objects of relatively recent origin. With respect to ship-wreck archaeology, the fixed period of 100 years qualifies as a reasonable time limit.

The notion of "archaeological" and "historical" as envisaged by other relevant rules of international law. The examination of international instruments protecting cultural property also indicates that the notion of archaeological let alone historical, is not confined to items that are many hundreds years old. The 1970 Convention and the 1985 Cultural Offences Convention establish a 100 years time-limit, while the 1976 San Salvador Convention includes relatively recent items within the ambit of the cultural property to be protected.[87] The same applies to the legally non-binding Recommendation 848 (1978) of the Council of Europe on the underwater cultural heritage, which covers objects that have been *beneath* the water for more than 100 years with potential discretionary exclusion of less important objects and inclusion of more recent ones,[88] and the Draft European Convention.[89] Finally, Council Regulation (EEC) No. 3911/92 of 9 December 1992 on the export of cultural goods and Council Directive 93/7 of 15 March 1993 on the return of cultural objects unlawfully removed from the territory of a Member State apply, *inter alia,* to "archaeological objects more than 100 years old which are the products of land or underwater excavations or finds".

National heritage laws. Although there is no uniformity in the definitions given or in the setting of time-limits when age is established as a qualifying factor of protection, a period of 100-200 years is rather common, especially amongst laws dealing with underwater remains.

Table One   Time limits provided by general antiquities legislation[90]

States	Time-Limits
Argentina	1860
Bahrain	1780
Belize	150 years old
Bolivia	1900
Brunei	1894
Canada	50 years old
Democratic Yemen	200 years old
Cyprus	1850
Egypt	100 years old
Gambia	1937
Ghana	1900
Gibraltar	1800
Honduras	1900
Hong Kong	1600
India	100 years old
Indonesia	50 years old
Iraq	200 years old
Israel	1700
Jordan	1700
Kenya	1895/1800
Kuwait	40 years old
Lebanon	1700
Lesotho	100 years old
Libya	100 years old
Luxembourg	100 years old
Madagascar	100 years old
Malaysia	1850
Malta	50 years old
The Netherlands	50 years old
Nigeria	1918
Pakistan	1857
Philippines	100 years old

Saudi Arabia	200 years old
Sri Lanka	1815
Sudan	1821
Syria	200 years old
Tanzania	1863
Tunisia	100 years old
United Arab Emirates	150 years old
United States	100 years old
Yemen, Arab Republic	500 years old
Zambia	1890

Table Two Time limits provided specifically for underwater remains[91]

States	Time-Limits
Australia	75 years old
Channel Islands	50 years old
China	1911
Denmark	100 years underwater
Finland	100 years old
Ireland	100 years old
New Zealand	60 years underwater
	100 years underwater
Norway	100 years old
South Africa	50 years old
	100 years old
Sweden	100 years underwater

Examination of the travaux préparatoires: An early version of article 149 had made reference to a 50-year limit as the qualifying factor for the protection of shipwrecks and their cargoes.[92] Although subsequently deleted, this time-limit indicates that the expression "objects of an archaeological and historical nature" intended to cover items of relatively recent origin.

In contrast, Oxman, who participated in the drafting of article 303, argues that:

> "The provision is not intended to apply to modern objects whatever their historical interest. Retention of the adjective 'historical' was insisted upon by Tunisian delegates,

who felt that it was necessary to cover Byzantine relics that might be excluded by some interpretations of the word 'archaeological'. Hence the term historical origin, lacking at best in elegance when used with the term 'archaeological objects' in an article that expressly does not affect the law of salvage, does at least suggest the idea of objects, that are many hundreds of years old. The article contains no express time limit. As time marches on, so does our sense of what is old. Nevertheless, given the purpose for using the term 'historical', it may be that if a rule of thumb is useful for deciding what is unquestionably covered by this article, the most appropriate of the years conventionally chosen to represent the start of the modern era would be 1453: the fall of Constantinople and the final collapse of the remnants of the Byzantine Empire. Everything older would clearly be regarded as archaeological or historical. A slight adjustment to 1492 for applying the article to objects indigenous to the Americas, extended perhaps to the fall of Tenochtitlan (1521) or Cuzco (1533) in those areas, might have the merit of conforming to historical and cultural classifications in that part of the world."[93]

Oxman's restrictive interpretation is based on the comments of Tunisian delegates who thought that the retention of the term "historical" was necessary for the inclusion of Byzantine relics within the scope of protection. In their opinion, it was debatable whether the latter would fall within the notion of "archaeological". However, there is nothing in article 303(2) or in its *travaux préparatoires* to indicate that the term "historical" is strictly confined to Byzantine relics or to objects originating before the fall of Tenochtitlan (1521) or Cuzco (1633).

There seem to be two approaches to interpreting the expression "objects of an *archaeological and historical nature*". A restrictive interpretation would cover items that are many hundreds of years old, while an extensive interpretation would allow the protection of objects of relatively recent origin. Within the general framework of the 1982 Convention, the second interpretation appears to be the most reasonable one. The underlying purpose of both article 303 and 149 is the protection of the cultural heritage of the oceans, which has recently been endangered by the development of advanced underwater technology. Once the importance and value of underwater cultural property has been acknowledged, it would absurd to ensure the safeguarding of very old items only. The increased interest of the international community in the protection of the underwater cultural heritage and the recent trend in the field of marine archaeology not to leave anything unprotected, call for a teleological interpretation allowing the preservation of relatively recent items. As already seen, the Draft European Convention offers a useful definition of underwater cultural property. In addition to the qualitative criteria of protection, a *fixed time period of 100 years* is established. The term "underwater cultural property" as defined by the Draft European Convention, has, no doubt, a wider scope than the expression "objects of an archaeological and historical nature". However, the latter is broad enough to include objects of 100 years old.[94] It is not argued here that the 1982 Convention should be interpreted in the light of the Draft European Convention. What is suggested, is that the 100 year limit, combined with the potential extension of protection to more recent items, provides a useful yardstick for interpreting the expression "objects of an archaeological and historical nature" and distinguishing the scope of application of heritage legislation from that of salvage law.

Interpretation of the term "object"

The distinction between movable and immovable cultural property appears in both national and international instruments, which often restrict protection to one or other category. However, this approach can be negative. For example, if protection is confined to movable property, immovable property will be protected only after being detached and turned into movable property. There is no reason why the 1982 Convention should exclude submerged settlements from its ambit. At first sight, article 303(2) appears to imply the mobility of the protected objects. Only movable goods can be removed, exported or imported. However, one should consider that article 303(2) is but an application of the general duty to protect archaeological and historical objects found at sea laid out by article 303(1). The underlying purpose of article 303(2) is the determination of coastal rights over archaeological objects in the contiguous zone, and not the restriction of the scope of protection to movable goods. It is notable that the 1985 Draft Convention, which adopts a provision similar to article 303(2) to determine the territorial scope of its application, specifically includes sites and installations within the protected underwater cultural property,[95] while the 1969 Archaeological Convention defines "archaeological *objects*" as "all *remains* and *objects* or any traces of human existence which bear witness to epochs...".

To conclude, the 1982 Convention is the first codification of the law of the sea to provide for underwater cultural property. It would be regrettable if the objects to be protected were interpreted on the basis of an old-fashioned understanding of the notion of archaeology that would enable the preservation of very old items only, or if their scope was limited to movable cultural property.

Delimitation of the contiguous/archaeological zone

Contrary to the TSC, the 1982 Convention does not provide for the delimitation of opposite or adjacent contiguous zones. Article 33 fails to refer to this issue without giving any explanation for this ommission. Nor does the examination of the records of the Conference offer any significant help in this respect. The only official document of the Conference that incorporates a delimitation provision is a Working Paper of the Second Committee, elaborated in Caracas in 1974 and entitled "Main Trends".[96] Provision 49 of Part II of this document adopts the median line as the boundary between adjacent or opposite contiguous zones[97] in the absence of agreement to the contrary. However, this provision was not included in the subsequently adopted ISNT. It is notable that in the early stages of the Conference, the limited number of proposals on the contiguous zone either included a delimitation formula identical to article 24(3) of the TSC or did not mention delimitation at all.[98] The explanation for the dirth of discussion on delimitation was that a number of delegations believed that in the light of the establishment of the 12-mile territorial sea and the EEZ, the institution of the contiguous zone should be abolished. While this approach did not ultimately prevail, it detracted attention from the delimitation issue. Only the Cypriot delegate argued in a number of instances that a delimitation formula had to be adopted.

The following arguments have been advanced in doctrine as possible explanations for the omission of a delimitation formula. First, there is no need for delimitation; since coastal powers in the contiguous zone are non-exclusive, they can be exercised concurrently in the same area.[99] Second, the delimitation of the contiguous zone is governed by the delimitation formula of the EEZ (c.f. article 74); article 33 does not include a provision on this issue on the basis that a delimitation of the contiguous zone would constitute a delimitation of the EEZ.[100]

It is debatable whether the first argument holds for the general contiguous zone.[101] However, it does not hold for the 24-mile archaeological zone, where the legislative jurisdiction of the coastal State has been recognised. Even under a restrictive interpretation of article 303(2), the coastal State would be entitled to adopt legislation under which the removal of archaeological objects from the bed of the contiguous zone without its permission is illegal. The concurrent exercise of these rights would inevitably lead to a conflict of legislative competence in that the same objects would fall within two different jurisdictions. As a result, the delimitation of the archaeological zone is necessary.[102] The second argument, i.e., that the delimitation formula of the EEZ is applicable, should also be rejected; this approach not only neglects the nature and the historic development of the contiguous zone, but it also assumes that both opposite or adjacent States have declared EEZs. The EEZ and the contiguous zone did not only develop separately, but they also have a different jurisdictional nature. The contiguous zone as elaborated both by the TSC and the 1982 Convention is an accompaniment to the territorial sea; its main purpose is to make the exercise of coastal jurisdiction in the territorial sea efficient. It is on these grounds that the application of the delimitation formula of the EEZ is neither justifiable nor desirable within the general framework of the 1982 Convention.

Which delimitation formula would then be applicable to adjacent or opposite contiguous/archaeological zones? One solution would be the application by analogy of article 15 dealing with the delimitation of the territorial sea. Alternatively, it has been argued that article 24(3) of the TSC is still binding, either as a rule of custom or conventionally on the basis of article 311(1) and (2) of the 1982 Convention.[103] Article 311(1) reads: "This Convention shall prevail, as between States parties .. over the Geneva Conventions on the Law of the Sea of 1958". According to Caflisch, the use of the word "prevail" signifies the fact that the Geneva Conventions will not be abrogated, when there is a total absence of incompatibility. This is confirmed by article 311(2): "The Convention shall not alter the rights and obligations of States parties which arise from other agreements compatible with this Convention." It can, thus, be inferred that article 24(3) of the TSC is still applicable as the 1982 Convention is silent on the delimitation of the contiguous zone, and there seems to be no contradiction with the formula adopted by the TSC.[104] Although the conventional application of article 24(3) is questionable,[105] the delimitation of opposite or adjacent contiguous/archaeological zones on the basis of the principle of equidistance, failing agreement to the contrary, may be justified either as a rule of custom[106] or as an application by analogy of article 15.

CUSTOMARY INTERNATIONAL LAW

State practice does not provide evidence for the recognition of the 24-mile archaeological zone as a customary rule. To date, three States, Denmark, France and Tunisia, have expanded their competence over this area. France and Tunisia have employed the concept of the contiguous zone as a legal basis to extend their competence,[107] while the Danish legislation combines the breadth of 24nm with the notion of the continental shelf. Section 49(1) of the Conservation of Nature Act as amended by Act No. 530 of 10 October 1984 reads:

> "Ancient monuments on or in the seabed such as megaliths, graves, settlement sites, ruins, blockades, defence constructions or bridges may not be damaged or removed without the consent of the National Agency for the Protection of Nature, Monuments and Sites, if they are situated in the territorial waters or the *continental shelf within 24 nautical miles* from the baselines, from which the breadth of the outer territorial waters is measured" (emphasis added).

The same applies for wrecks of ships, which are considered to have been wrecked for more than 100 years ago (section 49(2)).[108] Section 49(4), which entitles the Minister for the Environment to take all the necessary measures for the protection of the discovered remains, clearly indicates that Denmark has expanded its legislative jurisdiction over the 24-mile zone. The same applies for the French[109] and the Tunisian legislation. It may be recalled that the Draft European Convention specifically expands coastal jurisdiction over the archaeological (contiguous) zone. Finally, under articles 2(2) and 3 of the Chinese Regulation on Protection and Administration of Underwater Cultural Relics Law 1989, China exercises jurisdiction over underwater cultural relics "originating from China or from an unidentifiable country, which remain beyond China's territorial sea but within other sea areas under China's jurisdiction according to Chinese laws."[110] As argued, since enactment of the Law on the Territorial Sea and the Contiguous Zone (1992), the 1989 Regulation has become automatically effective in the Chinese 24-mile contiguous zone.[111]

So far as the general concept of the contiguous zone is concerned, as of 16 November 1993, forty-nine (49) States have claimed contiguous zones.[112] These claims are not always compatible with the regime envisaged by the TSC and the 1982 Convention.[113] None of the existing contiguous zones claims, however, make specific reference to the removal of underwater cultural property. This fact loses its significance if it is considered that the 24-mile archaeological zone has an independent nature from the contiguous zone. As previously indicated, coastal States do not have to declare a contiguous zone first in order to be entitled to control access to underwater cultural property found within the 24-mile limit. It is notable that Denmark, which has expanded its competence over this area, has not claimed a contiguous zone, while both the French and the Chinese legislation on the contiguous zone do not refer to the removal of cultural property. The relevant claims are to be found in the heritage legislation.[114]

NOTES

1   Paragraph 2 establishes the maximum breadth of the contiguous zone to 12 nm, while paragraph 3 deals with the delimitation of opposite or adjacent contiguous zones."Failing agreement to the contrary, neither of the two States is entitled to extend its contiguous zone beyond the median line every point of which is equidistant from the nearest points on the baselines from which the breadth of the territorial seas of the two States is measured." A comparison of article 24(3) with article 12 of the TSC dealing with the delimitation of adjacent or opposite territorial seas, shows that the former does not take into consideration the existence of "special circumstances". Article 12 reads: "The provisions of this paragraph shall not apply, however, where it is necesary by reason of its historic title or other special circumstances to delimit the territorial seas of the two States in a way which is at variance with this provision." It is difficult to understand the reason for the omission of the reference to "special circumstances" in article 24(3). According to Caflisch, a possible explanation is that the drafters of the TSC considered that even an "inequitable" delimitation of the contiguous zone would not cause serious problems to the "State-victim", as in these waters coastal States enjoy only limited powers of control. Caflisch, L., "La délimitation des espaces marins entre états dont les côtes se font face ou sont adjacente" in Dupuy, R.J., Vignes, D. (eds.), *Traité du nouveau droit de la mer*, Collection Droit International, Economica, Bruylant, 1985, pp. 373-440 at p. 392.

2   Lowe, A.V., "The development of the concept of the contiguous zone", 52 *B.Y.I.L.* (1981) pp. 109-169 at p. 141. See also Frommer, A.M., "A contribution to the study of the contiguous zone", 16 *Revue belge du droit international* (1981/82) pp. 434-458; Gidel, G., "La mer territorial et la zone contiguë", 48 *Hague Recueil* (1934-II) pp. 241-273; Masterson, W.E., *Jurisdiction in Marginal Seas*, Kennikat Press, Port Washington, New York, London 1929; McDougal & Burke, W.T., *The Public Order of the Oceans - A Contemporary International Law of the Sea*, Yale University Press, New Haven/London, 1962 pp. 565-608; O'Connell, D.P., *The International Law of the Sea,* vol. II, Clarendon Press, Oxford, 1984 at p. 1045; Oda, S., "The concept of the contiguous zone", 11

Int'l & Comp. L.Q. (1962) pp. 131-153; Rao, R.C., *The New Law of Maritime Zones,* Milind Publications Private Limited, New Delhi, 1983, pp. 301-316.

3   O'Connell, *ibid* at p. 1034.

4   Lowe, *op. cit.* note 2 at p. 147.

5   *Ibid* at p. 157. See also McDougal & Burke, *op. cit.* note 2 at pp. 606-607 and Oda, *ibid* at p. 153.

6   The restrictive nature of coastal rights is confirmed by the 1958 scheme, which forbids the arrest of ships passing through the territorial sea for offences committed before they enter these waters. If legislative jurisdiction were to exist in the contiguous zone, then foreign shipping that would commit an offence there would acquire in the territorial waters a greater degree of immunity than in high seas, as in this case they could be seized after hot pursuit. See Churchill, R.R. & Lowe, A.V., *The Law of the Sea,* 2nd revised edition, Manchester University Press, 1988 at p. 117. See also Fitzmaurice, G.G., "Some Results of the Geneva Conference on the Law of the Sea", 8 *Int'l & Comp. L.Q.* (1959) pp. 73-121, who adopts a very restrictive interpretation of coastal powers within the contiguous zone. In his view, since the basic object of the contiguous zone is anticipatory, i.e., to avoid an offence being committed subsequently when, by entering the territorial sea, the vessel comes within the jurisdiction of the coastal State, coastal rights are essentially supervisory and preventive. *Ibid* at p. 114. He admits, however, that the coastal State is entitled to punish an offence committed within its territory or territorial sea. The punitive aspect of coastal rights over the contiguous zone should be emphasised as Sir Gerald Fitzmaurice's restrictive interpretation has been used recently as a basis to oppose the adoption of article 2 of the Draft European Convention on the Protection of the Underwater Cultural heritage. See *supra* at pp. 170-171.

7   At the preventive level, the measures that the coastal State is entitled to undertake are limited to stopping, warning, inspecting and investigating at sea the vessel in question.

8   At the repressive level, the scope of coastal powers is more extensive since the infringement of coastal laws has already taken place. The additional powers of boarding and escorting the ship concerned into port are generally acceptable. Confiscation of the contraband at the port may also be justified, if it is permissible by domestic law. See further Economides, C., "The Contiguous Zone, Today and Tomorrow" in Rozakis, C.L., Stephanou, C.A. (eds.), *The New Law of the Sea,* Selected and Edited Papers of the Athens Colloquium on the Law of the Sea (September 1982), North Holland, Amsterdam, 1983, pp. 69-81 at p. 77: "In such cases, the coastal State directly imposes fines or more severe sanctions, such as seizure of the ship, confiscation of the property on board or imprisonment ... the State may exercise full jurisdiction in the contiguous zone; however, the existence of some link between the ship, which is at fault, and the coastal State is applicable here too and more strictly so, since the imposition of such sanctions presupposes that the infringements have been committed on the coastal State's territory or in its territorial sea." See also Fitzmaurice, *op. cit.* note 6.

9   28 *I.L.R.* (1963) p. 170.

10 *Ibid* at p.175. In the opinion of the court, article 24 is not declaratory of customary international law because the conditions surrounding the delimitation of the territorial sea and the contiguous zone were very different in State practice from those contained in this article. "States apply different rules according to their respective municipal laws, which fact in itselfprecludes recognition of any pre-existing custom in the matter... Italy has not accepted the limit of the contiguous zone in the form in which it is expressed in article 24. The rules of municipal law have therefore remained in force. In Italy it is the rule laid down in article 33 of the Customs Law, which was designated to give the widest possible powers to the Italian courts and not merely police powers to prevent smuggling." *Ibid* at pp. 173-174. Article 33 of the Customs Law of 25 September 1940 provides that Italy shall be entitled to exercise jurisdiction over a further six-mile zone, on top of the six miles territorial sea established by article 2 of the Italian Maritime Code, for the purpose of preventing and punishing smuggling along the Italian coast. The latter is referred to as a "zone of vigilance". It is notable that in 1951 the Italian court of Cassation held that violations of customs regulations within the 12-mile zone must be regarded as committed within Italian territory. See *Simpson Sones e altri,* IX *Annali di diritto internazionale* (1951) p. 203.

11 In McDougal's & Burke's view, "the coastal State is by the recognition of its competence to control access, in substance, authorised to extend its laws to the areas concerned for the purpose of prescribing, in relation to the particular interests, the behaviour by foreign vessels reasonably believed to be compatible with the preservation of these interests. In realistic observation, the prescription by the coastal State relates to the events occurring in the contiguous area and not merely to those within the waters, or upon the land, subject to its comprehensive authority." *Op. cit.* note 2 at p. 608. See also Oda, *ibid* at p. 153, Symonides, J., "Contiguous Zone", XVI *P.Y.I.L.* (1987) pp. 143-154, ID, "Origin and Essence of the Contiguous Zone", 20 *Ocean Dev. & Int'l L.* (1989) pp. 203-211, and Rao, *ibid* at pp. 323-325. Finally, O'Connel argues that the refusal of the legislative competence of the coastal State contracts the very notion which has underlain the contiguous zone and that, therefore, article 24 should be read so as to authorise the coastal State to make foreign ships subject to its laws in the contiguous zone. In this respect, he proposes an interpretation based on a perception of the contiguous zone as evidenced in State practice in an historical perspective. The laws that the coastal State is entitled to apply within the contiguous waters must be limited in scope as the hovering laws were, to prevent the evasion of other laws such as laws respecting customs duties, passport or health control, which are intrinsically laws to be administered at the frontier. Under this interpretation, the dichotomy between "prevention" and "punishment" of article 24 loses its significance, as punishment of an offence committed in contiguous waters, is in this context incidental to prevention. O'Connell, *op cit.* note 2 at p. 1060.

12 Oda, *ibid* at pp. 151-153.

13 An outgoing vessel is a vessel that has already violated coastal laws within the territorial sea and heads away to the high seas.

14   Most of the scholars, who are in favour of a right of hot pursuit arising from
      offences committed within the contiguous zone, base their arguments upon the
      rejection of the original ILC text and the adoption of a joint Polish/Yugoslavian
      proposal which attempted to modify the ILC draft by permitting pursuit to begin
      in the contiguous zone. Doc. A/CONF.13/C.2/L.20/Rev.1 and L.61/Rev.1,
      UNCLOS I, Off. Rec. vol. IV, p. 121 and p. 82 (statement by the Polish delegate
      in introducing the amendment). The ILC's Commentary on draft article 47 (right
      of hot pursuit) read: "The offence giving rise to hot pursuit must always have
      been committed in the internal waters or in the territorial sea: acts committed
      in the contiguous zone cannot confer upon the coastal State a right of hot
      pursuit." II *ILC Yearbook* (1956) at p. 285. See further Oda, *op. cit.* note 2 at
      p. 131; Poulantzas, N., *The Right of Hot Pursuit in International Law*, Leyden,
      1969 at pp. 163-167; Treves, T., "La Navigation" in Dupuy & Vignes (eds.),
      op. cit. note 1, pp. 687-808 at pp. 706-711; McDougal & Burke, *op. cit.* note
      2 at pp. 893-923, 920-923; Brownlie, I., *Principles of International Law*, 4th
      ed., Clarendon Press, Oxford, 1990 at p. 247.
      Since the restrictive interpretation of the contiguous zone has been adopted by
      the TSC, an extensive interpretation of article 23 of the CHS will result in a
      logical inconsistency. On the one hand, the coastal State would enjoy the right
      of hot pursuit for breaches of law which occurred within contiguous waters,
      while, on the other, it would lack the necessary jurisdictional powers to apply
      these laws. See further, Lowe, *op. cit.* note 2 at p. 167: "It might also be added
      that the conclusion that a right of hot pursuit might arise from offences actually
      committed within the contiguous zone would create a singular problem. Under
      article 19(5) of the TSC, a coastal State is prohibited from taking steps to arrest
      any person on board, or conduct an investigation, in connection with a crime
      committed before the ship enters the territorial sea, where the ship is only
      passing through the territorial sea without entering internal waters. This would
      clearly include crimes committed in the contiguous zone. Therefore, by fleeing
      into the territorial sea such a ship could achieve a greater degree of immunity
      from coastal State jurisdiction than it could by fleeing on to the high seas, where
      the right of hot pursuit would exist. Indeed, were the ship to pass through the
      territorial sea of the coastal State into that of a third State, any pursuit would
      necessarily be interrupted, so that the right of hot pursuit could not be exercised
      by the State in whose contiguous zone the 'offence' was committed, even when
      the ship eventually emerged on to the high seas."
15   The limited powers of control that the coastal State enjoys under the TSC
      scheme, cannot safeguard its interests in the prevention of smuggling, the
      protection of public health and the regulation of immigration. Moreover, the
      rigid conceptualism of article 24 does not allow the consideration of other
      emerging interests. According to McDougal & Burke, if a generalised contiguous
      zone had been adopted it could be used as a means "to permit other contempora-
      ry interests to be taken into account and to preserve a flexible device for the
      accommodation of continually emerging interests." *Op. cit.* note 2 at p. 77. In
      their opinion, the artificial distinction between the contiguous zone and the
      continental shelf and conservation zones "denies the fluidity of the general

concept and affords opportunity for irrational attempts to foreclose future claims to newly developed uses of the sea."

16 A/CONF.13/C.1/L.78, *UNCLOS I, Off. Rec.* vol. 3, p. 232. The Polish draft, which had been adopted by the First Committee, was rejected in the Plenary session and replaced by the original ILC text. According to Rao, the rejection of the First Committee text in the plenary was a surprise development in that a good majority of the States present at UNCLOS I were in favour of the Polish draft. *Op. cit.* note 2 at p. 332.

17 The following cases have been described by Caflisch as relevant to the archaeological issue: (i) A foreign vessel in the contiguous zone is attempting to import antiquities found outside the territorial sea into the territory or the territorial sea of the coastal State, contrary to the customs or fiscal regulations of that State; (ii) The attempt described under (i) has succeeded and the foreign vessel is present in the contiguous zone; (iii) A foreign vessel present in that zone has exported submarine antiquities from the territory or the territorial sea of the coastal State in violation of the latter's customs or fiscal regulations. Caflisch, L., "Submarine Antiquities and the International Law of the Sea", 13 *N.Y.I.L.* (1982) pp. 3-32 at p. 13.

18 See also Miller, who argues that "as the contiguous zone extends to high seas areas and not to the seabed and subsoil thereunder, the contiguous zone provisions of the TSC do not apply to the exploration and excavation of antiquities and to marine archaeology." Miller, H.C., *International Law and Marine Archaeology,* Academy of Applied Sciences, Belmont, Mass. 1973 at p. 20 and Pazarci, H., "Le concept de zone contiguë dans la convention sur le droit de la mer", XVIII *Revue belge de droit international* (1984/85) pp. 249-271 at p. 251. This argument is of no practical significance under the TSC, which recognises only the exercise of enforcement jurisdiction in contiguous waters. Since customs and fiscal laws cease to apply beyond the outer limit of the territorial sea, the scope *ratione loci* of coastal powers in the contiguous zone is not in question. Whatever falls within the scope of customs and fiscal laws may be governed by the regime of the contiguous zone, irrespective of its location. Traditionally, the contiguous zone has served the need of coastal States to protect their revenue from smuggling and defend their coasts beyond the territorial sea. Without being confined to a particular resource of the oceans, it attributed jurisdictional powers to the coastal State in respect of customs, defence and health matters. There is nothing in the TSC to indicate that the concept of the contiguous zone is strictly confined to the superjacent waters; indeed a restrictive interpretation could easily result in absurdities, e.g., that the coastal State is not entitled to seize contraband jettisoned by a foreign vessel in the contiguous zone.

19 The contiguous zone cannot be regarded as part of the national territory. In contrast, Miller argues that the coastal State "in order to comply with the 1970 Convention could clearly extend its customs laws to the contiguous zone". Miller, *ibid* at p. 20. See also Rigo, A., "Book Reviews: International Law and Marine Archaeology by H. Crane Miller", 5 *J. Mar. L. & Com.* (1973-74) pp. 141-142.

20 The reference to the high seas has been omitted as the area beyond the outer territorial sea limit may now be governed by the EEZ regime. See *infra* chapter 7.

21 On the contrary, Rao argues that: "There is no explicit indication in the Conference records whether those States which proposed the continuation of the contiguous zone regime on the model of article 24 of the TSC also shared the Fitzmaurice's interpretation of that provision". *Op. cit.* note 2 at p. 331.

22 Platzöder, R., *Third United Nations Conference on the Law of the Sea: Documents*, vol. IV, Oceana Publications Inc., Dobbs Ferry, New York, 1983 at p. 526. In the light of articles 56, 57 and 76 of the ICNT the parallel reference to the EEZ was unnecessary as both zones coincided up to the 200-mile line.

23 Doc.A/CONF.62/C.2/Inf.Meeting/43 (August 16, 1979). *Ibid*, vol. V at p. 50.

24 Doc.A/CONF.62/C.2/Inf.Meeting/43/Rev.1 (August 21, 1979). *Ibid.*

25 Doc.A/CONF.62/C.2/Inf.Meeting/43/Rev.2 (March 19, 1980). *Ibid* at p. 51. The only change was the omission of "salvaging" and "proper representation" from the purposes for which the sovereign rights of coastal States were recognised. In the light of article 303(3), which reserved the law of salvage, it can be seen to be significant that the term "salvaging" was replaced by the term "recovery"; even the slightest interference with this ancient maritime law was undesirable. In any case, the term recovery is more appropriate for archaeological operations.

26 Informal Proposal by Cape Verde, Greece, Italy, Malta, Portugal, Tunisia and Yugoslavia, Doc.A/CONF.62/C.2/ Inf.Meeting/43/Rev.3 (March 27 1980). *Ibid.*

27 The very use of the term "jurisdiction" indicates a change in the balance of principles. Jurisdiction, in contrast to sovereign rights, does not raise presumptions in its favour. It may be defined as "the power of a sovereign state to create or affect legal interests (legislative jurisdiction) and to enforce its laws (enforcement jurisdiction)".

28 In this respect see the statements of Mr. Varvesi (Italy), Mr. Stavropoulos (Greece), Mr. Mizzi (Malta), Mr. Abdel Meguid (Egypt) and Mr. de Lacharrire (France), *UNCLOS III, Off. Rec.*, vol. XIII at p. 14 (para. 44), p. 26 (para. 27), p. 26 (para. 31), p. 37 (para. 65) and p. 30 (para. 12) respectively. According to the Greek delegate: "After being revised, it [the proposal] now appeared to enjoy widespread and substantial support. The fact that delegations might not refer to it within the limited time allowed in the plenary meetings of the Conference should not militate against the inclusion of the proposal in the second revision of the negotiation text." *Ibid.* It is notable, however, that in the *Report of the Chairman of the Second Committee, Doc.A/CONF.62/L.51*, it was states that "in the case of the informal proposal on C2/Informal Meeting/43/Rev.2, the sponsors put forward a third revision which the Committee was unable to discuss".

29 *U.S. Delegation Report, Ninth Session of the Third United Nations on the Law of the Sea (1980)*. Text reprinted in Arend, A.C., "Archaeological and Historical Objects: The International Legal Implications of UNCLOS III", 22 *V.J.I.L.* (1982) pp. 777-803 at p. 795. See also the statement by Mr. Richardson (U.S.A.), *UNCLOS III, Off. Rec.* vol. XIII at p. 43 (para. 158).

30 See further Caflisch, *op. cit.* note 17 at p. 17; Oxman, B.H., "The Third UN Conference on the Law of the Sea: The Ninth Session (1980)", 75 *A.J.I.L.* (1981) pp. 211-256 at pp. 240-241; Treves, T., "La nona sezzione della Conferenza sul diritto del mare", 63 *Rivista di diritto internazionale* (1980) pp. 432-463 at pp. 440-442. The "creeping jurisdiction" argument is often employed by the major maritime powers as a defence against extensive coastal claims. It could be summarised as the "belief that maritime jurisdictional rights granted for one purpose are likely to expand either *ratione loci* or *ratione materiae* and that there is no guarantee that they will not 'creep' out further into the high seas or that the freedom of navigation will not be further eroded." Brown, E.D., "Maritime Zones: A Survey of Claims" in Churchill, R.R. and others (eds.), *New Directions in the Law of the Sea*, vol. III (1973), pp. 157-192 at p. 172. The tendency of "exclusive rights for some purposes" to become "exclusive rights for others, perhaps all purposes", has been described as an "undeniable law" of international life and a "valuable lesson of experience". Anand, R.P., *Legal Regime of the Sea Bed and the Developing Countries*, Sijthoff, Leyden, 1976 at p. 110. With respect to archaeological objects, the creeping jurisdiction argument may be thought to have a basis in reality since the attribution of sovereign rights over archaeological objects is additional to the already existing rights over the natural resources of the continental shelf and the EEZ. This is clearly not the case for the following reasons: (a) underwater archaeological remains are inevitably connected with the continental shelf in that they are located on and under the seabed. Whatever the legal regime of their protection, it will "overlap" with the continental shelf; (b) the continental shelf regime itself, introduced by Truman's Proclamation, was a departure from the freedom of the high seas, which presumably covered the vast ocean areas beyond the territorial sea boundary. The emergence of the need to protect and preserve the underwater cultural heritage should likewise have resulted in the enunciation of a legal regime shaped upon its nature and needs. Claims are creeping forward in any event. A major advantage of the conventional establishment of jurisdictional zones is that these trends are held to a reasonable limit. If a jurisdicional zone is well defined and the attributed rights properly specified, the possibilities of "creeping" jurisdiction are minimised and the prospects of a minimum public order of the oceans are increased. The attribution of jurisdiction alone would not turn the continental shelf into a territorial zone.

31 Doc.A/CONF.62/GP.4 of 27 March 1980 in Platzöder, *op. cit.* note 22, vol. XII at p. 299.

32 Doc.A/CONF.62/GP.10 of 18 August 1980 in Platzöder, *ibid*, vol. XII at p. 302.

33 The support of the Tunisian delegate, who was the general representative of the Group of 77 throughout the negotiations in the Conference, was influential, even though he stated that on the archaeological issue he was only representing his country.

34 Arend, *op. cit.* note 29 at p. 797.

35 Various solutions were put forward. One suggestion was to emphasise the right of the coastal State to make access to its ports conditional on requirements relating to the removal of archaeological resources. A second suggestion was to permit the coastal State to enact customs and fiscal laws and regulations with respect to archaeological objects found in the contiguous zone. See further Caflisch, *op. cit.* note 17 at pp. 18-19 and Treves, *op. cit.* note 30 at p. 441.

36 Doc.A/CONF.62/GP 11 of 19 August 1980 in Platzöder, *op. cit.* note 22 vol. XII at p. 303.

37 According to para. 13 of the Report of the President on the work of the informal plenary meeting of the Conference on general provisions: "The proposal in document GP/11 concerning archaeological objects and objects of historical value was taken up for consideration along with the other proposals on that subject ... It was decided that all these documents be considered together. After a brief discussion, however, it seemed that the proposal in GP/11 was closer to a compromise than any of the others. That text, with some amendments was eventually adopted." Doc. A/CONF.62/L.58, *UNCLOS III, Off. Rec.* vol. XIV 128 at p. 129. These amendments were: (a) the modification of the term "archaeological objects and objects of historical value" to "archaeological objects and objects of historical origin"; (b) the reservation of the rights of the identifiable owners in paragraph 3, and (c) the inclusion of paragraph 4. In the final text of the Convention, the term "archaeological objects and objects of an archaeological origin" was modified in "objects of an archaeological and historical nature", the formula employed by article 149. In this way, the unreasonable differentiation of the two terms was removed.

38 See also Caflisch, *op. cit.* note 17 at p. 19.

39 Oxman, *op. cit.* note 30 at p. 241.

40 This is illustrated by the statements made by the various delegations. For example, the compromise formula was acceptable to Greece, because it amounted to granting the coastal State legislative competence in the contiguous zone. It was regarded as "an acceptable minimum, although it would have preferred a more far-reaching provision". Statement by Mr. Stavropoulos (Greece), *UNCLOS III, Off. Rec.* vol. XIV at p. 38 (para. 107). To the United States it was acceptable, because it "permitted the coastal State to exercise jurisdiction over attempted removals of archaeological objects from the contiguous zone without expanding jurisdiction over the continental shelf and the EEZ and also without creating an archaeological zone." Oxman, *op. cit.* note 30 at p. 240.

41 Fuller, L.L., *Legal Fictions,* Stanford University Press, Stanford, California, 1967 at p. 40 *et seq.*

42 Even if the presumed fact is present in reality, but the party chooses to rely on the conclusive presumption either because proof would be difficult or because he does not know whether the fact ispresent or not, the conclusive presumption attributes to the facts "an artificial effect" beyond their natural tendency to produce belief. It knowingly gives an insufficient proof the value of a sufficient one. The same applies to rebuttal presumption to the extent that rebuttal is

limited. In this case, the *prima facie* rebuttal presumption has the same effect as a conclusive presumption. *Ibid* at p. 42.

43 *Ibid* at p. 44. Even within these limits, there is a fiction in the sense that we ordinarily treat as an "inference", what is in reality passive acceptance of an imposed principle (i.e., when the presumption is treated as a rule of law by the judge, it is clear that it is not an inference as to them).

44 *Ibid* at p. 47.

45 See also Caflisch, *op. cit.* note 17 at p. 20.

46 Oxman, *op. cit.* note 30 at p. 241.

47 Caflisch, *op. cit.* note 17 at p. 20. See further the Report of the President on the Informal Plenary Meeting of the Conference on General Provisions, *op. cit.* note 38: "It was agreed that the reference in paragraph 2 'to result in an infringement' was understood to mean that it would constitute or constitutes an infringement within its territory or territorial sea".

48 The explanation given for article 303(2) was the following: "With the aim of controlling traffic in objects found on the bottom within this zone, the new article would allow coastal States to presume that removing the article without their approval would result in infringement of their regulations committed within their territory or territorial waters. Thus, under such a presumption, the coastal State could act to prevent such removal or punish those responsible for it." United Nations, Information Service, "Law of the Sea Conference Accepts General Provisions, Including Article on Protection of Artifacts Found in Sea Bottom", *Press Release SEA/125*, 25 August 1980, p. 2.

49 Lauterpacht, H. Text quoted in O'Connell, D.P., *International Law,* vol. 1, 2nd ed. Stevens & Sons, London, 1970 at p. 251.

50 In the light of the *travaux préparatoires* of article 303(2), one could even question the existence of a common intention of the parties. According to Lauterpacht, where there is no common intention for the reason that the parties, although using identical language, did not intend the same result, "the judge may legitimately have recourse to what may be considered the common intention of the treaty taken in its entirety, by reference to the historical circumstances of its creation and to its object as ascertained by the general tendency of its clauses". Lauterpacht, H., "Restrictive interpretation and the principle of effectiveness of the interpretation of treaties", 26 *B.Y.I.L.* (1949) pp. 48-85.

51 As already seen, under normal circumstances, coastal powers would be limited to preventive measures. Since the vessel in question has not yet entered the territorial sea, it has not committed any crime.

52 According to article 111(1) of the 1982 Convention: "If the foreign ship is within a contiguous zone ... the pursuit may only be undertaken if there has been a violation of the rights for the protection of which the zone was established." If the other conditions of the right of hot pursuit are also fulfilled, the coastal State may pursue the vessel in question on the high seas. Implicit in article 111 is the notion of "constructive presence". Accordingly, a ship whose boats remove archaeological objects from the bed of the contiguous zone, would be pursued on the high seas, even if itself remains outside the 24 mile limit. This is the combined effect of articles 303(2) and 111.

53 There are an increasing number of scholars recognising the extension of the legislative powers of the coastal State over the 24-mile zone. In particular, see Caflisch, *op. cit.* note 17 at p. 20; Giorgi, M.C., "Underwater archaeological and historical objects" in Dupuy, R.-J. & Vignes, D. (eds), *A Handbook on the New Law of the Sea*, vol.1, Hague Academy of International Law, Martinus Nijhoff, 1991 at p. 569; Karagiannis, V., "Une nouvelle zone de jurisdiction: la zone archéologique maritime", *Espaces et ressources maritimes*, 1990, No. 4, pp. 1-26; Leanza, U., "The territorial scope of the Draft European Convention on the Protection of the Underwater Cultural Heritage" in Council of Europe, *International Legal Protection of Cultural Property, Proceedings of the Thirteenth Colloquy on European Law*, Delphi, 20-22 September 1983, Strasbourg, 1984, pp. 127-130 at p. 129; ID, *Nuovi Saggi di Diritto del Mare*, Giappichelli editore, 1988 at pp. 35-56; Roucounas, E., "Submarine Archaeological Research: Some Legal Aspects" in Leanza, U. (ed.), *The International Legal Regime of the Mediterranean Sea*, Università degli Studi di Roma, Pubblicazioni della Facoltà di Giurisprudenza, 2, Milano, Dott. A. Giuffrè editore, 1987, pp. 309-334 at pp. 324-325; Treves, *op. cit.* note 30 at p. 442; ID, "Stato costiero e archeologia sottomarina", *Rivista di diritto internazionale* (1993) pp. 698-719 at pp. 704-705. In contrast, Oxman, B.H., "Marine archaeology and the international law of the sea", 12 *Columbia - VLA Journal of Law & the Arts* (1988) pp. 353-372 at p. 364, argues that article 303(2) does not in any way expand the nature of coastal powers in the contiguous zone, but rather permits the coastal State to establish a presumption of smuggling.

54 Ronzitti, N., "Strato costiero e tutela del patrimonio storico sommerso", 86 *Il diritto maritimo* (1984) pp. 3-24 at p. 9.

55 *Ibid.*

56 See further Final Activity Report, *ibid* at pp. 5-10 and pp. 33-34 (Minority statement made by the Turkish expert); Pazarci, H., "Sur la recherche archéologique subaquatique en Mediteranée" in Leanza, (ed), *op. cit.* note 53, pp. 359-366. ID, *op. cit.* note 18. It has been argued that the expansion of coastal jurisdiction would inevitably lead to conflict of competence between opposite or adjacent States, since one State may adopt legislation under which the removal of underwater cultural property from the continental shelf of another State is illegal. The following example was used to illustrate the difficulties which are bound to be met by the creation of such archaeological zones. The Channel Islands, in the English Channel, are awarded a 12-mile enclave continental shelf boundary in the area to the north and northwest by the Court of Arbitration. If the United Kingdom claimed a 24-mile archaeological zone off the Channel Islands, this would extend over the continental shelf of France which lies beyond the 12-mile enclave boundary of the Channel Islands. The United Kingdom could then adopt legislation rendering the removal of archaeological objects from the continental shelf of France illegal. As will be discussed in chapter 7, the continental shelf regime is a natural resource regime, which does not apply, as such, to underwater cultural property. As a result there should be no room for conflict as the same objects do not fall within different jurisdictions despite the obvious

pratical difficulties. This should be contrasted with the possibility of conflict which would exist if the opposite or adjacent archaeological zones overlap in which case the delimitation of the two zones is essential. Similar difficulties may arise if one State chooses the continental shelf as the basis of its cultural heritage zone, while an adjacent State may choose a different basis resulting in an overlap of such zones. Such a situation may occur under the 1992 Archaeological Convention (revised), see *supra* at pp. 80-81. It is notable that Turkey did not object to the 1992 formula and signed the Convention.

57   It is noteworthy that the earlier drafts of article 2 did not employ the term "contiguous zone" in order to define the geographical scope of its application. The 1984 draft referred to "a maritime zone which does not extend beyond 24 nautical miles". See *Doc. CAHAQ(84)4, DIR/JUR (84)1*. As explained by the Chairman of the *Ad Hoc* Committee: "The article did not mention the zone by name in order to avoid giving the specific regime of the contiguous zone a new meaning (1983, Public Seminar, Syracuse University)", quoted in O'Keefe, P.J., "The Law and Nautical Archaeology. An International Survey" in Langley, S.B.M. & Unger, R.W. (eds.), *Nautical Archaeology: Progress and Public Responsibility*, BAR International Series, No. 220, 1984, pp. 9-17 at p. 11. On the territorial scope of application of the 1985 Draft Convention see further Halkiopoulos, Th., "Questions juridique de base de la Convention européenne pour la protection du patrimoine culturel subaquatique". Paper presented at the *Seminario: La protezione del patrimonio culturale subacqueo nel Mediterraneo*, organised by the Università degli Studi di Roma 'Tor Vergata', Anacapri, 1 October 1994; Gnagnarella, F. and (di) Fonzo, L., "La sfera di applicazione spaziale della Convenzione Europea sulla Protezione del Patrimonio Culturale Subacqueo", *ibid*, and Leanza, U., "The territorial scope of application of the Draft European Convention on the Protection of the Underwater Cultural Heritage" in Council of Europe, *International Legal Protection of Cultural Property*, Strasbourg, 1984, pp. 127-130.

58   Done at London, Moscow and Washington, 11 February 1971; *ST/LEG/SER.B/19* at pp. 455-459. Article II: "For the purpose of this Treaty, the outer limit of the sea-bed zone referred to in article I shall be coterminous with the twelve-mile limit of the zone referred in Part II of the Convention on the Territorial Sea and the Contiguous Zone, signed at Geneva on 29 April 1958, and shall be measured in accordance with the provisions of Part I, section II of that Convention and in accordance with international law."

59   Caflisch, *op. cit.* note 17 at p. 21.

60   See also Migliorino, L., "Submarine Antiquities and the Law of the Sea", 4(4) *Marine Policy Reports* (1982) at p. 4.

61   Ronzitti, *op.cit.* note 54 at p. 12.

62   Arend, *op. cit.* note 29 at p. 801.

63   *Ibid* at p. 779 (footnote 8).

64   It is notable that the Salvage Association has suggested the year 1860 as the cut-off point for protecting historic wrecks, after which commercial interests could take precedence. See further Dromgoole, S., "Protection of Historic Wrecks. The UK Approach. Part II: Towards Reform", 4 *International Journal*

of Estuarine and Coastal Law (1989) pp. 95-116 at p. 103, and Auburn, F.M., "Convention for Preservation of Man's Heritage in the Ocean", 185 *Science* (1974) pp. 763-767 at p. 764, who argues that "for purposes of the Continental Shelf Convention, the term 'natural resources' should be deemed to include archaeological and cultural artefacts and wrecks not less than 100 years old". The requirement of this period is specified in order to eliminate the possibility of interfering with nuclear submarines and other modern wrecks.

65　See also Roucounas, *op. cit.* note 53 at pp. 328-329.

66　See also Oxman, *op. cit.* note 30.

67　Under an extensive interpretation, the existence of an owner may nullify the jurisdictional rule of article 303(2) and/or the duty of protection established by article 303(1). According to Migliorino: "The rights of identifiable owners of archaeological objects removed from the seabed in the contiguous zone will not be affected. Although there might be a violation of the coastal State's custom and fiscal laws, proprietary rights of identifiable owners are not affected." *Op. cit.* note 60 at p. 4.

68　Otherwise, the owner may even be empowered to destroy the discovered cultural property.

69　It is notable that under the French Law No 89-874 of 1 December 1989 on Maritime Cultural Property, amending Law of 27 September 1941, United Nations, *Law of the Sea: Current Developments in State Practice,* No. III, Office for Ocean Affairs and the Law of the Sea, 1992, pp. 39-43, the provisions dealing with the aquisition of ownership of maritime cultural property by the State (i.e., articles 2 and 11) do not apply in the contiguous zone. In contrast, article 9, which provides that "where the owner of a maritime cultural property is known, his written consent shall be obtained before action is taken with respect to such property", is applicable within the 24 mile zone. See also article 3 of the Chinese Regulation on Protection and Administration of Underwater Cultural Relics Law 1989, which states that "the State has title to underwater cultural relics originating from China or from an unidentifiable country, which remain beyond China's territorial sea but within other sea areas under China's jurisdiction". As argued, China may clearly reclaim title to underwater cultural relics with original Chinese ownership. However, regarding cultural relics with original foreign ownership, if the foreign ownership is not abandoned by the foreign owner or the successor thereof, China's claim would be inconsistent with article 303(3) concerning the rights of the identifiable owners and might result in diplomatic disputes with the foreign country concerned over ownership. See Zhao, H., "Recent developments in the legal protection of historic shipwrecks in China", 23 *Ocean Dev. & Int'l L.* (1992) pp. 305-303 at pp. 320-321.

70　UNESCO has long urged the need for cultural co-operation as a factor of mutual understanding and progress of peoples and the promotion of cultural exchanges among nations. In particular, see the Declaration of the Principles of International Cultural Co-operation adopted by the General Conference at its fourteenth session (1966) and Recommendations No. 13 (International communication), No. 138 (International cultural relations), No. 141 (Equality of treatment in cultural exchanges), No. 142 (Cultural agreements and exchanges) and No. 144 (Developing countries and international cultural co-operation) adopted during the World Conference on Cultural Policies, Mexico City 26 July - 6 August 1982. UNESCO, Final Report, *World Conference on Cultural Policies, CLT/MD/1*, Paris, November 1982. Similarly, ICOM has encouraged short - and long term exchanges of cultural property with programmes such as the Museums Exchange Programme (MUSEP) and the *ICOM Guidelines for Loans*. See Monreal, L., "Problems and possibilities in recovering dispersed cultural heritages", 31 *Museum* (1979) pp. 49-57. See also the Agreement on the Importation of Educational, Scientific and Cultural Materials, also known as the "Florence Agreement", 31 *U.N.T.S.* 25, whose aim was to facilitate the free flow of educational scientific and cultural materials across national boundaries. The Agreement was adopted by the General Conference of UNESCO in Florence in 1950. For a discussion see Edwards, J.F., "Major global treaties for the protection and enjoyment of art and cultural objects", 22 *The University of Toledo Law Review* (1991) pp. 919-953 at pp. 930-939.

71 Article 5(a).

72 Article 15.

73 Article 8.

74 Adopted on 26 November 1976 by the General Conference of UNESCO at its nineteenth session, held in Nairobi. Text reprinted in UNESCO, *Conventions and Recommendations concerning the protection of cultural heritage*, 1985 pp. 181-190.

75 *Ibid*, article 3. It is notable that an early draft of the 1976 Recommendation (Preliminary Draft Recommendation on the International Exchange of Cultural Property) provided in section 3 that: "Member States, following the legislative procedures of their respective countries, should modify existing statutes or regulations or adopt new legislation or regulations regarding inheritance, taxation and customs duties in order to make it possible or easier to carry out the following operations solely for the purposes of international exchanges of cultural property and donations to cultural institutions or to governments: (c) acquisition of cultural property in *co-ownership* by cultural institutions belonging to different States" (emphasis added). UNESCO, *The Exchange of Original Objects and Specimens Among Institutions in Different Countries*. Preliminary report prepared in accordance with Article 10.1 of UNESCO's Rules of Procedure concerning Recommendations to Member States and International Conventions covered by the terms of Article IV, paragraph 4, of the Constitution, *SHC/MD/27 Annex*, Paris, 26 August 1975.

76 Article 1.

77 *Ibid.*

78 For a different approach see Ronzitti, *op. cit.* note 54 at p. 13.

79 See further Caflisch, *op. cit.* note 17 at p. 22; Migliorino, *op. cit.* note 60 at p. 4; Oxman, *op. cit.* note 53 at p. 364 and Ronzitti, *op. cit.* note 54 at p. 24. It is notable that the 1992 (revised) Convention specifically provides in article 11 that: "Nothing in this (revised) Convention shall affect existing or *future* bilateral or multilateral treaties between parties concerning the illicit circulation

of elements of the archaeological heritage or their restitution to the rightful owner" (emphasis added).

80 *Ibid.*

81 It is notable that the juxtaposition between "archaeological" and "historical" was always present even in the proposals made at the early stages of the Conference. According to Caflisch, the French Language Group of the Drafting Committee had proposed the deletion of the reference to "archaeological objects" or the amendment to "archaeological objects and other objects of historical origin". Since archaeological objects are a sub-category of objects of historical origin, there would be no case of an archaeological object that could not be considered of historical origin. Caflisch, *op. cit.* note 17 at p. 7, note 18. The French text notably refers to "objets de caractère historique *ou* archéologique" in the text of articles 149 and 303 and to "objets archéologiques et historiques" in the respective titles. See also Rosenne, S., and Sohn, L.B. (eds), *United Nations Convention on the Law of the Sea 1982: A Commentary*, vol. V, Center for Oceans Law and Policy, University of Virginia, Martinus Nijhoff Publishers, 1989 at p. 160: "It is not even clear whether the word 'and' is conjunctive, as it is in the Chinese, English and French texts, or disjunctive as in the Arabic, Russian and Spanish texts. In many countries archaeology (antiquities) is regulated by law, and for that reason it may be suggested that exceptionally, in this context, the word may be read disjunctively, 'historical' being more a matter of subjective appreciation (subject to the provisions of Part XV on the settlement of disputes)".

82 8 *ILM* (1969) p. 679. Article 31.

83 *Ibid.* Article 32.

84 Clarke, D.L., *Analytical Archaeology*, Methuen, London, 1968 at p. 12. "The archaeologist's facts are artefacts - and their context. The data of the discipline is the information observed about the attributes of these artefacts embracing their contextual attributes and their specific attributes." *Ibid* at p. 14.

85 Wilkes, B., *Nautical Archaeology*, David & Charles, Newton Abbot, 1971 at pp. 18-19.

86 Muckelroy, K., *Discovering a Historic Wreck*, Handbooks in Maritime Archaeology, No. 1, National Maritime Museum, 1981 at p. 1. According to article 36 of the Mexican Federal Law on Archaeological, Artistic and Historic Monuments and Zones, 1972, the term "historic" is confined to the period between the sixteenth to the nineteenth century. UNESCO, *The protection of movable cultural property. Collection of legislative texts, Mexico, CC.87/WS 12*, 1987. On the interpretation of the term 'historic' within the Australian Historic Shipwrecks Act, 1976 see Ryan, P., "Legislation on Historic Wreck" in *Papers from the First Southern Hemisphere Conference on Maritime Archaeology,* Australian Sports Publications, Perth, W. Australia, 1977, pp. 23-33 at p. 25.

87 Article 1 of the 1970 UNESCO Convention reads: "For the purposes of this Convention, the term 'cultural property' means property which ... belongs to the following categories: (e) antiquities *more than one hundred years old*, such as inscriptions, coins and engraved seals; (k) articles of furniture *more than*

one hundred years old and old musical instruments" (emphasis added); Article 1 of Appendix II of the 1985 Convention defines cultural property as: "(a) products of archaeological explorations and excavations (including regular and clandestine) conducted on land and underwater; (f) tools, pottery, inscriptions, coins, seals, jewellery, weapons and funerary remains, including mummies, *more than one hundred years old*; (g) articles of furniture, tapestries, carpets and dress *more than one hundred years old*; (h) musical instruments *more than one hundred years old*", and article 2 of the San Salvador Convention: "(b) monuments, buildings, objects of an artistic, utilitarian and ethnological nature, whole or in fragments, from the colonial era and the *nineteenth century*; (d) all objects originating *after 1850* that the States parties have recorded as cultural property, provided that they have given notice of such registration to the other parties to the treaty" (emphasis added).

88   The adoption of such a criterion, which is also employed by the Danish and Swedish legislation (see *infra* note 91) as well as the ILA Draft Convention on the Protection of the Underwater Cultural Heritage, has been criticised on the basis that it is the ship's age and not the date when it was wrecked that determines its antiquarian value. For example, an antique statue carried by a recently wrecked ship would not be considered as "antiquity", as the decisive criterion of protection would be the date of the shipwreck and not the age of the object considered. See further Caflisch, *op. cit.* note 17 at p. 8 and Braekhus, S., "Salvage of Wrecks and Wreckage - Legal Issues Arising from the Runde Find", 20 *Scandinavian Studies in Law* (1976) pp. 39-68 at pp. 62-63. It should be noted, however, that the establishment of such time limits is accompanied by the discretionary exclusion of less important objects and inclusion of more recent ones. As argued, the 100-year underwater rule avoids the undesirable situation where the owner of an old vessel that has sunk recently cannot salvage his property, unless permission is obtained from the competent authorities. See Prott, L.V. and O' Keefe, P.J., *The Law and the Cultural Heritage,* vol. 1, *Discovery and Excavation*, Professional Books Ltd, 1984 at p. 178.

89   Article 1(2) reads: "Underwater cultural property being *at least 100 years old* shall enjoy the protection provided by this Convention. However, any contracting State may provide that such property which is less than 100 years old shall enjoy the same protection".

90   *Argentina*, Law No. 9080 of 1911 declaring archaeological ruins and palaeontological remains of scientific interest to be the property of the State; Law No. 12.665 of 4 October 1940, Museums Monuments and Historic Places regulated by Decree No. 84.005 of 7 February 1941. National property is defined as ruins and remains of archaeological, palaeontological or scientific interest, and works of art executed before 1860 in the territory which is now Argentina, and presently within the country. Burnham, B., *The Protection of Cultural Property - Handbook of National Legislations*, ICOM, 1974, pp. 31-32.
     Bahrain: The Bahrain Antiquities Ordinance of 1 March 1970. Under article 2, "antiquity" means "any object whether movable or immovable which has been constructed, shaped, inscribed, erected, excavated or otherwise produced or modified by human agency earlier than the year A.D. 1780." This definition

also applies to human and animal remains of a date earlier than A.D. 600. Furthermore, the Minister of Information may declare an object of a date later than A.D. 1780 to be an antiquity. UNESCO, *The Protection of Movable Cultural Property. Compendium of Legislative Texts*, vol. II, 1984 pp. 15-22.

Belize: Ancient Monuments and Antiquities Ordinance, 1971 (Gazetted 31 December 1971). Under article 2, "antiquity" means any article manufactured or worked by man, whether of stone, pottery, metal, wood, glass or any other substance, or any part thereof - (i) the manufacture or workmanship of which belongs to the Mayan or other American civilisarion being of an age of one hundred and fifty years or more; or (ii) the manufacture or workmanship of which belongs to a civilization other than the Mayan or American civilisation being an article which is first discovered in the country of an age of one hundred and fifty years and more. 'Ancient Monument' means any structure or building erected by man or any natural feature transformed by or worked by man, or the remains or any part thereof, whether upon land or in any river, stream or watercourse or under the territorial waters of the country that has been in existence for one hundred years or more. UNESCO, *The Protection of Movable Cultural Property. Collection of Legislative Texts, CLT-85/WS 20*, 1985.

Bolivia: Supreme Decree No. 05918 of 6 November 1961 concerning the protection of artistic, historical and archaeological treasures. Under Bolivian legislation, monuments, museums and works and objects of artistic, historical and archaeological value constitute the cultural heritage of the nation. The year of 1900 is set up as the minimum age of protection of certain categories. UNESCO, vol. II, pp. 23-29.

Brunei: The Antiquities and Treasure Trove Enactment, 1967. An antiquity is defined as: (a) any object, movable or immovable or any part of the soil or of the bed of a river or lake or of the sea, which has been constructed, shaped, inscribed, erected, excavated or otherwise produced or modified by human agency at any date prior to or reasonably believed to be prior to January 1, 1984. Burnham, *ibid* at pp. 43-44.

Canada: Act of 19 June 1975, Canadian Cultural Property Export Control List. In defining the protected cultural property, article 3(3) provides that "no object shall be included in the Control List if that object (a) is less than fifty years old; or (b) was made by a natural person who is stil living." UNESCO, vol. II, pp. 55-69.

Cyprus: The Antiquities Law of 31 December 1935, as amended by the Antiquities (Amendment) Law No. 48 of 1964 and the Antiquities (Amendment) Law No. 32 of 1973. Section 2 provides that: "'Antiquity' means any objecty, whether movable or part of immovable property which is work of architecture, sculpture, graphic art, painting and any art whatsoever produced, sculptured,inscribed or painted by human agency, or generally made in Cyprus earlier than the year A.D. 1850 in any manner and from the sea within the territorial waters of Cyprus and includes any such object or part there of which has ar a later date been added, reconstructed, readjusted or restored: Provided that in the case of wuch works of ecclesiastical or folk art of the highest archaeological, artistic or historical importance, the year A.D. 1900 shall be taken into account in place of the year A.D. 1850". *CLT-85/WS 22*, 1985.

Democratic Yemen: Antiquities and Museum Law, 1970 defines "antiquity" as more than 200 years old; Prott and O'Keefe, *op. cit.* note 88 at p. 50. As from 22 May 1990, Democratic Yemen and Yemen Arabic Republic were unified.

Egypt: Law No. 117 of 1983 putting into force the Law on the Protection of Antiquities. Article 1: "An 'antiquity' is any movable or immovable property that is a product of any of the various civilisations or any of the arts, sciences, literatures and religions of the successive historical periods extending from prehistoric times down to a point one hundred years before the present and that has archaeological or historical value or significance as a relic of one of the various civilisations that have been established in the land of Egypt or historically related to it, as well as human and animal remains from any such period." *CLT-85/WS 27*, 1985.

The Gambia: The Monuments and Relics Act, No. 8 of 1974 (article 2).

Ghana: National Museaums Decree, 1969 (article 30).

Gibraltar: Museum and Antiquities Ordinance, No. 22 of 1966.

Honduras: Decree No. 81184 of 30 May 1984, published in the Official Gazette No. 24,387, 8 August 1984. According to article 5, the cultural heritage comprises (a) monuments: architectural works of great content and value from the anthropological, historical and artistic point of view, both of the colonial era and of the nineteenth century; (b) movable property: engravings, paintings, sculptures, furniture, jewellery ... of great content and value from the anthropological, historical and artistic point of view manufactured before 1900. *CLT-85/WS 28*, 1985.

Hong Kong: Antiquities and Monuments Ordinance, 1971.

India: The Antiquities and Art Treasures Act, 1972 as amended by the Antiquities and Art Treasures (Amendment) Act 1976 (sec. 2); the Ancient Monuments and Archaeological Sites and Remains Bill, 1958 as amended by the Antiquities and Art Treasures Act, 1972 (sec. 2). Both acts define "antiquity" as property that has been in existence for no less than 100 years. UNESCO, vol. I, pp. 164-187.

Indonesia: Indonesian Antiquities Act, Decree No. 238 of 13 June 1931. This legislation protects movable and immovable property more than fifty years old or belonging to a style which is no less than fifty years old (article 1). *Ibid*, vol. II, pp. 90-98.

Iraq: Antiquities Law, 1936, as amended in 1974 and 1975. According to article 1 "antiquities" means movable and immovable possessions, which were erected, made, produced, sculptured, written, drawn or photographed by man, if they are two hundred years old or more. *Ibid*, pp. 99-111.

Jordan: The Antiquities Law, Provisional law No. 12 of 1976. Article 2 defines as antiquity any movable or immovable property produced or altered by man before A.D. 1700. UNESCO, vol. II, pp. 149-157.

Kenya: The Antiquities and Monuments Act, No. 2 of 1983. Section 2: "Antiquity" means any movable object other than a book or document made in or imported into Kenya before the year 1895, or any human,faunal or floral remains of similar minimum age which may exist in Kenya; "monument" means any immovable structure built before the year 1895 ... or a place or immovable structure of any age which, being of historical interest, has been and remains declared by the Minister to be a monument; "object of archaeological or palaeontological interest" means an antiquity which was in existence before the year 1800; "object of historical interest" means an antiquity which came into existence in or after the year 1800." *CLT-85/WS 29*, 1985.

Kuwait: Princely Decree No. 11 of 1960 concerning Antiquities, amended by Ameer Decree No. 1 of 1976. Under the Decree of 1960, 'antiquity' means everything made, built or produced by man more than forty years ago. UNESCO, vol. II, pp. 158-166.

Lebanon: Regulation on Antiquities, Order No. 166 LR of 1933. Article 1 defines "'antiquity' as any product of human activity, dating from before 700 (1107 of the hegira) irrespective of the civilisation to which it belongs". *Ibid* at pp. 188-207.

Lesotho: The Historical Monuments, Relics, Fauna and Flora Act, No. 41 of 1967 (Date of Assent: 13 December 1967). Section 8: "the Minister may from time to time on the recommendation of the commission by notice in the Gazette, proclaim to be - (c) antiquity, any movable object (not being a monument or a relic) of aesthetic, historical, archaeological or scientific value or interest, the whole or more valuable portion whereof has for more than one hundred years been in any part of southern Africa, or which was made there in more than one hundred years before the publication of such notice." *CLT-85/WS 30*, 1985.

Libyan Arab Jamahiriya: The Antiquities Law (No. 40 of 1968), protects any construction of an immovable nature, any other product of human activity which are more than 100 years old, as well as human, animal or botanic remains dating earlier than A.D. 600. The competent authorities may declare that an item of property less than 100 years old is an antiquity. UNESCO, vol. II, pp. 250-263.

Luxembourg: Law of 12 August 1927 and Regulation of 26 April 1930 for National Sites and Monuments. Law of 21 March 1966 concerning Excavation and the Safeguard of Movable Cultural Property. A permit is required for the exportation of any object more than 100 years old or whose author has been deceased for more than 50 years. Burnham, *ibid,* p. 107.

Madagascar: Order No. 73-050 on the safeguarding, protection and preservation of cultural property (7 September 1973). According to article 20(c), items of artistic interest which are more than thirty years old are also protected as part of the national cultural heritage. UNESCO, vol. II, pp. 208-217.

Malaysia: The Antiquities and Treasures Trove Ordinance, No. 14, 1957. An antiquity is defined as (a) any object, movable or immovable, or any part of the soil or of the bed of a river or lake or of the sea, which has been constructed, shaped, inscribed, erected, excavated, or otherwise produced or modified by human agency at any date prior to or reasonably believed to be prior to January 1, 1850. Burnham, *ibid*, pp. 108-109.

Malta: Antiquities (Protection) Act-XI of 1925, as amended in 1974. Cultural property is defined as monuments and other movable and immovable objects of geological, archaeological, artistic or antiquarian interest, existant in Malta no less than 50 years, and relating to local art or history. *Ibid*, pp. 110-111.

The Netherlands: Monuments Act of 22 June 1961 as amended in 1988 by the Monuments Act, No. 622 of 1988. Under article 1(b)1, monuments are defined as artefacts, over 50 years of age and of importance because of their historic value, beauty or scientific meaning, and which are the products of official excavations. Monuments less than 50 years of age may also be protected under municipal regulations, while those which are not the products of excavations are governed by the provisions of the Civil Code. The 1988 Monuments Act explicitly regulates underwater sites for the first time.

Nigeria: National Commission for Museums and Monuments Decree, No. 77, 1979. "'Antiquity' means any object of archaeological interest or land in which any such object was discovered or is believed to exist, any relic of early human settlement or colonisation or any work of art or craftwork ... which is of indigenous origin or was made before 1918, and is of historical, artistic or scientific interest or has been used during a traditional ceremony." UNESCO, vol. II, pp. 229-241.

Pakistan: Antiquities Act, 1975. Article 2 (Definitions): "In this Act unless there is anything repugnant in the subject or context: (b) 'ancient' means belonging or relating to any perior prior to May 1857." *Ibid*, pp. 242-261.

Philippines: Cultural Properties Preservation and Protection Act No. 4846 of 18 June 1966, as amended by Presidential Decree No. 374 of 10 January 1974. According to section 3(d): "Antiques are cultural properties found locally which are one hundred years or more in age or even less, but their production having ceased, they have therefore, become or are becoming rare." *Ibid,* pp. 262-269.

Saudi Arabia: Regulations for antiquities, Royal Decree No. M/26, 3 August 1972. Article 5: "The term 'antiquities' shall mean property, movable or immovable, built, made, produced, adapted or designed by man over 200 years ago as well as property having acquired archaeological characteristics through ancient natural factors. The Department of Antiquities may classify as antiquities movable or immovable property attributed to a more recent date, if, in its opinion, such property has archaeological or artistic characteristics ...". *Ibid*, pp. 270-286.

Sudan: The Antiquities Ordinance (No. 2 of 1952). Section 3: "In this ordinance unless the context otherwise requires 'antiquity' means (a) any object, whether movable, immovable or a part of the soil, which has been constructed, shaped, inscribed, erected, excavated or otherwise produced or modified by human agency earlier than the year A.D. 1821 and includes any part of any such object which has at any later date been added, reconstructed or restored." *Ibid*, pp. 310-317.

Syrian Arab Republic: Decree-Law No. 222 of 26 October 1963 on the treatment of antiquities in the Syrian Arab Republic. Article 1 defines antiquity as any movable or immovable property that is more than 200 years old. *Ibid*, pp. 264-278.

Tanzania (United Republic of): Antiquities Act No. 10 of 1964, as amended by the Antiquities (Amendment) Act, No. 22 of 1979. Article 2 protects, *inter alia*, "monuments" and "relics" produced or modified by human agency in Tanganyika before the year 1863. *CLT-85/WS 25*, 1985.

Tunisia: Law No. 86-35 of May 1986 concerning the Protection of Archaeological Property, Historic Monuments and Natural and Urban Sites. *CC-88/WS 2*, 1988 (article 3).

United Arab Emirates: Law No. 8 of 1970 on antiquities and excavations. Article 2 protects objects, buildings and inscriptions more than 150 years old as well as human or animal remains at least 100 years old. UNESCO, vol. I, pp. 290-299.

United States: Archaeological Resources Protection Act of 1979. "Archaeological resource" is defined as "any material remains of past human life or activities which are of archaeological interest, as determined under uniform regulations promulgated pursuant to this Act [and which are] at least 100 years of age." 16 *U.S.C.A.* para. 470bb(1). In addition, a number of States have enacted specific legislation to protect underwater cultural resources. Among them, Arizona and Massachussetts have set a time limit of 100 years old, while Louisiana and Texas protect pre-20th century ships and wrecks of the sea, and Rhode Island and Vermont shipwrecks, vessel, cargo, tackle and archaeological specimens, unclaimed for 10 years. See further Throckmorton, P., "Introduction: Marine Archaeology", 28 *Oceanus*, No. 1, Spring 1985 pp. 2-12 at p. 5.

Yemen, Arab Republic: Antiquities Act 1972 defines "antiquity" as more than 500 years old.

Zambia: Natural and Historic Monuments and Relics Act (*ch.* 90, 1948 as amended in 1953) and By-laws 1957. Protected cultural property includes ancient monuments, ancient workings and relics, all of which are known or believed to have been in existence prior to the 1st day of January 1980. Burnham, *ibid*, pp. 154-155.

91 *Australia:* Australian Historic Shipwrecks Act, 1976, as amended by Statute Law (Miscallaneous Provisions) Act (No. 1) 1985. The 1985 Amendment enables the Minister to declare all remains of ships (whether or not the existence and location of the remains are known) situated in Australian waters which are at least 75 years old to be historic shipwrecks.

Channel Island of Guernsey (United Kingdom): The Wreck and Salvage (Vessels and Aircraft) (Bailiwick of Guernsey) Law 1986.

China: The Regulation on Protection and Administration of Underwater Cultural Relics Law 1989. Article 2: "The above provisions do not include underwater remains dating later than 1911 which are unrelated to a significantly historically event, revolutionary moments or renowned persons".

Denmark: Section 49 of the Conservation of Nature Act as amended by Act No. 530 of 10 October 1984 and section 28 of the Museum Act, Act No. 291 of 6 June 1984 with later amendments, protect objects and wrecks of ships which are considered to have been wrecked or lost more than 100 years ago.

It is notable that the earlier regulations on historic shipwrecks were based on the State's title to property being lost more than 150 years ago. C/f. Act No. 203 of 31 May 1963 on the Protection of Historic Wreck *ST/LEG/SER.B/15*, pp. 159-60.

Finland: Act on Archaeological Remains, 1963. Article 20: "Wrecks of ships or other craft discovered in the sea or in inland waters, which can be expecterd to be more than one hundred years old, or parts of such wrecks, are protected."

Ireland: National Monuments (Amendment Act) 1987, No. 17 of 1987. Section 3(4): "Subject to the provisions of this section, a person shall not, at the site of a wreck (being a wreck which is more than 100 years old), or of another object (being an archaeological object), that is lying on, in or under the seabed or on in land covered by water...".

Norway: Cultural Heritage Act of 1978. Article 14: "The State shall have the right of ownership of boats more than 100 years old, hulls, gear, cargo and all else that has been on board, or parts of such objects, when it is clear that it is no longer reasonably possible to find out if there is an owner or who is the owner." *CC-87/WS 7,* 1987.

New Zealand: The Historic Places Act, 1980. According to section 2 (a): "'archaeological site' means any place in New Zealand (b) which is the site of the wreck of any vessel where at any material time that wreck occurred more than 100 years before that time", UNESCO, *The protection of cultural property,* vol. II, pp. 220-228. Antiquities Act 1975. According to section 2(h): "'antiquity' means any ship, boat or aircraft, or any part of any ship, boat or aircraft in any case where that ship, boat or aircraft has been, or appears to have been, a wreck in New Zealand, or within the territorial waters of New Zealand, for more than 60 years."

South Africa: National Monuments Act 1969 as amended in 1979 and in 1981. National Monuments Amendment Act, No. 35 of 1979 (section 10a: declaration of a wreck to be a monument). Under section 12(2)b of the National Monuments Amendment Act, No. 13 of 1981, a permit is required for the excavation and removal of wrecks and artefacts more than 100 years old which have not been declared as national monuments. See further Meurs, (van) L., *Legal Aspects of Marine Archaeological Research,* Special Publication of the Institute of Marine Law, University of Cape Town, Publication No. 1, 1985, pp. 69-82.

Sweden: Act No. 350 of 12 June 1942 concerning ancient monuments and finds as amended by Act No. 77 of March 1967 and Act No. 589, 30 June 1971. According to section 9(a) shipwrecks and associated objects are protected "if at least one hundred years can be assumed to have lapsed since the ship was wrecked."

92 *UNCLOS III, Off. Rec.,* vol. I at p. 163.

93 Oxman, *op. cit.* note 30 at p. 241, footnote 152. See also Arend, *op. cit.* note 29 at pp. 779-780. It should be noted that both arguments were made before the modification of the formula "archaeological objects and objects of an historical origin" to "objects of an archaeological and historical nature".

94 In this context it is rather significant that the term "nature" employed by the 1982 Convention has a wider scope than the notion of "value", "significance" or "interest" which are normally used by national heritage in order to define the cultural property to be protected. See further Dromgoole, *op. cit.* note 64 at p. 103: "Were there to be some form of blanket protection of all wrecks over a certain age, as suggested by the Council of Europe, the opportunity would then be made available to investigate sites and assets whether or not they are of historical importance before interference takes place. Blanket designation has been the solution adopted by many countries to the problem of deciding which wrecks to protect. The *onus* could be put on commercial operators to undertake a survey of the area of the seabed in which they are interested to discover whether or not wrecks exist which may be of historical importance. If a site of historical interest was discovered, the principle of rescue archaeology could be applied whereby development or recovery is delayed while the site is surveyed or excavated." See also Del Bianco, H.P. (Jr.), "Underwater Recovery Operations in Offshore Waters: Vying for Rights to treasure", 5/6 *Boston University International Law Journal* (1987/88) pp. 153-176 at p. 171, who argues that under article 303, "the coastal State may exercise jurisdiction over the recovery of archaeological and historical objects, but it is not clear how to determine if the object has any archaeological or historical nature until after it has been recovered. One solution to this issue would be to construe article 303 broadly so as to include all objects older, say, fifty years".

95 See also chapter 1, note 25 at pp. 25-26. Similarly, the few States which have expanded their competence over the 24-mile zone specifically include submerged sites and settlements within the scope of the protected cultural property. For example, the 1989 French law covers immovable maritime cultural property, which was excluded from the scheme of protection of the 1961 law on shipwrecks. See Law No. 61-1262 of 24 of November 1961 on the Control of Shipwrecks and Decree No. 61-1547 of 26 December 1961.

96 *UNCLOS III, Off. Rec.*, vol. I, pp. 107-142 (Appendix I).

97 *Ibid* at p. 115. See also Platzöder, *op. cit.* note 22, vol. I at p. 398.

98 *Byelorussian Soviet Socialist Republic, Bulgaria, Czechoslovakia, German Democratic Republic, Hungary, Mongolia, Poland and Union of Soviet Socialist Republics:* Draft article on the contiguous zone, 29 July 1974, Doc. A/CONF.62/ C.2/L.27 in Platzöder, *ibid*, vol. V at p. 148; *Peru:* C.2/Blue Paper No. 10, 17 April 1975, *ibid*, vol. IV at p. 147. The only exception was a Turkish informal proposal in 1975 which stated: "The provision of this Convention relating to the delimitation of the territorial sea/marine spaces would be applicable for the delimitation of the contiguous zone." In other words, under the Turkish proposal "special circumstances" were also to be taken into consideration. C.2/Blue Paper No. 6, 17 April 1975, *ibid*, vol. IV at p. 129.

99 See further Caflisch, *op.cit.* note 1; ID, "Les zones maritimes sous juridiction nationale, leur limites et leur délimitation", 84 *R.G.D.I.P.* (1980) pp. 68-119 at pp. 83-85 as well as in Bardonnet, D., Virally, M. (eds.), *Le nouveau droit*

international de la mer, Publications de la R.G.D.I.P., Nouvelle série, No. 39, Pedone, A., éditions, Paris, 1983, pp. 35-139 at pp. 53-58.

100 This seems to be the most widespread explanation. In particular, see Churchill and Lowe, *op. cit.* note 6 at p. 104, and the statement of the Turkish delegate that: "The Convention is silent on the delimitation of contiguous zones between States with opposite or adjacent coasts. By analogy, the provisions on the delimitation of EEZs and continental shelves should also be applicable to the delimitation of contiguous zones". Statement by Mr. Kirca (Turkey) in *UNCLOS III, Off. Rec.* vol. XVII at p.77 (para. 170). See also Pazarci, *op. cit.* note 18 at pp. 265-266. Another possible explanation could be the unwillingness of the drafters to complicate further the negotiations on the controversial - and far more important - issues of the delimitation of the continental shelf and the EEZ. Caflisch, *op. cit.* note 1 at p. 392.

101 The necessity of the delimitation of the contiguous zone is obvious if it is considered that coastal States enjoy the right of hot pursuit from these waters. In order to determine whether the ship pursued is within the limits of the contiguous zone, the latter should be clearly defined. The asssumption that a delimitation provision is not necessary, not only contradicts the very use of the term "zone" (see also Caflisch, *op. cit.* note 1 at p. 392), but it also neglects the historical background and development of the contiguous zone.

102 All these complications stem from the manner in which the archaeolgical issue was dealt with by UNCLOS III. By the time the regime of the contiguous zone was discussed before the Second Committee, article 303(2) had not as yet been adopted. Even President Aguillar appeared to share the approach that a delimitation formula was not necessary. His statements, however, were made before the elaboration of article 303(2). Conversation with Dr. Th. Halkiopoulos, Special Legal Advisor to the Ministry of Foreign Affairs, Athens, Greece.

103 Caflisch, *op. cit.* note 1 at p. 393.

104 *Ibid*, footnote 41.

105 One could argue that the omission of the delimitation formula in an article identical to article 24 of the TSC implies the willingness to change the law on the issue. Furthermore, article 311(2) may be interpreted as referring to agreements *other* than the Geneva Conventions.

106 The 1982 Convention permits its application by providing in its Preamble that: "Matters not regulated by this Convention continue to be governed by the rules and principles of general international law". It is true that only a small number of the States that have claimed contiguous zones have made provision for a delimitation formula. However, the majority of those which have done so, establish the principle of equidistance, pending or failing agremeent to the contrary, as the delimitation formula of opposite or adjacent contiguous zones. See also the statement of the Cypriot delegate: "Similarly we note with satisfaction that the delimitation of the territorial sea between States with opposite or adjacent coasts is, in the ordinary case, based as in the past on the principle of equidistance and that in the absence of a specific provision in the present Convention it can be presumed that this principle is also the rule for the delimitation of the contiguous zone as prescribed in the 1958 Convention." Statement

by Mr. Jacovides (Cyprus), *UNCLOS III, Off. Rec.* vol. XVII at p. 71 (para. 71), and the declaration made by Yugoslavia at the time of the ratification of the Convention, which states, *inter alia,* that the *principles of customary law embodied* in article 24(3) of the TSC will apply to the delimitation of the contiguous zone between the parties to the 1982 Convention. In contrast, see Pazarci, *op. cit.* note 18 at p. 265. See also Treves, T., "Codification du droit international et pratique des états dans le droit de la mer", *Hague Recueil* (1990-IV) pp. 9-302 at p. 76, who argues that State practice is too limited to provide enough evidence to establish a rule of custom. The following States have incorporated delimitation formulas in their contiguous zone legislation:

Democratic Yemen: Act No. 45 of 1977 concerning the Territorial Sea, Exclusive Economic Zone, Continental Shelf and Other Marine Spaces. Article 17(b): "Pending agreement on the demarcation of the marine boundaries, the limits of the ... contiguous zone ... between the Republic and any State with coasts adjacent or opposite to it, the coast of the Republic shall not be extended to more than the *median or equidistance line*" (emphasis added). *ST/LEG/SER.B/19,* pp. 21-26. As from 22 May 1990, Democratic Yemen and Yemen Arabic Republic were unified.

Djibouti: Law 52/AN/78 concerning the Territorial sea, the Contiguous zone, the Exclusive Economic Zone, the Maritime Boundaries and Fishing. Article 15: "The maritime boundaries of the territorial sea, the contiguous zone and the economic zone between the Republic and a neighbouring State whose coastlines are adjacent to or opposite those of the Republic shall be determined by an agreement with that State. Pending the conclusion of an agreement for determining the maritime boundaries, those boundaries shall not extend beyond a *median line* between the two States or beyond a line all points of which are *equidistant* from the points closest to the baselines used to measure the breadth of the territorial seas of the Republic and the State concerned" (emphasis added). Text reprinted in Smith, R.W., *Exclusive Economic Zone Claims - An Analysis and Primary Documents,* Martinus Nijhoff Publishers, Dordrecht, 1986 at pp. 111-117.

France: Act of 31 December 1987 concerning the Campaign against Drug Trafficking and Amending Certain Provisions of the Penal Code provides in article 44bis: "In a contiguous zone lying between 12 and 24 nautical miles measured from the baselines, from which the territorial sea is measured and *subject to the delimitation agreements with neighbouring States...*" (emphasis added). United Nations, *The Law of the Sea: National Claims to Maritime Jurisdiction. Excerpts of Legislation and Table of Claims*, Office for Ocean Affairs and the Law of the Sea, 1992.

India: Territorial Waters, Continental Shelf, Exclusive Economic Zone and Other Maritime Zones Act, 1976. Article 9(1): "The maritime boundaries between India and any State whose coast is opposite or adjacent to that of Indiain regard to their respective ... contiguous zones ... shall be determined by agreement ... between India and such State and pending such agreement between India and any such State, and unless any other provisional arrangements are agreed to between them, the maritime boundaries between India and such State shall not extend beyond the line every point of which is *equidistant* from the nearest point from which the breadth of the territorial waters of India and of such State are measured" (emphasis added). *ST/LEG/SER.B/19* at pp. 47-54.

Saint Vincent and the Grenadines: Maritime Areas Act 1983 (Act No. 15). Article 17: "(1) Where the rights of Saint Vincent and the Grenadines in relation to (b) the contiguous zone, overlap with the ... contiguous zone ... of an adjacent State, until such a time as a delimitation agreement is reached the seaward limits of the affected offshore areas of Saint Vincent and the Grenadines shall extend to the *equidistance line* between the archipelagic baselines of Saint Vincent and the Grenadines and the territorial sea baselines of the other State" (emphasis added). Smith, *ibid* at pp. 399-403.

Finally, one should mention the *Portugese* Act No. 2130 of 22 August 1966, which provided in article IV that: "Failing agreement to the contrary with a State whose coasts are adjacent or opposite to those of the Portuguese State, the limit of the territorial sea or of the contiguous zone shall not extend beyond the *median line* every point of which is *equidistant* from the nearest points on the baselines from which the breadth of the territorial sea of the two States is measured" (emphasis added). *ST/LEG/SER.B/15* at p. 112. However, by virtue of article 11 of Law No. 33/77 of 28 May 1977, article III of Law No. 2130, 1966, which established a 12-mile contiguous zone, was revoked. Smith, *ibid* at p. 372.

107 *France:* Law No. 89-874 of 1 December 1989 on Maritime Cultural Property, amending Law of 27 September 194, *op. cit.* note 69. Article 1: "Maritime cultural property shall comprise deposits, wrecks, artefacts or in general all property of prehistoric, archaeological or historical interest which is situated in the maritime public domain or on the *seabed in the contiguous zone*" (emphasis added). Under article 12, "the present Act shall apply to maritime cultural property situated in the contiguous zone lying between 12 and 24 miles measured from the baselines of the territorial sea, subject to the provisions of delimitation agreements with neighbouring States"; *Tunisia:* Law No. 86-35 of 9 May 1988 on the Protection of Archaeological Property, Historic Monuments and Natural Urban Sites, *op. cit.* note 91. Article 3: "Excavations may involve: visible ruins; ruins buried under the ground; ruins submerged in any stretch of water, including inland water, territorial waters and the *contiguous zone to a distance of 24 nautical miles* from the base lines used to calculate the width of the territorial waters ..." (emphasis added). Under article 1, "Tunisia shall also protect and safeguard archaeological property and historic monuments which are located within its territorial and maritime boundaries, but which belong to other peoples, and shall secure respect for those outside its borders in accordance with approved international conventions and the rules of international law".

108 See also article 28 (1) of the Danish Museum Act, Act No. 291 of 6 June 1984 with later amendments. It has been argued that this solution was adopted in order to resolve questions of delimitation between Denmark and neighbouring

countries. See further Lund, C., "Beskyttelse af historiske skibsvrag og fortidsminder pa den danske havbund" in *Fortidsminder og kulturhistorie*, National Forestry and Nature Agency, Copenhagen, 1987; ID, "Protection of the underwater heritage" in Leanza (ed.), *op cit.* note 53, pp. 351-353. The present status of the archaeological zone is, however, unclear, as the new Act No. 9 of 3 January 1992 on the Protection of Nature extends Danish jurisdiction on matters of natural and cultural conservation to the 200 nm fishing zone. The 24-mile zone is not formally extended but the two bases of jurisdiction overlap. Information kindly provided by Mr. K. Bangert, Lecturer, University of Copenhagen.

109 The French law is very carefully drafted along the lines of article 303(2). However, provision is made for the obligation to leave the discovered cultural property *in situ* and to report it to the administative authority, to aquiring prior administrative authorisation for the carrying out of any exploration or excavation work and the rewarding of the persons who discover and report such property. Violation of these provisions may invoke payment of fines or even imprisonment up to two years. For a discussion see Firth, A., "Recent legislation in France", 20 *I.J.N.A.* (1991) pp. 65-71.

110 The 1989 Regulation asserts no jurisdiction over underwater cultural relics originating from an identifiable foreign country. See also *infra* chapter 10, note 38 at p. 367.

111 Zhao, *op.cit.* note 69 at p. 316.

112 United Nations, *The Law of the Sea: Practice of States at the time of entry into force of the United Nations Convention of the Law of the Sea,* 1994 at p. 215. Out of these claims, forty-four States claim a 24nm contiguous zone, one State claims a 15 nm contiguous zone, and four States claim 18 nm contiguous zones. In addition, a small group of States claim customs zones of varying widths, i.e., *Colombia*: Decree No. 3183 of 10 December 1952 [12 nm]; *Denmark*: Customs Act 1972 [4 nm]; *Finland*, Customs Regulations of 8 September 1939 as amended [6nm], *Norway*: Customs Act of 10 June 1966 [10 nm], and *Syrian Arab Republic:* Decree-Law No. 304 of 28 December 1963 [41 nm]. Finally, South Africa appears to have expanded its powers over a 200-mile zone: c.f. Territorial Waters Act, No. 87 of 1963 as amended by Act No. 98 of 1977.
Antigua and Barbuda, Proclamation No. 20, August 30, 1982; The Maritime Areas Act, 1982 (No. 18 of 1982) [24 nm];
Argentina, Act No. 23.968 of 14 August 1991 [24];
Bahrain, Decree-Law No. 8 of 1993 with respect to the territorial sea and contiguous zone of the State of Bahrain [24nm];
Bangladesh, Territorial Waters and Maritime Zones Act, 1974; Ministry of Foreing Affairs Declaration No. LT-I/3/74, April 13, 1974 [18 nm];
Burma (Myanmar), Territorial Sea and Maritime Zones Law, 1977 (No. 3 of 1977) [24 nm];
Brazil, Act concerning the Territorial Sea, the Contiguous Zone, the Exclusive Economic Zone and the Continental Shelf of Brazil and Other Provisions, Act No. 8617 of 4 January 1993 [24nm];

Bulgaria, Act of 8 July 1987 concerning ocean space of the People's Republic of Bulgaria [24nm];

China, Law on the Territorial Sea and the Contiguous Zone of 25 February 1992 [24nm];

Chile, Law No. 18.565 amending the Civil Code with regard to maritime spaces [24 nm];

Democratic Kampuchea (Cambodia), Decree of 13 July 1980 by the Council of State of Cambodia on Territorial Waters [24 nm];

Democratic Yemen, Act No. 45 of 1977 concerning the Territorial Sea, the Exclusive Economic Zone, the Continental Shelf and other Marine Spaces [24 nm]. As from 22 May 1990, Democratic Yemen and Yemen Arabic Republic were unified.

Djibouti, Law 52/AN/78 concerning the Territorial Sea, the Contiguous Zone, the Exclusive Economic Zone, the Maritime Frontiers and Fishing [24 nm];

Dominica, Territorial Sea, Contiguous Zone, Exclusive Economic Zone and Fishery Zones Act, 1981 (No. 26 of 1981) [24 nm];

Dominican Republic, Act No. 186 of 13 September 1967 on the Territorial Sea, the Contiguous Zone, the Exclusive Economic Zone and the Continental Shelf as amended by Act No. 573 of 1 April 1977 [24 nm];

Egypt, Decree concerning the Territorial Waters of the United Arab Republic (the Arab Republic of Egypt) of 15 January 1951 as amended by the Presidential Decree of 17 February 1958; Declarations (upon ratification of the United Nations Convention on the Law of the Sea, of December 19, 1982) [24 nm];

France, Act of 31 December 1987 concerning the Campaign against Drug Trafficking and Amending Certain Provisions of the Penal Code [24 nm];

Gabon, Law No. 9/84 establishing an Exclusive Economic Zone [24 nm];

The Gambia, Territorial Sea and Contiguous Zone Act, 1968, Act No. 4 of 19 April 1968 as amended by the Territorial Sea and Contiguous Zone (Amendments) Act 1969, Act No. 9 of 10 July 1969 [18 nm];

Ghana, Maritime Zone (Delimitation) Law 1986 [24 nm];

Haiti, Decree No. 38 [24 nm];

Honduras, Constitution (1982) [24 nm];

India, Territorial Waters, Continental Shelf, Exclusive Economic Zone and Other Maritime Zones Act, 1976 [24 nm];

Iran, Act on the Marine Areas of the Islamic Republic of Iran in the Persian Gulf and the Oman Sea (1993) [24 nm];

Madagascar, Ordinance No. 85-013 determining the limits of the maritime zones (territorial sea, continental shelf and exclusive economic zone) of the Democratic Republic of Madagascar, 16 September 1985 as amended and ratified by Law No. 85-013 of 11 December 1985 [24 nm];

Malta, Territorial Waters and Contiguous Zone (Amendment) Act, 1975 (No. XLVI of 1975, 21 October 1975) as amended by the Territorial Waters and Contiguous Zones (Amendment) Act, (No. XXIV of 18 July 1978) [24 nm];

Marshall Islands, The Marine Zones (Declaration) Act 1984 (Act of 13 September 1984) [24 nm];

Mauritania, Ordinance 88-120 of 31 August 1988 establishing the limits and the Legal Regime of the Territorial Sea, the Contiguous Zone, the Exclusive Economic Zone and the Continental Shelf of the Islamic Republic of Mauritania [24 nm];

Mexico, Federal Act Relating to the Sea, 9 January 1986 [24nm];

Morocco, Decree No. 1-81-179 (1981) promulgating Law No.1-81 establishing an exclusive economic zone extending 200 nautical miles off the Moroccan coast [24 nm];

Namibia, Territorial Sea and Exclusive Economic Zone of Namibia, Act No.3 of 1990, 30 June 1990 as amended by Amendment Act 1991 [24nm];

Oman, Declaration No. 4 on the Contiguous Zone (Declaration made at the time of the ratification of the UN Convention on the Law of the Sea, 17 August 1989) [24 nm];

Pakistan, Territorial Waters and Maritime Zones Act, 1976 [24 nm];

Qatar, Declaration by the Ministry of Foreign Affairs of 2 June 1974 [24 nm];

Romania, Act concerning the Legal Regime of the Internal Waters, the Territorial Sea and the Contiguous Zone of Romania, 7 August 1990 [24nm];

Saint Kitts and Nevis, Maritime Areas Act 1984 [24 nm];

Saint Lucia, Maritime Areas Act 1984 [24 nm];

Saint Vincent and the Grenadines, Maritime Areas Act, 1983 (Act No. 15) [24 nm];

Saudi Arabia, Royal Decree concerning the Territorial Waters, Royal Decree No. 33 of February 1958 [18 nm];

Senegal, Act No. 85-14 delimiting the territorial sea, the contiguous zone and the continental shelf of 25 February 1985 [24 nm];

Spain, Law 27/1992 of 24 November 1992 concerning national ports and merchant shipping, [24 nm];

Sri Lanka, Maritime Zones Act No. 22 of 1 September 1976; Presidential Proclamation of 15 January 1977 in pursuance of Maritime Zones Act No 22 of 1 September 1976; [24 nm];

Sudan, Territorial Waters and Continental Shelf Act, 1970 [18 nm];

Trinidad and Tobago, Archipelagic Waters and Exclusive Economic Zone Act, 1986 [24 nm];

Tunisia, op. cit. note 107 [24 nm];

Tuvalu, Marine Zones (Declaration Ordinance 1983 [24 nm];

United Arab Emirates, Federal Law No. 19 of 1993 concerning the Maritime Areas of the United Arab Emirates [24 nm];

Vanuatu, Marine Zones Act No. 23 of 1981 [24 nm];

Venezuela, Territorial Sea Law (1956) [15 nm];

Vietnam, Statement on the Territorial Sea, the Contiguous Zone, the Exclusive Economic Zone and the Continental Shelf of 12 May 1977 [24 nm];

113 See, for example, *compatible claims:* Democratic Kampuchea, Djibouti, Dominican Republic, Gabon, Ghana, Malta, Morocco, Saint Lucia, Saint Vincent and the Grenadines, Senegal, Tuvalu, *Non-combatible claims:* Antigua and Barbuda, Bangladesh, Burma, China, Chile, Dominica, Egypt, The Gambia, Haiti, India,

Iran, Madagascar, Mexico, Pakistan, Saudi Arabia, Sri Lanka, Sudan, Vanuatu, Venezuela, Vietnam, Yemen. The latter have either extended their *legislative competence* over contiguous waters (i.e., Antigua and Barbuda, Bangladesh, India, Iran, Pakistan, Venezuela) or include *security* among the protected interests (i.e., Bangladesh, Burma, China, Haiti, India, Iran, Saudi Arabia, Sri Lanka, Sudan, Venezuela). Honduras and Saint Christopher and Nevis have not made known the purposes for which they have established a contiguous zone. See also *Limits in the Seas*, No. 112, *United States Response to Excessive National Maritime Claims*, March 9, 1992, pp. 34-35.

114 For example, China's claim for jurisdiction over underwater cultural remains within the contiguous zone was also expressed in the Third Draft Law on the Territorial Sea and the Contiguous Zone of P.R. China. However, these provisions were omitted in the Law of the Territorial Sea and the Contiguous Zone of 1992, because they have been already included in the Underwater Cultural Remains Regulation of 1989. Zhao, *op. cit.* note 69 at p. 316.

CHAPTER 6

The High Seas

THE GENEVA CONVENTION ON THE HIGH SEAS (1958)

The principle of the freedom of the high seas

Article 1 defines the term "high seas" as "all parts of the sea that are not included in the territorial sea or the internal waters of a State", while article 2 advocates the nature and scope of the regime of the high seas:

> "The high seas being open to all nations, no State may validly purport to subject any part of them to its sovereignty. Freedom of the high seas is exercised under the conditions laid down by these articles and by the other rules of international law. It comprises, *inter alia*, both for coastal and non-coastal States:
> (1) freedom of navigation
> (2) freedom of fishing
> (3) freedom to lay submarine cables and pipelines
> (4) freedom to fly over the high seas.
> These freedoms, and others which are recognised by the general principles of international law, shall be exercised by all States with reasonable regard to the interests of other States in their exercise of the freedom of the high seas."

Since the enumeration of these freedoms is not exhaustive, the right to use the high seas may be exercised for any purpose not expressly prohibited by international law.[1] Confirmation of this can be found in paragraph 2 of the ILC's Commentary on draft article 27 (now article 2)[2] which reads: "The list of freedoms of the high seas contained in this article is not restrictive. The Commission has merely specified four of the main freedoms, but it is aware that there are other freedoms such as freedom to undertake scientific research on the high seas - a freedom limited only by the general principle stated in the third sentence of paragraph 1 of the Commentary of the present article, i.e., that States are bound to refrain from any acts which might adversely affect the use of the high seas by nationals of other States." The ILC did not specifically mention the freedom to explore or exploit the subsoil of the high seas since "apart from the case of the exploitation or exploration of the soil or subsoil of a continental shelf ... such exploitation had not yet assumed sufficient practical importance to justify special regulation."[3] It would seem, therefore, that uses of the seabed, such as the removal of artefacts, which are now possible due to the development of advanced underwater technology may be exercised as a freedom of the high seas, if they satisfy the criteria set by the CHS.[4]

Criteria for the legitimate exercise of a freedom of the high seas
The CHS provides two criteria for the legitimate exercise of a freedom of the high seas: (a) the positive criterion of "reasonableness"; (b) the negative criterion of "non-prohibition" by the rules of international law (both customary and conventional). With the exception of the general prohibition of the appropriation of any part of the high seas, article 2 does not offer guidance as to the meaning of "reasonable regard", which each State has to pay to the interests of other States when exercising its right of free use of the seas.[5] Consequently, what is "reasonable" can only be decided on an individual case basis. The prohibition of the exclusive appropriation of the high seas has been argued to be "a matter of degree, reasonableness and proportionality".[6] Since all ocean uses involve an element of exclusivity, even sea uses with an exclusive character can be regarded as being "reasonable", if they do not involve a disproportionate appropriation of a given sea area.[7]

Jurisdictional powers on the high seas
Under article 6, on the high seas the sole applicable jurisdiction is that of the flag State: "Ships shall sail under the flag of one State only save in exceptional cases expressly provided for in international treaties or in these articles and shall be subject to its exclusive jurisdiction." In other words, the flag State exercises quasi-territorial jurisdiction over the vessels that sail under its flag. Exceptions to this fundamental rule are the cases of slavery and piracy *jure gentium*, where international law recognises the exercise of universal jurisdiction, as well as the exercise of the right of hot pursuit and self-defence.[8]

Another form of applicable jurisdiction on the high seas which, however, is not specifically regulated by the CHS, is that of the national State. All States are entitled to exercise their jurisdiction over their nationals in international waters. The nationality principle as a basis of jurisdiction is well established in international law.[9]

Marine archaeology as an exercise of a freedom of the high seas

Marine archaeology constitutes an independent use of the oceans, distinct from both traditional salvage and marine scientific research.[10] It has a multi-disciplinary nature that covers a broad range of activities related to the identification, preservation, documentation and interpretation of the human remains of the oceans. In the absence of a prohibitory rule of international law, marine archaeology should be regarded as a legitimate freedom of the seas, if it is exercised with reasonable regard to the interests of other States.[11]

Degree of exclusivity of underwater archaeological activities
For the successful operation of an archaeological project underwater, a substantial degree of control of the area in question is necessary. The area of the seabed involved varies considerably from site to site, while the exclusive use of the water column between the water-surface and the ocean floor is also required. In case excavation takes place, the degree of exclusivity and interference increases substantially. The lifting of submerged archaeological objects is a delicate and time-consuming operation that often involves the erection of artificial structures on the seabed and/or the removal of sediments covering archaeological deposits. In order to consider whether marine archaeology constitutes a "reasonable" use of the oceans in terms of *locus* and operation, the size of the area claimed, the period of time needed and the degree of interference with other sea uses need to be examined in each case. In this context, the existence of nearby fishing grounds, oil/gas provinces or sea lanes used for international navigation as well as the adequacy of the means to warn about possible hazards will be significant factors to be assessed.[12] Due to the temporary and peaceful nature of archaeological projects and the lack of a prohibitory rule of international law, marine archaeology should be considered as a *prima facie* legitimate exercise of a freedom of the high seas.[13] However, it will be a matter of examining each individual case in order to determine whether the particular project is exercised with reasonable regard to the interests of other States.

Legitimacy of the designation of marine archaeological reserves
The designation of marine archaeological reserves is essential in cases where there are no visible remains, but certain sea areas are suspected to contain items of archaeological interest, where the location of a site has not been adequately defined, and, finally, for the *in situ* preservation of underwater

cultural property.[14] Does their creation constitute a legitimate exercise of the freedom of the high seas? To date, all the international and regional instruments providing for the designation of specially protected areas limit their scope of application to the territorial sea.[15] The only exception is the 1992 Archaeological Convention (revised), which allows the creation of archaeological reserves beyond the territorial sea in any area within the jurisdiction of the parties; whether this coincides with the territorial sea, the contiguous zone, the continental shelf or the EEZ. The designation of marine archaeological reserves in international waters does not appear to be permissible, as such claims will inevitably result in the appropriation of a part of the high seas, which is expressly prohibited by article 2 of the CHS. However, since uses with an exclusive character, such as the construction of artificial islands,[16] have been advanced as an exercise of a freedom of the high seas, provided they are kept within the limits of reasonableness, the creation of marine archaeological reserves could also be justified. This argument is valid only in so far as temporary delimitations of areas of archaeological interest are concerned, e.g., during exploration and excavation activities. The creation of permanent reserve zones cannot be justified as an exercise of the freedom of the high seas; foreign nationals and vessels flying the flag of a third State would not be obliged to comply with such measures, as the only applicable jurisdiction on the high seas is that of the flag/national State.

The problem associated with the designation of archaeological reserves on the high seas is highlighted by the British Protection of Military Remains Act 1986[17], which attempts to secure the protection of the remains of military aircraft and vessels that have crashed, sunk or been stranded and of associated human remains from unauthorised interference. Even though the 1986 Act extends its scope so as to include military remains found in international waters, the exercise of extraterritorial jurisdiction is limited to offences committed on board British-controlled ships and to offenc ~ committed by British citizens and subjects.[18] Similarly, the U.S. Marine Protection, Research and Sanctuaries Act 1972, which enables the designation of marine sanctuaries "for the purpose of preserving or restoring such areas for their conservation, recreational, ecological or esthetic value" as far as the outer limit of the continental shelf,[19] limits its application to foreign citizens "only to the extent consistent with recognised principles of international law or authorised by international agreement."[20]

Sanctions against illegal interference

In cases where marine archaeology is exercised as a freedom of the high seas, what kind of protection would it be granted against interference, theft and other damaging acts? The 1958 Geneva Conventions failed to provide for a compulsory dispute settlement procedure. Instead, an Optional Protocol of Signature concerning the Compulsory Settlement of Disputes was appended.[21] Article II of the 1958 Protocol provides that:

> "Disputes arising out of the interpretation or application of any Convention on the Law of the Sea shall lie within the compulsory jurisdiction of the International Court of Justice, and may accordingly be brought before the Court by an application made by any party to the dispute being a Party to this Protocol."

In any case, States would be entitled, on the basis of self-defence to take on the high seas "whatever action, including the use of force, as might be necessary" to protect from interference by foreigners the exercise by their nationals of the freedom of the high seas.[22] Consequently, if an archaeological team is interfered with or prevented from operating by the nationals of another State unjustifiably, the home State of the archaeologists may step into the dispute and take the necessary "practical" measures, always within the limits of reasonableness and proportionality. If such interference amounts to an act of piracy, the exercise of universal jurisdiction on the basis of the rules of piracy *jure gentium* may also be justified.

Conflict between marine archaeology and other sea uses

The CHS fails to establish criteria for the reconciliation of legal, but conflicting, uses. This is true both for conflicts over the same activities and conflicts over different, but incompatible, uses.[23] The two aforementioned criteria of "reasonableness" and "non-prohibition by the rules of international law" concern exclusively the legitimate exercise of a sea-use. It will, therefore, be a matter of examining each individual case in order to determine whether the operation of an archaeological project underwater would acquire priority over another sea use, or whether the operators of a sea project would be obliged to take protective measures for the safeguarding of cultural property accidentally discovered.

An evaluation in socio-economic terms of the different interests involved would seem a necessary prerequisite for establishing priorities and for providing a fair solution to the dispute.[24] Obviously, the protection of underwater cultural property cannot always be expected to have priority. What is important, is to take into consideration its value when establishing priorities. If marine archaeology is in conflict with the freedom of navigation, that is, if archaeological activities take place near "recognised sea lanes essential to international navigation" and create navigational hazards, the priority will almost certainly lie in favour of the latter, which has traditionally been the essence of the freedom of the high seas. Among the factors to be taken into account in resolving the conflict would be the time of the conflict, the severity of the hazard, the adequacy of means to warn shipping and the availability and the cost of alternative routes.[25] Provisions, such as article 18 of the Convention on the International Regulations for Preventing Collisions at Sea (1972), which requires that vessels underway shall keep out of the way of vessels restricted in their ability to manoeuvre, may also be taken into account in the reconciliation of conflicts.[26] The same evaluation of interests will probably take place in relation to conflicts with the traditional freedoms of fishing and laying of cables and pipelines.[27]

Flag State jurisdiction and the removal of historic shipwrecks

The question of whether a sunken vessel retains its status as "ship" and so is subject to the exclusive jurisdiction of its flag State is particularly relevant when its removal is considered. The issue of jurisdiction over wrecked vessels and their cargoes is a controversial political issue, one which goes well beyond the narrow field of the protection of the underwater cultural heritage. There are many economic, scientific, military and security interests involved especially with respect to sunken warships and nuclear submarines. There are two schools of thought on this issue. The first claims that all sunken vessels, whether State-owned or not, have ceased to be "ships" and, therefore, are not subject to the exclusive jurisdiction of their flag States.[28] The second asserts that sunken vessels retain their legal status as ships with all the subsequent implications.[29] It is notable that, in the course of the negotiations of UNCLOS III, a number of proposals, mainly made by eastern European countries, suggested that ships and aircraft sunk beyond the limit of the territorial sea, as well as equipment and cargo on board, may be salvaged only by the flag State or with the flag State's consent.[30] As explained: "A customary rule has come into being in international law whereby a flag State and the owner of a ship or aircraft do not forfeit their rights to a ship or aircraft sunk at sea or to equipment and property on board.

Such rights are absolute and are not subject to any time-limit, provided that the ship, the aircraft or the equipment and property on board sunk beyond the limits of the territorial waters of States."[31] With the passage of time, the scope of these proposals was restricted to sunken warships and vessels owned or operated by a State and used only for government non-commercial purposes.[32] However, none of these suggestions found their way into the Final Text of the Convention. Even the amendments which reserved to the coastal State the prior right to carry out salvage operations in case the services of a third State were required for the salvaging of ships and aircraft sunk in the EEZ, were not acceptable.[33]

It is beyond doubt that warships and State-owned or operated vessels, used only on government non-commercial service, enjoy complete immunity from the jurisdiction of any State other than the flag State on the high seas (c.f. articles 8(1) and 9 of the CHS and articles 95 and 96 of the 1982 Convention respectively). As a corollary to the rule of immunity, they are exempted from the application of numerous international treaties, such as the Brussels Convention for the Unification of Certain Rules with Respect to Assistance and Salvage at Sea (1910)[34] or the International Convention on Salvage (1989).[35] It is debatable, however, whether *sunken* warships and State-owned vessels used for government non-commercial purposes still qualify as ships submitted to the exclusive jurisdiction of their flag State and enjoying immunity. The *rationale* of flag State jurisdiction is to facilitate the needs of international navigation and other legitimate uses of the seas undertaken by ships. Since there is a lack of an overall authority on the high seas, the flag State is the only State competent to exercise jurisdiction over the ships sailing under its flag. Sunken vessels lying on the sea-floor cannot qualify as "ships", as they are not used for navigation nor are they capable of being so.[36] The most common characteristic of the definition of "ships" is their ability to navigate; if they cannot navigate, they are not considered as ships with all the consequent implications. The same applies to warships.[37]

However, the fact that recovery operations on the high seas may be undertaken by any State does not mean that the *ownership* of sunken vessels is impaired or lost. For such a situation to occur, abandonment of the ship in question must be proven first. With respect to warships and other State-owned vessels, abandonment is very difficult to prove, especially when national law requires the explicit renunciation of title. It has been suggested that sunken warships and public State vessels retain their status as public State property and, therefore, "the State can prohibit any physical interference with that property even to the point of allowing its remains to lie on the bottom of the sea".[38] This conclusion is confirmed by a number of cases where coastal States had even asked the permission of the flag State to recover warships from their territorial sea.[39] After having been denied permission, they did not recover the sunken warships. It seems, however, that in these instances in question was not the legality of the recovery operations, but the right of disposal of the wrecks concerned.[40]

To sum-up, existing public international law does not appear to recognise the priority of the flag State in relation to the removal of shipwrecks. *A fortiori*, therefore, *historic wrecks* found on the high seas will not be submitted to the exclusive jurisdiction of their identifiable flag State; recovery operations would rather be subject to the jurisdiction of the removing vessel. This consideration is more than obvious in relation to shipwrecks lying for hundreds of years on the bottom of the seas. It would be absurd to refer to such remains as "ships" subject to the exclusive jurisdiction of their flag State as in certain cases even the distinction between them and the seabed is difficult.[41] With respect to sunken State-owned vessels and warships, it must be accepted that they do retain their status as public State property so that their recovery may[42] require the consent of the flag State.

Conclusion

On the high seas the sole applicable jurisdiction being that of the flag/ national State, any activity related to cultural property found in this area is subject to its exclusive jurisdiction. However, the latter provides one of the most inefficient bases for protecting the underwater cultural heritage. First, the flag/national State is incapable of ensuring effective control over its vessels/nationals when they operate in distant waters. Even if it had the appropriate legislation, it would almost certainly lack the means of enforcement. Having at its disposal only the limited sanctions provided for by international law, it is very difficult for the flag State to prohibit interference from ships sailing under the flag of third States. Second, the designation of archaeological reserves, which undoubtedly constitute the most effective means of protecting underwater cultural property, does not appear to be permissible under the doctrine of the freedom of the high seas. Inevitably, such claims will result in the appropriation of a part of the high seas, which is expressly prohibited by article 2 of the CHS. Third, the doctrine of the freedom of the high seas entitles everyone to proceed to the removal and aquisition of underwater cultural property. This free-for-all system does not acknowledge any priority to the flag State or, as the case may be, to the State of origin, nor does it impose on potential salvors the obligation to take protective measures.

Unless precise and definite rules on marine archaeology are adopted, the depredation of the cultural heritage of the oceans will continue to take place as an exercise of the right of free use of the seas.[43] Marine archaeology can only survive as a regulated freedom. It is an activity which has assumed sufficient practical importance to justify special legal regulation.

THE UN CONVENTION ON THE LAW OF THE SEA (1982)

Legal status

The establishment of the 200-mile EEZ and the Area by the 1982 Convention introduced fundamental changes to the legal regime of the high seas. Within the 200-mile EEZ, the freedom of the high seas has ceased to exist; it has retreated *ratione loci*. At the same time, however, it has survived as the exercise of a right to use the seas for certain purposes. This right is functional, in the sense that it is strictly confined to its content[44] and it does not raise presumptions in its favour. Article 86 reads:

> "The provisions of this part (high seas) apply to all parts of the sea which are not included in the exclusive economic zone, in the territorial sea or in the internal waters of a State, or in the archipelagic waters of an archipelagic State. This article does not entail any abridgment of the freedoms enjoyed by all States in the exclusive economic zone in accordance with article 58".

With respect to activities that do not feature among the freedoms enumerated by article 58, i.e., freedoms of navigation and overflight and of the laying of submarine cables and pipelines and other international uses of the sea related to these freedoms, nor have been attributed as a right to coastal States, the 1982 Convention provides in article 59 that all States have an interest in their exercise. Article 59 will be examined in detail in Chapter 7.

Beyond the outer limit of the continental shelf, the principle of the freedom of the high seas has been advanced as a new species of *res communis*; the common heritage of mankind. Article 87(2) reads :

> "These freedoms shall be exercised by all States with due regard for the interests of other States in their exercise of the freedom of the high seas and also with due regard for the rights under this Convention with respect to activities in the Area".

Other than that, the elaboration of the principle of the freedom of the high seas by article 87 of the 1982 Convention is almost identical to that provided for by article 2 of the CHS. However, notable differences between the two are: (a) the addition of the "freedom to construct artificial islands and other installations permitted under international law" and "the freedom of scientific research" in the enumerated freedoms, and (b) the modification of the term "reasonable regard" to "due regard".[45] Since marine archaeology does not qualify as scientific research, the inclusion of the latter in the permissive list of freedoms of article 87 is of no importance to the international regime of underwater cultural property.

Effect of article 303 on archaeological and historical objects found on the high seas

Duty to protect objects of an archaeological and historical nature and to co-operate therefor (article 303(1))
In exercising their right of free use of the high seas, States are under the obligation to protect archaeological and historical objects and to co-operate therefor. This is the combined effect of article 303(1), which establishes the duty to protect archaeological and historical objects found at sea, and article 87(1) which reads: "Freedom of the high seas is exercised under the conditions laid down by this Convention and by other rules of international law". The establishment of these duties undoubtedly recognise the protection of the underwater cultural heritage as an objective of the contemporary law of the sea. As argued, they should be given the broadest possible meaning so as to embrace the whole sprectrum of activities related to the underwater cultural heritage, including the safeguarding of those operations against other legitimate uses of the seas. However, article 303(1) cannot form the legal basis for claims to any part of the high seas.[46]

Article 303(1) does not specify the measures to be taken in its implementation. This raises the question as to whether the obligation to suspend
operations until proper protective measures are taken is also included within
its scope.[47] In the light of the vague language of article 303(1) and the huge
investments made in offshore operations, it would be difficult to give a
positive answer to this question. The substantial loss of profit that deep sea
operators may suffer from the suspension of activities will play a decisive
role in the final settlement of the issue. Nevertheless, as the only applicable
jurisdiction on the high seas is that of the flag/national State, it will be a
matter for each individual State to impose on the ships flying its flag or on
its nationals the obligation to undertake such measures.

*Reservation of the rights of the identifiable owners, the law of salvage and
other rules of admiralty, and laws and practices with respect to cultural
exchanges (article 303(3))*
With respect to archaeological objects found on the high seas, the reservations of article 303(3) can only be read to mean that whatever law is
applicable, it should not abolish the rights of the identifiable owners, the
law of salvage and the laws and practices with respect to cultural exchanges.
It has been emphasised throughout this work that this provision must not
be interpreted in a way that would overrule the duty of protection established
by article 303(1). In this context, it is suggested that salvors should be
obliged to carry out recovery operations in an archaeologically responsible
manner. As argued, the reservation of salvage and admiralty law by article
303(3) should be confined to cases in which archaeological and historical
objects are not involved, i.e., objects which are less than 100 years old and
which are eligible for salvage. If, however, salvage law is deemed to be
applicable to wrecks falling within the ambit of article 303(1), recovery
operations should be conducted in accordance with archaeological standards.
The application of archaeological principles in salvage operations is essential,
if it is considered that national heritage laws are not applicable on the high
seas. Flag States are no doubt entitled to oblige their nationals or the ships
flying their flag to respect their heritage laws when operating on the high
seas. However, such measures are not applicable to foreign-flag ships and
nationals. Within the general framework of the 1982 Convention, the expansion of coastal competence beyond the 24-mile limit is not permissible.
Unless States enact specific legislation to apply their heritage laws to underwater cultural property brought within their jurisdiction regardless of the
nationality of the finder, the activities of foreign subjects on the high seas

are not affected by coastal legislation. An illustrative example is provided by France which applies its laws to wrecks found on the high seas and brought within the territorial sea.[48]

In contrast, admiralty courts appear to have jurisdiction over salvage operations on the high seas even in the case of derelict of foreign origin. In *Treasure Salvors Inc. v. The Unidentified Wrecked and Abandoned Sailing Vessel* (*Treasure Salvors III*), the U.S. Court of Appeals, Fifth Circuit, stated that: "Since the admiralty jurisdiction of United States courts is not limited by the nationality of the ships, sailors or seas involved and since the principles of the law of salvage are part of the *jus gentium*, i.e., the international maritime law, U.S. courts have long adjudicated salvage claims involving foreign vessels, alien salvors and salvage operations occurring on the high seas".[49] The court recognised that it had *in personam* jurisdiction over the competing salvors and, therefore, could rule on the competing claims to the portion of the wreck remaining outside the courts' territorial jurisdiction.[50] In *Colombus-Discovery Group v. the Unidentified, Wrecked and Abandoned Sailing Vessel, S.S. Central America in Rem*, the district court of Virginia asserted *in rem* jurisdiction over the wreck of *Central America* which was located in international waters. In the court's view the presence of certain pieces of the vessel brought into the jurisdiction was sufficient to give constructive possession of the wreck, so that for the purpose of *in rem* jurisdiction the *res* was within the territory of the court.[51] *Colombus-America* appears to be the first case in which a U.S. admiralty court has asserted *in rem* jurisdiction over a shipwreck in international waters.[52]

In *Simon v. Taylor,* the Supreme Court of Singapore held that if a wreck is found on the high seas and it, or its cargo, is brought within the territorial jurisdiction of the Receiver, rights to salvage depend upon the law of the forum (*lex fori*).[53] In the English case of *The Tubantia,*[54] the High Court of Admiralty held that an action in respect of injurious acts done on the high seas had always been within its jurisdiction. The court applied the law of salvage as to salvors in possession and ruled that the plaintiffs were sufficiently in occupation of the wreck to exclude third parties from interfering with the property.[55] However, the court did not address the question of the prerogative rights of the Crown: "Nor need I come to any conclusion as to the limits which international right may impose upon any claim under the prerogative of the British Crown to *bona vacantia* lying on the ocean floor."[56] This issue was discussed in *The Lusitania* where it was held that the Crown had no right to unclaimed wrecks found in extraterritorial waters and consequently chattels found in 1982 in the Lusitania, which was torpedoed in 1915, belonged to the finders.[57] Mr. Justice Sheen admitted that there was a *lacuna* in the provisions for the disposal of "extraterritorial wrecks" if unclaimed by the owner.[58] Nevertheless, the finder was considered to have a better claim to the discovered wreck than anyone else. Even if the wreck was classified as historic, the court would not have ruled otherwise since the scope of application of the Protection of Wrecks Act 1973 is also confined exclusively to areas landward of the outer limit of the territorial sea.[59]

To sum up, on the high seas the implementation of the duty to protect archaeological and historical objects is inevitably left to the individual States. If the flag/national State has not enacted specific legislation to protect them, historic wrecks and their cargoes will be governed by admiralty law, while the finder would be considered as having a good right to such property. Obviously, in most cases a choice of law problem will not be avoided. In practice, it will be the choice-of-law rules of the *forum* to determine which substantive law is applicable to cultural property found on the high seas.[60] The applicable law could be the law of the flag of either the sunken or the salving vessel, the *lex fori* or the law of the owner. There may be also cases where the coastal State on whose continental shelf the wreck lies has extended its heritage lagislation over this area or cases, such as that of the statue *Melqart di Sciacca*, which was found on the high seas approximately 24 nm off the coast of Sicily.[61] According to the Tribunal of Sciacca, the statue of Melqart entered Italian territory when it was caught in the nets of the Italian boat which discovered it. Since the net forms part of the boat which, in turn, is being treated as part of Italian territory by article 4 of the Italian Code of Navigation, the discovery of the statue took place on "Italian territory". As a result Law No. 1089 of 1 June 1939 on the Protection of Objects of Artistic and Historic Interest applied, article 49 of which vests title of ownership of fortuitously discovered objects to the State.[62] In other words, the acquisition of underwater cultural property by the flag State of the removing vessel was based on a maritime law treating ships flying that State's flag as part of its territory, and a heritage law vesting title of ownership of accidentally discovered archaeological objects to the State.[63]

Reservation of other international agreements and rules of international law regarding the protection of archaeological and historical objects (article 303(4))

The vast majority of the international instruments dealing with the protection of the cultural heritage are territorially confined. Notable exceptions are the 1985 Cultural Offences Convention, the 1992 Archaeological Convention (revised) and the UN General Assembly Resolutions on the Return or Restitution of Cultural Property to the Countries of Origin. As already seen, the 1992 Convention applies to all elements of the archaeological heritage which are found in any area of the jurisdiction of the parties and thus appears to exclude high seas areas. However, to the extent that it includes the continental shelf problems may arise as to the application of coastal laws in this area. Under article 13 of the 1985 Convention, each party is entitled to take the necessary measures in order to prosecute any offence relating to cultural property committed on board a ship or an aircraft registered in it, or committed outside its territory by one of its nationals, or by a person having his/her habitual residence on its territory (article 13 (1) b, c, d). In addition, it may prosecute offences committed outside its territory when the cultural property against which that offence was directed belongs to the said Party or one of its nationals (article 13 (1) e), and, finally, when the offence was directed against cultural property originally found within its territory (article 13 (1) f). With the exception of the general right to prosecute offences committed on board a ship, the effectiveness of this jurisdictional provision is limited by two factors. First, it concerns exclusively the offences provided for by the Convention, and second, it refers to property that "belongs" to the State concerned or it was found, or believed to be, in its territory in modern times.[64] The same applies for the restitution of cultural property, which is restricted to cases where cultural property found on the territory of States parties, has been removed from the territory of another party subsequent to an offence relating to cultural property committed in the territory of a party (article 6). Consequently, even if the scope of the 1985 European Convention is broad enough to permit its applicability to international waters, its effectiveness is considerably limited with regard to cultural property found seaward of the outer limit of the territorial sea.

Finally, the UN General Assembly Resolutions on the Return or Restitution of Cultural Property to the Countries of Origin include within their scope cultural property found on the high seas. Without attempting to modify existing international law, the UN Resolutions promote the conclusion of bilateral or even multilateral agreements so as to enable the participation of the State of origin in archaeological excavations underwater. Such a regulation is obviously in accordance with the duty of co-operation established by article 303(1) of the 1982 Convention.

Conclusion

The establishment of the general duty to protect objects of an archaeological and historical nature is the most important innovation of the 1982 Convention with respect to cultural property found on the high seas. The main disadvantage of this scheme is that its implementation is left to individual States. Since the only applicable legal order on the high seas is that of the national/flag State, the enactment of protective measures lies entirely at its discretion. In discussing the CHS, it was argued that the doctrine of the freedom of the high seas provides one of the most inefficient schemes of protection. Regrettably, the adoption of a general duty to protect archaeological objects at sea cannot guarantee a much better result. Nevertheless, it is hoped that States will implement the obligation to protect archaeological objects in the broadest possible sense so as: (a) to embrace the whole spectrum of activities related to the underwater cultural heritage, and (b) to elaborate it to specific rights and obligations in relation to its nationals or ships flying its flag.

Under the 1982 Convention, the freedom of the high seas has retreated *ratione loci* and *ratione operae* due to the establishment of the EEZ and the Area. In case the coastal State has declared an EEZ, marine archaeology will be exercised as a freedom of the high seas only in the area defined between the outer limit of EEZ and that of the continental shelf.

CUSTOMARY INTERNATIONAL LAW

The CHS provides in its preamble that the States parties "adopted the following provisions as generally declaratory of established principles of international law". Nevertheless, the recently established concepts of the EEZ and the Area have introduced substantial alterations to the traditional principle of the freedom of the high seas.[65] It has been argued that "nowadays we are faced with a paradoxical situation where on the one hand the freedom of the high seas has retreated as a result of the expansion of the principle of sovereignty while on the other it has advanced as a 'new species of *res communis'*, a common heritage of mankind."[66] Others take a more extreme view and argue that "the absence of sovereignty that characterised in the past the high seas has been substituted by the triptych - sovereignty of the coastal State - common exploitation - freedom of navigation",[67] or that "no longer do we have a freedom of the high seas. There is only a functional right in the sense that States other than the coastal one may now carry on those activities which are strictly indispensable for communications, transportation, marine and air traffic."[68] It has been admitted, however, that "theoretically the freedom of the high seas is not abolished. Most of the States refer to restrictions and designations of this freedom rather than to its abolition and substitution by another regime."[69]

At this stage, it would be premature to argue that the freedom of the high seas has been substituted wholly by a new regime. Contemporary State practice does not provide sufficient evidence for the creation of a rule of custom, especially with respect to residual rights. In order to assess the status of underwater cultural property in international waters under customary law, it is necessary to examine the concepts of the EEZ and the Area.

NOTES

1   This approach, however, is not shared by all as a number of scholars argue that the freedom of the high seas covers only a limited number of long established uses. For a discussion of the different approaches in interpreting article 2 of the CHS see, among others, Momtaz, D., "The High Seas" in Dupuy, R.-J. & Vignes, D. (eds), *A Handbook on the New Law of the Sea*, vol. 1, Hague Academy of International Law, Martinus Nijhoff, 1991, pp. 383-422; Papadakis, N., *The International Legal Regime of Artificial Islands*, Sijthoff, Leyden, 1977, pp. 57-60; Soons, A.H.A., *Marine Scientific Research and the Law of the Sea*, T.M.C. Asser Institute - The Hague, Kluwer Law and Taxation Publishers 1982, pp. 53-54. Momtaz argues that "the Conference finally opted for the British formula: in order to accede to the rank of freedoms of the high seas, the other uses of the high seas must be recognised by general legal principles. This was, however, only a makeshift solution, as subsequent difficulties in interpretation were to prove. Would it be up to each user to prove that a given freedom complied with general legal principles, or would the mere fact that the intended use did not violate any general legal principle suffice? If one were to opt for the first interpretation, the freedom of the high seas would in short be reduced to those freedoms for which proof could be furnished; it goes without saying that the difficulty of this undertaking would involve the risk of closing the door

for evermore on any development in the use of the high seas which was not the subject of the express or tacit agreement of the collectivity of States. At the other extreme, taking the lack of incompatibility between a projected use of the high seas and general legal principles as the sole basis on which to assert the legality of this use could become a source of abuse... It is, however, true to say that since the jurisdiction of coastal States has been extended over both the adjacent waters and the subjacent seabed, the question of identifying the other freedoms has become much less urgent". *Ibid* at p. 393.

2 II *ILC Yearbook* (1956) at p. 278.

3 *Ibid*. The Commentary refers only to the subsoil of the high seas and not to the seabed. As a result, certain authors distinguish between the legal regime of the seabed and the subsoil, the former being described as *res nulllius* and the latter *res communis*. This distinction has been of cardial importance. Howe-ver, this theory is not well-founded in State practice. See further Henchoz, A-D., *Réglementations nationals et internationales de l' exportation et d' exploitation des grands fonds marins*, Etudes suisses de droit international, vol. 76, Schul-thess Polygraphischer Verlag, Zürich, 1992, pp. 641-643, 649 and Papadakis, *op. cit.* note 1 at pp. 55-56.

4 Van Dyke and Yuen argue that the definition of the high seas under the CHS includes only the waters, thus excluding the deep seabed. In their opinion the recognition of the laying of cables and pipelines as freedom of the high seas does not imply that the seabed is part of the high seas for all uses. Cable-laying is a classic example of an activity that is a high seas freedom because of the nature of the activity. To the ILC, the nature of the activity was controlling, not the region in which it ocurred; cable-laying on the continental shelf is a freedom of the high seas, but mineral exploiotation on the continental shelf is the rihgt of the coastal nation alone. Similarly, the high seas freedom to lay cables on the deep seabed in no way implies that the mineral exploitation of the deep seabed is a freedom of the high seas. Van Dyke, J. & Yuen, Ch., "Common heritage v. freedom of the high seas; which governs the seabed?", 19 *San Diego L. Rev.* (1981/82) pp. 493-551 at pp. 507-508. For further discussion see Hen-choz, *op. cit.* note 3 at p. 644 *et seq.*

5 Others argue that the "criterion of reasonableness embodied in the CHS is invoked only when there is a legal conflict between two recognised standards". Fischer, G., "Droit international et expérimentation des armes nucleaires", *AFDI*, 1956 at p. 312. Text quoted by Momtaz, *op. cit.* note 1 at p. 398. "This criterion should enable us to establish an order of priority between two or several free-doms of the high seas and to safeguard the principle of equality between States. This order of priority would be drawn up taking into account the manner in which the various freedoms were exercised. However, it must be recognised that the major disadvantage of reasonable use is its subjectivism." *Ibid.*

6 Brown, E.D., "Freedom of the high seas versus the common heritage of man-kind: fundamental principles in conflict", 20 *San Diego L. Rev.* (1983) pp. 521-560 at p. 535.

7 *Ibid* at pp. 535-536. See also Henchoz, *op. cit.* note 3 at p. 709 *et seq.*

8 See further articles 13 and 22 (prevention and punishment of slavery), articles 14-21 and 22 (piracy *jure gentium*) and article 23 (right of hot pursuit). Under customary international law, all States are entitled on the basis of self-defence to enforce their rights subject to the limits of the use of force, i.e., reasonableness and proportionality.

9 Brownlie, I., *Principles of Public International Law*, Clarendon Press, 4th edition, Oxford, 1990 at p. 303.

10 Marine archaeology should not be considered as an exercise of the so-called "fifth freedom" of the high seas, the freedom of scientific research, but as a subject of its own right. In contrast, Arend argues that: "Archaeological exploration is 'scientific research on the high seas' and, therefore, qualifies as a freedom of the high seas". Arend, C.A., "Archaeological and Historical Objects: The International Legal Implications of UNCLOS III", 22 *V.J.I.L.* (1982) pp. 777-803 at p. 786.

11 See also Miller, H.C., *International Law and Marine Archaeology*, Academy of Applied Sciences, Belmont, Mass., 1973 at pp. 26-29.

12 Due notice of the construction of any installations necessary for the exploration or excavation of a marine archaeological site and adequate means of warning of their presence are essential in this respect. According to article 5(5) of the CSC, the coastal State must give due notice of the construction of installations and other devices necessary for the exploration and the exploitation of its natural resources and maintain permanent means for giving warning of their presence. *A fortiori*, therefore, these measures should be taken by States, while exercising the right of free use of the high seas.

13 As noted, the right of use of the high seas may be exercised for any purpose not expressly prohibited by international law. "There is no need to positively establish the existence of a right of use". Brown, *op. cit.* note 8 at p. 536. This approach, however, is not shared by all. See above note 1 and Van Dyke & Yuen, *op. cit.* note 4.

14 See also Prott, L.V. and O'Keefe, P.J., *The Law and the Cultural Heritage*, vol. 1, *Discovery and Excavation*, Professional Books Ltd., Abingdon, 1984 at p. 201 and Migliorino, L., "La protezione *in situ* del patrimonio culturale subacqueo". Paper presented at the *Semiranio: La Protezione del patrimonio culturale subacqueo nel Meditteraneo,* organised by the Università degli Studi di Roma 'Tor Vergata', Anacapri, 1 October 1994. At national level, it is rather common for legislation dealing specifically with underwater sites to provide for the creation of a protective zone. States have long recognised the establishment of marine archaeological reserves as an effective means of protecting underwater cultural property, in particular historic wrecks. In this respect, laws realted to national parks and environmental protection have also been employed. For example, in Tasmania, the *National Parks and Wildlife Act 1970* was used by the Tasmanian Government to protect the wreck of Sydney Cove. In South Australia, the *Aboriginal and Historic Relics Preservation Act 1965* allows the declaration of areas of historical or scientific significance as either prohibited areas or historic reserves. The latter has been used more than once to cover areas of the seabed of historic significance. See further O'Keefe, P.J. & Prott,

L.V. "Australian Protection of Historic Shipwrecks", 6 *A.Y.B.I.L.* (1978) pp. 119-138 at p. 137.

15 At international level, the 1968 UNESCO Recommendation concerning the Preservation of Cultural Property Endangered by Public or Private Works provides for the protection of important immovable cultural property endangered by public or private works by zoning or scheduling. At regional level, the 1982 Protocol concerning Mediterranean Specially Protected Areas provides for the designation of specially protected areas to safeguard "sites of scientific, aesthetic, historical, archaeological, cultural or educational interest", while the 1969 Archaeological Convention for the delimitation and protection of sites and areas of archaeological interest, and the creation of reserve zones for the preservation of material evidence to be excavated by later generations of archaeologists.

16 See article 87(1)d of the 1982 Convention, which includes among the freedom of the high seas "the freedom to construct artificial islands and other installations permitted under international law" as well as Papadakis, *op. cit.* note 2 at p. 60 and Henchoz, *op. cit.* note 7 at pp. 712-713. Some scholars argue that deep seabed mining also qualifies as freedom of the high seas. See, for example, Brown, E.D., *Sea-Bed Energy and Mineral Resources and the Law of the Sea*, vol. 2, *The Area Beyond the Limits of National Jurisdiction,* Graham & Trotman, London 1986 at II.2.16 and II.2.40-II.2.42. In contrast, see Van Dyke and Yuen, *op. cit.* note 4.

17 Protection of Military Remains Act, 1986, *c.35.*

18 Section 1(6) reads: "For the purposes of this Act a place (whether in the United Kingdom, in United Kingdom or in international waters) is a protected place if: (a) it comprises the remains of, or of a substantial part of, an aircraft, or vessel to which this Act applies; and (b) it is on or in the sea bed or is the place, or in the immediate vicinity of the place, where the remains were left by the crash, sinking or stranding of the aircraft or vessel; but no place in international waters shall be a protected place by virtue of its comprising remains of an aircraft or vessel which has crashed, sunk or been stranded while in service with, or while being used for the purposes of, any of the armed forces of a country or territory outside of the United Kingdom."
    Under section 3(1): "Where a contravention of subsection (2) of section 2 above occurs in international waters or an excavation or operation prohibited by subsection (3) of the section is carried out in international waters, a person shall be guilty of an offence under that section in respect of that contravention, excavation or operation only: (a) if the acts or omissions which constitute the offence are committed in the United Kingdom, in United Kingdom waters or on board a British-controlled ship; or (b) in a case where those acts or omissions are committed in international waters but not on board a British-controlled, if that person is: (i) a British citizen, a British Dependent Territories citizen or a British Overseas citizen; (ii) a person who under the British Nationality Act 1981 is a British subject; or (iii) a British protected person (within the meaning of that Act); (iv) a company within the meaning of the Companies Act 1985 or the Companies Act (Northern Ireland) 1960."

19 16 *U.S.C.A.* paras. 1431-1439 as amended in 1984 (Marine Sanctuaries Amendment Act 1984). According to para. 1432(3): "'Marine environment' means those areas of coastal and ocean waters, the Great Lakes and their connecting waters, and submerged lands over which the United States exercises jurisdiction consistent with international law".

20 15 *C.F.R.* para. 922.10 (1977). For a discussion of the 1972 Marine Sanctuaries Act, see Lawrence, A., "State Antiquity Laws and Admiralty Salvage: Protecting our Cultural Resources", 33 *U. Miami L. Rev.* (1977) pp. 291-338 at pp. 317-320. On the basis of Title III of this Act, the United States has designated the wreck site of the USS Monitor, located approximately 16 miles south-southeast of Cape Hatteras, North Carolina, as a national marine sanctuary. See further Miller, E.M., "The Monitor National Marine Sanctuary", 28 *Oceanus,* No. 1, Spring 1985, pp. 66-71.

21 450 *U.N.T.S.* 169. As at 31 December 1990, 39 States were parties to the Protocol. See *Multilateral Treaties Deposited with the Secretary General, United Nations,* 1990, ST/LEG/SER.E/19 at p. 768.

22 Brown, E.D., *The Legal Regime of Hydrospace,* Stevens & Sons, London, 1972 at p. 102. As noted by Prof. Brown, the political factors which would militate against action in accordance with these rules except in very exceptional circumstances, hardly need to be stressed. For the settlement of disputes between salvors, in case salvage law applies to historic or archaeological wrecks, see *supra* at pp. 225-227, in particular notes 51-53.

23 "The most general blackletter provision, article 2, could hardly offer less guidance to particular decision". See McDougal, M.C. and Burke, W.T., *The Public Order of the Oceans: A Contemporary International Law of the Sea,* Yale University, New Haven/London, 1962 at p. 87.

24 On the reconciliation of conflicting users under both the CHS and customary international law, see Brown, *op. cit.* note 22 at p. 102 *et seq.*

25 Brown, *ibid* at p. 100.

26 Text reproduced in Churchill, R. & Nordquist, M. (eds.), *New Directions in the Law of the Sea,* vol. IV at p. 245. However, if it is considered that the underlying purpose of article 18 is the facilitation of international navigation and not the establishment of priorities between different users of the high seas, its significance is limited. In contrast, Migliorino attributes particular importance to article 18 as a criterion for resolving conflicts between vessels engaged in the removal of archaeological objects and other conflicts between vessels engaged in the removal of archaeological objects and other ships. See Migliorino, L., *Il recupero degli oggetti storici ed archeologici sommersi nel diritto internazionale,* Studi e documenti sul diritto internazionale del mare 15, Dott. Giuffrè, A. editore, Milano, 1984 at pp. 66-67, 123 and 141.

27 If archaeological operations conflict with mineral exploration and exploitation, a distinction should be made between areas which are and areas which are not subjected to national jurisdiction. Conflicts with coastal sovereign rights over the continental shelf will be examined in Chapter 7. Conflicts with mineral exploration and exploitation activities in the Area are discussed in Chapter 8.

28 In particular see Caflisch, L., "Submarine Antiquities and the International Law of the Sea", 13 *N.Y.I.L.* (1982) pp. 3-32 at pp. 24-25; Eustis III, F.A., "The Glomar Explorer Incident: Implications for the Law of Salvage", 16 *V.J.I.L.* (1975) pp. 117-185; Gelberg, L., "Rechtsprobleme der Bergung auf Hoher See", 15 *Jahrbuch für Internationales Recht* (1971) pp. 429-447 at pp. 445-446; Gidel, G., *Le droit international de la mer*, vol. 1, Sirey, Paris, 1932, pp. 70-71; Migliorino, L., "The Recovery of Sunken Warships in International Law" in Vukas, B. (ed.), *Essays on the Law of the Sea*, Sveucilisna naklada Liber, Zagreb, 1985, pp. 244-258; Nafziger, J.A.R., "Finding the Titanic: beginning an international salvage of derelict law at sea", 12 *Columbia - VLA Journal of Law & the Arts* (1988) pp. 339-351 at p. 345, and Roucounas, E., "Submarine archaeological research: some legal aspects" in Leanza, U. (ed.), *The International Legal Regime of the Mediterranean Sea*, II Università degli Studi di Roma, Pubblicazioni della Facolta di Giurisprudenze, 2 Dott. Giuffrè A. editore, Milano, 1987, pp. 309-334 at pp. 330-331. See also Riphangen who argues that: "Turning now to *sunken* ships it is understandable that such 'objects' cannot simply retain indefinetely the status under international law of a ship, even though in several cases, such "objects" have been salvaged, repaired and operated again as 'ships'". Riphagen, W., "Some Reflections on 'Functional Sovereignty'", 6 *N.Y.I.L.* (1975) pp. 121-165 at p. 128.

29 In particular see Collins, M.G., "The Salvage of Sunken Military Vessels", 10 *International Lawyer* (1976) pp. 681-690; Colombos, C.J., *Law of the Sea*, 6th rev.ed., Longmans, London, 1967 at p. 310; Münch (von), I. "Shiffwracks Völkerrechtliche Probleme", 20 *Archiv des Völkerrechts* (1982) pp. 183-198 at pp. 194-198; O'Connell, D.P., *The International Law of the Sea*, vol. II, Clarendon Press, Oxford, 1984 at pp. 913-914; Quéneudec, J-P., "Chronique du droit de la mer", 23 *Annuaire français de droit international* (1977) pp. 730-744 at pp. 734-735. Even under this approach, however, opinions vary considerably. According to Colombos, "the shipwrecked persons and property do not thereby lose the protection of the flag State of the shipwrecked vessel". Queneudec argues that immunity continues to apply to sunken warships, *ibid* at p. 735, while von Münch favours a qualified application of flag State jurisdiction. Finally, in O'Connell's view: "Whatever be its characterisation in municipal law, a sunken ship must be presumed·to retain the law of the flag as it remains a ship. But the question whether the site of a wreck remains a wreck, so that artefacts found there are presumed to follow the law of the flag is a different question." *Ibid* at pp. 913-914. On the salvage of sunken ships see further Mensbrugghe (van der), Y., "Réflexions sur la definition du navire dans le droit de le mer" in Societé française pour le droit international, *Actualités du droit de la mer*, Pedone, A. éditions, Paris, 1973, pp. 62-754 at pp. 66-67, and Starkle, G., "Les épaves de navires en haute mer et le droit international. Le cas du 'Mont-Louis', 18 *Revue belge de droit international* (1984/84) pp. 496-528. Starkle argues that from the point of view of public international law, the important issue is not whether the wreck qualifies as a ship, but whether the flag State claims to exercise its jurisdiction on the wreck, whether this is or

this is not a ship. In his view, under article 5 of the CHS, the flag State is the one which accords nationality and the one to say whether a wreck is a ship or not as well as to establish the conditions under which a vessel may lose its nationality. The sinking of the vessel itself is not sufficient to deprive the flag State of its jurisdiction. *Ibid* at pp. 506-507. It is the national legislation which will determine the moment beyond which the wreck will not be protected by the flag State.

30 Informal suggestion by the USSR (C.2/Informal Meeting/39, 16 May 1978); Revised informal suggestion by the USSR (A/CONF.62/C.2/Informal Meeting/39/ Rev.1, 1 September 1978), "New article or paragraph 3 of article 98" in Platzöder, R., *Third United Nations Conference on the Law of the Sea: Documents*, vol. V at p. 45. These proposals were prompted by the *Glomar Explorer incident* (1971) which caused deep concern to the international community. In 1974, the United States raised a section of a Soviet submarine from the deep seabed with a specially built deepwater salvage ship, the Glomar Explorer. The Glomar incidence appears to be the first time where a country attempted to salvage a foreign military vessel in international waters. Obviously, it raised a lot of discussions on both the legality of the operations and the manner in which they were carried out. The Glomar Explorer was disguised as a commercially operated oceanographic vessel, while the Central Intelligence Agency (CIA) seemed to have played an important role in the operation. For further discussion see Collins, *ibid*; Eustis III, *op. cit.* note 28; Rubin, A.P., "Sunken Soviet Submarines and Central Intelligence: Laws of Property and the Agency", 69 *A.J.I.L.* (1975) pp. 855-858.

31 See the explanatory note attached to the revised informal suggestion. *Ibid.*

32 Informal proposal by Bulgaria, Byelorussian Soviet Socialist Republic, Czechoslovakia, German Democratic Republic, Hungary, Poland, Ukrainian Soviet Socialist Republic, Union of Soviet Socialist Republics (A/CONF.62/C.2/Informal Meeting/50, 14 March 1980), *ibid* at p. 57.

33 Informal proposal by the Socialist Republic of Vietnam (A/CONF.62/C.2 Informal Meeting/52, 19 March 1980); Informal proposal by the Socialist Republic of Vietnam (A/CONF.62/C.2/ Informal Meeting/53, 19 March 1980). *Ibid* at pp. 58-59. See also the informal proposal by the Democratic Yemen, which suggested that: "The provisions of article 95 and 96 of this Convention apply to sunken warships, as well as sunken vessels, which are owned or operated by a State and which are only on goverment non-commercial service", (C.2/Informal Meeting/57, 20 March 1980). In Migliorino's view: "It is not easy to ascertain the reason for the failure of the Soviet block proposals, since official records make no mention of it. It has been argued that the coastal State could complain of the long presence of foreign vessels in its EEZ due to recovery operations. Furthermore, the coastal State could be interested, in case of dangerous or polluting wrecks, in intervening rapidly". *Op. cit.* note 28 at p. 249.

34 37 *Stat.* 1658, *T.S.* No 516. Article 14. The 1926 Brussels Convention on State-owned Vessels (Societé des Nations, *Recueil des Traités*, vol. 176, p. 199), distinguishes between government-owned vessels in public service and those

in commercial service and accords immunity for arrest and seizure only to the former. See furter Eustis III, *op. cit.* note 28 and Migliorino, *ibid* at p. 250.

35 *LEG/CONF.7/27*, May 2, 1989. Text reprinted in *Lloyd's Maritime and Commercial Quartely* (1990) p. 54. Article 4(1) states: "Without prejudice to article 5, this Convention shall not apply to warships or other non-commercial vessels owned or operated by a State and entitled, at the time of salvage operations, to sovereicn immunity under generally recognised principles of international law unless that State decides otherwise." For further discussion see Neilson, W.L., "The 1989 International Convnetion on Salvage", 24 *Connecticut Law Review* (1992) pp. 1203-1252. The Convention is not as yet in force.

36 Relevant to this issue is the arbitral award of Martens (de) in the *Costa Rica Packet Case (1897) (Great Britain v. The Netherlands)*, Moore, 5 *International Arbitrations* 4948; *R.G.D.I.P.* (1987) p. 736, note 1. Crew from the Costa Rica Packet, a British merchant ship boarded a derelict prauw (a native Malaysian boat) on the high seas and took goods from it. When the Costa Rica Packet entered a Dutch port in the East Indies the captain was arrested on charges related to the seizure of the goods. The Arbitrator held that the Netherlands had no jurisdiction to act as it had done as "the appropriation of the cargo of the derelict prauw has incontrovertibly taken place on the high seas; where only the flag State has jurisdiction. Consequently, the alleged appropriation was only justiciable by the respective national authorities, i.e., by English tribunals." According to Gidel, Marten's award was based on the assumption that a floating assemblage which has the form of a ship does not qualify as a ship if there is no intention to be used for maritime navigation under the control of a State. See further Gidel, *op. cit.* note 28 at p. 71; Caflisch, *ibid* at p. 25, footnote 81; Harris, D.J., *Cases and Materials on International Law*, 3rd edn, Sweet & Maxwell, London, 1983 at p. 218; Lazaratos, G., "The Definition of Ship in National and International Law", 22/23 *Revue hellenique de droit international* (1969/70) pp. 57-99 at pp. 91-92. See also Starkle, *op. cit.* note 30 at p. 509. In *United States v. Smiley* it was held that: "The constructive territory of the United States embraces vessels sailing under their flag; wherever they go they carry the laws of their country, and for a violation of them their officers and men may be subjected to punishment. But when a vessel is destroyed, and goes to the bottom, the jurisdiction of the country over it necessarily ends, as much so as it would over an island which should sink into the sea". 27 *Fed. Cas.* 1133 [6 *Sawy.* 640], Case No. 16317 at p. 1135.

37 Under both the CHS and the 1982 Convention, "warship means a ship belonging to the armed forces of a State bearing the external marks distinguishing such ships of its nationality under the command of an officer duly commissioned by the government of a State and whose name appears in the appropriate service list or its equivalent and manned by a crew which is under regular armed forces discipline" (c.f. article 8(2) of the CHS and article 29 of the 1982 Convention). This definition can hardly apply to sunken warships. Migliorino, *op. cit.* note 28 at p. 251.

38 Eustis III, *op. cit.* note 28 at p. 186. See also Galenskaya, L.N., "International co-operation in cultural affairs", *Hague Recueil* (1986-III) pp. 265-331 at p. 302: "In particular, naval ships are the property of a State and under the rules of State succession those States have all the rights to the wrecked ships. We cannot consider them as a prize of war or a war victim because these ships were lost in battle". See also *U.S. v. Steinmetz,* 1991 *AMC* 2099, aff'd 973 *F2d* 212 (3rd Cir. 1992), where the Court of Appeals held that the U.S. had not abandoned title which it acquired at the close of the Civil War, to the Confederate raider C.S.S. Alabama which was sunk off the coast of France in 1864. The U.S. claimed title as successor to the Confederacy. As argued, in doing so, the U.S. followed "its longstanding position that title to warships is not lost in the absence of capture or abandonment, and that abandonment could not be implied merely by long passage of time". See Letter from Department of State to Maritime Administration, reprinted in 8 *Digest of United States Practice in International Law,* pp. 999-1066, and Dromgoole, S. and Gaskell, N., "Who has a right to historic wrecks and wreckage", 2 *International Journal of Cultural Property* (1993) pp. 217-273, at p. 236. "Salvors should not presume that sunken U.S. warships have been abandoned by the United States. Permission must be granted from the United States to salvage sunken U.S. warships, and as a matter of policy, the U.S. Government does not grant such permission with respect to ships that contain the remains of deceased servicemen... In the absence of an express transfer or abandonment of a U.S. warship sunk in the near past (e.g. in the World War II era), it should be presumed that title to such vessels remains in the U.S. Title to vessels sunk in the more distant past (such as during the 17 and 18th centuries) would, of course, still be determined by the more conventional interpretation of abandonment of that period", *ibid* at p. 1004.

39 See further Migliorino, *op. cit.* note 28 at pp. 253-254; ID, *op. cit.* note 27 pp. 45-54 and pp. 106-113, where salvage operations on the high seas are being discussed. Special mention should be made to the case of *Admiral Nakhimov,* a Czarist warship which sunk in the strait of Korea during the Russo-Japanese war of 1904-1905. In 1905, the area where the warship sunk was part of the high seas. Today, since the extention of the Japanese territorial sea to 12 miles, this area is subject to Japanese sovereignty. When a Japanese private firm announced in 1980 that it planned to recover the sunken warship, the Soviet Union protested on the grounds that the warship belonged to it, as the successor of the Czarist Empire. Being a warship, it retained sovereign immunity so that the recovery operation would amount to an act of piracy. The Japanese government rejected this assertion by arguing that since the warship sunk during the Russo-Japanese war, it should be considered as booty. Rousseau, Ch., "Chronique des faits internationaux", 85 *R.G.D.I.P.* (1981) pp. 406-409. See also the 1952 Agreement between the United Kingdom and Italy regarding the salvage of *H.M.S. Spartan,* under whose terms the United Kingdom agreed to accept the Italian Government's offer of 50% of the amount received by the Italian State from the firm SARMAD for the sale of scrap salvaged from the wreck. The Italian Government shall relieve the UK Government of any liability in respect of ownership of the wreck and shall indemnify it against any claim

that might be preferred in respect of the wreck. Furthermore, it undertook to hand over to the British Embassy in Rome all documents and correspondance, cyphers, cypher machines, books, safes, steel chests, steel boxes and cash, which may be recovered from the wreck as well as to deliver the bodies of any British Naval personnel which may be found in the course of the salvage operations. See *No. 2076 Exchange of Notes Constituting an Agreement between the Government of the United Kingdom of Great Britain and Northern Ireland and the Government of Italy Regarding the Salvage of H.M.S. Spartan, Rome, 6 November 1952, U.N.T.S.* 432 (1953). Finally, Galenskaya, *ibid*, refers to a 1984 joint Egyptian-French expedition to lift the ships of Napoleons fleet which sunk in the region of Cape Abukir in the Mediterranean. Under the agreement concluded between the Ministries of Culture of Egypt and France, all the treasures which would be lifted from the seabed, would be tranferred to the ownership of Egypt, but other finds would be divided between the two States.

40 *Ibid* (1985) at p. 254. "Not having obtained permission to dispose of the wrecks from the flag State, the requesting State found no benefit in recovering them and giving them to the flag State". In Starkle's view, the jurisdiction of the flag State does not extend beyond the moment of abandonment by the owner. Ownership and jurisdiction are inextricably linked in the case of public vessels, where there seems to be a presumption of non-abandonment. This presumption should also apply to private vessels. Starkle, *op. cit.* note 29 at p. 508. See also Gelberg, *op. cit.* note 28, who argues that the goods which have sunk on the high seas are considered to be *res nullius* after the passage of a given time.

41 In *Robinson v. The Western Australian Museum,* Gibbs, J. argued that: "It would be relevant to inquire to what extent it [the Gilt-Dragon] remained distinguishable from the seabed and to what extent it had retained its original character as a ship." [1977] 51 *A.L.J.R.* 806 at p. 816. The pleadings in the case, however, did not permit an answer to be given to such enquiries. Finally, in von Münch's opinion, *op. cit.* note 29 at p. 195, the recognition of flag State jurisdiction over wrecks should be limited, *inter alia*, to cases where the flag State has knowledge of the place where the wreck lies. Although knowledge of the precise location of the wreck-site is not required, wrecks of the 16th or the 18th century do not appear to fall within this category of sunken vessels.

42 See also Roucounas, *op. cit.* note 28 at p. 331, who argues that: "It would therefore be more cogent with the interests at stake to say that, depending on the circumstances of each case, the flag State would have to relinquish ownership in the case of warships. Some writers maintain that States must indeed relinquish their ownership over warships but we do not have enough evidence to support this position".

43 Even Miller who is in favour of the protection of marine archaeology as one of the freedoms of the high seas, admits that such a regulation "would nevertheless leave a gap with respect to protection of marine archaeological sites from treasure hunters and marauders who might wreak irreparable damage on the site and archaeological objects. But this gap, I submit, would be better filled through international agreement than by extension of national sovereign rights". *Op. cit.* note 11 at p. 34.

44 See further Conforti, B., "Does freedom of the seas still exist?", *I.Y.I.L.* (1975) pp. 5-24 at p. 12.

45 "The most likely explanation is that the text in the Draft (then) Convention is based on a proposal inspired by the Spanish version of the Geneva Convention and translated into the other languages without looking at the official text of the Geneva Convention in these languages". Treves, T., "Drafting the LOS Convention", 5 *Marine Policy* (1981) pp. 273-276 at p. 274. In contrast, it has been argued that the wording of article 87 is more precise and, therefore, more suitable. See Momtaz, *op. cit.* note 1 at p. 398.

46 This is revealed in both article 89 and article 241, which state respectively that: "No State may validly purport to subject any part of the high seas to its sovereignty", and "marine scientific research activities shall not constitute the legal basis for any claim to any part of the marine environment or its resources." Although archaeological research does not qualify as marine scientific research, in this context it appears sufficiently analagous to justify the application of article 241 to archaeological operations.

47 Existing international instruments and national heritage laws providing for the suspension or the cessation of work in case of accidental discovery of cultural property in the course of construction projects, limit, in their majority, their scope of application to cultural property found landward of the outer limit of the territorial sea. See, for example, article 9 of the 1968 UNESCO Recommendation concerning the Preservation of Cultural Property Endangered by Public or Private Works, which reads: "Member States should give due priority to measures required for the preservation *in situ* of cultural property endangered by public or private works in order to preserve historical associations and continuity. When overriding economic or social conditions require that cultural property be transferred, abandoned or destroyed, the salvage or rescue operations should always include careful study of the cultural property involved and the preparations of detailed records." So far as finance is concerned, article 15 offers the following alternatives: "(a) The national or local authorities responsible for the safeguarding of cultural property should have adequate budgets to undertake the preservation or salvage of cultural property endangered by private or public works; or (b) the costs of preserving or salvaging cultural property endangered by public or private works, including preliminary archaeological research, should form part of the budget of construction costs; or (c) the possibility of combining the two methods mentioned in sub-paragraphs (a) and (b) above should be provided for." In the event of unusual costs due to the size or the complexity of the operations required, which will be the case in underwater operations "there should be possibilities of obtaining additional funds through enabling legislation, special subventions, a national fund for monuments or other appropriate means." See also the *Finnish* Act of Archaelogical Remains No. 295 of 17 June 1963 (sec. 13,14,15) and the *Swedish* Act No. 350 of 12 June 1942 concerning Ancient Monuments and Finds, as amended by Act No. 17/1967 and Act No. 589/ 1971. Section 8 of the latter provides that if an ancient monument or shipwreck not previously known is found "in the course of digging or other works" work must be immediately suspended. Under section 9, if an ancient

monument or shipwreck not previously known is affected by a "public or a large private work project" and a special investigation of it has to be undertaken or special measures taken in order to preserve it "the cost thereof shall be borne by those responsible for the project unless this is found to be unreasonable in view of special circumstances". Council of Europe, Parliamentary Assembly, *The Underwater Cultural Heritage*, Doc. 4200-E, Strasbourg 1978, Appendix III: "Analysis of Legislation in Individual Countries", pp. 91-135 at pp. 125-256. See also Prott, L.V. and O'Keefe, P.J., "Final Report on Legal Protection of the Underwater Cultural Heritage", *ibid* at pp. 72-96. So far as licensees of exploration or exploitation activities on the continental shelf are concerned, it must be noted that a number of coastal States oblige them to report the discovery of archaeological objects and to respect their national laws. Such practices are being discussed in chapter 7. Finally, articles 5 and 6 the 1992 Archaeological Convention (revised) provide for the conservation *in situ*, when feasible, of the archaeological heritage found during development work and the covering, from public sector or private sector resources, as appropriate, of the total costs of any necessary related archaeological operations. As noted, the revised Convention expands its scope of application to any area subject to the jurisdiction of the parties, including the continental shelf. The same applies to those national heritage laws which expand their scope of application to the outer limit of the continental shelf, and which are also discussed in chapter 7.

48 Decree No. 61-1547 of 26 December 1961 establishing the regime of shipwrecks. According to article 1: "Subject to international convention in force, the following shall constitute wrecks to which the present decree shall be applicable: (1) Vessels and aircraft abandoned as unseaworthy, together with their cargoes; (2) Abandoned ship's boats, gear, tackle, anchors, chains and fishing tackle and wreckage; (3) Goods jettisoned or lost overboard and generally all objects, *including those of ancient origin*, of which the owner has lost possession and which are either stranded on State-owned shore, or flotsam or jetsam found in territorial waters, *or flotsam and jetsam found in the high seas and brought back into territorial waters or onto the national seaboard"* (emphasis added). The translated text appears in Chabert, J. "How underwater archaeology is regulated in France" in UNESCO, *Underwater Archaeology: A Nascent Discipline*, Museums and Monuments XIII, Paris 1972, Appendix, pp. 297-306 at p. 300. Article 1 was not amended by the Decree No. 85-632 of 1985 which modified Decree No. 61-1547. C/f 59 *Semain Juridique* (1985) Pts. 2-4 [para. 57335]. Similarly, in *Spain* the Regulations in Matters of Salvage and Findings approved by Decree of 30 April 1967 applies to all salvors and to the owners of the vessels salvaged, when the ship or wreck in question enters a Spanish port, irrespective of the geographical place of the event. The same rule applies to "findings" i.e. to anything found or washed up, or floating in territorial waters or beyond which is brought in to a Spanish port. See Decree No. 984/67 of April 1967 approving Regulations for the Application of Law of 24 December 1962. (Mo. Marina, B.O. 17 Mayo) in XXI *Arranzadi - Nueve Diccionario de Legislacion RENT-SEGU*, (26404-27245) Editorali Aranzadi, Pamplona, 1977, para. 27008, pp. 759-764 and article 86(5) of Act No 27/1992

concerning national ports and merchant shipping: "In particular, the Ministry of Public Works shall be responsible for: Assistance, rescue and towing, maritime findings and removals, except in the case of military equipment or materials that may affect defense... without prejudice to any powers of the competent authorities in respect of findings or removals of historical, artistic or archaeological value". In *Australia,* the 1912 Navigation Act provides that any person who has found and taken possession of any wreck outside Australian territory and who brings it to Australia must give notice to the Receiver of Wreck. Where no owner establishes a claim to any wreck found in or brought into Australia and in the possession of a Receiver, within a year after it comes into the possession of the Receiver, the Receiver must sell it, deducting the expenses of sale and salvage, and pay the proceeds into a governmental fund. As argued, an Australian court would likely decide that the Receiver of Wreck is entitled to claim possession and to sell items recovered from wreck in areas outside the jurisdiction established by the Historic Shipwrecks Act 1976 that are brought to Australia. See International Committee on Cultural Heritage Law, *Report and Draft Convention on the Protection of the Underwater Cultural Heritage,* International Law Association 65th Conference, Cairo, Egypt 20-26 April 1992 at p. 6. As will be discussed below, the 1976 Act asserts control over historic shipwrecks situated "in Australian waters or in waters above the continental shelf". The same applies for the 1985 Law on the Spanish Historic Heritage, which expands Spanish jurisdiction over the archaeological and historical heritage found on the continental shelf. See *infra* chapter 7 at pp. 259-279, 289-290.

49   640 *F2d* 560, 567 (5th Cir. 1981). "The courts of the United States take jurisdiction, subject to some reservations imposed by their own application of the doctrine of *forum non conveniens,* of suits on maritime claims arising out of transactions and occurrences anywhere in the world." Gilmore, G. and Black, G., *The Law of Admiralty,* 2nd ed., The Foundation Press, Inc., Mineola, New York, 1975, at pp. 51-52. *Ibid* at pp. 566-567. See also *Treasure Salvors Inc. v. The Unidentified Wrecked and Abandoned Sailing Vessel ("Treasure Salvors I"),* 569 *F2d* 330 (5th Cir. 1978) at pp. 334-335. See further *Sobonis v. Steam Tanker Defencer,* 298 *F. Supp.* 631 (S.D.N.Y. 1969); *Barkas v. Cia Naviera Coronado, S.A.,* 126 *F. Supp.* 532 (S.D.N.Y. 1954); *The Bee,* 3 *F. Cas.* No. 1219 (D. Me. 1836). Federal courts have jurisdiction of all cases involving admiralty or maritime claims. Claims arising out of salvage operations - efforts to rescue or recover ships disabled or abandoned at a sea or to retrieve their cargo - are unquestionably within the admiralty jurisdiction of the federal courts. The subject matter jurisdiction granted by 28 *U.S.C.* para. 1333 is not limited to causes of action arising from events or occurrences on the territorial waters of the United States.

50   "The fact that the property which is the subject of the salvage effort is not within the territorial jurisdiction of the court, and thus not subject to an *in rem* decree, is irrelevant because the salvor's claim is not one *in rem,* seeking to recover against the vessel for salvage in which the *in rem* fiction is used to personify the vessel and treat it as party to the litigation. Although rights to the vessel

may be the subject of the dispute, the adverse parties in this situation are the competing salvors. Thus, since the court has jurisdiction over them, and the subject matter involves claims based on the maritime law of salvage and of finds, the court is fully competent to adjudicate the dispute regardless of the location of the salvage operations." *Ibid* at pp. 567-568. In *Treasure Salvors Inc. v. The Unidentified Wrecked and Abandoned Sailing Vessel*, 546 F. Supp. 919 (S.D. Fla. 1982) at pp. 928-929, the U.S. district court recognised a *quasi-in-rem* jurisdiction over the wreck of the Atocha as the contents of the ship, recovered from outside the district, were brought within the district, where several artifacts from the ship earlier had been arrested. Each artifact brought ashore was placed in the custody of the Court. The Court reasoned that eventually the entire contents of the ship would be placed in its custody within the district and so retained a *quasi-in-rem* jurisdiction over the contents of the vessel that would ripen into *in rem* jurisdiction as the salvors brought the last items ashore. Thus, the court had *in personam* jurisdiction over competing salvors, combined with vast array of artifacts properly arrested within district amounted to a qualified jurisdiction *in rem* which was likely to ripen into full *in rem* jurisdiction. See also *Indian River Recovery Co. v. The China, Her Appurtenances, Etc v. Ocean Watch, Intervenor*, 645 F. Supp. 141 (S.D. Fla. 1986); 1989 *AMC* 50, 52, where the district court held that it had no *in rem* jurisdiction over the vessel and its contents, since no items recovered from the China Wreck were arrested within the district of Delaware. Similarly, in *Platoro Limited, Inc. v. The Unidentified Remains of a Vessel*, 508 F.2d 1113, 1114 (5th Cir. 1975), the U.S. Court of Appeals, Fifth Circuit, held that the trial court did not have *in rem* admiralty jurisdiction where the salvaged articles were not located within the district and had not been located there at any time during pendency of the suit. In *Marex Titanic, Inc. and Titanic Ventures v. the Wrecked and Abandoned Vessel, Her Engines Etc., Believed to be the RMS Titanic, In Rem*, 1993 *AMC* 2798, the U.S. Court of Appeals, Fourth Circuit, reversed the decision of the district court and held that the district court erred in allowing competing salvors to intervene, vacating plaintiff salvor's warrant of arrest, and enjoining plaintiff salvor from interfering with intervening salvor after plaintiff had filed a voluntary dismissal. Titanic Ventures had agreed to the Court exercising *in personam* jurisdiction over it, and both parties agreed that this gave the court the authority to determine who had exclusive salvage rights to the *Titanic*. As already indicated, in 1985 a joint French/American expedition discovered the *Titanic*. In 1987, Titanic Ventures (a private American corporation) and IFREMER conducted a joint salvage operation that recovered 1.800 items from the wreck site. On August 7, 1992, Marex filed an action seeking to be named the sole and exclusive owner of any objects recovered from the *Titanic* or alternatively that it be granted a salvage award. In order to establish jurisdiction, he deposited two objects taken from the wreck. Titanic Ventures argued that Marex had obtained the warrant through factual misrepresentation and that the court should dismiss the case in deference of the French Government's prior exercise of jurisdiction.

51   1989 *AMC* 1955. The district court held that the salvor, Columbus-America, maintained a reasonable presence at the site during the three-month seasonal window for salvage operations, given the rough seas, sailing distances to a safe port, remoteness from repair facilities and assistance and the complexity of technology. It also achieved "telepossession" of the wreck by real time imaging and the use of robots, thus entitling it to the exclusive right of ownership of the salved artifacts. *Ibid* at p. 1958.

52   See King, M., "Admiralty Law: Evolving Legal Treatment of Property Claims to Shipwrecks in International Waters", 31 *Harvard J. Int'l L.* (1990) pp. 313-321, who argues that courts should carefully consider the international implications of the approach of the court before adopting it wholesale. However, even before Columbus-America, several commentators had argued that under the current jurisdictional rules, admiralty courts may base an assertion of exclusive *in rem* jurisdiction over wrecks in international waters on the doctrines of constructive presence and necessity: "When a court has personal jurisdiction over the intervenor, it can protect the first salvor's priority. But if the court does not have personal jurisdiction and the entire *res* cannot be brought into the territory, the court will be unable to protect the first salvor unless it can issue an injunction based upon its control of part of the vessel. At issue is whether a court may assert limited control over a vessel in international waters and enjoin interference with effort to bring it within the territorial jurisdiction of the court after the plaintiff has property filed a claim and has brought some portion of the *res* into the jurisdiction. Courts that have been presented with this quandry thus far have been able to issue the injunction by asserting *in personam* jurisdiction. Since, however, *in personam* jurisdiction is not often likely to be available where the wreck is in international waters, eliminating the territorial presence requirement may be justified under a theory of constructive presence or jurisdiction by necessity". Fry, J.P., "The Treasure Below: Jurisdiction over Salving Operations in International Waters", 88 *Columbia Law Review* ((1988) pp. 863-881 at p. 869. If the plaintiff salvor were not able to secure an injunction to protect its right as first salvor because the court lacked jurisdiction over the vessel or the intervenor, it would be forced to litigate in the home *forum* of every intervenor. The cost of multiple-forum litigation could lead the first salvor to abandon the salving operation. *Ibid* at p. 865. See also Alexander, B.E., "Treasure Salvage Beyond the Territorial Sea: An Assessment and Recommendations", 20 *J. Mar. L & Com.* (1989) pp. 1-19. As undersea world recovery operations have increased, competition between rival parties has led to conflict and inevitably to a surge of litigation concerning rights in offshore wrecks. In *Indian River, op. cit.* note 50, two parties sought the exclusive right to salvage a wreck lying outside State territorial waters but within the U.S. contiguous zone. The court allowed one party to continue non-commercial salvage operations and permanently enjoined opposing party from commercially salvaging the wreck. See also Del Bianco, H.P. (Jr.), "Underwater Recovery Operations in Offshore Waters: Vying for Rights to Treasure", 5/6 *Boston University International Law Journal* (1987/88) pp. 153-176 at p. 154. Finally, in *Martha's Vineyard Scuba Headquarters, Inc. v. The Unidentified, Wrecked and Abandoned*

Steam Vessel Etc., 1988 *AMC* 1109, the U.S. Court of Appeals, Fifth Circuit, held that the rules of the Convention on the International Regulations for Preventing Collisions at Sea (COLREGS) do not apply to a Panamanian-flag vessel in international waters, where Panamanian authorities did not object to her conducting salvage operations inside established traffic seperation lane leading to N.Y. It is immaterial that a U.S. domestic company may have benefited from those operations. The court held that there was no misconduct of the salvor which would preclude its right to receive objects salved from sunken wreck. In this case, one of the salvors commissioned a vessel flying the flag of Panama and sent it to the locus of the wreck. The vessel anchored in at an outbound lane of the NY Traffic Separation Scheme (TSS), a delineated international shipping route, in breach of the rules of the COLREGS.

53 [1975] 2 *Lloyd's Rep.* 338; 56 *I.L.R.* (1980) 40. See also Ress, G., "Die Bergung Kriegsversunkter Schiffe im Lichte der Rechtslage Deutschlands", *ZaöRV* (1975) pp. 363/374, who is critical of this decision, in particular of the choice of *lex fori* than the law of the flag State to determine the conditions of abandonment.

54 [1924] *P.* 78.

55 *Ibid* at p. 79. In O'Connell's view, *op. cit.* note 29 at p. 917, *The Tubantia* reveals that the law of salvage is applicable on the high seas even in the case of derelict of foreign origin, where there is jurisdiction over the defendant. The Tubantia was a Dutch ship found fifty miles from land and claimed by rival salvors. The plaintiffs were four aliens and one British subject, while the defendants were British subjects and were salving from a British ship. In contrast, see Fry, *op. cit.* note 52 at p. 869, footnote 44, who argues that: "Arguably, the court asserted some control over the unrecovered portion lying in international waters when it held that the vessel was in the first salvor's possession". Although the salvor had actual possession of only a portion of the *res*, the court concluded that the first salvor had possession of the unrecovered portion of the wreck, because "they were dealing with it as a whole".

56 *Ibid* at p. 87. In the court's opinion, HMS Thetis had shown that property could be derelict without being *a droit* of Admiralty. (1835) 3 *Hagg.* 228; 166 *Eng. Rep.* 390.

57 [1985] *T.L.R.*, November 30; [1986] 1 *Lloyd's L.R.* 132; *Pierce v. Bernis*, (1986) 2 *W.L.R.* 501 (Q.B. 1985); [1986] 1 *All Eng. Rep.* 1011. At the time of sinking, the Lusitania was the property of Cunard Steamship Company Ltd. The insurers had paid the owners in respect of the total loss and had acquired legal title to the ship. At the time of her loss the Lusitania contained two further categories of chattel - the personal property of the passengers and a quantity of general cargo - the contents. In 1982 salvage operations were performed on the wreck and about 94 items salved. Some of the items were agreed to be part of the vessel and others to the the the contents.

58 The court held that the relevant statutory provisions the Merchant Shipping Act 1894 paras. 518-522 and the Merchant Shipping Act 1906, s.72, contained no suggestion that the Crown had any interest in wreck found outside the territorial waters of the United Kingdom, since no such right was stated, nor any duty prescribed to deliver it to the Receiver of wreck. Since unclaimed wreck found

outside territorial waters did not vest in the Crown, there was a gap in the provisions for its disposal. The judge held that the contents of the Lusitania were wreck for the purpose of Part IX of the 1894 Act and that one had to turn to paras. 518-522 to discover how they should be dealt with. Section 72 of the Merchant Shipping Act 1906 provided that s.518 of the principal Act (that of 1894) shall apply to wreck found or taken possession of outside the limits of the United Kingdom, as it applies to wreck found or taken possession of within the limits of the United Kingdom. (But) it was clear that s.518 was concerned with the duties of a person who finds or takes possession of any wreck. It has no bearing on possessory title any more than on the title of the true owner. Before 1854, it appeared that a *droit* of admiralty was recognised in respect of all wreck ... wherever found. But this did not appear to have survived the 1894 Act. The old *droit* appeared to have been abandoned. On the implications of *The Lusitania* see Nash, M.L., "The Lusitania and its Consequences", 136 *New L.J.* (1986) pp. 317-319 and Lillington, S.D., "Wreck or wrecuum maris?" *Lloyd's Maritime and Commercial Law Quartely* (1987) pp. 267-273 at p. 272: "The effect of the *The Lusitania* has real practical significanca for maririme treasure hunters. Prior to it any such person raising property from under international waters and bringing it within the U.K. would have to comply with s.72 of the 1906 Act and deliver it up to the Receiver. Indeed, that remains true. However, formely he would then have received a salvage reward in an amount at the discretion of the Crown, but the Crown would have assserted a *droit* of Admiralty over the property. The situation now appears to be that salvage may not always be a relevant factor. Such a finder may now choose between asserting a finder's title or, alternatively, seeking out the true owner and claiming salvage."

59   Protection of Wrecks Act, 1973, *c. 30.* In particular see sections 1 and 3(1).

60   "When there is a competition between these several legal systems, the resulting questions are to be resolved by the choice of law rules of the *forum.* The problem is that in most legal systems these rules are silent on the subject, and so they must be inferred from basic principles". O'Connell, *op. cit.* note 29 at p. 911. In Eleazer's view: "Reduced to its essential context, salvage of vessels and cargoes concerns relationships between individual owners on the one hand and salvors on the other. Recovery of property at sea then, is a problem of private international law. The core issue of private international law is what approach to dispute resolution is most effective, resort to conflicts of law solutions, giving wide play to the divergencies in municipal law, or multilateral convention by which nations agree to bring their own law into conformity with internationally established norms ... In salvage disputes arising over transactions on the high seas, international uniformity is a desirable goal". Eleazer, H., "The Recovery of Vessels, Aircraft and Treasure in International Waters" in Wurfel, S.W. (ed.), *Some Current Sea Law Problems*, University of North Carolina, Sea Grant Publication, 1975, UNC-SG-75-06, pp. 26-38 at p. 28.

61   Tribunale di Sciacca, Sentenza 9 gennaio 1963, reprinted in 86 *Foro Italiano* (1963) pp. 1317-1320 as well as in 30 *Rivista de diritto della navigazione* (1964) No. 2 pp. 352-363.

62 *Ibid* at p. 1317.
63 The reasoning of the Tribunal raised a lot of discussions among legal scholars in Italy. In particular see Cartei, R., "Rinvenimento di oggetti archeologici in alto mare", 30 *Rivista de diritto della navigazione*, (1964) pp. 352-363 and Martini, G., "Ritrovamenti in mare di relitti e di cose di interesse artistico o storico", 64 *Il diritto marittimo* (1964) pp. 284-319 at pp. 308-314.
64 See Council of Europe, *Explanatory Report of the European Convention on Offences relating to Cultural Property*, Strasbourg, 1985 at p. 16: "Sub-paragraph *f* refers to cultural property reported or believed to be in the territory of the State in question at the time when attention was first given to it in modern times".
65 Even in 1959, the reduction in the field of application of the regime of the high seas was described as its "decomposition". See further Cocatre-Zilgien, A., "La répression des infractions commises en haute mer en temps de paix", XV *Revue egyptienne de droit international* (1959) pp. 71-90.
66 Brown, *op. cit.* note 6 at pp. 522-523.
67 See Rozakis, C.L., *The Law of the Sea as Developed through the Claims of the Coastal State*, Papazisis Publishing Co., Athens, 1976 at pp. 46-47 (in Greek).
68 Conforti, *op. cit.* note 44 at p. 12. See also Dupuy, R.J., "The Convention on the Law of the Sea and the New International Economic Order", 3/4 UNESCO, *Impact of science on society* (1984) pp. 313-325 (special issue on "Research, international law and the sea in man's future") and Negreponte, J.D., "Who Will Protect Freedom of the Seas?" 86 *Department of State Bulletin* (1986) No. 2115, pp. 41-43. Negreponte, who is in favour of the freedom of the seas, argues that: "The freedom of the seas was not given to mankind; it was won – through scholarly and legal debate and in naval engagements".
69 Rozakis, *op. cit.* note 67.

CHAPTER 7

The Continental Shelf and
the Exclusive Economic Zone

THE GENEVA CONVENTION ON THE CONTINENTAL SHELF (1958)

The right to conduct archaeological research over the continental shelf

The CSC does not deal specifically with the underwater cultural heritage. Nevertheless, articles 2 and 5 are of interest in so far as the right to conduct archaeological research over the continental shelf is concerned.

Exclusion of underwater cultural property from the notion of "natural resources" and the sovereign rights of the coastal State
Article 2 of the CSC determines the nature and the scope of coastal rights over the continental shelf. Paragraphs 1 and 4 read respectively:

> "(1) The coastal State exercises over the continental shelf sovereign rights for the purpose of exploring it and exploiting its natural resources.
> (4) The natural resources ... consist of the mineral and other non-living resources of the seabed and subsoil together with living organisms belonging to sedentary species..."

A primary question to be discussed is whether underwater cultural property qualifies as a "natural resource" of the seabed and thus come within the ambit of the Convention. The meaning to be attached to natural resources gave rise to lengthy discussions in the course of the preparatory work of the Fourth Committee of the First UN Conference on the Law of the Sea (UNCLOS I), where proposals of a most different character and scope had been submitted.[1] Amongst others, the question was asked whether the definition could be interpreted to include inanimate objects, such as cargoes and wrecks of ships which might be found on the seabed. The answer was that such an interpretation was ruled out by the use of the term "non-living resources". Wrecks and cargoes could on no account be described as "resources".[2] This interpretation is confirmed by the ILC's Commentary on draft article 68 (now article 2), which refers to "natural resources" without, however, defining the term. The Commentary reads: "It is clearly understood that the rights of the coastal State do not cover objects, such as wrecked ships and their cargoes (including bullion) lying on the seabed or covered by the sand of the subsoil."[3] Although the quoted text refers exclusively to wrecks and their cargoes, the latter appear "sufficiently analogous to archaeological objects to justify an inference that the drafters intended to exclude them from the category of natural resources."[4]

The majority of legal scholars favour a restrictive interpretation of the term. There are commentators, however, who argue that an extensive interpretation of "natural resources" so as to include underwater cultural property is permissible. Castagné[5] offers one of the earliest and most discussed proposals. In his opinion, the general terms employed by the CSC serve perfectly the needs of underwater archaeology; nothing is opposed to the inclusion of archaeological remains in the notion of "natural resources" as defined in article 2(4) nor to the interpretation of archaeological research as "exploitation" of these resources. The enrichment of the cultural heritage is a factor of both economic development and social and intellectual progress, not to count the educational and touristical perspectives.[6] Meenan argues that natural resources should be liberally construed to include archaeological resources[7], while in Auburn's view they should be deemed to include archaeological and cultural artefacts and wrecks not less than 100 years old.[8]

One should also mention *Treasure Salvors Inc. v. Abandoned Sailing Vessel Believed to be the Nuestra Señora de Atocha*[9], which is the first US case to discuss the legal issues surrounding the removal of relics from the continental shelf. Treasure Salvors Inc., a Florida corporation, sued for possession and confirmation of title to an unidentified wrecked and abandoned vessel, thought to be the Nuestra Señora de Atocha, a Spanish vessel which sank in the sea off the Marquesas Keys in 1622. The wreck was located on the continental shelf outside the territorial waters of the United States. The United States intervened, and claimed title to the wreck upon the following grounds: (a) application of the Antiquities Act[10] to objects located on the outer continental shelf area of the United States through the operation of the Outer Continental Shelf Lands Act (OCSLA)[11]; (b) exercise of sovereign prerogative through either the Abandoned Property Act[12] or the aforementioned Antiquities Act. The district court rejected both claims. With respect to the rule of sovereign prerogative it held that although it is recognised by American courts, it must be explicitly asserted in legislation. In the court's opinion, neither the Abandoned Property Act nor the Antiquities Act provided the basis for such an assertion.[13] Since "the property of the wreck involved in this case is neither within the jurisdiction of the United States nor owned and controlled by our government",[14] the application of both Acts was rejected. With respect to the Federal Government's claim that the site in question was located on lands within the jurisdiction and control of the United States by operation of the OCSLA, the court stated that the latter "asserts jurisdiction over the minerals in and under the continental shelf"[15] and rejected the claim. The court read the OCSLA in the light of the subsequently ratified CSC and relied on the ILC's 1956 Commentary to exclude wrecks from the definition of natural resources. In the court's opinion, the CSC supersedes any incompatible terminology in the OCSLA as it was adopted by the United States after the passage of the latter. More specifically, it became effective as law in the United States eleven years after the passage of the OCSLA. The same conclusions were reached by the Court of Appeals.[16]

The importance of *Treasure Salvors* is twofold. First, it supports the view that under the CSC coastal jurisdiction is confined to the exploration and exploitation of the natural resources of the seabed, which exclude wrecks and their cargoes from their scope, and second, it establishes that abandoned shipwrecks found on the outer continental shelf of the United States are governed by the traditional law of salvage.[17] It is not surprising, therefore, that it raised a lot of discussions in the United States. A number of scholars agreed with the approach, reasoning and the holding of the court.[18] Others considered it as an obstacle to the protection of cultural resources. It has been argued that "although the court drew acceptable inferences from the law it cited, it inexplicably failed to discuss relevant and significant trends towards the protection of cultural property in the international sector"[19] and that "through its interpretation of the CSC the court in the instant case reasonably rejects the government's attempt to provide substantial protection of the public interest in antiquities on the outer continental shelf reserving such protection to specific congressional legislation. While the Congress may be reluctant to weaken the Geneva accord, the realisation that other nations have expanded jurisdiction despite it and that such legislation would not strike at the heart of the Convention, may overcome this reluctance."[20] Finally, Butler argues that the court made a substantive addition to the CSC by elevating Commentary which is not part of the official Convention to the status of law.[21] In his opinion, the court did not consider shipwrecks as a judicially adopted exception to the general jurisdiction over the seabed, but it implicitly treated them as part of the superjacent waters from which they come.[22]

To sum-up, under the CSC and in the light of the preparatory work of the ILC, underwater cultural property cannot be interpreted as a "natural resource" of the seabed. As a result, it does not fall within the scope of the sovereign rights of the coastal State. Recourse to the ILC's Commentary does not amount, as argued, to a substantive addition to the CSC by elevating it to the status of law. On the contrary, this approach is in absolute consistency with the Vienna Convention on the Law of Treaties (1969), which states in article 32 that recourse may be taken to supplementary means of interpretation when the meaning of a term is ambiguous or obscure.[23]

Exclusion of archaeological research from the sovereign right to explore the continental shelf
As already seen, article 2(1) recognises the sovereign right of the coastal State to explore its continental shelf. Under a literal interpretation, the coastal State would enjoy the sovereign right to explore its continental shelf for any purpose, including archaeological research. This would mean that archaeological research on the continental shelf would require the permission of the coastal State, while the removal of the discovered items would remain open to everyone, as these are not natural resources. *Vice versa*, foreign vessels would be entitled to remove underwater relics from the continental shelf, but they would not have the right to search for them. One would, therefore, agree with Caflisch that "this interpretation is absurd and must be rejected: if third States are permitted to recover antiquities from the shelf, they must *a fortiori* be entitled to discover them."[24] This interpretation may also be rejected if it is considered in the light of the *travaux préparatoires* of the CSC. Draft article 68 read: "The coastal State exercises over the continental shelf sovereign rights for exploring and exploiting its natural resources ...".[25] The change in the wording of article 2(1) was made by the Drafting Committee and was not therefore debated by the Fourth Committee itself. On this basis, Prof. Brown argues that the ILC Commentary on draft article 68 would appear to be still valid: "[The Commission] was unwilling to accept the sovereignty of the coastal State over the seabed and subsoil of the continental shelf... the text as now adopted leaves no doubt

that the rights conferred upon the coastal State cover all rights necessary for and connected with the exploration and exploitation of the natural resources of the continental shelf".[26] In contrast, Castagné asserts that underwater operations for archaeological purposes undoubtedly constitute "exploration" of the seabed.[27]

Denial of the consent regime of the coastal State
Article 5(1) and (8) read respectively:

> "(1) The exploration of the continental shelf and the exploitation of its natural resources must not result in any unjustifiable interference with navigation, fishing or the conservation of the living resources of the sea, nor result in any interference with fundamental oceanographic or other scientific research carried out with the intention of open publication.
>
> (8) The consent of the coastal State shall be obtained in respect of any research concerning the continental shelf and undertaken there. Nevertheless, the coastal State shall not normally withhold its consent if the request is submitted by a qualified institution with a view to purely scientific research into the physical or biological characteristics of the continental shelf, subject to the provision that the coastal State shall have the right, if so desired, to participate or to be represented in the research, and that in any event the results shall be published."

The interpretation problems that arise here concern the interaction of the two provisions[28] and the meaning to be attributed to the terms "fundamental oceanographic or other scientific research" and "research concerning the continental shelf and undertaken there". Can they be construed in such a way so as to include archaeological research within their scope?

Fundamental oceanographic and other scientific research. The CSC fails to define the terms "fundamental oceanographic" and "other scientific research". However, a close examination of the records of the debate in the Fourth Committee shows that both concepts refer to research related to the physical and biological characteristics of the continental shelf.[29] The distinction between "fundamental oceanographic" and "other scientific" was never intended to include research unrelated to the natural environment. As explained, the reason for the addition of the term "other scientific research" was the following: "In a number of instances marine research of great value had combined biological and meteorological as well as oceanographic elements."[30] In other words, the term "other scientific research" is also confined to the biological, geological and physical characteristics of the marine environment and should not be interpreted extensively so as to include archaeological research. Does this mean that in the exercise of its sovereign rights over the continental shelf the coastal State is entitled to interfere with archaeological operations conducted by third States? If this conclusion is correct, the latter would be granted extensive powers over the conduct of archaeological activities in this area. However, such an interpretation would contradict the nature of coastal powers over the continental shelf, which are expressed to be confined to the exploration and exploitation of the natural resources of the seabed. Article 3 of the CSC emphasises the residual status of the area as high seas by providing that:

> "The rights of the coastal State over the continental shelf do not affect the legal status of the superjacent waters as high seas, or that of the airspace above those waters."

Since marine archaeology is an exercise of a freedom of the high seas, it would be reasonable to assume that the exercise of coastal rights over the continental shelf should not result in any unjustifiable interference with archaeological research undertaken by third States. By the time of the adoption of the Geneva Conventions, the lack of adequate underwater technology made the search for, and removal of, underwater cultural property far too remote to create juridical problems. Consideration was thus taken only for the interference of coastal sovereign rights with the traditional freedoms of the seas, such as navigation, fishing, conservation of the living resources, marine scientific research and laying of submarine cables or pipelines.[31] It seems, therefore, that in the exercise of its resource-related jurisdiction, the coastal State must not interfere unjustifiably with the conduct of archaeological research by third States. So far as the exercise of the rights of flag States over the continental shelf is concerned, the CSC is silent. Unlike coastal States, flag States are not required to avoid interference with the resource-related activities of the coastal State in the exercise of their right of free use of the seas. This obligation, however, can be inferred from the principle that the coastal State enjoys over its continental shelf sovereign rights for the purpose of exploring it and exploiting its natural resources. In case conflict between the two activities is unavoidable, the priority would lie in favour of the latter. The very use of the term "sovereign right" raises strong presumptions in its favour.[32]

Research concerning the continental shelf and undertaken there. Article 5(8) requires the consent of the coastal State for "any research concerning the continental shelf and undertaken there". Once again, the Convention fails to define the terms employed. At first sight, archaeological research conducted on the continental shelf appears to fall within the ambit of article 5(8) which refers to "any" research. A literal interpretation of paragraph 8 would also be in accordance with article 2(1) which attributes sovereign rights for the purpose of exploring the continental shelf ("exploring it"). Nevertheless, in the light of the general scheme of the CSC, which confines coastal rights to natural resource-exploration and exploitation, the above interpretation should be rejected.[33] Since archaeological objects are not considered "natural resources" of the seabed, the drafters of the Convention could not have intended to submit to coastal jurisdiction activities related to them and, therefore, "the word research cannot be interpreted as including their discovery."[34] In discussing the exercise of archaeological research over the continental shelf, Prof. Brown called for conventional clarification of the language of article 5(8), the vagueness of which leaves many issues unsettled. Clearly, however, "an argument can be made for differentiating research concerning the archaeological remains from research concerning the continental shelf *simpliciter* on the basis that archaeological research is not in fact at all concerned with the continental shelf or its natural resources."[35]

In contrast, Castagné argues that archaeological research is "purely scientific research", if it is considered in the light of the knowledge acquired and the advanced techniques employed; an extensive interpretation of the CSC is, therefore, logically required.[36] Along the same lines, Michael claims that even if their assimilation to "natural resources" is accepted with difficulty, archaeological and historical objects represent economic wealth so that the consent of the coastal State will always be required.[37] These arguments are not valid within the general framework of the CSC, where there is nothing to indicate that everything that has economic value and is situated on the continental shelf is subject to the sovereign rights of the coastal State. Vallat's argument that "anything of value might be included in 'natural resources', and any use or interference with the subsoil or sea bed might equally be regarded as a use of or interference with their natural resources",[38] was made in 1946 before the adoption of the CSC. Finally, in Korthals Altes' view, a marginal control can at most be read in article 5. The control envisaged consists "in refusing consent only if the requested research is prone to interfere with normal exploration and exploitation of the continental shelf or in stopping research if such interference has already taken place."[39]

As a general rule, the consent of the coastal State will not be required for the conduct of archaeological research over the continental shelf. The position may become complicated in relation to devices that are employed both in archaeological research and in other oceanographical surveys, such as the photographic sonar.[40] If it is considered that marine archaeology is a multi-disciplinary science which derives from and contributes to a wide range of applied sciences, it will be very difficult to draw the line between archaeological research and research concerning the continental shelf *simpliciter*. Most importantly, which will be the criteria on the basis of which the nature of research will be determined? The capacity of installation or its declared purpose? There is obviously room for conflict, as coastal States would insist upon the capacity-criterion, while flag States would assert the declared purpose as the determining factor. The coastal State may, therefore, require its prior authorisation for the operation of devices that are capable of providing data on the resources of the continental shelf. It can easily prove that it has a legitimate interest in controlling such research under article 5(8). In this context, the demand of the coastal State to be informed in advance of all the scientific research to be conducted on its continental shelf and to express its consent on the methods to be employed is regarded as being justifiable, even if the research in question takes place in principle in the superjacent waters.[41] Due to the vague language of article 5(8) there is a diversity of opinion on whether *physical* contact with the continental shelf is the only interpretation of the expression "research concerning the continental shelf and undertaken there".[42] With respect to archaeological research, this debate is of limited importance as the former does not fall within the notion of "research" under article 5(8).[43] Nevertheless, the coastal State should be *informed* about the nature of operations due to take place on its continental shelf.[44]

Further complications may arise from the fact that most underwater remains are half buried under sand and concretion. Although the ILC's Commentary made it clear that all wrecks, regardless of their position on the seabed, are excluded from coastal rights, the location of archaeological remains in marine deposits leaves room for arguments that the search for their discovery or their removal interferes with the resource-related rights of the coastal State. It has thus been argued that: "Legislators have a simple weapon to control the activities of marine archaeologists on the continental shelf, and that is to regulate the disturbance of the seabed. So, a wreck site embedded in coral could be immunised by the expedient of forbidding interference with the coral, which is a 'natural resource' of the continental shelf."[45]

In conclusion, the fact that archaeological research entails contact with the seabed could create difficulties in practice. Coastal States may claim that archaeological operations interfere with their resource-orientated rights and deny the right of flag States to conduct archaeological research on their continental shelf without their consent. The practice of some Latin-American States which confiscate every man-made object recovered from their continental shelf as evidence of illegitimate exercise of exploration activities in the area, is illustrative of this attitude.[46]

Unilateral expansion of coastal jurisdiction over underwater cultural property on the continental shelf

Legitimacy of claims

Attempts have been made to justify the exercise of coastal jurisdiction over underwater cultural property on the outer continental shelf either on the assumption that coastal States enjoy rights of ownership over their submerged lands or by advancing the legal vacuum theory in the field of cultural heritage law. The first argument was made in relation to U.S. law, in particular the Submerged Lands Act (SLA) and the OCSLA. Since these acts grant plenary control over the seabed and subsoil of the continental shelf, "it is not unreasonable to conclude that jurisdiction over the seabed and the subsoil should include jurisdiction over the underwater archaeological resources located therein. At any rate, it is a fundamental tenet of property law that abandoned property lodged in the soil belongs to the owner of the soil."[47] This argument is of limited practical significance as, first, it exclusively concerns U.S. law, and, second, it has been discounted both by *Treasure Salvors*, which ruled that the CSC supersedes any incompatible terminology of the OCSLA by being a later statute, and the ASA, which excludes shipwrecks found on the continental shelf from its scope. The assertion of federal ownership over shipwrecks on the outer continental shelf proposed in a number of earlier bills, was rejected on the basis that it would raise substantial international and federal law questions.[48] Nevertheless, as an argument it warrants attention as it may be employed as a basis for justifying coastal claims over archaeological objects on the continental shelf. As noted, the

CSC attributes to the coastal State sovereign rights to explore its continental shelf and to exploit its natural resources; it does not confer rights of ownership nor does it recognise the exercise of coastal sovereignty over the area. Rights of ownership are of a fundamentally different nature and are accorded by domestic law. The notion of sovereign rights is less comprehensive than the notion of sovereignty, which could justify the vesting of the property in the State as a vesting of the sovereign right of dominion. Even within the territorial sea, the competence of the coastal State to regulate access to underwater cultural property is regarded as a corollary of the exercise of its sovereignty over the area; it is not related in any way to rights of ownership over the seabed and the subsoil.[49] Consequently, arguments, such as "abandoned property lodged in the soil belongs to the owner of the soil", based on analogies from the theory of property regarding land antiquities, are of no importance with regard to relics found on the continental shelf.

Under the second line of reasoning, "the drafters of the Conventions intended to leave regulation of activities concerning submerged antiquities to other legal processes. If this conclusion is valid it would be entirely appropriate for a State to unilaterally legislate regulation of exploitation of underwater archaeological resources."[50] This statement appears to advance the legal vacuum theory in the field of cultural heritage law; "if there is an occurrence that is not covered by existing international law, then the State affected by this transpiration is free to formulate rules to meet the problems created."[51] However, the high seas is not an area where a legal vacuum exists and which is to be filled by the legal order of the coastal State. The applicable legal order on the high seas is the legal order of the flag or the national State. All States are free to use the high seas for peaceful purposes. "Since international authority does not exist in any visible form, all authority which is actually exercised must in fact be national, but on the high seas it is not as it is within State territory, the expression of uncontrolled or sovereign power. It is exercised, as it were, by delegation from a higher law to which the national law of every particular State must conform."[52] Since the sovereign rights of the coastal State do not cover underwater cultural property, recovery operations are subject to the legal regime of the high seas (see the residuary rule of article 3 of the CSC).

A broad interpretation of the term "natural resources" would also grant the coastal State the necessary jurisdictional powers to control access to marine archaeological sites on the continental shelf. This interpretation is not permissible within the general framework of the CSC. However, given the fact that only a few States have become parties to the Optional Protocol of Signature concerning the Compulsory Settlement of Disputes, and the vaguenesss of articles 2 and 5 of the CSC, a State which is not a party to the said Protocol may interpret these provisions virtually at will. It is notable that the Australian Historic Shipwrecks Act 1976, which extends Australia's competence to the continental shelf, provides in section 28 that: "Subject to the obligations of Australia under international law, including obligations under any agreement between Australia and another country or countries, this Act extends according to its tenor to foreigners and to foreign ships (including foreign hovercraft and any similar foreign craft)".[53] Since international law prohibits the application of national heritage legislation in this area, it has been argued that section 28 in effect nullifies the application of the Act on the continental shelf.[54]

Unilateral claims to jurisdiction over cultural property found on the continental shelf can only be justified as part of the more general process of the creation of a rule of customary law. Under the CSC, the assertion of such claims may provoke an international controversy, the consequences of which could spread at different levels.

International and national implications
At international level, the coastal State will not be responsible simply by asserting jurisdiction over underwater cultural property on the continental shelf. As a rule, the mere act of passing legislation is not creative of responsibility. The responsibility of a State for acts or omissions of the legislature arises from the *implementation* of legislation which is in breach of international law. Normally, in the case of injury to aliens a claimant must establish damage consequent on the implementation of legislation. Nevertheless, as argued by Prof. Schwarzenberger: "It is a matter of argument whether the mere existence of such legislation or only action under it constitutes the breach of an international obligation. Sufficient relevant *dicta* of the World Court exist to permit the conclusion that the mere existence of such legislation may constitute a sufficient proximate threat of illegality to establish a claimant's legal interest in the proceedings for at least a declaratory judgment."[55] In practice, as with most maritime claims, the validity of claims over cultural property on the continental shelf is ultimately a question of opposability. They will still be valid *vis-à-vis* States which have aquiesced in them.[56]

At national level, the issue arises whether and, if yes, to what extent, domestic courts will give effect to such claims. The obligation of domestic courts to apply international law can be dealt with only within the national legal system of each State. In exercising their competence to determine the manner of giving effect to international obligations on the municipal level, States use different methods which are influenced by monist or dualist doctrines.[57] In most States, treaties have the same status as national statutes so that the relation between them is governed by the traditional rules of statute interpretation. The "incorporated", in case of a convention, ratified international law prevails over existing laws which might be opposed to it; a later law, however, may nullify or modify the international law on the basis of the principle of *lex posterior derogat legi priori*. In *Treasure Salvors*, the court applied traditional rules of statute interpretation[58] and held that the CSC superseded any incompatible terminology in the OCSLA on the basis that it was a later statute, i.e., the CSC became law in the USA eleven years later and repealed prior statutes on the same subject. The OCSLA was interpreted in a way that was compatible with the CSC, namely the jurisdictional provision of the OCSLA was limited to natural resources rights on and under the continental shelf.[59] In other States, the Constitution provides for the priority of treaties over national law so that the ratified international conventions, when entering into force, have a superior legal status to other domestic statutes, i.e., they supersede both prior and later domestic statutes.[60] The majority of the States, however, apply the "doctrine of incorporation" in its original form.

So far as the application of foreign law by domestic courts is concerned, it appears that there is no rule of international law which forbids a court to examine the international validity of a foreign law.[61] The situation may, therefore, arise where the courts of a third State would have to consider whether they should recognise or apply the extended heritage legislation of the coastal State, i.e., the court of a third State has jurisdiction on a contract made by one of its nationals to sell artefacts raised illegally from the continental shelf of a State which has expanded its antiquities legislation over this area. Will it consider the contract as contrary to public policy or will it hold that such legislation - the one that the contract is in violation of - should not be recognised as contrary to international law?[62] Although this issue can only be answered on the basis of the national law of each State and the therein applicable legal order, it seems unlikely that courts will uphold such a legislation.[63]

Obligation to report the accidental discovery of cultural properties during mineral exploration and exploitation activities

A small group of States oblige the licencees of oil and mineral exploration and exploitation activities to report the accidental discovery of cultural property on the continental shelf to the competent authorities and to respect relevant national laws. Such practices should not be considered as a unilateral extension of the heritage legislation of the States concerned, but rather as the undertaking of protective measures in the exercise of their resource-related rights. Only the licencees of petroleum exploration and exploitation projects are obliged to respect such regulations; other sea-users operating in the continental shelf area are not affected as they do not operate under the municipal law of the coastal State.

According to section 44 of the Royal Decree of 8 December 1972 relating to Exploration and Exploitation of Petroleum in the Seabed and Substrata of the Norwegian Continental Shelf:

> "Any discovery having historical interest, such as shipwrecks etc. made during exploration for the exploitation of petroleum, shall immediately be reported to the Ministry. The activity must not damage or destroy any such discovery (see Act of 29th June 1951 No. 3 relating to antiquities). The Ministry may issue orders as to the procedure to be observed in treatment of such discovery."[64]

Similarly, Greek Law No. 468 of 10/12 November 1976 on Prospecting, Exploration and Exploitation of Petroleum (Hydrocarbons) and the Settlement of Related Matters enables the Greek State to oblige the licencees of mineral exploration or exploitation projects to respect its antiquities legislation.[65] In the Netherlands, all licences for the exploration and exploitation of mineral resources of the Dutch part of the continental shelf include clauses for protecting the cultural heritage,[66] while in the United States, the Department of the Interior has sponsored surveys for the location of prehistoric sites in the process of gas and oil exploration on the outer continental shelf.[67] Similar protective measures have been adopted by Denmark, Israel, Libya and Thailand.[68]

THE UN CONVENTION ON THE LAW OF THE SEA (1982)

The Continental Shelf

Legal status
The 1982 Convention introduced substantial alterations to the legal regime
of the continental shelf, especially with respect to definition and delimitation.[68a] However, regarding coastal rights over the underwater cultural
heritage, the identical language of article 77(1) and (4) to that of article 2(1)
and (4) of the CSC indicates that no change took place. The sovereign rights
of the coastal State do not cover objects of an archaeological and historical
nature which are excluded from the notion of "natural resources" of the
seabed. This is confirmed by the *travaux préparatoires* of article 303 which
initially concerned the attribution of sovereign rights over the continental
shelf for the purpose of protecting archaeological and historical objects. The
examination of the records of the Conference leaves no doubt that the latter
do not fall within the continental shelf regime or that of the EEZ.[69]

The same applies to archaeological research which is excluded from the
scope of marine scientific research and the consent regime. Article 246(2)
of the 1982 Convention reads: "Marine scientific research in the exclusive
economic zone and on the continental shelf shall be conducted with the
consent of the coastal State". In discussing the CSC, it was pointed out that
article 5(8) creates interpretational problems due to its vague language.
Interpreted extensively, archaeological exploration could fall within the
notion of "research concerning the continental shelf and undertaken there"
and the consent regime of the coastal State. These problems appear to have
been avoided under article 246, which simply refers to "marine scientific
research". Within the framework of the 1982 Convention, archaeological
research does not fall within this notion and is thus excluded from the
consent regime of article 246. Nevertheless, as previously indicated, problems
may appear in practice as most States require their consent for the undertaking of any research on the continental shelf.

It would seem, therefore, that beyond the 24-mile line and up to the outer
continental shelf limit, marine archaeology would be exercised as a freedom
of the high seas. However, the situation is not as clearcut since, under the
1982 Convention, the seabed under national jurisdiction is not only governed
by the continental shelf provisions, but also by the 200 EEZ which has

replaced the regime of the high seas. A distinction should thus be drawn between the legal regime of the seabed that falls within and beyond the EEZ.

Duty of States to protect archaeological and historical objects found on the continental shelf

Under article 303(1), States have the duty to protect archaeological and historical objects found at sea. The establishment of this duty may be used by coastal States as a basis for justifying the enactment of protective legislation in the exercise of their resource-related jurisdiction on the continental shelf. Along these lines, the Draft European Convention reads in article 17:

> "Each Contracting State, in the exercise of its jurisdiction over the exploration and exploitation of the natural resources of its continental shelf, shall take appropriate measures for the protection of underwater cultural property in accordance with the objectives of this Convention."

The adoption of this provision has been criticised on the following grounds: (a) it enables contracting States to take protective measures on the continental shelf, despite the fact that the Draft Convention does not apply in this area; (b) the entitlement of the coastal State to take such measures in exercising its resource-jurisdiction over the continental shelf will exacerbate the difficulties created by the establishment of the 24-mile "contiguous" archaeological zone. Under this view, the expansion of coastal jurisdiction is bound to lead to a conflict of competence between adjacent or opposite States, as in certain cases an object within the contiguous zone of one State would be located on the continental shelf of another State.[70] In the first place, draft article 17 does not extend the scope of application of the Draft Convention over the continental shelf.[71] The obligation of contracting States to take appropriate measures to protect underwater cultural property is confined to specific operations, and not to the actual area where these operations take place. It should, therefore, be regarded as an application of the general duty to protect the underwater cultural heritage. Furthermore, the expansion of an archaeological "contiguous" zone over the continental shelf should not automatically result in a conflict of competence, as coastal States do not, as a matter of positive law, enjoy any rights over archaeological objects situated on the continental shelf. The continental shelf regime is a natural resource regime, which does not apply, as such, to underwater cultural property, nor is it affected by its protection. In short, there should be no room for conflict as the same objects do not fall within different jurisdictions. Nevertheless, practical difficulties remain.

The Exclusive Economic Zone

Legal status

The EEZ is a concept of recent origin, which originally purported to put an end to the exploitation of the fisheries resources of developing countries by the long-distance fleets of the maritime powers. As elaborated by the 1982 Convention, the EEZ is an area beyond and adjacent to the territorial sea, whose breadth cannot exceed the 200nm limit and which is subject to a specific legal regime under which the rights and jurisdiction of the coastal State and the rights and freedoms of other States are governed by the relevant provisions of the Convention. The EEZ is a *sui generis* regime; it is subsumed neither under coastal sovereignty nor the freedom of the high seas.[72] The lack of a residual regime means that in this vast ocean area there are no presumptions in favour of either of the two fundamental principles of the law of the sea. The allocation of rights between coastal and flag States is now governed by the specific provisions of the 1982 Convention, which make a clear distinction between the resolution of conflicts regarding the attribution of residual rights[73] and conflicts between the exercise of rights which have been accorded to coastal and third States.[74]

Under article 56(1), the coastal State has sovereign rights for exploring and exploiting, conserving and managing the natural resources, whether living or non-living, of the waters superjacent to the seabed and of the seabed and its sub-soil, and with regard to other activities for the economic exploitation and exploration of the zone, such as the production of energy from the water, currents and winds. In addition, the coastal State has jurisdiction over artificial islands; marine scientific research; the protection of the marine environment, and other rights and duties provided for in the Convention (article 56(2)). In the light of article 56(3) which reads: "The rights set out in this article with respect to the seabed and subsoil shall be exercised in accordance with Part IV [continental shelf]", and the fact that archaeological research cannot be interpreted as marine scientific research nor does it fall within the scope of the "other rights and duties provided for in the Convention", the EEZ does not appear to have a direct effect on archaeological and historical objects found at sea.[75] However, there is an important difference between the legal regimes of the seabed within and beyond the 200 mile

EEZ. *Within the 200 mile limit*, there is no residual regime; both the allocation of rights between coastal and flag States and the reconciliation of conflicts takes place in accordance with the provisions of the 1982 Convention. *Beyond the 200 mile limit, and up to the outer limit of the continental shelf*, the residual regime is that of the freedom of the high seas. The issue, therefore, arises as to the conditions under which archaeological research would be exercised within the EEZ. Do flag States enjoy the right to undertake such operations?

Right to conduct archaeological research in the EEZ
Only the exercise of a limited number of freedoms in the EEZ are recognised by the 1982 Convention. According to article 58(1):

> "In the exclusive economic zone, all States whether coastal or land-locked, enjoy, subject to the relevant provisions of this Convention, the freedoms referred to in article 87 of navigation and overflight and of the laying of submarine cables and pipelines and other internationally lawful uses of the sea related to these freedoms, such as those associated with the operation of ships, aircraft and submarine cables and pipelines, and compatible with the other provisions of this Convention."

Marine archaeology is not included in the comprehensive list of freedoms, which all States enjoy in the EEZ.[76] This does not mean, however, that flag States are deprived of the right to conduct archaeological research. Any State may search for and remove archaeological objects in an EEZ, if no other State intends to undertake the same operations. Article 59 recognises the interests of *all* States in using the EEZ for purposes not specifically provided for in the Convention. In case of conflict between the interests of the coastal State and any other State or States, the consideration of equity and the evaluation of the interests involved will be employed to reconciliate the conflicting parties.

The content of article 59 is mainly procedural. First, it establishes the duty[77] to negotiate and, second, it adopts the criteria on the basis of which the reconciliation of conflicts over the allocation of rights within the EEZ should[78] be attempted. So far as the actual exercise of the activities in question is concerned, this "procedural rule" is not helpful. The only qualification to be read in article 59 is that the interests[79] of the States conducting such activities should not conflict with the interests of other States. In this context and in relation to the emplacement of military devices to the seabed, it has been argued that: "The State which emplaces military objects on the bed of the economic zone of another State is in a relatively better position than the other State. While it cannot be presumed that the emplacement of these objects conflicts with the interest of the coastal State, it is obvious that their removal or destruction by the coastal State conflicts with the interest of the emplacing State. Consequently, emplacement of objects may precede negotiations ... while objects may be removed or destroyed only if it is agreed or decided that they cannot be emplaced on the basis of equity and in the light of other factors indicated in article 59."[80]

These interesting observations are but one of the factors to be taken into account by the negotiators. The ICJ held in the *North Sea Continental Shelf Cases* that: "In fact, there is no legal limit to the considerations which States may take account of for the purpose of making sure that they apply equitable procedures and more often than not it is the balancing-up of all such considerations that will produce this result rather than reliance on one to the exclusion of all others. The problem of the relative weight to be accorded to different considerations naturally varies with the circumstances of the case."[81] With respect to the exercise of archaeological research and the right to control access to underwater sites, the following factors will be relevant to the settlement of the issue: (a) the existence of a cultural link between the cultural property in question and one of the parties of the dispute; (b) in case of relatively recent wrecks, the qualification of one of the parties as the flag State of the sunken vessel;[82] (c) the accommodation of the interests of the international community in the protection and preservation of the underwater cultural property; (d) interference with the exercise of the rights of the coastal or flag States. It should be emphasised that each case will be decided on its own merits and that there will be no room for the creation of precedents for the resolution of future conflicts. The underlying purpose of article 59 is, precisely, the ruling out of a residual regime in the EEZ.[83]

The effect of articles 60 and 80 upon the conduct of archaeological research in the EEZ/continental shelf
Article 60(1) reads:

> "In the exclusive economic zone the coastal State shall have the exclusive right to conduct and to authorise the construction, operation and uses of:

(b) installations and structures for the purposes provided in article 56 and other economic purposes.
(c) installations and structures which may interfere with the exercise of the rights of the coastal State in this zone",

while article 80 allows its *mutatis mutandis* application to the continental shelf. These provisions may provide a basis for coastal control over the removal of archaeological and historical objects, in the few cases where the conduct of the relevant operations requires the use of an installation or a structure. According to Migliorino[84], the term "other economic purposes" may be interpreted in such a way as to include the removal of underwater relics, the economic value of which is often high. However, such an interpretation is questionable within the general framework of the 1982 Convention. First, the *travaux préparatoires* of article 303 confirm that the expansion of coastal jurisdiction over archaeological objects on the continental shelf and/or the EEZ was not acceptable. Second, economic profit is not the main aim in preserving and protecting the limited cultural resources of the oceans. Third, an extensive interpretation of article 60(1)b would in effect subject under coastal control any activity involving the construction of installations on the continental shelf.[85] Article 60(1)c would appear to provide a more realistic basis for asserting control over archaeological operations involving the construction of installations which may interfere with coastal rights. Contrary to article 5(2) of the CSC, which refers exclusively to coastal control over installations and devices necessary for the natural-resource exploration and exploitation, the 1982 Convention expands coastal control over structures *potentially* capable of interfering with its rights. This makes the challenge of coastal competence even more difficult. It should always be borne in mind that, if the coastal State has not declared an EEZ, article 60 will not be applicable. However, the coastal State will still enjoy the right to control installations that may interfere with its rights, as prescribed by the continental shelf regime.[86]

To conclude, articles 60(1) and 80 grant the coastal State a wide range of powers over structures and installations on the EEZ/continental shelf.[87] Even if the direct application of these articles is not acceptable, article 60(1)c will be taken into consideration as a factor relevant to the exercise of archaeological research in the EEZ under article 59. Needless to say that those archaeological operations which do not involve the use of structures and installations on the continental shelf will not be affected.

Conflict between marine archaeology and other sea uses in the EEZ
As already seen, marine archaeology falls within the "grey" area over which
the Convention does not attribute rights or jurisdiction. The reconciliation
of *conflicts between rights attributed to coastal or flag States and such
activities* is not specifically regulated by the Convention. The reciprocal "due
regard rule" of articles 56(2) and 58(3) is applicable only to rights and duties
governed by the Convention, while article 59 deals with the attribution of
residual rights. It seems, however, that even such conflicts should be solved
on the basis of the latter which considers the rule of equity[88] as the fundamental criterion for the reconciliation of conflicing interests. The scope of
article 59 is broad enough to include cases other than those limited to the
allocation of residual rights as it appears in its title: "Basis for the resolution
of conflicts regarding the attribution of rights and jurisdiction in the exclusive economic zone." Conflicts between the latter and other rights provided
for by the Convention may well fall within its ambit.[89]

In case of conflict between marine archaeology and coastal rights or rights
allocated to flag States, the negotiators will proceed to an evaluation of the
different interests involved and the consideration of the rules of equity.
Inevitably, the priorities established by the 1982 Convention will be taken
into account as relevant factors to the dispute under article 59. Thus, the
very use of the term "sovereign rights" and the fact that certain freedoms
have been accorded as a right to flag States imply a priority in their favour.
It will, therefore, be very difficult for equitable considerations to restore
the balance.[90] However, even if the protection of archaeological objects
may not acquire priority in a particular case, there will at least be an obligation on the parties concerned to take the necessary measures to avoid unreasonable interference with them and, possibly, to undertake rescue operations
(c.f. article 303(1)).

Article 59 should also be deemed to be applicable in cases of *conflict
between marine archaeology and other activities over which the Convention
does not attribute rights or jurisdiction*. There is indeed only a limited
number of sea uses which are not regulated by the 1982 Convention. However, in the light of the recent development of underwater technology this
number could easily increase. Possible examples include the emplacement
of acoustic devices on the seabed, mainly for the location of submarines
and jurisdiction over buoys used for pure scientific research.[91] There is
nothing in the text of article 59 to exclude conflicts between non-allocated

rights and/or conflicts between such rights and rights attributed to flag or coastal States from its ambit. In any case, in the absence of a more relevant rule of law, the application by analogy of article 59 would appear to provide the best solution.[92]

Conclusion

The replacement of the freedom of the high seas by the EEZ has significant implications for the legal regime of underwater cultural property. *Within the 200 mile EEZ*, there is no presumption in favour of either coastal or flag-State jurisdiction; each case should be decided on its own merits. In case of doubt, the issue will be resolved on the basis of equity and in the light of all the relevant circumstances. Overall, it will be more difficult for third States to oppose the expansion of coastal jurisdiction over archaeological objects in the EEZ.[93] In this context, Australia's claim over historic wrecks on the continental shelf has been regarded as compatible with article 59.[94] Furthermore, coastal States may take advantage of their extensive rights over the EEZ and exercise control over underwater cultural property indirectly, i.e., by claiming that archaeological research conducted by third States interferes with their resource-related rights. There is nothing in the 1982 Convention to prevent coastal States from undertaking protective measures in the exercise of their resource jurisdiction over the EEZ. The adoption of such measures should be considered as an application of the general duty to protect archaeological and historical objects by article 303(1). *Beyond the EEZ and up to the outer continental shelf limit*, marine archaeology will be regarded as a legitimate freedom of the high seas, if it is not prohibited by a rule of international law and is exercised with due regard to the interests of other States.

CUSTOMARY INTERNATIONAL LAW

The limited number of States (Australia, Ireland, Portugal, Spain and Yugoslavia)[95] which have expanded their jurisdiction over underwater cultural property on the continental shelf, cannot provide the basis for the creation of a customary rule. At present, archaeological and historical objects found in this area are governed by the freedom of the high seas.[96] The same would seem to apply to cultural property found in the EEZ. As of 16 November 1993, ninety-two (92) States have proclaimed EEZs.[97] The general concept of the EEZ and the basic rules governing it have undoubtedly become part of customary law.[98] However, it is debatable whether its elaboration into specific rights and obligations by the 1982 Convention reflects customary law, since a number of national laws diverge from the EEZ provisions of the Convention.[99] Morocco and Jamaica are the only States to date to claim jurisdiction over the conduct of archaeological research in the EEZ, while Denmark has recently expanded its jurisdiction over archaeological and historical objects found within its 200 nm exclusive fishing zone.[100] In addition, a number of States claim sovereign rights over "all resources"[101] and/or jurisdiction over "any research" conducted in the EEZ.[102] Under an extensive interpretation of these terms, archaeological research and in general underwater cultural property found in the area could fall within coastal jurisdiction.[103] Other States claim jurisdiction over the construction of structures, installations and devices "for any other purose",[104] while a group of mainly Latin-American countries claim 200 nm territorial seas.[105] Cultural property found in these waters would fall within coastal sovereignty. The future will show whether these States will alter the status of such waters to an EEZ.

So far as the accommodation of residual rights is concerned, none of the analysed national legislation includes a provision similar to article 59 so that it may safely be assumed that this provision does not reflect customary law. Only Comoros' Law No. 82-005 relating to the delimitation of the maritime zones of the Islamic Federal Republic of the Comoros of 6 May 1982 provides in article 8(c) that "where a conflict arises between the interests of the Comoros and any other State or States, the conflict shall be resolved on the basis of equity, taking into account the respective importance of the interests involved to the parties as well as to the international community as a whole".

Juda has attempted to classify the different residual clauses employed by national EEZ legislation into four groups:

> "One group of States specifically asserts in addition to those enumerated rights, rights and obligations of an unspecified nature 'for which provision is made by international law' or which is recognised by international law. The important point is that these States explicitly recognise international law as the standard and determinant of any additional rights or duties which they may possess beyond the rights specifically provided in article 56. A second and much smaller group of States refers not to an international law standard, but rather to what might be termed functional principles. Guatemala, for

example, 'claims other rights and obligations as may derive from jurisdiction over the zone'. Honduras refers to 'such other rights and obligations as derive from the sovereign rights over the resources of the area'. A third group make no specific reference to rights other than those explicitly enumerated in their national proclamations and/or legislation. Finally, a fourth group, presently only three countries, maintain that residual rights in the EEZ fall within the competence of the coastal State."[106]

This approach has been criticised on the basis that it misinterprets the respective clauses providing for "other rights and jurisdiction" of the coastal State. As argued by Kwiatkowska: "One should avoid drawing the misleading conclusion, as Juda does, from those provisions of State legislation which place the clause of 'other' rights and jurisdiction at the end of the article listing the competence of the coastal State in its EEZ. Such a clause is modelled upon article 56(1)c referring to 'other rights and duties provided for in this Convention' and in no way prejudices the resolution of the question of residual rights in the future practice of States in accordance with article 59."[107] It is notable that the legislation of a small number of States, such as Ghana and Indonesia, specifically refers to other rights and jurisdiction provided for in the 1982 Convention. Nevertheless, Juda's classification is still useful in that it illustrates the lack of regulation of residual rights by national EEZ legislation.[108] Furthermore, such clauses may function as residual clauses in case a State is not a party to the Convention and is, therefore, not bound by its provisions, in particular article 59.

Since contemporary international law does not recognise coastal jurisdiction over archaeological objects in the EEZ, it would be reasonable to conclude that, at present, all States are entitled to undertake archaeological research within the 200-mile zone even if there is no specific mention of it as a right.[109]

NOTES

1   See further Garcia Amador, F.V., *The exploitation and conservation of the resources of the sea*, Second Enlarged Printing, Leyden, 1963 at pp. 126-128.
2   Statement made on 26 March 1958 by Mr. Jhirad (India) before the Fourth Committee, *UNCLOS I, Off. Rec.*, vol. VI at p. 51 (20th meeting). This clarification was made in relation to the proposed definition of "natural resources" by six States (Australia, Ceylon, Federation of Malaya, India, Norway, United Kingdom), Doc.A/CONF.13/C.4/L.36 of 24 March 1958, *ibid* at p. 136. See

also Caflisch, L., "Submarine Antiquities and the Law of the Sea", 13 *N.Y.I.L.* (1982) pp. 3-22 at p. 14, footnote 44.

3   II *ILC Yearbook* (1956) at p. 298.

4   Arend, A.C., "Archaeological and Historical Objects: The International Legal Implications of UNCLOS III", 22 *V.J.I.L.* (1982) pp. 777-803 at p. 784. Still, one could raise the question whether immovable underwater cultural property is also excluded from the notion of natural resources. Could the omission to refer to submerged setttlements be interpreted as an indication that they fall within the sovereign rights of the coastal State? The answer should be in the negative. First, the ILC's Commentary deals with wrecks and their cargoes in general without any specific reference to historic shipwrecks. There was no intention to differentiate the regime of shipwrecks from other cultural property found underwater. Most likely, the underlying purpose of its drafters was to avoid interference with the law of salvage. By the time of the drafting of the CSC, the removal of underwater remains seemed far too remote to create jurisdictional problems. Little attention was thus paid to this issue. Second, there is nothing in the *travaux préparatoires* or in the text of the CSC to indicate that sunken cities and submerged harbour works are "natural resources" of the seabed. A literal interpretation would also result in the same conclusion. Third, under the CSC, coastal States are entitled to exercise sovereign rights for specific purposes over the continental shelf. Everything that does not fall within the scope of these rights is governed by the residual freedom of the high seas. The continental shelf falls under neither the *imperium* nor the *dominium* of the coastal State. The fact that sunken settlements are immovable property and in a sense form part of the seabed, does not mean that they, nevertheless, "belong" to the coastal State. However, one may, distinguish wrecks which have become petrified or fossilised. In *Elwes v. Brigg Gas Co. (1886)*, 33 *Ch.D* 56, a boat embedded in the riverbank was held to be the property of the owner of the land where it was found, whether regarded as a mineral or as part of the soil in which it was embedded when discovered, or as a chattel. The court did not consider it necessary to decide whether the boat was a mineral. However, if it were required to decide the question, it should hold that it was not a mineral as it had not become petrified or fossilised and was always indistinguishable from the seabed.

5   Castagné, A., "L'archéologie sous-marine et le droit" in Société française pour le droit international, *Actualités du droit de la mer*, Colloque de Montpellier, 25-27 Mai 1972, Pedone, A. éditions, Paris, 1973, pp. 164-183.

6   *Ibid* at p. 171.

7   Meenan, J.K., "Note: Cultural Resources Preservation and Underwater Archaeology - Some Notes on the Current Legal Framework and a Model Underwater Antiquities Statute", 15 *San Diego L. Rev.* (1978) pp. 623-662 at p. 644. "Although archaeological resources are not natural resources, perhaps natural resources should be liberally construed to include them". Finally, Korthals Altes argues that wrecks are "resources" though not "natural resources of the seabed". Korthals Altes, K., "Submarine Antiquities and the Law: A Legal Labyrinth", 4 *Syracuse J. Int'l. L. & Com.* (1977) pp. 77-96 at p. 80. This argument is of

no practical significance as it does not subject wrecks under the sovereign rights of the coastal State. See also Caflisch, *op. cit.* note 2 at p. 14, footnote 44.

8   Auburn, F.M., "Convention for Preservation of Man's Heritage in the Ocean", 185 *Science* (1974) pp. 763-765 at p. 764.

9   408 *F. Supp.* 907 (S.D. Fla. 1976).

10   16 *U.S.C.* paras. 431-433.

11   43 *U.S.C.* para. 133 (1976).

12   40 *U.S.C.* para. 310.

13   *Ibid* at pp. 909-910.

14   These were the necessary prerequisites for the application of the Acts. With respect to the Abandoned Property Act, the court held that it applies only to property which was abandoned as a result of the Civil War and therefore it could not be used to assert sovereign prerogative in this case. The court relied on *Russel v. Forty Bales Cotton*, 21 *F.Cas.* 42 (S.D. Fla. 1872) (No. 12, 54). *Ibid.*

15   *Ibid* at p. 910.

16   569 *F.2d* 330 (5th Cir. 1978) ("Treasure Salvors I"). The Fifth Circuit adopted the district court's view that the Atocha was not situated on lands owned or controlled by the United States (i.e., it rested on the continental shelf outside the U.S. territorial sea) and that, therefore, the Antiquities Act was not applicable to its recovery. "We note that even were we to find that the Antiquities Act did cover this salvage operation, its enforcement provision, 16 *U.S.C.* para. 433, has been held unconstitutionally vague." *United States v. Diaz*, 499 *F.2d* 113 (9th Cir. 1974). The Court reached that conclusion, i.e., that the U.S. had limited control over the wreck site of Atocha, after discussing in detail the history of the OCSLA, the Submerged Lands Act, 43 *U.S.C.* para. 1301 (1976), and the subsequently ratified CSC. It held that OCSLA consists almost exclusively of specific measures to facilitate exploitation of natural resources on the continental shelf, and that "an extension of the natural resources of the continental shelf is not necessarily an extension of sovereignty." *Ibid* at p. 339. So far as the Government's claim on the treasure as successor to the prerogative rights of the King of England was concerned, the court held that the United States could not assert such a claim. *Ibid* at p. 330. The same conclusion was reached in relation to the claim that a legislative assertion of sovereign prerogative was passed through the Abandoned Property Act. *Ibid* at pp. 341-342. "Since the United States has no claims of equitable ownership in a Spanish vessel wrecked more than a century before the American Revolution, and the wreck is not 'within the jurisdiction of the United States', the Abandoned Property Act has no application to the present controversy". Contrary to the district court the Court of Appeals rejected the Abandoned Property Act on the basis that it applies only to property to which the U.S. has an equitable claim. See also *United States v. Tyndale*, 116 *F.2d* 820 (1st Cir. 1902). As already seen, the district court had rejected this Act on the basis that it applies only to abandoned civil war property. See above footnote 14.

After affirming the district court's decision that Treasure Salvors was entitled to possession of the vessel and its cargo, the Fifth Circuit remanded the case to the district court for further action. In the district court, Treasure Salvors attempted successfully to issue an ancillary warrant to compel the State of Florida to release to the court that portion of the treasure which was in its possession as a result of prior contacts between Treasure Salvors and the State, 459 *F. Supp.* 507 (S.D. Fla. 1978). Florida appealed to the Fifth Circuit, which affirmed the district court's opinion apart from the privity issue which it declined to affirm or modify. *Florida Department of State v. Treasure Salvors Inc.*, 621 *F.2d* 1340 (5th Cir. 1980) *("Treasure Salvors II")*. Florida subsequently appealed to the United States Supreme Court, which reviewed only the issue of the Eleventh Amendment, *Florida Department of State v. Treasure Salvors Inc*, 458 *U.S.* 670, 682 (1982). See further Bowers, D.L., "Maritime Law - Salvage Operations - Eleventh Amendment not a Bar to Admiralty in Rem Actions against Property seized by State Officials acting Outside their Authority". Florida Department of State v. Treasure Salvors Inc *("Treasure Salvors II")*, 7 *Suffolk Transnational Law Journal* (1983) pp. 601-613.

17   "The Convention does not change the law of salvage as it applies to *res derelictae* even though the recovery of such property might involve contact with the seabed or removal of sand and other material". 408 *F. Supp.* 907 (S.D. Fla. 1976) at p. 910. See also *supra* at pp. 226-227, chapter 6.

18   Balinsky, D.A., "Treasure Salvors Inc. v. Abandoned Sailing Vessel Believed to be the Nuestra Señora de Atocha", 5 *Brooklyn J. Int'l L.* (1979) pp. 178-190; Jones, J.E., "Admiralty - Possessory Rights in Abandoned Vessels: Salvor of Abandoned Vessels on the Continental Shelf is Entitled to Ownership Because Neither Does the Outer Continental Shelf Lands Act Extend American Territorial Jurisdiction to the Continental Shelf for the Purpose of Antiquities Act Claim to the Vessel Nor Did Congress Incorporate into American Law the Sovereign Prerogative of the English King to Ownership of Such a Vessel", 19 *V.J.I.L.* (1979) pp. 473-487.

19   Lawrence, A., "State Antiquity Laws and Admiralty Salvage Protecting our Cultural Resources", 32 *U. Miami L. Rev.* (1977) pp. 291-338 at p. 316.

20   DeLanis, J.A., "Jurisdiction: Salvage of Abandoned Vessels on the Continental Shelf", 9 *V. and J. Transnat'l L.* (1976) pp. 915-927 at p. 926. See also McDonald, B., "Admiralty - Salvage: The United States has Not Asserted Sovereign Prerogative Over Abandoned Property on the Outer Continental Shelf", 4 *U. Fla. L. Rev.* (1976) pp. 561-568.

21   Butler, J.S., "Admiralty: Salvage Rights - Sovereign Claims on the Outer Continental Shelf do not Extend to Abandoned Vessels?", 7 *Georgia J. Int. Comp. L.* (1977) pp. 169-176 at p. 174.

22   *Ibid.*

23   8 *ILM* (1969) at p. 679.

24   Caflisch, *op. cit.* note 2 at p. 14.

25   II *ILC Yearbook* (1956) at p. 298.

26   Brown, E.D., "Freedom of Scientific Research and the Legal Regime of Hydrospace", 9 *Indian J. Int'l L.* (1969) pp. 327-380 at pp. 349-350. The quoted text appears in II *ILC Yearbook* (1956) at p. 297 (para. 2 of Commentary on article 68).

27   Castagné, *op. cit.* note 5 at p. 171.

28   Article 5 creates interpretation problems as, on the one hand, paragraph (1) guarantees the freedom of "fundamental oceanographic or other scientific research", while, on the other, paragraph (8) requires the consent of the coastal State "in respect of any research concerning the continental shelf and undertaken there". For the reconciliation of these *prima facie* conflicting provisions see Caflisch, L. & Piccard, S., "The Legal Regime of Marine Scientific Research and UNCLOS", 38 *ZaöRV* (1978) pp. 848-901 at p. 861 and Brown, *op. cit.* note 26 at p. 353 *et seq.*

29   See also Miller, H.C., *International Law and Marine Archaeology*, Academy of Applied Sciences, Belmont, Mass., 1973 at p. 23. "It is clear that the conferees were primarily concerned with classical oceanographic research - the physical, biological and geological characteristics of the sea, seabed and subsoil".

30   Statement made by Admiral Mouton, on whose suggestion the phrase "or scientific research" was added. Doc.A/CONF.13/C.4/L.50 at p. 82, para. 18. See further Brown, *op. cit.* note 26 at p. 352, note 101: "And it seems clearly from Admiral Mouton's intervention that submarine archaeological research was not envisaged as falling within the term 'other scientific research'".

31   See also Brown, *ibid* at p. 357. "Even if archaeological research can hardly be classified as 'other scientific research' protected by Article 5(1), it is still the exercise of a freedom of the high seas and, as such, protected from unreasonable interference." A confirmation of this conclusion is provided by article 78(2) of the 1982 Convention which states expressly that: "The exercise of the rights of the coastal State over the continental shelf must not infringe or result in any unjustifiable interference with navigation and other rights and freedoms of other States provided for in this Convention".

32   In Prof. Brown's view, the sovereign rights of the coastal State constitute an exception to the predominant principle of the freedom of the seas and, like all legal exceptions, must be restrictively interpreted in the event of conflict with one of the pre-existing freedoms. In case of conflict between the coastal State's sovereign rights over the continental shelf and one of the freedoms of the sea, there would thus be a legal presumption in favour of the various freedoms of the sea. This is not to say, however, that the traditional freedoms are to be given undue weight. Clearly, there would be little point in recognising a sovereign right to exploit the continental shelf, if its existence were to be unreasonably curtailed by reference to other interests. Brown, E.D., *Sea-Bed Energy and Mineral Resources and the Law of the Sea*, vol. 1, *The Areas Within National Jurisdiction*, Graham & Trotman, London, 1984 at I.11 2-3.

33   A confirmation of this conclusion can be found in the ILC's Commentary on draft article 68 that "consent of the State will only be required for research relating to the exploration and exploitation of the seabed or subsoil", II *ILC Yearbook* (1956) at p. 298 (para. 10 of Commentary on article 68), and in article 5(8) which states that: "The coastal State shall not normally withhold its consent ... with a view to purely scientific research into the physical or biological characteristics of the continental shelf." These passages leave no doubt that the term "research" is confined to the natural environment and its resources.

34 Caflisch, *op. cit.* note 2 at p. 15.

35 Brown, *op. cit.* note 26 at pp. 357-358. See also Miller, *op. cit.* note 29 at p. 25.

36 Castagné, *op. cit.* note 5 at p. 171.

37 Michael, M.D., *The Archaeological and Historical Objects of the Continental Shelf. International Law and the Aegean*, Saccoulas, Publishing Co., Athens, 1983 at p. 39 (in Greek). See also Apollis, G., *L'emprise maritime de l'état côtier*, Pedone, A. éditions, Paris, 1981 at pp. 187-188.

38 Vallat, F.A., "The Continental Shelf", 23 *B.Y.I.L.* (1946) pp. 333-338 at pp. 336-337.

39 Korthals Altes, *op. cit.* note 7 at p. 81. "Unilateral State control implied by article 5(8) on research expeditions might stop destructive treasure hunters. But I judge such use of article 5(8) *malplacé* - resorting to it for a purpose for which it was never intended. Pleas, however, plausible, for the coastal State's consent to archaeological research seem to neglect the very background of the Convention."

40 Burke, W.T., "Law and the New Technologies" in Alexander, L.M. (ed.), *The Law of the Sea Offshore Boundaries and Zones*, The Ohio University Press, 1967, pp. 204-227 at pp. 216-217. There are numerous devices of this kind. A well-known method of surveying is scanning the bottom in parallel adjacent strips, using a specially designed vehicle and a high capacity camera system. Its typical applications are: undersea cable, pipeline and fixed installations surveys, stereophotogrammetric mapping of the bottom, photography of large ships and marine life, archaeological surveys, landing beach and approach surveys. See Rebikoff, D., "Photogrammetry in dirty water by mosaic and strip scanning" in UNESCO, *Underwater archaeology: a nascent discipline*, 1972, pp. 223-230 at p. 223 and, for more recent techniques, Green, J., *Maritime Archaeology: A Technical Handbook,* Academic Press Ltd, 1990.

41 Roucounas, E., "Submarine Archaeological Research: Some Legal Aspects" in Leanza, U. (ed.), *The International Legal Regime of the Mediterranean Sea*, II Università degli Studi di Roma, Pubblicazioni della Facoltà di Giurisprudenza 2, Dott A. Giuffrè, A. editore, Milano, 1987, pp. 309-334 at p. 323.

42 Some scholars argue that the consent of the coastal State is limited to research concerning the continental shelf *and* undertaken there. "It would seem reasonable to conclude that the intention was to make clear that the requirement of prior consent was limited to research concerning the continental shelf, which involved physical contact with the seabed or subsoil of the shelf." Brown, *op. cit.* note 26 at p. 356. In Menzler's view, in the light of article 3 of the CSC and the fact that the latter refers only to the seabed and the subsoil, "the decisive criterion should be 'the touching of the ground'". Menzler, E., "Scientific Research on the Seabed and its Regime" in Sztucki, J. (ed.), *Symposium on the International Regime of the Seabed. Proceedings*, Academia Nazionale Dei Lincei, Rome, 1970 (hereinafter cited as Rome Proceedings), pp. 619-647 at p. 623.

Others claim that conduct of research by acoustic, vision or electronic means must be considered as "undertaken there", if its object concerns the continental shelf, its bed and the subsoil. According to Prof. Revelle: "A surface ship making gravity measurements or an aircraft towing a magnetometer are certainly investigating the properties of the seafloor and the sediments and rocks beneath it, as is a ship making recording echo-soundings or operating a sonic sub-bottom profiler, and it is likely that most States will interpret the Convention as requiring their consent for such activities." Revelle, R., "Scientific Research on the Seabed - International Co-operation in Scientific Research and Exploration of the Seabed" in *Rome Proceedings, ibid*, pp. 649-663 at p. 660. Prof. Roucounas suggests the application of the general principles of "constructive presence" in cases where there is no "physical" contact between the research vessel and the seabed, but there is no doubt that the research "concerns" the continental shelf within the meaning of article 5(8). "But even if the purpose of the research is to increase scientific knowledge, it still infringes the coastal State's sovereign rights over the seabed and subsoil, because one of these rights is the right to the exclusive knowledge of mineral resources." *Ibid* at pp. 322-323. Under an extensive interpretation, the presence of each one condition only may be sufficient for the coastal consent to be required. In this context, the only research activities which would remain free would be those which are undertaken in the superjacent water column or air space and are not related to the continental shelf. "It seems, therefore, that article 5(8) should be interpreted as requiring coastal State consent for any marine scientific research related to the shelf's resources, even if the research is to take place in the superjacent water or air space." Caflisch & Piccard, *op. cit.* note 28 at p. 862, note 47.

43 See, however, Miller, who argues that: "Archaeological research can be conducted either from the superjacent waters or on the shelf itself. Research conducted on the shelf is clearly 'undertaken there', even though it is unconnected with the exploitation of the shelf's natural resources." *Op. cit.* note 29 at p. 33.

44 In practice most States require their consent for the conduct of *any research* on or over their continental shelf. See, for example, article 132 of the Federal Mining Law of 13 August 1980 of the *(former) Federal Republic of Germany,* which states that: "Whoever intends, for investigation of the continental shelf on the spot, to carry out research activities which by their very nature are obviously not suited for the exploration for or the discovery of mineral resources, shall require a permit to be issued by the Deutsches Hydrographisches Institut (German Institute of Hydrography) to provide a ruling regarding the utilization and the use of the waters covering the continental shelf and the airspace above these waters", United Nations, *The Law of the Sea: National Legislation, Regulations and Supplementary Documents on Marine Scientific Research in Areas under National Jurisdiction*, Division for Ocean Affairs and the Law of the Sea, Office of Legal Affairs, 1989, at p. 117; *Greek* Diplomatic Note No. 6257.1/207/AS from the Ministry of Foreign Affairs, 31 January 1978: "Any request concerning permission to carry out marine scientific research in the Greek territorial sea or continental shelf should be addressed to the Department of International Organisations and Conferences, Ministry of Foreign Affairs", *ibid* at p. 123; article 11 of *Guyana's* Maritime Boundaries Act, 1977: "No person (including a foreign Government) shall, except under and in accor-

dance with the terms of a licence or a letter of authority granted by the Minister responsible for natural resources, explore the continental shelf or exploit its resources or carry out any search or excavation or conduct any research within the continental shelf or drill therein or construct, maintain or operate any artificial island, offshore terminal, installation or other structure or device therein for any purpose whatsoever". *The Law of the Sea: National Legislation on the Continental Shelf*, Division for Ocean Affairs and the Law of the Sea, Office of Legal Affairs, 1989 at p. 118 and article 9 of *Haitian* Decree No. 38 of 8 April 1977: "No one may engage in exploration or exploitation of this platform as referred to above without the explicit consent of the Haitian State, even if no such activities are being carried out by the Haitian State itself", *ibid* at p. 123.

45   O'Connell, D.P., *The International Law of the Sea*, vol. II, Clarendon Press, Oxford, 1984 at p. 918. See also note 86.

46   Roucounas, *op. cit.* note 41 at p. 323 and Michael, *op. cit.* note 37 at p. 65, who suggests that Greek courts should adopt a similar approach. See also article 19 of the *Chilean* Supreme Decree No. 711 of 22 August 1975 Approving Regulations Governing the Supervision of Marine Scientific and Technological Research Conducted in the Maritime Zone under National Jurisdiction, which states that: "Any breach of these regulations shall be punished by the maritime authority; this does not preclude the confiscation of the articles and data obtained through research and the suspension of the authorization to proceed with the research", *The Law of the Sea: National Legislation, Regulations and Supplementary Documents on Marine Scientific Research in Areas under National Jurisdiction*, Division for Ocean Affairs and the Law of the Sea, Office of Legal Affairs, 1989 at p. 68. It must be noted that Chile is not a party to the CSC.

47   Meenan, *op. cit.* note 7 at pp. 643-644. In Meenan's view: "Notwithstanding the report of the ILC on the CSC, it might be reasonable to conclude that the seabed of the continental shelf is owned or controlled by the Government of the United States. Therefore, the provisions of the Antiquities Act should be applicable to underwater archaeological resources on the continental shelf." *Ibid* at p. 648. See also Kenny, J.K. and Hrusoff, R.R., "The Ownership of the Treasures of the Sea", *Wm. & Mary L. Rev.* (1967) pp. 383-401 at p. 401, who argue that "property recovered in areas far beyond the three mile limit may be regarded as within the sovereignty of the coastal power if they are withdrawn from its continental shelf".

48   For a discussion of those bills, see Giesecke, A., "New Legislation Introduced to Protect Historic Shipwrecks", 10 *JFA* (1983) pp. 488-490; ID, "Management of Historic Shipwrecks in the 1908s", 12 *JFA* (1985) pp. 108-112; Herscher, E., "97 Congress, 1st session, HR 132", 10 *JFA* (1983) pp. 107-113; ID; "Hearings Held on Historic Shipwreck Legislation", 11 *JFA* (1984) pp. 79-96; "House Passes Historic Shipwreck Legislation", 12 *JFA* (1985) pp.112-116; Szypszak, C.A., "The Protection, Salvage and Preservation of Underwater Cultural Resources in the Chesapeake Bay", 4 *Virginia Journal of Natural Resources Law*

(1983) pp. 373-395 at pp. 391-394; Throckmorton, P., "Introduction: Marine archaeology", 28 *Oceanus*, No. 1, Spring 1985, pp. 2-12.

49 It is noteworthy that in the United States, the States which have asserted sovereign prerogative have premised their claims upon ownership of the submerged lands beneath the territorial sea. Such regulation, however, concerns exclusively the U.S. legal system and the relation between the Federal Government and the States. So far as international law is concerned, the United States exercises sovereignty over its territorial sea. The determination of the respective rights of the States and the Federal Government in this area will be decided on the terms of U.S. law. See for example *Jupiter Wreck, Inc. v. Unidentified, Wrecked and Abandoned Sailing Vessel*, 691 *F. Supp.* 1377 (S.D. Fla 1988), 1988 *AMC* 2705, where the court applied the common law of finds with the result that the owner of the soil has title to abandoned property found beneath it. "Since the *res* is embedded in soil, which is owned by the State, it belongs to the latter. Under the common law of finds, ownership of abandoned property is generally assigned without regard to where the property is found."

50 Meenan, *op. cit.* note 7 at p. 646. Meenan's argument is based on a statement made by Korthals Altes that: "A sound interpretation would be that the CSC is only concerned with the non-living mineral resources of the continental shelf, while research on any other items is beyond its scope". *Ibid,* footnotes 124 and 125.

51 Walker, C.W., "Jurisdictional Problems Created by Artificial Islands", 10 *San Diego L. Rev.* (1973) pp. 638-663 at p. 657. See further Papadakis, N., *The International Legal Regime of Artificial Islands*, Sijthoff Publications on Ocean Development, vol. 2, Sijthoff-Leyden, 1977 at p. 127 *et seq.*

52 Smith, H.A., *The Law and Custom of the Sea*, 3rd ed., Stevens & Sons Ltd., London, 1959 at p. 46.

53 Historic Shipwrecks Act, 1976, No. 190 of 1976, *Acts of the Parliament of the Commonwealth of Australia* 1976 at p. 1596, as amended in 1980 by the Historic Shipwrecks Amendement Act, No. 88 of 1980, *Acts of the Parliament of the Commonwealth of Australia* 1980 at p. 912. See also the Protection of Movable Cultural Heritage Act, No. 11 of 1986. Australia has ratified both the CSC and the CHS.

54 Ronzitti, N., "Stato costiero e tutela del patrimonio storico sommerso", 86 *Il diritto marittimo* (1984) pp. 3-24 at p. 20. As already seen, the U.S. Marine Protection, Research and Sanctuaries Act of 1972, which enables the designation of marine sanctuaries as far as the outer limit of the continental shelf, limits its application to foreign citizens "only to the extent consistent with recognised principles of international law or authorised by international agreement." See *supra* at p. 215.

55 Schwarzenberger, G., *International Law*, vol. I, 3rd edition, Stevens & Sons Ltd, 1957 at p. 614. See also Brownlie, I., *Principles of Public International Law*, 4th edition, Clarendon Press, 1990 at p. 449 and Smith, B.D., *State Responsibility and the Marine Environment: The Rules of Decision*, Clarendon Press, 1988 at pp. 24-25.

56 For example, to date, there has been no protest against Australia on the basis of the extension of its jurisdiction over the continental shelf. On the contrary, the latter has concluded two bilateral Agreements, one with the Netherlands and one with Papua-New Guinea, which assume the extension of its competence over the outer continental shelf area. See Australia/Netherlands Agreement concerning Old Dutch Shipwrecks. Schedule 1 to the Historic Shipwrecks Act, 1976, *op. cit.* note 53, pp. 1613-1616, and Australia/Papua New Guinea: Treaty on Sovereignty and Maritime Boundaries in the Area Between the Countries, 18 *ILM* (1979) at p. 291. Article 9 of the latter states that: "(1) Wrecks of vessels and aircrafts which lie on, in or under the seabed in an area of seabed jurisdiction of a Party shall be subject to the jurisdiction of that Party; (2) If a wreck of historical or special significance to a Party is located or found in an area between the two countries under the jurisdiction of the other Party, the Parties shall consult with a view to reaching agreement on the action if any to be taken with respect to that wreck ...". Under article 1(1)i, "seabed jurisdiction" is defined as "sovereign rights over the continental shelf in accordance with international law".

57 Under the "monist theory", the two systems of law are parts of one legal order; international law is either superior or inferior to municipal law. All monist doctrines are based on the theoretical postulate that the "law" has to be understood as a unity and that its validity has to be derived from one common source. Under the "dualist" school, international and municipal law are two distinct and self-contained systems; they are part of several legal orders existing independently from each other and needing special provisions in order to be brought into a reciprocal relationship. Neither legal order has the power to create or alter the rules of the other. In case of conflict, a municipal court would apply municipal law, while in international courts, international law would have primacy. See further Brownlie, *op cit.* note 55 at pp. 32-57; Heiskanen, V., *International Legal Topics*, Harvard University, 1992, pp. 1-200; O'Connell, D.P., *International Law*, 2nd ed., vol. I, Stevens & Sons, London, 1970 at pp. 38-79; Partsch, K. J., "International Law and Municipal Law", 10 *E.P.I.L.* (1987), pp. 238-257; Schwarzenberger, G., *A Manual of International Law*, 6th ed., Professional Books Ltd., Abingdon, 1976 at pp. 36-41 and Virally, M., "The Sources of International Law" in Sørensen, M. (ed), *Manual of Public International Law*, The Macmillan Press Ltd., London and Basingstoke, 1968, pp. 116-174 at pp. 165-171. Under the "theory of transformation", international agreements must be specifically incorporated into domestic law by legislation so as to become municipal law. "Transformation" is understood to mean the domestic act whereby the norm of international law is incorporated into the domestic legal system. Partsch, *op. cit.* note 57 at p. 245. In the United Kingdom, for example, a treaty, though internationally binding, will not thereby alone become part of the law of the land, unless an enabling Act of Parliament has been passed. So far as the application of customary international law is concerned, the predominant rule is that of "incorporation" or "adoption". Customary rules will be considered part of the law of the land and enforced as such, unless they are inconsistent with Acts of Parliament or prior judicial decisions

of final authority. Brownlie, *ibid* at pp. 43-47. Under the theory of "incorporation", treaties duly concluded shall take effect as municipal law. The concept of "incorporation" is used for all forms of implementing international obligations in the domestic sphere. One of these ways is "adoption", whereby a treaty or other norm is declared applicable internally without changing its content or character as sources of international law. Partsch, *ibid* at p. 245.

58 In the United States, treaties approved by the Senate have the same legal status as the laws of the U.S. According to article VI, clause 2 of the U.S. Constitution: "This Constitution, and the Laws of the United States which shall be made in Pursuance thereof; and all Treaties made, or which shall be made under the Authority of the United States shall be the Supreme Law of Land; and the Judges in every State shall be bound thereby, any Thing in the Constitution or Laws of Any State to the Contrary notwithstanding." C.f. *Constitution of the United States, National and State*, Published for Legislative Drafting Research Fund of Columbia University, 2nd ed., Oceana Publications Inc., Dobbs Ferry, New York, 1987 at p. 9. In other words, they override conflicting State law and prior federal legislation, but they can be nullified by subsequent federal legislation.

59 "The laws of Congress are always to be construed so as to conform to the provisions of a treaty, if it be possible to do so without violence to their language ... the treaty will retain its force, till otherwise ordered by congress or the President". *United States v. Forty-Three Gallons of Whiskey*, 108 *U.S.* 491 (1883). Accordingly, both the Antiquities Act and the Abandoned Property Act were held inapplicable as they depend on U.S. jurisdiction, ownership and control. In the court's view, even if the OCSLA was interpreted to grant jurisdiction over archaeological objects on the seabed, the CSC signed after the passage of the Act superseded any incompatible terminology in OCSLA and nullified its jurisdictional effect. In support of its reasoning the district court cited *United States v. Ray* where it was held that: "To the extent that any of the terms of the [OCSLA] are inconsistent with the later enacted CSC, they should be superseded". 423 *F.2d* 16 (5th Cir. 1970) at 21. In Meenan's view, the holding of *United States v. Ray* does not support this part of Treasure Salvors. As the court itself admitted: "There is nothing in the pertinent language of the CSC which detracts from or is inconsistent with the OCSLA. To the contrary, the CSC confirms and crystallises the exclusiveness of those rights" (*ibid* at p. 21). In addition, says Meenan, when the U.S.A. ratified the CSC, the Senate gave its advice and consent with the understanding that no federal law would be superseded by their ratification. *Op. cit.* note 7 at pp. 645-646 and footnote 122. "If federal legislation intends to assert substantial governmental control over antiquities, Congress must specifically repudiate the Convention provisions prohibiting this exercise of jurisdiction." A statute is not repealed by a later affirmative statute which contains no repealing clause, unless the conflict between them cannot be reconciled or the latter covers the same ground as the former, and is clearly intended as a substitute thereof. *Red Rock v. Henry*, 106 *U.S.* 596, 601. See further *Frost v. Wenie*, 157 *U.S.* 46 (1895), *King v. Cornell*, 106 *U.S.* 395, 396, *United States v. Tynen*, 11 *Wall.* 88-95 (78 *U.S.*) (1871) 20 *Law Ed.*

153; *"Henderson's Tobacco"*, 11 *Wall.* 652-659 (78 *U.S.*) (1871) 20 *Law Ed.*
235. In other words, the enactment of a statute attributing jurisdiction over
archaeological objects on the continental shelf will supersede the CSC so long
as this is expressed or clearly indicated.

60   Examples are the Netherlands' Constitution of 1956, the French Constitution
     of 1958 and the Greek Constitution of 1975.

61   See further Rambaud, P., "International Law and Municipal Law: Conflicts and
     their Review by Third States", 10 *E.P.I.L.* (1987) pp. 257-262.

62   See Prott, L.V. & O'Keefe, P.J., "Final report on legal protection of the under-
     water cultural heritage" in Council of Europe, Parliamentary Assembly, *The
     underwater cultural heritage,* Report of the Committee on Culture and Education
     (Rapporteur Mr. J. Roper) Doc. 4200-E, Strasbourg, 1978, pp. 45-88 at p. 56.

63   In its judgment of June 22, 1972, *Allgmeine Versicherungsgesselschaft v. E.K.*,
     59 *BGHZ* 83, the German Federal Supreme Court (Bundesgerichtshof), declared
     void a contract which aimed at the export of cultural property from Nigeria
     in contravention of its exports laws, at a time when the Federal Republic of
     Germany was not a party to the 1970 UNESCO Convention on the Means of
     Prohibiting and Preventing the Illicit Import, Export and Transfer of Ownership
     of Cultural Property. According to article 138 of the German Civil Code, the
     courts should not enforce contracts contrary to public policy (*ordre public*).
     The court found that the UNESCO Convention represented international public
     policy and refused to enforce a contract which was contrary to public policy
     and the international need for understanding between nations. In the court's
     view, an act violating international law becomes *ipso facto* contrary to the *ordre
     public* of the Federal Republic of Germany. For a discussion of this decision
     and its significance for the protection of the cultural heritage, see Bleckmann,
     A., "Sittenwidrigkeit wegen Verstosses gegen den *ordre public* international",
     34 *ZaöRV* (1974) pp. 112-132; Church, D., "Evaluating the effectiveness of
     foreign laws on national ownership of cultural property in U.S. Courts", 30
     Columbia Journal of Transnational Law (1992) pp. 179-229 at pp. 211-212;
     Prott, L.V., "Problems of private international law for the protection of the
     cultural heritage", *Hague Recueil* (1989-V) pp. 215-317 at pp. 289-290, Prott
     and O'Keefe, *ibid* at p. 57 (fn 18), Seidl-Hohenveldern, I., "Artefacts as national
     cultural heritage and as common heritage to mankind" in Bello, E.G. et Prince
     Bola, A. Ajibolo, *Essays in Honour of Judge T.D. Elias,* Dordrecht, 1992, pp.
     163-168, and Wyss, M.Ph., *Kultur als eine Dimension der Völkerrechtsordnung,*
     Schweizer Studien zum Internazionalen Recht, Bd 79, Schulthess Polygraphi-
     scher Verlag, Zürich, 1992, pp. 158-160. See also Reichelt, G., "International
     protection of cultural property", *Uniform Law Review* (1985-I) pp. 43-153 at
     p. 131 *et seq.;* ID, "International protection of cultural property (second study)"
     Uniform Law Review (1988-I) pp. 53-131 at pp. 113-125, who stresses the
     importance of the recognition of foreign *ordre public* and the role of mandatory
     rules in the international protection of cultural property. Nevertheless, it should
     be recalled that the expansion of coastal jurisdiction over underwater cultural
     property on the continental shelf is in contravention of current international law,

and may itself be regarded as a breach of the international *ordre public*. Courts have generally been reluctant to enforce the cultural heritage legislation of other States; see, for example, *Attorney-General of New Zealand v. Ortiz and others*, (1983) 2 *All E.R.* 93 (H.L.); 2 *W.L.R.* at 809.

64 Text reprinted in Prott, L.V. & O'Keefe, P.J., *Law and the Cultural Heritage*, vol. 1, *Discovery and Excavation*, Professional Books Ltd., Abingdon, 1984 at p. 96.

65 Article 16(6): "In carrying out the work of exploration, the contractor must observe the laws and regulations in force, including the regulations referred to in Article 39 hereof, relating to archaeological sites and monuments in general, places of historical interest and outstanding natural beauty"; Article 39(1): "Presidential decrees issued by motion of the Ministry of Industry and Energy shall prescribe regulations for the execution of any and all works and projects for the prospecting, exploration, and exploitation of hydrocarbons including ... cultural property and other activities in the exploitation area". *Official Gazette* A'302/1976.

66 Information provided by Dr. Th.J. Maarleveld, Department of Underwater Archaeology, National Service of Archaeological Research, Ministry of Culture.

67 See Executive Order No. 11593 "Protection and Enhancement of the Cultural Environment", 3 *C.F.R.* (1971/1975 Compilation), 36 *Fed. Reg.* 8921 (1971) and the National Historic Preservation Act of 1966 as amended in 1980, 16 *U.S.C.* para. 470(f) (Supp. IV, 1980). Section 106: "The head of any Federal agency having direct or indirect jurisdiction over a proposed Federal or federally assisted undertaking in any state and the head of any Federal department or independent agency having authority to licence any undertaking, shall prior to the approval of the expenditure of any Federal funds on the undertaking or prior to the issuance of any licence, as the case may be, take into account the effect of the undertaking on any district, site, building, structure, or object that is included in the National Register." In *Treasure Salvors*, the United States claimed that it had listed "several sites of historic and archaeological importance located on the outer continental shelf ... on the National Register of Historic Places". C.f. Pretrial Memorandum of Law of the United States, Intervenor-defendant at p. 39 cited in McDonald, *op. cit.* note 20 at p. 568. See further Riess, W.C., "Cultural Resources on the Northeast Continental Shelf" in Cockrell, W.A. (ed.), *In the Realms of Gold: The Proceedings of the Tenth Conference and Underwater Archaeology*, Fathom Eight Special Publication, No. 1, Fathom Eight, California, 1981, pp. 226-228 and Glasier, G.E., "Cultural Resource Preservation: A Consideration before Mineral Development", 28 *Rocky Mountain Mineral Law Institute* (1982) pp. 635-670 at pp. 654-656.

68 On the Danish law see Lund, C., "Beskyttelse af historiske skibsvrag og fortisminder pa den danske havbund" in *Fortidsminder og kulturhistorie*, National Forestry and Nature Agency, Copenhagen, 1987, pp. 135-150; *Israel:* Submarine Areas Law No 5713 of 10 February 1953. Article 177: "The holder of a preliminary permit or a petroleum right shall not, save with the consent of the Minister of Religions, carry out any operation within 100 meters from a holy site; where a doubt arises as to whether a particular site is a holy site, the Minister of

Religions shall decide. The holder of a preliminary permit or a petroleum right shall not, save with the consent of the Director of the Department of Antiquities, carry out any operation within 100 meters from an historical site within the meaning of the Antiquities Ordinance; such consent shall not derogate from the obligations imposed by that Ordinance"; *Libyan Arab Jamahirya:* Petroleum Law of 21 April 1955 (No 25 of 1955). Article 9: "The concession shall not confer upon the concession holder the right to do any work within the pricincts of cemeteries, places used for religious worship and places of antiquity as defined in the Antiquities Laws in force. Any works of art or antiquity discovered by the concession holder shall be subject to the law in force"; *Thailand:* Petroleum Act of 26 March 1971. Section 73: "If historical objects, fossils, economic minerals, or those minerals which are of significant value in geological studies are discovered in the conduct of his petroleum exploration or production operations, the concessionaire shall report such discovery to the Department of Mineral Resources within thirty days from the date of discovery." *ST/LEG/ SER.B/16* at p. 105.

Finally, article 72 of the Mines Act of the *Socialist Republic of Bosnia and Herzegovina* of 15 April 1980 reads: "Exploitation of mineral substances may not be performed in an area where there are concentrations of ... cultural monuments and natural wonders ... so designated in particular provisions ... If industrial mineral substances of particular social concern are at issue, the Executive Council of the Assembly of the Socialist Republic of Bosnia and Herzegovina may authorise their exploitation even in the areas or zones stipulated in the preceding paragraph, with provision made by decree relative to measures to be taken to protect such works or zones". Similar provisions are to be found in the relevant legislation of the other constituent republics of *Yugoslavia,* such as the Mines Act of the *Socialist Republic of Croatia* of 12 May 1983 (article 30) and the Mines Act of the *Socialist Republic of Montenegro* of 19 April 1985 (article 60).

68a Article 76(1) reads: "The continental shelf of a coastal State comprises the sea-bed and subsoil of the submarine areas that extend beyond its territorial sea throughout the natural prolongation of its land territory to the outer edge of the continental margin, or to a distance of 200 nautical miles from which the breadth of the territorial sea is measured where the outer edge of the continental margin does not extend up to that distance."

69 On the contrary see Michael, *op. cit.* note 37 at pp. 62-66; Fry, E.M., "Synopsis. Recent Developments in the Law of the Sea 1984-1985", 23 *San Diego L. Rev.* (1986) pp. 701-722 at pp. 720-722. "International law permits coastal nations to assert jurisdiction and control over subsoil and seabed natural resources of the continental shelf, which encompasses archaeological resources". A similar approach is adopted by Cycon, D.E., "Legal and Regulatory Issues in Marine Archaeology", 28 *Oceanus,* No. 1, Spring 1985, pp. 78-84. See also Alexander, B.E.,"Treasure salvage beyond the territorial sea: an assessment and recommendations", 20 *J. Mar. Law & Com.* (1989) pp. 1-19 at p. 12, who argues that "even though coastal nations do not have sovereign rights to abandoned shipwrecks on the continental shelf, a treasure salvor should not necessarily presume

that coastal nations will not attempt to assert some control over treasure salvage operations on their continental shelf. Since it is possible for treasure salvage operations to affect natural resources or exploitation activities on the continental shelf, the admiralty court in the adjacent coastal nation should adjudicate treasure salvage claims over abandoned shipwrecks located on the adjacent continental shelf."

Finally, it has been argued that within the general framework of the 1982 Convention coastal jurisdiction over archaeological objects on the continental shelf is implicitly recognised. According to Lund: "The limits of the Area [seabed beyond national jurisdiction] are clear as far as the exploitation of minerals and other natural resources is concerned. The Area begins beyond the continental shelf. But does Article 149 refer to the same area? If it does it would mean that the coastal State has jurisdiction for the purpose of protection of underwater cultural heritage on the continental shelf. Otherwise there would be a gap between the jurisdiction of the coastal States and the regime set up in Part XI of the Convention or the Area would stretch in on the continental shelf, when talking about underwater cultural heritage, but not when talking about minerals and natural resources." Lund, C., "Report on Protection of the Underwater Cultural Heritage - The Rules of UN Law of the Sea Protection" in Council of Europe, Parliamentary Assembly, *Parliamentary Conference on the UN Convention on the Law of the Sea*, Palermo, 2-4 November 1983, *AS/JUR/MAR/CONF(35)* 7, pp. 1-10 at p. 8. There can be no doubt that the 1982 scheme of protection is incoherent and incomplete. However, the desire "to fill the gaps" should not result in the advancement of interpretations that do not take into consideration the fundamental principles of the 1982 Convention and the law of the sea in general. It would be absurd to argue that "the Area would stretch in on the continental shelf, when talking about underwater cultural heritage", or that alternatively "the coastal State has jurisdiction for the purpose of protection of underwater cultural heritage on the continental shelf".

70   *Ibid* at pp. 8-9. These arguments mainly represent the Turkish views on the Draft European Convention on the Protection of the Underwater Cultural Heritage. See further "Minory statement made by the Turkish expert" in Council of Europe, *Ad Hoc* Committee of Experts on the Underwater Cultural Heritage (CAHAQ), "Final Activity Report", *Doc. CAHAQ(85)5*, Strasbourg, 23 April 1985, Appendix V, pp. 33-34. See also *supra* chapter 5 at pp. 195-196.

71   In an attempt to clarify the precise meaning to be attributed to article 17, the Explanatory Report on the Draft Convention emphasises the fact that "the Convention does not otherwise apply to the continental shelf." See "Draft Explanatory Report on the Convention on the Protection of the Underwater Cultural Heritage", *ibid,* Appendix IV, pp. 24-32 at p. 32.

72   On the legal status of the EEZ see also Kwiatkowska, B., *The 200 mile Exclusive Economic Zone in the New Law of the Sea*, Martinus Nijhoff Publishers, 1989 at pp. 230-235, who argues that the provisions of the Convention supply arguments in favour of both a high seas and a *sui generis* status of the EEZ.

73 Article 59: "In cases where the present Convention does not attribute rights or jurisdiction to the coastal State or to other States within the exclusive economic zone, and a conflict arises between the interests of the coastal State and any other State or States, the conflict should be resolved on the basis of equity and in the light of all the relevant circumstances, taking into account the respective importance of the interests involved to the parties as well as to the international community as a whole."

74 Concerning rights attributed by the Convention, the reciprocal "due regard rule" as envisaged in articles 56(2) and 58(3) is applicable. Article 56(2): "In exercising its rights and performing its duties under this Convention in the exclusive economic zone, the coastal State shall have due regard to the rights and duties of other States and shall act in a manner compatible with the provisions of this Convention." Article 58(3): "In exercising their rights and performing their duties under this Convention in the exclusive economic zone, States shall have due regard to the rights and duties of the coastal State and shall comply with the laws and regulations adopted by the coastal State in accordance with the provisions of this Convention and other rules of international law in so far as they are not incompatible with this Part."

75 In the view of Lucchini and Voekkel: "on constate ici une lacune du droit de la mer". Lucchini, L., Voekkel, M., *Droit de la mer*, Pedone A. éditions, 1990 at p. 219. See, however, Zhao, H., "Recent developments in the legal protection of historic shipwrecks in China", 23 *Ocean Dev. & Int'l. L.* (1992) pp. 305-303 at pp. 316-317, who argues that "even though historic shipwrecks may not be regarded as natural resources, the words 'such as', which refer to 'the production of energy from the water, currents and winds' do not exhaust all of the examples of 'other activities for economic exploration and exploitation of the zone' and treasure hunting and economic salvage activities may be construed as 'other activities for economic exploration and exploitation of the zone'. Accordingly, the coastal State might be able to exercise jurisdiction over such activities in the EEZ." He also argues that marine archaeology is clearly a form of marine scientific research and that most provisions of Part XIII may apply to archaeological research. See also Alexander, *op. cit.* note 69 at pp. 9-10, who argues that if treasure salvage is an economic exploitation of the EEZ, a U.S. admiralty court is the logical and appropriate forum in which that question should be adjudicated. However, even if treasure salvage in the EEZ is a high seas freedom, an appropriate admiralty court should be able to assert jurisdiction over an abandoned shipwreck in the EEZ, if the court's *in rem* jurisdiction is properly invoked and perfected.

76 It is obvious from the discussion of the right of innocent passage in Chapter 4 that archaeological research cannot be justified either as an exercise of the freedom of navigation or as a related use.

77 The establishment of this duty is implicit in the text of article 59, which provides criteria for the settlement of disputes, in particular, in concepts such as "equity", "relevant circumstances" and "the respective importance of the interests involved". A similar approach was adopted by the ICJ in the *Fisheries Jurisdiction* and the *North Sea Continental Shelf cases*, where the duty to negotiate was

established from: (a) the concept of preferential rights, and (b) article 33 of the UN Charter. *Fisheries Jurisdiction C.f. (United Kingdom v. Iceland) (Merits)* Judgment, *I.C.J. Reports* (1974) 3 at p. 32, para. 74 and *North Sea Continental Shelf Cases (Federal Republic of Germany v. Denmark, Federal Republic of Germany v. The Netherlands)*, Judgment of 20 February 1969, *I.C.J. Reports* (1969) 3 at pp. 46-47, paras. 85 and 86. See also Brown, *op. cit.* note 26 at pp. 343-344, Treves, T., "Military Installations, Structures and Devices on the Seabed", 74 *A.J.I.L.* (1980) pp. 808-852 at p. 844, and *infra* at pp. 305-306.

78 The use of the word "should" implies that the criteria in article 59 are optional. In other words, there is no obligation to follow the criteria indicated for settling the dispute. See further Migliorino, L., *Il recupero degli oggetti storici ed archeologici sommersi nel diritto internazionale*, Studi e documenti sul diritto internazionale del mare 15, Dott. Giuffrè, A. editore, Milano, 1984 at p. 166; ID, "The Recovery of Sunken Warships in International Law" in Vukas, B. (ed.), *Essays on the Law of the Sea*, Sveucilisna naklada Liber, Zagreb, 1985, pp. 244-258 at p. 257.

79 The recognition of these interests as "rights" will occur after the conclusion of the negotiations and the attribution of jurisdiction to the coastal or flag State.

80 Treves, *op.cit.* note 77 at p. 845.

81 *Op. cit.* note 77 at p. 50 (para. 93).

82 Migliorino, *op. cit.* note 78, argues that in relation to sunken warships, the interests of the flag State should receive more consideration than the interests of the coastal State.

83 Article 59 safeguards to a considerable extent the *sui generis* nature of the EEZ. However, this approach is not shared by all States; for example, see the Interpretative Declarations made by Cape Verde and Uruguay. *Cape Verde*: "IV. The regulations of the uses or activities which are not expressly provided for in the Convention but are related to the sovereign rights and to the jurisdiction of the coastal State in such zone, falls within the competence of the said State provided that such regulation does not hinder the enjoyment of the freedoms of international communications". *Uruguay*: "C. Regulation of the uses and activities not provided for expressly in the Convention (residual rights and obligations) relating to the rights of sovereignty and to the jurisdiction of the coastal State in its exclusive economic zone falls within the competence of that State provided that such regulation does not prevent enjoyment of the freedom of international communication which is recognised to other States". In contrast, *Italy*, declared that: "According to the Convention, the coastal State does not enjoy residual rights in the exclusive economic zone...". *Law of the Sea Bulletin*, No. 5, July, 1985 at pp. 45-46.

84 Migliorino, *op. cit.* note 78 at pp. 154-156. See also Giorgi, M.C., "Underwater archaeological and historical objects" in Dupuy, R-J. & Vignes, D. (eds), *A Handbook on the New Law of the Sea*, vol. 1, Hague Academy of International Law, Martinus Nijhoff, 1991, pp. 561-575 at pp. 571-572.

85 It is notable that during UNCLOS III, the proposals that would have made *all* installations for *any purpose* subject ot coastal State jurisdiction wer not accepted. See Nandan, S.N., Rosenne, S. and Grandy, N.R. (eds), *United Nations Convention on the Law of the Sea. A Commentary*, vol. II, Center for Oceans Law and Policy, University of Virginia, Martinus Nijhoff, 1993 at pp. 584-585.

86 C.f. articles 77 to 82 of the 1982 Convention. See also Zhao, *op. cit.* note 75 at p. 319, who argues that a coastal State may have jurisdiction over any exploration and excavation of historic shipwrecks that involve drilling on the continental shelf. Under article 81, the coastal State shall have the exclusive right to authorize and regulate drilling on the continental shelf. Similarly, a coastal State can exercise jurisdiction over any salvage activities involving the use of explosives to salvage historic shipwrecks on the continental shelf, since explosions may endanger the marine environment and living and non-living resources surrounding the historic shipwreck site. In recent years, many historic shipwrecks have been damaged with explosives. For example, *Geldermalsen* is said to have been dynamited after the chinaware was salvaged so that the location of the shipwreck in the South China Sea would remain unknown to the concerned governments. In 1986, when information about the auction of the chinaware salvaged from the wreck was released, China considered the *Geldermalsen* to be Chinese cultural property, despite the fact that at the time of sinking it was owned by the Dutch East Indian Company on the grounds that the chinaware originated in China. The Chinese government, however, did not make any claim to ownership as the location of the wreck remained unknown.

87 In this respect, consider the declarations made by Brazil, Cape Verde, Italy and Uruguay upon signature of the 1982 Convention on the application of article 60. *Brazil:* "The Brazilian Government understands that, in accordance with the provisions of the Convention, the coastal State has, in the exclusive economic zone and on the continental shelf, the exclusive right to construct and to authorise and regulate the construction, operation and use of all types of installations and structures without exception, whatever their nature or purpose." The same provision appears in the declaration made by Brazil while ratifying the 1982 Convention on 22 December 1988. *Cape Verde:* "This Convention does not entitle any State to construct, operate or use installations or structures in the exclusive economic zone of another State, either those provided for in the Convention or those of any other nature, without the consent of the coastal State." Cape Verde reiterated this statement in its declaration upon ratification of the Convention on 10 August 1987. *Italy:* "Moreover, the rights of the coastal State to build and to authorise, the construction, operation and the use of installations and structures in the exclusive economic zone and on the continental shelf is limited only to the categories of such isntallations and structures as listed in article 60 of the Convention." *Uruguay:* "This Convention does not empower any State to build, operate or utilise installations or structures in the exclusive economic zone of another State, neither those referred to in the Convetion not any other kind, without the consent of the coastal State." *Law of the Sea Bulletin*, No. 5, July 1985 at p. 46.

88 Equity is implicit in the notion of the "due regard rule" of articles 56(2) and 58 (3). See also footnote 77.

89 In contrast, Migliorino, argues that the rule of article 59 is not applicable in cases in which a conflict arises between two or more States, none of which is the coastal State. *Op. cit.* note 78 at p. 257.

90 In contrast, in case of conflict with coastal "rights" and "jurisdiction", the employment of these terms indicates that there is no room for raising priorities in their favour. The negotiators will proceed to an evaluation of the different interests involved and the consideration of the rules of equity. See also Nandan, Rosenne, Grandy (eds), *op.cit.* note 85, at p. 569: "Given the functional nature of the EEZ, wher economic interests are the princiipal concern this formula would normally favor the coastal State. Where conflicts arise on issues not involving the exploration for and exploitation of resources, the formula would tend to favor the interests of other States or the international community as a whole".

91 See also Churchill, R.R. and Lowe, A.V., *The Law of the Sea*, 2nd revised edition, Manchester University Press, 1988 at p. 144.

92 In contrast, Migliorino suggests the application of the concept of "reasonable-ness" (ragionevolezza). *Op. cit.* note 78 at pp. 170-172.

93 According to Apollis: "Le développement des compétences exclusive de l'état côtier en matière de recherches scientifiques a incidence économique et de protection du 'patrimoine national' par la zone économique et le plateau conti-nental n'autorise en aucune manière une interprétation restrictive concernant les gisement archéologiques". *Op. cit.* note 37 at p. 188.

94 Migliorino, *op. cit.* note 78 at p. 182.

95 *Australia:* Australian Historic Shipwrecks Act 1976, *op. cit.* note 53; *Ireland:* National Monuments (Amendment) Act, 1987, Number 17 of 1987. Section 3(1) provides that "where the Commissioners are satisfied in respect of any place on, in or under the seabed of the territorial waters of the State or on, in or under the seabed to which section 2(1) of the Continental Shelf Act, 1968, applies or on or in land covered that - (a) it is or may prove to be the site where a wreck or an archaeological object lies or formely lay, and (b) on account of the historical or artistic importance of the wreck or the object the site ought to be protected, they may by order designate an area of the seabed, or land covered by water, around and including the site as a restricted area"; *Portugal:* Law No 289/93 of 21 August 1993; *Spain:* Law 16/1985 of 25 June 1985 on the Spanish Historical Heritage. Article 40: "(1) In accordance with the provisions of Article 1 of this law, movable or immovable items of a historical nature that lends themselves to archaeological study, whether they have been excavated or not or whether they be found above ground or below ground, in territorial waters *or on the continental shelf*, shall constitute the Spanish His-torical Heritage. Similary, geological and palaeontoligal features that are related to the history of humanity its origins and its ancestry shall be a part of that heritage; (2) Caves, shelters and sites containing examples of rock art are declared property of cultural interest by virtue of this law" (emphasis added). *Yugoslavia:* Article 24 of the 1987 Law of Yugoslavia on the Coastal Sea and the Continental Shelf proclaims sovereign rights not only over natural resources,

but also over "other resources", i.e., "archaeological and other buried articles". United Nations, *The Law of the Sea: Current Developments in State Practice*, No III, Office for Legal Affairs, Division for Ocean Affairs and the Law of the Sea, 1992 at pp. 129-144. For a discussion of the 1987 Act see Skrk, M., "The 1987 Law of Yugoslavia on the Coastal Sea and the Continental Shelf", 20 *Ocean Dev. & Int'l. L.* (1989) pp. 501-514 at p. 508. A similar provision is to be found in article 3 of the Decree of the Council of State concerning the establishment of the Exclusive Economic Zone of the *Socialist Republic of Romania* in the Black Sea, No. 142 of 25 April 1986. However, article 3 of the 1986 Decree does not clarify what is meant with the expression "other resources of the seabed". See also Franckx, E., "Romania's Proclamation of a 200-mile Exclusive Economic Zone", 2 *International Journal of Estuarine and Coastal Law* (1987) pp. 144-153. *China* may also be considered to have expanded its jurisdiction over the continental shelf. As already seen, the 1989 Regulation on Protection and Administration of Underwater Relics enables China to exercise jurisdiction over underwater relics found in areas under its jurisdiction according to Chinese laws. Since China enjoys *ab initio* and *ipso jure* sovereign rights over the continental shelf, it is argued that the Regulation became effective upon its entry into force, even before the enactment of the relevant continental shelf legislation. It is notable that the Third Draft Underwater Cultural Relics Regulation, referred specifically to the continental shelf and the EEZ. However, since the Chinese laws concerning these areas were still in draft form and under examination, the Regulation employed the broad term "other sea areas under China's jurisdiction" instead of distinguishing those zones yet to be claimed formally. Zhao, *op.cit.* note 75 at p. 315 *et seq.* Finally, see the declaration made by *Cape Verde* while ratifying the 1982 Convention, where it is stated that, without prejudice to article 303 any object of archaeological and historical nature found within marine spaces under its sovereignty or jurisdiction shall not be removed without its prior authorisation. United Nations, *Law of the Sea: Current Developments in State Practice*, vol. II, Office for Oceans Affairs and the Law of the Sea, 1989 at p. 89.

96   In the *North Sea Continental Shelf Cases,* the ICJ held that articles 1 to 3 of the CSC have acquired the status of a customary rule. *Op. cit.* note 77 at p. 42. As noted, these articles confine coastal rights over the continental shelf to natural-resource exploration and exploitation, the notion of which excludes underwater cultural property. More recently in the *Libya/Malta Continental Shelf Case* (1985), see below note 98, para. 39, the ICJ asserted that current law allows all States to claim a 200-mile continental shelf and took article 76(1) of the 1982 Convention to represent customary international law. For further discussion see Evans, M.D., *Relevant Circumstances and Maritime Delimitation*, Clarendon Press, Oxford, 1989 at pp. 52-55.

97   United Nations, *The Law of the Sea: Practice of States at the Time of Entry into Force of the United Nations Convention on the Law of the Sea,* Division for Ocean Affairs and the Law of the Sea, Office of Legal Affairs, 1994 at p. 216.

98 In 1982, in the *Tunisia/Libya Continental Shelf Case, I.C.J. Reports* (1982) p. 18 at p. 74, para. 100, the ICJ referred to the concept of the EEZ as "part of modern international law", while in the *Libya/Malta Continental Shelf Case, I.C.J. Reports* (1985) p. 13 at p. 33, it held that: "It is incontestable that the institution of the exclusive economic zone with its rule on entitlement by reason of distance, is shown by the practice of States to have become a part of customary law." See also the Restatement (Third) of the Foreign Relations Law of the United States and Simmonds, K.R., "The Law of the Sea: Restatement (Third) and the UN Convention on the Law of the Sea", 24 *International Lawyer* (1990) pp. 931-956 at pp. 947-950. It would be correct to say that the EEZ acquired customary status even before the adoption of the 1982 Convention. By the time of the RSNT, the concept of the EEZ had been recognised by the international community; in 1977 and 1978, 55 claims had already been implemented. Smith, R.W., *Exclusive Economic Zone Claims: An Analysis and Primary Documents,* Martinus Nijhoff Publishers, Dordrecht, 1986 at p. 30.

99 See also Caminos, H. & Molitor, R., "Progressive Development of International Law and the Package Deal", 79 *A.J.I.L.* (1985) pp. 871-890 at p. 888: "The customary rule does not derive from the EEZ provisions of the Convention but rather from the practice of States reflected in the combined effect of the numerous municipal laws establishing such zones and the numerous bilateral fisheries agreements concluded during the last 10 years. Clearly, EEZs as they now exist under customary international law may not resemble in all respects the EEZ regime embodied in the 1982 Convention", Brown, E.D., "The Legal Regime and the United Nations Convention on the Law of the Sea (UNCLOS)" in *Exclusive Economic Zones - Resources, Opportunities and the Legal Regime,* vol. 8, Advances in Underwater Technology, Ocean Science and Offshore Engineering, Graham & Trotman Ltd., London, 1986, pp. 15-35 at p. 18, and Attard: "Indeed, the provisions relating to the EEZ's basic character, particularly those relevant to the coastal State's competence, remain substantially the same at least from the ICNT until their incorporation into the 1982 Convention. This stability, and the evolving consensus at the Conference encouraged States to establish EEZs and to make their legislation conform with the relevant provisions of the UNCLOS III text prevailing at the time. Even before the Conference's conclusion, this widespread practice had already crystallised elements of the UNCLOS III model. Consequently, the 1982 Convention EEZ model, which incorporates these elements may be considered, at least in its essentials, to reflect customary law. The EEZ provisions of the 1982 Convention, such as articles 69 and 70, which do not reflect customary law remain purely conventional values. Whether they will acquire a broader basis remains to be seen; *qua* conventional rules, however, they are not opposable to non-parties". Attard, D.J., *The Exclusive Economic Zone in International Law,* Clarendon Press, Oxford, 1987 at p. 308. See also Treves, T., "Codification du droit international et pratique des états dans le droit de la mer", 223 *Hague Recueil* (1990-IV) pp. 9-302 at p. 83-89.

For these reasons a number of scholars were opposed to the recognition of the EEZ as part of customary law at least on a general level. See Burke, W.T., "National legislation on ocean authority zones and the contemporary law of the sea", 9 *Ocean Dev. & Int'l L.* (1983) pp. 289-322 at pp. 311-313; the dissenting opinion of Judge Oda in the *Tunisia/Libya Continental Shelf Case, ibid* at p. 142 *et seq.*, Charney, J.L., "The Exclusive Economic Zone and Public International Law", 15 *Ocean Dev. & Int'l L.* (1985) pp. 233-288 at p. 239 and citations in footnote 33; Smith, *ibid* at p. 32, and Soons, A.H.A., *Marine Scientific Research and the Law of the Sea*, T.M.A. Asser Institute, Kluwer Law and Taxation Publishers, The Hague, 1982 at p. 266, who states: "It can be argued, however, that among those States which have established exclusive economic zones of an identical or similar nature, the concept of the exclusive economic zone as defined by them has become part of international law." For a discussion of the EEZ as customary international law, see further Kwiatkowska, *op. cit.* note 72 at pp. 27-37.

100 *Jamaica:* Act 33 of 1991 entitled the Exclusive Economic Zone Act 1991. Article 4(c)i: "In the Zone there is vested in the Crown .... jurisdiction in respect of ...... the recovery of archaeological or historical objects"; *Morocco:* Act No. 1-81 of 18 December 1980, promulgated by Dahir No. 1-81-179 of 8 April 1981. Article 5: "Any archaeological research or exploration undertaken by a foreign State or by nationals of a foreign State in the exclusive economic zone shall be subject to the prior authorisation of the Moroccan administration"; *Denmark:* Article 1(2) of the Act No. 9 of 3 January 1992 on the Protection of Nature. See also *infra* chapter 5 at p. 211, note 108.

101 *States asserting sovereign rights over "all resources":* Democratic People's *Republic of Korea:* Decree by the Central People's Committee establishing the Economic Zone of the People's Democratic Republic of Korea, 21 June 1977; *Iceland:* Law No 41 of 1 June 1979 concerning the Territorial Sea, the Economic Zone and the Continental Shelf (article 4); *Mauritius:* Maritime Zones Act, 1977, Act No 13 of 3 June 1977 (article 7(1)a); *Pakistan:* Territorial Waters and Maritime Zones Act, 1977 (article 6(2)a); *Seychelles:* Maritime Zones Act, 1977 (article 7(1)a); *Vanuatu:* Maritime Zones Act No 23 of 1981 (article 10(a). *States requiring their permit for the exploration or exploitation of "any resources":* Barbados: Marine Boundaries and Jurisdiction Act, 1978 (article 6(1)a); *Grenada:* Marine Boundaries Act, 1978 (article 6(1)a); *Guyana:* Maritime Boundaries Act, 1977 (article 17); *Mauritius: ibid* (article 7(2)a); *Pakistan: ibid* (article 6(3); *Philippines:* Presidential Decree No 1599 of 11 June 1978 establishing an Exclusive Economic Zone and for Other Purposes (article 3(a)); *Seychelles: ibid* (article 7(2)a); *Tanzania (United Republic of):* Territorial Sea and Exclusive Economic Zone Act 1989 (article 10(1)a); *Vanuatu: ibid* (article 11(a)).

102 *States requiring their permit for the conduct of "any research":* Barbados: ibid (article 6(1)c); *Democratic People's Republic of Korea, ibid; Grenada: ibid* (article 6(1)c); *Guyana: ibid* (article 17); *Iran:* Act on the Marine Areas of the Islamic Republic of Iran in the Persian Gulf and the Oman Seas (article 14); *Malaysia:* Exclusive Economic Zone Act 1984, Act No 311 (article 5(b)); *Mauritius: ibid* (article 7(2)c); *Pakistan: ibid* (article 6(3); *Philippines: ibid* (sec.3(b).(c)); *Seychelles: ibid* (article 7(2)b); *Trinidad & Tobago:* Archipelagic

Waters and Exclusive Economic Zone Act, 1986 (article 22(f)): consent required for the carrying out of any other such activity; *Tanzania (United Republic of): ibid* (article 10(1)c); *Vanuatu: ibid* (article 11(c)).

103 For example, consider section 7 of *Mauritius'* Maritime Zones Act, 1977. Under section 9: "The Prime Minister may, by Order published in the Gazette: (a) declare any area of the continental shelf or the exclusive economic zone to be a designated area; and (b) make such provisions as he considers necessary with respect to - (i) the exploration, exploitation and protection of the resources within the designated areas; (v) customs and other fiscal matters in relation to the designated areas." Guyana, India, Iran, Pakistan and Seychelles have enacted similar provisions with respect to the declaration of designated areas. It is also reported that in Seychelles antiquities are classified as 'non-living' resources of the seabed. See further Prott and O'Keefe, *op. cit.* note 64 at p. 95.

Finally, section 7(7) of *India's* Territorial Waters, Continental Shelf, Exclusive Zone and Other Maritime Zones Act 1976 provides that: "The Central Government may by notification in the official Gazette: (a) extend, with such restrictions and modifications as it thinks fit, any enactment for the time being in force in India or any part thereof to the exclusive economic zone or any part thereof; and (b) make such provisions as it may consider necessary for facilitating the enforcement of such enactment, and any enactment so extended shall have effect as if the exclusive economic zone or the part thereof to which it had been extended is a part of the territory of India." It has been argued that: "Though the provision apparently gives authority to the Central Government to extend any enactment to the EEZ, the intention seems to be to extend only such enactments as are relatable to the EEZ and are in keeping with the rights and jurisdiction claimed by India under the Maritime Zones Act 1976, for it is well settled that not all Indian enactments could be extended to the EEZ, since it is not unlike the territorial waters and the continental shelf, part of the territory of India." Rao, P.C., *The New Law of Maritime Zones*, Milind Publications Private Ltd., New Delhi, 1983 at p. 283. Nevertheless there is nothing in sec. 7 to prevent the Indian Government from extending its antiquities legislation over the EEZ.

104 See, for example, *Mauritius, ibid* (article 7(1)b), *India, ibid* (article 7(4)b); *Pakistan, op. cit.* note 101, (article 6(2)b); *Guyana, ibid* (article 16(b)), *Grenada*, Marine Boundaries Act, Act No. 20 (article 5(a)(ii). Article 6(1)c requires permitt for drilling in, or constructing, maintaining or operating any structure or device. Finally, Iceland claims jurisdiction with regard to the establishment and use of man-made structures.

105 These are: Benin, Congo, Ecuador, El Salvador, Liberia, Nicaragua, Panama, Peru, Sierra Leone, Somalia, Uruguay. See *Law of the Sea Bulletin*, No. 23, June 1993 at p. 78.

106 Juda, L., "The Exclusive Economic Zone: Compatibility of National Claims and the UN Convention on the Law of the Sea", 16 *Ocean Dev. & Int'l L.* (1986) pp. 1-58 at pp. 16-20. On the acccommodation of residual rights see also Treves, *op. cit.* note 99 at pp. 213-217.

107 Kwiatkowska, *op. cit.* note 72 at p. 230.

108 *States asserting rights and duties for which provision is made in international law or is recognised in international law:* Antigua and Barbuda; Barbados; Bulgaria; Burma; Democratic Yemen; Dominica; Equatorial Guinea; France; Grenada; Guyana; Iceland; India; Jamaica; Kenya; Malaysia; Marshal Islands; Mauritania; Mauritius; Micronesia; Pakistan; Philippines; Poland; Romania; Seychelles; Spain; Sri Lanka; Thailand; Tuvalu; USSR; Vanuatu; Saint Vincent and Grenadines.

Functional test for residual rights (without reference to international law standard): Guatemala; Honduras.

States silent on question of residual rights: Argentina; Bangladesh; Brazil; Belize; Cambodia; Colombia; Cook Islands; Costa Rica; Cuba; Dominican Republic; Fiji; Gabon; Ghana; Indonesia; Guinea-Bissau; Maldives; Mexico; Morocco; Mozambique; Namibia; Nieu; New Zealand; Nigeria; Norway; Oman; Qatar; São Tomé and Príncipe; Suriname; Togo; Portugal; Samoa; Senegal; Saint Kitts and Nevis; Saint Lucia; Tonga; Trinidad and Tobago; Turkey; Viet Nam; United States; United Arab Emirates; Venezuela.

States claiming possession of residual rights: Cape Verde; Haiti; Korea; Uruguay. For *Uruguay* see Interpretative Declaration, *Law of the Sea Bulletin*, No. 5 July, 1985 at pp. 45-46, as it has not as yet declared on EEZ. Haiti appears to claim sovereignty over the air space and waters of the EEZ, while Korea claims sovereignty over all living and non-living resources of the waters, the seabed and the subsoil. *Source:* Juda, *op.cit.* note 106, pp. 16-20, *updated and amended by the author.*

109 See, however, section 10 of the Swedish Economic Zone Act of 16 December 1992, which reads: "The Act, as well as the regulations and conditions that are published on the basis of this Act, shall not include any restrictions of the rights, existing under international law... nor of any other rights that follow from the generally recognised principles of international law". As argued, the burden of proof lies on the flag State to show that the enjoyment of a certain right has in fact been recognised as a general principle of international law. Mahmoudi, S., "Current legal developments: Sweden", 8 *The International Journal of Marine and Coastal Law* (1993) pp. 524-529 at p. 528.

CHAPTER 8

The International Deep Seabed (The Area)

THE GENEVA CONVENTION ON THE HIGH SEAS (1958)

Under the scheme of the 1958 Geneva Conventions, the deep seabed is governed by the freedom of the high seas. Marine archaeology may be exercised as a legitimate use of the seabed, if it is kept within the limits of reasonableness and it is not prohibited by a rule of international law.[1] In this context, the 1970 Declaration of Principles Governing the Sea-Bed and the Ocean Floor, and the Subsoil thereof, Beyond the Limits of National Jurisdiction may be of interest: "The sea-bed and and ocean floor and the subsoil thereof, beyond the limits of national jurisdiction (hereinafter referred to as the area), as well as the resources of the area are the common heritage of mankind."[2]

The question that arises here is whether deep seabed cultural property falls within the notion of "resources" and the common heritage of mankind principle. *Prima facie*, the answer seems to be in the negative. Despite the absence of a definition of the term "resources", there is little doubt that the Declaration refers to mineral-resource exploration and exploitation. UN Resolution 2749 was the result of the desire of the majority of States to preserve the riches and wealth of the deep seabed as the common heritage of mankind and to provide economic assistance to developing countries.[3] A further confirmation of this conclusion is provided by the fact that the international deep seabed regime, adopted by the 1982 Convention on the basis of the 1970 Declaration, does not encompass archaeological and historical objects within the notion of "resources". While it could be argued that the text of the Declaration is wide enough to include them within its scope,[4] such an interpetation would not significantly alter their legal regime. The reason is that the Declaration does not specify the manner in which the common heritage principle is to be implemented; it simply declares the responsibility of States to ensure that activities in the Area shall be carried out in conformity with the international regime to be established on the basis of the principles of the Declaration. It was article 149 of the 1982 Convention which introduced the cultural aspect of the common heritage of mankind principle as applied on the deep seabed.[5]

THE UN CONVENTION ON THE LAW OF THE SEA (1982)

Article 149 of the Convention states:

> "All objects of an archaeological and historical nature found in the Area shall be preserved or disposed of for the benefit of mankind as a whole, particular regard being paid to the preferential rights of the State or country of origin, or the State of cultural origin or the State of historical and archaeological origin."

Genesis and development of article 149

The Sea-Bed Committee. On 26 May 1970, in a Report submitted by the Secretary-General on the Potential Role of the International Machinery to be Established, "the exploration and recovery of sunken ships and lost objects" was foreseen as a use of the seabed, "which might be accompanied by the performance of related functions and powers by international machinery (both from point of view of archaeology and as regards salvage operations)."[6] The submission of underwater relics to the jurisdiction of the International Machinery was considered independently of their interpretation as resources of the seabed; if their recovery was regarded as a legitimate use of the seabed, they would fall within the regulatory powers of the Machinery. As explained, "perhaps [the wrecks, relics or lost objects lying on the seabed] are not resources or at least not natural resources. Nevertheless, they may fall under the jurisdiction of the machinery if the recovery of such objects is regarded as another use of the seabed."[7] On 9 August 1970, the United States proposed a draft Convention to the Sea-Bed Committee.[8] Although the draft text did not provide specifically for marine archaeological sites,[9] article 25 was of some relevance. It read: "The International Seabed Resource Authority may designate as international marine parks and preserves specific portions of the international seabed area that have unusual educational, scientific or recreational value."

In 1971, Greece submitted a working paper in Sub-Committee I and proposed the inclusion of "Archaeological and Historical Treasures of the
Sea-Bed and the Ocean Floor Beyond the Limits of National Jurisdiction"
in the list of topics for discussion.[10] Eventually, the legal regime of the
underwater cultural heritage was placed on the agenda of the Sea-Bed
Committee in the "List of Subjects and Issues Relating to the Law of the
Sea"[11] under the aforementioned title. It was numbered twenty-third on
a list of 25 items. The archaeological issue was raised again in 1972 by a
Greek proposal, which provided that "the archaeological and historical
treasures of the seabed and the ocean floor beyond the limits of national
jurisdiction should be protected as a common heritage of mankind."[12] The
proposal provided, *inter alia*, for: (a) the obligation to report to the Authority
the discovery of any item of archaeological or historical value, (b) the
establishment of regional supervisory organs, (c) the temporary suspension
of operations as soon as an item of antiquity was "spotted" in the international seabed area, (d) the notification of the State or States of origin and
the consideration of their rightful interests, and (e) the prohibition of the
selling of the recovered items to unauthorised persons. It also included a
criminal clause, stating that each State should make it an offence for its
nationals and vessels to violate the relevant regulations. The proposal was
revised in 1973 by a less comprehensive text,[13] which, however, retained
the main features of the initial draft in that all objects of archaeological or
historical value in the deep seabed were considered to be part of the common
heritage of mankind; the Authority was empowered to take measures for
the identification, protection and conservation of such items, while the State
of cultural origin was granted the preferential right to salvage and acquire
them under procedures to be established by the Assembly, including compensation to be paid to the Authority. In case the State of cultural origin omitted
to exercise its preferential rights, the Authority would dispose of the object
in question in accordance with the principle that it forms part of the common
heritage of mankind.

A similar proposal was drafted by Turkey in 1973.[14] The Turkish proposal,
which was submitted four months before the revised Greek proposal,
regarded archaeological and historical treasures discovered during the exploration and exploitation of the Area as constituting part of the common
heritage of mankind and, thus, enjoying the protection of the International
Authority. The latter was required to bring such discoveries to the notice
of member States and, in case the State of the country of origin did not

exercise its right to acquire the treasure against payment, to sell it to authorised third parties or keep it in a museum belonging to the International Authority or to the United Nations. The Authority was also entitled to draw up, in consultation with specialised agencies of the United Nations, rules for regulating the discovery, identification, protection, acquisition and disposal of the items in question.

To sum-up, all the proposals recognised the Authority as the competent international organ to deal with deep seabed archaeological treasures. However, there were a number of differences in the specific rights attributed to the Authority. For example, under the Turkish proposal, the International Authority had the right to sell the discovered treasures to authorised third parties in case the State of the country of origin did not exercise its rights to acquire the treasure. Under the revised Greek proposal, the Authority would only dispose of the objects in conformity with the principle of the common heritage of mankind, while the initial Greek proposal prohibited the selling to unauthorised persons. The consideration of the rights of the State(s) of origin was also common. Although the precise scope of these rights was not specified, it can be assessed that they were mainly confined to the salvaging and the acquisition of the items discovered against compensation to be paid to the Authority/finder. In an attempt to define the rightful holder of these rights, the initial Greek proposal used the expression "State of historical origin", while the revised draft employed the formula "State of cultural origin". In contrast, the Turkish proposal referred to the "State of the country of origin". According to the Turkish representative, the latter was preferable as it was more precise than the Greek expression, which, in his opinion, was unable to face the problem of the same culture being shared in the past by several countries.[15] The Turkish proposal attempted to overcome the considerable difficulties in identifying the State of origin by giving preference to the State that exercises sovereignty over the country of origin.[16] It seems, therefore, that at these early stages of the negotiations, the Authority was seen as a sort of *custodian* of archaeological treasures for the benefit of mankind as a whole; an approach that did not challenge the rightful interests of the State(s) of origin.

The debate on the archaeological issue ended with the elaboration of article 20 which was subsequently passed on to the first substantive session of UNCLOS III. It read:[17]

"1. Particular regard being paid to the preferential rights of [the State of country of] [the State of cultural] [the State of historical and archaeological] origin, all objects of an archaeological and historical nature found in the area shall be preserved [or disposed of by the Authority] for the benefit of the international community as a whole.

2. The recovery and disposal of wrecks and their contents more than [fifty] years old found in the Area shall be subject to regulation by the Authority without prejudice to the rights of the owner thereof."

The bracketed language indicates that the archaeological issue was still pending.

The Third UN Conference on the Law of the Sea (First Committee). The first substantive session of UNCLOS III (the 1974 Caracas session) did not deal with the archaeological issue. Committee I considered the articles as they appeared in the Report of Sub-Committee I of the Seabed Committee and did not issue a new text. The text that was prepared by the Sub-Committee was labelled variant (A) and this was put together with a variant (B), which suggested its omission.[18] The 1975 Gevena session added a new paragraph (3) to the mentioned variant (A), subjecting all disputes relating to a preferential right or a right of ownership to the procedure of settlement of disputes of the Convention. The resulting text formed article 19 of the ISNT adopted at that session.[19]

"1. All objects of an archaeological and historical nature found in the Area shall be preserved or disposed of by the Authority for the benefit of the international community as a whole, particular regard being paid to the preferential rights of the State of country of origin, or the State of cultural origin, or the State of historical and archaeological origin.

2. The recovery and disposal of wrecks and their contents more than 50 years old found in the Area shall be subject to regulation by the Authority without prejudice to the rights of the owner thereof.

3. Any dispute with regard to a preferential right under paragraph 1 or a right of ownership under paragraph 2, shall, on the application of either party, be subject to the procedure for settlement of disputes provided for in this Convention."

The 1976 New York session produced the RSNT, which modified article 19 of the ISNT considerably. Article 19 of the RSNT[20] read:

"All objects of an archaeological and historical nature found in the Area shall be preserved or disposed of for the benefit of the international community as a whole, particular regard being paid to the preferential rights of the State or country of origin, or the State of cultural origin or the State of historical and archaeological origin."

By deleting paragraphs (2) and (3) of article 19 of the ISNT and by failing to designate an international body to implement the proposed regime, the drafters of this article produced a vague provision of limited practical significance. However, the modification of the term "State of country of origin" to "State or country of origin" was helpful in that it attributed some meaning to the, otherwise, incomprehensible text.[21] Article 19 of the RSNT remained unchanged[22] until the 1980 Geneva session (resumed ninth), which substituted "benefit of mankind as a whole" for "benefit of the international community as a whole" and incorporated the amended text as article 149 of the Draft Convention on the Law of the Sea (Informal Text).[23] This modification was preserved in the Final Text of the Convention adopted in the 1982 Caracas session.

Analysis of article 149

Failure to designate an appropriate international body to implement article 149

The significance of article 149 is limited to a considerable extent by the failure to establish an international agency to implement the proposed regime. The Authority, which had appeared in the early proposals as the regulating organ, is not mentioned in article 149, arguably on the basis that it was not qualified to undertake the task of protecting archaeological objects.[24] Another reason would seem to be the determination of some States, notably the United States, to restrict the scope of the powers of the Seabed Authority to activities relating to mineral resources.[25] In the light of of article 157(2), which states that the "powers and functions of the Authority shall be those expressly conferred upon it by this Convention. The Authority shall have such incidental powers consistent with this Convention, as are implicit in and necessary for the exercise of those powers and functions with respect to activities in the Area", the Authority does not appear to enjoy any jurisdictional powers over archaeological and historical objects. Deepwater archaeological operations do not qualify as "activities in the Area" which are confined to mineral resource exploration and exploitation.[26] In contrast, the initial Greek proposal had even suggested the establishment of regional organs for the exploration and utilisation of the archaeological and historical treasures of the international seabed in closed or semi-closed seas. The nomination of one of the departments of the Authority as competent to address the archaeological issue would have avoided all these problems. Since the latter is the overall regulating body in the Area, it would have been entirely appropriate for it to deal with the protection of archaeological and historical objects.[27]

As things now stand, there are two alternatives:

a. To establish a qualified international body to deal with the protection of deep seabed cultural property.
b. To leave the implementation of the proposed regime to individual States.

Despite the obvious difficulties in designating an international or a regional agency to implement the proposed regime,[28] the establishment of an international agency is essential as "mankind" as such can hardly exercise any rights or implement any duties. It must be represented legally by an international organisation. In this respect, UNESCO appears to be the most appropriate body to deal with the task of establishing an effective regime of protection. Not only does it have the legislative and the operative powers, it has also shown an increased interest in underwater archaeology and the protection of the cultural heritage of the oceans.[29] The second alternative is for the proposed regime to be implemented by individual States. The effectiveness of this solution is doubtful, especially when it is considered that the text of article 149 is vague enough to allow more than one interpretation. Flag State jurisdiction has been proved to be unable to accommodate the needs of the protection of the underwater cultural heritage. The abandonment of the implementation of the concept of the common heritage of mankind on the same principles cannot guarantee a fair result.

Substantive meaning of article 149
In addition to the lack of an appropriate body to implement article 149, the proposed regime suffers from vagueness and ambiguity. First, article 149 does not specify how and where the objects in question will be "preserved or disposed of" for the benefit of mankind as a whole, nor does it provide for the funding of such activities. What does "disposal" mean within the ambit of article 149? Does it include the "selling" of the objects in question to third parties? If yes, how is "mankind as a whole" to be benefited from such transactions? Second, under article 149, archaeological and historical objects receive the attention of the international community only when found. Is the right to search for such items also to be carried for the mankind as a whole or is archaeological research to be exercised as a freedom of the high seas? Third, article 149 fails to establish the obligation to report the

accidental discovery of archaeological objects and/or notify the interested parties. Finally, the accommodation of "preferential rights" is far from satisfactory. Article 149 recognises three different categories of States as claimants to these rights without defining the employed terms and without establishing priorities. Inevitably, conflicts will arise as to which State has priority over the items discovered. With shipwrecks, the additional problem may arise as to whether the right of the State of origin of the ship prevails over the right of the State of origin of individual artefacts from its cargo. All these questions must first be answered if the proposed scheme is to be put into practice.

Preservation and disposal of objects of an archaeological and historical nature for the benefit of mankind as a whole. With regard to deep seabed cultural property, the concept of "benefit of mankind as a whole" should be viewed in terms of the universal importance of culture. In the light of the recently increased concern of the international community in the protection of the cultural heritage of the twentieth century, deep seabed cultural property must not be appropriated by individual States or privately operating salvors. Both the artefacts themselves and the information they provide form part of the common heritage of mankind.

Article 149 breathed new life into the abstract notion of "the right to equal enjoyment of the common cultural heritage" that appears in the Banjul Charter on Human and Peoples Rights (1981).[30] Many questions, however, remain unanswered: what does the "right to equal enjoyment of the common cultural heritage" mean? Does aricle 149 refer to cultural exchanges or to the sending on loan of collections of artefacts to individual States? Is it possible to consider the "benefit of mankind as a whole" in economic terms? The answer to this last question should be in the negative. The notion of the benefit of mankind as a whole under article 149 differs in nature from this concept when used generally in the Area, where it is mainly confined to the distribution of wealth acquired by the exploitation of mineral resources and the transfer of technology. Despite the fact that the "common heritage of mankind" priniciple has often been described as the legal counterpart of the attempt to establish a New International Economic Order, as elaborated by the 1982 Convention, the deep seabed regime is limited to mining operations alone. The declaration that not only the mineral resources but the Area itself belongs to the common heritage of mankind (Article 136), does not appear to have further implications on the exercise of other activities. The international deep seabed regime did not replace the freedom of the high seas by a new management system encompassing all activities in the Area.

According to Pinto, the mineral resources of the seabed are *res publicae*. "The common heritage of mankind is the common property of mankind. The commonness of the common heritage is a commonness of ownership and benefit."[31] However, it is debatable whether article 149 can be read in terms of "commonness of ownership". The early Greek and Turkish proposals had, indeed, referred to sunken archaeological and historical treasures as part of the common heritage of mankind. The subsequent drafts, however, simply advocated the preservation and disposal of archaeological objects for the benefit of the international community as a whole. The declaration of the Area and its resources as the common heritage of mankind does not affect *per se* archaeological objects. The latter are not minerals, while their regime is distinguishable from the seabed. The international deep seabed regime is primarily confined to mineral-resource exploration and exploitation. At the same time, consideration has been given to the presence of archaeological objects in the Area. Under article 149 the benefit of mankind as a whole should primarily be regarded as cultural and educational.[32]

However, there is nothing in the 1982 Convention to prohibit the elaboration in the future of the principle of the common heritage of mankind in a more concrete form. As already seen, its application in the cultural field differs from its application to natural-resource regimes, such as the deep seabed and the outer space. Since archaeological remains on land are always situated within State territories, one of the fundamental elements of the notion of the common heritage of mankind, the prohibition of appropriation by individual States, is lacking. It is on these grounds that the cultural common heritage of mankind has been described as "patrimoine commun de l'humanité 'par l'affectation'".[33] Recently, the need to protect deep seabed archaeological remains, which are endangered by the development of advanced underwater technology, has broadened the scope of the common heritage of mankind so as to include remains found on the seabed beyond national jurisdiction. It is with regard to these sites that the elaboration of the notion of the common heritage of mankind in a more concrete form is needed. In this context, the notion of *trust* would appear to provide the best solution. The establishment of an international organ as a *trustee* of humanity, accompanied by the recognition of the rightful interests of the State(s) of origin of the objects discovered may ensure a fair and satisfactory scheme of protection.[34]

Furthermore, article 149 does not specify the manner in which archaeological objects are to be "preserved or disposed of". The only reference to this issue was made by the 1973 Turkish proposal, which provided for the keeping of the recovered items in a museum belonging to the International Authority or to the United Nations in case the State of origin neglected to exercise its rights. This is an interesting suggestion that could guarantee the protection of the recovered cultural property under the aegis of the international community. If, however, under the circumstances, the *in situ* preservation of underwater cultural property is possible, it should be preferred. According to Prott and O'Keefe: "The phrase shall be 'preserved or disposed of' writes an unfortunate conflict into the article - the question whether to preserve a shipwreck requiring the suspension of exploration or construction projects at enormous cost, or 'dispose of' it in some other way."[35]

Funding is another important but neglected issue. Since the Authority does not enjoy any powers over archaeological objects, it is very unlikely that deep seabed archaeological projects will be sponsored by its funds (article 171). The enormous costs of underwater operations would have to be covered by other sources, such as the UN Environmental Fund or the International Fund for the Promotion of Culture of UNESCO.[36] The situation is far from satisfactory, as those States which are not parties to the 1982 Convention, may oppose the use of their contributions to the budget the said organisations for archaeological purposes.[37] Nevertheless, unless an international organisation is designated to implement the proposed regime, the undertaking of archaeological projects on the international deep seabed is entirely at the discretion of individual States.

Right to search for objects of an archaeological and historical nature. Article 149 fails to provide for the search of archaeological objects. The question, therefore, arises whether archaeological exploration should be carried out for the benefit of mankind as a whole. In the light of the UNESCO Recommendation on International Principles Applicable to Archaeological Excavations (1956), which defines archaeological excavations as "any research aimed at the discovery of objects of archaeological character whether such research involves digging of the ground, or systematic *exploration* of its *surface* or is carried out on the bed or in the sub-soil of inland or territorial waters of a member State" (emphasis added)[38], the answer appears to be in the positive even if article 149 does not refer specifically to "excavations". Since the search for and location of underwater sites are inextricably linked with their preservation and protection, the conduct of such activities should also fall within the scope of article 149.

This is confirmed by article 143, which reads: "Marine scientific research in the Area shall be carried out exclusively for peaceful purposes and for the benefit of mankind as a whole". In other words, a necessary prerequisite for the exercise of scientific research is its conduct for the benefit of mankind as a whole. *A fortiori*, archaeological exploration which aims at the discovery of artefacts that are to be preserved or disposed of for the benefit of mankind, should be undertaken under the same conditions. The fact that archaeological research does not qualify as marine scientific research[39] is of no importance in this context.

It is very unlikely that the drafters of article 149 intended to subject the search for and location of archaeological objects to the principle of the freedom of the high seas. The status of archaeological exploration is, in this respect, similar to the status of activities in the Area undertaken before the approval of plans of work by the Authority. Article 1 of Annex III of the 1982 Convention provides that "title to minerals shall pass upon recovery in accordance with this Convention", while article 2(1)b emphasises the fact that "prospecting shall be conducted only after the Authority has received a satisfactory written undertaking that the proposed prospector shall comply with this Convention".

The notion of preferential rights under article 149. The notion of preferential rights is not new in the law of the sea. Indeed, the preferential rights for the coastal State in a situation of special dependence on coastal fisheries originated in proposals submitted by Iceland at the Geneva Conference of 1958.[40] The ICJ had the opportunity to discuss their nature and scope in the *Fisheries Jurisdiction Cases (1974)*[41] In the Court's opinion, the notion of preferential rights "necessarily implies the existence of other legal rights in respect of which that preference operates... The characterisation of the coastal State's rights as preferential implies a certain priority, but cannot imply the extinction of the concurrent rights of other States".[42] Finally, "it is implicit in the concept of preferential right that negotiations are required in order to define or delimit the extent of those rights".[43]

In applying the Court's *rationale* to the concept of preferential rights envisaged by article 149, the following may be assessed:

a. Legal right in respect of which preference operates: The recognition of the preferential rights of the State(s) of origin is based on the intimate cultural and historical link between those States and the cultural property discovered. More specifically, it implies that the latter forms part of a State's cultural heritage. As already seen, a number of UN General Assembly Resolutions on the Restitution of Cultural Property to the Countries of Origin, invite States seeking the recovery of cultural and artistic treasures from the seabed to facilitate the participation of the States having a historical and cultural link with those treasures by mutually acceptable conditions. With respect to deep seabed archaeological objects, the 1982 Convention advanced the interests of those States into preferential rights.

b. The notion of preferential rights is non-exclusive: The recognition of the preferential rights of the State(s) of origin does not exclude other States or the international community from acquiring the recovered archaeological material. As has already been seen, the early proposals on archaeological treasures recognised the right of the Authority to dispose of the recovered items in conformity with the principle of the common heritage of mankind and even to sell them to authorised third parties in case the State of origin did not exercise its right to acquire "the sunken treasure". Article 149 is silent on this issue.

c. Duty to negotiate: In the Court's view, the obligation to negotiate "flows" from the very nature of the preferential rights and corresponds to the principles and provisions of the UN Charter concerning Peaceful Settlement of Disputes. The negotiations should be conducted "on the basis that each party must in good faith pay reasonable regard to the legal rights of the other. It is not a matter of finding simply an equitable solution, but an equitable solution derived from the applicable law."[44] All disputes relating to a preferential right under article 149 will be resolved on the basis of the General Provisions of the 1982 Convention on Dispute Settlement (Part XV) and *not* on the specific provisions dealing with disputes in the Area (Part XI, section 5). This is by reason of article 187 which provides that: "The Sea-Bed Dispute Chamber shall have jurisdiction under this Part and the annexes relating thereto in disputes with respect to *activities in the Area*" (emphasis added). As already mentioned, deep seabed archaeological operations do not qualify as "activities in the Area".

To sum up, the Court's ruling on the *Fisheries Jurisdiction Cases* provides some useful evidence as to the scope of the "preferential rights" envisaged by article 149. However, further development is required if the latter are to be recognised as an emerging concept of the law of the sea. The only information provided by the *travaux preparatoires* of article 149 is that, originally, these rights included both the salvaging and the acquisition of archaeological and historical treasures. There is no specific indication of either their nature[45] or the range of items which they cover. *Prima facie*, it seems that their scope covers *all* objects of an archaeological and historical nature. However, it may be advisable to limit their exercise to items that are particularly representative of the cultural identity of the people who created it. In this way, unnecessary over-fragmentation of recovered archaeological material will be avoided. This interpretation is also consistent with the underlying purpose of article 149 which is the protection of cultural property under the aegis and for the benefit of the international community, without, however, depriving the State of origin of its rightful interests.

It should be recalled that the concept of preferential rights had also appeared in a number of proposals concerning the attribution of sovereign rights over the continental shelf for the purpose of protecting archaeological and historical objects. In that context, their scope was restricted to the sale or disposal of the recovered items resulting in their removal *out of the coastal State.*[46] A similar provision was included in the 1980 U.S. draft proposal, which declared the duty of States to protect objects of an archaeological and historical nature found in the marine environment in general.[47] None of these suggestions made its way into the Final Text of the Convention.

Determination of the State(s) of origin. Three formulas have been employed to identify the State(s) of origin: (a) "State or country of origin"; (b) "State of cultural origin"; and (c) "State of historical and archaeological origin". The formulation of these terms raises many interpretational problems. Which criteria distinguish the "State of origin" from the "State of cultural origin"? What are the differences between "cultural origin" and "historical and archaeological origin"? How could one define or even distinguish a "State" from a "country"?[48]

It is difficult to give an answer to these questions as these formulas were never intended to be used accumulatively. For example, the term "State of cultural origin" gives emphasis to the cultural link between an object and a State, while the term "State of the country of origin", as it appeared in the original Turkish proposal, gave preference to the State that exercises sovereignty over the country of origin of the discovered cultural property.[49] The reason for the initial inclusion of the three expressions, in brackets, in draft article 20 (prepared by the Seabed Committee) was the fact that agreement had not been achieved and the issue was remitted to the first session of UNCLOS III for further discussion. Only one of these terms should have been chosen; otherwise[50] guidance should have been given as to which State would acquire priority in case of conflicting claims.

The identification problem is acute, since in most cases, the determination of the State of origin is extremely difficult.[51] However, even if it is possible to identify traces of origin, the qualification of more than one State as claimants to the recovered items might create considerable difficulties.[52] It is interesting to note that the Intergovernmental Committee for Promoting the Return of Cultural Property to its Countries of Origin or its Restitution in the Case of Illicit Appropriation defines the "country of origin" as that "to whose cultural tradition the object is linked."[53] In this context, the distinction between the "State of origin" and the "State of cultural origin" introduced by article 149 may be confusing. Even if the expression "State of origin" is still to be interpreted as the State that exercises sovereignty over the country of origin, there is no reason why the balance should weigh in its favour. The argument of the Turkish representative that this expression resolves the problem of the same culture being shared in the past by several countries does have a basis in reality. It does not always ensure a fair result, however. What is needed is the establishment of *criteria* on the basis of which the decision can be made whether a particular item *belongs* to the cultural heritage of one State or another.

Article 4 of the 1970 Convention reads:

> "The States Parties to this Convention recognise that for the purpose of the Convention property which belongs to the following categories forms part of the cultural heritage of each State:
> (a) Cultural property created by the individual or collective genius of *nationals* of the *State concerned*, and cultural property of importance to the State concerned *created*

within the territory of that State by *foreign nationals* or stateless persons resident within such territory;

(b) cultural property *found* within the national territory" (emphasis added).

Similarly, article 5 of the San Salvador Convention states:

"The cultural heritage of each State consists of property mentioned in Article 2, *found* or *created* in its territory and legally acquired items of foreign origin" (emphasis added).

The significance of these provisions is limited in that they deal with cultural property found within national territories, while deep seabed archaeological objects are situated on the seabed beyond national jurisdiction. In this context, the decisive criterion for determining the property that constitutes part of the cultural heritage of each State would seem to be that of *nationality* rather than the territorial link of cultural property.[54] In case of conflict, the "effective link" of nationality envisaged by the ICJ in the *Nottebohm Case* in 1955 may be useful as a criterion for resolving the dispute. Preference should be given to "the *real* and *effective* nationality, that which accords with the facts, that based on stronger factual ties between the person concerned and one of the States whose nationality is involved" (emphasis added).[55] In other words, preference should be given to the State to whose cultural heritage the property in question is more closely linked.[56]

Finally, the drafters of article 149 failed to provide for potential conflicts between the State of origin of a sunken vessel and the State of origin of individual items of its cargo. In the light of the language of article 149, which refers to *objects* of an archaeological and historical nature in general, without differentiating between the hull of a ship and its contents, there seems to be no room for the raising of priorities in favour of either. Both categories of cultural property are equally valued. However, this interpretation should not result in the overfragmentation of the material recovered. Archaeologists have often emphasised the fact that when the legislation does not provide for the preservation of the material of the wreck in a collection, it does not, in fact, protect the wreck. Individual items, even those of outstanding value, are of marginal significance outside their context. It is important, therefore, that the already mentioned Australia/Netherlands Agreement regards the sharing of material from an archaeological site as the accommodation in several localities of a corporate entity rather than its division into parts. In case the contents of an archaeological site are to be apportioned, the total assemblage should be capable of re-assembly for further research. Where unique or rare objects themselves form a meaningful assemblage within the whole, this assemblage should not be split or, if split, perfect replicas be made to complete the assemblage. The incorporation of these principles can ensure that important collections of archaeological material from shipwrecks will not be overfragmented and that future research will be possible.[57]

In conclusion, article 149 allows more than one State to qualify as claimants to deep seabed archaeological objects. The drafters of the Convention having failed to provide guidelines for the reconciliation of potential conflicts between them, both the determination of their scope and the attribution of priorities will have to take place on a case-by-case basis.

Limitations in the scope of article 149. It has been argued that the scope of article 149 should be limited to objects of exceptional value, especially if the Authority is to be granted any rights over their preservation and protection. The reason is twofold:

> First, article 149 refers to objects that are of interest to mankind as a whole. "The language used in relevant texts drafted by UNESCO would be confined to exceptionally valuable and rare items of cultural heritage. I am referring, by way of comparison, to the wording used in Article I of the Convention for the Protection of the World's Cultural and Natural Heritage (1972), which speaks of objects of exceptional value, while the preamble of the Convention stresses the 'unique' character of the objects to which it refers."
>
> Second, this interpretation is the only plausible interpretation within the general framework of the 1982 Convention. Otherwise, it would be difficult to understand why "all the archaeological and historical objects found up to 24 miles from the coast belong to the coastal State, then there is a void next to what the objects are falling within the competence of an international organ".[58]

Such an approach may prove to be detrimental to the protection of deep seabed archaeological sites. First, for the archaeologist, the commonplace has the same value as the spectacular. What is important is not the recovery of spectacular items, but the acquisition of information. With this in mind, what criteria should be used to determine whether underwater cultural property is of exceptional value? Second, the overall scheme of protection of the 1972 Convention relates to the attribution of *additional assistance* to the preservation of sites of outstanding universal value. Other than that, the State on whose territory the cultural property is situated has the main responsibility for the protection of cultural property that does not fall within the ambit of the Convention. On the high seas, where no State has jurisdiction over archaeological objects, the protection of all cultural property should take place under the aegis of the international community. The adoption of outstanding universal value as criterion for determining the scope of objects of archaeological and historical nature, may leave a number of sites unprotected. Third, article 149 refers to the preservation and disposal of *all* objects of an archaeological and historical nature for the benefit of mankind as a whole. There is nothing in the text of article 149 or in its *travaux préparatoires* to indicate that the objects in question must be of exceptional value.

The 1982 scheme is, no doubt, incoherent and incomplete. Archaeological and historical objects found on the continental shelf, beyond the 24-mile limit, are "free for all", while those found on the deep seabed are to be preserved for the benefit of mankind as a whole. This does not mean, however, that the scope of the protected objects should be interpreted restrictively so as to give some meaning to the otherwise incomprehensible regime. The inability of the 1982 Convention to provide an efficient scheme of protection is the result both of the manner in which the archaeological issue was dealt with during the negotiations of UNCLOS III and of the determination of the maritime powers to prevent the expansion of coastal competence over archaeological objects on the continental shelf. The examination of the records of the Conference in no way indicates that the scope of the deep seabed archaeological objects is limited to items of outstanding universal value. However, there might be a need for qualification in the exercise of the preferential rights of the State(s) of origin, whose potential abuse may easily lead to the dispersal of significant collections in different parts of the world. It may be advisable to limit their scope to items which are particularly representative of the cultural identity of a specific people.

Interaction between article 149 and article 303(3)

At first sight, there seems to be a conflict between article 149, which provides for the preservation and disposal of the archaeological and historical objects of the international deep seabed for the benefit of mankind, and article 303(3) which reserves the law of salvage and the rights of the identifiable owners; the latter is also applicable to the Area since it forms part of the General Provisions of the 1982 Convention. However, under closer examination this *prima facie* conflict loses its significance. The reservation of salvage law by article 303(3) may be read as referring to objects which do not qualify for protection under article 303(1) and are eligible for salvage, i.e., objects which are less than 100 years old. Since article 149 itself may be regarded as an application of article 303(1), the reservation of admiralty law is limited to those cases where it does not apply. Alternatively, the priority of article 149 over article 303(3) may be justified under the maxim *lex specialis derogat legi generali*. Article 303(3) forms part of the General Provisions of the 1982 Convention, while article 149 deals specifically with archaeological objects found on the deep seabed.[59]

So far as the rights of the identifiable owners are concerned, a different approach should be adopted in that they should be reserved even with respect to protected deep seabed cultural property. This is confirmed by the *travaux préparatoires* of article 149, where at some stage provision was made for their reservation. The reservation appeared together with the establishment of a 50-year limit as the qualifying factor of protection of shipwrecks. In other words, with respect to cultural property of relatively recent origin, where the possibilities of identifying the original owner are increased, provision was made for the protection of his rights.

Duty of the Authority to protect archaeological and historical objects

There is nothing in the 1982 Convention to prevent the Authority from undertaking protective measures in exercising its resource-jurisdiction in the Area. Such measures should not be regarded as an expansion of its competence over archaeological objects, but as an application of the duty to protect archaeological and historical objects found at sea established by article 303(1). These may include the obligation to report the accidental recovery of archaeological remains, the undertaking of *interim* protective measures or even the suspension of operations until the arrival of archaeologists. Users other than those engaged in "activities in the Area" will not be affected by these regulations as they do not operate under the jurisdiction of the Authority. They will still, however, be under the duty to protect deep seabed archaeological remains, on the basis of article 303(1).[60]

Conflicting uses in the Area

The 1982 Convention distinguishes between "activities in the Area" and "other activities in the marine environment", the notion of which appears to include deep seabed archaeology.[61] Their accommodation, under article 147(1) and (3), is based on a reciprocal reasonable regard rule;[62] no priority is given to either activity, as, in both cases, the sole criterion is that of "reasonableness." However, if it is considered that the rights of the States/entities engaged in "activities" in the Area are exclusive and that they have been granted by the Authority on behalf of mankind as a whole, the balance should weigh in their favour.[63]

Conflict between marine archaeology and "activities in the Area"
Since "activities in the Area" enjoy a higher status than "other activities in the marine environment", the question arises as to whether they also enjoy priority over the preservation of deep seabed cultural property. *Prima facie*, the answer seems to be in the negative as, under article 149, archaeological and historical objects must also be preserved or disposed of "for the benefit of mankind as a whole". In other words, the State that undertakes archaeological operations on the international deep seabed does not act in its national interest alone; it acts in the wider interest of the international community in the protection of the underwater cultural heritage. There is, however, an important difference between deepwater archaeology and mineral exploration and exploitation in the Area. The States engaged in mineral--related activities do not only act for "the benefit of mankind", but they have also been granted the exclusive right to do so by an international organisation acting on its behalf. In contrast, the States involved in archaeological research will implement the common heritage principle virtually at will. It would, therefore, be reasonable to conclude that in case of unavoidable conflict between the preservation of deep seabed cultural property and "activities in the Area", the priority would lie in favour of the latter. Only the Authority can offer protection to deep seabed archaeological objects under these circumstances.

Conflict between marine archaeology and "other activities in the marine environment"
The accommodation of conflicts *between* activities qualifying as "other activities in the marine environment" falls outside of the scope of article 147. Inevitably, such disputes fall within the residual high seas regime.

Potential conflicts between archaeological operations and such will be resolved on the basis of article 87(2) and the criterion of "reasonableness".[64]

Conclusion

The proposed preservation or disposal of objects of an archaeological or historical nature found in the Area by article 149 is of limited practical significance. First, the Convention fails to establish an international agency to put the proposed regime into practice. As the Authority does not enjoy any powers over the protection of such objects, implementation of the common cultural heritage of mankind principle is left, at the present stage, to individual States. Second, the vague text of article 149 allows more than one interpretation. There being no international organisation to specify the measures to be taken for the preservation and disposal of deep seabed archaeological objects, the whole issue lies at the absolute discretion of the flag States. Third, the Convention fails to define the scope of the preferential rights of the State of origin. In case of conflict over the allocation of these rights and the determination of their nature, the negotiators or the competent tribunal or court will enjoy quasi-legislative powers. Nevertheless, both the recognition of the interest of the international community in the preservation of deep seabed cultural property and the acknowledgement of the preferential rights of the State of origin constitute an important landmark in the development of the law. The future will show whether the regime envisaged will be put into practice or pale into insignificance.

CUSTOMARY INTERNATIONAL LAW

So far as deep seabed cultural property is concerned, there is an overall lack of evidence both in State practice and in law. It is notable that twelve years after the adoption of the 1982 Convention nothing has been said or agreed upon the regime of deep seabed archaeological objects. Neither do the national laws regulating deep seabed mining ("reciprocating States regime") provide for cultural property found in the Area.[65] The same applies to the 1994 Agreement relating to the Implementation of Part XI of the 1982 United Nations Convention on the Law of the Sea. The only exception is a U.S. law providing for the designation of the remains of the *Titanic* as an International Maritime Memorial.[66] The 1986 Act directs the U.S. Government to enter into negotiation and consultations aimed at developing international guidelines for research, exploration and, if appropriate, salvage. However, consultations with the United Kingdom, France, Canada and other interested nations mandated under the Titanic Memorial Law, revealed little or no interest in an international agreement.[67] The main interest of States, so far as the Area is concerned, is in the implementation of the international deep seabed regime, while the technological capacities in excavating and preserving deep water archaeological sites are still limited. On top of this, marine archaeological projects involve huge investments.

Nevertheless, despite this lack of evidence in State practice, there seems to be room for the recognition in the future of the cultural riches of the deep seabed as the common heritage of mankind. First, during the negotiations of UNCLOS III, the few States that were against the adoption of such a principle simply opposed the expansion of the powers of the Authority over non-resource-related activities.[68] Second, the very notion of "common heritage of mankind", which has already been developed in the field of cultural heritage law, paves the way for the elaboration of a similar concept in relation to deep seabed sites. At present, the protection and preservation of deep seabed cultural property for the benefit of mankind as a whole may be addressed only as a general principle. Even if one accepts the view that the deep seabed regime laid down in the 1982 Convention reflects customary law[69] its significance to cultural property is limited. Archaeological objects are not included within the notion of "resources", while the implementation of article 149, which forms part of the conventional regime of the deep seabed, is left to the discretion of individual States. The same applies to the 1970 Declaration of Principles Governing the Seabed and the Ocean Floor, and the Subsoil thereof, Beyond the Limits of National Jurisdiction which simply declares the responsibility of States to ensure that activities in the Area shall be carried out in conformity with the international regime *to be established* on the basis of its principles. It seems, therefore, that under customary law, deep seabed cultural property is still governed by the principles of the freedom of the high seas and flag State jurisdiction. It is notable that despite the U.S. attempt to designate the *Titanic* as a maritime memorial, salvage operations have already began.[70]

NOTES

1   See *supra* pp. 217-219. This chapter is an updated version of a part of my PhD
    thesis originally published under the title "Deep Seabed Cultural Property and
    the Common Heritage of Mankind" in 40 *ICLQ* (1991) pp. 859-894, published
    by the British Institute of International and Comparative Law, 17 Russel Square,
    London WC1B 4DR.

2   The area shall not be subject to appropriation by any means by States or persons,
    while all activities regarding the exploration and exploitation of the area and
    other related activities shall be governed by the international regime to be
    established. The area shall be open to use exclusively for peaceful purposes.
    Its exploration and the exploitation of its resources shall be carried out for the
    benefit of mankind as a whole, taking into particular consideration the interests
    and needs of the developing countries. A/RES/2749 (XXV) December 17, 1970,
    25 *UN GAOR Supp.* No. 28 (A/8028) at p. 28.

3   There was no reference to deep seabed archaeological objects either in the
    discussions by non-governmental organisations or in the deliberations at the
    UN between 1968-1970. The same applies to the developments prior to the
    adoption of the Maltese proposal in 1967 and the establishment of the *Ad hoc*
    Seabed Committee. For a discussion of "The Dawn of a regime of the deep
    ocean floor", see Oda, S., *The Law of the Sea in our Time - I New Developments
    1966-1975*, Sijthoff Publications on Ocean Development, vol. 3, Leyden, 1977,
    pp. 1-112. The only exception was Ambassador Pardo's statement: "There are
    more objects of archaeological value lying on the bottom of the Mediterranean
    than exist in the museums of Greece, Italy, France and Spain combined". Doc.
    A/C.1/PV. 1515, p. 3, *UN GAOR* vol. I, A/C.1/PV. 1494-1537 (1967).

4   Rao argues that the 1970 UN Resolution may be interpreted so as to submit all
    the activities that require physical occupation of the seabed and ocean floor
    to the regulation of an international regime. Rao, P.C., *The Public Order of
    Ocean Resources: A Critique of the Contemporary Law of the Sea,* The MIT
    Press, Massachussetts, 1975 at p. 157 *et seq.*

5   In the past, it had been argued that the recovery of historic shipwrecks should
    fall within the ambit of the deep seabed regime, still then under consideration,
    on the basis that submarine archaeology is an eminently peaceful use of the
    oceans, and sunken wrecks qualify as "resources" of the seabed. See Castagné,
    A., "L'archéologie sous-marine et le droit" in *Société française pour le droit
    international, Actualités du droit de la mer.* Colloque de Montpellier, 25-27
    Mai 1972, Pedone, A. édition, Paris, 1973, pp. 164-183 at p. 172. However,
    as will be seen, the drafters of the 1982 Convention did not share this approach
    and confined the international deep seabed regime to mineral exploration and
    exploitation alone. At the same time, provision was made for archaeological
    and historical objects found in the Area.

6   Doc. A/AC.183/23, 25 *UN GAOR Supp. No. 21 (A/8021)*, at pp. 110-111.

7   *Ibid* at p. 96.

8 "Draft UN Convention on the International Seabed Area", Doc. A/AC.138/25 (1970), 25 *UN GAOR Supp. No. 21 (A/8021)* at p. 29. The U.S. draft, which dealt mainly with mineral exploration and exploitation, proposed a division of the seabed in three areas: (i) an area subjected to national sovereignty; (ii) a "trusteeship area", an intermediate area of coastal State jurisdiction; (iii) the area beyond the "trustee-ship area" where total control would be placed with an international body. It was in this third area that article 25 would apply.

9 According to Auburn: "It is significant that this document, the proposal of one of the super-powers, contains no provision for safeguarding archaeological artefacts". Auburn, F.M., "Archaeology and the Law", 2 *I.J.N.A.* No. 1 (1973) pp. 159-162 at p. 160.

10 Working paper submitted by Greece, Doc. A/AC.138/54 (1971) 26 *UN GAOR Supp.* No. 21 (A/8421) at p. 194.

11 In the explanatory note it was made clear that "the present list has been prepared in accordance with General Assembly Resolution 2750 and that the list should serve as a framework for discussion and drafting of necessary articles until such time as the agenda of the Conference is adopted." C/f "List of Subjects and Issues to be Dealt with by the Seabed Committee", Doc. A/AC.138/66 of 16 August 1972, 27 *UN GAOR Supp.* No. 21 (A/8721) p. 146, footnote 22.

12 "Archaeological and Historical Treasures of the Sea-bed, and the Ocean Floor Beyond the Limits of National Jurisdiction", Doc. A/AC.138/SC.I/L.16 of 2 August 1972. Text reprinted in Oda, S., *The International Law of the Ocean Development - Basic documents*, vol. II, Sijthoff, Leyden, 1975 pp. 328-330.

13 "Draft Article on Protection of Archaeological and Historical Treasures", Doc.A/AC.138/SC.I/L.25 of 14 August 1973. *Ibid* at pp. 330-331.

14 "Archaeological and Historical Treasures on the Sea-Bed and Ocean Floor Beyond the Limits of National Jurisdiction", Doc. A/AC.138/SC.I/L.21 of 28 March 1973. *Ibid* at p. 330.

15 Statement made on 23 March 1973 by Mr. Akyamac before Sub-Committee I. Committee on the Peaceful Uses of the Sea-bed and the Ocean Floor Beyond the Limits of National Jurisdiction, 62nd to 68th Meetings, held at New York from 7 March to 5 April 1973, *Doc.A/AC.138/SC.I/SR.62-68* at p. 43.

16 See also Caflisch, L., "Submarine Antiquities and the International Law of the Sea", 13 *N.Y.I.L.* (1982) pp. 3-32 at p. 26, footnote 89.

17 "Texts Illustrating Areas of Agreement and Disagreement on Items 1 and 2 of the Subcommittee's Programme of Work", Report of Subcommittee I, Appendix III to the Report of the Committee on the Peaceful Uses of the Sea-Bed and the Ocean Floor Beyond the Limits of National Jurisdiction to the General Assembly of the United Nations, 28 *UN GAOR Supp.* No. 21 (A/9021), vol. 2 at p. 69. According to the accompanying Report of Subcommittee I: "One delegation expressed the view that it was not appropriate to deal with the subject of archaeological and historical objects in the context of these articles ... and the above text should be omitted." *Ibid* at p. 169, n. 33. In the light of article 149 which did not designate the Authority as the competent body to deal with the regime of archaeological objects, it can be seen to be significant that the U.S. delegation had opposed the expansion of the competence of the Authority

on archaeological matters. According to the U.S., the power of the Authority should be confined to the control of resource exploration and exploitation. See below footnote 25 and Arend, A.C., "Archaeological and Historical Objects: The International Legal Implications of UNCLOS III", 22 *V.J.I.L.* (1982) pp. 777-803 at p. 790, footnote 66.

18 *UNCLOS III, Off. Rec.*, vol. III, at p. 163. In footnote 27 it was mentioned that "one delegation expressed the view that the first part of this paragraph up to the word 'origin' should be deleted".

19 Doc. A/CONF.62/WP.8, Informal Single Negotiating Text of 7 May 1975 (ISNT), *UNCLOS III, Off. Rec.*, vol IV, p. 137 at p. 140. It is noteworthy that article 19 of ISNT retained the three expressions describing the States of origin. Its drafters abstained from choosing or giving preference to one of these States. They simply provided that any dispute arising from the nature or the exercise of a preferential right would be solved on the basis of the provisions of the Convention dealing with dispute settlement, i.e., articles 57-65 of ISNT. The bracketed language, which indicated that the issue was still under consideration, has been removed.

20 RSNT of 6 May 1976, Doc. A/CONF.62/WP.8/Rev.1, *UNCLOS III, Off. Rec.*, vol. V, p. 125 at p. 131 (article 19).

21 According to Caflisch, this verbal modification was made on "the assumption that the word 'of' was the result of a typographical error". *Op. cit.* note 16 at p. 30, footnote 98. The underlying purpose of the original Turkish formula was the determination of the State that was to enjoy the preferential rights in cases where more than one State shared the same culture. The State preferred was the State that exercises sovereignty over the country of origin of the recovered items. Obviously, this fact was not considered by the drafters of article 19, who by including the word *or* might have given some meaning to the otherwise incomprehensible text, but this was different from the original purpose of the Turkish draft, which read "State of the country of origin".

22 The 1977 New York (sixth) session produced the Informal Composite Negotiating Text (ICNT) which included article 149 on archaeological and historical objects. The article was identical to article 19 of RSNT: Doc. A/CONF.62/WP.10, 15 July 1977, *UNCLOS III, Off. Rec.*, vol. VIII at p. 25. The 1979 Geneva session (eighth) produced Revision 1 of ICNT. There was no change in the text of article 149. The 1980 New York session (ninth) did not introduce any modifications to article 149 either.

23 Doc. A/CONF.62/WP.10/Rev.3, *UNCLOS III, Off. Rec.*, vol. XIII, p. 245.

24 No one would deny the fact that other international agencies were better qualified to deal with archaeological matters. However, no provision was made for UNESCO or for any other appropriate body to undertake such activities. See further Caflisch, *op. cit.* note 16 at p. 29 and Arend, *op. cit.* note 17 at p. 800.

25 See the statement of the U.S. delegate (Mr. Ratiner) during the 21st meeting of the third session of the First Committee in Geneva in 1975 (Monday, 28 April). "First, the competence of the Authority should be restricted to activities directly related to the exploration and the exploitation of the resources of the international area. The term 'activities', as it was being used in the work of

the Committee, needed to be defined in such a way that other activities to be conducted in the area, such as basic or fundamental scientific research, did not fall within the regulatory powers of the Authority. Second, the powers and functions to be conferred on the Authority and its organs by the Convention should be those specifically provided for and not implied from the general provisions of the treaty." *UNCLOS III, Off. Rec.* vol. IV, p. 61.

26 According to article 1(3) of the 1982 Convention: "'Activities in the area' means all activities of exploration for, and exploitation of, the resources of the Area", which in turn are defined by article 133(a) as "all solid, liquid or gaseous mineral resources *in situ* in the Area at or beneath the seabed, including polymetallic nodules". Deep seabed archaeological operations would rather be considered as "other activities in the marine environment" (see article 147).

27 According to Caflisch: "The present text of article 149 constitutes the worst possible solution, for it amounts to abandoning the implementation of that principle (e.g. the common heritage principle) to individual states." Caflisch, *op. cit.* note 16 at p. 29.

28 For example, which will be its relationship with the Authority? Since both entities would be dealing with deep seabed issues there may be cases of conflicting competence. Furthermore, will its structure be similar to that of the existing international and regional management commissions, whose effectiveness depends upon the voluntary co-operation of States, or will it be granted a greater degree of autonomy? On the status of the various international marine organisations, see Bekiashev, K.A., Serebriakov, V.V. *International Marine Organisations*, Martinus Nijhoff Publishers, The Hague, 1981 and for relevant documentation see *International Organisations and the Law of the Sea, Documentary Yearbooks*, 1985 to date, edited by the Netherlands Institute for the Law of the Sea (NILOS), Graham & Trotam/Martinus Nijhoff/NILOS, 1993.

29 UNESCO has undertaken a two-year programme to prepare an international survey of the underwater cultural heritage through the Scientific Committee of the Confédération Mondiale des Activités Subaquatiques. See further Gifford, J.A., Redknap, M. and Flemming, N.C. "The UNESCO international survey of underwater cultural heritage", 16 *World Archaeology* (1984/85) pp. 373-376. UNESCO's experience in the protection of cultural property was mentioned during the very early stages of the negotiations. C.f Mr. Akyamac's statement before Sub-Committee I of the Seabed Committee, *op. cit.* note 15. It is notable that at its 141st session in May 1993, the Executive Board of UNESCO invited the Director-General to make a study of the technical and legal aspects of an instrument on the underwater cultural heritage.

30 21 *ILM* (1982) at p. 58. Article 22(1).

31 Pinto, M.C.W. "Emerging concepts of the law of the sea: some social and cultural aspects", 3/4 UNESCO *Impact of Science and Technology*, 1984, (Special Issue, "Research, international law and the sea in the man's future"), pp. 335--345 at p. 339. See also Goldie, L.F.E., "A Note on Some Diverse Meaning of the Common Heritage of Mankind", 10 *Syracuse J. Int'l L. & Com.* (1983) pp. 69-110 at p. 81.

32 According to para. 10 of the 1972 Greek proposal: "The Authority should promote, in co-operation with the regional organ, the universal sharing of the cultural benefits derived from the discovery of such treasures, taking into particular consideration the rightful interests of the State of historical origin of the discovered treasures." *Op. cit.* note 12. See, however, the initial Greek proposal, which reads: "11. The State of historical origin of the archaeological or historical discovery possesses preferential rights to acquire this item by compensating the finder. If such a right to aquire is not exercised within a reasonable time, the object will be disposed of at the discretion of the finder". It is noteworthy that the Turkish representative had interpreted this text as attributing to the State of the cultural origin of the treasure a preferential right to buy it from the international authority and, if that right was not exercised, the treasure would be sold to third parties. He also presumed that the proceeds from the sale would be treated in the same way as those from the sale of commercial commodities: statement by Akayamac, *op. cit.* note 15.

33 Kiss, A-Ch., "La notion de patrimoine commune de l'humanité", 175 *Hague Recueil* (1982-II), pp. 99-256 at pp. 229-232. In contrast, Kiss describes the concept of the "common heritage of mankind" applied to natural-resource regimes, as "patrimoine de l'humanité 'par nature'". On the concept of the "common heritage of mankind" see further Danilenko, G., "The concept of the common heritage of mankind in international law", XIII *Annals of Air and Space Law* (1988) pp. 247-265; Dupuy, R-J., "The Notion of Common Heritage of Mankind Applied to the Seabed", VIII *Annals of Air and Space Law* (1983) pp. 347-355; Goldie, L.F.E., "A note on some diverse meanings of the common heritage of mankind", 10 *Syracuse Journal of International Law and Commerce* (1983) pp. 69; Joyner, C.C., "Legal Implications of Mankind", 35 *Int'l & Comp. L.Q.* (1986) pp. 190-199; Larschan, B. and Brennan, B.C., "The Common Heritage of Mankind Principle in International Law", 21 *Colum. J. Transnat'l L.* pp. 305-307; Perrakis, S.E., "The right to enjoyment of the common heritage of mankind as a solidarity right" *Legal Studies* vol. 3, Law School, University of Thrace, Saccoulas Publishing Company, 1982 pp. 164-184 (in Greek); Reiley, E.H., "The common heritage of mankind", 5(3) *California Lawyer* (1985) pp. 15-26; Stocker, W., *Das Prinzip des "Common Heritage of Mankind" als Ausdruck des Staatengemeinschaftsinteresses im Völkerrecht,* Schweizer Studien zum Internazionalen Recht, Band 81, Schulthess Polygraphischer Verlag, Zürich, 1993; White, M.V. "The Common Heritage of Mankind: An Assessment", 14 *Case W. Res. J. Int'l L.* (1982) pp. 509-542; Wolfrum, R. "The principle of the common heritage of mankind", 43 *ZaöRV* (1983) pp. 312-337; ID, "Common heritage of mankind", 11 *E.P.I.L.* (1989) pp. 65-69. On the application of the concept of the common heritage of mankind in the cultural field see also the bibliography cited in chapter 1, footnote 9.

34 "A fiduciary relationship with respect to property, subjecting the person by whom the property is held to equitable duties to deal with the property for the benefit of another person". *Restatement (Second) of Trusts*, para. 2 (1959), quoted in Dukerminier, J. and Johanson, S.M. *Family Wealth Transactions:*

Wills, Trusts, Future Interests and Estate Planning (1972) at p. 379. See also Kiss, *ibid* at pp. 128-133 and Gechman, J., "Rescuing cultural treasures: the need for an incentive generating doctrine", 25 *Houston Law Review* (1987) pp. 577-603 at pp. 582-583, who argues that the creation of a trust requires clear manifestation of intent to seperate legal and equitable interest. In the case of a charitable trust, the trustee is given discretion to select among charitable beneficiaries.

35 Prott, L.V. & O'Keefe , P.J., *The Law and the Cultural Heritage,* vol. 1, *Discovery and excavation,* Professional Books Ltd., Abingdon, 1984 at p. 98.

36 The "International Fund for the Promotion of Culture" was established in 1977 by resolution 3.322 adopted by the General Conference at its eighteenth session. Its main sources are contributions by member States, voluntary contributions by private institutions and income derived from the investment of resources. For example from 1977 to 1985, it contributed to the implementation of 198 projects in 74 countries: "Report by the Director-General on the Activities of the International Fund for the Promotion of Culture, Item 3.5 of the provisional agenda", *UNESCO 23 C/88,* 18 July 1985.

37 It is notable that the United States withheld its *pro rata* share of the costs of the UN budget for funding the Preparatory Commission. This was a reaction to a UN General Assembly Resolution, on December 3, 1982, to finance the Preparatory Commission under the Law of the Sea Treaty from the regular UN budget. See further "Funding the Law of the Sea Preparatory Commission - President's Statement, Dec. 30 1982"; 83 *Department of State Bulletin* (1983) at p. 82. The United States pays 25% of the regular UN budget. In the light of recent developments concerning the adjustment of Part XI, the U.S. is reconsidering its position.

38 UNESCO, *Conventions and Recommendations of UNESCO concerning the protection of the cultural heritage,* 1985, pp. 101-114. Article 1.

39 See chapter 1 at pp. 34-35. For a discussion of article 143 and its scope *ratione materiae,* see Brown, E.D., *The Area Beyond the Limits of National Jurisdiction,* vol. 2, *Seabed Energy and Mineral Resources and the Law of the Sea,* Graham & Trotman, London, 1986 at pp. II.3 39-II.3 41.

40 C.f. "Iceland: revised proposal", Doc. A/CONF.13/C.3/L.79/Rev.1, 14 April 1958, *UNCLOS I, Off.Rec.,* vol. V at p. 158.

41 *Fisheries Jurisdiction (United Kingdom v. Iceland),* Merits Judgment, *I.C.J. Reports* (1974) p. 3; *Fisheries Jurisdiction (Federal Republic of Germany v. Iceland), ibid* at p. 175.

42 *Ibid* at p. 24, para. 54 and pp. 27-28, para. 62.

43 *Ibid* at p. 32, para. 74.

44 *Ibid.*

45 According to Oxman: "The various 'States of origin' obtain an exhortation that 'particular regard' be paid to their 'preferential rights', but fell short of confirming any particular right of proprietary interests." Oxman, B.H. "The Third UN Conference on the Law of the Sea: The Ninth Session (1980)", 75 *A.J.I.L.* (1981) pp. 211-256 at p. 240, footnote 143. Prof. Roucounas argues that "article

149 institutes a kind of right of preemption, but there is no clear indication as to whom this right belongs". Roucounas, E., "Submarine archaeological research: some legal aspects" in Leanza, U. (ed.), *The International Legal Regime of the Mediterranean Sea*, II Università degli Studi di Roma, Pubblicazioni della Facoltà di Giurisprudenza 2, Dott. Giuffrè A. editore, Milano, 1987, pp. 309-334 at p. 327.

46 See *supra* chapter 5 at pp. 162-165. The only drafts that did not limit the exercise of the preferential rights to the sale or disposal of the recovered items "out of the coastal State", were the 1979 Greek proposal and the joint proposal by Cape Verde, Italy, Malta, Portugal, Tunisia and Yugoslavia. *Ibid* at pp. 162-163.

47 "Particular regard shall be given to the State of origin ... in the case of sale or any other disposal resulting in the removal of such objects from a State which has possession of such objects". Doc.A/CONF.62/GP.4 of 27 March 1980 in Platzöder, R., *Third United Nations Conference on the Law of the Sea: Documents*, vol. XII at p. 299. See also *supra* chapter 5, at p. 164.

48 See further Caflisch, *op. cit.* note 16 at p. 30 and Galenskaya, who argues that the "State of origin" is the State where the objects were produced, while the "State of cultural origin" is the State where the cultural treasures were sold, presented, etc, that is where the owner had its domicile. Galenskaya, L.N., "International co-operation in cultural affairs", *Hague Recueil* (1986-III) pp. 265-331 at p. 303.

49 By referring to the "State or country of origin" the final draft does not ensure preference to the State that exercises sovereignty over the country of origin, while it raises a lot of interpretation problems. The drafters of article 149 neglected these differences as they did not only retain both formulas, but they also failed to establish priorities between them. In addition, they included a third formula referring to the "State of historical and archaeological origin".

50 In Prof. Roucounas' view, the reason for the inclusion of the three formulas in article 149 was to ensure that all States having a "spatial or qualitative" link with the discovered objects have a legal basis to promote their interests. *Op. cit.* note 45 at p. 328.

51 This is due to the following factors: (a) absence of the necessary evidence, (b) the geographical distribution/configuration of States might have changed, (c) the case may arise of objects originating from a territory which was not at that time a subject of international law, (d) State succession, (e) claims may be made by entities which have not yet attained statehood, (f) finds might even belong to civilisations long dead so that no living group can feasily claim direct connections, (g) the same culture might be shared by several countries.

52 This is one of the main reasons that the inclusion of the preferential rights in article 149 has been criticised. In particular see Watters, D.R., "The Law of the Sea Treaty and Underwater Cultural Resources", 48 *American Antiquity* (1983) pp. 808-816 and Bass, G.F., "Marine Archaeology: A Misunderstood Science", 2 *Ocean Yearbook* (1980) pp. 137-152, at p. 151: "Suggestions that antiquities found in international waters should belong to the country of historical or cultural origin are meaningless. If scholars cannot agree on the origins

of the Cape Calidonya wreck and its cargo, some holding that it is Syrian, other that it is Greek, and still others that it is either Cypriot or of mixed nationality, how could claims to modern ownership be argued in courts of law? Similarly it is known that classical Greek statues were cast not only in what is modern Greece, but also in Italy, Asia Minor, and elsewhere. Ancient cargoes of raw metals found in the Mediterranean show that analyses of trace elements in the bronze might eventually suggest only the sources of the ores mined, and not where the statues eventually were made."

53 CLT/CH/4.82, Paris, 11 June 1982. "Return and Restitution of Cultural Property - A Brief Resumé" at p. 3.

54 For a discussion of the "territorial link" of cultural property in general see Becher, K., "On the obligation of subjects of international law to return cultural property to its permanent place", 44 *Annuaire de l'AAA* (1974) pp. 96-90 and Schulze, D., *Die Restitution von Kunstwerken - Zur Völkerrechtlichen Dimension der Restitutionresolutionen der Generalversammlung der Vereinten Nationen,* Reihe D. Band 12, Bremen 1983 (im Selbstverlag des Museums), pp. 31-38. With respect to deep seabed cultural property, the whole issue acquires a different character in that the cultural property in question lies in international waters. For example, archaeological objects found within national boundaries would be considered as part of that State's cultural heritage, even if they were created by nationals of another State (c/f article 4 of the 1972 Convention). In contrast, archaeological objects found on the deep seabed would raise questions as to "origin" and "State succession". For a critical view of the concept of "cultural heritage" under the 1970 Convention, see Gonzalez, M.A.,"New Legal Tools to Curb the Illicit Traffic in Pre-Columbian Antiquities", 12 *Colum. J. Transnat'l L.* (1973) pp. 316-341; Gordon, J.B., "Comment: The UNESCO Convention on the Illicit Movement of Art Treasures", 12 *Harvard Int'l L.J.* (1971) pp. 537-556.

55 *Nottebohm Case (Liechtenstein v. Guatemala)* (second phase), Judgment of April 6th, 1955; *I.C.J. Reports* (1955) p. 4 at p. 22.

56 "It is not easy to determine the strongest historic link. Each case must be seperately examined on its merits with regard to the person for whom the object was made, by whom it was made and for what purpose and place it was made - and, if aquired, the manner of aquisition. The strongest link would determine the most appropriate home for the treasure." Messenger, Ph.M.(ed), *The Ethics of Collecting Cultural Property: Whose Culture, Whose Property?*, University of New Mexico Press, Albuquerque, 1990. See further Jayme, E., "Die Nationalität des Kunstwerks als Rechtsfrage" in Reichelt, G. (Hrgb.), *Internazionaler Kulturgüterschutz,* Wiener Symposium 18-19 Oktober 1990, Manzsche Verlags- und Universitätsbuchhandlung, Wien, 1992, pp. 7-29, and Nahlik, S.E., "Book Review: Halina Niec, Ojzyzna dzielsztuki. Miedzynarodowa ochrona integralnos- ci naradowej spuscizny kulturalnej [The Proper Country of the Work of Art. International Protection of the Integrity of the National Cultural Heritage], 1980", XI *P.Y.I.L.* (1981/82) pp. 258-261. According to Nahlik, the most important conclusion of Dr. Niec is that some kind of nationality of the cultural property in question should be established to settle conflicting claims. Finally, Jayme

suggests that one criterion should be the nationality of the artist who created the art object. However, one should also consider situations where the art object has been exported legally or created specifically for a certain place. *Ibid.*

57 Schedule I to the Australian Historic Shipwrecks Act, 1976, No. 190 of 1976. Australia, *Acts of the Parliament of the Commonwealth* 1976, pp. 1613-1616.

58 Roucounas, *op. cit.* note 45 at pp. 326-327.

59 On the contrary, Caflisch argues that: "Owing to the general lack of effectiveness of the regime proposed in Article 149 ... it seems that this issue will be solved in favour of the applicability of the general clauses of Article 303 to the Area". *Op. cit.* note 16 at p. 29.

60 See also Roucounas, *op. cit.* note 45 at pp. 326-327, who discusses three possible interpretations of the rights of the Authority over deep seabed archaeological objects, and Verlaan, who argues that the marine scinetific research of Part XI provide sufficient basis for assigning responsibilities to the Authority for objects of an archaeological and historical nature found in the Area. Verlaan, Ph.A., "Marine Archaeology: A Trojan (Sea) Horse?", 8 *Ocean Yearbook* (1989) pp. 231-253 at p. 237.

61 See above footnote 26.

62 Article 147(1) and (3) read respectively: "Activities in the Area shall be carried out with reasonable regard for other activities in the marine environment." "Other activities in the marine environment shall be conducted with reasonable regard for activities in the Area."

63 Treves, T., "Military Installations, Structures and Devices of the Seabed", 74 *A.J.I.L.* (1980) pp. 808-857 at p. 854. A distinction should also be made between operations conducted before and after the approval of the plan of work by the Authority. In the early stages, where "prospecting is the most relevant activity", there is no reason why mineral exploration activities should acquire priority over "other activities in the marine environment". *Ibid.* Potential conflicts will be resolved solely on the basis of the reciprocal "reasonable regard rule". In other words, it will be a matter of each individual case to determine which activity will acquire priority over the other.

64 The criterion of reasonableness is also employed by article 147, which provides in paragraph (2) that: "(a) [D]ue notice must be given of the erection, emplacement and removal of installations used for carrying out activities in the Area and permanent means for giving warning of their presence must be maintained; (b) such installations may not be established where interference may be caused to the use of recognised sea lanes essential to international navigation or in areas of intense fishing activity; (c) safety zones shall be established around such installations with appropriate markings to ensure the safety of both navigation and the installations. The configuration and location of such safety zones shall not be such as to form a belt impeding the lawful access of shipping to particular maritime zones or navigation along international sea lanes." If "activities in the Area" must comply with the aforementioned measures in order to qualify the reasonable regard test, *a fortiori*, archaeological operations should be undertaken under the same conditions.

65 See further Brown, E.D., *Sea-bed Energy and Mineral Resources and the Law of the Sea*, vol. 3, *Selected Documents, Tables and Bibliography*, Graham & Trotman, London 1986.

66 RMS Titanic Memorial Act of 1986. PL 99-513-Oct. 21, 1986, 100 *Stat.* 2082. Contrary to what was thought, the *Titanic* may not be located on the international deep seabed, but on the continental shelf of Newfoundland (Canada), as defined by article 76 of the 1982 Convention. See further Gault, I.T. and Vander Zwaag, D., "Legal Jurisdiction over the Titanic", *Lighthouse*, Edn 37, Spring 1988.

67 Timpany argues that "the nations of the world are challenged to produce an agreement, perhaps similar to the "common heritage of mankind" concept, that the *Titanic* is everyone's and should be held in trust for all the people in the world" Timpany, M.S., "Ownership rights in the *Titanic*", 37 *Case Western Reserve Law Review* (1986) pp. 72-102 at p. 102.

68 As argued: "The United States has repeatedly made it clear that its own objections to Part XI are due exclusively to the economic regime and machinery established for the natural resources of the Area. I have seen no reference to a United States objection to this particular article [149] or its subject matter". Ratiner, L., "Unfinished Business", *LOS Lieder* 1 (1987) pp. 1-2. See also Verlaan, *op. cit.* note 60 at p. 238.

69 One of the most controversial issues of contemporary international law is whether the international deep seabed regime, as envisaged by the 1982 Convention, constitutes customary law. The views are diametrically opposed. On the one hand, there are States regarding the principle of common heritage as *jus cogens*, while on the other, States notably the industrialised ones, recognising only the obligation to undertake deep seabed mining operations in accordance with the common heritage of mankind principle advocated by the 1970 Declaration. In their opinion, an acceptable international machinery to implement the common heritage principle has not yet been established so that mining operations can still be exercised as a freedom of the high seas. On this point see Brown, E.D., *The Area Beyond the Limits of National Jurisdiction*, vol. 2, *Seabed Energy and Mineral Resources and the Law of the Sea*, Graham & Trotman, London, 1986 at II.2-35 *et seq.* In contrast, see Chile's declaration: "With regard to the international sea-bed regime [the delegation of Chile wishes] to reiterate the statement made by the Group of 77 at [the April 1982] meeting regarding the legal concept of the common heritage of mankind, the existence of which was solemnly confirmed by consensus by the General Assembly in 1970 and which the present Convention defines as a part of *jus cogens*. Any action taken in contraversion of this principle and outside the framework of the seabed regime would as [the April 1982] debate showed, be totally invalid and illegal." *Law of the Sea Bulletin*, No. 5, July 1985 at p. 54. The litterature on this issue is abundant. See, *inter alia*, Harry, M.A., "The deep seabed: the common arena of mankind or arena for unilateral exploitation?", XL *Naval Law Review* (1992) pp. 207-228; Henchoz, A-D., *Réglementations nationales et internationales de l'exploration et d'exploitation des grands fonds marins*, Etudes suisses de droit

international, vol. 76, Schulthess Polygrahischer Verlag, Zürich 1992; Van Dyke, J. & Yuen, Ch., "Common heritage v. freedom of the high seas; which governs the seabed?", 19 *San Diego L. Rev.* (1981/82) pp. 493-551, and citations in note 33. The situation should change after the adoption of the 1994 Agreement relating to the Implementation of Part XI of the 1982 Convention on the Law of the Sea, which appears to represent an acceptable implementation of the common heritage principle to the industrialised States.

70   See *supra* chapter 6, note 50, for recent litigation concerning salvage rights over the wreck.

CHAPTER 9

Conclusions

THE 1958 GENEVA CONVENTIONS

The Geneva Conventions of 1958, which are still in force, do not provide a satisfactory basis for the protection of the underwater cultural heritage. Under their scheme the outer limit of the territorial sea determines the area within which archaeological sites are or, at least, can be protected, and the area where protection is minimal. Landward of the territorial sea boundary, underwater cultural property falls within the sovereignty of the coastal State, which is responsible for its protection. Flag States cannot demand, as a matter of strict law, any rights for their vessels, while archaeological research is excluded from the notion of innocent passage. So far as the right of entry to ports is concerned, ships are entitled to use designated foreign ports, if their use is not expressly restricted or prohibited. In this context, the coastal State may make entry to its ports dependent on conditions concerning the removal of artefacts. Even though of limited practical significance, this scheme provides a basis for regulating access to cultural property found in extraterritorial waters.

Seaward of the territorial sea boundary, the protection lies at the absolute discretion of flag States which, even if willing to take the appropriate measures, lack the necessary means of enforcement. Anyone has the right to remove archaeological remains on the high seas. This "free-for-all" system does not acknowledge any priorities to the flag State or, as the case may be, to the State of origin, nor does it impose any obligation to protect archaeological sites. Potential salvors may proceed to recover cultural property as underwater relics are not excluded from the scope of the law of salvage. In the contiguous zone, the maximum breadth of which is 12 nautical miles, the coastal State may exercise limited powers of control over foreign vessels that attempt to import, or export, underwater cultural property into, or from, the territory or the territorial sea of the coastal State in contravention of its customs and fiscal laws.

The sovereign rights of the coastal State over the continental shelf do not cover underwater cultural property. According to the ILC's 1965 Commentary, shipwrecks and their cargoes cannot be interpreted as "natural resources" of the seabed. Similarly, archaeological research falls under neither the sovereign right to explore the continental shelf nor the consent regime of the coastal State. Nevertheless, the vague language of article 5(8) of the CSC, which requires coastal consent for "any research concerning the continental shelf and undertaken there", leaves room for different interpretations. Under an extensive construction of the term "research", the permission of the coastal State will be required for the search for archaeological remains on the outer continental shelf.

THE UN CONVENTION ON THE LAW OF THE SEA (1982)

The 1982 Convention, which will enter into force on 16 November 1994, is the first law of the sea convention to provide for underwater cultural property. It, therefore, constitutes an important landmark in the protection of the cultural heritage of the oceans. There is no difference in the legal regime of underwater cultural property found landward of the outer limit of the territorial sea under either the TSC or the 1982 Convention. In exercising its sovereignty, the coastal State can impose whatever conditions it thinks necessary for the protection and preservation of the underwater cultural heritage. The establishment of the right of transit passage through straits used for international navigation does not affect the exercise of the sovereignty of the riparian State(s) over these waters; nor is the conduct of archaeological research during passage permissible. The same applies to the new concept of "archipelagic waters". The archipelagic State is the only State competent to undertake and/or to authorise the undertaking of archaeological operations. However, under the 1982 Convention, coastal States are not only entitled to regulate access to archaeological sites found within the territorial sea boundary, but they also have the duty to protect them and to co-operate therefor.

The main innovation of the 1982 Convention with respect to underwater archaeological remains is the establishment of a *24-mile archaeological zone*. Despite the limiting language of article 303(2), which confines coastal rights to the "control of traffic" of archaeological and historical objects found on the bed of the contiguous zone, in substance, far more extensive rights are recognised. The combination of article 303(1), which advocates the general duty to protect archaeological objects, and the fiction established by article 303(2), allows the expansion of coastal legislation over the 24-mile zone.

Beyond the 24-mile limit and up to the outer limit of the continental shelf, marine archaeology will be exercised as a freedom of the high seas subject to the general provisions of article 303(1), (3) and (4). However, in case the coastal State has declared an EEZ, a distinction should be made between marine spaces falling within and beyond the outer limit of the EEZ. *Beyond the 24 mile line and up to the outer limit of the EEZ*, the exercise of marine archaeology falls within the "grey area", where the 1982 Convention does not attribute rights and jurisdiction to either coastal or flag States. In case of doubt, the issue will be solved on the basis of equity and in the light of all the relevant circumstances. *Beyond the outer limit of the EEZ and up to the outer limit of the continental shelf*, marine archaeology will be exercised as a freedom of the high seas under the conditions described above. Similarly to the CSC, the 1982 Convention excludes archaeological objects from the scope of coastal rights over the continental shelf and the EEZ. The same applies to archaeological research which is excluded from the scope of "marine scientific research" and the consent regime. Nevertheless, coastal States may take advantage of their extensive, almost territorial, rights in the 200-mile zone and exercise control indirectly, i.e., by claiming that archaeological research conducted by third States interferes with their resource-related rights or by employing articles 60 and 80, which grant them a wide range of powers over the construction and use of installations on the seabed. Furthermore, the establishment of the general duty to protect archaeological objects found at sea by article 303(1) may be used by coastal States as a basis to enact protective measures in the exercise of their resource-jurisdiction over the continental shelf. Such a regulation should not be regarded as an extension of coastal jurisdiction over archaeological resources in this area, but as an application of article 303(1). The undertaking of such measures is confined to specific operations and not to the actual area where these operations take place.

Finally, archaeological objects found in the *Area* are to be "preserved or disposed of" for the "benefit of mankind as a whole", while taking into consideration the preferential rights of the "State or country of origin", the "State of cultural origin" or the "State of archaeological and historical origin".

In chapter 2 of this book, the *desiderata* of underwater archaeology that should be reflected in the international regime of the protection of underwater cultural property were discussed. Unfortunately, only a small percentage of these principles has been incorporated in the protective measures of the 1982 Convention. The establishment of the general duty to protect objects of an archaeological and historical nature alone cannot restore the balance. In implementing this duty, States are recommended to take all the appropriate measures so as to embrace the whole spectrum of activities related to the underwater cultural heritage. However, a lot of questions, both jurisdictional and substantive, remain to be addressed.

Negative factors

Restriction of protection to the 24-mile limit: The main disadvantage of the 1982 scheme is the "abandonment" of cultural property found seaward of the 24-mile line to flag State jurisdiction. Even if a coastal State has claimed an EEZ, the exercise of marine archaeology under article 59 cannot ensure an effective regime of protection. In this area, the implementation of the general duty to protect archaeological objects lies upon the absolute discretion of individual States.

Use of a legal fiction to justify the extension of coastal jurisdiction in the 24-mile zone: The use of a fiction as a means of expanding coastal jurisdiction over archaeological objects found in the 24-mile zone creates interpretation problems as to its precise scope and nature.

Failure to designate an international body to implement article 149: The 1982 Convention failed to establish an international machinery to put the proposed regime of protection of deep seabed cultural property into practice. Since the Authority does not enjoy any powers over it, there is an urgent need to either nominate an existing international organisation, such as UNESCO, or designate a new one to undertake this responsibility. Otherwise, the proposed scheme will pale into insignificance.

Failure to define the State of origin of the recovered cultural property: reference to three States claimants: The formulation of the terms "State or country of origin", "State of cultural origin" and "State of historical and archaeological origin" under article 149 raises significant interpretational problems. What are the criteria for distinguishing the "State of origin" and the "State of cultural origin"? Which are the differences between "cultural" and "historical and archaeological origin"? How can one define or even distinguish between a State and a country? The identification problem is, no doubt, acute, as in most cases the determination of the State of origin is extremely difficult. However, even if under the circumstances, it is possible to identify traces of origin, the qualification of more than one State as claimant to the recovered property may create considerable difficulties.

Failure to provide for the right to conduct archaeological exploration: Both articles 149 and 303(2) fail to provide for the right to search for and locate marine archaeological remains. Article 149 refers to their preservation and disposal, while article 303(2) to their removal and traffic.

Reservation of the law of salvage: Since national heritage legislation often conflicts with salvage law, the reservation of the latter by article 303(3) is unfortunate. Under an extensive interpretation of article 303(3), both coastal jurisdiction over archaeological objects in the 24-mile zone and the protection of archaeological remains in international waters would be considerably limited.

Lack of definition of the protected cultural property: The 1982 Convention does not define the formula "objects of an archaeological and historical nature". As a result, both the meaning of "archaeological" and "historical", and the question of whether immovable cultural property is included within the scope of protection are left open to debate.

Failure to pay the required degree of attention to the archaeological issue: The 1982 Convention reveals a lack of an understanding of the notion of underwater cultural property, or to use the formula employed by the Convention, of "objects of archaeological and historical nature". This is illustrated by: (a) the co-existence of marine spaces where archaeological research is "free-for-all", and the Area where archaeological remains are to be preserved or disposed of for the "benefit of mankind as a whole", and (b) the recognition of the preferential rights of the State(s) of origin only in relation to remains found on the international deep seabed. One may, therefore, raise the following questions. Is there no need for the protection and preservation of archaeological objects found on the outer continental shelf area for the benefit of mankind as a whole? Does the international community lose its interest in the protection of cultural property found within marine spaces under coastal jurisdiction? Which is the reason for the failure to recognise the preferential rights of the States of origin in relation to cultural property found on high seas areas?

Regrettably, the drafters of the 1982 Convention did not pay the required attention to the archaeological issue and its peculiarities. It is notable that a number of the informal proposals, such as those submitted by Greece, envisaged a more coherent scheme of protection: (a) due to the proposed expansion of the coastal jurisdiction over the continental shelf, there was no area where marine archaeology would be exercised as a freedom of the high seas; (b) the State of cultural origin was granted preferential rights in respect of objects located on the outer continental shelf; (c) the Authority was designated as the responsible body to put the regime of deep seabed archaeological objects into practice. It is obvious, therefore, that a more satisfactory scheme could have been adopted. The reasons for the failure to do so were the opposition of the maritime powers to the expansion of coastal jurisdiction over the continental shelf and the desire to limit the international deep seabed regime to mineral-resource exploration and exploitation. The result was inevitable to the extent that the existing natural-resource based delimitation of the seabed was used to determine the regime of archaeological and historical objetcs, while they were excluded from the notion of the natural resources of the seabed. Archaeological objects always appeared to be the exception to the overall applicable regime of the seabed.

Positive factors

Extension of coastal jurisdiction over archaeological objects beyond the territorial sea limit: Even though coastal jurisdiction is limited to the 24-mile zone, the mere fact that it surpasses the traditional territorial sea limit constitutes an important development.

Establishment of the duty to protect "objects of an archaeological and historical nature" found at sea and to co-operate therefor: Despite their general language, these duties form the basis for recognising extended coastal rights over marine archaeological remains. For example, consider the positive role of article 303(1) in the recognition of the 24-mile zone as a fully-fledged archaeological zone and the acknowledgement of the right of coastal States to adopt protective legislation in the exercise of their resource-related jurisdiction over the continental shelf and/or the EEZ. Most importantly, States have the discretion to implement these duties into specific rights and obligations, which may embrace the whole spectrum of the protection of the underwater cultural heritage.

Article 303(1) may be read as establishing:

·   the obligation to report the accidental discovery of marine archaeological sites;
·   the obligation to take the appropriate *interim* measures for the preservation of underwater cultural property before the arrival of archaeologists or even the suspension of construction projects:
·   the need for the *in situ* protection of archaeological objects;
·   the need for conservation, proper presentation, and restoration of the recovered items;
·   the promotion of the exchange of scientific information;
·   the undertaking of joint archaeological projects, and
·   the co-ordination of the fight against the illicit trade of artefacts.

Introduction of the cultural aspect of the concept of the common heritage of mankind: Article 149 introduced the cultural aspect of one of the fundamental concepts of contemporary law of the sea: "the common heritage of mankind". Despite the fact that the Authority is given no rights over the protection of archaeological objects, their preservation for "the benefit of mankind as a whole" constitutes an important landmark in the development of the law of cultural heritage.

Recognition of the preferential rights of the State(s) of origin: By recognising the preferential rights of the State(s) of origin of the discovered archaeological material, the 1982 Convention emphasises the fact that the preservation of the cultural heritage of the oceans for the benefit of mankind as a whole should not deprive the State of origin of its rightful interests.

It is obvious from the above analysis that, on balance, the negative factors outweigh the positive. Could one then argue that the 1982 Convention failed in its attempt to regulate underwater cultural property? The answer could be yes, in that it failed to provide a sound regime of protection, or, on the other hand, no because it introduced new concepts, established the duty to protect the limited cultural resources of the oceans, and left room for the development of more comprehensive regimes in the future. To adopt a negative attitude towards the protective measures of the 1982 Convention does not help the protection of the underwater cultural heritage. In contrast, positive criticism is helpful, and may even result in the elaboration of more comprehensive schemes of protection. For example, consider the attitude of Turkey in the Council of Europe, which proposed the extension of coastal jurisdiction over the continental shelf, or alternatively, its restriction within the territorial sea boundary. In a few words, if the expansion of coastal competence over the outer continental shelf was not acceptable, coastal jurisdiction should retreat to the outer limit of the territorial sea. In the light of the lengthy negotiations of UNCLOS III and the fact that the establishment of a 24-mile zone constitutes a progressive development of the law, this solution appears defeatist. The few protective measures of the 1982 Convention should not be refused; coastal States should take advantage of these regulations and ensure the extension of their jurisdiction in the 24-mile zone. At the same time, however, there is need to develop new principles and concepts in order to provide a sound regime of protection of the cultural resources of the oceans.

CUSTOMARY INTERNATIONAL LAW

In the field of international customary law, two legal regimes of underwater cultural property may be identified: cultural property found within marine spaces falling under coastal sovereignty, and cultural property found in extraterritorial waters and subject to the high seas regime. Even if a state had declared an EEZ, the conduct of archaeological research falls within the ambit of residual rights, the accommodation of which varies under existing national legislation. Since most EEZ laws are silent on this issue, it must be accepted that all States are entitled to undertake archaeological activities in this area. At the same time, a tendency to extend coastal jurisdiction beyond the traditional territorial sea limit is distinguishable. This is revealed in: (a) articles 303(2) of the 1982 Convention and 2 of the Draft European Convention, which expand coastal competence over the 24-mile archaeological (contiguous) zone. To date three States, Denmark, France and Tunisia, have expanded their competence over this area: France and Tunisia have employed the concept of the contiguous zone as a legal basis to extend their competence, while the Danish legislation combines the breadth of 24nm with the notion of the continental shelf; (b) the practice of a small group of States, such as Australia, Ireland, Jamaica, Morocco, Portugal, Spain and Yugoslavia which claim jurisdiction over cultural property found on the continental shelf or the EEZ, and (c) Recommendation 848 (1978) of the Council of Europe, which proposes the creation of 200 mile cultural protection zones. At present, it is not possible to confine this tendency to a certain area. It is notable that the most recent international instrument to protect the archaeological heritage, the 1992 Archaeological Convention (revised), determines the territorial scope of its application by reference to all existing jurisdictional zones, without any preference. Along the same lines, China claims jurisdiction over underwater cultural relics found within sea areas under its jurisdiction according to Chinese laws. Finally, in Denmark there are overlapping bases of jurisdiction since the enactment of Act No. 9 of 3 January 1992, which expands Danish jurisdiction over archaeological and historical objects found within the 200 nm fishing zone.

So far as the recognition of deep seabed cultural property as the common heritage of mankind is concerned, the whole issue appears to be more a matter of attitude than of evidence. To be more specific: The RMS Titanic Maritime Memorial Act is the only instrument to date other than the 1982 Convention to deal with the cultural resources of the deep seabed. The other exception is a series of UN General Assembly Resolutions on the Return or Restitution of Cultural Property to the Countries of Origin, whose general language permits their application to cultural property found on the seabed beyond national jurisdiction. However, despite the lack of evidence in State practice and in law, the recognition of the cultural resources of the deep seabed as the common heritage of mankind is widely acceptable. As noted, during the negotiations of UNCLOS III, the few States that were against the adoption of such a principle, simply opposed the extension of the powers of the Authority over non-resource related purposes. It should always be remembered that at the early stages of the Conference, the Authority was designated as the competent body to deal with the archaeological issue. Similarly, in the course of the negotiations of the Council of Europe, the cultural heritage in extraterritorial waters was considered to be more of a common heritage of mankind than the land archaeological heritage or that in territorial waters.

At present the preservation of deep seabed cultural property does not appear to be high in the priorities of States. The recent salvaging of the *Titanic* despite the U.S.' intervention and the public outcry indicates that, unless an international body is designated to deal with deep seabed archaeological sites, their protection, if any, rests with the goodwill of individual States. There may be cases where the States having a historical and cultural link with the discovered cultural property will not take the initiative to protect it, and cases where the identification of the relics will not be possible. Most important, the residual regime being that of the high seas, only the flag national State can prevent the ships flying its flag or its nationals from interfering with a marine archaeological site. Under these circumstances, deep seabed cultural property will remain unprotected. This state of affairs contrasts sharply with the underlying purpose of article 149 of the 1982 Convention for the creation of a comprehensive scheme of protection under the aegis of the international community as a whole.

PART THREE

CHAPTER 10

Future Developments

NEED TO PROTECT CULTURAL PROPERTY FOUND IN MARINE SPACES BEYOND
THE 24-MILE LIMIT

The regulation of rights of access to and the safeguarding of archaeological
sites in extraterritorial waters constitute major problems for the international
protection of the underwater cultural heritage. Under both the 1958 Geneva
Conventions and customary law, cultural property found beyond the territorial sea is governed by the high seas regime. Under the 1982 Convention,
this area is limited to marine spaces lying beyond the 24-mile archaeological
zone up to the outer limit of the continental shelf. Beyond the outer continental shelf limit, deep seabed cultural property will be preserved or disposed
of for the benefit of mankind as a whole, while taking into consideration
the preferential rights of the State(s) of origin. Even if a coastal State has
declared an EEZ, the situation will not be substantially different, as the
pursuit of marine archaeology falls within the ambit of residual rights, the
accommodation of which under article 59 cannot guarantee an effective
scheme of protection.

There are two extreme solutions to the archaeological issue: (a) to regulate
the exercise of archaeological activities as a "freedom" of the seas by establishing international or regional Committees, or (b) to extend coastal jurisdiction over cultural property beyond the 24-mile limit to the outer limit of
the continental shelf.[1] In the light of the many disadvantages of the doctrine
of the freedom of the high seas as a basis for protecting underwater cultural
property, even a "regulated" freedom could not ensure a satisfactory scheme
of protection. As the area in question is the continental shelf, coastal States
may oppose the undertaking of protective measures on the basis that they
interfere with their resource-related rights. The effectiveness of the international or regional regulation of archaeological activities in extraterritorial
waters would thus be limited. The same applies for the suggested creation
of a *uniform law* for submarine antiquities, encompassing the territorial sea,

the contiguous zone and the high seas: "In principle, the competence to deal with this matter should be entrusted to that coastal State from or to whose territory the salvage or research operations are to be directed. The coastal State should be authorised to deal with licences."[2] This proposal offers an unrealistic solution to the protection of underwater cultural property. It not only assumes the creation of a uniform law, but it also requires good will and co-operation between States. For example, which coastal State will be given priority over the salvaging of antiquities in extraterritorial waters, if there is more than one State interested in the undertaking of the relevant operations? In contrast, moderate solutions, such as the proposed declaration of the Mediterranean as a "sea of human civilisation", through adoption of a regional convention, would seem to provide a more realistic alternative.[3] However, as yet, no positive step has been taken in this regard.

Finally, special mention should be made to the work of the International Law Association's Cultural Heritage Law Committee in drafting an International Convention on the Protection of the Underwater Cultural Heritage.[4] The ILA's Draft Convention allows each State party to establish a "cultural heritage zone" coextensive with the continental shelf[5], while, at the same time it employs nationality as a principal jurisdictional basis to enforce its provisions in areas which are not within a cultural heritage zone or a territorial sea of another State party.

EXTENTION OF COASTAL JURISDICTION OVER THE CONTINENTAL SHELF

Adequacy of the existing legal definition of the continental shelf

The expansion of coastal competence over cultural property found beyond the 24-mile limit can take place on the basis of one of the following concepts: (a) The legal continental shelf; (b) The EEZ; (c) The 200-mile cultural protection zone proposed by Recommendation 848 (1978) of the Parliamentary Assembly of the Council of Europe. It has been argued that the legal continental shelf is inadequate for the protection of the underwater cultural property as it was originally limited to the exploitation of mineral and other non-living resources of the seabed and the subsoil and is, therefore, associated with the morphology of the seabed. Alternatively, the EEZ has been considered to offer a more suitable basis of protection; since the minimum 200-mile breadth is measured on the surface, irrespective of the geomorphology of the seabed, the disadvantages of an abrupt continental shelf are avoided.[6] These arguments, no doubt, hold true for the definition of the continental shelf as elaborated by the CSC.[7] It is doubtful, however, whether they are valid for the continental shelf definition of the 1982 Convention, since the continental shelf and the EEZ coincide up to the 200-mile limit. As previously indicated, the ICJ accepted in the *Libya-Malta Continental Shelf Case* (1985) that the 200 nm continental shelf is part of international customary law.[8] Nevertheless, the majority of States still employ the CSC formula to define the outer limit of their continental shelf (see table 1). This is presumably due to the fact that, in most cases, the legislation on the EEZ covers the coastal State's rights with respect to the continental shelf, and also due to the complexity of the definition of the continental shelf contained in article 76 of the 1982 Convention.[9] If one considers together: claims to a 200 nm continental shelf as such (6); claims to the outer edge of the continental margin or breadth of 200 nm (CM/200) (22); claims to a 200 mile EEZ where no precise claim is made to a continental shelf (27); claims to a 200 mile territorial sea where no precise claim is made to a continental shelf (9); claims to 200 nm or to 100 nm from the 2500 m isobath (2); claims to 200nm/350nm continental shelf (1), and claims to 200nm/natural prolongation continental shelf (1), the number of States claiming a 200nm continental shelf goes up to sixty-eight (68) (see table 2).

Table 1: Outer limit of the continental shelf

Criteria	Number of States
Exploitability	5
Continental margin	1
Depth (200 metres) plus exploitability	40
Breadth (200 nautical miles)	6
Outer edge of the continental margin or breadth of 200 nautical miles (CM/200)	22
Breadth (200 nautical miles or 100 nautical miles from the 2,500 metre isobath)	2
Breadth (200/350 nautical miles)	1
Breadth (200nm) + natural prolongation	1

Source: Law of the Sea Bulletin, No. 23, June 1993 at p. 80.

Table 2: States claiming a minimum 200 mile continental shelf

States claiming a 200 mile continental shelf

Democratic Kampuchea	Peru
Ghana	Solomon Islands
Ivory Coast	Saint Vincent and the Grenadines

States claiming a 200 mile continental shelf or to the outer edge of the continental margin

Antigua and Barbuda	Mexico
Argentina	New Zealand
Burma (Myanmar)	Pakistan
Dominican Republic	Saint Lucia
Canada	Saint Kitts and Nevis
Cook Islands[a]	Senegal
Guyana	Seychelles
Iceland	Sri Lanka
India	Vanuatu
Mauritania	Vietnam
Mauritius	Yemen

States claiming a 200 mile EEZ with no precise claim to a continental shelf

Barbados	Kiribati
Brazil	Marshall Islands
Belize	Micronesia (Federal States of)
Cape Verde	Mozambique
Comoros	Namibia
Cuba	Niue[a]
Democratic People's Republic of Korea	Oman
	São Tomé & Príncipe
Djibouti	Samoa
Dominica	Suriname
Equatorial Guinea	Togo
Gabon	Tuvalu
Grenada	United Republic of Tanzania
Guinea	Zaire
Guinea-Bissau	

States claiming a 200 mile territorial sea with no precise claim to a continental shelf

Benin	Panama
Congo	Sierra Leone[b]
El Salvador	Somalia
Liberia	Uruguay[b]
Nicaragua	

States claiming a 200 mile continental shelf or 100 miles from the 2,500 metre isobath

Ecuador	Madagascar

States claiming a 200/350 mile continental shelf

Chile

States claiming a 200 mile continental shelf/natural prolongation

Norway

a Self-governing associated States and territories entitled to become members to the 1982 Convention under article 305(1)
b These States have claimed a 200m/EXP continental shelf

Source: Law of the Sea Bulletin, No. 23, June 1993.

The extension of coastal jurisdiction over the basis continental shelf, in the *form of a cultural heritage zone,* would provide the best means for protecting underwater cultural property. Since the outer continental shelf limit forms the baseline of the Area, the extension of coastal competence over the continental shelf will leave no ocean area unprotected or where marine archaeology would be exercised as a freedom of the high seas.

Archaeological potential of the continental shelf

The archaeological potential of the continental shelf was questioned in the course of the negotiations of UNCLOS III by the U.S. delegation, which asserted that only the area immediately beyond the territorial sea was relevant for

the protection of archaeological objects. As noted, the political motive behind
these allegations was the U.S.'s wish to restrict legal control of underwater
cultural property to the contiguous zone so that undesired expansion of
coastal competence over the continental shelf would be avoided.

Shipwrecks: In the past, the majority of vessels wrecked were sunk as a
result of some accident in connection with the shore.[10] However, the pro-
portion of ships sunk in the open sea is not negligible. From a study of 19th
century losses at Lloyd's of London, Bascom asserted that about 20% of
all sinkings occured well away from the coast.[11] In applying this figure
to the Mediterranean shipping in classical times, he estimated that there are
150,000 ships down offshore. To these figures an additional number of 5000
warships should be considered, many of them in deep water.[12] The significance of Bascom's estimations has been pointed out by Muckelroy:
"Although Bascom dealt with the Mediterranean shipping in classical times,
his figures probably represent the correct order of the magnitude for all
sinkings in the open sea at any period."[13]

The virtual absence of oxygen together with other chemicals and biological
reasons means that the deep water is likely to contain the best preserved
wrecks of all. Even wrecks below 200m, which is approximately the edge
of the geological continental shelf, could be found in "wonderful condition".[14] First, the temperature on the bottom is near freezing and chemical
reactions proceed slowly. Second, deepwater shipwrecks are well beneath
wave action, trawlnets and divers; it is, therefore, likely that their cargo
would not be scattered about as much as it is in ships wrecked in shallow
water. Third, the absence of currents allows the accumulation of protective
silt on the upper surface.[15] The most uncertain aspect of wreck preservation
in deep water is the destructive action of marine borers. It is notable that
the exploration of the wreck site of the *Titanic* revealed that almost no
wooden parts survived. The effectiveness of these biological agents, however,
varies according to the region. Marine borers are totally absent in
oxygen-free waters.

Submerged sites: Prehistoric archaeological material may also be found on
the continental shelf.

"The area of the continental shelf is 5% of the entire area of the Earth equivalent to
a continent the size of North America. This continent was once available for exploitation

by Stone Age peoples, and its exploitation contributed mightily to the growth of early technology, marine skills, the origins of agriculture, and of civilization itself up to the start of the Bronze Age in the Middle East. It is unscientific to go on saying: 'This must have happened ...That must be so.' Now is the time for earth scientists, oceanographers and archaeologists to combine in the exploration of the drowned continent and to obtain reliable scientific evidence."[16]

Technological capabilities for undertaking archaeological operations on the continental shelf

The development of advanced underwater technology which has taken place recently in an attempt to meet the needs of deep seabed mining and the off-shore oil industry has made the deep sea more accesible to archaeologists.[17] At present, commercial and naval mixed-gas-breathing ranges down to 400-450 m.[18] Below this, waters are visited only by submersibles, manned or unmanned. One-atmosphere diving suits and lock-out submersibles provide the archaeologist with direct access to increased depths. In contrast, few sites deeper than 50-60 metres can be regarded as accessible to archaeological teams using SCUBA (self-contained underwater breathing apparatus).[19] Unmanned, remotely operated vehicles have already performed television and photographic inspections of several sites. In the location and investigation of the remains of the *Titanic* at 12.500 feet (4100m) beneath the Atlantic, a manned submersible, an unmanned survey vehicle, capable of operating to 6,000m depth and a remotely controlled underwater robot (Jason) played a very important role.[20] Jason, was also employed in the discovery and exploration of the wreck site of Isis, a 4th century A.D. African *amphora* wreck in 818m at the west end of the Strait of Sicily. Isis is the deepest wreck and the only one found by deliberate archaeological research.[21] However, as argued: "It would be improper to comment on the effectiveness of Jason as a survey and excavation tool until an archaeological report appears".[22]

Although the location and the removal of archaeological remains from the continental shelf is now possible, whether technical developments will become available to archaeologists before they become available to commercial interests is a different issue. It is very unlikely that a similar attempt by archaeologists to recover a Roman wreck from deep water would either attract the attention of the public or raise the funds required as did the expedition for the location of the *Titanic*.[23] Meanwhile, technological advances in locating and recovering artefacts are occurring rapidly and it can realistically be expected that many more sites will be interfered with and salvaged, without proper documentation or preservation. The development of advanced underwater technology should not result in unscientific or incomplete excavations of deepwater sites. It would be wise to protect and keep underwater remains for future study at a time when there would be a more developed underwater archaeological methodology.[24]

Funding of archaeological projects and enforcement of national heritage laws

The magnitude of the budget of offshore archaeological projects is comparable with the budget of mineral exploration and exploitation projects. The budget of underwater search and exploration is between twenty and fifty times the budget required for a similar period along the coastline.[25] The question, therefore, arises as to whether coastal States have the financial means and/or the scientific and technological capabilities to promote and back-up this field of research.

One may argue that the wider the ocean area, the less capable the coastal State is to achieve this goal, especially when considering that the majority of coastal States are developing countries. This argument has a basis in reality. However, the following factors should also be considered. First, the potential inability of coastal States to carry out archaeological operations may be addressed by the granting of licences to foreign archaeological teams. This practice is already popular with land sites. Second, projects such as the 1977-79 wreck excavation in Mombasa, Kenya, indicate that even developing countries are capable of successfully completing offshore archaeological projects.[26] This particular project received grants from both the British Council and the National Museum of Kenya. Third, the extension of coastal jurisdiction over cultural property on the continental shelf will secure the legal position of archaeological operations, which are presently governed by the freedom of the high seas. Potential sponsors may, thus, be less reluctant to co-operate.

The extended ocean area covered by the legal continental shelf will, no doubt, create considerable enforcement problems. Even a maritime power has been reported to declare that its naval forces are able to effectively control only an area between 12-20 miles.[27] The reason is that, in practice, the detection of foreign vessels engaged in illicit operations is extremely difficult. Exploration activities carried out by sonars and visual search systems are almost undetectable. The same applies to the operation of small craft and divers. In shallow waters, the removal of *amphorae* and other isolated objects often takes place unnoticed by coastal authorities. The situation is significantly different with respect to deepwater activities due to the nature of the operations involved. Excavation and, in general, salvaging in deep water are time-consuming activities which involve the exclusive use of a sea area for a considerable period of time. It is, therefore, very unlikely that they could take place unnoticed by the coastal State. However, illicit excavations do not constitute the only danger to underwater sites. Illegitimate appropriation of chance discoveries during offshore operations should also be confronted. In short, the enforcement of national heritage laws over the outer continental shelf is not an easy task to undertake. Coastal States should be prepared to undertake all the necessary measures and practices in order to avoid the plundering of the limited cultural resources of the oceans. In this respect, a judicious programme of education of the public is also important.[28]

Justification of coastal claims over cultural property on the continental shelf

Coastal interest in the protection of underwater cultural property situated on the continental shelf

The coastal State on whose continental shelf the cultural property is situated has an increased interest in its preservation and protection. As previously indicated, the safeguarding of cultural remains discovered accidentally during resource-related activities falls within coastal responsibility. The coastal State will be entitled to undertake protective measures in the exercise of its resource-related jurisdiction as an expression of the duty to protect the underwater cultural heritage. However, coastal interest is not only limited to the preservation of property accidentally discovered. Underwater cultural property found on the continental shelf provides evidence of the *history* of the coastal State, even if it does not originate from that particular country.

The significance of shipwrecks for the history of the coastal State on whose continental shelf they are situated was questioned in *Robinson v. The Western Australian Museum* in 1977.[29] In Judge Barwick's view:

"After all these wrecks, but particularly the Gilt Dragon were wrecks of Dutch ships which were in the course of commerce between Holland and the East Indies. They were not even bent upon or in any way instrumental in the exploration of the Australian coastline: less, indeed, were they engaged in doing anything with particular historical significance for the Colony of Western Australia. The most it can be said about them is that they rest on the bed of the sea 'off' the north-western coast of Australia and that the coastline of that coast now forms the boundary of Western Australia ... With a degree of artistry these ancient wrecks were described as 'historic'. So they might properly be styled in the history of navigation but scarcely in the history of the colony or State of Western Australia."[30]

Judge Barwick's views have been criticised on the grounds that they could prove to be detrimental for underwater archaeology and the protection of the cultural resources of the oceans. As argued:

"To suggest that Australian history developed in total isolation from anything which may have taken place beyond the low-water mark at Rottnest - all this would be a recipe for the grossest provincialism and barbarism. And indeed, in an era which places stress on Australia's multi-cultural origins, it would be odd to overlook the shipping which provided Australia's lines of trade and communication with the rest of the world. Once this is admitted, it is easy to accept that maritime archaeology is at least as legitimate and exciting a source of evidence as anything we may gather from the printed or manuscript record."[31]

These arguments hold true for any coastal State. Maritime archaeology provides useful evidence of both the naval and the general history of States by revealing contacts between different societies over water. It would be absurd to argue that of significance to a coastal State are only those remains which originate from it. Such an attitude, combined with the lack of adequate heritage legislation, may exclude important underwater sites from the scope of protection even within coastal waters. Other scholars stress the *intimate link* between the archaeological riches of the continental shelf and the coastal State. It has been argued that Greece should be entitled to unilaterally extend its antiquities legislation over its continental shelf, in particular, over the Aegean Sea. The claim is based on the special geographical position of Greece in relation to the sea, the physical unity between the Greek continent and the Greek islands, and the fundamental importance of the Aegean Sea to Greek history and civilisation in general.[32] The latter, which has been inhabited by Hellenic populations since 7000 BC, has always played an important role in the social, political and economic development of Greece. According to Michael, Greece has both the right and the moral duty to preserve and protect its cultural heritage.[33] The cultural development of coastal States may, therefore, play an important role in the recognition of their claims over archaeological remains on the continental shelf.

Effectiveness of coastal claims
Probably the less controversial basis of coastal claims over archaeological objects on the outer continental shelf is their effectiveness. Only the recognition of the juridical and judicial competence of the coastal State can ensure an effective scheme of protection of underwater cultural property. For the successful completion of archaeological projects underwater a substantial degree of control of the area in question is required, which cannot be guaranteed by flag State operations in extraterritorial waters. It is noteworthy that in the course of the negotiations of the Council of Europe, even those countries which emphasised the role of the flag State in protecting the underwater cultural heritage, admitted that the coastal State was "in a better position to monitor activities the purpose of which was to gain possession of the objects in question."[34] In many cases it is impossible to determine at a sufficiently early stage whether those activities relate to the flag or the coastal State, while, in others, the flag State cannot be identified.[35]

In conclusion, the recognition of coastal claims over underwater cultural property on the continental shelf should be based on their effectiveness and the increased concern of coastal States in the protection of underwater sites which reveal their history and the creativity of the past. However, the coastal State that preserves the limited cultural resources of the oceans does not act only in its own national interest. It also acts in the interest of the international community in the safeguarding of the cultural heritage which provides useful information about past civilisations and promotes the understanding between nations. In this context, both the dissemination of the information acquired and the co-operation of States throughout the different stages of archaeological research are essential. Although at present, States are recommended to implement article 303(2) and create 24-mile archaeological zones, the elaboration in the future of a more comprehensive regime should not be neglected. The holding of a *world conference on underwater archaeology* would appear to provide the best means of achieving this goal. Article 303(4) which reserves international conventions protecting historical and archaeological objects allows such a development.[36] The proposed expansion of coastal jurisdiction over the continental shelf, in the form of a cultural protection zone, would not give rise to creeping jurisdiction because the proposed zone will be coextensive with the geographical area covered by the continental shelf, but not subject to its legal regime. Instead, the legal basis for such expansion in international law will be the Convention itself. To adopt a provision along the lines of the 1992 Archaeological Convention (revised), which encompasses all jurisdictional zones, i.e., the territorial sea, the contiguous zone, the continental shelf, the EEZ or the cultural heritage zone, within its scope, without indicating a preference for one or the other, would result in unsurmountable difficulties being met in practice. In view of the discretion which States will possess to choose the jurisdictional zone/ geographical area with which the cultural heritage zone would be coextensive, the situation may arise where one State chooses the continental shelf as the basis of its cultural heritage zone, while an adjacent State may choose a different basis resulting in an overlap of such zones. For example, which delimitation formula will be used in such cases?

RECOGNITION OF THE INTERESTS OF THE STATE(S) OF ORIGIN IN THE DIS-
COVERED CULTURAL PROPERTY

The present state of the law

The accommodation of the interests of the State of origin of cultural property found on the continental shelf is not a new concept within the law of the sea. As already seen, in the course of the negotiations of UNCLOS III, provision was made for the preferential rights of the State(s) of origin over archaeological and historical objects found in this area. The exercise of these rights, which featured in a number of proposals expanding coastal competence over the continental shelf, was limited to the sale or disposal of the recovered objects resulting in their removal out of the coastal State. Although these proposals did not find their way into the Final Text of the Convention, they reveal a tendency not only to recognise the interests of the States of origin, but also to provide a legal basis for the exercise of their rights. Since the extension of coastal jurisdiction over this area was not acceptable, no provision was taken for the interests of the State of origin.[37] Similarly, the UN General Assembly Resolutions on the Restitution or Return of Cultural Property to the Countries of Origin invite States seeking the recovery of cultural and artistic treasures from the seabed to facilitate the participation of States having a historical and cultural link with those treasures.

The Draft European Convention does not make any specific reference to the State(s) of origin. It simply states in article 4 that "where underwater cultural property is of particular interest to other contracting States, contracting States should consider providing information about the discovery of such property and collaborating in the investigation, excavation, documentation, conservation, study and cultural promotion of the property to the extent permitted by their legislation". In view of the fact that the number of States which provide for the notification of, or the co-operation with, the State of origin of the discovered underwater cultural property is small, the practical significance of article 4 is limited.[38] Furthermore, the concept of restitution under the Draft Convention is restricted to cultural property illegally recovered or exported from the "area" of contracting States, namely the territorial sea and, for the parties that have established it, the contiguous zone. In other words, as State of origin is considered to be the coastal State in whose "area" the underwater cultural property is situated. No provision is made for the accommodation of the interests of the State of cultural origin.

Special mention should once more be made to the Dutch proposal to grant the identifiable flag State a similar competence to that of the coastal State in respect of flag State objects.

> "Neither competence would be exclusive. Anybody wishing to search for and salvage objects of either the flag State or the coastal State would have to apply to both for authorisation. In practice, the two States would be compelled to reach mutual agreement on the ultimate destination of any objects removed from the sea zone."[39]

Apart from the obvious difficulties in applying this scheme, its significance is limited to relatively recent wrecks, as it is very unlikely that the country of origin of a Roman wreck could qualify as its flag State.[40] It is notable that the Dutch proposal referred specifically to the 1976 Australia/Netherlands Agreement concerning V.O.C. wrecks lying off the coast of Western Australia. One should not overlook, however, that, in the case of V.O.C. wrecks, there were certain factors which made the conclusion of an agreement between the interested parties simple. First, the geographical position of Western Australia and, more specifically, the lack of neighbouring countries reduces the number of States on whose continental shelf the wrecks are situated. In contrast consider the Mediterranean, where, in a similar case, there would be a number of coastal States involved. Given that not all continental shelf boundaries are settled, the conclusion of an agreement, or better agreements, between the coastal States concerned and the State of origin would be a rather difficult task to undertake. Second, the Netherlands is not only the undisputed State of origin, but also the present legal successor to the V.O.C. as the owner of the wrecked vessels.[41] Third, the Netherlands did not object to the extension of the competence of Australia over the continental shelf. Under the circumstances, the creation of a Committee to overesee the deposition of representative collections in the museums of the Netherlands and Australia was possible.

Need to attribute specific rights

Although few would object to the recognition of the continuing interest of the identifiable State of origin in the discovered cultural property, the attribution of specific rights is not always welcomed. Even the use of the term "participation" in the UN General Assembly Resolutions has been criticised. This objection is mainly based on the fact that the identification of a *modern* State as the State of origin of submerged cultural property is often difficult and authoritative.[42] For example, which State is to be considered as the successor of a past civilisation, which overlays contemporary national boundaries? Most of the difficulties arise in respect of ancient relics. Relatively recent property presents less problems in relation to the identification of the State of origin, as the geographical distribution of States remains similar. Furthermore, one could argue that the accommodation of claims made by the State of origin is of minimal importance. What matters most, is the preservation of the limited cultural resources of the oceans and the acquisition of the valuable information they can provide about past societies and civilisations.

While these arguments have some basis in reality, it is not possible to deny a particular State the enjoyment of its identifiable cultural heritage. The cultural heritage is the product of given socio-economic and political processes and should, therefore, be considered in terms of social realisations rather than aesthetic appreciations. To the people who created it, cultural property has not only artistic and historical value, but also spiritual and religious significance. It is on these grounds that the State of origin of cultural property found underwater should be granted a juridical basis to advance its legitimate interests when this is feasible. It would be unrealistic to expect the recognition of such rights over archaeological material found landward of the outer limit of the territorial sea. At most, the conclusion of bilateral agreements along the lines of the UN General Assembly Resolutions should be endeavoured.

However, the whole issue acquires a completely different character with respect to cultural remains found on the continental shelf. First, the continental shelf occupies a vast ocean area. The further from the coast, the more likely it is that remains will originate from countries other than the coastal State. Second, it may be recalled that the aim is to secure the accommodation of the interests of the State of primary origin by the coastal State, whose competence is to be expanded over the continental shelf. Since international law will act as an enabling force in respect of the extension of coastal jurisdiction over this area, there is no reason why certain rights could not be attributed to the State of origin at the same time. The recognition of such rights is essential for two reasons: (a) the concept of cultural heritage implies the existence of a right related to it;[43] (b) the attribution of specific rights to the State of origin will enable it to qualify as an active participant instead of a passive beneficiary of someone else's obligation. The recognition of a right will facilitate access to a range of legal norms and enforcement mechanisms. Otherwise, the whole issue will be left to the discretion of the State, which is in possession of the requested items.[44] On the other hand, it is true, both the identification of the "State of origin" and the determination of the objects which form part of the national cultural heritage are extremely difficult. As time goes on, it can become difficult to link an art object with a specific nation let alone a specific State. Nevertheless, an attempt will be made to justify a legal basis for the identifiable State of origin to promote its interests in the field of public international law.

Legal nature of claims by the State(s) of origin

In the context of the preferential rights of the State(s) of origin under article 149, it was argued that their recognition was based on the intimate cultural and historical link between those States and the discovered objects. More specifically, the legal right in respect of which preference operates would appear to be the right of a State to its cultural heritage. Can the so-called "sovereign right to cultural property" form the basis for claims made by the State of origin of cultural property found on the continental shelf of another State? The former is often described as the right of each State to keep any object belonging to the national heritage within its territory as well as to claim its restitution, if it leaves the territory.[45]

Restitution or return of cultural property to the country of origin
Up to the present time, the notion of restitution or return of cultural property
is confined to property that has been either stolen, lost, or illicitly exported
and property removed from former colonies.[46] The term "restitution" is
used in circumstances when the cultural property has been removed from
the territory of the State, without its consent or in contravention of its export
laws, while the term "return" is used for cases where the property was
removed before such legislation existed, i.e., removal during the colonial
period.[47] It is obvious, therefore, that their significance for the accommodation of claims made by the State of origin of cultural property found underwater is limited. First, no illegal transaction or appropriation of the cultural
property in question took place, unless, of course, it forms part of looted
collections of works of art, contained in the cargoes of wrecks, and second,
the property concerned was not found within the territory of the claimant
State in modern times. Although certain items have originated from a particular State, they now rest on the bed of the continental shelf of another State.
Under these circumstances, it would be very difficult to legally justify the
obligation of the coastal State to "return" the recovered material to its State
of origin.[48] As previously indicated, the 1985 Cultural Offences Convention
adopts the passive personality principle as a basis for expanding jurisdiction
over offences committed outside the territories of States parties, restricts
the notion of "restitution" to the return of cultural property from the territory
of one to that of another Party with a view to being handed over to its lawful
owners. A similar approach has been adopted by the Draft European Convention. In this context, it is very unlikely that the State of primary origin would
be given any consideration. The coastal State on whose continental shelf
the cultural property is situated is more likely to be considered as the State
of origin.[49]

However, Dorothee Schulze made some interesting suggestions in respect
of the general question of restitution envisaged by the UN General Assembly
Resolutions, which are worthy of consideration:

> "The normative phrasing of the restitution order confirms in this concrete area tendencies
> towards the positive establishment in law of a *general right to development* as a legit-
> imate claim of the developing countries. At the same time, the concrete order can refer
> back to a general right to development. The constructive problems of the actual form
> of the declared obligation of restitution as an obligation not only of the former colonial
> powers but of all countries in possession of the reclaimed works of art, which are being
> reclaimed on the basis of the laws of tort and inheritance, do not arise when they are

placed in this particular legitimisation of claim. The basis for the claim is here solely the actual possession of such objects, which at least now are of fundamental importance for the cultural heritage of the claimant State. Here, however, wider examination and the preparation of an appropriate register of claims by the States concerned are necessary" (emphasis added).[50]

Such a consideration is of extreme importance to the legitimisation of claims over underwater cultural property. First, it avoids the constructive problems of the actual form of the obligation to return cultural property found underwater to its State of origin. Second, since the basis of these claims is the *possession* of underwater cultural property, they may also encompass archaeological material presently found on the high seas. The fact that the UN General Assembly Resolutions on the Restitution or Return of Cultural Property to the Countries of Origin make specific reference to underwater remains, provides another confirmation of this conclusion. Even though there is no provision for the return of the recovered underwater cultural property to its State of origin, the consideration of the interests of the States which have historical and cultural links with the discovered treasures as part of the general question of restitution is essential.

This school of thought has been criticised by some scholars on the basis that the right to development[51] often runs directly counter to the right to preserve or develop a culture.[52] Although it is true that in certain instances not only archaeological sites but also social traditions have been destroyed in the name of development, economic progress is not the only dimension of the right to development. Development is a comprehensive economic, social, cultural and political process.

Right to development and to self-determination
Culture constitutes a fundamental part of the life of each individual and of each community. Development, whose ultimate aim is man, must have a cultural dimension.[53] The integration of the cultural dimension of development has been one of the fundamental aims of UNESCO in the last years[54] and features together with the preservation and presentation of the cultural heritage among the objectives assigned to the World Decade for Cultural Development (1988-1997).[55] "The notions of cultural identity and development are complementary ... Development should therefore not be received as a transformation imposed from without disrupting the traditional values and compromising the identity of a people, but should on the contrary take

the fullest account of local circumstances and have recourse to flexibly adjusted strategies."[56] In this context, the employment of the right to development as the basis for the claims of the State of origin of underwater cultural property appears to be both plausible and permissible.

Nevertheless, such an approach may enable only the less-developed or developing countries to satisfy their claims. *Prima facie*, this argument appears to have a basis in reality. However, the following factors should also be considered. First, recent years have seen a tendency to expand the notion of development and related rights:

> "Il y a intérêt a élargir la désignation du sujet du droit au développement. Du droit des uns, les peuples sous-développes, l'encontre des autres, les peuples développes, if faut passer un droit universel, concernant les uns et les autres, pour des raisons d'ailleurs différents (au reste, complémentaires). Il semble opportun d'inclure le droit des peuples sous-développes au développement au sein du droit de tout homme et de toute communauté à être soi et, le devenir, entre autre choses par le développement."[57]

Second, the notion of cultural development has a wider scope which cannot be restricted to certain categories of peoples.[58] The right of development is closely related to the *right of peoples to self-determination*. According to the International Covenant on Economic, Social and Cultural Rights[59], the International Covenant on Civil and Political Rights[60] and the Declaration on the Granting of Independence to Colonial Countries and Peoples:[61]

> "All peoples have the right to self-determination. By virtue of that right they freely determine their political status and freely pursue their economic, social and cultural development."

The right of peoples to self-determination presupposes in the sphere of culture the right to an original civilisation which has not only to be preserved, but to be developed.[62] "No universal obligation to return illicitly exported cultural property has yet been established. However, when analysing the practice of the States in detail, it appears that a new customary rule is in a phase of advanced positivation and will establish a universal obligation of restitution. The principle of unjust enrichment and, above all, the principle of self-determination of peoples, contribute to the crystallisation of this new customary rule to its integration into international law."[63]

In this context of crucial importance is the definition of the term "people". It may be interpreted restrictively so as to be synonymous with the State, or extensively so as to refer to those who share a culture. It seems that a generally acceptable definition of peoples is not possible. One would, there-fore, agree with Crawford that the notion of a people is context-dependent; what constitutes a people for the purpose of one right does not necessarily satisfies the requirements of another.[64] Without accepting the restrictive interpretation of "people", there is no reason why a State should not be entitled to the right to self-determination. "The entity recognised by interna-tional law for purposes of self-determination ... is a people at the commence-ment of the process and a State at the end, even though the composition of the entity does not change. There appears to be no reason why human rights law should recognise this entity under one name but not under another".[65] "Rights of self-determination and thus rights to follow policies designed to preserve a culture, are fullest when a people is sovereign".[66] In this context, both the people who possess a State and those who have not yet attained statehood should qualify as subjects to the right to self-determination and/or development.[67] As argued by Williams: "To go one step further and to submit that there is today a case for cultural self-determination by States is not beyond the pale, as national culture enhances a people's ability to understand their origins and development. Cultural objects designated by a State as of intrinsic importance to its people's heritage and prohibited from export should be amenable to restitution in fullfilment of this right".[68]

Cultural rights of peoples

Recent years have seen an expansion of cultural rights from the individual to peoples. In addition to the rights to education, participation in cultural life, communication and information, one refers to collective rights such as: (a) the right to develop a culture;[69] (b) the right to preserve and develop a culture;[70] (c) the right of a people to its own artistic, historical and cul-tural wealth.[71] It has been argued that: "An assertion of a 'people's right' to its own artistic and cultural heritage in this kind of context may be more in the manner of an assertion of some permanent right to decide on its location, or even an assertion of the primacy of a spiritual claim over a commercial one".[72]

Conclusion

Law should anticipate and accommodate the legitimate interests of the State of origin of cultural property found on the continental shelf by attributing specific rights to it. However, the right of the State of origin to recover underwater cultural property cannot always find its legal justification as a property right or as a corollary of its sovereignty. It should rather be considered as a patrimonial right or as an expression of the right to cultural self-determination and development. This is confirmed by the recently emerged "cultural rights" of peoples, in particular the right of a people to its own artistic, historic and cultural wealth. It can be argued that States in fullfilment of their search for cultural identity and self-determination should be able to recover the most significant items of their patrimony. The State of origin should be entitled to the enjoyment of cultural property which is of particular importance to its people and reveals specific national features. The notion of cultural identity is central to the question of the recognition of the interests of the State of origin. Only those objects that reveal the cultural identity of the people who created them should be returned.[73] Otherwise, it would be absurd to expand coastal jurisdiction over the continental shelf as an effective scheme of protection, if every discovered object of foreign origin was to be returned. Inevitably, such an approach would result in an unnecessary over-fragmentation of the discovered archaeological material.

At present, the recognition of the rightful interests of the State of origin of underwater cultural property, or even the, still rather unlikely, "return" of some of the objects discovered can only take place on a bilateral basis by agreement between the State which is in possession of the claimed cultural property and the State of origin.[74] It is hoped that States will conclude agreements similar to the 1972 Australia/Netherlands Agreement, which adopts principles that can ensure that the recovered material is kept in a collection.

THE ILA DRAFT CONVENTION ON THE PROTECTION OF THE UNDERWATER CULTURAL HERITAGE

The Draft Convention on the Protection of the Underwater Cultural Heritage is the result of the work of the International Law Association's Cultural

Heritage Law Committee over the last six years. As explained in the Commentary,[75] the main purpose of the Draft Convention is to provide basic protection beyond the territorial seas of coastal States for a very sensitive and precious heritage that is subject to growing threats of damage and destruction, while, at the same time, offering help to avoid and resolve jurisdictional issues involving underwater cultural heritage. The Draft Convention allows each State party to establish a "cultural heritage zone" coextensive with its continental shelf. Under article 1(3), "cultural heritage zone" means all the area beyond the territorial sea of the State up to the outer limit of its continental shelf as defined in accordance with relevant rules and principles of international law. A State party shall take measures to ensure that activities within its zone affecting the underwater cultural heritage comply at a minimum with the provisions of the Charter.[76] Even though the territorial sea is excluded from the notion of the cultural heritage zone, under article 6, States parties are encouraged to apply the provisions of the Convention and the criteria of the Charter to this area.[77] In addition, article 7 prohibits the use of the territory of States parties or any other areas over which it exercises jurisdiction to be used in support of activities violating the Charter.

The Draft Convention employs nationality as a principal jurisdictional basis to enforce its provisions in areas which are not subject under the jurisdiction of the parties. Under article 8, each State party shall prohibit its nationals and ships of its flag from activities affecting the underwater cultural heritage in respect of any area which is not within a cultural heritage zone or a territorial sea of another State party; this prohibition shall not apply to activities complying with the criteria contained in the Charter. The Draft Convention also provides for the issuance of permits allowing entry into its territory of underwater cultural heritage excavated or retrieved after its entry into force so long as the State has determined that the excavation and retrieval activities have complied or will comply with the Charter (article 9); the seizure of heritage brought within its territory, directly or indirectly,[78] after having been excavated or retrieved in a manner not conforming with the Charter (article 10), and, finally, penal sanctions for importation of underwater cultural property which is subject to seizure (article 11). After seizure, each State party undertakes to record, protect and take all reasonable measures to conserve underwater cultural heritage, and keep it in display or otherwise ensure the fullest reasonable access to it for the benefit of the public (article 12). It is notable that the Draft Convention makes no reference to article 149 of the 1982 Convention providing for the preservation of deep seabed cultural property for the benefit of mankind as a whole. It simply refers to article 3 that States parties shall take all reasonable measures to preserve the underwater cultural heritage for the benefit of humankind. Nevertheless, as stated in the Preamble, the Draft Convention intends "to codify and progressively develop the law, in conformity with international rules and practice, including provisions in the 1982 United Nations Convention on the Law of the Sea".

Furthermore, article 13 provides for collaboration with States which have expressed a patrimonial interest in particular underwater cultural heritage in the investigation, documentation, conservation, study and cultural promotion of the heritage as well as information-sharing with other States parties. This is a rather modest solution to the question of the accommodation of claims made by the State of origin along the lines of article 4 of the Draft European Convention. However, discussions at the working sessions of the Committee reveal that a more far-reaching provision was not acceptable. At the same time, it was thought that the accommodation of preferential rights under article 149 was not satisfactory and should not serve as a model for a rule on the continental shelf. An additional reference to the State of origin is to be found in the Preamble, where it is emphasised that the underwater cultural heritage belongs to the common heritage of mankind and that responsibility for protecting it rests not only with the State(s) more directly concerned with a particular activity affecting the cultural heritage or having an historical or cultural link with it, but with all States and other subjects of international law. Educating the public is advanced as a major objective of the Convention,[79] while disputes concerning its interpretation or application are submitted to arbitration, under the procedure envisaged in article 16. States parties also undertake to establish internal procedures for resolving disputes concerning the compliance of activities affecting the underwater heritage with the Charter.

As already indicated in chapter 1, the ILA Draft adopts a rather extensive definition of the underwater cultural heritage, which includes all underwater traces of human existence together with their archaeological and natural context (article 1(1)). However, the scope of the Convention is limited to underwater cultural heritage which has been lost or abandoned[80] and is submerged underwater for 100 years, with potential inclusion of more recent objects (article 2(1)). The Convention does not apply to warships, military remains and other vessels or aircraft owned or operated by a State and used for government, non-commerial services (article 2(2). Finally, and most importanly, the Convention excludes the law of salvage from its ambit.

In conclusion, the ILA Draft constitutes an ambitious attempt to deal with the complex problems posed in the protection of underwater cultural property found in international waters in a responsible and scientific manner. Its adoption is an important development in the sphere of the law of cultural heritage and reflects hightening awareness of the need to preserve this significant source of historical material. Nevertheless, one would have liked to see a more radical approach in accommodating the interests of the State(s) of origin as well as acknowledgment of the recently emerged 24-mile archaeological zone.[81]

NOTES

1 See also Lund, C. "Patrimoine culturel subaquatique", 12 *Jus Gentium* (1985) pp. 60-74 at pp. 65-67 and pp. 73-74; ID; "Report on Protection of the Underwater Cultural Heritage - The Rules of UN Law of the Sea Protection" in Council of Europe, Parliamentary Assembly, *Parliamentary Conference on the UN Convention on the Law of the Sea*, Palermo, 2-4 November 1983, *AS/JUR/MAR/ CONF(35) 7*, pp. 1-10 at p. 4; Del Bianco, H.P.(Jr.), "Underwater recovery operations in offshore waters: vying for rights to treasure", 5/6 *Boston University International Law Journal* (1987/88) pp. 153-176 at pp. 172-176.

2 Del Bianco, *ibid* at p. 139.

3 See *supra* chapter 1 at p. 11-12. According to Roper, Rapporteur of the Committee on Culture and Education, Council of Europe: "I would not want the Assembly to think that we have a dogmatic view on this. We looked at various solutions, including that of the 'sea of human civilisation', a fascinating and imaginative idea put forward by our Greek colleagues, and the 200 miles of cultural protection zone with median line where appropriate, and show a preference on balance for the latter rather than the former, but we would be delighted if it proved possible for the countries of the Mediterranean, as suggested in the recommendation, to reach agreement amongst themselves about anappropriate arrangement to create a 'sea of human civilisation'. That is by no means excluded from what we suggest". See "Underwater cultural heritage (Debate on the Report from the Committee on Culture and Education, Doc. 4200 and amendments and vote on the draft recommendation), 18th Sitting, 4 October 1978" in Council of Europe, Parliamentary Assembly, *Official Records of Debates*, Thirtieth Ordinary Session (Second Part), 27 September - 5 October 1978, Strasbourg 1979, vol. II at pp. 696-713 at p. 709.

4   The final version was adopted at the 66th Conference of the ILA in Buenos Aires and will be forwarded to UNESCO for consideration. See *infra* Appendix at pp. 437-444.

5   It is notable that the previous drafts employed a formula similar to the one adopted by the 1992 Archaeological Convention (revised), which left the breadth of the cultural heritage zone to the State concerned. For a discussion see O'Keefe, P.J., "The International Law Association Draft Convention on the Protection of the Underwater Cultural Heritage", paper presented at a seminar on the underwater cultural heritage organised by the Italian Association of ex-Parliamentarians and the European University, 25 May 1993. See also International Committee on Cultural Heritage Law, *Report and Draft Convention on the Protection of the Underwater Cultural Heritage,* International Law Association 65th Conference, Cairo, Egypt 20-26 April 1992. The discussions at the Working Session of the Committee, of which the author is a member, illustrate the different approaches in dealing with the archaeological issue. Some members were against the expansion of coastal jurisdiction beyond the contiguous zone. See, for example the comments made by Professor Hibeo Takabayashi (Japan), who said that he understood the necessity of international co-operation for the protection of underwater cultural heritage and, for this reason, it is important to establish common definitions, common criteria for the punishment of offender and free exchange of information between States. However, he was unable to support the idea of establishing a "cultural heritage zone" of 200 miles as cultural heritage found on the seabed outside the territorial sea is not a natural resource. He felt that the coastal State could regulate and punish offenders found within its territory by application of the universality principle. Professor Shigeru Kosai (Japan) thought that the determination of whether objects constitute "cultural heritage" should be referred to an international agency within UNESCO or some other appropriate international organisation which would be composed of multinational experts. To this end, he recommended that an Article should be included in the draft Convention to the effect that: "Any entity, individual or State which wishes to undertake any activity affecting the underwater cultural heritage outside the territorial waters of any Party shall inform the International Agency of its intended project in advance and the International Agency, after investigation, shall determine whether the said objects are of such scientific or historical significance and, if it is so determined, the excavation shall be undertaken under the authorization and supervision of the agency in conformity with the criteria laid down in the Appendix." In his view, maritime activities outside the national limits of maritime waters, such as territorial sea, archipelagic waters and contiguous zone (as referred to in Article 303 of the 1982 United Nations Convention on the Law of the Sea) are governed by the principle of the freedom of the sea. Nevertheless, it was eventually agreed that the cultural heritage zone should coincide with the continental shelf.

6   Prott, L.V. and O'Keefe, P.J., *Law and the Cultural Heritage*, vol. 1, *Discovery and Excavation*, Professional Books Ltd., Abingdon, 1984 at p. 99.

7   Article 1 of the CSC defines "the 'continental shelf' as seabed and subsoil of the submarine areas adjacent to the coast but outside the area of the territorial sea, to a depth of 200 metres or, beyond that limit, to where the depth of the superjacent waters admit of the exploitation of the natural resources of the said areas". The breadth of the continental shelf is thus associated with the morphology of the seabed, while "exploitability" is adopted as a fundamental criterion of delimitation. See further Roper, J., "Explanatory Memorandum" in Council of Europe, *The Underwater Cultural Heritage*, Report of the Committee on Culture and Education (Rapporteur Mr. John Roper), Doc. 4200-E, Strasbourg 1987, pp. 1-26 at p. 17.

8   See *supra* chapter 7, note 96 at p. 290.

9   United Nations, *The Law of the Sea: Practice of States at the Time of Entry into Force of the United Nations Convention on the Law of the Sea*, 1994 at p. 13.

10 "If only one craft had sunk in each year since Palaeolithic seafarers reached Melos, 12,000 wrecks would have taken place in the Mediterranean alone". Bass, G.F. "Marine Archaeology: A Misunderstood Science", 2 *Ocean Yearbook* (1980) pp. 137-151 at p. 139. See further Muckelroy, K., *Maritime Archaeology*, Cambridge University Press, 1978 at p. 150 and Bascom, W., "Deepwater Archaeology", 174 *Science* (1971) pp. 261-269 at p. 265.

11 Bascom, *ibid* at p. 266. ID; *Deep water, Ancient Ships: The Treasure Vault of the Mediterranean*, David & Charles, Newton Abbot, 1976 at p. 84.

12 More specifically, there must be one ship in 4 sq.nm of bottom along trade routes. *Ibid* at p. 266.

13 Muckelroy, *op. cit.* note 10 at p. 150. In contrast, Marx argues that approximately 98% of all shipping losses in the western hemisphere prior to 1825 occurred in waters less than 10m deep. *Ibid.* See also Gibbins, who argues that although ancient records and medieval analogy suggest that most routes were coastal, there are some unavoidable open-sea passages, and some coast-bugging ships must have been swept offshore to founder. Gibbins, D., "Archaeology in deep water - a preliminary view", 20 *I.J.N.A.* (1991) pp. 163-165 at p. 163.

14 Bascom, *op. cit.* note 10 at p. 262. See also Muckelroy, *ibid.* "Any wooden ship reaching the seabed is likely to do so intact ... those which have are likely to be of great archaeological significance. This is because a wooden structure can only be sunk with the aid of its ballast and other contents; if a vessel has broken up on the surface and spilt much of its cargo far and wide, its constituent parts will wallow about on the surface until eaten by marine creatures."

15 *Ibid.*

16 Flemming, N.C., "Ice Ages and Human Occupation of the Continental Shelf", 28 *Oceanus*, No. 1, Spring 1985 pp. 18-25 at p. 25; ID, "More on the Outer Continental Shelf", 8 *JFA* (1981) at p. 505; Patterson, L.W., "OCS Prehistoric Site-Discovery Difficulties", 8 *JFA* (1981) pp. 231-232 and "Comments I and II" by Stickel, E.G. and Roberts, M. respectively, *ibid* at pp. 232-235. Patterson argues that at present there are no reliable techniques to locate prehistoric sites on the OCS and that, therefore, future environmental regulations should not

require any expenditure for their location until reliable and cost-effective detection methods are available. *Ibid* at p. 232. As noted, the Department of the
Interior has sponsored such surveys in the process of gas and oil exploration
in an attempt to guide decision making about issuing oil and gas leases and
about the need for site-specific surveys in advance of oil and gas drilling,
pipelaying, and other activities affecting the seabed. In commenting on Patterson's arguments, Roberts emphasises the fact that "the number of sites may
be less important than the discovery of a single site", the archaeological value
of which would be great, *ibid* at p. 234, while Flemming deals with the question
"whether or not the right methods are being used in the search for prehistoric
archaeological material on the outer continental shelf." In his opinion there are
several groups in Europe using simple techniques, and extrapolation of them,
to discover palaeolithic sites in deeper water. "I anticipate that significant
palaeolithic discoveries will be made in water depths of 30-50m within the next
three or four years." *Ibid* at p. 505.

17   Back in 1970, a Japanese submersible capable of reaching 300m was used in
an archaeological study off Kyushu. See further Auburn, F.M., "Deep Sea
Archaeology and the Law", 2 *I.J.N.A.* (1973) pp. 159-162 at p. 159. It seems,
therefore, that with minor amendments deepwater salvage equipment could be
useful for marine archaeologists. In commenting on the salvage operations of
the Oceaneer, which recovered the wreckage of a Boeing 727 at 1000 ft. (300m),
Bascom stated that: "The operation was salvage, not archaeology, but it indicates
the possibilities at depths between 300 and 1500 ft. (90 and 460m). There was
need for delicacy in handling the wreckage or for removing a mud or sand cover
from artefacts. But we have no doubt that, with the addition of a 'soft' grasper
and aducted blower, similar equipment would be most useful for marine archaeologists." Bascom, *op. cit.* note 10 at p. 225. Bascom had also suggested
the use of a remote-controlled articulated arm extending from a pipe dropped
down by a specially designed ship, for the initial sampling of a site and the
removal of all loose artefacts as well as a kind of giant grab for the lifting of
complete hulls. *Ibid* at p. 261 and pp. 266-268; ID, "A Tool for Deepwater
Archaeology", 1 *I.J.N.A.* (1972) pp. 180-184. The importance of *Alcoa Seaprobe*
consisted in the potential recovery of entire small ships in one piece: "Since
the principal significance of deepwater sites lies in the fact that they are substantially intact, it would seem to be infinitely preferable to work towards means
of encapsulating such remains and lifting them complete, together with the
surrounding seabed for controlled excavation is shallow and shelter water."
Muckelroy, *op. cit.* note 10 at p. 153. The *Alcoa Seaprobe* was scrapped after
damage caused by inexperienced operators. Nevertheless, her sea tests demonstrated the feasibility of deepwater search and recovery. See further Bascom,
W., "Deepwater salvage and archaeology" in Throckmorton, P. (ed.), *History
from the Sea: shipwrecks and archaeology*, Mitchell Breazley Publishers, 1987,
pp. 222-225 at p. 225 and *Sea Technology,* December 1986 (special issue:
"Diving and submersibles").

18 Working at these depths requires extensive support facilities designed to keep the diver at the local pressure. The facilities are placed on the seabed or on the surface vessel. The greatest depth reached to date is 460m. Verlaan, Ph.A., "Marine Archaeology: A Trojan (Sea) Horse?", 8 *Ocean Yearbook* (1989) pp. 231-253 at p. 248.

19 Blackman, D.J., "Archaeological Aspects" in Council of Europe, *op. cit.* note 8, pp. 27-44 at p. 35. See also Muckelroy, *op. cit.* note 10 at pp. 149-150.

20 See also Bowen, F.M., "Jason's Med Adventure", 33 *Oceanus* (1990) pp. 61-69 at p. 63: "The main technological event was the debut of our fiber-optic cable (f/o) Argo-Jason system: two deep ocean, search-survey-and-sampling robots controlled from the surface. Argo-Jason was chained to the deck beside the original coaxial-cable Argo, the discoverer of the *Titanic* and the soon to be discovered *Bismarck*." This was the first time where a deep-water antiquarian site has been approached and probed by a robot's mechanical arm. Jason had to display a diver's co-ordination in safely recovering the artefacts while disrupting the site as little as possible. See further Ballard, R.D., *The discovery of the Titanic: exploring the greatest of all ships,* A Hodder & Stoughton/Madison Press Book, 1987, pp. 59-85; Golden, F., "A Quarter-century under the sea", 31 *Oceanus* (1988/89) pp. 2-9; Harris, S.E. & Abers, K., "Argo: Capabilities for Deep Ocean Exploration", 28 *Oceanus*, No. 4, Winter 1985/86; Ryan, P.R., "The quest to find the Bismarck" 32 *Oceanus* (1988/89) pp. 27-35 and Wachsmann, S., "Ships of Tarshish to the Land of Ophir: Seafaring in Biblical times", 33 *Oceanus* (1990) pp. 70-82.

21 Gibbins, *op.cit.* note 13 at p. 164.

22 *Ibid.*

23 It is notable that the British financial backers of the salvaging of the Titanic, Ocean Research and Exploration Ltd., paid IFREMER 13.5 million francs (1.35 million) to carry out the first 54-day phase of the operation. A second phase lasting 17 days cost 2.5 million francs. *The Times*, Wednesday, July 29, 1987, p. 7, c. 3.

24 See Osaki, E., "A Proposal on Ways for Keeping Underwater Cultural Assets in Fair Preservation" in Arnold, J.B. (ed.), *Beneath the Waters of Time: The Proceedings of the Ninth Conference on Underwater Archaeology*, Texas Antiquities Committee Publication No. 6, 1978, pp. 191-197 at p. 192.

25 Muckelroy, *op. cit.* note 10 at p. 153. It should be considered, however, that in underwater expeditions the work goes on twenty-four hours a day, and that, therefore, the actual operation time is equivalent to twenty weeks of a land expedition. See also Nelson, R.H., "Guiding the Ocean Search Process: Applying Public Land Experience to the Design of Leasing and Permitting Systems for Ocean Mining and Ocean Shipwrecks", 20 *Ocean Dev. & Int'l L.* (1989) pp. 577-600 at p. 596, who discusses the wide diversity of exploration methods and experiences in deep sea salvaging. Using as examples the discovery in 1985 of the *Titanic* and Fisher's long search for the *Atocha* he concludes: "Any proposed leasing and permitting system for ocean resources could well be examined from the perspective of how this system would have affected concrete

past searches, such as those for the *Atocha* or the *Titanic*. As these examples indicate, the answers could also differ substantially from one case to another".

26 See Piercy, B.C.M., "The Mombasa Wreck Excavation", 137 *Museum* (vol. xxxv, No. 1) 1983 pp. 27-29 and Muckelroy, *ibid.* at p. 7.

27 Roucounas, E., "Cultural Treasures on the Seabed", 23 *Review of Public and Administrative Law* (1979) pp. 10-37 (in Greek).

28 Prott & O'Keefe, *op.cit.* note 6 at p. 14.

29 51 *A.L.J.R.* (1977) at p. 806.

30 *Ibid* at pp. 811-812.

31 Bolton, G.C., "Maritime Archaeology and Australian History" in Jeffery, W. and Amess, J. (eds.), *Proceedings of the Second Hemisphere Conference on Maritime Archaeology*, published by the South Australian Department of Environment and Planning and the Commonwealth Department of Home Affairs and Environment, Adelaide, South Australia, 1983, pp. 37-45. See also the criteria suggested by the Australian Department of Arts, Heritage and Environment for deciding whether particular wrecks should be declared historic: (a) a wreck significant in the discovery, early exploration, settlemnt or early development of parts of Australia; (b) relevance of a wreck to the opening up or development of parts of Australia; (c) relevance of a wreck to a particular person or event of histotical importance; (d) the wreck is a possible source of relics of historical significance; (e) the wreck is representative of a particular maritime design or development; (f) naval wrecks, other than those deliberately scrapped or sunk and having no particular or emotional interest; (g) wrecks of an outstanding recreational or educational potential. Henderson, G., *Maritime Archaeology in Australia*, University of Western Australia Press, 1986 at p. 68.

32 Michael, M.D., *The Archaeological and Historical Objects of the Continental Shelf. International Law and the Aegean*, Saccoulas Publishing Co., 1983 at pp. 15-16 and 106-116 (in Greek).

33 *Ibid* at p. 100.

34 Letter by the Government of the Netherlands, dated 5 November 1982 and addressed to the Direction of Legal Affairs of the Council of Europe at p. 2.

35 Nevertheless, as argued, there is no reason why a similar competence should not be exercised by an "identifiable flag State" in respect of flag State objects. *Ibid.*

36 As already indicated, this provision may be interpreted so as to refer to future international conventions. In this respect see the ILA Draft Convention on the Protection of the Underwater Cultural Heritage, *op. cit.* note 4.

37 The failure of article 303 to include a similar provision in relation to objects found within the 24-mile zone has been explained by Oxman as follows: "There is no reference to disposal and accordingly no reference either to the benefit of mankind or to the rights of various States of origin as in article 149". Oxman, B.H., "The Third United Nations Conference on the Law of the Sea: The Ninth Session (1980)", 75 *A.J.I.L.* (1981) pp. 211-256 at p. 241, footnote 153. Oxman's observations are well-founded with the exception of the extremely restrictive interpretation of the concept of "benefit of mankind". Within UNCLOS III, the rights of the States of origin were, indeed, limited to cases of sale or disposal

of the objects recovered. However, the failure of the 1982 Convention to provide for the rights of the various States of origin within the 24-mile zone should not be read so as to imply their rejection. To a certain extent, this omission was the result of the drafting of the compromise formula of article 303(2). Although the latter can be interpreted extensively so as to establish a full-fledged archaeological zone, the text itself refers to the control of traffic of archaeological and historical objects by the coastal State. As already seen, article 303(2) was a "last-minute" solution. After long and unsuccessful negotiations, the President of the Plenary of the Conference asked the interested parties to negotiate with each other and present a commonly acceptable draft within two days. Under these circumstances, the controversial issue was the expansion of coastal competence beyond the territorial sea limit and not the accommodation of claims made by the State(s) of origin.

38 It is notable that in Denmark the Keeper of National Antiquities was obliged under a special official instruction of the Danish 1963 Protection of Historic Shipwrecks Act, to negotiate with the proper authorities of any country connected with the wreck which was to be excavated and raised. Although the instruction was not renewed under the new legislation expanding the Danish jurisdiction over the 24-mile zone, it is still a practice to contact other countries with an interest in a specific wreck. The most recent example is the wreck of Lord Nelson's ship, St. George, wrecked in 1811 on the west coast of Jutland. Some of the items recovered from the wreck have been sent to the National Maritime Museum in Greenwich. See also article 3 of the Chinese Regulation on Protection and Administration on Underwater Relics of 1989, which asserts neither jurisdiction nor claim for title to underwater cultural relics originating from an identifiable foreign country found within other sea areas under China's jurisdiction. As commented by Zhao: "The reason why these claims are not asserted in the UCR Regulation is unclear. It is possible that the drafters of the Regulation neglected this kind of UCR or considered that UCR originating from an identifiable foreign country is equivalent to UCR with identifiable owners". See Zhao, H., "Recent developments in the legal protection of historic shipwrecks in China", 23 *Ocean Dev. & Int'l L.* (1992) pp. 305-333 at pp. 321-322. Under the same provision, China reserves the right to identify UCR which originates from China, but remains within high seas areas or areas of foreign jurisdiction (excluding the territorial sea).

39 *Op. cit.* note 34 at pp. 2-3.

40 It should be recalled that contemporary international law does not recognise the exclusiveness of flag State jurisdiction over wrecks even on the high seas. In the few cases where coastal States have asked the permission of the flag State to recover public-owned ships or aircraft sunk within their territorial sea, this was done to facilitate the disposition of State-owned property and not the legality of the salvage operations.

41 Under the terms of the Agreement, the Netherlands as the present legal successor to the V.O.C., "transfers all its rights, title and interest in and to wrecked vessels of the V.O.C. lying on or off the coast of the State of Western Australia and in and to any articles thereof" to Australia, which recognises the continuing

interest of the latter, particularly for historical and other cultural purposes, in articles removed from any of the vessels. Although it is not clear whether, under the aforementioned terms, Australia acknowledges the Netherlands as the legal owner of the V.O.C. wrecks or it simply recognises its cultural and historical interests in those vessels, According to O'Keefe and Prott: "The Agreement does not state that The Netherlands had title to the wrecks and thus does not constitute an acknowledgement of this claim by the Australian Government. Rather, whatever title The Netherlands did in fact have under its own law and/or any other system of law is transferred to Australia." O'Keefe, P.J. and Prott, L.V., "Australian Protection of Historic Wrecks", 6 *A.Y.B.I.L.* (1978) pp. 119-138 at p. 124.

42   Conversation with Prof. A.J. Parker, Department of Classics, University of Bristol, June 1987.

43   "Heritage is something to be claimed as a right, something to be defended." UNESCO, *Pictures from a living past*, Paris, 1978 at p. 3.

44   "The moral question is much harder to resolve than the legal question because moral norms are imprecise and their applicability is controversial. That is one reason for legal rules: to provide definitive and practically workable solutions to otherwise troubling and unruly questions." Merryman, J.H., "Thinking About the Elgin Marbles", 83 *Mich. L. Rev.* (1985) pp. 1880-1923. See further Donnelly, J., "In Search of the Unicorn: The Jurisprudence and Politics of the Right to Development", 15 *Calif. W. Int'l L.J.* (1985) pp. 473-509 at p. 490, who attributes particular importance to the conceptual distinction between rights and righteousness, having a right and being right, entitlement and obligation: "Not all moral 'oughts' are grounded in and give rise to rights: one does not have a right to everything that is or would be right for one to do or possess; we do not have rights, in the string and strongsense of titles and claims, to everything that is right." *Ibid* at p. 490.

45   Nahlik, S.E., "Book Review: Niec, H. [The Proper Country of the Work of Art. International Protection of the Integrity of the National Cultural heritage], Panstwowe Wydawnictwo Naukowe, Krakow, 1980 [In Polish]", XI *P.Y.I.L.* (1981/82) pp. 258-261 at pp. 260-261. See also Nieciowna, H., "Sovereign Rights to Cultural Property", 4 *Polish Yearbook of International Law* (1971) pp. 239-253.

46   The literature on the controversial issue of restitution of works of art to their countries of origin is abundant. In particular, see Fraoua, R., *Le trafic illicit des biens culturels et leur restitution - Analyse des réglementations nationals et internationals critiques et propositions*, Travaux de la Faculté de Droit de l'Université de Fribourg, Suisse 68, Editions Universitaires Fribourg, 1985; Freedman, P., "Lost Heritage: Symposium takes up Return of Cultural Treasures", *UNESCO Features* No. 766 (1981) pp. 1-5; Goy, R., "La retour et la restitution des biens culturels à leur pays d'origine en cas de appropriation illégale", 83 *R.G.D.I.P.* (1979) pp. 962-985; Kinnane, D., "Committee Urges Co-operation in Returning Art Works", *UNESCO Features* No. 755 (1980) pp. 1-4; Nafziger, J.A.R., "The New International Legal Framework for the Return, Restitution or Forfeiture of Cultural Property", 15 *N.Y.U.J. Int'l L. & Pol.* (1985) pp.

789-812; Paczensly, (von) G., *"Cultural Riches from the Third World Treasures which Do not Belong to Us" (translation of an article that appeared in the German magazine Art No. 4, April 1981)*, Mimeographed paper, ICOM; Prott, L.V. and O'Keefe, P.J., *Law and the Cultural Heritage*, vol. 3, *Movement*, Butterworths, 1989 at pp. 802-862; Schulze, D., *Die Restitution von Kunstwerken - Zur Völkerrechtichen Dimension der Restitutionsresolutionen der General Versammlung der Vereinten Nationen*, Band 12, Bremen, 1982 (Im Selbstverlag des Museums); Stétié, S., "The Intergovernmental Committee Mechanisms for a New Dialogue", *Museum* (vol. XXXIII, No. 2) 1981, pp. 116-117; Williams, S.A., "Recent Developments in Restitution and Return of Cultural Property", 3 *The International Journal of Museum Management and Curatorship* (1984) pp. 117-129. See also *Lost Heritage - The Question of the Return of Cultural Property*, The Commonwealth Arts Association, London, 1981, and 31 *Museum* (1979) (special issue dedicated to the "Return and Restitution of Cultural Property").

47 See further Intergovernmental Committee, *1986 Guidelines* at p. 11; Prott & O'Keefe, *ibid* at p. 834 *et seq* and Williams, *ibid* at p. 118. The Draft Unidroit Convention on Stolen or Illegally Exported Cultural Goods uses the term "restitution" in cases of stolen cultural objects and the term "return" in cases where a cultural object has been removed from the territory of a contracting State contrary to its export legislation. The Convention has no retroactive force and applies only when a cultural object has been stolen or removed from the territory of a State after the entry into force of the Convention. See Draft Unidroit Convention, Fourth Session of the Committee of Governmental Experts on the International Protection of Cultural Property, Rome, 29/9-8/10/1993.

48 The following arguments have been raised against the return of cultural property to its country of origin by the countries which are in possession of the requested items. First, there is the *legal argument* that the cultural property was legally acquired. Second, there is a *museological argument* that the objects in question are well conserved and that, if removed, they may be damaged either in transit or in the rather poor conditions in the State or origin. Third, there is the *technical argument* that the whole issue should be addressed by the competent museum authorities in the countries involved. Fourth, there is the *universalist argument* that the objects in question would be given wider publicity in the large national museums where they are kept. UNESCO, *ibid* at pp. 8-9 and Williams, *ibid* at p. 125. Along these lines, Merryman, *op. cit.* note 44 at p. 1881, rejects cultural nationalism as a basis for the disposition of the Parthenon marbles and their return to Greece. He argues that cultural nationalism expresses dubious values and is founded on sentiment, while the concerns of cultural internationalism, preservation, integrity and distribution/access do not clearly support the Greek position. See further Merryman, J.H., "The protection of partimony" in Duboff, L.D. (ed), *Art Law: Domestic and International*, F.B. Rothman & Co, 1975, pp. 255-261; ID, "The retention of cultural property", 21 *University of California Davis Law Review* (1988) pp. 477-513; ID, "The public interest in cultural policy", 77 *California Law Review* (1989) pp. 339-364; Nafziger, J.A.R., "Com-

ments on the relevance of law and culture to cultural property law", 10 *Syracuse J. Int'l L. & Com.* (1983) pp. 323-331; Warren, K.J., "A philosophical perspective on the ethics and resolution of cultural properties issues" in Messenger, Ph. M. (ed), *The Ethics of Collecting Cultural Property: Whose culture, Whose Property?* Albuquerque, 1990, pp. 1-25 at pp. 3-10.

49 Especially if the national heritage legislation vests title of ownership of underwater relics to the State, the justification of such claims would be even more difficult. See also Byrne-Sutton, Q., *Le traffic international des biens culturels sous l' angle de leur revendication par l'état d'origin*, Schulthess Polygraphischer Verlag, Zürich, 1988 at p. 61, who argues that there are two possible definitions of the State of origin. The first one, which exists always, is the one given by the national heritage legislation; the State of origin is simply the State which considers itself the owner of a cultural object. The second refers to a State which considers itself as having *heritage rights* over the object. In his view, the international community should attempt to establish uniform criteria for the determination of the second notion of the State of origin through the adoption of an international convention. This approach allows for multiple States of origin. As already seen, in the context of article 149 of the 1982 Convention and the accommodation of the preferential rights of the various States of origin envisaged therein, the "effective link" of nationality proposed by the ICJ in *the Nottebohm case* was suggested as a criterion for resolving conflicts between them. Thus, the State, to whose cultural tradition the objects in question are more closely linked, should be entitled to their enjoyment. Obviously, each case will be decided on its own merits. See further Prott & O' Keefe, *op. cit.* note 46 at p. 36, and Seidl-Hohenveldern, I., "La protection internationale du patrimoine culturel national", 97 *R.G.D.I.P.* (1993) pp. 395-409, who suggests two criteria for the determination of the State of origin: the physical presence of the object and ideological links ("liens ideologique"). Article 5 of the Unidroit Draft, *op. cit.* note 47, provides that a court or other competent authority in the requested State shall order the return of an object if the requesting State proves significant impairment of its interests in the physical preservation of an object or its context; the integrity of a complex object; the preservation of information; the use of the object by a living culture or the outstanding historical importance of the object for the requesting State.

50 Schulze, *op. cit.* note 46 at p. 229.

51 See further Alston, P., "The Shortcomings of a 'Garfield Cat' Approach to the Right to Development", 15 *Calif. W. Int'l L. J.* (1985) pp. 510-518; ID, "The Right to Development at the International Level" in Dupuy, R.-J. (ed.), *The Right to Development at the International Level*, Hague Academy of International Law, United Nations University, Workshop, The Hague, 16-18 October 1979, pp. 99-114; Brietzke, P.H., "Consorting with the Chameleon, or Realising the Right to Development", 15 *Calif. W. Int'l L. J.* (1985) pp. 560-606; Chowdhury, S.R., Denters E.M.G. & de Waart, P.J.I.M. (eds), *The Right to Development in International Law*, Martinus Nijhoff Publishers, 1992. Donnelly, J., "In search of the Unicorn: the jurisprudence and politics of the right to development", 15

Calif. W. Int'l L.J. (1985) pp. 473-509; ID, "The theology of the right to development - A reply to Alston", 15 *Calif. W. Int'l L.J.* (1985) pp. 519-523; Nanda, V.P., "Introduction. The Right to Development under International Law: Challenges Ahead", 15 *Calif. W. Int'l L.J.* (1985) pp. 431-440; Reich, R.V., "The Right to Development as an Emerging Human Right", 23 *V.J.I.L.* (1983) pp. 287-328; Shelton, D., "A Response to Donnelly and Alston", 15 *Calif. W. Int'l L. J.* (1985) pp. 524-527; Umbricht, V., "Right to Development" in Dupuy (ed.), *ibid* at pp. 94-98; Zacklin, R., "The Right to Development at the International Level", *ibid* at pp. 115-120.

52 Prott, L.V., "Cultural Rights as People's Rights in International Law" in Crawford, J. (ed), *The Rights of Peoples*, Clarendon Press, 1988, pp. 93-106 at pp. 102-103.

53 "Mexico City Declaration on Cultural Policies", UNESCO, *Final Report, World Conference on Cultural Policies*, Mexico City, 26 July-6 August 1982, CLT/MD/1 pp. 41-46 at p. 42.

54 Even in 1967, it was considered preferable that "certain criteria for cultural development should be defined, and that culture should be linked to the fulfilment of personality and to economic and social development." See Round-Table Meeting on Cultural Policies, Monaco, 18-22 December 1967, *SHC/CS/188/19*, Paris, 7 May 1968 at p. 7.

55 "Report by the Director-General on the World Decade for Cultural Development", Executive Board, *124 EX/18*, 5 May 1986 at p. 8. See also 23/C Resulution 11.10 on the World Decade for Cultural Development, and Resolution 41/187 of the UN General Assembly proclaiming the Decade.

56 Recommendation No. 26 "Cultural basis of development", UNESCO, *op. cit.* note 54 at p. 78.

57 Sanson, H., "Du droit des peuples sous-développes au développement au droit des hommes et des communautes à être soi, non seulement par soi, mais aussi par les autres" in Dupuy (ed.), *op. cit.* note 51, pp. 192-232 at p. 201.

58 This does not mean, however, that the peculiarities of cultural rights in underdeveloped countries should be neglected. "Self-determination, rehabilitation, development, all are motive forces that will dominate and fashion the content of cultural rights in underdeveloped areas ... It would therefore be a great mistake if in order to preserve the myth of universality, we were to frame a general concept of cultural rights out of keeping with the present international combination of circumstances." Boutros-Ghali, B., "The right to culture and the Universal Declaration of Human Rights" in UNESCO, *Cultural rights as human rights*, Studies and documents on cultural policies, 1970, pp. 73-75 at p. 75.

59 A/RES/2200, 21 *UN GAOR Supp.* No. 16 (A/6316) at p. 49. Text reprinted in Brownlie, I. (ed.), *Basic Documents on Human Rights*, 2nd ed., Clarendon Press, Oxford, 1981, pp. 118-127.

60 21 *UN GAOR Supp.* 16 (A/6316) at p. 52; Brownlie, *ibid*, pp. 128-145.

61 A/RES/1514, 15 *UN GAOR Supp.* No. 16 (A/4684) pp. 66-67. A similar provisi-
    on is included in the African Charter on Human and People's Rights (Banjul
    Charter) 1981. According to article 22(1): "All people shall have the right to
    their economic social and *cultural development* with due regard to their freedom
    and identity and in the equal enjoyment of the common heritage of mankind",
    21 *ILM* (1982) at p. 58. Under article 1 of the Declaration on the Right to
    Development: "(1) The right to development is an inalienable human right by
    virtue of which every human person and all peoples are entitled to participate
    in, contribute to, and enjoy, economic, social and political development, in which
    all human rights and fundamental freedoms can be fully realize; (2) The human
    right to development also implies the full realization of the right of peoples
    to self-determination ..." Resolution 41/128 of the UN General Assembly; 41
    UN GAOR Supp. No. 53 (A/41/53), p. 186. See also Resolution 48/130 of 20
    December 1993, 48 *UN GAOR Supp.* No. 49 (A/48/49) at p. 389.
62 N'Daw, A., "Universal culture and national culture" in UNESCO, *op. cit.* note
    58, pp. 28-30 at p. 28. It is notable that during the World Conference on Cultural
    Policies in Mexico, one delegate stressed that "the foremost cultural right was
    the right of peoples to self-determination." *Op. cit.* note 54 at p. 9.
63 Fraoua, *op. cit.* note 46. See also Williams, S.A., "Protecting the Archaeological
    Heritage: Can the New World Order Protect the Old?". Paper presented at the
    Athens Conference on the Protection of the Archaeological Heritage, organised
    by the Institute of Hellenic Constitutional History and Constitutional Law,
    November 26-27, 1992.
64 Crawford, J., "The rights of peoples: some conclusions" in Crawford (ed), *op.
    cit.* note 52 at pp. 168-169.
65 Reich, *op. cit.* note 51 at p. 319.
66 VanDyke, V., "The Cultural Rights of Peoples", 2(3) *Universal Human Rights*
    (1980) pp.1-21 at p. 3. Nevertheless, the interpretation of the "people" as the
    "State" can be authoritarian. "[T]hrough the intermediary of so-called people's
    rights it becomes possible to misconstrue human rights as rights of the State
    which can be invoked against the person, instead of human rights which can
    be invoked against the State". Leuprecht, P., "Which human rights? ... a distres-
    sing spectacle of cynicism and hypocrisy?'" in *Forum* (Council of Europe) pp.
    5-6 at p. 6. Makinson defines a people as a kind of collectivity, or group of
    human beings and a State as a kind of governing or administering apparatus.
    Even when a State serves as representative or spokesman for a people, the two
    are never identical. Makinson, D., "Right of peoples: the point of view of a
    logician" in Crawford (ed), *op cit.* note 54 at p. 73. Within given society one
    may distinguish between a predominant culture and "sub-culture", while ethnic
    minorities should also be entitled to their own cultural heritage. Nevertheless,
    claims for return or restitution between cultures in the same State, where the
    legality of the original taking usually cannot be questioned under the national
    law concerned, are not dealt with by the international mechanism set up to deal
    with inter-State claims. Prott & O' Keefe, *op. cit.* note 46 at p. 834. See further
    Salerno, F., "Sulla tutela internazionale dell'identita culturale delle minoranze
    straniere", 73 *Rivista di diritto internazionale* (1990) pp. 257-293; Haibronner,

K., "The legal status of population groups in a multinational State under public international law", 20 *Israeli Yearbook on Human Rights* (1991) pp. 127-154; Capotorti, F., "Are minorities entitled to collective international rights?", 20 *Israeli Yearbook on Human Rights* (1991) pp. 351-357; Moustakas, J., "Group rights in cultural property: justifying strict inalienability", 74 *Cornell Law Review* (1989) pp. 1179-1227.

67 The right of development of States poses development not as a new right of States, but as a principle of international law urging States to co-operate. The right of development of States withdraws development co-operation from the ambit of charity. Chowdhury, S.R., and De Waart, P.J.I.M., "Significance of the right to development: an introductory view" in Chowdhury et al, *op. cit.* note 44, pp. 7-23 at p. 13.

68 Williams, *op.cit.* note 63 at pp. 7-8. In contrast Wyss argues that existing State practice does not recognize sufficient attributes to justify the establishment of a right to cultural self-determination. Wyss, M.Ph., *Kultur als eine Dimension der Volkerrechtsordnung*, Schweizer Studien zum Internazionalen Recht, Band 79, Schulthess Polygraphischer Verlag, Zürich, 1992 at p. 232.

69 See Declaration of the Principles of International Cultural Co-operation, 1966, article 1(2) UNESCO, *op. cit.* note 58 at pp. 123-125; Banjul Charter, 1981, Article 22(1), *op. cit.* note 61; Universal Declaration of the Rights of Peoples, 4 July 1976 (Algiers Declaration). Article 13: "Every people has the right to speak its own language and preserve and develop its own culture, thereby contributing to the enrichment of the culture of mankind". Text reprinted in Rigaux, F., "The Algiers Declaration of the Rights of Peoples" in Cassese, E. A. (ed.), *UN Law/Fundamental Rights. Two Topics in International Law,* Sijthoff & Noordhoff, Alpen aan Rijn, pp. 219-223 (Appendix). See further Falk, R., "The Algiers Declaration of the Rights of Peoples and the Struggle for Human Rights", *ibid* at pp. 225-235. For a discussion of the African Charter on Human and Peoples' Rights see Gittleman, R. "The African Charter on Human and People's Rights: A Legal Analysis", 22 V.J.I.L. (1982) pp. 667-714.

70 Algiers Declaration. Article 2.

71 *Ibid.* Article 14.

72 Prott, *op. cit.* note 52 at p. 100. In Prof. Prott's view the formulation of this right was primarily intended to shore up the restitution of movable cultural property.

73 The determining criterion should be the social, cultural and spiritual importance of the property which is to be returned to its State of origin. This is also the approach adopted by the Intergovernmental Committee for Promoting the Return of Cultural Property to its Countries of Origin or its Restitution in Case of Illicit Appropriation, with respect to the more general question of restitution of works of art. "Return and restitution of cultural property - a brief resumé", C.f. *CLT/ CH/4.82*, Paris, 11 June 1982 at p. 3. See further Ganslmayr, H. *et al*, "Study on the principles, conditions and means for the restitution or return of cultural property in view of reconstituting dispersed heritages", 31 *Museum* (1979) pp. 62-66.

74   The promotion of bilateral negotiations for the return or restitution of cultural property has been one of the fundamental objectives of the Intergovernmental Committee. In this respect a "standard form concerning requests for return or restitution" has been prepared. UNESCO, *Final Report of the Intergovernmental Committee for Promoting the Return of Cultural Property to its Countries of Origin or its Restitution in Case of Illicit Appropriation*, Second Session, Paris, 14-18 September 1981, *CC-81/CONF.203/10*, Paris, 12 March 1982. Appendix I.

75   See International Committee on Cultural Heritage Law, *Report and Draft Convention on the Protection of the Underwater Cultural Heritage,* International Law Association 66th Conference, Buenos Aires, 14-20 August 1994.

76   "Charter" means the "Charter for the Protection and Management of the Underwater Cultural Heritage" prepared by the International Council for Monuments and Sites (ICOMOS) and annexed to the Draft Convention. ICOMOS has already produced a Charter for the Protection and Management of the Archaeological Heritage. Article 15 allows ICOMOS to revise the Charter and any revision shall be deemed to be a revision "in the annexed Charter" subject to specific objections by the parties. This provision was adopted to avoid subjecting Charter amendments to the procedure for amending the Convention; the criteria of the Charter should reflect technology changes and other developments in the discipline of archaeology.

77   The same applies for internal waters. It must be noted, however, that under the scheme of the ILA Draft Convention, there is no obligation on a State to adopt a "cultural heritage zone". If a State wants to limit its control over underwater cultural heritage to a three- or twelve-mile territorial sea, it can do so and still become a party to the Convention.

78   The "directly or indirectly" language is an attempt to expand the scope of the Convention. As explained in the Commentary: "An intervening sale of excavated material can create problems. Suppose that European excavators of material excavated off the Malaysian coast proceed directly from the Far East to the Netherlands and suppose that the Netherlands is not a party to the Convention. There the excavated material is sold by auction. One of the purchasers is France and brings his ceramics home. Under the Convention, if France was a party, it could have an obligation to seize the ceramics. This obligation exists whatever the number of intervening transaction in an object".

79   Article 14. As explained in the Commentary, educational means may include formal training but also many other activities, such as promotion of exhibitions, production of leaflets, provision of background material to journalists and sponsorship of essay competitions against students.

80   The Convention employs a presumption of abandonment in article 1(2).

81   The only reference to article 303 of the 1982 Convention is to be found in the commentary to the Preamble.

BIBLIOGRAPHY

SELECTED DOCUMENTS

UNITED NATIONS

(i) General Assembly

'Draft UN Convention on the International Seabed Area', Doc. A/AC.138/25 (1970); 25 *UN GAOR Supp.* No. 21 (A/8021) at p. 29.

Informal proposal by Greece: 'Archaeological and Historical Treasures of the Sea-Bed and the Ocean Floor Beyond the Limits of National Jurisdiction', Doc. A/AC.138/SC.I/ L.16 of 2 August 1972.

Informal proposal by Greece: 'Draft Article on Protection of Archaeological and Historical Treasures'; Doc. A/AC.138/SC.I/L.25 of 14 August 1973.

'List of Subjects and Issues to be Dealt with by the Seabed Committee', Doc. A/AC.138/ 66 of 16 August 1972; 27 *UN GAOR Supp.* No. 21 (A/8721) at p. 146.

'Report of the International Law Commission on the Work of its Thirty-eighth Session'; 41 *UN GAOR Supp.* No. 10 (A/41/10) at pp. 98-99.

Report of the Secretary General: 'Study on International Machinery', Doc. A/AC.183/23; 25 *UN GAOR Supp.* No. 21 (A/8021) at pp. 61-123.

Report of the Committee on the Peaceful Uses of the Sea-bed and the Ocean Floor Beyond the Limits of National Jurisdiction, Appendix III (Report of Sub-Committee I): 'Texts Illustrating Areas of Agreement and Disagreement on Items 1 and 2 of the Subcommittee's Programme of Work'; 28 *UN GAOR Supp.* No. 21 (A/9021), vol. 2 at p. 69.

Resolution 2749 (XXV) of December 17, 1970: 'Declaration of Principles Governing the Seabed and the Ocean Floor, and the Subsoil thereof, Beyond the Limits of National Jurisdiction'; 25 *UN GAOR Supp.* No. 28 (A/8028) at p. 24.

Resolution 2750 (XXV) 1970; 25 *UN GAOR Supp.* No. 28 (A/8028) at p. 26.

Resolution 41/128: 'Declaration on the Right to Development'; 41 *UN GAOR Supp.* No. 53 (A/41/53) at p. 186.

Resolution 41/187: 'Proclamation of the World Decade for Cultural Development'; 41 *UN GAOR Supp.* No. 53 (A/41/53) at p. 142.

Resolution 48/15 of 2 November 1993: 'Return or Restitution of Cultural Property to the Countries of Origin'; 48 *UN GAOR Supp.* No. 49 (A/48/49) at p. 19.

Statement by Mr. Akyamac (Turkey) before Sub-Committee I, on 23 March 1973. Committee on the Peaceful Uses of the Seabed and the Ocean Floor beyond the Limits of National Jurisdiction. Sub-Committee I: Summary Records of the Sixty-Second to Sixty-Eighth Meetings held at New York from 7 March to 5 April 1973. Doc. A/AC.138/SC.I/SR.62-68 at p. 43.

Statement by Ambassador Pardo (Malta); Doc. A/C.1/PV. 1515 p. 3; 22 *UN GAOR (A/C1/PV. 1494-1537)* vol. I (1967).

'Working Paper submitted by Greece concerning the Law of the Sea', Doc. A/AC.138/54 (1971); 26 *UN GAOR Supp.* No. 21 (A/8421) at p. 194.

(ii) International Law Commission

Report of the International Law Commission to the General Assembly: 'Commentary on article 18. Duties of foreign ships during their passage', Doc. A/3159; II *ILC Yearbook* (1956) at p. 274.

Report of the International Law Commission to the General Assembly: 'Commentary on article 27 (freedom of the high seas)', Doc. A/3159; II *ILC Yearbook* (1956) at p. 278.

Report of the International Law Commission to the General Assembly: 'Commentary on article 47 (right of hot pursuit)', Doc. A/3159; II *ILC Yearbook* (1956) at p. 285.

Report of the International Law Commission to the General Assembly: 'Commentary on article 68 (para. 2)', Doc. A/3159; II *ILC Yearbook* (1956) at p. 297.

Report of the International Law Commission to the General Assembly: 'Commentary on article 68 (para. 10)', Doc. A/3159; II *ILC Yearbook* (1956) at p. 298.

(iii) UNCLOS I

'Iceland: revised proposal', Doc. A/CONF.13/C.3/79/Rev.1 (14 April 1958); *UNCLOS I, Off. Rec.*, vol. V at p. 158.

'Poland: proposal (Article 36)', Doc. A/CONF.13/C.1/L.78 (29 March 1958); *UNCLOS I, Off. Rec.*, vol. III at p. 232.

'Poland and Yugoslavia: proposal', Doc. A/CONF.13/C.2/L.20/Rev.1 and L.61/Rev.1; *UNCLOS I, Off. Rec.*, vol. IV at p. 121.

'Statement by Mr. Jhirad (India) on 26 March 1958, before the Fourth Committee of the 1958 Conference'; *UNCLOS I, Off. Rec.*, vol. VI at p. 51.

(iv) UNCLOS III

'Draft article 20: Archaeological and Historical Objects', Doc. A/CONF.62/C.1/L.3 (5 August 1974); *UNCLOS III, Off. Rec.*, vol. III at p. 163.

Delegation of Turkey: 'Contiguous Zone (Item 3). Provision 49'; C.2/Blue Paper No. 6 (19 April 1975); Platzöder, R., *Documents*, vol. IV at p. 129.

ICNT/Article 149, Doc. A/CONF.62/WP.10 (15 July 1977); *UNCLOS III, Off. Rec.*, vol. VIII at p. 25.

ISNT/Article 19, Doc. A/CONF.62/WP.8 (7 May 1975); *UNCLOS III, Off. Rec.*, vol. IV at p. 140.

Informal proposal by Austria, Belgium, Bolivia, Botswana, Denmark, Germany (Federal Republic of), Laos, Lesotho, Liberia, Luxembourg, Nepal, Netherlands, Paraguay, Singapore: 'Draft articles on marine scientific research', Doc. A/CONF.62/C.3/L.19 (23 August 1974); *UNCLOS III, Off. Rec.*, vol. III at p. 267.

Informal proposal by Bulgaria, Byelorussian Soviet Socialist Republic, Czechoslovakia, German Democratic Republic, Hungary, Mongolia, Poland, Ukrainian Societ Socialist Republic and Union of Socialist Republics: 'Draft articles on marine scientific research'. Doc. A/CONF.62/C.3/L.26(3 April 1975); *UNCLOS III, Off. Rec.*, vol. IV at p. 213.

Informal proposal by Bulgaria, Byelorussian Soviet Socialist Republic, Czechoslovakia, German Democratic Republic, Hungary, Poland, Ukrainian Soviet Socialist Republic, Union of Soviet Socialist Republics: 'Article 96-bis. Immunity of sunken warships as well as vessels whichare only on government non-commercial service', Doc. A/CONF.62/C.2/ Informal Meeting/50 (14 March 1980); Platzöder, R., *Documents*, vol. V at p. 57.

Informal proposal by Byelorussian Soviet Socialist Republic, Bulgaria, Czechoslovakia, German Democratic Republic, Hungary, Mongolia, Poland and Union of Soviet Socialist Republics: 'Draft article on the contiguous zone', Doc. A/CONF.62/C.2/L.27 (27 July 1974); Platzöder, R., *Documents*, vol. V at p. 148.

Informal proposal by Cape Verde, Greece, Italy, Malta, Portugal, Tunisia and Yugoslovia. 'Article 77: Add a new paragraph 5', Doc. A/CONF.62/C.2/Informal Meeting/43/Rev.1 (21 August, 1979); Platzöder, R., *Documents*, vol. V at p. 50.

Informal proposal by Cape Verde, Greece, Italy, Malta, Portugal, Tunisia and Yugoslavia. 'Article 77: Add a new paragraph 5', Doc. A/CONF.62/C.2/Informal Meeting/43/Rev.2 (19 March, 1980); Platzöder, R., *Documents*, vol. V at p. 51.

Informal proposal by Cape Verde, Grece, Italy, Malta, Portugal, Tunisia and Yugoslavia. 'Article 77: Add a new paragraph 5', Doc. A/CONF.62/C.2/Informal meeting/43/Rev.3 (27 March 1980); Platzöder, R., *Documents*, vol. V at p. 51.

Informal proposal by Colombia, El Salvador, Mexico and Nigeria: 'Draft article on marine scientific research', Doc. A/CONF.62/C.3/L.29 (6 May 1975); *UNCLOS III, Off. Rec.*, vol. IV at p. 216.

Informal proposal by Greece: 'Article 77 (ICNT/Rev.1)'; Platzöder, R., *Documents*, vol. IV at p. 526.

Informal proposal by Greece: 'General Principles and Provisions. Article: Objects of Archaeological or Historical Value', Doc. A/CONF.62/GP/10 (18 August 1980); Platzöder, R., *Documents*, vol. XII at p. 302.

Informal suggestion by the USSR: 'New article or paragraph 3 of article 98'; Platzöder, R., *Documents*, vol. V at p. 45.

Informal proposal: 'General Provisions', Doc. A/CONF.62/GP/11 (19 August 1980); Platzöder, R., *Documents*, vol. XII at p. 303.

Informal proposal by the Socialist Republic of Vietnam.,Doc. A/CONF.62/C.2/Informal Meeting/53 (19 March 1986); Platzöder, R., *Documents*, vol. V at p. 58.

Informal proposal by the Socialist Republic of Vietnam, Doc. A/CONF.62/C.2/Informal Meeting/53 (19 March 1980); Platzöder, R., *Documents*, vol. V at p. 59.

Informal proposal by Trinidad and Tobago: 'Draft articles on marine scientific research'. Doc. A/CONF.62/C.3/L.9 (5 August 1974); *UNCLOS III, Off. Rec.*, vol. III at p. 252.

Informal proposal by Turkey: 'Archaeological and Historical Treasures on the Sea-Bed and Ocean Floor Beyond the Limits of National Jurisdiction', Doc. A/AC.138/SC.I/L.21 (28 March 1973).

Informal proposal by the United States of America: 'General Provisions. Article: Archaeological and Historical Objects', Doc. A/CONF.62/GP/4(27 March 1980); Platzöder, R., *Documents*, vol. XI at p. 299.

Peru, C.2/Blue Paper No. 10 (17 April 1975); Platzöder, R., *Documents*, vol. IV at p. 147.

'Report of the President on the Work of the Informal Plenary Meeting of the Conference on General Provisions', Doc. A/CONF.62/L.58; *UNCLOS III, Off. Rec.,* vol. XIV at p. 128.

RSNT/Article 19, Doc. A/CONF.62/WP.8/Rev.1 (6 May 1976); *UNCLOS III, Off. Rec.*, vol. V at p. 131.

Statement by Mr. Ratiner (U.S.A.); *UNCLOS III, Off. Rec.*, vol. IV at p. 61.

Statement by Mr. Richardson (U.S.A.); *UNCLOS III, Off. Rec.*, vol. XIII at p. 43 (para. 158).

Statement by Mr. Stavropoulos (Greece); *UNCLOS III, Off. Rec.*, vol. XIV at p. 38 (para. 107).

Working Paper by the Second Committee: Main Trends, Doc. A/CONF.62/L.8/Rev.1, *UNCLOS I, Off. Rec.*, vol. I pp. 93-146 at pp. 107-142.

UNESCO

Declaration of the Principles of International Cultural Co-operation, 1966, adopted at the fourteenth session of the General Assembly, 4 November 1966.

Mexico City Declaration on Cultural Policies. World Conference on Cultural Policies, Final Report. CLT/MD/1, Paris, 1982, pp. 41-46.

'Desirability of Adopting an International Instrument on the Protection of the Cultural Heritage against Natural Disasters and their Consequences: Report of the Director General'. 22 C/26, 5 August 1983.

'The Exchange of Original Objects and Specimens Among Institutions in Different Countries. Preliminary Report'. SHC/MD/27, Paris, 26 August 1975.

Intergovernmental Committee for Promoting the Return of Cultural Property to its Countries of Origin or its Restitution in the Case of Illicit Appropriation: 'Final Report'. Second session, Paris, 14-18 September 1981. CC-81/CONF.203/10, Paris, 12 March 1982.

Intergovernmental Committee for Promoting the Return of Cultural Property to its Countries of Origin or its Restitution in the Case of Illicit Appropriation: 'Preliminary Study of Three National Situations with Regard to the Return of Cultural Property to its Country of Origin'. CC 79/CONF.206/5, Paris, 14 March 1980.

Intergovernmental Committee for Promoting the Return of Cultural Property to its Countries of Origin or its Restitution in the Case of Illicit Appropriation: 'Return and restitution of cultural property - a brief resumé'. CLT/CH/4.82, Paris, 11 June 1982.

Intergovernmental Committee for Promoting the Return to its Country of Origin or its Restitution in Case of Illicit Appropriation: 'Final Report', Third session, Instabul, Turkey, 9-12 May 1983. CLT-83/CONF.216/8, Paris, 10 November 1983.

IOC Summary Report of Working Groups on Legal Questions Related to Scientific Investigations of the Ocean. First meeting, Paris 16-20 September 1968. AVS/9/89 M(8), December 1968.

Preliminary Report of the Director-General of UNESCO on the 1956 UNESCO Recommendation on International Principles Applicable to Archaeological Excavations. UNESCO/CUA/68, 9 August 1955.

Recommendation on International Principles Applicable to Archaeological Excavations adopted at the eighth session of the General Assembly, 5 December 1956.

Recommendation on the Means of Prohibiting and Preventing the Illicit Export, Import and Transfer of Ownership of Cultural Property adopted at the thirteenth session of the General Assembly, 19 November 1964.

Recommendation concerning the Preservation of Cultural Property Endangered by Public or Private Works adopted at the fifteenth session of the General Assembly, 19 November 1968.

Recommendation concerning the Protection at National Level of the Cultural and Natural Heritage adopted at the seventeenth session of the General Assembly, 16 November 1972.

Recommendation concerning the International Exchange of Cultural Property adopted at the nineteenth session of the General Assembly, 26 November 1976.

Recommendation on Participation by the People at Large in Cultural Life and their Contribution to It, adopted at the nineteenth session of the General Conference, Nairobi, 26 November 1976.

Recommendation for the Protection of Movable Cultural Property adopted at the twentieth session of the General Conference, 28 November 1978.

Recommendations: No. 13 'International Communication'; No. 15 'Coexistence of Different Cultural Groups Within a State and their Relations With Other Countries'; No. 26 'Cultural Basis of Development'; No. 27 'World Decade for Cultural Development'; No. 45 'The Mediterranean'; No.138 'International Cultural Relations'; No. 141 'Equality of Treatment in Cultural Exchanges'; No.142 'Cultural Agreements and Exchanges' and No. 144 'Developing Countries and International Cultural Cooperation'. Adopted during the World Conference on Cultural Policies, Mexico City, 26 July - 6 August 1982. Final Report, CLT/MD/1, Paris, November 1982.

'Report of the Special Committee of Governmental Experts to Examine the Draft Convention on the Means of Prohibiting and Preventing the Illicit Import, Export and Transfer of Ownership of Cultural Property', 9 *ILM* (1970) p. 1038.

'Report by the Director-General on the Activities of the International Fund for the Promotion of Culture'. 22 C/92, 5 August 1983.

'Report of the Intergovernmental Committee for Promoting the Return of Cultural Property to its Countries of Origin or its Restitution in Case of Illicit Appropriation'. 21 C/83, 11 August 1980.

'Report of the Intergovernmental Committee for Promoting the Return of Cultural Property to its Countries of Origin or its Restitution in Case of Illicit Appropriation'. 22 C/88, 22 September 1983.

'Report by the Director-General on the World Decade for Cultural Development'. Executive Board, 124 EX/18, 5 May 1986.

'Report by the Director-General on the Activities of the International Fund for the Promotion of Culture'. 23 C/88, 18 July 1985.

Resolution 3.322 adopted at the eighteenth session of the General Conference and establishing the 'International Fund for the Promotion of Culture'.

Resolution 4/7.6/5: 'Statutes of the Intergovernmental Committee for Promoting the Return of Cultural Property to its Countries of Origin or its Restitution in Case of Illicit Appropriation' adopted at the twentieth session of the General Conference.

Resolution 11.10 on the World Decade for Cultural Development adopted by the General Conference at its twenty-third session in Sofia. *Records of the General Conference, Resolutions*, Twenty-third Session, vol. 1 at pp. 67-68.

Round-table Meeting on Cultural Policies, Monaco, 18-22 December 1967, SHC/CS/188/19, Paris, 7 May 1968.

World Conference on Cultural Policies, Mexico City, 26 July - 6 August 1982. Problems and Prospects. CLT-82/MONDIA CULT/3, Paris, 21 June 1982.

World Conference on Cultural Policies, Final Report, CLT/MD/1, Paris, November 1982.

COUNCIL OF EUROPE

Draft Convention on the Protection of the Underwater Cultural Heritage, *Ad Hoc* Committee of Experts on the Underwater Cultural Heritage, Fifth Meeting (19-23 March 1984); *DIR/JUR(84)1,* Strasbourg, 24 June 1984.

Draft Convention on the Protection of the Underwater Cultural Heritage, *Ad Hoc* Committee on the Underwater Cultural Heritage: 'Final Activity Report'; *Doc. CAHAQ (85)5,* Strasbourg, 23 April 1985.

Explanatory Report on the European Convention on Offences relating to Cultural Property, Strasbourg 1985.

Explanatory Report on the revised European Convention on the Protection of the Archaeological Heritage, Strasbourg 1992.

'Movement of art objects and return of works of art' (Joint debate on the report on the return of works of art and the report on the movement of art objects), 19th Sitting, 3 October 1983; Parliamentary Assembly, *Official Report of Debates*, vol. II, Thirty-fifth Ordinary Session (Second Part), 29 September - 6 October 1983, Strasbourg 1984, pp. 537-547.

'Order No. 421 (1983) on the movement of art objects'; *Texts Adopted by the Assembly*, Thirty-fifth Ordinary Session, (Second Part), 26 September - 6 October 1983, Strasbourg 1983.

Recommendation 848 (1978) on the underwater cultural heritage; *Texts Adopted by the Assembly*, Sessions 30-32 (1978/81) [Thirtieth Ordinary Session].

Recommendation 921 (1981) on metal detectors and archaeology; *Texts Adopted by the Assembly*, Thirty-third Ordinary Session, (Second Part) 30 September - 8 October 1981, Strasbourg 1981.

Recommendation 883 (1984) of the Parliamentary Assembly on the United Nations Convention on the Law of the Sea.

Recommendation 997 (1984) of the Parliamentary Assembly on regional planning and protection of the environment in European coastal regions.

Recommendation 1133 (1990) on European tourism policies; *Texts Adopted by the Assembly*, Fourth-second Ordinary Session (Second Part) 26/28 September-4 October 1990, Strasbourg 1990.

'Reply from the Committee of Ministers to Written Question No. 264 by Mr. Beith on archaeology', Doc. 5072; Parliamentary Assembly, *Documents*, Working Papers, vol. I, Thirty-fifth Ordinary Session.

'Report on the movement of art objects (Rapporteur: Mr. Beith)', Doc. 5110; Parliamentary Assembly, *Documents - Working Papers*, vol. I, Thirty-fifth Ordinary Session (Second Part), 29 September - 6 October 1983, Strasbourg 1983.

'Report on the return of works of art (Rapporteur: Mr. Tummers)', Doc. 51, 15th September 1983; Parliamentary Assembly, *Documents - Working Papers*, vol. I, Thirty-fifth Ordinary Session (Second Part), 26 September - 6 October 1983.

'Report on protecting the cultural heritage against disasters (Rapporteur: Mr. Ross)', Doc. 5624; Parliamentary Assembly, *Documents - Working Papers*, vol. IV, Thirty-eighth Ordinary Session (Second Part) 17-25 September 1986, vol. IV Doc. 5616-5624, Strasbourg 1986.

Resolution adopted by the participants in the European Symposium 'Greek, Carthaginian and Etruscan navies and trade in the Tyrrhenian Sea' held at the European University Centre for the Cultural Heritage in Ravello, 25 January 1987, Italy; European Parliamentary Assembly, Committee on Culture and Education, Sub-Committee of the Architectural and Artistic Heritage. AS/CULT/AA(38)

Resolution 808 (1983) on the return of works of art; *Texts Adopted by the Assembly*, Thirty-fifth Ordinary Session (Second Part), 26 September - 6 October 1983, Strasbourg, 1983.

'Written Question No. 264 by Mr. Beith on archaeology', Doc. 5033; Parliamentary Assembly, *Documents - Working Papers*, vol. VI, Thirty-fourth Ordinary Session, Nos. 4983-5036, 1982/83.

'Underwater Cultural Heritage' (Debate on the Report from the Committee on Culture and Education, Doc. 4200, and amendments and vote on the draft recommendation), 18th Sitting, 4 October 1978; Parliemantary Assembly, *Official Records of Debates*, vol. II, Thirtieth Ordinary Session (Second Part), 27 September – 5 October 1978, Strasbourg 1979, pp. 696-713.

EUROPEAN UNION

Council Regulation (EEC) No. 3911/92 of 9 December 1992 on the export of cultural goods; *OJ L* 395 of 31.12.1992 at p. 1.
Commission Regulation (EEC) No 752/93 of 30 March 1993 laying down provisions for the implementation of Council Regulation (EEC) No 3911/92 on the export of cultural goods; *OJ L* 77 of 31.3.1993 at p. 24.
Council Directive 93/7/EEC of 15 March 1993 on the return of cultural objects unlawfully removed from the territory of a Member State; *OJ L* 74 of 27.3.1993 at p. 74.

ICOM

Ethics of Aquisition, 1970. Reprinted in Burnham, B. (1974), pp. 194-197.
Recommendations on the Protection of Cultural Property, Malacca, 1972.
'Study on the principles, conditions and means for the restitution of cultural property in view of reconstructing dispersed heritage', ICOM 77/SEC.8, Paris, August 1977. Reprinted in UNESCO, CC-78/CONF.609/3 Annex 1.
Code of Professional Ethics adopted at the fifteenth General Assembly held in Buenos Aires, 4 November 1986.
Resolution No. 1 of the fifteenth General Assembly: 'The Contribution of Cultural Exchange to Mutual Understanding Amongst Peoples'; 39 *Bulletin of the International Council of Museums*, No. 4, 1986 at p. 13.
Statutes adopted at the sixteenth General Assembly held in the Hague, 5 September 1989.

OTHER DOCUMENTS

Universal Declaration of the Rights of Peoples, Algiers 4 July 1976.
Conference on Security and Co-operation in Europe (CSCE), Document of the Cracow 'Symposium on the cultural heritage of the CSCE Participating States, 6 June 1991, 19 *H.R.L.J.* (1991) pp. 279-282.

COLLECTION OF DOCUMENTS AND LEGISLATIVE TEXTS

Burnham, B.,
  The Protection of Cultural Property. Handbook of National Legislations, ICOM, 1974.
Churchill, R.R. and others (eds.),
  New Directions in the Law of the Sea, Oceana Publications Inc., Dobbs Ferry, New York.
Leanza, U. and Sico, I. (eds.),
  Mediterranean Continental Shelf: Delimitation and Regimes. International and National Sources, vols I-IV, Oceana Publications, 1988.

Oda, S.,
  The International Law of Ocean Development - Basic Documents, vol. II, Sijthoff,
  Leyden, 1975.
Platzöder, R.,
  The Third United Nations Conference on the Law of the Sea. Documents, Dobbs Ferry,
  New York, Oceana Publications Inc., vols. 1-13, 1982-87.
Smith, R.W.,
  Exclusive Economic Zone Claims: An Analysis and Primary Documents, Martinus
  Nijhoff Publishers, Dordrecht 1986.
Simmonds, K.R.(ed.)
  New Directions in the Law of the Sea (New Series), Oceana Publications Inc., Dobbs
  Ferry, New York.
UNESCO,
  · *The Protection of Movable Cultural Property. Compendium of Legislative Texts*,
    vols. I and II, 1984.
  · *The Protection of Movable Cultural Property. Collection of Legislative Texts*, 1985
    and 1987.
  · *Conventions and Recommendations of UNESCO concerning the Protection of the
    Cultural Heritage*, 1983 and 1985.
United Nations,
  · *Laws and Regulations on the Regime of the High Seas*, United Nations Legislative
    Series, ST/LEG/SER.B/1, 1951.
  · *Laws and Regulations on the Regime of the Territorial Sea*, United Nations Legis-
    lative Series, ST/LEG/SER.B/6, 1957.
  · *National Legislation and Treaties Relating to the Territorial Sea, the Contiguous
    Zone, the Continental Shelf, etc.,* United Nations Legislative Series, ST/LEG/SER.B/
    15, 1970.
  · *National Legislation and Treaties Relating to the Law of the Sea*, United Nations
    Legislative Series, ST/LEG/SER.B/16, 1970.
  · *National Legislation and Treaties Relating to the Law of the Sea*, United Nations
    Legislative Series, ST/LEG/SER.B/18, 1976.
  · *National Legislation and Treaties Relating to the Law of the Sea*, United Nations
    Legislative Series, ST/LEG/SER.B/19, 1980.
  · *The Law of the Sea: National Legislation on the Exclusive Economic Zone, the
    Economic Zone and the Exclusive Fisheries Zone*, 1986 (Sales No. E.85.V.10).X
  · *Law of the Sea: National Legislation on the Continental Shelf,* Office for Ocean
    Affairs and the Law of the Sea, 1989
  · *Law of the Sea: Current Developments in State Practice,* Office for Ocean Affairs
    and the Law of the Sea, No. I (1987), No. II (1989), No. III (1992).
  · *The Law of the Sea, National Claims to Maritime Jurisdiction, Excerpts of Legis-
    lation and Table of Claims,* Office for Ocean Affairs and the Law of the Sea, 1992.
  · *Le droit de la mer: revendications d'extentions de la jurisdiction nationale à des
    zones maritimes*, Bureau des affaires maritimes et du droit de la mer, 1992.

· *The Law of the Sea: Practice of Archipelagic States*, 1992.
· *The Law of the Sea: National Legislation on the Exclusive Economic Zone*, Division for Ocean Affairs and the Law of the Sea, 1993.

United States Department of State,
Limits in the Seas, No. 36, *National Claims to Maritime Jurisdictions*, 6th Revision, Office of the Geographer, 1990.

BOOKS AND PERIODICAL LITERATURE

This selected bibliography is arranged in two parts, covering respectively archaeological and legal aspects of the protection of the underwater cultural heritage.

ARCHAEOLOGICAL ASPECTS

Aarons, G.A.,
'Port Royal Jamaica from cataclysm to renaissance', 138 *Museum* (vol. XV, No. 2) 1983.

Alpozen, O.,
'The Bodrum Museum of underwater archaeology', 137 *Museum* (vol. XV, No. 1) 1983 pp. 61-63.

Amess, J.,
'Operation of the Commonwealth Historic Shipwrecks Act' in Jeffery, W. and Amess, J. (eds.), *Proceedings of the Second Southern Hemisphere Conference on Maritime Archaeology*. Published by the South Australian Department of Home Affairs and Environment and Planning, 1983.

Anuskiewicz, R.J.,
'The Exorbitant Cost of Underwater Remote Sensing and Research: A Public and Federal Government Cultural Resource Dilemma' in Arnold, J.B. (ed.), *Beneath the Waters of Time: Proceedings of the Ninth Conference on Underwater Archaeology*, Texas Antiquities Committee Publication No. 6, Austin, 1978, pp. 183-185.

Arnold, J.B.,
'Underwater site testing: results of the Texas Antiquities Committees 1977 field season' in Arnold, J.B. (ed.), *Beneath the Waters of Time: Proceedings of the Ninth Conference on Underwater Archaeology*, Texas Antiquities Committee Publication, No. 6, Austin, 1978, pp. 205-210.

Arnold, J.B. & Hudson, J.,
'A preliminary report on remote sensing data litigation' in Cockrell, W.A. (ed.), *In the Realms of Gold: The Proceedings of the Tenth Conference on Underwater Archaeology*, Fathom Eight Special Publication No. 1, 1981, pp. 3-15.

Azcarraga, J.L.,
'El concepto de plataforma continental ante la arqueologia submarina', 4/5 *Boletin de la Junta Municipal de Arqueologia de Cartagena* (1974) pp. 19-24.

Bacon, C.,
'Underwater exploration at Dunwich, Suffolk', 3 *I.J.N.A.*(1974) pp. 314-318.

Ballard, R.D.,
- The Discovery of the Titanic: Exploring the Greatest of All Ships. A Hodder & Stoughton/Madison Press Book, London, 1987.
- *The Lost Wreck of the Isis*, London, Hodder & Stoughton, 1990.
- *Exploring the Titanic*, edited by Cream, P., Scholastic/Madison, London, 1993.

Barinov, M.M.,
'The new worlds of underwater archaeology - diving into the past', *UNESCO Courier*, May 1972 'Underwater Archaeology' (special issue), pp. 5-7.

Barker, P.,
Techniques of Archaeological Excavation, Batsford, London, 1977.

Barnes, M.R.,
'A response to Raab and Klinger on archaeological site significance', 45 *American Antiquity* (1980) p. 551.

Basch, L.,
'Ancient wrecks and the archaeology of ships', 2 *I.J.N.A.* (1972) pp. 1-58.

Bascom, W.,
- 'The archaeologist in deep water', *UNESCO Courier*, May 1972, pp. 34-36.
- 'Deepwater archaeology', 174 *Science* (1974) at pp. 261-269.
- *Deep Water, Ancient Ships: the Treasure Vault of the Mediterranean.* David & Charles, Newton Abbot, 1976.
- 'Deepwater salvage and archaeology' in Throckmorton, P. (ed.), *History from the Sea: Shipwrecks and Archaeology,* Mitchell Breazley Publishers, London, 1987, pp. 222-225.

Bass, G.F.,
- 'The promise of underwater archaeology in retrospect', 137 *Museum* (vol. XV, No. 1) 1983, pp. 5-8.
- 'The promise of underwater archaeology' (from the Smithsonian Report for 1963), Publication 4583, Smithsonian Institution, Washington, 1964, pp. 461-471.
- 'The Asherah, a submarine for archaeology', 18 *Archaeology* (1965) pp. 7-15.
- *Archaeology under Water - Ancient Peoples and Places* (General Editor Daniel, G.), Thames & Hudson, London, 1966.
- *A History of Seafaring based on Underwater Archaeology*, Thames & Hudson, London, 1972.
- 'Eighteen Mediterranean wrecks investigated between 1900 and 1968' in UNESCO, *Underwater Archaeology: A Nascent Discipline*, Paris, 1972, pp. 35-51.
- 'The trials of an underwater archaeologist', *UNESCO Courier*, May 1972, pp. 8-15.
- 'Marine archaeology: a misunderstood science', 2 *Ocean Yearbook* (1980) pp. 137-152.
- 'A plea for historical particularism in nautical archaeology' in Gould, R.A. (ed.), *Shipwreck Anthropology.* A School of American Research Book, University of New Mexico Press, Albuquerque, 1983, pp. 91-104.
- *Ships and Shipwrecks of the Americas: A History based on Underwater Archaeology*, Thames and Hudson, 1988.

Bass, G.F. & Rozencrantz, D.M.,
'Submersibles in underwater search and photogrammetric mapping' in UNESCO, *Underwater Archaeology: A Nascent Discipline,* Museums and Monuments XI, Paris, 1972, pp. 271-283.

Beith, A. & Flanagan, O.J.,
'Explanatory Memorandum' in Council of Europe, *Metal Detectors and Archaeology* Doc. 4741-E, Strasbourg, 1981 at p.1.

Biasotti, A.,
'Remote surveillance of underwater archaeological sites', 15 *I.J.N.A.* (1986) pp. 185-188.

Binford, L.R.,
'Archaeological perspectives' in Binford, L.R. (ed.), *An Archaeological Perspective,* New York, Seminar Press, 1972.

Blackman, D.J.,
· 'Archaeological aspects' in Council of Europe, Parliamentary Assembly, *The Underwater Cultural Heritage,* Report of the Committee on Culture and Education (Rapporteur Mr. John Roper), Doc. 4200-E, Strasbourg, 1978, pp. 27-44.
· (ed.), *Marine Archaeology.* Proceedings of the Twenty-third Symposium of the Colston Research Society held in the University of Bristol, April 4th-8th, 1971, Colston Papers, vol. XXI, Butterworths, London, 1973.

Blawatsky, V.D.,
'Submerged sectors of towns on the Black Sea coast' in UNESCO, *Underwater Archaeology: A Nascent Discipline,* Paris, 1972, pp. 115-122.

Bolton, G.C.,
'Maritime archaeology and Australian history' in Jeffery, W. and Amess, J. (eds.), *Proceedings of the Second Southern Hemisphere Conference on Maritime Archaeology.* Adelaide, South Australia, 1983, pp. 37-45.

Booda, L.L.,
· 'Underwater expeditions produce mixed results', 21 *Sea Technology,* No. 10, October 1980, pp. 40-41.
· (editor emeritus) 'Mariner's museum leads USS Monitor preservation project', 28 *Sea Technology,* No. 4, April 1987, pp. 29-30.

Borhegyi (de), S.F.,
'The challenge, nature and limitations of underwater archaeology' in Holmquist, J.D. and Wheeler, A.H. (eds.), *Diving into the Past: Theories, Techniques and Applications of Underwater Archaeology,* Minnesota Historical Society and the Council of Underwater Archaeology, 1964, pp. 1-9.

Borrell, P.J.,
'Riches on the Caribbean sea-bed', 137 *Museum* (vol. XV, No. 1) 1983, pp. 41-43.

Broadwater, J.D.,
'The York Rover shipwreck project: results from the 1978 Survey' in Cockrell, W.A. (ed.), *In the Realms of Gold: The Proceedings of the Tenth Conference on Underwater Archaeology,* San Marino, California, Fathom Eight, 1981, pp. 33-44.

Bound, M. & Vallintine, R.,
'A wreck of possible Etruscan origin off Giglio Island', 12 *I.J.N.A.* (1983) pp. 113-122.
Bowen, F.M.,
'Jason's Med Adventure', 33 *Oceanus* (1990) pp. 61-69.
Chabert, J.,
'How underwater archaeology is regulated in France' in UNESCO, *Underwater Archaeology: A Nascent Discipline,* Museums and Monuments XI, Paris, 1972, Appendix, pp. 297-306.
Childress, F.,
'The National Marine Sanctuaries Programme as a cultural resource management tool for the U.S.S. Monitor' in Arnold, J.B. (ed.), *Beneath the Waters of Time. Proceedings of the Ninth Conference of Underwater Archaeology,* Texas Antiquities Committee Publication No.6, Austin, 1978, pp. 187-189.
Clarke, D.L.,
Analytical Archaeology, Methuen, London 1968.
Cleere, H.,
'Review: Nautical archaeology: progress and public responsibility by Langley, S.B.M. and Unger, R.E.,' 15 *I.J.N.A.* (1986) pp. 350-351.
Cockrell, W.A.,
'The trouble with treasure - a preservationist view of the controversy', 45 *American Antiquity* (1980) pp. 3-339.
Cockrell, W.A. and others,
'Crisis in underwater archaeology' in Cockrell, W.A. (ed.), *In the Realms of Gold: The Proceedings of the Tenth Conference on Underwater Archaeology.* Fathom Eight Special Publication No. 1, 1981, pp. 243-255.
Cockrell, W.A. (ed),
In the Realms of Gold. The Proceedings of the Tenth Conference on Underwater Archaeology. Fathom Eight Special Publication No. 1, 1981.
Cowan, R., Cowan, Z. & Marsden, P.,
'The Dutch East Indiaman Hollandia wrecked on the Isles of Scilly in 1743', 4 *I.J.N.A.* (1975) pp. 267-300.
Croome, A.,
"The United States' Abandoned Shipwrecks Act goes into action - a report", 21 *I.J.N.A.* (1992) pp. 39-53.
Crumlin-Pederson, O.,
'Wrecks in the North Sea and the Baltic' in UNESCO, *Underwater Archaeology: A Nascent Discipline,* Paris 1972, pp. 65-75.
Cummings, C.R. (ed.),
Underwater Archaeology: The Proceedings of the Fourteenth Annual Conference on Underwater Archaeology, Fathom Eight, California, 1983.
Davies, P.N.
'The Mary, Charles II's Yacht: the discovery of the wreck', 2 *I.J.N.A.* (1973) pp. 59-60.

Davies, F.L.,
'The antiquities and artifacts market: facts from the other side' in Cockrell, W.A. (ed.), *In the Realms of Gold. The Proceedings of the Tenth Conference on Underwater Archaeology,* Fathom Eight Special Publication No. 1, 1981, pp. 221-2.

Dean, M.,
· *Guidelines on Acceptable Standards in Underwater Archaeology,* Scottish Institute of Maritime Studies, University of St. Andrews, 1988.
· (ed.), *Archaeology Underwater,* 1992.

Department of Environment and Planning,
Conserving our Historic Shipwrecks, South Australia Government Publications, 1987.

Dodd, E.,
Polynesian Seafaring, Nautical Publishing Company Ltd., Lymington, 1972.

Drewry, J.M.,
'Sea search for history: project Bonhomme Richard', 17 *Sea Technology,* No. 5, May 1976, pp. 18-20.

Drocourt, D.,
'The Roman ship of Marseilles: a world première', 35 *Museum* (vol. XV, No. 1) 1983 pp. 49-53.

Dumas, F.,
· *Deep-water Archaeology,* Routledge & Kegan Paul, London, 1962.
· *Epaves antiques: introduction à l'archéologie sous-marine méditerranée,* Maison-neuve GP et Larose, Paris, 1964.
· 'Ancient wrecks' in UNESCO, *Underwater Archaeology: A Nascent Discipline,* Paris, 1972, pp. 27-34.

Earle, P.
· *The Wreck of the Almiranta.* Sir William Phips and the Search for the Hispaniola Treasure, Macmillan London Ltd., 1979.

Editorial
· 2 *I.J.N.A.* (1973) pp. 2-5.
· 7 *I.J.N.A.* (1978) pp. 1-2.

Fenwick, V.,
"Editorial", 16 *I.J.N.A.* (1987) p. 1.

Flemming, N.C.,
· *Cities in the Sea.* New English Library, London, 1972.
· 'More on the outer continental shelf', 8 *JFA* (1981) p. 505.
· 'Ice ages and human occupation of the continental shelf', 28 *Oceanus,* No. 1, Spring 1985, pp. 18-25.
· (ed.), *The Undersea,* Cassel & Company Ltd., London, 1977.

Franzen, A.,
'The salvage of the Swedish warship Wasa' in UNESCO, *Underwater Archaeology: A Nascent Discipline.* Museums and Monuments XI, Paris, 1972, pp. 77-83.

Frost, H.,
· *Under the Mediterranean,* Routledge & Kegan Paul, London, 1963.

· 'Ancient harbours and anchorages in the eastern Mediterranean' in UNESCO, *Underwater Archaeology: A Nascent Discipline*. Museums and Monuments XI, Paris, 1972, pp. 95-114.

· 'Museums from the depths', 137 *Museum* (vol. XV, No.1) 1983, p. 11.

Gathercole, P.,

'Recording ethnographic collections: the debate on the return of cultural property', 151 *Museum* (1986) p. 189.

Giesecke, A.G.,

'The future underwater' in Throckmorton, P. (ed.), *History from the Sea: Shipwrecks and Archaeology*. Mitchel-Breazley Publishers, London, 1987, pp. 226-227.

Gifford, J.A. *et al*,

'The UNESCO international survey of underwater cultural heritage', 16 *World Archaeology* (1984/85) pp. 373-376.

Golden, F.,

'A Quarter-century under the sea', 31 *Oceanus* (1988/89) pp. 2-9.

Goodwin, D.V.,

'Search for Hunley Produces Other Wrecks', 21 *Sea Technology*, No. 10, October 1980, pp. 42-46.

Gould, R.A.,

· 'Looking Below the Surface: Shipwreck Archaeology as Anthropology' in Gould, (ed.), *Shipwreck Anthropology*. A School of American Rersearch Book, University of New Mexico Press, Albuquerque, 1983, pp. 3-22.

· (ed), *Shipwreck Anthropology*. A School of American Research Book, University of New Mexico Press, Albuquerque, 1983.

· 'The USS Monitor Project research design' in Cogar, W.B. and Sine, P. (eds), *Naval History,* Willmington, Del. 1988, pp. 83-88.

Graham, D.M.,

'Quest for the R.M.S. Titanic: the search and recovery of the elusive luxury liner involved U.S. and French instrument equipment makers', 26 *Sea Technology*, No. 10 October 1985, pp. 70-75.

Green, J.N.,

· *Australia's Oldest Wreck, BAR Supplementary Series* 27, 1977.

· *The loss of the Vereenigde Oostindische Compagnie Jacht Vergulde Draeck, Western Australia 1656, BAR Supplementary Series* 36(i) and 36(ii), 1977.

· 'The excavation and reconstruction of the Batavia, Western Australia', 137 *Museum* (vol. XV, No. 1) 1983, pp. 30-33.

· 'Book review: The treasure of the Atocha by Mathewson, D.', 16 *I.J.N.A.* (1987) pp. 73-75.

· *Maritime Archaeology: A Technical Handbook*, Academic Press, 1990.

Greenfield, J.,

The Return of Cultural Treasures, Cambridge University Press, 1989.

Gruel, K. & Buchsenschutz, O.,

'Informatique et archéologie', 153 *Les dossiers d'archéologie* (1990) pp. 80-83.

390   *Bibliography*

Hale, J.R.,
  'The value of sea trials in experimental archaeology' in Cogar, W.B. & Sine, P. (eds),
  Naval History, Wilmington, Del., 1988, pp. 13-17.
Hall, E.J.,
  'Wreck prospecting by magnometer' in UNESCO, *Underwater Archaeology: A Nascent
  Discipline,* Museums and Monuments XI, Paris, 1972, pp. 285-293.
Hangrove, T.R.,
  'Submerged Spanish Era towns in Lake Taal, Philippines: An underwater and archival
  investigation of a legend', 15 *I.J.N.A.* (1986) pp. 323-337.
Harris, S.E. & Abers, K.,
  'Argo: Capabilities for Deep Ocean Exploration', 28 *Oceanus* (1985/86) pp. 99-101.
Harrison, R.F.,
  · 'Museological problems associated with the underwater heritage' in UNESCO,
     Protection of the Underwater Heritage. Technical handbooks for museums and
     monuments, 4, 1981, pp.135-163.
  · 'The Mary Rose Tudor Ship Museum', 137 *Museum* (vol. XV, No. 1) 1983, pp.
     44-49.
Heide (van der), G.D.,
  'Wrecks as ancient monuments' in UNESCO, *Underwater Archaeology: A Nascent
  Discipline.* Museums and Monuments XI, Paris, 1972, pp. 161-168.
Henderson, G.,
  · 'Maritime Archaeology in Australia' in *Maritime Australia: Exploring the Scientific
     and Technological Base*, Canberra, 1987, pp. 113-127.
  · *Maritime Archaeology in Australia*, University of Western Australia Press, 1986.
Heyerdahl, Th.,
  Early Man and the Ocean - The Beginning of Navigation and Seaborne Civilisations.
  George Allen & Unwin Ltd., London, 1978.
Holmquist, J.D. & Wheeler, A.H.(eds.)
  Diving into the Past: Theories and Applications of Underwater Archaeology. The
  Minnesota Historical Society and the Council of Underwater Archaeology, 1964.
Jeffery, W. and Amess, J. (eds.),
  Proceedings of the Second Southern Hemisphere Conference on Maritime Archaeology.
  Published by the South Australian Department of Environment and Planning and the
  Commonwealth, 1983.
Johnstone, P.E.,
  · *The Archaeology of Ships.* The Bodley Head, London, 1974.
  · (ed.), *Proceedings of the Sixteenth Conference on Underwater Archaeology.* Special
     Publication Series No. 4, Society of Historical Archaeology, 1985.
Johnston, P.F.,
  'Treasure salvage, archaeological ethics and maritime museums', 22 *I.J.N.A.* (1993)
  pp. 53-60.

Karo, G.,
- · 'Antikythera' in Taylor, J. du Plat (ed.), *Marine Archaeology,* Hutchinson of London, 1965, pp. 35-39.
- · 'Art salvaged from the sea', I *Archaeology* (1948) pp. 180-185.

Katsev, M.,
'The Kyrenia ship restored' in Throckmorton, P., *History from the Sea: Shipwrecks and Archaeology.* Mitchell Beazley Publishers, 1987, pp. 55-59.

Keith, D.H.,
'Excavation of a third century B.C. shipwreck at La Secca di Capistello, Italy: A pioneer application of saturation diving techniques in nautical archaeology', *Proceedings of the Ninth Conference on Underwater Archaeology,* Texas Antiquities Committee Publ. No. 6, 1978, pp. 3-14.

Kerber, J.E.,
Coastal and Maritime Archaeology: A Bibliography, The Scarecrow Press Inc., 1991.

Ki-Woong, K.,
'The Shinan shipwreck', 137 *Museum* (vol. XXXV, No. 1) 1983 pp. 35-37.

Krarning, L-A.,
'The Wasa: museum and museum exhibit', 142 *Museum* (1984) pp. 75-80.

Lanitzi, G.,
Amphoren Wracks, Versunkene Städte. Brockhaus VEB F.A Verlag, Leipzig, 1980.

Lawson, E.,
'In between: the case of artifacts from the seabed to the conservation laboratory and some reasons why it is necessary' in Arnold, J.B. (ed.), *Beneath the Waters of Time: Proceedings of the Ninth Conference on Underwater Archaeology.* Texas Antiquities Committee Publication, No. 6, Austin, 1978, pp. 69-91.

Lenihan, D.J.,
'Rethinking shipwreck archaeology: A history of ideas and considerations' in Gould, R.A. (ed.), *Shipwreck Anthropology.* A School of American Research Book, University of New Mexico Press, 1983, pp. 37-64.

Leone, M.P.,
'Land and water, urban life and boats: underwater reconnaissance in Chesapeake Bay' in Gould, R.A. (ed.) *Shipwreck Anthropology,* A School of American Research Book. University of New Mexico Press, 1983, pp. 173-188.

Linder, E. & Raban, A.,
Marine Archaeology. Cassel's Introducing Archaeology Series, No. 7, Cassel & Company Ltd., 1975.

Lycett, A.,
'Sea gives up its treasures', *The Times,* Tuesday, April 28, 1987, p. 12, col. 3.

Marsden, P.,
- · 'Archaeology at sea', 46 *Antiquity* (1972) pp. 198-202.
- · 'The wreck of the Dutch East Indiaman Amsterdam near Hastings, 1749: an *interim* report', 1 *I.J.N.A.* (1972) pp. 73-96.

· *The Wreck of the Amsterdam,* Hutchinson of London, 1974.
· 'The Challenge of Nautical Archaeology', 137 *Museum* (vol. XV, No. 1) 1983, pp. 12-14.
· 'The origin of the Council for Nautical Archaeology', 15 *I.J.N.A.* (1986) pp. 179-183.

Martin, C.,
· 'Archaeology in an underwater environment' in UNESCO, *Protection of the Underwater Heritage,* Technical handbooks for museums and monuments 4, 1981, pp. 13-76.
· *Full Fathom Five. Wrecks of the Spanish Armada,* Chatto & Windus, London, 1975.

Martin, C. and Flemming, N.C.,
'Underwater Archaeologists' in Flemming, N.C. (ed.), *The Undersea,* Cassel & Company Ltd., London, 1971, pp. 202-229.

Martin, C. & Long, A.N.,
'Use of explosives on the Adelaar wreck site 1974', 4 *I.J.N.A.* (1975) pp. 345-352.

Marx, R.F.,
· 'The drowned city of Port Royal: excavating underwater sites in Jamaica', *UNESCO Courier,* May 1972, pp. 28-30.
· 'The submerged remains of Port Royal, Jamaica' in UNESCO, *Underwater Archaeology: A Nascent Discipline,* 1972, pp. 139-145.
· *Underwater Dig - An Introduction to Marine Archaeology,* London, 1975.
· 'The disappearing underwater heritage', 137 *Museum* (vol. XV, No. 1) 1983, pp. 9-10.

Masters, P.M. & Flemming N.E.,
Quaternary Coastlines and Maritime Arcaeology: Towards the Prehistory of Map Bridges and Continental Shelves, Academic Press, 1983.

Mazel, C.,
· 'Technology for marine archaeology', 28 *Oceanus* No. 1, Spring 1985, pp. 85-99.
· 'Technology and the marine archaeologist', XL *Unesco Courier* (1987) pp. 15-18

McCarthy, M.,
· 'Wrecks and recreation' in Jeffery, W. and Amess, J. (eds.), *Proceedings of the Second Hemisphere Conference in Maritime Archaeology.* Adelaide, South Australia, 1983, pp. 381-390.
· 'Wreck Inspection Techniques' in Jeffery, W. and Amess, J. (eds.), *Proceedings of the Second Hemisphere Conference in Maritime Archaeology.* Adelaide, South Australia, 1983, pp. 349-361.

McGrail, S. (ed),
Aspects of Maritime Archaeology and Ethnography, Trustees of the National Maritime Museum, Greenwich, 1984.

Merlin, A.,
'Submarine discoveries in the Mediterranean', 4 *Antiquity* (1930) pp. 405-414.

Mikliaev, A.M.,
'The Hermitage Museum underwater', 137 *Museum* (vol. XV, No. 1) 1983, pp. 676-69.
Molaug, S.,
'The Norwegian Maritime Museum organises underwater archaeology', 137 *Museum* (vol. XV, No. 1) 1983, pp. 57-61.
Morcos, S.A.,
'The birthplace of submarine archaeology', XXXVIII *Unesco Courier* (1985) pp. 42-45.
Morrison, J.,
'An Athenian warship recreated' in Throckmorton, P., *History from the Sea: Shipwrecks and Archaeology*, Mitchell Beazley Publishers, 1987, pp. 44-49.
Morrison & Coates, J.P.,
The Athenian Trireme - The history and reconstruction of an Ancient Greek Warship, Cambridge University Press, 1986.
Muckelroy, K.,
· 'Introduction' in Muckelroy, K. (ed.), *Archaeology Under Water: An Atlas of the World's Submerged Sites*, McGraw-Hill, New York, 1980, pp. 6-11.
· 'Techniques and approaches' in Muckelroy, K. (ed.), *Archaeology Under Water: An Atlas of Submerged Sites*, McGraw-Hill, New York, 1980, pp. 12-31.
· *Discovering an Historic Wreck*, Handbooks in Maritime Archaeology No. 1, National Maritime Museum, London, 1981.
· (ed.), *Archaeology Under Water: An Atlas of the World's Submerged Sites*, McGraw-Hill, New York, 1980.
Murphy, L.,
'Shipwrecks as data base for human behavioural studies' in Gould, R.A. (ed.), *Shipwreck Anthropology*. A School of American Research Book, University of New Mexico Press, 1983, pp. 65-89.
Murray, J.,
'HMS Pandora: on the trail of the bounty', 35 *Sea Frontiers* (1989) pp. 328-335.
Museum,
Underwater Archaeology, No. 137 (vol. XV, No. 1) 1983 (special issue).
Oceanus,
Marine Archaeology, No. 28, Winter 1985/1986 (special issue).
Oleson, J.P. (ed),
The Harbours of Caesaria Maritima: Results of the Caesarea Ancient Excavation Project, 1980-1985. BAR International Series 491, 1989.
Parkes, P.A.,
Current Scientific Techniques in Archaeology, Croom Helm, 1986.
Parker, A.J.
· *Ancient shipwrecks of the Mediterranean and the Roman Provinces, BAR International Series* 580, 1992.
· 'The Mediterranean, an underwater museum', XL *Unesco Courier* (1987) pp. 8-10.

Papers

First Southern Hemisphere Conference on Maritime Archaeology, Australian Sports Publications, 1978.

Patterson, L.W.,

'OCS prehistoric site-discovery difficulties', 8 *JFA* (1981) pp. 231-232.

Pearson, C.,

· 'On-site conservation requirements for marine archaeological excavation', 6 *I.J.N.A.* (1977) pp. 37-46.

· 'Conservation of the underwater heritage' in UNESCO, *Protection of the underwater heritage*. Technical handbooks for museums and monuments, 4, 1981, pp. 77-133.

· (ed), *Conservation of Marine Archaeological Objects*, Butterworths, London, 1987.

Peterson, M.,

· *History under the Sea*. A Handbook for Underwater Exploration. Published by the Smithsonian Institution, City of Washington, 1965.

· 'Wreck sites in the Americas' in UNESCO, *Underwater Archaeology: A Nascent Discipline*, Paris, 1972, pp. 85-93.

Piercy, R.C.M.,

'Mombasa wreck excavation', 137 *Museum* (vol. XV, No. 1) 1983, pp. 30-33.

Pirazzoli, P.A.,

'Submerged remains of Ancient Megisti in Castellorizo Island (Greece)', 16 *I.J.N.A.* (1987) pp. 57-66.

Pryor, F.,

'Flag Fen', 96 *Current Archaeology*, April 1985, pp. 6-8.

Raab, M.L. & Klinger, T.C.,

· 'A critical appraisal of "significance" in contract archaeology', 42 *American Antiquity* (1977) pp. 629-634.

· 'A reply to Sharrock and Grayson on archaeological significance', 44 *American Antiquity* (1979) pp. 328-329.

Raban, A.,

· 'Archaeology in Israel', 28 *Oceanus* No. 1, Spring 1985, pp. 59-64.

· (ed.), *Harbour Archaeology, Proceedings of the First International Workshop on Ancient Mediterranean Harbours, BAR International Series* 257, 1985.

· (ed.), 'Archaeology of coastal changes' in *Proceedings of the First International Symposium 'Cities on the Sea - Past and Present', BAR International Series* 404, 1988.

Rebikoff, D.,

'Photogrammetry in dirty water by mosaic and strip scanning', in UNESCO, *Underwater Archaeology: A Nascent Discipline*. Museums and Monuments XI. 1972, pp. 223-230.

Roberts, M.,

'Comment II', 8 *JFA* (1981) pp. 233-235.

Romero, P.B.,

'The sacred well of Chichén-Itzá', UNESCO *Courier* May 1972, pp. 30-33.

Roper, J.,
'Explanatory Memorandum' in Council of Europe, Parliamentary Assembly. *The Underwater Cultural Heritage*. Report of the Committee on Culture and Education (Rapporteur Mr. John Roper). Doc. 4200-E, Strasbourg, 1978, pp. 1-26.

Rosencrantz, D.M., Klein, M. and Edgerton, H.E.,
'The uses of sonar' in UNESCO, *Underwater Archaeology: A Nascent Discipline*, Museums and Monuments XI, 1972, pp. 257-270.

Rule, M.,
The Mary Rose - The Excavation and Raising of Henry VI's Flagship, Conway Maritime Press, London, 1982.

Ruoff, U.,
· 'Archaeological discoveries in lakes and rivers', 137 *Museum* (vol. XV, No. 1) 1983, pp. 64-67.
· 'Palafittes and underwater archaeology' in UNESCO, *Underwater Archaeology: A Nascent Discipline*. Museums and Monuments XI, 1972, pp. 123-127.

Ryan, P.R.,
'The quest to find the Bismarck', 32 *Oceanus* (1988/89) pp. 27-35;

Schmidt, P.R. and Mrozowski, R.A.,
'History, smugglers, change and shipwrecks' in Gould, R.A. (ed.), *Shipwreck Anthropology*, University of New Mexico Press, 1983, pp. 143-171.

Sea Technology,
Diving and submersibles (special issue), December, 1986.

Sharrock, F.W. and Grayson, D.K.,
"'Significance' in contract archaeology", 44 *American Antiquity* (1979) pp. 327-328.

Shiner, J.L.,
'Underwater archaeology, european vs american' in Arnold, J.B. (ed.), *Beneath the Waters of Time: The Proceedings of the Ninth Conference on Underwater Archaeology*. Texas Antiquities Committee Publication No. 6, Austin, 1978, pp. 199-203.

Sinoto, V.H.,
'Huahine: heritage of the great navigators', 137 *Museum* (vol. XV, No. 1) 1983, pp. 70-73.

Smith, K.C.,
· 'A remarkable discovery: the bronze age shipwreck at Kas' 12(1) *I.N.A. Newsletter* 1985, pp. 2-5.

Smith, R.C., Keith, D.H., Lakey, D.,
'The Highborn Cay wreck: further explorations of a 16th century Bahaman shipwreck', 14 *I.J.N.A.* (1985) pp. 63-72.

Smolaret, P.,
'From Polish waters', 137 *Museum* (vol. XV, No. 1) 1983, pp. 37-40.

Stengel, R.,
'Bounty from the oldest shipwreck', *Time Magazine*, December 17, 1984, p. 54.

Sténuit, R.,
Treasures of the Armada. David & Charles, Newton Abbott, 1974.

Stickel, E.G.,
'Comment I', 8 *JFA* (1981) pp. 232-235.

Tarlton, R.,
'Electronic navigation and search techniques' in Arnold, J.B. (ed.), *Beneath the Waters of Time: The Proceedings of the Ninth Conference on Underwater Archaeology.* Texas Antiquities Committee Publication No. 6, Austin, 1978, pp. 337-348.

Taylor, J. du Plat
- 'The Future' in Taylor, J. du Plat (ed.), *Marine Archaeology*, Hutchinson of London, 1965, pp. 190-201.
- 'Archaeology'. Reprinted from Woods, J.D. & Lythgoe, J.N. (eds.), *Underwater Science*, Oxford University Press, 1971.
- (ed.), *Marine Archaeology*. Edited for C.M.A.S. (World Underwater Federation), Hutchinson of London, 1965.

Throckmorton, P.,
- *The Lost Ships - An Adventure in Undersea Archaeology*, Jonathan Cape, London 1965.
- *Shipwrecks and Archaeology: The Unharvested Sea*, Victor Gollancz Ltd., London 1970.
- 'The future of the past - the promise of archaeology'. Oceans 20 - Third World Congress of Underwater Activities, 1973, pp. 38-41.
- 'Ships and shipwrecks: the archaeology of ships' in Blackman, D.J. (ed.), *Marine Archaeology*, Butterworths, London, 1973, pp. 493-516.
- 'Discussion' in Blackman, D.J. (ed.), *Marine Archaeology,* Butterworths, London 1973, pp. 517-520.
- *Diving for Treasure*, Thames & Hudson Ltd., London, 1977.
- 'Future sites' in Throckmorton, P. (ed.), *History from the sea : shipwrecks and archaeology.* Mitchell Beazley Publishers, London, 1987, pp. 220-221.
- 'The age of discovery/introduction' in Throckmorton, P. (ed.), *History from the Sea: Shipwrecks and Archaeology.* Mitchell Beazley Publishers, London, 1987, pp. 171-173.
- (ed.), *History from the Sea: Shipwrecks and Archaeology*, Mitchell Beazley Publishers, London 1987.
- 'The battle of Lepanto: search and survey mission (Greece) (1971-72)', 2 *I.J.N.A.* (1973) pp. 121-130.
- *Surveying in Archaeology.* Underwater Monograph Series, 5, Colt Archaeological Institute, Bernard Quaritch Ltd., London, 1969.
- 'Introduction: Marine archaeology', 28 *Oceanus*, No. 1, Spring 1985, ppp. 2-12.

Tirvengadum, D.D.,
'The Saint-German: from literary myth to museum object', 137 *Museum* (vol. XV, No. 1, 1983, pp. 54-56.

Trenerry, W.N.,
'Some legal problems in the field of underwater archaeology' in Holmquist, J.D. & Wheeler, A.H. (eds.), *Diving into the Past: Theories, Techniques and Applications of Underwater Archaeology,* Minnesota Historical Society, St. Paul, 1963, pp. 37-43.

Underwater Research Group,
Techniques in Underwater Research (From the bottom to the book), in memory of Taylor, J.- du Plat, Hassle-free Productions, 1986.

UNESCO,
· *Underwater Archaeology: A Nascent Discipline.* Museums and Monuments XI, Paris, 1972.
· *Protection of the Underwater Heritage.* Protection of the cultural heritage. Technical handbooks for museums and monuments, 4, 1981.

Various Authors,
· 'Ports, harbours and other submerged sites' in Taylor, J. du Plat (ed.), *Marine Archaeology,* Hutchinson of London, 1965, pp. 160-189.
· 'Some notable wreck excavations' in Taylor, J. du Plat (ed.), *Marine Archaeology,* Hutchinson of London, 1965, pp. 35-146.

Wachsmann, S.,
'Ships of tarshish to the land of Ophir: seafaring in Biblical times', 33 *Oceanus* (1990) pp. 70-82.

Watters, D.R.,
'Terms and concepts related to marine archaeology', 28 *Oceanus,* No. 1, Spring 1985, pp. 13-17.

Watts, G.P.,
Underwater Archaeology: the Challenge before Us, San Marino, Fathom Eight, 1981.

Watson, P.J.,
'Method and theory in shipwreck archaeology' in Gould, R.A. (ed.), *Shipwreck Anthropology,* University of New Mexico Press, 1983, pp. 23-36.

Weissmann, G.,
'Titanic and Leviath', 31 *Oceanus* (1988/89) pp. 68-77.

Wilkes, W.,
Nautical Archaeology, David & Charles, Newton Abbot, 1971.

Williams, J.C.C.,
'Underwater surveying by simple graphic photogrammetry with obliques' in UNESCO, *Underwater Archaeology: A Nascent Discipline.* Museums and Monuments XI, 1972, pp. 211-212.

Yoerger, D.,
'Historical and archaeological treasures - The Titanic - a case study in technical implications' in Lewis A., Scott, A. and Carter, H.L. (eds), *New Developments in Marine Science and Technology,* Honolulu, 1989, pp. 80-83.

LEGAL AND CULTURAL ASPECTS

Abi-Saab, G.,
'The legal formulation of a right to development (subjects and content)' in Dupuy, R.-J. (ed.), *The Right to Development at the International Level*, Hague Academy of International Law, 1979, pp. 159-175.

Abramson, R., Huttler, S.B.,
'The legal response to the illicit movement of cultural property', 5 *Law & Pol. Int'l Bus.* (1973) pp. 932-970.

Akinsaya, A.,
'The law of the sea: unilateralism or multilateralism?' 34 *Revue egyptienne de droit international* (1978) pp. 39-99.

Alexander, B.E.,
'Treasure salvage beyond the territorial sea: an assessment and recommendations', 20 *J. Mar. Law & Com.* (1989) pp. 1-19.

Alexander, L.M.,
The Law of the Sea. Offshore Boundaries and Zones, The Ohio University Press, 1967.

Allott, P.,
'*Mare nostrum*: a new international law of the sea', 86 *A.J.I.L.* (1992) pp. 764-787

Alpizar, O.J.,
'Sovereign rights and sunken treasure: Treasure Salvors Inc. v. Unidentified and Abandoned Sailing Vessel', 7 *Capital University L. Rev.* (1977/78) pp. 75-87.

Alston, P.,
· 'The right to development at the international level' in Dupuy, R.-J (ed.), *The Right to Development at the International Level*, Hague Academy of International Law, 1979, pp. 99-114.
· 'The shortcomings of a 'Garfield the Cat' approach to the right to development', 15 *Calif. W. Int'l L.J.* (1985) pp. 510-518.

Anand, R.P.,
Legal Regime of the Seabed and the Developing Countries, Sijthoff A.W., Leyden 1976.

Anderson, D.,
'Legal effects of mechanisms for adjusting Part XI'. Paper presented to the *18th Annual Seminar of the Center for Oceans Law and Policy, University of Virginia, School of Law*, Rhodos 22-25 May 1994.

Anghie, A.,
'Human rights and cultural identity: new hope for ethnic peace?', 33 *Harvard International Law Journal* (1992) pp. 341-352.

Aoyagi, K.,
'Community of group rights' in UNESCO, *Cultural Rights as Human Rights*. Studies and documents on cultural policies, 1970, pp. 25-27.

Apollis, G.,
L'emprise maritime de l'état côtier. Pedone, A. editions, Paris, 1981.

Arauze (de), R.T.,
  'Museums and the containment of illicit traffic', 136 *Museum* (vol. XIV, No. 2) 1982
  pp. 134-135.
Arend, A.C.,
  'Archaeological and historical objects: the international legal implications of UNCLOS
  III', 22 *V.J.I.L.* (1982) pp. 777-803.
Arnold, J.B.,
  · 'Some thoughts on salvage law and historic preservation', 7 *I.J.N.A.* (1978) pp.
    173-176.
  · 'Underwater cultural resources and the antiquities market', 5 *JFA* (1978) p. 232.
  · 'The Platoro lawsuit revisited' in Cummings, C.R. (ed.), *Underwater Archaeology:
    The Proceedings of the Fourteenth Annual Conference on Underwater Archaeology*,
    Fathom Eight, California 1983.
  · 'The Platoro lawsuit: The final chapter', in Johnston, P.E. (ed.), *Proceedings of
    the Sixteenth Conference on Underwater Archaeology*, Special Publication Series,
    No. 4, Society of Historical Archaeology, 1985, pp. 1-8.
  · 'U.S. federal level historic shipwreck legislation: development and status', 16
    I.J.N.A. (1987) pp. 3-5.
Asamoah, H.,
  'Rights of self-determinaiton of peoples in established States: Southern Africa and
  the Middle East', *The American Society of International Law Proceedings* (1991)
  pp. 541-561.
Ashburner, W.,
  The Rhodian Sea-Law, Clarendon Press, Oxford, 1909.
Atkinson, D.,
  'Returning works of art', 4 *Forum (Council of Europe)* (1983) pp. 2-3.
Attard, D.J.,
  The Exclusive Economic Zone in International law, Clarendon Press, Oxford, 1987.
Auburn, F.M.,
  · 'Deep sea archaeology and the law', 2 *I.J.N.A.* (1973) pp. 159-162.
  · 'Convention for preservation of man's heritage in the ocean', 185 *Science* (1974)
    pp. 763-767.
Balinsky, D.A.,
  'Treasure Salvors Inc. v. The Unidentified Wrecked and Abandoned Sailing Vessel,
  Believed to be Nuestra Señora de Atocha', 5 *Brooklyn J. Int'l L.* (1979) pp. 178-190.
Ballarino, T.,
  "La problematica dei beni culturali rubati o illecitamente esportati al vaglio del sistema
  di diritto internazionale privato". Paper presented at the *Seminario: La protezione
  del patrimonio culturale subacqueo nel Mediterraneo,* organized by the Università
  degli Studi di Roma 'Tor Vergata', Anacapri, 1 October 1994.
Bardonnet, D., Virally, M. (eds),
  Le nouveau droit international de la mer, Nouvelle Série No. 39, Pedone, A. éditions,
  Paris, 1983.

Barrowman, E.,
'The recovery of shipwrecks in international waters: a multilateral sulution', 8 *Michigan Yearbook of International Legal Studies* (1987) pp. 231-246.

Barrows, R.T.,
'Ownership of submerged lands and rights to articles found thereon', 66 *The Michigan Bar Journal* (1987) pp. 886-893.

Bassiouni, M.C.,
· 'Theories of jurisdiction and their application in extradition law and practice', 4/5 *Calif. W. Int'l L.* (1973/75) pp. 1-71.
· 'Reflections on criminal jurisdiction in international protection of cultural property', 10 *Syracuse J. Int'l L. & Com.* (1983) pp. 281-322.

Bator, P.M.,
· 'An essay on the international trade in art', 34 *Stanford L. Rev.* (1982) pp. 275-384.
· 'Regulation and deregulation of international trade' in Duboff, L.D. (ed), *Art Law: Domestic and International*, Rothman & Co, 1975, pp 299-307.

Baxter, R.R.,
'Treaties and custom', 129 *Hague Recueil* (1970-I) pp. 31-105.

Beall, K.S.,
'State regulation of search and salvage of sunken treasures' 4 *Natural Resources Lawyer* (1971) pp. 14-17.

Beaucourt, C.,
'Le secret de l'épave ou l'étrange évolution du régime de sa propriété', 38 *Droit maritime français* (1986) pp. 451-463.

Becher, K.,
'On the obligation of subjects of international law to return cultural property to its permanent place', 44 *Annuaire de l'AAA* (1974) pp. 96-99.

Bekkouche, M.A.,
'La récupération du concept de partimoine commun de l'humanité par les pays industrielles', XX *Revue belge de droit international* (1987) pp. 124-137.

Bekiashev, K.A., Vitali, V.S.,
International Maritime Organisations, Martinus Nijhoff Publishers, The Hague, 1981.

Bersin, J.E.,
'The protection of cultural property and the promotion of international trade in art', 13 *New York Law School of International & Comparative Law* (1992) pp. 125-151.

Bettini, E.,
'Possible future regimes on the seabed resources' in Szyucki, J. (ed.) *Symposium on the International Regime of the Sea-Bed*, Proceedings, Academia Nazionale dei Linzei, 1970, pp. 319-342.

Beurier, J.-P.,
'Pour un droit international de l'archéologie sous-marine', 93 *R.G.D.I.P.* (1989) pp. 45-68.

Black's
Law Dictionary, 5th ed., St. Paul Minn. West Pub. Company, 1979.

Blackstone, N.,
Commentaries on the Laws of England, Clarendon Press, M. CLXV, vol. I, ch. 7, pp. 280-284.

Bleckmann, A.,
'Sittenwidrigkeit wegen Verstobes gegen den *ordre public* international', 34 *ZaöRV* (1974) pp. 112-132.

Boer, B.,
'Protection of Movable Cultural Heritage Property Act 1986' (1987), 4 *Environmental and Planning Law Journal* 63.

Boutros-Ghali, B.,
'The right to culture and the Universal Declaration of Human Rights' in UNESCO, *Cultural Rights as Human Rights.* Studies and documents on cultural policies, 1970, pp. 73-75.

Bowers, D.L.,
'Maritime law - salvage operations - Eleventh Amendment not a bar to admiralty *in rem* actions against property seized by State officials acting outside their authority', Florida Department of State v. Treasure Salvors, Inc, 7 *Suffolk Transnational Law Journal* (1983) pp. 601-613.

Braekhus, S.,
'Salvage of wrecks and wreckage: legal issues arising from the Runde find', 20 *Scandinavian Studies in Law* (1976) pp. 39-68.

Brice, G.,
Maritime Law of Salvage, Stevens & Sons Ltd., London, 1983.

Brierly, J.L.,
The Law of Nations. An Introduction to the International Law of Peace, 6th edition, Clarendon Press, Oxford, 1963.

Bridwell, J.,
'The Texas Antiquities Code: an historical commentary in a contemporary context', 24 *Southwestern L.J.* (1970) pp. 326-338.

Brietzke, P.H.,
'Consorting with the chameleon, or repraising the right to development', 15 *Calif. W. Int'l L.J.* (1985) pp. 560-606.

Brown, E.D.,
· 'Freedom of scientific research and the legal regime of hydrospace', 9 *Indian J. Int'l Law* (1969) pp. 327-380.
· *The Legal Regime of Hydrospace.* The Library of World Affairs, No. 70, Stevens & Sons, London, 1971.
· 'Maritime zones: a survey of claims' in Churchill, R. and others (eds.), *New Directions in the Law of the Sea,* vol. III, 1973, pp. 157-192.
· *Passage Through the Territorial Sea, Straits Used for International Navigation and Archipelagos,* David Davies Memorial Institute of International Studies, 1973.

· 'The exclusive economic zone: criteria and machinery for the resolution of international conflicts betrween different users of the EEZ', 4 *Marit. Pol. Mgmt.* (1978) pp. 325-350.

· 'Freedom of the high seas versus the common heritage of mankind: fundamental principles in conflict', 20 *San Diego L. Rev.* (1983) pp. 521-560.

· 'Exclusive economic zones: the legal regime and the UN Convention on the Law of the Sea' in *Advances in Underwater Technology*, Ocean Science and Offshore Engineering, vol. 8, Graham & Trotman, London, 1986.

· *Sea-Bed Energy and Mineral Resources and the Law of the Sea*, vol. 1, *The Areas Within National Jurisdiction*, Graham & Trotman, London, 1984.

· *Sea-Bed Energy and Mineral Resources and the Law of the Sea*, vol. 2, *The Area Beyond the Limits of National Jurisdiction*, Graham & Trotman, London, 1986.

· *Sea-Bed Energy and Mineral Resources and the Law of the Sea*, vol. 3, *Selected Documents, Tables and Bibliography*, Graham & Trotman, London, 1986.

· *Sea Bed Energy and Minerals: The International Legal Regime*, Martinus Nijhoff Publishers, 1992.

Brownlie, I.,

· *Principles of International Law*, 4rd ed., Clarendon Press, Oxford, 1990.

· *Basic Documents in International Law*, 2nd ed., Clarendon Press, Oxford, 1982.

Burhenne, W.E. (ed.),

International Environmental Law - Multilateral Treaties, Berlin, 1982.

Burgers J.H.,

'Introduction item: the right to cultural identity' in Berting, J. et al, *Human Rights in a Pluralist World*, Westport, 1990.

Burke, K., DeLeo, D.,

'Innocent passage and transit passage in the United Nations Convention on the Law of the Sea', 9 *Yale Journal of World Public Order* (1983) pp. 389-408.

Burke, W.T.

· *A Report on International Legal Problems of Scientific Research in the Oceans*, Clearinghouse for Federal, Scientific and Technical Information, Doc. BP-177-724.

· 'Law and new technologies' in Alexander, L.M. (ed.) *The Law of the Sea. Offshore Boundaries and Zones*, The Ohio University Press, 1967, pp. 204-227.

· 'National legislation on ocean authority zones and the contemporary law of the sea', 9 *Ocean Dev. & Int'l L.* (1983) pp. 289-322.

· 'Customary law of the sea: advocacy or disinterested scholarship?', 14 *Yale Journal of International Law* (1989) pp. 508-527 and

· 'Remarks' in 'The Law of the Sea: Customary Norms and Conventional Rules', 81 *American Society of International Law Proceedings* (1987) pp. 75-104 at pp. 75-84.

Byrne-Sutton, Q.,

Le traffic international des biens culturels sous l' angle de leur revendication par l'état d'origin, Schulthess Polygraphischer Verlag, Zürich, 1988.

Bustamente, Y.,

The Territorial Sea. Published by University Microfilms International, Ann Arbor, Michigan, London, 1978.

Butler, J.S.,

'Admiralty - salvage rights - sovereign claims on the outer continental shelf do not extend to abandoned vessels', 7 *Georgia J. Int. & C.L.* (1977) pp. 169-176.

Butler, W.E.,

'Custom, treaty, State practice and the 1982 Convention', 12 *Marine Policy* (1988) pp. 183-186.

Caflisch, L.,

· 'Les zones maritimes sous jurisdiction nationale, leurs limites et leur jurisdiction', 84 *R.G.D.I.P.* (1980) pp. 68-119, and in Bardonnet, D. et Virally, M. (eds.), *Le nouveau droit international de la mer*, Publications de la R.G.D.I.P., Nouvelle Série No. 39, Pedone, A. éditions, Paris 1983, pp. 35-139.

· 'Submarine antiquities and the international law of the sea', 13 *N.Y.I.L.* (1982) pp. 3-32.

Caflisch, L. & Piccard, S.,

'The legal regime of marine scientific research and UNCLOS', 38 *ZaöRV* (1978) pp. 848-901.

Caminos, H. & Molitor, M.R.,

'Progressive development of international law and the package deal', 79 *A.J.I.L.* (1985) pp. 871-890.

Capotorti, F.,

'Are minorities entitled to collective international rights?', 20 *Israeli Yearbook on Human Rights* (1991) pp. 351-357.

Cartei, R.,

'Rinvenimento di oggetti archeologici in alto mari', 30 *Rivista de diritto della navigazione* (1964) pp. 352-363.

Carty, A.,

'Towards a critical theory of general custom as a source of international law', 12 *Marine Policy* (1988) pp. 211-218.

Cassese, A.,

· 'Progressive transnational promotion of human rights' in Ramcharan, B.G. (ed.), *Human Rights - Thirty Years After the Universal Declaration*, Martinus Nijhoff, 1979, pp. 249-262.

· (ed.), *UN Law/Fundamental Rights. Two Topics in International Law*. Sijthoff & Noordhoff, Alpen aan den Rijn, 1979.

Cassese, A. & Jouve (eds.)

Pour un droit des peuples, Paris, Berger, Levrault, 1978.

Castagné, A.,

'L'archéologie sous-marine et le droit' in Société française pour le droit international, *Actualités du droit de la mer*. Colloque de Montpellier, 25-27 Mai 1972, Pedone, A. éditions, Paris, 1973, pp. 164-183.

Cerise, C.A.,
  'Treasure Salvors: the admiralty court 'finds' old law', 28 *Loy. L. Rev.* (1982) pp. 1126-1145.
Charney, J.I.,
  'The exclusive economic zone and public international law', 15 *Ocean Dev. & Int'l L.* (1985) pp. 233-288.
Chowdhury, S.R. Denters E.M.G. & de Waart, P.J. (eds),
  The Right to Development in International Law, Martinus Nijhoff Publishers, 1992.
Church, D.,
  'Evaluating the effectiveness of foreign laws on national ownership of cultural property in US Courts', 30 *Columbia Journal of Transnational Law* (1992) pp. 179-229.
Churchill, R.R. & Lowe, A.V.,
  The Law of the Sea, 2nd revised edition, Manchester University Press,1988.
Clark, I.C.,
  'Illicit traffic in cultural property: Canada seeks a bilateral agreement', 151 *Museum* (1986) pp. 182-187.
Cockrell, W.A.,
  'Some moral, ethical and legal considerations in underwater archaeology' in Cockrell, W.A. (ed.), *In the Realms of Gold. The Proceedings of the Tenth Conference on Underwater Archaeology*. Fathom Eight Special Publication, No. 1, 1981, pp. 215-220.
Cohen, Y.A.,
  'From nation State to international community' in UNESCO, *Cultural Rights as Human Rights*. Studies and documents on cultural policies, 1970, pp. 76-79.
Collins, M.G.,
  'The salvage of sunken military vessels', 10 *International Lawyer* (1976) pp. 681-690.
Colombos, C.J.,
  The International Law of the Sea. 6th ed., Longman Group Ltd., London 1967.
Comacho, E.D.,
  'Ecuadorian law', 30 *Oceanus*, No. 2, Summer 1987 pp. 16-19.
Conforti, B.,
  'Does freedom of the seas still exist?', *I.Y.I.L.* (1975) pp. 5-24.
Council of Europe,
  · *The Underwater Cultural Heritage*. Report of the Committee on Culture and Education (Rapporteur Mr. John Roper), Doc. 4200-E, Strasbourg 1987.
  · *International Legal Protection of Cultural Property*. Proceedings of the Thirteenth Colloquy on European Law, Delphi, 20-22 September 1983, Strasbourg 1984.
  · *Parliamentary Conference on the UN Convention on the Law of the Sea*, Palermo, 2-4 November 1983. AS/JUR/MAR/CONF.35(7).
Crawford, J. (ed.),
  The Rights of Peoples, Clarendon Press, Oxford, 1988.
Cycon, D.E.,
  · 'Who owns the Titanic?', 28 *Oceanus*, Winter 1985-1986, pp. 94-95.

· 'Legal and regulatory issues in marine archaeology', 28 *Oceanus,* No. 1, Spring 1985, pp. 78-84.

Daniele, L.,

"La nozione di 'stato d'origine' negli strumenti internazionali e comunitari concernenti il traffico di beni culturali". Paper presented at the *Seminario: La protezione del patrimonio culturale subacqueo nel Mediterraneo,* organised by the Università degli Studi di Roma 'Tor Vergata', Anacapri, 1 October 1994.

Danilenko, G.,

· 'The concept of the common heritage of mankind in international law', XIII *Annals of Air and Space Law* (1988) pp. 247-265

· *Law Making in the International Community,* Martinus Nijhoff, 1993.

Davies, P.,

· 'Salvage on the New Zealand coast', *N.Z.L.J.* (1982) pp. 39-42.

· 'Wrecks on the New Zealand coast', *N.Z.L.J.* (1983) pp. 202-205.

Davis, A.J.,

'Beyond repatriation: a proposal for the equitable restitution of cultural property', 33 *U.C.L.A.L. Rev.* (1985) pp. 642-663.

DeLanis, J.A.,

'Jurisdiction - continental shelf - abandoned vessel salvaged from the surface of the United States continental shelf beyond territorial waters is not under jurisdiction of United States Government', 9 *V. and J. Transnat'l L.* (1976) pp. 915-926.

Del Bianco, H.P. (Jr.),

'Underwater recovery operations in offshore waters: vying for rights to treasure', 5/6 *Boston University International Law Journal* (1987/88) pp. 153-176.

Department of Trade,

Historic Shipwrecks: The Role of the Department of Trade, London, 1979.

Dicke, D.C.,

'The instruments and the agencies of the international protection of cultural property' in Council of Europe, *International Legal Protection of Cultural Property.* Proceedings of the Thirteenth Colloquy on European Law, Delphi, 20-22 September 1983, Strasbourg, 1984.

Djordjevic, J.,

'The social property of mankind' in Borgese, E.M. (ed.), *Pacem in Maribus,* Dodd, Mead & Company, New York, 1972, pp. 166-182.

Donelly, J.,

· 'In search of the Unicorn: the jurisprudence and politics of the right to development', 15 *Calif. W. Int'l L.J.* (1985) pp. 473-509.

· 'The theology of the right to development - A reply to Alston', 15 *Calif. W. Int'l L.J.* (1985) pp. 519-523.

Doris, E.P.,

The Law of Antiquities. Legislation - Jurisprudence - Interpretation. Saccoulas Publishing Co., Athens, 1985 (in Greek).

Dromgoole, S.,
- 'Protection of Historic Wrecks: The UK Approach. Part I: The Present Legal Framework', 4 *International Journal of Estuarine and Coastal Law* (1989) pp. 26-51.
- 'Protection of Historic Wrecks. The UK Approach. Part II: Towards Reform', 4 *International Journal of Estuarine and Coastal Law* (1989) pp. 95-116.

Dromgoole, S. and Gaskell, N.,
"Who has a right to historic wrecks and wreckage?", 2 *International Journal of Cultural Property* (1993) pp. 217-273.

DuBoff, L.D.,
- 'The protection of cultural property in time of peace', 44 *Annuaire de l'AAA* (1974) pp. 45-62.
- (ed), *Art Law: Domestic and International,* Rothman, F.B. & Co, 1975.
- *et al.*, 'Proceedings of the Panel on the U.S. Enabling Legislation of the UNESCO Convention on the Means of Prohibiting and Preventing the Illicit Import, Export and Transfer of Ownership of Cultural Property', 4 *Syracuse J. Int'l L. and Comm.* (1976) pp. 97-139.

Dupuy, R.-J.,
- 'The notion of the common heritage of mankind applied to the seabed', VIII *Annals of Air and Space Law* (1983) pp. 347-355 and in Rozakis, C.L. & Stephanou, C.A. (eds.), *The New Law of the Sea.* Selected and Edited Papers of the Athens Colloquium on the Law of the Sea, September 1982. North Holland, Amsterdam, 1983, pp. 199-208.
- 'The Convention on the Law of the Sea and the New International Economic Order', 3/4 UNESCO - *Impacts of Science on Society* (1984) pp. 313-325 (Special issue on 'research, international law and the sea in man's future').
- (ed.), *The Right to Development at the International Level.* Hague Academy of International Law, United Nations University Workshop, The Hague, 16-18 October 1979.
- *The Management of Humanities Resources: The Law of the Sea,* Hague Academy of International Law, United Nations University Workshop, The Hague, 29-31 October 1981.
- *The Future of International Law in a Multicultural World.* Hague Academy of International Law, United Nations University Workshop, The Hague, 17-19 November 1983.

Dupuy, R.-J., Vignes, D. (eds),
- *Traité du nouveau droit de la mer.* Collection 'Droit Internationale', Economica, Bruylant, 1985.
- *A Handbook on the New Law of the Sea*, Vols 1 and 2, Hague Academy of International Law, Martinus Nijhoff, 1991.

Dyke (van), J.M. (ed.),
Consensus and Confrontation: The United States and the Law of the Sea Convention, Honolulu, Law of the Sea Institute, Honolulu, 1985.

Economides, C.,
'The contiguous zone: today and tomorrow' in Rozakis, C.L., Stephanou, C.A. (eds.), *The New Law of the Sea*. Selected and Edited Papers of the Athens Colloquium on the Law of the Sea (September 1982), North Holland, Amsterdam 1983, pp. 69-81.

Edwards, J.F.,
'Major global treaties for the protection and enjoyment of art and cultural objects', 22 *The University of Toledo Law Review* (1991) pp. 919-953.

Eide, A.,
'Maldevelopment and 'the right to development' - a critical note with a constructive intent' in Dupuy, R.-J. (ed.), *The Right to Development at the International Level.* Hague Academy of International Law, 1979, pp. 397-417.

Eisen, L.E.,
'The missing piece: a discussion of theft, statutes of limitations and title disputes in the art world', 81 *The Journal of Criminal Law & Criminology* (1991) pp. 1067-1101.

Eleazer, H.,
'The recovery of vessels, aircraft and treasure in international waters' in Würfel, S.W.(ed.), *Some Current Sea Law Problems,* University of North Carolina, Sea Grant Publication 1975, UNC-SG-75-06, pp. 26-38.

Eustathiades, C.,
· 'La protection des bien culturel en cas de conflit armé et la Convention de la Haye de 14 mai 1954', *Etudes de droit international*, vol. III, Athènes, 1959, p. 395.
· *International Law,* University of Athens, 2nd ed., 1979 (In Greek).

Eustis, III, F.A.,
'The Glomar Explorer incident: implications for the law of salvage', 16 *V.J.I.L.* (1975) pp. 177-185.

Evans, M.D.,
Relevant Circumstances and Maritime Delimitation, Clarendon Press, Oxford, 1989.

Eyo, E.,
'Nigeria', 31 *Museum* (1970) pp. 1821.

Falk, R.A.,
· *The Role of Domestic Courts in the International Legal Order.* Syracuse University Press, New York 1964.
· 'Comparative protection of human rights in capitalist and socialist third world countries', 1(2) *Universal Human Rights* (1979) pp. 3-29.
· 'The Algiers Declaration of the Rights of Peoples and the struggle for human rights' in Cassese, A. (ed.), *UN Law/Fundamental Rights. Two Topics in International Law*, Sijthoff & Noordhoff, Alpen aan den Rijn, 1979 pp. 225-235.

Fee, F.H.,
'Abandoned property: title to treasure recovered in Florida's territorial waters', 21 *U. Fla. L. Rev.* (1968/69) pp. 360-375.

Firth, A.,
'Recent legislation in France', 20 *I.J.N.A.* (1991) pp. 65-71.

Fish, P.R.,
'Federal policy and legislation for archaeological conservation', 22 *Arizona L. Rev.* (1980) pp. 677-699.

Fisher, M.A.,
'The Abandoned Shipwreck Act: the role of private enterprise', 12 *Columbia - VLA Journal of Law & the Arts* (1988) pp. 373-377.

Fitzmaurice, G.G.,
'Some results of the Geneva Conference on the Law of the Sea', 8 *Int'l L. & Comp. L.Q.* (1959) pp. 73-121.

Franckx, E.,
'Romania's proclamation of a 200-mile exclusive economic zone', 2 *International Journal of Estuarine and Coastal Law* (1987) pp. 144-153.

Frankowska, M. (ed.),
Scientific and Technologial Revolution and the Law of the Sea. Warsawa, Ossolineum, 1974.

Fraoua, R.,
Le traffic illicite des biens culturels et leur restitution: Analyse des réglementations nationals et internationals critique et propositions. Travaux de la Faculté de Droit de l'Université de Fribourg, Suisse, 1985, pp. 163-166.

Frigo, M.,
La protezione dei beni culturali nel diritto internazionale, Universita di Milano, Pubblicazioni della Facolta di Giurisprudenza, Serie II, Studi di diritto internazionale, No. 7, Dott. A. Giuffrè editore, 1986.

Freedman, P.,
'Lost heritage: symposium takes up return of cultural treasures', *UNESCO Features* No. 776 (1981) pp. 1-5.

Frommer, A.M.,
'The British hovering acts: a contribution to the study of the contiguous zone', 16 *Revue belge du droit international* (1981/82) pp. 434-458.

Fry, E.M.,
'Marine archaeology', 23 *San Diego Law Review* (1986) pp. 701-722.

Fuller, L.L.,
Legal Fictions. Stanford University Press, 1967.

Galenskaya, L.N.,
'International co-operation in cultural affairs', 198 *Hague Recueil* (1986-III) pp. 265-331.

Galgano, F.,
'Legal aspects of trade in art in Italy', *International Sales of Works of Art* (1985) 125.

Gamble, J.K.,
'Where trends the law of the sea?', 10 *Ocean Dev. & Int'l L.* (1981/82) pp. 61-91.

Gamble, J.K. & Frankowska, M.,
'The 1982 Convention and customary law of the sea: observations, a framework and a warning', 21 *San Diego L. Rev.* (1984) pp. 491-511.

Ganslmayr, H.,
· 'Federal Republic of Germany', 31 *Museum* (1979) pp. 12-13.
· *et al.*, 'Study on the principles, conditions and means for the restitution or return of cultural property in view of reconstituting dispersed heritages', 31 *Museum* (1979) pp. 62-66.

Garcia-Amador, *et al.*,
The Exploitation and Conservation of the Resources of the Sea. Second enlarged printing, Sijthoff, Leyden, 1963.

Gault, I.T. and Vander Zwaag, D.,
'Legal jurisdiction over the Titanic', *Lighthouse, Edition 37*, Spring 1988.

Gechman, J.,
'Rescuing cultural treasures: the need for an incentive generating doctrine', 24 *Houston Law Review* (1987) pp. 577-603.

Gelberg, L.,
'Rechtsprobleme der Bergung auf Hoher See', 15 *Jahrbuch für Internationales Recht* (1971) pp. 429-447

Gibson, J.,
'The ownership of the sea bed under British territorial waters', 6 *International Relations* (1978) pp. 474-499.

Gidel, G.,
· *Le droit international de la mer*, vol. 1, Sirey, Paris, 1932.
· 'La mer territorial et la zone contiguë', 48 *Hague Recueil* (1934-II) pp. 241-273.

Giesecke, A.G.,
· 'New legislation introduced to protect historic shipwrecks', 10 *JFA* (1983) pp. 488-490.
· 'Management of historic shipwrecks in the 1980s', 12 *JFA* (1985) pp. 108-115.
· 'Shipwrecks: The past in the present', 15 *Coastal Management* (1987) pp. 176-195.
· 'The Abandoned Shipwreck Act: affirming the role of the States in historic preservation', 12 *Columbia - VLA Journal of Law & the Arts* (1988) pp. 379-389.

Gilmore, C. & Black, G.,
The Law of Admiralty, 2nd ed., The Foundation Press Inc., Mineola, New York 1975.

Gittleman, R.,
'The African Charter on Human and People's Rights: a legal analysis', 22 *V.J.I.L.* (1982) pp. 667-714.

Giorgi, M.C.,
'Underwater archaeological and historical objects' in Dupuy, R-J. & Vignes, D. (eds), *A Handbook on the New Law of the Sea*, vol. 1, Hague Academy of International Law, Martinus Nijhoff, 1991, pp. 561-575.

Clasier, G.E.,
   'Cultural resource preservation: a consideration before mineral development', 28 *Rocky Mountain Mineral Law Institute* (1982) pp. 635-670.
Gnagnarella, F. and (di) Fonzo, L.,
   "La sfera di applicazione spaziale della Convenzione Europea sulla Protezione del Patrimonio Culturale Subacqueo". Paper presented at the *Seminario: La protezione del patrimonio culturale subacqueo nel Mediterraneo,* organized by the Università degli Studi di Roma 'Tor Vergata', Anacapri, 1 October 1994.
Goddard, K.S.,
   'Is there a right to wreck?', *Lloyd's Maritime and Commercial Law Quarterly* (1986) pp. 625-630.
Goldie, L.F.E.,
   'A note on some diverse meanings of the common heritage of mankind', 10 *Syracuse J. Int'l L. & Com.* (1983) pp. 69-110.
Gonzalez, M.A.,
   'New legal tools to curb the illlicit traffic in pre-Columbian antiquities', 12 *Colum. J. Transnat'l L.* (1973) pp. 316-341.
Gordon, J.B.,
   'Comment: The UNESCO Convention on the Illicit Movement of Art Treasures', 12 *Harvard Int'l L.J.* (1971) pp. 537-556.
Gounaris, E.,
   · 'The salvage of wrecks from the seabed', *Kathimerini* 24 July 1977, p. 3, col. 1.
   · 'The extension and delimitation of sea areas under the sovereignty, sovereign rights and jurisdiction of coastal States' in Vukas, B. (ed), *Essays on the New Law of the Sea,* Zagreb, 1985, pp. 85-97.
Goy, R.,
   · 'Les objets de musée en droit international', 44 *Annuaire de l'AAA* (1974) pp. 22-33.
   · 'Rapport de synthese', 44 *Annuaire de l'AAA* (1974) pp. 149-156.
   · 'La retour et la restitution des biens culturels à leur pays d'origin en cas de appropriation illégale', 83 *R.G.D.I.P.* (1970) pp. 962-985.
   · 'Le regime internationale de l'importation, de l'exportation et du transfert de propriété des biens cultures', 16 *Annuaire français de droit international* (1970) pp. 605-
Graham, G.M.,
   'Protection and reversion of cultural property: issues of definition and justification', 21 *International Lawyer* (1987) pp. 755-793.
Grandall, J.I.,
   'Extending admiralty jurisdiction over non-maritime property: ascertaining the salvor's possessory and proprietary rights to sunken aircraft', 15 *Pacific Law Journal* (1984) pp. 977-1012.
Green, J. & Henderson, G.,
   'Maritime archaeology and legislation in Western Australia: a case for legislation', 6 *I.J.N.A.* (1977) pp. 245-248.

Green, J. *et al*,
'Notes and news: maritime archaeology and legislation in Western Australia', 10 *I.J.N.A.*, (1981) pp. 145-160.

Grigg, J.W.,
'The Michigan Aboriginal Records and Antiquites Act: a constitutional question', 65 *The Michigan Bar Journal* (1986) pp. 432-437.

Gibson, J.,
'United Kingdom: The Lusitania and the ownership of wreck', 1 *International Journal of Estuarine and Coastal Law* (1986) 323-324.

Gross-Espiell, H.,
'The right to development as a human right', 16 *Texas Int'l L.J.* (1981) pp. 189-205.

Hailbronner, K.,
'The legal status of population groups in a multinational State under public international law', 20 *Israeli Yearbook on Human Rights* (1991) pp. 127-154.

Haile, M.,
'Human rights, stability and development in Africa: some observations on concept and reality', 24 *V.J.I.L.* pp. 575-615.

Halkiopoulos, Th.,
"Questions juridique de base de la Convention européenne pour la protection du patrimoine culturel subaquatique". Paper presented at the *Seminario: La protezione del patrimonio culturale subacqueo nel Mediterraneo,* organised by the Università degli Studi di Roma 'Tor Vergata', Anacapri, 1 October 1994.

Hamzah, B.A.,
'Indonesia's archipelagic regime: implications for Malaysia', 8 *Marine Policy* (1984) pp. 30-43.

Hardin, G.,
'The tragedy of the commons', 162 *Science* (1968) pp. 1243-1248.

Harris, D.J.,
Cases and Materials on International Law, 3rd ed., Sweet & Maxwell, London, 1983.

Harry, M.A.,
'The deep seabed: the common arena of mankind or arena for unilateral exploitation?', XL *Naval Law Review* (1992) pp. 207-228.

Haquani, Z.,
'Le droit au développement: fondements et sources' in Dupuy, R.-J. (ed.), *The Right to Development at the International Level.* Hague Academy of International Law, 1979, pp. 22-69.

Heide (van der), D.,
'Maritime archaeology and problems of legislation in Europe' in *Papers from the First Southern Hemisphere Conference on Maritime Archaeology,* Perth, W. Australia, 1977. Australian Sports Publication, 1978, pp. 15-20.

Heiskanen, V.,
International Legal Topics. Finish Lawyers' Publishing Company, 1992.

Henchoz, A-D.,

Réglementations nationales et internationales de l'exploration et d'exploitation des grands fonds marins, Etudes suisses de droit international, vol. 76, Schulthess Polygrahischer Verlag, Zürich, 1992.

Hermann, L.L.,

'The modern concept of the off-lying archipelago in international law', 23 *Canadian Yearbook of International Law* (1985) pp. 172-200.

Herscher, E.,

· '97 Congress, 1st session H.R. 132', 10 *JFA* (1983) pp. 107-113.

· 'Hearings held on Historic Shipwreck Legislation', 11 *JFA* (1984) pp. 79-96.

Hewitt, N.M.,

'The proposed Abandoned Shipwreck Acts of 1987 - archaeological preservation and maritime law', 12 *Suffolk Transnational Law Journal* (1989) pp. 381-393.

Hitchens, G.,

The Elgin Marbles. Should they be returned to Greece? Chatto & Windus, London 1987.

Houseman, L.A.,

'Current practices and problems in combating illegality in the art market', 12 *Seton Hall L. Rev.* (1982) pp. 506-567.

Hoyle, B.J.,

· 'U.S. position on Titanic Memorial Site', 28 *Oceanus,* No. 4, Spring 1985, pp. 45-46.

· 'Historical and Archaeological Treasures' in Alexander L., Allen, S. and Hanson, C.L. (eds), *New Developments in Marine Science and Technology: Economic, Legal and Political Aspects of Change,* Proceedings of the 22th Annual Conference of the Law of the Sea Institute (1988) Honolulu, 1989, pp. 84-88.

Hurst, C.J.B.,

'Whose is the bed of the sea? sedentary fisheries outside the three-mile limit', 4 *B.Y.I.L.* (1923/24) pp. 34-43.

Ibler, V.,

'The importance of the exclusive economic zone as a non-resource zone' in Vukas, B. (ed.), *Essays on the New Law of the Sea,* Zagreb, 1985, pp. 118-140.

ILA,

· 'Committee on Cultural Heritage Law: First Report', *Report of the 64th Conference, Broadbeach, Queensland, Australia,* 1990, pp. 208-222.

· *Report and Draft Convention on the Protection of the Underwater Cultural Heritage,* International Committee on Cultural Heritage Law, International Law Association 65th Conference, Cairo, Egypt 20-26 April 1992.

· *Draft convention on the Protection of the Underwater Cultural Heritage: Final Report,* International Committee on Cultural Heritage Law, International Law Association 66th Conference, Buenos Aires, 14-20 August 1994.

Johnson, G.M.,
'Historical perspectives on human rights and U.S. foreign policy', 2 *Universal Human Rights* No. 3, July/September 1980, pp. 1-18.

Jones, C.,
'Marine archaeology in the U.K.: a pattern of development', 2 *Marine Policy* (1978) pp. 321-330.

Jones, J.E.,
'Admiralty - possessory rights in abandoned vessels', 19 *V.J.I.L.* (1979) pp. 473-3487.

Joyner, C.C.,
'Legal implications of mankind', 35 *Int'l & Comp. L.Q.* (1986) pp. 190-199.

Juda, L.,
'The exclusive economic zone: compatibility of national claims and the UN Convention on the Law of the Sea', 16 *Ocean Dev. & Int'l L.* (1986) pp. 1-58.

Jayme, E.,
'Die Nationalität des Kunstwerks als Rechtsfrage', in Reichelt, G. (Hrgb), *Internazionaler Kulturgüterschutz,* Wiener Symposium 18/19 Oktober 1990, Manzsche Verlags- und Universitätsbuchhandlung, Wien, 1992, pp. 7-29.

Karagiannis, V.,
'Une nouvelle zone de jurisdiction: la zone archéologique maritime', *Espaces et ressources maritimes,* No. 4, 1990, pp. 1-26.

Kartashkin, V.,
'Economic, social and cultural rights' in Vasak, K. (ed.), *The International Dimensions of Human Rights,* vol. 1, Greenwood Press, Westport, Connecticut, UNESCO, Paris, 1982.

Kazazis, A.,
'Thefts, donations or sales?', 76 *UNESCO Courier* (1984) p. 91.

Kennedy, W.R.,
Law of Salvage, 5th ed. (British shipping Laws), Stevens & Sons, London, 1985.

Kenny, J.J. & Hrusoff, R.R.,
'The ownership of the treasures of the sea', 9 *Wm. & Mary L. Rev.* (1967) pp. 383-401.

King, M.,
'Admiralty law: evolving legal treatment of property claims to shipwrecks in international waters', 31 *Harvard International Law Journal* (1990) pp. 313-321.

King, J.L.,
'Cultural property and national sovereignty' in Messenger Ph.M. (ed), *The Ethics of Collecting Cultural Property: Whose Culture, Whose Property?*, University of Mexico Press, Albuquerque, 1990, pp. 199-214.

Kinnane, D.,
'Committee urges co-operation in returning art works', *UNESCO Features*, No. 755 (1980) pp. 1-4.

Kiss, A-Ch.,
- 'La notion de patrimoine commune de l'humanité', 175 *Hague Receuil* (1982-I) pp. 99-256.
- 'Conserving the common heritage of mankind', 59 *Revista Juridica de la Universidad de Puerto Rico* (1990) pp. 773-777.

Kluckhohn, C.,
'Cultural anthropology' in Izumi, S. (ed.), *American Study Seminar,* Tokyo, 1954.

Knauss, A.J.,
- 'Development of freedom of scientific research issue of the Third Law of the Sea Conference', 1 *Ocean Dev. & Int'l L.* (1973) pp. 93-120.
- 'Creeping jurisdiction and customary international law', 15 *Ocean Dev. & Int'l L.* (1985) pp. 209-216.

Knudson, S.J.,
Culture in Retrospect. An Introduction to Archaeology, Rand McNally College Publishing Company, Chicago, 1978.

Koenig, R.A.,
'Property rights in recovered sea treasure', 3 *N.U.U.L. Int'l & Comp. L.* (1982) pp. 271-305.

Kolodkin, A.L., Andrianov, V.V. and Kiselev, V.A.,
'Legal implications of participation or non-participation in the 1982 Convention', 12 *Marine Policy* (1988) pp. 187-191.

Korthals Altes, A.,
- *Prijs der Zee,* Raakvlak van Redding, Strandrecht en wrakwetgeving. W.E.J. Tjeenk Willink, Zwolle 1973.
- 'Submarine antiquities and the law', 44 *Annuaire de l'AAA* (1974) pp. 127-141.
- 'Submarine antiquities: a legal labyrinth', 4 *Syracuse J. Int'l L. and Comm.* (1976) pp. 77-96.

Koumantos, G.,
'International legal protection of cultural property: introductory report' in Council of Europe, *International Legal Protection of Cultural Property*, Proceedings of the Thirteenth Colloquy on European Law, Delphi, 20-22 September 1983, Strasbourg, 1984, pp. 12-16.

Ku, Ch.,
'The archipelagic States concept and regional stability in Southeast Asia', 23 *Case W. Res. J. Int'l Law* (1991) pp. 463-478.

Kwiatkowska, B.,
The 200 mile Exclusive Economic Zone in the New Law of the Sea, Martinus Nijhoff Publishers, 1989.

Larschan, B. & Berman, B.C.,
'The common heritage of mankind principle in international law', 21 *Colum. J. Transnat'l L.* (1983) pp. 305-337.

Larsen, D.P.,
'Ownership of historic shipwreck in U.S. law', 9 *The International Journal of Marine and Coastal Law* (1994) pp. 31-56.

Larson, A., Jenks, C. & others,
Sovereignty within the Law. Oceana Publications Inc., Dobbs Ferry, New York, 1965.

Larson, D.L,
'When will the UN Convention on the Law of the Sea come into effect?', 20 *Ocean Dev. & Int'l L.* (1989) pp. 175-202.

Lauterpacht, H.,
· 'Restrictive interpretation and the principle of effectiveness of the interpretation of treaties', 26 *B.Y.I.L.* (1949) pp. 48-85.
· 'Sovereignty over submarine areas' 27 *B.Y.I.L.* (1950) pp. 376-433.

Lawrence, A.,
'State antiquity laws and admiralty salvage: protecting our cultural resources', 32 *U. Miami L. Rev.* (1977) pp. 291-338.

Lazaratos, G.,
'The definition of ship in national and international law', 22/23 *Revue hellenique de droit international* (1969/70) pp. 57-99.

Leach, R.A.,
'Effective enforcement of the law of nations: a proposed international human rights organisation', 15 *Calif. W. Int'l L.J.* (1985) pp. 705-731.

Leanza, U.,
· 'The territorial scope of the Draft European Convention on the Protection of the Underwater Cultural Heritage' in Council of Europe, *International Legal Protection of Cultural Property,* Proceedings of the Thirteenth Colloquy on European Law, Delphi 20-22 September 1983, Strasbourg, 1984, pp. 127-130.
· (ed), *The International Legal Regime of the Mediterranean Sea,* II Università degli Studi di Roma, Pubblicazioni della Facoltà di Giurisprudenza 2, Dott. A. Giuffrè editore, 1987.
· *Nuovi saggi di diritto del mare,* Giappicheli editore, Torino, 1988.

Lee, L.T.,
'The Law of the Sea Convention and third States', 77 *A.J.I.L.* (1983) pp. 541-568.

Lentsch (de Vries), P.,
'The right of overflight over strait States and archipelagic States: developments and prospects', 14 *N.Y.I.L.* (1983) pp. 165-225.

Leo (de), G.,
'Appunti sul ritrovamento in alto mare di cose di interesse artistico o storico', *Diritto e giurisprudenza* (1965) pp. 263-265.

Leuprecht, P.,
'Which human rights?..."a distressing spectacle of cynicism and hypocrisy."', *Forum (Council of Europe)* 1984, No. 2, pp. 5-6.

Leyendecker, R.S.,
'Une organisation internationale pour la sauvegarde et la récuperation des oeuvres d'art', 44 *Annuaire de l'AAA* (1974) pp. 89-95.

Lillington, S.D.,
'Wreck or wrecuum maris? The Lusitania', *Lloyd's Maritime and Commercial Law Quartely* (1987) pp. 267-273.

Lindsay, M.F.,
'The recovery of cultural artifacts: the legacy of our archaeological heritage', 22 *Case W. Res. J. Int'l Law* (1990) pp. 165-82.

Lindbloom, S.J.,
'Historic shipwreck legislation: rescuing the Titanic from the law of the sea', 13 *Journal of Legislation* (1986) pp. 92-111.

Lipka, L.J.,
'Abandoned property at sea: who owns the salvage 'finds'?', 12 *Wm. & Mary L. Rev.* (1970) pp. 97-110.

Lohrey, T.E.,
'Sunken vessels, their cargoes and the casual salvor', 20 *JAG Journal* (1964) pp. 25-29.

Lo Monaco, A.,
'Sulla restituzione di beni culturali rubati all'estero secondo la convenzione dell'UNESCO', 71 *Rivista di diritto internazionale* (1988) pp. 842-855.

Lorenzo, J.L.,
Approaches to the Archaeological Heritage. A Comparative Study of World Cultural Management Systems (edited by Henry Cleere), Cambridge University Press.

Lowe, A.V.,
· 'The right of entry into maritime ports in international law', 14 *San Diego L. Rev.* (1977) pp. 597-622.
· 'The development of the concept of the contiguous zone', 52 *B.Y.I.L.* (1981) pp. 109-169.

Lucchini, L., Voekkel, M.,
· *Les états et la mer: le nationalisme maritime,* Notes et études documentaires, la documentation française, Paris, 1977.
· *Droit de le mer*, Pedone A. éditions, 1990.

Luksic, B.,
'Limitation of liability for the raising and removal of ships and wrecks: a comparative survey', 12 *J. Mar. Law & Com.* (1981) pp. 50-64.

Lumb, R.D.,
'The Law of wrecks in Australia: Robinson v. the Western Australian Museum', 52 *Australian L.J.* (1978) pp. 198-207.

Lund, C.,
· 'Report on protection of the underwater cultural heritage - the rules of UN Law of the Sea Protection' in Council of Europe, Parliamentary Assembly, *Parliamentary*

Conference on the UN Convention on the Law of the Sea, Palermo, 2-4 November 1983, AS/JUR/MAR/CONF.35(7) pp. 1-10.
- 'Patrimoine culturel subaquatique', 12 *Jus Gentium* (1985) pp. 60-74.
- 'Protection of the under-water heritage', in Leanza, U. (ed), *The International Legal Reime of the Mediterranean Sea,* Dott.A. Giuffrè editore, 1987, pp. 351-353.
- 'Beskyttelse af historiske skibsvrag og fortidsminder pa den danske havbund', Fortidsminder og kulturhistorie, National Forestry and Nature Agency, Copenhagen 1987, pp. 135-150.

Mangone, G.J.,
'Straits used for international navigation', 18 *Ocean Dev. & Int. L.* (1987) pp. 391-409.

Martini, G.,
'Ritrovamenti in mare di relitti e di cose di interesse artistico o storico', 64 *Il diritto marittimo* (1964) pp. 284-319.

Masterson, W.E.,
Jurisdiction in Marginal Seas. Kennikat Press, Port Washington, New York, London 1929.

Matysik, S.,
'Legal problems of recovery of historical treasures from the sea-bed' in Frankowska, M. (ed.), *Scientific and Technological Revolution and the Law of the Sea,* Warsawa, Ossolineum, 1974, pp. 141-153.

M'Bow, A-M.,
'Plea for the return of an irreplaceable cultural heritage to those who created it', 31 *Museum* (1979) p. 58.

MacRae, L.,
'Customary international law and the United Nations of the Law of the Sea Treaty', 13 *Cal. W. Int'l L.J.* (1983) pp. 181-222.

Marston, G.,
'The evolution of the concept of sovereignty over the bed and the subsoil of the territorial sea', 48 *B.Y.I.L.* (1976/77) pp. 321-332.

Marx, R.,
'Legislation in U.S.A.' in *Papers from the First Southern Hemisphere Conference on Maritime Archaeology,* Australian Sports Publications 1978, pp. 8-15.

Mason, H.,
'Salvaging a sense of values' *Sunday Times,* 2 August 1987, p. 39, cols. 3-7.

McDonald, B.,
'Admiralty - abandoned property on outer continental shelf', 4 *Fla. L. Rev.* (1976) pp. 561-568.

McDougal, M.A. & Burke, W.T.,
The Public Order of the Oceans. A Contemporary Law of the Sea, Yale University Press, New Haven/London 1962.

McKinlay, J.R.,

'The New Zealand Historic Places Trust and the laws concerning marine archaeology in New Zealand' in *Papers from the First Southern Hemisphere Conference on Maritime Archaeology,* Australian Sports Publications, 1978, pp. 20-23.

McWilliams, D.L.,

'Salvage of ancient treasure ships', *Lloyd's Maritime and Commercial Law Quarterly* (1986) pp. 16-21.

Meenan, J.K.,

'Cultural resources preservation and underwater archaeology - some notes on the current legal framework and a model underwater antiquities statute', 15 *San Diego L. Rev.* (1978) pp. 623-662.

Melikan, R.,

'Shippers, salvors and sovereigns: competing interests in the Medieval law of shipwreck', 11 *The Journal of Legal History* (1990) pp. 163-182.

Mendelson, M.H.,

'Fragmentation of the law of the sea', 12 *Marine Policy* (1988) pp. 193-200.

Mensbrugghe, Y. (van der),

'Réflexions sur la définition du navire dans le droit de la mer' in Société française pour le droit de la mer, *Actualités du droit de la mer,* Pedone A. éditions, Paris, 1973, pp. 62-75.

Menzler, E.,

'Scientific research on the seabed and its regime' in Sztucki, J. (ed.), *Regime of the Seabed - Proceedings.* Academia Nazionale dei Linzi, Rome, 1970, pp. 619-647.

Merryman, J.H. Elsen, A.E.,

'Hot art: a re-examination of the illegal international trade in cultural objects', 12(3) *J. Arts. Mgmt. & L.* (1982) pp. 5-31.

Merryman, J.H.,

· 'The protection of partimony' in Duboff, L.D. (ed), *Art Law: Domestic and International,* F.B. Rothman & Co, 1975, pp. 255-261.

· 'International art law: from cultural nationalism to a common cultural heritage', 15 *N.Y.U.J. Int'l L. & Pol.* (1983) pp. 771-787.

· 'Thinking about the Elgin marbles', 83 *Mich. L. Rev.* (1985) pp. 1881-1923.

· 'The retention of cultural property', 21 *University of California Davis Law Review* (1988) pp. 477-513.

· 'The public interest in cultural policy', 77 *California Law Review* (1989) pp. 339-364.

· 'Protection of cultural "heritage?"', 38 *American Journal of Comparative Law* (1990) p. 513.

· 'The nation and the object', 3 *International Journal of Cultural Property* (1994) pp. 61-76.

Messenger, Ph.M. (ed.),

The Ethics of Collecting Cultural Property: Whose Culture, Whose Property?, University of New Mexico Press, Albuquerque, 1990.

Meyer, K.E.,

The Plundered Past, Atheneum, New York 1973.

Michael, M.D.,

The Archaeological and the Historical Objects of the Continental Shelf. International Law and the Aegean. Saccoulas Publishing Co., 1983 (in Greek).

Migliorino, L.,

· 'Submarine antiquities and the law of the sea', 4(4) *Marine Policy Reports* (1982) pp. 1-5.

· *Il recupero degli oggetti storici ed archeologici sommersi nel diritto internazionale.* Studi e documenti sul diritto internazionale del mare 15, Dott. Giuffrè, A., editore, Milano, 1984.

· 'The recovery of sunken warships in international law' on Vukas, B. (ed), *Essays on the New Law of the Sea*, Zagreb, Svencilisna naklada Liber, 1985, pp. 244-258.

· 'La protezione *in situ* del patrimonio culturale subacqueo'. Paper presented at the *Seminari: La protezione del patrimonio culturale subacqueo nel Meditteraneo,* organised by the Università degli Studi di roma 'Tor Vergata', Anacapri, 1 October 1994.

Miles, E.L.

Preparing for UNCLOS IV?, Special Report, Council on Ocean Law, June 1988.

Miller, E.M.,

'A time for decision on submerged cultural resources', 31 *Oceanus*, Nov. 1988, pp. 25-34.

Miller, H.C.,

International Law and Marine Archaeology. Academy of Applied Sciences, Belmont, Massachusetts, 1973.

Momtaz, D.,

'The High Seas' in Dupuy, R.-J. & Vignes, D. (eds), *A Handbook on the New Law of the Sea*, vol. 1, Hague Academy of International Law, Martinus Nijhoff, 1991, pp. 383-422.

Monden, A. & Wils, G.,

'Art objects as common heritage of mankind', XIX *Revue belge de droit international* (1986) pp. 327-338.

Monreal, L.,

'Problems and possibilities in recovering dispersed cultural heritages', 31 *Museum* (1979) pp. 47-57.

Moore, J.S.,

'Enforcing foreign ownership claims in the antiquities market', 97 *The Yale Law Journal* (1988) pp. 466-487.

Morris, R.A.,

'Legal and ethical issues in the trade in cultural property', *The New Zealand Law Journal* (1990) pp. 40-42.

Moulefera, T.,

'Algeria', 31 *Museum* (1979) pp. 10-11.

Moustakas, J.,
  'Group rights in cultural property: justifying strict inalienability', 74 *Cornell Law Review* (1989) pp. 1179-1227.
Mshrenieradze, V.,
  'Cultural interaction as a factor influencing cultural rights as human rights' in UNES-CO, *Cultural rights as human rights,* Studies and documents on cultural policies, 1970, pp. 42-45.
Münch, (von) I.,
  'Schiffwracks - Völkerrechtliche Probleme', 20 *Archiv des Völkerrechts* (1982) pp. 183-198.
Museum,
  · *Museum and the thefts of art* (Vol. XXXVI, No. 1) 1974 (special issue).
  · *Return and Restitution of Cultural Property,* Vol. 31, 1979 (special issue).
Nandan, S.N., Anderson, D.H.,
  'Straits used for international navigation: a commentary on Part III of the United Nations Convention on the Law of the Sea', 60 *B.Y.I.L.* (1989) pp. 159-204.
Nash, M.L.,
  · 'The law of treasure and treasure hunters', 128 *New L.J.* (1978) pp. 1163-1166.
  · 'The Lusitania and its consequences', 136 *New L.J.* (1986) pp. 317-319.
Nafziger, J.A.R.,
  · 'Regulation by the International Council of Museums: an example of the role of non-governmental organisations in the transnational legal process', 2 *Denv. J. Int'l L.* (1972) pp. 231-253.
  · 'I like it, but is it international law?' in Duboff, L.D. (ed), *Art Law: Domestic and International,* F.B. Rothman & Co, 1975, pp. 309-314.
  · 'UNESCO-centred management of international conflict over cultural property', 27 *Hastings L.J.* (1976) pp. 1051-1067.
  · 'Legal protection of America's archaeological heritage', 22 *Arizona L. Rev.* (1980) p. 675.
  · 'Comments on the relevance of law and culture to cultural property law', 10 *Syracuse J. Int'l L. & Com.* (1983) pp. 323-331.
  · 'The new international legal framework for the return, restitution or forfeiture of cultural property', 15 *N.Y.U. J. Int'l L. & Pol.* (1985) pp. 789-812.
  · 'International penal aspects of protecting cultural property', 19 *The International Lawyer* (1985) pp. 835-852.
  · 'Protection of cultural property', 17 *Calif. W. Int'l L. J.* (1987) pp. 283-289.
  · 'Finding the Titanic: beginning an international salvage of derelict law at sea', 12 *Columbia - VLA Journal of Law & the Arts* (1988) pp. 339-351.
  · 'Repose legislation: a threat to the protection of the world's cultural heritage', 17 *Calif. W. Int'l L. J.* (1987) pp. 250-265.
  · 'Protection of the Archaeological Heritage under the United States Constitution'. Paper presented at the *Athens Conference on the Protection of the Archaeological*

Heritage, Institute of Hellenic Constitutional History and Constitutional Law, November 26-27, 1992.

Nahlik, S.E.,
- 'On some deficiencies of the Hague Convention of 1954 on the Protection of Cultural Property in the Event of Armed Conflict', 44 *Annuaire de l'AAA* (1974) pp. 100-108.
- 'International law and the protection of cultural property in armed conflicts', 27 *Hastings L.J.* (1975/76) pp. 1069-1087.
- 'L'interêt de l'humanité à protéger son patrimoine culturel', 37/38 *Annuaire de l'AAA* (1967/68) pp. 156-165.
- 'Book review: The Proper Country of the Work of Art. International Protection of the Integrity of the National Cultural heritage, by Niec, H.' (in Polish). XI *P.Y.I.L.* (1981/82) pp. 258-261.
- 'International co-operation to prevent illicit traffic of cultural property', 51/52/53 *Annuaire de l'AAA* (1981/82/83) pp. 73-81.

Nanda, V.P.,
'Introduction - the right to development under international law: challenges ahead', 15 *Calif. W. Int'l L. J.* (1985) pp. 431-440.

Nandan, S.N., Rosenne, S. and Crandy, N.R. (eds),
United Nations Convention on the Law of the Sea - A Commentary, vol. II, Center for Oceans Law and Policy, University of Virginia, Martinus Nijhoff, 1993.

N'Daw, A.,
- 'Universal culture and national cultures' in UNESCO, *Cultural Rights as Human Rights.* Studies and documents on cultural policies, UNESCO 1970, pp. 28-30.
- *et al.,* 'Towards a definition of culture - Discussion' in UNESCO, *Cultural rights as human rights.* Studies and documents on cultural policies, UNESCO 1970 pp. 15-23.

Nelson, R.H.,
'Guiding the ocean search process: applying public land experience to the design of leasing and permitting systems for ocean mining and ocean shipwrecks', 20 *Ocean Dev. & Int'l L.* (1989) pp. 577-600.

Neilson, W.L.,
'The 1989 International Convention on Salvage', 24 *Connecticut Law Review* (1992) pp. 1203-1252.

Negreponte, J.D.,
'Who will protect freedom of the seas?', 86 *Department of State Bulletin* (1986) No. 2115, pp. 41-43.

Niec, H.,
- 'Human right to culture', 44 *Annuaire de l'AAA* (1974) pp. 109-115.
- 'Legislative models of protection of cultural property', 27 *Hastings L.J.* (1976) pp. 1089-1122.

Nieciowna, H.,
  'Sovereign rights to cultural property', 4 *Polish Yearbook of International Law* (1971)
  pp. 239-253.
Nonnenmacher, G.G.,
  'De la protection internationale du patrimoine culturel', 44 *Annuaire de l'AAA* (1974)
  pp. 142-148.
Norris, M.J.,
  · 'Misconduct of salvors', 18 *Brooklyn L. Rev.* (1952) pp. 247-262.
  · *The Law of Salvage,* Baker, Voorhis & Co., Mount Kisco, New York, 1958.
Northey, L.D.,
  'The Archaeological Resources Protection Act of 1979: protecting prehistory for the
  future', 6 *Harvard Environmental Law Review* (1982) pp. 61-115.
O'Connel, D.P.,
  The International Law of the Sea. Clarendon Press, Oxford, vol. I (1982), vol. II
  (1984).
Oda, S.,
  · 'The concept of the contiguous zone', 11 *Int'l & Comp. L.Q.* (1962) pp. 131-153.
  · *The Law of the Sea in our Time - I. New Developments 1966-1975.* Sijthoff
  Publications on Ocean Development vol. 3, Leyden, 1977.
  · *The Law of the Sea in our Time - II. The United Nations Seabed Committee, 1968-
  1973.* Sijthoff Publications on Ocean Development, vol. 4, Leyden, 1977.
O'Keefe, P.J.,
  · 'Maritime archaeology and salvage laws - some comments following Robinson v.
  The Western Australia Museum', 7 *I.J.N.A.* (1978) pp. 3-7.
  · 'International developments in legislation regulating maritime archaeology' in
  Jeffery, W. and Amess, J. (eds.), *Proceedings of the Second Southern Hemisphere
  Conference on Maritime Archaeology.* Published by the South Australian Department
  of Environment and Planning and the Commonwealth, 1983, pp. 175-181.
  · 'Export and import controls on movement of the cultural heritage: problems at the
  national level', 10 *Syracuse J. Int'l L. & Com.* 91983) pp. 352-370.
  · 'The law and nautical archaeology: an international survey' in Langley, S.B.M.
  & Unger, R.W. (eds.), *Nautical Archaeology: Progress and Public Responsibility.*
  BAR International Series No. 220, 1984, pp.9-17.
  · 'The International Law Association Draft Convention on the Protection of the
  Underwater Cultural Heritage', paper presented at a seminar on the underwater
  cultural heritage organised by the Italian Association of ex-Parliamentarians and
  the European University, 25 May 1993.
O'Keefe, P.J. & Prott, L.V.,
  · 'Australian protection of historic shipwrecks', 6 *A.Y.B.I.L.* (1978) pp. 119-138.
  · *Existing Legislative Protection of the Cultural and Natural Heritage of the Pacific
  Region,* UNESCO, Doc. CLT/82/WS-35 (1982).
  · 'Cultural Property', 9 *E.P.I.L.* (1986) pp. 62-64.

· *Protection of the Cultural Heritage within the Commonwealth: Consultative Document.*

Owen, D.R.,

·   'Some legal troubles with treasure: jurisdiction and salvage', 16 *Mar. Law & Com.* (1985) pp. 139-179.

·   'The Abandoned Shipwreck Act of 1987: good-bye to salvage in the territorial sea', 19 *J. Mar. Law & Com.* (1988) pp. 499-516.

Oxman, B.H.,

·   'The Third United Nations Conference on the Law of the Sea: The Ninth Session (1980)', 75 *A.J.I.L.* (1981) pp. 211-256.

·   'Marine archaeology and the international law of the sea', 12 *Columbia - VLA Journal of Law & the Arts* (1988) pp. 353-372.

Paczensly (von), G.,

'Cultural riches from the third world treasure which do not belong to us', *Art* No. 4, April 1981.

Paizis, D.,

'Problems related to the existing legislation on antiquities', *Penal Annals* (1968) pp. 315-210 (in Greek).

Palmer, N.E.,

'Treasure trove and the protection of antiquities', 44 *Mod. L. Rev.* (1981) pp. 178-187.

Papadakis, N.,

The International Legal Regime of Artificial Islands. Sijthoff, Leyden, 1977.

Papathanasopoulos, G.,

'Information memorandum on the protection, excavation and study of the underwater heritage in Greece. Measures exposed for the protection of the underwater cultural heritage (2 March 1978)' in Council of Europe, Parliamentary Assembly. *The Underwater Cultural heritage.* Report of the Committee on Culture and Education (Rapporteur Mr. John Roper), Strasbourg, 1978, pp. 152-157.

Passalacqua (de), J.L.A.,

·   'Propriedad del partimonio cultural sumergido bajo las aguas territoriales del Estado Libre Asociado de Puerto Rico', 21 *Revista Juridica de la Universidad Interamericana de Puerto Rico* (1987) pp. 597-604.

·   'Delito cultural: el partimonio cultural y la arqueologia subaquatica', 60 *Revista Juridica de la Universidad de Puerto Rico* (1991) pp 1231-1253.

Pazarci, H.,

·   'Sur la recherche archéologique subaquatique en Mediterranée' in Leanza, U. (ed), *The International Regal Regime of the Mediterranean Sea,* Dott.A. Giuffrè editore, 1987, pp. 359-366.

·   'Le concept de zone contiguë dans la convention sur le droit de la mer', XVIII *Revue belge de droit international* (1984/85) pp. 249-271

Pearson, C.,

'Legislation for the protection of shipwrecks in Western Australia', 5 *I.J.N.A.* (1976), pp. 171-180.

Pecoraro, Th.W.,
'Choice of law in litigation to recover national cultural property: efforts at harmonisation in private international law', 31 *V.J.I.L.* (1990) pp. 1-51.

Perisic, Z.,
'Common heritage of mankind in the United Nations Convention on the Law of the Sea' in Vukas, B. (ed.), *Essays on the New Law of the Sea*, Zagreb, 1985, pp. 289-300.

Perrakis, S.E.,
'The right to enjoyment of the common heritage of mankind as a solidarity right', *Legal Studies*, vol. 3, University of Thrace, Saccoulas Publishing Co., 1982, pp. 164-184 (in Greek).

Perry, R.M.,
'Sovereign rights in sunken treasures', *Land and Natural Resources Division Journal* (1969) pp. 89-113.

Phelan, M.,
'A synopsis of the laws protecting our cultural heritage', 28 *New England Law Review* (1993) pp. 63-108.

Philippaki, B.,
'Greece', 31 *Museum* 1979, pp. 15-17.

Pinto, M.C.W.,
'Emerging concepts of the law of the sea: some social and cultural aspects', 3/4 UNESCO *Impact of Science and technology* (1984) pp. 335-345 (Special issue on 'research, international law and the sea in man's future').

Post, H.H.G.,
'The protection of archaeological property and community law: framework and new developments'. Paper presented at the *Athens Conference on the Protection of the Archaeological Heritage*, Institute of Hellenic Constitutional History and Constitutional Law, November 26-27, 1992.

Potter, B.,
The Freedom of the Seas. London, 1924.

Poulantzas, N.,
The Right of Hot Pursuit in International Law, Sijthoff, Leyden, 1969.

Prisbe, J.T.,
'Law determining ownership of shipwreck in the United States: Klein v. Unidentified and Abandoned Sailing Vessel', *Lloyd's Maritime & Commercial Law Quartely* (1987) pp. 24-29.

Prott, L.V.,
· 'International penal aspects of cultural protection law', 7 *Criminal Law Journal* (1983) pp. 207-217.
· 'International control of illicit movement of the cultural heritage: the 1970 UNESCO Convention and some possible alternatives', 10 *Syracuse J. Int. L. & Com.* (1983) pp. 333-351.
· 'Problems of private international law for the protection of the cultural heritage', *Hague Recueil* (1989-V) pp. 215-317.

· 'The preliminary draft UNIDROIT Convention on stolen or illegally exported cultural objects', 41 *Int'l & Comp. L.Q.* (1992) pp. 160-170.

· 'Cultural rights as people's rights in international law' in Crawford, J. (ed), *The Rights of Peoples,* Clarendon Press, 1988, pp. 93-106.

· 'The definition of the archaeological heritage'. Paper presented at the *Athens Conference on the Protection of the Archaeological Heritage,* organised by the Institute of Hellenic Constitutional History and Constitutional Law, 26-27 November 1992.

Prott, L.V. & O'Keefe, P.J.,

· 'Final report on the legal protection of the underwater heritage' in Council of Europe, Parliamentary Assembly, *The Underwater Cultural Heritage,* Report of the Committee on Culture and Education (Rapporteur Mr. John Roper), Doc. 4200-E, Strasbourg, 1978 pp. 45-90.

· 'Analysis of legislation in individual countries' in Council of Europe, Parliamentary Assembly, *The Underwater Cultural Heritage,* Strasbourg, 1978, pp. 91-135.

· 'International legal protection of the underwater cultural heritage', 14 *Revue belge de droit international* (1978/1979) pp. 85-102.

· 'Law and the underwater heritage' in UNESCO, *Protection of the underwater heritage.* Protection of the cultural heritage. Technical handbooks for museums and monuments, 4, 1981 pp. 165-200.

· *'National Legal Control of Illicit Traffic in Cultural Property'.* A Report commissioned by UNESCO and discussed at a Consultation of Experts on Illicit Traffic, Paris, 1-4 March 1983. UNESCO, Doc. CLT/83/WS.16.

· *Law and the Cultural Heritage,* vol. 1, *Discovery and Excavation,* Professional Books Ltd., Abingdon, 1984.

· *Handbook of National Regulations concerning the Export of Cultural Property,* UNESCO, 1988.

· 'Maritime Archaeology', 11 *E.P.I.L.* (1989) pp. 210-212.

· *Law and the Cultural Heritage,* vol. 3, *Movement,* Butterworths, 1989.

· '"Cultural heritage" or "cultural property"?', 1 *International Journal of Cultural Property* (1992) pp. 307-320.

Punty, A.P.,

'Towards establishing an international tribunal for the settlement of cultural property disputes: how to keep Greece from losing its marbles', 72 *The Ceorgetown Law Journal* (1984) pp. 115-82.

Putnam, J.E.,

'Common markets and cultural identity: cultural property export restrictions in the European Community', *University of Chicago Legal Forum* (1992) pp. 457-476.

Quéneudec, J.-P.,

'Chronique du droit de la mer', 23 *Annuaires français du droit international* (1977) pp. 730-744.

Quinby, C. & Owen, D.R.,
 'Recent amendments to the US Wreck Removal Act', *Lloyd's Maritime and Commercial Law Quartely* (1989) pp. 15-20.
Ramakrishna, K.,
 'International issues', 30 *Oceanus*, No. 2, Summer 1987, pp. 16-19.
Rambaud, P.,
 'International law and municipal law', 10 *E.P.I.L.* (1987) pp. 238-262.
Ramcharan, B.G. (ed),
 Human Rights - Thirty Years After the Universal Declaration. Commemorative Volume on the Thirtieth Anniversary of the Universal Declaration of Human Rights, Martinus Nijhoff, 1979.
Rao, P.C.,
 · *The Public Order of Ocean Resources: A Critique of the Contemporary Law of the Sea.* The MIT Press, Massachussetts, 1975.
 · *The New Law of Maritime Zones*, Milind Publications Private Limited, New Delhi, 1983.
Read, B.,
 'Open season on ancient shipwrecks: implications of the treasure salvors decisions in the fields of archaeology, history, and property law', 4 *Nova Law Journal* (1980) p. 213.
Reat, D.J.,
 'The Elevent Amendment surfaces in Florida: Dept. of State v. Treasure Salvors, Inc.', 12 *Houston Journal of International Law* (1989) pp. 143-158.
Redfield, M.,
 'The legal framework for oceanic research' in Wooster, W.S. (ed.), *Freedom of Oceanic Research,* Crane Russak & Company Inc., New York 1973.
Reeves, J.S.,
 'The codification of the law of territorial waters', 24 *A.J.I.L.* (1930) pp. 486-499.
Reich, R.V.,
 'The right to development as an emerging human right', 23 *V.J.I.L.* (1983) pp. 287-328.
Reichelt, G.,
 · 'International protection of cultural property', *Uniform Law Review* (1985-I) pp. 43-153.
 · 'International protection of cultural property (second study)', *Uniform Law Review* (1988-I) pp. 53-131.
Reiley, E.H.,
 'The common heritage of mankind', 5 *California Lawyer* (1985) pp. 15-18.
Ress, G.,
 'Die Bergung kriegsversenkter Schiffe im Lichte der Rechtslage Deutschands. Bemerkungen zum einen Urteil des High Court von Singapur vom 24 Oktober 1974', 35 *ZaöRV* (1975) pp. 364-374.

Revelle, R.,
'Scientific research on the seabed. International co-operation in scientific research and exploration of the seabed' in Sztucki, J. (ed.), *Symposium on the International Regime of the Seabed - Proceedings.* Academia Nazionale dei Linzei, Rome 1970, pp. 649-663.

Riess, W.C.,
'Cultural resources on the northeast continental shelf' in Cockrell, W.A. (ed.), *In the Realms of Gold: The Proceedings of the Tenth Conference and Underwater Archaeology*, Fathom Eight Special Publication, No. 1, 1981.

Rigaux, F.,
'The Algiers Declaration of the Rights of Peoples' in Caseese, A. (ed.), *UN Law/ Fundamental Rights. Two Topics in International Law.* Sijthoff & Noordhoff, Alpen aan den Rijn, 1979, pp. 211-223.

Rigo, A.,
'Book review: International Law and Marine Archaeology by Miller, H.C.', 5 *J. Mar. L. & Com.* (1973) pp. 141-142.

Riphagen, W.,
'Some reflections on 'functional sovereignty'', 6 *N.Y.I.L.* (1975) pp. 121-165.

Roberts, E.L.,
'Cultural policy in the European Community: a case against extensive national retention', 28 *Texas Int'l L. J.* (1993) pp. 191-228.

Rodière, R.G.,
La mer. Droit des hommes ou proie des états, Paris, 1980.

Rodotà, S.,
'The civil law aspects of the international protection of cultural property' in Council of Europe, *International Protection of Cultural Property,* Proceedings of the Thirteenth Colloguy on European Law, Delphi, 20-22 September 1983, Strasbourg, 1984, pp. 99-111.

Ronzitti, N.,
'Stato costiero archeologica sottomarina e tutela del patrimonio storico sommerso', 86 *Il diritto marittimo* (1984) pp. 3-24.

Rosenberg, R.H.,
'Federal protection for archaeological resources', 22 *Arizona L. Rev.* (1980) pp. 701-735.

Rosenne, S. and Sohn, L.B. (eds),
United Nations Convention on the Law of the Sea - A Commentary, vol. V, Center for Oceans Law and Policy, University of Virginia, Martinus Nijhoff, 1989.

Roucounas, E.,
· 'Cultural treasures on the seabed', 23 *Review of Public and Administrative Law* (1979) pp. 10-37 (in Greek).
· 'Laws protecting underwater finds', 8 *Archaeology,* August 1983, pp. 8-15 (in Greek).

· 'General Report' in Council of Europe, *International Legal Protection of Cultural Property,* Strasbourg, 1984 pp. 136-147.
· 'Submarine archaeological research: some legal aspects' in Leanza, U. (ed.), *The International Legal Regime of the Mediterranean Sea,* II Università degli Studi di Roma, Pubblicazioni della Facoltà di Giurisprudenze 2, Dott. A. Giuffrè editore, Milano, 1987, pp. 309-334.

Rousseau, C.,
'Chronique des faits internationaux', 91 *R.G.D.I.P.* (1987) pp. 915-983.

Rubin, A.P.,
'Sunken soviet submarines and central intelligence: laws of property and the agency', 69 *A.J.I.L.* (1975) pp. 855-858.

Rozakis, C.L.,
The Law of the Sea as Developed through the Claims of Coastal States. Papazisis Publishing Co., Athens, 1976 (in Greek).

Rozakis, C.L. & Stephanou, C.A. (eds),
The New Law of the Sea. Selected and Edited Papers of the Athens Colloquium on the Law of the Sea, September 1982, North Holland, Amsterdam, 1983.

Runyan, T.J.,
'Shipwreck legislation and the preservation of submerged artifacts', 22 *Case W. Res. J. Int'l L.* (1990) pp. 31-45.

Ryan, P.,
'Legislation on historic wreck' in *Papers from the First Southern Hemisphere Conference on Maritime Archaeology,* Australian Sports Publications, 1978, pp. 23-33.

Sanson, H.,
'Du droit des peuples sous-développes au développement au droit des hommes et des communautes à être soi, ma non seulement pa soi, mais aussi par les autres' in Dupuy, R.-J. (ed.), *The Right to Development at the International Level,* Hague Academy of International Law, 1979, pp. 192-203.

Scheepers, G.P.J.,
'South African law of shipwrecks: contemporary and international law perspectives', 10 *Sea Changes* (1989) pp. 41-66.

Schreuer, Ch.,
'International law in municipal law: law and decisions of international organisations and courts', 10 *E.P.I.L.* (1987) pp. 262-268.

Schulze, D.,
Die Restitution von Kunstwerken - Zur Völkerrechtichen Dimension der Restitutionsresolutionen der Generalversammlung der Vereinten Nationen, Reihe D, Bd 12, Bremen, 1983 (Im Selbstverlag des Museums).

Schutter (de), B.,
'The harmonisation of criminal law and international criminal co-operation as instruments of protection' in Council of Europe, *International Protection of Cultural Property*, Strasbourg, 1984, pp. 72-98.

Schwarzenberger, I.G.,
- *International Law*, 1957, Stevens & Sons, London, vol. I, 3rd ed.
- *A Manual of International Law*, 6th ed., Professional Books Ltd., Abingdon, 1976.

Seabrook, J.B.,
'Legal approaches to the trade in stolen antiquities', 2 *Syracuse J. Int'l L. & Com.* (1974) pp. 51-66.

Seanor, D.,
'The case with Midas touch', 76 *ABA Journal* (1990) pp. 50-55.

Seferiades, S.,
'La question du rapatriement des 'Marbres d'Elgin' considerée plus specialment au point de vue du Droit de Gens' X *Revue de droit international* (1932) pp. 52-81.

Seidl-Hohenveldern, I.,
- 'Artefacts as national cultural heritage and as a common heritage of mankind' in Bello, E.G. & Prince Bola, A., Ajibolo, *Essays in Honour of Judge T.O. Elias,* Dordrecht, 1992, pp. 163-168.
- 'La protection internationale du partimoine culturel national', 97 *R.G.D.I.P.* (1993) pp. 395-409.

Shallcross, D.B. & Giesecke, A.G.,
'Recent developments in litigation concerning the recovery of historic shipwrecks', 10 *Syracuse J. Int'l L. and Com.* (1983) pp. 371-404.

Shaw, T.,
'Whose heritage?', 149 *Museum* (1986) p. 46.

Shelton, D.,
'A response to Donnelly and Alston', 15 *Calif. W. Int'l L.J.* (1985) pp. 524-527.

Shore, H.H.,
'Marine archaeology and international law: background and some suggestions', 9 *San Diego L. Rev.* (1972) pp. 668-700.

Sico, L.,
'Le norme internazionali e comunitarie concernenti l'illecita rimozione dei beni culturali rinvenuti sul fondo marino'. Paper presented at the *Seminario: La protezione del patrimonio culturale subacqueo nel Mediterraneo,* organised by the Università degli Studi di Roma 'Tor Vergata', Anacapri, 1 October 1994.

Silva (de), P.H.D.H.
'Sri Lanka', 31 *Museum* (1979) pp. 22-24.

Simmonds, K.R.,
- 'The law of the sea: Restatement (Third) and the UN Convention on the Law of the Sea', 24 *International Lawyer* (1990) pp. 931-956.
- 'The Law of the Sea', 24 *The International Lawyer* (1990) pp. 930-956.

Skrk, M.,
'The 1987 Law of Yugoslavia on the coastal sea and the continental shelf', 20 *Ocean Dev. & Int. L.* (1989) pp. 501-514

Smith, H.A.,

  The Law and the Custom of the Sea. 3rd ed., Number 9, The Library of World Affairs, Stevens & Sons Ltd., London, 1959.

Smith, R.W.

  Exclusive Economic Zone Claims: An Analysis and Primary Documents, Martinus Nijhoff Publishers, 1986.

Solf, W.A.,

  'Cultural Property, Protection in Armed Conflict', 9 *E.P.I.L.* (1986) pp. 64-68.

Soons, A.H.A.,

  Marine Scientific Research and the Law of the Sea, T.M.C. Asser Institute - The Hague, Kluwer Law and Taxation Publishers, 1982.

Sørensen, M.,

  Manual of Public International Law. The Macmillan Press, London and Basingstoke, 1968.

Spencer, T.C.,

  'International economic justice as a right of mankind', 37/38 *Annuaire de l' AAA* (1967/68) pp. 166-175.

Starkle, G.,

  'Les épaves de navires en haute mer et le droit international: le cas de "Mont-Louis"', 18 *Revue belge de droit international* (1984/85) pp. 496-528.

Stetié, S.,

  'The Intergovernmental Committee mechanisms for a new dialogue', *Museum* (vol. XXXIII, No. 2) 1981, pp. 116-117.

Stevens, T.T.,

  'The Abandoned Shipwreck Act of 1987: finding the proper ballast for the States', 37 *Villanova Law Review* (1992) pp. 573-617.

Stocker, W.,

  Das Prinzip des 'Common Heritage of Mankind' als Ausdruck des Staatengemein-schaftsinteresses im Völkerrecht, Schweizer Studien zum Internazionalen Recht, Band 81, Schulthess Polygraphischer Verlag, Zürich, 1993

Strahl, R.,

  'The retention and retrieval of art and antiquities through international and national means: the tug of war of cultural property', 5 *Brooklyn J. Int'l L.* (1979) pp. 103-128.

Strati, A.,

  · 'Deep seabed cultural property and the common heritage of mankind', 40 *Int'l & Comp. L.Q.* (1991), pp. 859-894.

  · 'The right to the common heritage of mankind: cultural dimension', in Perrakis, S.E. (sous la direction de), *Les droit des peuples et des minorités: une problematique en mutation,* Sakkoulas, 1993, pp. 145-165 (in Greek).

Sutcliffe, R.,

  'Formal submission of the Council for Nautical Archaeology' in Council of Europe, Parliamentary Assembly, *The Underwater Cultural Heritage.* Report of the Committee on Culture and Education (Rapporteur Mr. John Roper) Doc. 4200-E, Strasbourg, 1978, pp. 178-182.

Syatauw, J.J.G.,
'The protection of cultural heritage: a heritage of colonial expansion', 44 *Annuaire de l'AAA* (1974) pp. 34-44.

Symonides, J.,
- 'Contiguous Zone', 16 *P.Y.I.L.* (1987) pp. 143-154.
- 'Origin and Essence of the Contiguous Zone', 20 *Ocean Dev. & Int'l L.* (1989) pp. 203-211.

Symposium,
- 'Legal protection of America's archaeological heritage', 22 *Arizona L. Rev.* (1980) p. 675.
- *Lost Heritage - The Question of the Return of Cultural Property.* Report on the Symposium held in London in 1981. The Commonwealth Arts Association, London 1981.
- 'Jurisdictional issues in the international movement of cultural property', 10 *Syracuse J. Int'l L. & Com.* (1983) p. 281.
- 'International art law', 15 *N.V.U.J. Int'l L. & Pol.* (1983) p. 757.
- 'Development as an emerging human right' 15 *Calif. W. Int'l L.J.* (1985) p. 429.
- 'The best in State historic shipwreck programs' in Johnston, P.F. (ed.), *Proceedings of the Sixteenth Conference on Underwater Archaeology.* Special Publication Series, No. 4, Society of Historical Archaeology, Boston, 1985, p. 138.

Szabo, I.,
Cultural Rights, Sijthoff, Leyden, 1974.

Sztucki, J.(ed)
Symposium on the International Regime of the Seabed - Proceedings. Academia Nazionale dei Linzei, Rome, 1970.

Szypszak, C.A.,
'The protection, salvage and preservation of underwater cultural resources in the Chesapeake Bay', 4 *Virginia Journal of Natural Resources Law* 373-395 (1985).

Téson, F.R.,
'International human rights and cultural relativism', 25 *V.J.I.L.* (1985) pp. 869-898.

Thomason, D.N.,
'Rolling back history: The United Nations General Assembly and the right to cultural property', 22 *Case W. Res. J. Int'l L.* (1990) pp. 47-96.

Timpany, M.S,
Ownership rights in the Titanic', 37 *Case Western Reserve Law Review* (1986) pp. 72-102.

Townsend, G.I. Vander Zwaag, D.,
'Now that Pandora's Box is open could Canada assume responsibility for the wreck of the Titanic?', 1 *New Directions* (IITOPS) 6-7 (Nos 2/3 1987).

Treves, T.,
- 'Na nona sessione della conferenza sul diritto del mare', 63 *Rivista di diritto internazionale* (1980) pp. 432-463.
- 'Drafting the LOS Convention', 5 *Marine Policy* (1981) pp. 273-276.

- 'Military installations, structures and devices on the seabed', 74 *A.J.I.L.* (1980) pp. 808-857.
- 'La navigation' in Dupuy, R.-J., Vignes, D. (eds.), *Traite du nouveau droit de la mer*. Collection 'Droit International', Economica, Bruylant, 1985.
- 'Codification du droit international et pratique des états dans le droit de la mer', 223 *Hague Recueil* (1990-IV) pp. 9-302.
- 'The Agreement completing the Law of the Sea Convention: formal and procedural aspects'. Paper presented to the *18th Annual Seminar of the Center for Oceans Law and Policy, University of Virginia, School of Law*, Rhodos 22-25 May, 1994.
- 'Stato costiero e archeologia sottomarina', *Rivista di diritto internazionale* (1993) pp. 698-719.
- 'La protezione del patrimonio culturale subacqueo nella Convenzione di Montego Bay del 1982 sul diritto del mare: in particolare, il nuovo instituto della zona archeologica'. Paper presented at the *Seminario La protezione del patrimonio culturale subacqueo nel Mediterraneo,* organised by the Università degli Studi di Roma 'Tor Vergata', Anacapri, 1 October 1994.

Tubman, M.,
'Submarine archaeological and historical objects: a watery legislative limbo', 2 *International Insights* (1986) pp. 85-90.

Turak, D.C.,
'The African Charter on Human and Peoples' Rights: some preliminary thoughts', 17 *Akron L. Rev.* (1984) pp. 365-381.

Turner, M.,
Shipwrecks and Salvage in South Africa: 1505 to Present, Cape Town, C. Struik, 1988.

Umbricht, V.,
'Right to development' in Dupuy, R.-J. (ed.), *The Right to Development at the International Level.* Hague Academy of International Law, 1979, pp. 94-98.

UNESCO,
- *Cultural Rights as Human Rights,* Studies and documents on cultural policies, Paris, 1970.

United Nations
The Law of the Sea: Archipelagic States - Legislative History of Part IV of the United Nations Convention on the Law of the Sea, Office for Ocean Affairs and the Law of the Sea, 1989.

Vallat, F.A.,
'The Continental shelf', 23 *B.Y.I.L.* (1946) pp. 333-338.

Van Dyke, V.,
'The cultural right of peoples', (2) *Universal Human Rights,* (1980) pp. 1-21.

Van Dyke & Yuen
'Common heritage v. freedom of the high seas: which governs the seabed?' 19 *San Diego L. Rev.* 493 (1982).

Van Meurs, L.,
- 'Legal aspects of marine archaeological research', *Acta Juridica* (1986) pp. 83-124.

· *Legal Aspects of Marine Archaeological Research*. Special Publication of the Institute of Marine Law, University of Cape Town, Publication No. 1 (1985).

Vasak, K. (ed.),
The International Dimensions of Human Rights, vol. 1., Greenwood Press, Westport, Connecticut, UNESCO, 1982.

Vedovato, G.,
'La tutele du patrimoine archéologique subaquatique dans une Convention du Conseil de l'Europe'. Paper submitted at the *66th ILA Conference in Buenos Aires,* 14-20 August 1994.

Vicuña, F.O.,
· 'The deep seabed mining regime: terms and conditions for its re-negotiations', 20 *Ocean Dev. & Int'l L.* (1989) pp. 531-532.
· *The Exclusive Economic Zone: Regime and Legal Nature under International Law,* Cambridge, University Press, 1989.
· 'The deep seabed mining regime: terms and conditions for its renegotiation', 20 *Ocean Dev. Int'l L.* (1989) pp. 531-539.

Villeneau, J.,
'Réparation des dommages à la terre: traitement de l'épave', 5 *Annuaire de droit maritime et aérien* (1980) pp. 281-827.

Villiger, M.K.,
Customary International Law and Treaties, 1985.

Virally, M.,
'The sources of international law' in Sørensen, M. (ed.), *Manual of Public International Law,* The Macmillan Press Ltd., London and Basingstoke, 1968, pp. 116-174.

Vitelli, K.D.,
'To remove the double standard: historic shipwreck legislation', 10 *J.F.A.* (1983) pp. 105-113.

Vischer (de), C.,
Theory and Reality in Public International Law. Revised edition. Translated from the French by Corbett, P.E., Princeton University Press, Princeton, New Jersey, 1968.

von Bittner, W.T.R.
'The Louisiana Removal of Sunken Vessels Act of 1985 - state wreck removal statutes in perspective', 11 *The Maritime Lawyer* (1986) pp. 49-70.

Vranesh, G. & Musick, J.D.,
'Finders keepers?! - Or the new statutory laws of treasure trove and related subjects', *Natural Resources Lawyer* (1972) pp. 1-12.

Voudouri, D.,
'The idea of a common European cultural heritage in view of the abolition of the internal frontiers'. Paper presented at the *Athens Conference on the Protection of the Archaeological Heritage,* Institute of Hellenic Constitutional History and Constitutional Law, November 26-27, 1992.

Vukas, B. (ed.),
Essays on the Law of the Sea, Publisher: Sveucilisna Naklada Liver, Zagreb, 1985.

Wainright, R.,
  'Navigation through three straits in the Middle East: effects on the United States of being a non-party to the 1982 Convention on the Law of the Sea', 18 *Case W. Res. J. Int'l L.* (1986) pp. 361-414,
Walker, C.W.,
  'Jurisdictional problems created by artificial islands', 10 *San Diego L. Rev.* (1973) pp. 638-663.
Warren, K.J.,
  'A philosophical perspective on the ethics and resolution of cultural properties issues' in Messenger, Ph. M. (ed), *The Ethic of Collecting Cultural Property: Whose culture, Whose Property?* Albuquerque, 1990, pp. 1-25.
Watters, D.R.,
  'The Law of the Sea Treaty and underwater cultural resources', 48 *American Antiquity* (1983) pp. 808-816.
Weissmann, G.,
  'Titanic and Leviath', 31 *Oceanus* (1988/89) pp. 68-77.
White, M.V.,
  'The common heritage of mankind: an assessment', 14 *Case W. Res. J. Int'l L.* (1982) pp. 509-542.
Whiteman, M.M.,
  Digest of International Law, 15 vols., 1963-1974.
Williams, S.A.,
  · *The International and National Protection of Movable Cultural Property: A Comparative Survey,* Oceana Publications Inc., Dobbs Ferry, New York, 1978.
  · 'Protection of cultural property: the Canadian approach', 22 *Arizona L. Rev.* (1980) pp. 737-751.
  · 'Recent developments in restitution and return of cultural property', 3 *International Journal of Museum Managements and Curatorship* (1984) pp. 117-129.
  · 'Protecting the archaeological heritage: can the 'new world order' protect the old?'. Paper presented at the *Athens Conference on the Protection of the Archaeological Heritage,* Institute of Hellenic Constitutional History and Constitutional Law, November 26-27, 1992.
Wolfrum, R.,
  · 'The principle of the common heritage of mankind', 43 *ZaöRV* (1983) pp. 312-337.
  · 'Common heritage of mankind', 11 *E.P.I.L.* (1989) pp. 65-69.
  · *Law of the Sea at the Crossroads: The Continuing Search for a Universally Accepted Regime,* Duncker & Humblot, 1991.
  · 'Entry into force of the Law of the Sea Convention: legal effect for parties and non-parties'. Paper presented to the *18th Annual Seminar of the Center for Oceans Law and Policy, University of Virginia, School of Law,* Rhodos 22-25 May 1994.

Wooster, W.S. (ed.)

Freedom of Oceanic Research. A study conducted by the Center for Marine Affairs of the Scripps Institution of Oceanography, University of California, San Diego. Crane, Russak & Company Inc., New York, 1973.

Wyss, M.Ph.,

Kultur als eine Dimension der Völkerrechtsordnung, Schweizer Studien zum Internazionalen Recht, Band 79, Schulthess Polygraphischer Verlag, Zürich, 1992.

Yokaris, A.,

'American Experience in the Protection of Cultural Property' in Council of Europe, *International Legal Protection of Cultural Property.* Proceedings of the Thirteenth Colloquy in European Law, Delphi 20-22 September 1983, Strasbourg, 1984, pp. 131-133.

Young, R.L.,

'Supreme Court report - admiralty cases raise interesting questions', 68 *A.B.A. Jour.* (1982) pp. 1478-1493.

Yusuf, A.,

'Differential treatment as a dimension of the right to development' in Dupuy, R.-J. (ed.), *The Right to Development at the International Level,* Hague Academy of International law, 1979, pp. 233-245.

Zacklin, R.,

'The right to development at the international level: some reflections on its sources, content and formulation' in Dupuy, R.-J. (ed.), *The Right to Development at the International Level,* Hague Academy of International Law, 1979, pp. 115-120.

Zhao, H.,

'Recent developments in the legal protection of historic shipwrecks in China', 23 *Ocean Dev. & Int'l L.* (1992) pp. 305-333.

Zuleta, B.,

'The Law of the Sea after Montego Bay', 20 *San Diego L. Rev.* (1983), pp. 475-488.

ANNEX

The ILA draft convention on the protection of the underwater cultural heritage

PREAMBLE

States party to the present Convention,

Acknowledging the importance of the underwater cultural heritage as an integral part of the cultural heritage of humanity and a particularly important element in the history of peoples, nations, and their relations with each other concerning their shared heritage;

Noting growing public interest in the underwater cultural heritage;

Perceiving that growing threats to the underwater cultural heritage include increasing construction activity, advanced technology that enhances identification of and access to wreck, exploitation of marine resources, and commercialization of efforts to recover underwater cultural heritage;

Determining that the underwater cultural heritage may be threatened by irresponsible activity and that therefore cooperation among States, salvors, divers, their organizations, marine archaeologists, museums and other scientific institutions is essential for the protection of the underwater cultural heritage;

Considering that exploration, excavation, and protection of the underwater cultural heritage necessitates the application of special scientific methods and the use of suitable techniques and equipment as well as a high degree of professional specialization, all of which indicates a need for uniform governing criteria;

Recognizing that the underwater cultural heritage belongs to the common heritage of humanity, and that therefore responsibility for protecting it rests not only with the State or States most directly concerned with a particular activity affecting the heritage or having an historical or cultural link with it, but with all States and other subjects of international law;

Bearing in mind the need for more stringent supervision to prevent any clandestine excavation which, by destroying the environment surrounding underwater cultural heritage would cause irremediable loss of its historical or scientific significance:

Realizing the need to codify and progressively develop the law in conformity with international rules and practice, including provisions in the 1982 United Nations Convention on the Law of the Sea;

Convinced that information and multidisciplinary education about the underwater cultural heritage, its historical significance, serious threats to it, and the need for responsible diving, deep-water exploration and other activity affecting the underwater cultural heritage, will enable the public to appreciate the importance of the underwater cultural heritage to humanity and the need to preserve it; and

Committed to improving the effectiveness of measures at international and national levels for the preservation in place or, if necessary for scientific or protective purposes, the careful removal of the heritage that may be found beyond the territorial sea;

Have agreed as follows:

Article 1: Definitions

For the purpose of this Convention:

1.   "Underwater cultural heritage" means all underwater traces of human existence including;

(a) sites, structures, buildings, artifacts and human remains, together with their archaeological and natural contexts; and
(b) wreck such as a vessel, aircraft, other vehicle or any part thereof, its cargo or other contents, together with its archaeological and natural context.

2.   Underwater cultural heritage shall be deemed to have been "abandoned":

(a) whenever technology would make exploration for research or recovery feasible but exploration for research of recovery has not been pursued by the owner of the heritage within 25 years after discovery of the technology; or
(b) whenever no technology would reasonably permit exploration for research or recovery and at least 50 years have elapsed since the last assertion of interest by the owner in the underwater cultural heritage.

3. "Cultural heritage zone" means an area beyond the territorial sea of the State up to the outer limit of its continental shelf as defined in accordance with relevant rules and principles of international law.

4. "Charter" means the "Charter of the Protection and Management of the Underwater Cultural Heritage" prepared by the International Council for Monuments and Sites (ICOMOS) and annexed to this Convention.

Article 2 : Scope of the Convention

1. This Convention applies to underwater cultural heritage which has been lost or abandoned and is submerged underwater for at least 100 years. Any State Party may, however, protect underwater cultural heritage which has been submerged underwater for less than 100 years.

2. This Convention does not apply to any warship, military aircraft, naval auxiliary, or other vessels or aircraft owned or operated by a State and used for the time being only on government non-commercial service, or their contents.

Article 3 : General Principle

States Party shall take all reasonable measures to preserve underwater cultural heritage for the benefit of humankind.

Article 4 : Non-Applicability of Salvage Law

Underwater cultural heritage to which this Convention applies shall not be subject to the law of salvage.

Article 5 : Cultural Heritage Zone

1. A State Party to this Convention may establish a cultural heritage zone and notify other States Party of its action. Within this zone, the State Party shall have jurisdiction over activities affecting the underwater cultural heritage.

2. A State Party shall take measures to ensure that activities within its zone affecting the underwater cultural heritage comply at a minimum with the provisions of the Charter.

Article 6 : Internal and Territorial Waters

States Party shall transmit a copy of the Charter to all relevant authorities within their jurisdiction, requiring them to take appropriate measures to apply the Charter, at a minimum, to activity within their internal and territorial waters.

Article 7 : Prohibition of the Use of Territory in Support of Activities Violating the Charter

No State Party shall allow its territory or any other areas over which it exercises jurisdiction to be used in support of any activity affecting underwater cultural heritage and inconsistent with the criteria of the Charter. This provision shall apply to any such activity beyond that State's territorial sea but not within a territorial sea or cultural heritage zone of another State Party.

Article 8 : Prohibition of Certain Activities by Nationals and Ships

Each State Party shall undertake to prohibit its nationals and ships of its flag from activities affecting underwater cultural heritage in respect of any area which is not within a cultural heritage zone or territorial sea of another State Party. The prohibition shall not apply to activities affecting the underwater cultural heritage that comply with the Charter.

Article 9 : Permits

A State Party to this Convention may provide for the issuance of permits allowing entry into its territory of underwater cultural heritage excavated or retrieved after the effective date of this Convention so long as the State has determined that the excavation and retrieval activities have complied or will comply with the Charter.

Article 10 :Seizure of Heritage

1. Subject to Article 9, on the request of any Party or on its own initiative, each State Party shall, in accordance with its constitutional procedures, shall seize any underwater cultural heritage brought within its territory, directly or indirectly, after having been excavated or retrieved in a manner not conforming with the Charter.

2. A State shall seize underwater cultural heritage known to have been excavated or retrieved from a cultural heritage zone or territorial sea of another State Party only after obtaining the consent of that State.

Article 11 : Penal Sanctions

1. Each State Party undertakes to impose penal sanctions for importation of underwater cultural heritage which is subject to seizure under Article 10.

2. Each State Party agrees to cooperate with other Parties in the enforcement of these sanctions. Such cooperation, consistent with national procedures, shall include but not

be limited to, production and transmission of documents, making witnesses available, service of process and extradition.

Article 12 : Notification Requirements and
Treatment of Seized Heritage

1.   Each State Party undertakes to notify the State or States of origin, if known, of its seizure of underwater cultural heritage under this Convention.

2.   Each State Party undertakes to record, protect and take all reasonable measures to conserve underwater cultural heritage seized under this Convention.

3.   Each Party undertakes, wherever possible, to keep underwater cultural heritage seized under this Convention on display or otherwise ensure the fullest reasonable access to it for the benefit of the public.

Article 13 : Collaboration and Information-Sharing

1.   Whenever a State has expressed a patrimonial interest in particular underwater cultural heritage to another State Party, the latter shall consider collaborating in the investigation, excavation, documentation, conservation, study and cultural promotion of the heritage.

2.   To the extent compatible with the purposes of this Convention, each State Party undertakes to share information with other States Party concerning underwater cultural heritage, such as but not limited, to discovery of heritage, location of heritage, heritage excavated or retrieved contrary to the Charter or otherwise in violation of international law, pertinent scientific methodology and technology, and legal developments relating to heritage.

3.   Whenever feasible, each State Party shall use appropriate international databases to disseminate information about underwater cultural heritage excavated or retrieved contrary to the Charter or otherwise in violation of international law.

Article 14 : Education

Each State Party shall endeavour by educational means to create and develop in the public mind a realization of the value of the underwater cultural heritage as well as the threat to this heritage posed by violations of this Convention and non-compliance with the Charter.

Article 15 : Revision of the Charter

Revisions in the Charter by the International Council for Monuments and Sites shall be deemed to be revisions in the annexed Charter, binding on States Party except for those State Parties that notify their non-acceptance to the Director-General of the United Nations Educational, Scientific and Cultural Organization within six months after the effective date of a revision. Unesco shall inform the States Party of such revisions prior to the effective date of the revision.

Article 16 : Dispute Resolution

1.   States, on becoming Parties to this Convention, undertake to establish an internal procedure or procedures for resolving disputes concerning whether an activity resulting in excavation or retrieval of the underwater cultural heritage did or did not comply with the Charter.

2.   Any dispute between two or more States Party concerning the interpretation or application of the present Convention that is not settled by negotiation shall, at the request of one of them, be submitted to arbitration. If, within six months from the date of the request for arbitration, the States Party are unable to agree on the organization of the arbitration, any one of those States Party may refer the dispute to the International Court of Justice, or a special chamber thereof, by a request in conformity with the Statute of the Court.

Article 17 : Official Languages

This Convention is drawn up in Arabic, Chinese, English, French, Russian and Spanish, the six texts being equally authoritative.

Article 18 : Ratification or Acceptance

1.   This Convention shall be subject to ratification or acceptance by States Members of the United Nations Educational, Scientific and Cultural Organization, in accordance with their respective constitutional procedures.

2.   The instruments of ratification or acceptance shall be deposited with the Director-General of the United Nations Educational, Scientific and Cultural Organization.

Article 19 : Applicability to Territorial Units

1.   If a State Party has two or more territorial units in which different systems of law are applicable in relation to the matters dealt with in this Convention, it may, at the time of ratification, acceptance, approval or accession, declare that this Convention is

to extend to all its territorial units or only to one or more of them, and may substitute its declaration by another declaration at any time.

2. These declarations are to be notified to the depository and are state expressly the territorial units to which the Convention extends.

Article 20 : Reservations, Understandings and Declarations

1. The Director-General of the United Nations Educational, Scientific and Cultural Organization shall receive and circulate to all States Party the text of reservations, understandings and declarations made by States at the time of ratification or accession.

2. A reservation incompatible with the objects and purposes of the present Convention shall not be permitted.

3. Reservations may be withdrawn at any time by notification to that effect addressed to the Director-General of the United Nations Educational, Scientific and Cultural Organization, who shall then inform all States. Such notification shall take effect on the date on which it is received by the Director-General of the United Nations Educational, Scientific and Cultural Organization.

Article 21 : Accession by Non-Member States

1. This Convention shall be open to accession by all States not Members of the United Nations Educational, Scientific and Cultural Organization.

2. Accession shall be effected by the deposit of an instrument of accession with the Director-General of the United Nations Educational, Scientific and Cultural Organization.

Article 22 : Entry into Force

This Convention shall enter into force three months after the date of the deposit of the tenth instrument of ratification, acceptance or accession, but only with respect to those States which have deposited their respective instruments of ratification, acceptance or accession on or before that date. It shall enter into force with respect to any other State three months after the deposit of its instrument of ratification, acceptance or accession.

Article 23 : Denunciations

1. Each State Party to this Convention may denounce the Convention.

2. The denunciation shall be notified by an instrument in writing, deposited with the Director-General of the United Nations Educational, Scientific and Cultural Organization.

3. The denunciation shall take effect six months after notification.

The foregoing is the authentic text of the Convention duly adopted by the General Conference of the United Nations Educational, Scientific and Cultural Organization during its ... session, which was held in ... and declared closed on the ... day of ... .

IN FAITH WHEREOF we have appended our signatures this ... day of ... .

The President of the   The Director-General
General Conference

TABLE OF CASES

TABLE OF TREATIES

*   References under this heading cover Treaty provisions where cited in the text specifically as provisions of the EC Treaty as formulated by the Treaty on European Union. Despite the fact that the EC Treaty is an amended version of the EEC Treaty, using seperate headings seems the most convenient solution.

TABLE OF NATIONAL LEGISLATION

South Australia

1965   Aboriginal and Historic Relics Preservation Act, p. 232

Tasmania

1970   National Parks and Wildlife Act, p. 232

Bahrain

1970   The Bahrain Antiquities Ordinance of 1 March 1970, p. 200
1993   Decree-Law No. 8 of 1993 with respect to the territorial sea and the contiguous zone
         of Bahrain, p. 211

Bangladesh

1974   Territorial Waters and Maritime Zones Act; Ministry of Foreign Affairs Declaration
         No. LT-I/3/74, April 13, 1974, p. 212

Barbados

1978   Marine Boundaries and Jurisdiction Act, p. 293

Belize

1971   Ancient Monuments and Antiquities Ordinance (Gazetted 31 December 1971), p.
         201

Bolivia

1961   Supreme Decree No. 05918 of 6 November 1961 concerning the protection of artistic,
         historical and archaeological treasures, p. 201

Brunei

1967   The Antiquities and Treasure Trove Enactment, p. 141

Brazil

1993   Act concerning the Territorial Sea, the Contiguous Zone, the Exclusive Economic
         Zone and the Continental Shelf of Brazil and Other Provisions, Act No. 8617 of
         4 January 1993, p. 211

Bulgaria

1987   Act of 8 July 1987 concerning ocean space of the People's Republic of Bulgaria, p. 211

Burma (Myanmar)

1977   Territorial Sea and Maritime Zones Law, No. 3 of 1977, p. 211

Canada

1975   Act of 19 June 1975, Canadian Cultural Property Export Control List, p. 201

Cape Verde

1977   Decree No. 126/77 of 31 December 1977, p. 154

Channel Islands

1986   The Wreck and Salvage (Vessels and Aircraft) Bailiwick of Guernsey) Law, p. 205

China

1982   Protection of Cultural Relics Law of 1982, p. 152
1989   Regulation on Protection and Administration of Underwater Cultural Relics, pp. 152, 185, 197, 205, 211, 289, 367
1992   Law on the Territorial Sea and the Contiguous Zone of 25 February 1992, p. 185, 212, 214

Cayman Islands

1977   The Abandoned Wreck Law, p. 151

Chile

1970   Law No. 17.288 of 27 January 1970 on National Monuments, amended by Laws No. 17.341 of 9 September 1970 and No. 17.577 of 14 December 1970 and by Decree-Law No. 1 of 5 May 1979, p. 140
1975   Supreme Decree No. 711 of 22 August 1975 approving Regulations governing the Supervision of Marien Scientific and Technological Research Conducted in the Martime Zone, p. 278
1986   Law No. 18.565 amending the Civil Code with regard to maritime spaces, p. 212

Colombia

1952   Decree No. 3183 of 10 December 1952, p. 211

Comoros

1982   Law No. 82-005 relating to the delimitation of the maritime zones of the Islamic Federal Republic of the Comoros, pp. 155, 270

Cyprus

1935   Antiquities Law as amended by Laws No. 48 of 1964 and No. 32 of 1973, pp. 140, 141, 201-2

Democratic Kampuchea (Cambodia)

1982   Decree of 13 July 1980 by the Council of State of Cambodia on Territorial Waters, p. 212

Democratic People's Republic of Korea

1977   Decree by the Central People's Committee establishing the Economic Zone of the People's Democratic Republic of Korea, 21 June 1977, p. 292

Democratic Yemen*

1970   Antiquities and Museum Law, p. 202
1977   Act No. 45 of 1977 concerning the Territorial Sea, Exclusive Economic Zone, Continental Shelf and Other Maritime Zones, pp. 210, 212

*   As from 22 May 1990, Democratic Yemen and Yemen Arabic Republic were unified.

Denmark

1963   Protection of Historic Shipwrecks Act, Act No. 203 of 31 May 1963, p. 206, 367
1972   Customs Act, p. 211
1976   Order No. 598 of 21 December 1976 on the Fishing Territory of the Faroes, p. 157
        Order No. 599 of 21 December 1976 on the Boundary of the Sea Territory of the Faroes, p. 157
1978   Conservation of Nature Act, Consolidated Act No. 435 of 1 September 1978 as amended by Act No. 530 of 10 October, 1984, pp. 185, 206
1984   Museum Act No. 291 of 6 June 1984 with later amendments, pp. 152, 206, 210
1992   Act No. 9 of 3 January 1992 on the Protection of Nature, pp. 211, 292, 335

Djibouti

1978   Law 52/AN/78 concerning the Territorial Sea, the Contiguous Zone, the Exclusive Economic Zone, the Maritime Boundaries and Fishing, pp. 209, 212

Dominica

1981   Territorial Sea, Contiguous Zone, Exclusive Economic Zone and Fishery Zones Act, No. 26 of 1981, p. 212

Dominican Republic

1977   Act No. 186 of 13 September 1967 on the Territorial Sea, the Contiguous Zone, the Exclusive Economic Zone and the Continental Shelf as amended by Act No. 573 of 1 April 1977, p. 212

Ecuador

1971   Supreme Decree No. 959-A of 28 June 1971 establishing archipelagic baselines for Galapagos Archipelago, p. 157
1986   President's Decree on Galapagos Marine Resource Reserve, The Official Register of Ecuador, No. 434, May 13 1986, p. 158

Egypt

1951   Decree concerning the Territorial Waters of the United Arab Republic (the Arab Republic of Egypt) of 15 January 1951, as amended by the Presidential Decree of 17 February 1958, p. 212
1982   Declarations (upon ratification of the United Nations Convention on the Law of the Sea) of December 19, 1982, p. 212
1983   Law No. 117 of 1983 putting into force the Law on the Protection of Antiquities, pp. 141, 202

Fiji

1977   Marine Spaces Act; Interpretation (Amendement) Act, 1977; Marine Spaces (Amendment) Act, 1977, p. 155
1981   Marine Spaces (Archipelagic Baselines and Exclusive Economic Zone) Order, 1981, and Marine Spaces (Territorial Seas) (Rotuma and its dependencies) Order 1981, p. 155

Finland

1939   Customs Regulations of 8 September 1939, as amended, p. 211
1963   Act of Archaeological Remains, No. 295 of 17 June 1963, pp. 142, 152, 206, 240

France

1958   Constitution, p. 282
1961   Law No. 61-1262 of 24 November 1961 on the Control of Shipwrecks, p. 207

Haiti

1977   Decree No. 38 of 1977, p. 212, 298

Honduras

1982   Constitution, p. 212
1984   Decree No. 81184 of 30 May 1984, p. 202

Hong Kong

1971   Museum and Antiquities Ordinance, p. 202

Iceland

1979   Law No. 41 of 1 June 1979 concerning the Territorial Sea, the Economic Zone and the Continental Shelf, p. 292

India

1958   The Ancient Monuments and Archaeological Sites and Remains Bill as amended by the Antiquities and Art Treasures (Amendment) Act 1972, p. 202
1972   The Antiquities and Art Treasures Act as amended by the Antiquities and Art Treasures (Amendment) Act 1972, p. 202
1976   Territorial Waters, Continental Shelf, Exclusive Economic Zone and Other Maritime Zones Act, pp. 209, 212, 293

Indonesia

1931   Indonesian Antiquities Act, Decree No. 238 of 13 June 1931, p. 202
1960   Act No. 4 concerning the Indonesian Waters of 18 February 1960, p. 155

Iran

1993   Act on the Marine Areas of the Islamic Republic of Iran in the Persian Gulf and the Oman Sea, pp. 212, 293

Iraq

1936   Antiquities Law as amended in 1974 and 1975, p. 202

Ireland

1930   National Monuments Act as amended in 1954 and in 1987 by the National Monuments (Amendment) Act, 1987, No. 17 of 1987, pp. 142, 152, 206, 290

Lesotho

1967   The Historical Monuments, Relics, Fauna and Flora Act, No.41 of 1967 (Date of Assent: 13 December 1967), p. 203

Libyan Arab Jamahiriya

1955   Pertroleum Law of 21 April 1955 (No. 25 of 1955), p. 284
1968   Antiquities Law, No. 40 of 1968, pp. 141, 203

Luxembourg

1927   Law of 12 August 1927, p. 203
1930   Regulation of 26 April 1930 for National Sites and Monuments, p. 203-4
1966   Law of 21 March 1966 concerning Excavation and the Safeguard of Movable Cultural Property, p. 203

Madagascar

1973   Order No. 73-050 on the safeguarding, protection and preservation of cultural property 7 September 1973, p. 203
1985   Ordinance No. 85-103 determining the limits of the maritime zones (territorial sea, continental shelf and exclusive economic zone) of the Democratic Republic of Madagascar, 16 September 1985, p. 212

Malaysia

1957   The Antiquities and Treasure Trove Ordinance, No. 14 of 1957, pp. 203, 293

Malta

1925   Antiquities (Protection) Act, No. XI of 1925 as amended in 1974, p. 204
1975   Territorial Waters and Contiguous Zone (Amendment) Act 1975 No. XLVI of 1975, 21 October 1975 as amended by the Territorial Waters and Contiguous Zones (Amendment) Act, No. XXIV of 18 July 1978, p. 212

Marshall Islands

1984   The Marine Zones (Declaration) Act 1984, Act of 13 September 1984, pp. 155, 212

Mauritania

1988   Ordinance No. 88-120 of 31 August 1988 establishing the Limits and the Legal Regime of the Territorial Sea, the Contiguous Zone, the Exclusive Economic Zone and the Continental Shelf of the Islamic Republic of Mauritania, pp. 212-213

Mauritius

1977   Maritime Zones Act, Act No. 13 of 3 June 1977, p. 213.

Mexico

1972   Federal Law on Archaeological, Artistic and Historic Monuments and Zones, p. 199
1986   Federal Act Relating to the Sea, p. 213

Morocco

1981   Dahir No. 1-81-179, promulgating Law No. 1-81 Establishing an Exclusive Economic
        Zone extending 200 nautical miles off the Moroccan Coast, pp. 213, 292

Namibia

1990   Territorial Sea and Exclusive Economic Zone of Namibia, Act No. 3 of 1990 as
        amended by Amendment Act 1991, p. 213

The Netherlands

1956   Constitution, p. 282
1961   Monuments Act as amended in 1988 by the Monuments Act, No. 622 of 1988, p.
        204

New Zealand

1975   Antiquities Act, p. 206
1980   The Historic Places Act, p. 206

Nigeria

1979   National Commission for Museums and Monuments Decree, No. 77 of 1979, p. 204

Norway

1966   Customs Act of 10 June 1966, p. 211
1972   Royal Decree of 8 December 1972 relating to Exploration and Exploitation of
        Petroleum in the Seabed and Substrata of the Norwegian Continental Shelf, p. 261
1978   Cultural Heritage Act, No. 50 of 9 June 1978, pp. 142, 152, 206

Oman

1989   Declaration No. 4 on the Contiguous Zone (Declaration made at the time of the
        ratification of the UN Convention on the Law of the Sea, 17 August 1989), p. 213

Pakistan

1975　Antiquities Act, p. 204
1976　Territorial Waters and Maritime Zones Act, pp. 213, 292, 293

Papua New Guinea

1977　National Seas Act, p. 155

Philippines

1961　Act No. 3046 of 17 June 1961 to define the Baselines of the Territorial Sea of
　　　Philippines as amended by Act No. 5446 of 18 September 1968, pp. 155, 157
1966　Cultural Properties Preservation and Protection Act No. 4846 of 18 June 1966 as
　　　amended by Presidential Decree No. 374 of 10 January 1974, p. 204
1978　Presidential Decree No. 1599 of 11 June 1978 establishing an Exclusive Economic
　　　Zone and for Other Purposes, p. 293

Portugal

1966　Act No. 2130 of 22 August 1966, p. 210
1977　Law No. 33/77 of 28 May, 1977, p. 210
1985　Decree-Law No. 495/85 of 29 November 1985, p. 157
1993　Law No. 289/93 of 21 August 1993, p. 290

Qatar

1974　Declaration by the Ministry of Foreign Affairs of 2 June 1974, p. 213
1980　Law No. 2 of 1980 on Antiquities, p. 141

Romania

1986　Decree of the Council of State concerning the Establishment of the Exclusive Eco-
　　　nomic Zone of the Socialist Republic of Romania in the Black Sea, No. 8 of 25
　　　April 1986, p. 290
1990　Act concerning the Legal Regime of the Internal Watras, the Territorial Sea and
　　　the Contiguous Zone of Romania, 7 August 1990, p. 213

Saint Kitts and Nevis

1984　Maritime Areas Act, p. 213

Saint Lucia

1984　Maritime Areas Act, p. 213

Saint Vincent and Grenadines

1983   Maritime Areas Act, No. 15 of 1983, pp. 155, 210, 213

São Tomé e Príncipe

1978   Decree-Law No. 14/78 of 16 June 1978, p. 155
1982   Decree-Law No. 42/82 of 2 December 1983, p. 155

Saudi Arabia

1958   Royal Decree concerning the Territorial Waters, Royal Decre No. 33 of February
        1958, p. 213
1972   Regulation for antiquities, Royal Decree No. M/26 of 3 August 1972, p. 204

Senegal

1985   Act No. 85-14 delimiting the Territorial Sea, the Contiguous Zone and the Continen-
        tal Shelf, 25 February 1985, p. 213

Seychelles

1977   Maritime Zones Act, p. 292, 293

Solomon Islands

1979   Delimitation of Marine Waters Act, Act No. 32 of 1979, p. 155

South Africa

1963   Territorial Waters Act, No. 87 of 1963 as amended by Act No. 98 of 1977, p. 211
1979   National Monuments Act as amended by in 1979 by the National Monuments
        Amendment Act, No. 35 of 1979 (promulgated on 11 April 1979) and in 1981 by
        the National Monuments Amendment Act, No. 13 of 1981, p. 206

Spain

1962   Law 60/1962 of 24 December 1962 on the Regime of Salvage and Findings, p. 150,
        241
1967   Decree 984/1967 of 30 April 1967 approving Regulations for the Application of
        Law of 24 December 1992, pp. 151, 241
1977   Royal Decree 2510/1977, p. 157
1978   Law 15/1978 of 20 February 1978 on the Economic Zone, p. 157
1985   Law 16/1985 of 25 June 1985 on the Spanish Historical Heritage, pp. 242, 290
1992   Law 27/1992 of 24 November 1992 concerning National Ports and Merchant Ship-
        ping, pp. 213, 241-242

Sri Lanka

1976   Maritime Zones Law, No. 22 of 1 September 1976, p. 213
1977   Presidential Proclamation of 15 January 1977 in pursuance of Martime Zones Act No. 22 of 1 September 1976, p. 213

Sudan

1952   The Antiquities Ordinance, No. 2 of 1952, p. 204
1970   Territorial Waters and Continental Shelf Act, p. 213

Sweden

1942   Act No. 350 of 12 June 1942 concerning Ancient Monuments and Finds as amended by Act No. 77 of 17 March 1967 and Act No. 589 of 30 June 1971, pp. 142, 240-241
1992   Economic Zone Act of 16 December 1992, p. 294

Syrian Arab Republic

1963   Decree-Law No. 222 of 26 October 1963 on the treatment of antiquities in the Syrian Arab Republic, pp. 204-205
        Decree-Law No. 304 of 28 December 1963, p. 211

Tanzania (United Republic of)

1964   Antiquities Act, No. 10 of 1964 as amended by the Antiquities (Amendment) Act, No. 22 of 1979, p. 205
1989   Territorial Sea and Exclusive Economic Zone Act 1989, pp. 292, 293

Thailand

1971   Petroleum Act of 26 March 1971, p. 284

Trinidad and Tobago

1983   Ministry of Foreign Affairs Notice, No. 500 of 1983, p. 155

1986   Act No. 24 of 1986, Archipelagic Waters and Exclusive Economic Zone Act, pp. 155, 213, 293

Tunisia

1986   Law No. 86-35 of 3 May concerning the Protection of Archaeological Property, Historic Monuments and Urban Sites, p. 210

1989   Law No. 89-21 of 22 February 1989 on Maritime Wrecks, p. 210

Venezuela

1956 Territorial Sea Law, p. 214

Vietnam

1977 Statement on the Territorial Sea, the Contiguous Zone, the Exclusive Economic Zone and the Continental Shelf of 2 May 1977, p. 214

Yemen (Arab Republic)*

1972 Antiquities Act, p. 205

* As from 22 May 1990, Democratic Yemen and Yemen Arabic Republic were unified.

Yugoslavia

1987 Law of Yugoslavia on the Coastal Sea and the Continental Shelf, pp. 289-290

Socialist Republic of Bosnia and Herzegovina

1980 The Mines Act of 15 April 1980, p. 284

Socialist Republic of Croatia

1983 The Mines Act of 12 May 1983, p. 284

Socialist Republic of Montenegro

1985 The Mines Act of 19 April 1985, p. 284

Zambia

1948 Natural and Historic Monuments and Relics Act 1948 as amended in 1953 and By-Laws 1957, p. 205

INDEX

(see also Table of Cases, Table of Treaties and
Table of National Legislation)